Higher Level Language Processes in the Brain

Inference and Comprehension Processes

Higher Level Language Processes in the Brain

Inference and Comprehension Processes

EDITED BY

Franz Schmalhofer
University of Osnabrück

Charles A. Perfetti
University of Pittsburgh

LEA LAWRENCE ERLBAUM ASSOCIATES, PUBLISHERS
2007 Mahwah, New Jersey London

Senior Acquisitions Editor: Lori Handelman
Editorial Assistant: Anthony Messina
Cover Design: Tomai Maridou
Full-Service Compositor: MidAtlantic Books and Journals, Inc.

Lawrence Erlbaum Associates, Inc., Publishers
10 Industrial Avenue
Mahwah, New Jersey 07430
www.erlbaum.com

CIP information for this volume can be obtained by contacting the Library of Congress.

ISBN 978-0-8058-5262-2—0-8058-5262-X (case)
ISBN 978-1-4106-1591-6—1-4106-1591-X (e book)

Books published by Lawrence Erlbaum Associates are printed on acid-free paper, and their bindings are chosen for strength and durability.

Printed in the United States of America

10 9 8 7 6 5 4 3 2 1

Contents

Higher Level Language Processes in the Brain

Inference and Comprehension Processes

1

Editors' Introduction: Mind and Brain in Higher Level Comprehension

Charles A. Perfetti
University of Pittsburgh

Franz Schmalhofer
University of Osnabrück

The study of text comprehension has developed from its fundamental but highly general question—how do people understand what they read?—to include more refined questions about the components and mechanisms of comprehension. What are the conditions that enable inferences and related processes that involve going beyond the literal text information? How do readers immediately link the meaning of a word in relation to its context? How does understanding proceed from a text-propositional level to a situation model level? (Or does it?) Is comprehension grounded in biological experience? What kinds of explicit models can account for comprehension processes?

Such questions have become compelling partly as a consequence of research progress in comprehension (and cognition generally) and partly because more methods have been brought to bear on comprehension. Computational modeling and neuroimaging methods have emerged to complement experimental behavioral methods (and these methods have expanded themselves) in the study of comprehension. Together, these three general methods have the potential to provide converging evidence for the components of comprehension and their mechanisms. This volume is a reflection of how this potential is being realized. In bringing together this small sample of work, we aimed both to assess the state of the art and to illustrate the kinds of new studies that are advancing the study of comprehension.

STATES OF THE ARTS

The first section is three state-of-the-art chapters. Singer and Leon review the state of the art in experimental behavioral studies. Their review leads them to conclude that behavioral-empirical studies have led to much progress in a relatively short time, while also exposing controversies that are resistant to simple resolution. One of their more intriguing conclusions is that text and discourse research has paved the way for broader generalizations concerning the principles of cognition. Singer and Leon establish a strong foundation for the recurring themes of this volume, including the nature of situation models, propositional representations, conditions on inference making, perceptual symbols, and limitations of various methods of discourse study.

Goldman, Golden, and Van den Broek review the state of the art in computational modeling, detailing its usefulness for explaining comprehension processes. As they define it, "a *model* refers specifically to a representation of the psychological processes that comprise a component or set of components involved in human text comprehension." A computational model is then a representation that is expressed in forms that can be run on a computer. They explain the value of computational modeling for developing theories of text comprehension, for testing explanations and accounting for unexpected findings, and for supporting communication within the comprehension field and with other areas. In making the case for these values, Goldman et al. provide some interesting comparisons of the some of the best-known models of comprehension.

Ferstl reviews the state of the art in neuroimaging research on comprehension. Keeping with integrative focus of the volume, the chapter does not merely review results of neuroimaging studies, but rather establishes a general framework for comprehension based on the class of models proposed by Walter Kintsch. The chapter provides a relatively nontechnical review of brain imaging studies that can be related to this framework and establishes results that are relevant for the work of later chapters on neuroimaging studies of integration, inferences, and cerebral functions. Ferstl concludes that the main value of neuroimaging is a better understanding of how cognitive processes work together to produce comprehension. She concludes that for this to happen, research will move from identifying single brain regions to discovering the contributions of components of a discourse comprehension network.

COMPUTATIONAL MODELS

The second section presents two chapters on computation models. Dennis and Kintsch demonstrate the application of string theory to inference rule generation for simple texts. This application, the Syntagmatic Paradigmatic (SP) model, is based on simple comparison processes across unstructured (no syntax) strings of words stored in memory through experience. The SP model is intended to capture the relations that are usually represented in propositions, but without extracting explicit relationships. It provides a new inference mechanism, inference by coincidence, which allows inference-like retrieval process based on a corpus of similar strings. Dennis and Kintsch point out limitations of SP as a general language model.

Frank, Koppen, Noordman, and Vonk present a model of multiple levels of text representation, the Distributed Situation Space (DSS) model. The DSS creates situation models without first extracting propositions and allows the emergence of inferences from knowledge applied to story statements. The chapter extends the model with a simple recurrent network to simulate word-by-word reading. Multiple levels of discourse representation automatically arise from learning to transform sentences from a textual representation of a sentence into a situational one. Frank et al. note various limitations of the current DSS model that prevent it from creating an overall interpretation of a story from the incremental transformation of word sequences.

INTEGRATIVE PROCESSES IN TEXT COMPREHENSION

The third section shifts to studies of integrative processes in comprehension, with a special emphasis on inferencing as a kind of integration process. Schmalhofer and Perfetti combine ERP, fMRI, and behavioral studies of word-to-text integration. They report evidence with strong convergence across fMRI (German) and ERP (English) studies that forward inferences produce less immediate integration compared with text-based integration. For example, in the ERP results, integrating a word with a preceding sentence is less likely when the integration depends on an inference in the preceding sentence than when the preceding sentence contains a paraphrased antecedent of the word. This conclusion is reinforced by results of a parallel fMRI study. Theoretically, Schmalhofer and Perfetti suggest that the process of linking a word to a representation of the prior text includes a resonance process that compares the word with semantic contents (as opposed to the verbatim words) of recent text memory.

Singer and Remillard emphasize a distinction between explicit and implicit text ideas. They show that the process dissociation method can be used to clear up discrepancies between the distinction in text processing between explicit and implicit ideas and the failure of behavioral evidence to capture this distinction and to address the role of automaticity in inference processing. Singer and Remillard compare the retrieval profiles for explicit text ideas, bridging inferences, and elaborative inferences, examining the contributions of recollection and familiarity. Their experiments indicate that there are measurable differences between people's representation of explicit and implicit text ideas.

The chapter by Reichle and Mason exemplifies the goal of cross-method integration that can bring progress to theories of comprehension. They combine computational modeling and neuroimaging in developing a model to explain results from behavioral and fMRI studies of causal inferences. They demonstrate how the results of an fMRI experiment can inform understanding of the cognitive processes that lead readers to make causal inferences during reading. Their strategy is to link the patterns of fMRI-measured activation during the reading of short texts with the functional roles that have been attributed to the observed brain areas. From this, Reichle and Mason develop a small number of simple computational principles to make predictions about the outcomes of both brain-imaging and behavioral experiments.

McNamara, de Vega, and O'Reilly examine individual differences in comprehension skill, reviewing both behavioral and ERP studies. They conclude that ERP data show that less skilled readers rely more on superficial aspects of reading and do not efficiently manage the use of background knowledge. They conclude also that this picture from ERP data corresponds well with behavioral results that poor readers are less likely to make inferences during reading.

COGNITIVE REPRESENTATIONS

Section IV is six chapters that concern the cognitive representations of comprehended language. The new look in comprehension—that comprehension is grounded in experience and embodied in biological systems—is seen in the chapter by Kaup, Zwaan, and Lüdtke. They hypothesize that understanding negation requires two mental simulations, one of which is the actual state of affairs as described by a text, and the other of which is a simulation of the pragmatically expected state of affairs; they report four experiments testing this hypothesis. Kaup et al. propose a mechanism by which negation is implicitly represented in the experiential simulations created during language comprehension and argue that this mechanism is necessary if the experiential program is to produce a general theory of language comprehension.

In their chapter, Graesser, Louwerse, McNamara, Olney, Cai, and Mitchell examine the link between computational linguistics and the cognitive processes that create a reader's situation model. Because the construction of a situation model is heavily influenced by a text's linguistic features, including text cohesion, Graesser et al. identify the factors that contribute to text cohesion and thus to psychological coherence.

They describe a computer system, Coh-Metix, that organizes measures of text properties and allows their application for research that links text properties to comprehension.

Therriault and Rinck examine the general representational issue of the nature of the reader's situational model for narrative texts. They conclude that, contrary to its privileged position in demonstrations of situation models, space is not a fundamental dimension of a reader's situation models. Instead, readers are sensitive to fundamental aspects of narrative events, including time, which provides the critical information about the duration, order, and progression of unfolding events. They argue also that goals and causality, which have been accorded privileged status in some accounts, are actually derivative dimensions, dependent upon protagonist information (in the case of goals) and time (in the case of causality). Therriault and Rinck suggest that two relatively neglected dimensions, emotion and perspective, are important in situation models, but leave open the possibility that these dimensions may also be derivative rather than basic.

Long, Baynes, and Prat examine the representation issue through a highly integrative perspective on hemispheric functions. Building on research that has established an important role for the right hemisphere in understanding language, they summarize their priming experiments, which use divided visual-field presentation and which were guided by important distinctions in current theories of discourse processing. Their priming results across four studies show left hemisphere effects at the level of propositional relations, except for left-hemisphere-damaged aphasics. Based on both patient and nonpatient populations, Long et al. conclude that each hemisphere represents explicit information from a text, but each organizes the information differently—within-sentence relations are coded in the left hemisphere only, whereas the right, as well as the left, hemisphere codes lexical-semantic information.

The question of hemisphere functions is taken up as well by Tapiero and Fillon, who address emotional inferences. Like Long et al., Tapiero and Fillon used divided visual field presentation, with lexical decisions made on words that were either congruent or incongruent with an emotional state that could be inferred from a passage that was being read at the time of the decision. Their results confirmed hemisphere differences, with the right hemisphere showing more priming by emotional words. Whether a word was congruent with the inferred emotion and whether the emotional valence was positive or negative had differential effects on the two cerebral hemispheres.

Magliano, Radvansky, and Copeland address the representation issue from the perspective of autobiographical memory. They argue that situation models are general mechanisms that function across a variety of experiences that people have beyond written texts. They develop their argument through examples from movies and virtual reality settings. They argue that among the shared properties of situational models across various experiences are causal relationships. They conclude with the generalists' proposition that "there are a myriad of ways that the humans can experience events, and it seems reasonable that a common mental apparatus underlies the comprehension of all of them."

FINAL WORDS

Most of the authors of this volume participated in a conference (Higher Level Language Processes in the Brain: Inference and Comprehension Processes) held at the Hanse Advanced Study Institute in Delmenhorst, Germany, and organized by the editors of this volume. The conference focused on interaction and research integration around comprehension issues and included several specific steps (prior circulation of critical questions, discussion sessions on conference topics) to bring this about. A distinctive outcome was the emergence of several joint chapters from individual participants. For example, Paul van den Broek joined with Susan Goldman and Richard Golden to write a state-of-the-art modeling chapter, turning two conference presentations into one well-integrated chapter. Erik Reichle and Robert Mason also teamed up for a collaborative chapter, specifically choosing to combined their respective expertise in neuroimaging and computational modeling for an integrative chapter that neither would have been inclined to write individually. Following separate presentations at the conference, Franz Schmalhofer and Charles Perfetti came to agree that their differences on inferences had been significantly reduced, allowing them to work on a collaborative chapter that could become more integrative than their separate chapters could have been.

Charles Perfetti
Franz Schmalhofer

I

STATE OF THE ART

2

Psychological Studies of Higher Language Processes: Behavioral and Empirical Approaches

Murray Singer
University of Manitoba

Jose Leon
Universidad Autonoma de Madrid

During the past 35 years, higher language processes have been subjected to intensive study within an information-processing framework. This brief time span has witnessed remarkable progress in the discovery of basic phenomena of language comprehension; the identification of cognitive mechanisms underlying these phenomena; and the proposal of detailed, testable theories in this domain. Much of this progress has been driven by the development and application of behavioral methods for the scrutiny of people's comprehension of spoken and written language. These techniques have generated a steady stream of empirical evidence to challenge cognitive scientists.

This chapter documents and elaborates on the conversations of the Behavioral/Empirical discussion group at the International Hanse-Conference on Higher Level Language Processes in the Brain. The group focused on areas of distinct progress within this realm, and qualifications and constraints of the behavioral approach. This chapter addresses these issues, using a parallel structure.

PROGRESS IN THE STUDY OF LANGUAGE PROCESSES

Information-processing research concerning language comprehension has been characterized by the identification, reconsideration, and regular refinement of the understanding of numerous phenomena central to this domain. Furthermore, these advances have been continuously guided by detailed theoretical formulations. In this section, several phenomena and the pertinent theoretical constructs are reviewed.

Propositional Representations

Early in the enterprise, there was agreement that progress in language comprehension research required a well-defined system of semantic analysis. What emerged from this consensus was the proposal that one or more elementary ideas, or propositions, underlie each clause or sentence (e.g., Clark, 1969; Kintsch, 1972; Schank, 1972; Winograd, 1972). According to Kintsch's (1972) influential analysis, each proposition consists of a predicate plus one or more arguments. Predicates typically correspond to a verb or other relational term, and arguments correspond to nouns. Accordingly, the propositions underlying sentence (1) are shown in (2), with the predicate of each proposition appearing first:

1. The car pulling the trailer climbed the steep hill.
2. a. (PULL, CAR, TRAILER)
   b. (CLIMB, CAR, HILL)
   c. (STEEP, HILL)

Equally importantly, these propositions were proposed to be organized in networks (Anderson & Bower, 1973) or propositional schemas (van Dijk & Kintsch, 1983).

Propositional analysis was an effective tool for identifying units of meaning. However, a considerable body of empirical work was needed to establish that propositions functioned as psychological elements. Kintsch and Keenan (1973) showed that reading time for complex sentences varied systematically as a function of (a) their number of propositions rather than word length and (b) the number of propositions that the readers recalled from those sentences. Likewise, reading time varies with the number of *different* arguments underlying a message (Haberlandt & Graesser, 1985; Kintsch, Kozminsky, Streby, McKoon, & Keenan, 1975).

Other investigations exposed subtle features of propositional organization. Words from a previously-encountered sentence are more effective recall cues for words that stem from the same proposition than they are for words that stem from different propositions underlying the sentence (Weisberg, 1969). Even more strikingly, the speed of recognizing that a word that has appeared in a recent sentence is faster when it is immediately preceded by a word from the same proposition than when it is preceded by a word from a different one (Ratcliff & McKoon, 1978). The structures of propositional networks, as well as individual propositions, were established to be reflected by readers' behavior. For example, people's recall of text statements varies systematically with the level at which they appear in hierarchical propositional networks

(Kintsch et al., 1975), and recognition judgments about words from text are speeded more by preceding words that are close in the network than they are by those that are distant (McKoon & Ratcliff, 1980).

This body of empirical work sanctioned the central role that propositions were to play in the development of theories of language comprehension (e.g., Kintsch, 1988). Furthermore, the propositional representation, or "textbase," is widely viewed as one of at least three critical representational levels that result from discourse comprehension, along with representations of the surface details of discourse and of the situations to which the discourse refers (van Dijk & Kintsch, 1983; Schmalhofer, McDaniel, & Keefe, 2002). The role of such situation models is addressed later.

Factors Promoting and Constraining Inference Processing

Throughout the brief history of the field, advances in inference-processing research have closely paralleled those in the broader realm of language comprehension. Progress in inference research has been characterized by the tension resulting from the inevitability that discourse comprehension depends on inferential access to pertinent world knowledge on the one hand, and the constraints imposed on inference processing by limited cognitive resources on the other. In this regard, having heard that the delicate vase fell to the floor, people incorrectly report recognizing a test sentence that replaces *fell* with *smashed* virtually as often as they recognize the original sentence (Johnson, Bransford, & Solomon, 1973). This suggested that, during the course of reading, the understander may have computed the "elaborative inference" that the vase smashed. However, results converging from a variety of procedures indicated that the crucial inference might well have been drawn only at the time of the subsequent test. These results indeed tended to favor the latter alternative over the online inference view (Corbett & Dosher, 1978; Singer, 1979).

In the wake of these findings, the construct of discourse coherence played a central role in the delineation of the inferences that routinely accompany comprehension. Haviland and Clark (1974) had shown that people read the sentence *The beer was warm* more quickly in the context of *We got the beer out of the trunk. The beer was warm*, than for *We got the picnic supplies out of the trunk. The beer was warm.* They presented convincing evidence that the time difference could be attributed to the need to infer, in the latter sequence, that beer is a sensible ingredient of picnic supplies. This inference is necessary to preserve the coherence of its sequence, because the first sentence makes no mention of beer. Haviland and Clark labeled the inference that the beer formed part of the picnic supplies a "bridging inference."

These principles were shown to fruitfully distinguish between those plausible knowledge-based inferences that reliably accompany comprehension and those that do not. Consider the status of the idea, THE TOURIST USED A CAMERA, with reference to the three versions of the passage of Table 2–1 (Singer, 1980). This idea is stated explicitly in the first version, enhances

TABLE 2–1.
Three Versions of a Sample Experimental Passage Plus Test Sentence of Singer (1980)

Explicit
The tourist took the picture with the camera. The scene was more beautiful than he remembered.

Bridging Inference
The tourist took the picture of the church. The camera was the best he had ever owned.

Elaborative Inference
The tourist took the picture of the church. The scene was more beautiful than he remembered.

Test sentence
The tourist used a camera.

coherence by inferentially bridging the two sentences of the second version, and constitutes a sensible elaboration in the third. Readers of these passages in the explicit and the bridging conditions took virtually identical amounts of time to subsequently verify the test sentence, *The tourist used a camera* ("true"); but verification time was approximately a quarter-second longer in the elaborative inference condition. It was concluded that coherence requirements guide the reader to compute bridging inferences during the course of comprehension (Singer, 1980). The scrutiny of different categories of coherence-preserving inferences, using a variety of methodologies, tended to corroborate that proposal (Keenan, Baillet, & Brown, 1984; McKoon & Ratcliff, 1986; Myers, Shinjo, & Duffy, 1987; Potts, Keenan, & Golding, 1988; Singer & Ferreira, 1983).

The latter studies collectively tended to suggest that elaborative inferences are encoded either weakly or not at all, but researchers proceeded to focus on conditions that might promote the online derivation of elaborative inferences. One general principle that emerged from this work was that elaborative inferences may be encoded in a text representation when they are highly constrained. These constraints include circumstances in which the elaborative inference (a) represents a highly probable feature of a text concept (e.g., *ripe tomato* implies *red*; McKoon & Ratcliff, 1988), (b) represents a highly constrained category instantiation (e.g., *bird for Thanksgiving* implies *turkey*; O'Brien, Shank, Myers, & Rayner, 1988), and (c) is based on a recently mentioned concept (Lucas, Tanenhaus, & Carlson, 1990).

Theorists have strived to account for these results in terms of general principles of cognition. In this regard, Schmalhofer and McDaniel (2002) derived a unified analysis of these effects, using Kintsch's (1988) *construction-integration* model. Most briefly, they proposed that whereas explicit text ideas are encoded at surface, propositional, and situational levels of representation, inferences are initially constructed primarily or exclusively in the situation model. According to construction-integration, encoded elements at any representational level will endure only if they receive relatively high degrees of activation, which in turn depends on their degree of interconnection with other elements. Bridging inferences generally exceed elaborative inferences in their connections to other text ideas and pertinent knowledge. However, high constraint, as discussed earlier, can augment the interconnections of elaborative inferences. In this circumstance, elaborative inferences may become a lasting part of the text representation.

Discourse Situation Models

For 20 years or more, the border between language-processing investigations of inference processes and those of situation models has steadily blurred. As mentioned earlier, the situation model refers to the understander's representation of the circumstances to which a discourse refers (van Dijk & Kintsch, 1983; see also Johnson-Laird, 1983). Several factors influenced researchers to place a high priority on clarifying the situation model. First, it was a recognized axiom that memory for discourse gist overrides memory for surface detail (Sachs, 1967). However, these gist influences could not be explained simply in terms of the semantics of the propositional textbase. To cite just one example, in the stories of Potts (1972), readers encountered sentences such as *The squirrel was older than the fox. The fox was older than the bear. The bear was older than the owl.* After reading, people needed less time to correctly verify the new sentence, *The squirrel was older than the owl,* than any sentence that had appeared verbatim in the story. This outcome could be explained only in terms of a situational ordering such as squirrel > fox > bear > owl. In particular, it is generally easiest to distinguish entities that are the most different. Neither surface nor textbase analyses could account for this sort of result (see also Bransford, Barclay, & Franks, 1972; Sanford & Garrod, 1998).

Second, situational influences increasingly dominate surface and textbase representations with increasing delay between comprehension and retrieval (Kintsch, Welsch, Schmalhofer, & Zimny, 1990; Kintsch & van Dijk, 1978; Reder, 1982; Sachs, 1967). This further enhanced the need to specify the details of situational representations.

The Nature of Situation Models. From an information-processing perspective, at least two influential characterizations of the situation model have emerged. According to the first, situational representations comprise complex referential models that interrelate discourse entities with one another and with relevant world knowledge (e.g., Sanford & Garrod, 1998). This analysis again particularly emphasizes the construct of coherence. Thus, when a text is read that refers to someone using the alternative terms "the lawyer," "the attorney," "Susan," and "she," comprehension depends on the recognition that terms have the identical referent. The resulting representation must attribute all of the relevant traits and actions to the same entity. Any other representation would be incoherent.

A second general treatment emphasizes the multidimensional character of the situation model. From this perspective, the situation model consists of the integrated representations of single events. Those events have qualities, in the form of values on dimensions such as cause, motive, space, time, and narrative characters. Readers are proposed to monitor these dimensions during comprehension. As a result, the ease of integrating event representations either with another one or with the current situation model varies with the number of dimensions on which the two representations match (Zwaan, Langston, & Graesser, 1995; Zwaan, Magliano, & Graesser, 1995; Zwaan & Radvansky, 1998; Zwaan, Radvansky, Hilliard, & Curiel, 1998). Clauses describing events that mismatch on all dimensions will strike the reader as incoherent. One remedy in this circumstance is for the reader to initiate the construction of an entirely new structure (Gernsbacher, 1990).

Dimensions of Situation Models. Much of the research concerning the dimensions of situational representations has focused on individual dimensions. A detailed analysis of the *causal structure* of text representations initially emerged from the inspection of text inference processing. In this regard, considerable evidence indicated that causal bridging inferences predictably accompany reading comprehension (Black & Bern, 1981; Singer & Ferreira, 1983) and that the time needed to compute these inferences increases systematically with the semantic distance between an outcome and its antecedent cause (Keenan, Baillet, & Brown, 1984; Myers, Shinjo, & Duffy, 1987). Concomitantly, theorists advanced detailed models of the causal structures underlying text (Trabasso & Sperry, 1985; Trabasso, van den Broek, & Suh, 1989). According to this analysis, readers detect those causes which, with regard to a specific outcome, are "necessary in the circumstances" (van den Broek, 1990). Within this theoretical framework, it was shown that readers' recall and importance judgments of text ideas are influenced by the degree of causal connectivity among those ideas and by whether an idea appears in the main causal chain of the message (Trabasso & van den Broek, 1985). The causal status of text ideas influences whether they are retained in working memory for further processing (Fletcher & Bloom, 1988). Furthermore, causal structures affect the reader's ability to detect the relations among text ideas that may be separated by appreciable text distances (Long, Seely, & Oppy, 1996; Suh & Trabasso, 1993; van den Broek & Lorch, 1993).

More recently, the *spatial and temporal dimensions* of the situation model have been subjected to careful inspection. In one extensively used paradigm for examining spatial situations, people first memorize the layout of rooms and objects of a rather complex setting. When they then read a story set in that location, the current location of the narrative protagonist affects their judgment times about various locations and objects in the setting (Morrow, Greenspan, & Bower, 1987). These result patterns tend to reflect people's encoding of ordinal locations along paths rather than Euclidean distances (Rinck, Hahnel, Bower, & Glowalla, 1997). The patterns also depend on the precise nature of the participants' assigned experimental task (Wilson, Rinck, McNamara, Bower, & Morrow, 1993). It has been proposed that constraints on the derivation of spatial situations (e.g., Zwaan & van Oostendorp, 1994) may reflect the relevance, or functionality, of text information. In this regard, phrases such as *standing under the bridge* were read more quickly and remembered better in a functional context, such as *starting to rain*, than in a less relevant one, such as *blocking the moonlight* (Radvansky & Copeland, 2000). Under ordinary circumstances, comprehenders are very sensitive to at least the coarse spatial relations underlying discourse (Bransford et al., 1972; O'Brien & Albrecht, 1992; Sanford & Garrod, 1998).

There is likewise considerable evidence that people encode the temporal relations underlying discourse. This is not surprising—the time relations of texts are indicated in each clause, by means of linguistic markers such as adverbs, adverbial phrases, and verb tense. Certainly, readers' judgments of text ideas reflect their awareness of anomalies of the semantics of time, such as Markus waiting for Claudia on the station platform when prior text indicated that her train had arrived before his (Rinck, Hahnel, & Becker, 2001). Moreover, even subtle text characteristics such as whether an event is ongoing or completed, as signaled by verb aspect (*she was-changing/changed the flat tire*), affect the reader's access to other text events and episodes (Magliano & Schleich, 2000; see also Madden & Zwaan, 2003).

Conclusions. Advances in this domain warrant some general conclusions. First, the dimensions of the situation model interact closely. For example, theoretical analysis and empirical evidence indicate that the *motivational* structures underlying text are very *causal* in character (Schank & Abelson, 1977; Singer & Halldorson, 1996; Trabasso et al., 1989). Likewise, temporal and causal text relations are inherently intertwined: Assigning an event or action to the role of "cause" requires that it temporally precede its outcome (Trabasso et al., 1989). These regularities are hardly surprising, considering that the situation model characterizes complex events rather than isolated dimensions.

Second, the qualities of situation models are not specific to discourse comprehension but pertain to understanding stemming from any sort of sensory stimulation (Graesser, Singer, & Trabasso, 1994). In this regard, investigating the referential and multidimensional character of situation models constitutes a general issue of cognition. Whereas the thorough comprehension of discourse will result in situational representations, situation models need not arise from text comprehension.

THE BEHAVIORAL APPROACH TO LANGUAGE PROCESSES: QUALIFICATIONS AND CONSTRAINTS

Embodiment and Perceptual Symbols in Language Comprehension

The discussion group addressed the implications for language comprehension of the embodied cognition theoretical framework. This position stems from the proposal that representations of perception and action form the basis of meaning, and, more generally, cognition (e.g., Barsalou, 1999). A central tenet of this analysis is that language comprehension theories have neglected the relationship between propositional representations and the meaningful perceptual experiences to which these symbols refer. Indeed, embodiment theorists consider propositional analysis to appreciably misrepresent the fundamentals of meaning (e.g., Glenberg, 1997; Kaup, Zwaan, & Lütdke, this volume).

Considerable empirical support has already been invoked as supporting the embodiment analysis. Readers have been shown to exhibit faster recognition and naming of pictures that match the implied perceptual orientation and shape of objects than for mismatching ones (Stanfield & Zwaan, 2001; Zwaan, Stanfield, & Yaxley, 2002). In this regard, it takes less time to produce the name *eagle* for a picture of an eagle with its wings folded than unfolded after reading *The ranger saw the eagle in the nest* (Zwaan et al., 2002). This is despite the fact that a propositional analysis, such as (SEE, AGENT:RANGER, PATIENT:EAGLE, LOCATION:IN-NEST) in no way makes reference to the eagle's wings. Glenberg and Robertson (2000) showed that people assign higher plausibility judgments to unusual sentences whose concepts are experientially congruent than for incongruent ones (e.g., *As a substitute for her pillow, she filled up an old sweater with CLOTHES/WATER*, respectively). Glenberg and Robertson also presented evidence that high-dimensional semantic space computational models (e.g., Latent Semantic Analysis; Landauer, 1997), the meaning units of which are amodal rather than perceptually based, could not capture this effect. From a somewhat different perspective, Sanford and Garrod (1998) argued that readers' tendency to overlook the anomalies of trick sentences such as *The authorities were trying to decide where to BURY THE INJURED* (Barton & Sanford, 1993) suggests that important aspects of language comprehension involve the fit between a crucial word (e.g., *injured*) and the current situation (e.g., a plane crash). They proposed that this tends to refute the assumption that global representations are derived from lower-level propositional ones, because the latter ought to readily expose the anomaly.

The discussion group considered these proposals to offer an important challenge to existing formulations of language comprehension. A variety of interrelated observations and tests for the embodiment position were raised. First, the fact that propositional representations cannot account, on their own, for effects such as the eagle-wing matching result is not an entirely new revelation. To the contrary, it has long been realized that propositional representations must be augmented by situational ones to address people's awareness of the ordinal (Potts, 1972), spatial (Bransford et al., 1972), and other semantic connotations (McKoon & Ratcliff, 1988) of messages.

Second, and further to the first observation, coherent situational representations have long been accepted as the critical goal of language comprehension (van Dijk & Kintsch, 1983). From this perspective, evidence stemming from the embodiment framework might be viewed as clarifying a considerably neglected dimension of the situation model rather than denying the role of propositional representations. Third, proposals that cognitive psychological theories of meaning are dominated by propositional analyses (Glenberg, 1997) may overstate the current state of affairs. For example, the ACT theory (Anderson, 1983, 1993) clearly embraces linear, spatial, imaginal, and propositional representations as fundamental to human thought and behavior. Fourth, the proposal that comprehension depends on relating linguistic symbols to underlying perceptual experiences constitutes a form of semantic decomposition. However, empirical evidence tends to deny that comprehension requires the decomposition of symbols into semantic primitives (Fodor, Garrett, Walker, & Parkes, 1980; see also van Dijk & Kintsch, 1983, pp. 41–42). Fifth, Burgess (2000) noted that it remains for embodiment theories to be expressed in forms as detailed and well defined as certain competing theories that have been instantiated as computational models.

The application of the principles of embodied cognition in the domain of language comprehension is a novel undertaking. Empirical studies derived from this analysis are claimed to challenge the widely held multilevel analysis of discourse representation. Much work will be needed to determine whether multilevel discourse representation and embodiment are compatible analyses, or, alternatively, whether one or the other will dominate in language processing theory.

Interdisciplinary Approaches to Discourse Comprehension

The study of discourse processing is an interdisciplinary endeavor involving theories and techniques from computer science, computational linguistics, cognitive psychology (involving both behavioral and neuroscientific approaches), linguistics, sociolinguistics, rhetoric, and education (see Foltz, 2003, for a review). These complementary approaches highlight important constraints on the form of theories of discourse. For example, cognitive psychology imposes constraints on theories of representations, clarifies the interrelation between memory and comprehension, and identifies when and where specific cognitive processes may occur in the brain. Linguistics, sociolinguistics, and rhetoric provide examples of the types of language or social contexts that must be processed and constraints on how they are processed. Educational studies of reading and comprehension inform theories of (a) learning from text, (b) instructional design, and (c) the strategies that promote comprehension processes. Computer science and computational linguistics offer analyses of parsing, computer-generated semantic/syntactic representations, and computer simulations.

However, theoretical perspectives, whether interdisciplinary or not, are not always congruent. In this regard, connectionist approaches (e.g., McClelland, 1991) generally assume the unconstrained interaction and collaboration among lower and higher language processes. Modular theories, in contrast, postulate the relative independence of the contributing processes, such as word recognition and parsing (e.g., Fodor, 1983). These analyses posit fundamentally different architectures of language processing.

More recently, theorists have advanced general frameworks of language processing, including the minimalist (McKoon & Ratcliff, 1992), constructionist (Graesser et al., 1994), memory-based (O'Brien, Lorch, & Myers, 1998), and, as discussed earlier, embodied cognition. These positions converge and clash in almost kaleidoscopic fashion. *Minimalism* and *constructionism* advanced different views of the extent of inference processing in language comprehension. The minimalist proposal that the ready availability of relevant knowledge is a necessary condition for routine inference computation contributed to the *memory-based* articulation of the contribution of resonance processes to comprehension. In spite of the latter two trends, investigators are seriously considering the possibility that comprehension requires a close collaboration between *memory-based* and constructionist processes (Guéraud & O'Brien, 2005). The *embodied-cognition* view rejects (Glenberg, 1997) the propositional representations embraced by constructionism and possibly the role of resonance principles advocated by memory-based theorists as well (Zwaan & Madden, 2004). Nevertheless, these controversies enrich the theoretical landscape and create a scientific agenda of problems that demand scrutiny.

Methods

Another constraining factor of the behavioral approach is related to the available methodology. In general, experimental methods are constrained by theoretical assumptions about discourse and comprehension processes. It is well known that the choice of method is often guided by the investigator's theoretical framework. This is all the more true when one considers the methodologies that distinguish different disciplines. It is not surprising, therefore, that some debates turn on the application of a method that is central to one discipline but inimical to another. Indeed, debates about methodology are often as critical to the development of the field as ones about theoretical principles.

In this regard, empirical researchers employ a wide variety of tasks and measures. These include a considerable range of memorial tasks (free recall, cue recall, recognition); reading times for words, sentences, and other linguistic units; timed judgments about text-related concepts, including naming, lexical decision, speeded recognition, and verification; and the prompting of participants to provide speak-aloud protocols or to answer open-ended questions during reading. Different theoretical conclusions are sometimes suggested by online measures (e.g., priming, sentence reading times, eye tracking) versus post-reading measures (recognition, verification, and memory recall tasks).

This diversity of methods sometimes gives rise to ostensibly contradictory results. A good example is the length of the texts used for experiments in inference research. Text length is directly related to the number and type of inferences that the reader can generate. Thus, if elaborative inferences are to be studied, longer sections of text must be presented. This might explain, at least in part, why those investigators who prefer working with few sentences and who focus on anaphoric or referential inferences do not usually detect more complex inferences in their experiments.

In spite of this situation, there is a search for integrated and universal methodologies. For example, the three-pronged method proposed by Magliano and Graesser (1991; Graesser & Kreuz, 1993; Graesser & Zwaan, 1995) is designed to provide converging evidence concerning language-processing phenomena. It coordinates (a) readers' verbal protocols about text (e.g., thinking aloud, guided question answering) and (b) timed judgments about the implications of text with (c) theories of discourse processing that generate predictions in this domain. The application of the three-pronged method is arduous but can produce evidence that appreciably illuminates a scientific problem (e.g., Suh & Trabasso, 1993). The rapidly advancing coordination of behavioral and neuroscientific investigations of language processes is similarly likely to produce significant advances in the field (e.g., Ferstl, this volume).

Text Genres: Artificial Versus Natural

Naturalistic discourse typically conveys an informative or interesting message to the comprehender. Experimenter-generated materials, which are sometimes assigned the pejorative label of "textoid," serve to manipulate independent variables, control for extraneous variables, and satisfy counterbalancing constraints. Augmenting experimental control in this manner may sacrifice the information and meaning of the message and prompt the reader to consider superficial features of the text rather than its deeper significance. The study of artificial texts may uncover representations and processing strategies that are unnatural. The problem is the extent to which the results obtained through the study of artificial texts generalize to more natural reading situations and vice versa. Conversely, is it possible for the study of natural texts to offer the degree of control conditions required by a rigorous experiment?

Much of the early research on comprehension focused on narrative texts. Natural narratives, such as folktales, stories, and everyday scripts, are easy to comprehend because their content is similar to the settings, events, and actions that people experience in everyday life (Graesser et al., 1994; Schank, 1999). Furthermore, it was relatively easy to create artificial texts that satisfactorily resembled natural instances of those genres. More recently, however, discourse researchers have carefully scrutinized expository texts, such as scientific articles (Lorch & van den Broek, 1997; Otero, León, & Graesser, 2002). There are a number of reasons for this (Graesser, León, & Otero, 2002). First, individual differences among readers arguably affect expository comprehension more than narrative comprehension. Readers vary dramatically in their knowledge of content areas, their cognitive strategies of coping with difficult and unfamiliar content, their criteria for what it means to comprehend, and their motivation to persevere in mastering the science content. A thorough comprehension of scientific discourse fundamentally requires an excellent domain of highly specialized language, discourse, and world knowledge (Lemke, 1990; McKeown, Beck, Sinatra, & Loxterman, 1992; Means & Voss, 1985). In contrast, there is more uniformity among adult readers when they comprehend narrative text, at least narratives that do not have sophisticated literary forms (Graesser, Kassler, Kreuz, & McLain-Allen, 1998).

A second reason for investigating science texts is that their difficulty level pushes the comprehension skills of the reader to the limit. Third, the content of the material is useful for the reader to master. The content is not arbitrary or trivial, as in the case of many of the narrative text materials that are written by experimental psychologists. Promoting science education fits a mission that is prominent in virtually all countries and cultures. The importance of textbooks as a component of science instruction has also been emphasized by other researchers (Gottfried & Kyle, 1992; Yore, 1991), in spite of the trend to minimize textbooks in some circles in science education. Fourth and last, expository text has a distinctive way of organizing and explaining material (Black, 1985; Miller, 1985). It is frequently assumed that coherence and comprehension are closely related (Leon & Peñalba, 2002). Overall, although not in all circumstances, a coherently organized text facilitates the readers' comprehension and the subsequent task performance. However, sometimes the text per se is not sufficient for communicating about complex mechanical, biological, and physical systems. The text needs to be enriched by adjunct illustrations, diagrams, tables, figures, or photographs. Furthermore, in this electronic age, there are multimedia, hypermedia, simulation, and other computer technologies that are posited to facilitate more active learning and, it is hoped, deeper comprehension. However, there is very little empirical research on the effectiveness of these nontextual technologies, so this is an important direction for future research.

CONCLUSION

Our discussions suggested that the behavioral-empirical approach to higher-level language processes has produced considerable progress over a short period but has simultaneously highlighted debates and controversies that will demand scientific attention during the coming years. They also suggested that advances in the understanding of language processing carry broader implications concerning the principles of cognition. It is at least arguable that regularities of memory distortions were grasped in the field of discourse comprehension (Barclay et al., 1972; Loftus, 1975) long before they were more widely appreciated (Koriat, Goldsmith, & Pansky, 2000). In contrast, it is likely that the general implications of the encoding of situation models, as revealed by language processing studies, *will* be promptly applied to more general issues of cognition. Indeed, Kintsch (1998) proposed that comprehension, scrutinized predominantly in the realm of higher language processes, will likely function as an effective framework for achieving progress concerning many other important issues of cognition.

REFERENCES

Anderson, J. R., & Bower, G. H. (1973). Recognition and retrieval processes in free recall. *Psychological Review, 79,* 97–123.

Barsalou, L. W. (1999). Perceptual symbol systems. *Behavioral and Brain Sciences, 220,* 577–660.

Barton, S. B., & Sanford, A. J. (1993). A case study of anomaly detection: Shallow semantic processing and cohesion establishment. *Memory & Cognition, 21,* 477–487.

Black, J. B. (1985). An exposition on understanding expository text. In B. Britton & J. Black (Eds.), *Understanding expository text* (pp. 249–267). Hillsdale, NJ: Lawrence Erlbaum Associates.

Black, J. B., & Bern, H. (1981). Causal inference and memory for events in narratives. *Journal of Verbal Learning and Verbal Behavior, 20,* 267–275.

Bransford, J. D., Barclay, J. R., & Franks, J. J. (1972). Semantic memory: A constructive versus interpretive approach. *Cognitive Psychology, 3,* 193–209.

Clark, H. H. (1969). Linguistic processes in deductive reasoning. *Psychological Review, 76,* 387–404.

Corbett, A. T., & Dosher, B. A. (1978). Instrument inferences in sentence encoding. *Journal of Verbal Learning and Verbal Behavior, 17,* 479–492.

Fletcher, C. R., & Bloom, C. P. (1988). Causal reasoning in the comprehension of simple narrative texts. *Journal of Memory and Language, 27,* 235–244.

Fodor, J. A. (1983). *The modularity of mind.* Cambridge, MA: MIT Press.

Foltz, P. W. (2003). Quantitative cognitive models of text and discourse processing. In A. C. Graesser, M. A., Gernsbacher, & S. Goldman (Eds.), *Handbook of discourse processes* (pp. 487–523). Mahwah, NJ: Lawrence Erlbaum Associates.

Gernsbacher, M. A. (1990). *Language comprehension as structure building.* Hillsdale, NJ: Lawrence Erlbaum Associates.

Glenberg, A. M. (1997). What memory is for. *Behavioral and Brain Sciences, 20,* 1–55.

Glenberg, A. M., & Robertson, D. A. (2000). Symbol grounding: A comparison of high-dimensional and embodied theories of meaning. *Journal of Memory and Language, 43,* 379–401.

Gottfried, S. S., & Kyle, W. C. (1992). Textbook use and the biology education desired state. *Journal of Research in Science Teaching, 29,* 35–49.

Graesser, A. C., Kassler, M. A., Kreuz, R. J., & Mclain-Allen, B. (1998). Verification of statements about story worlds that deviate from normal conceptions of time: What is true about Einstein's dreams. *Cognitive Psychology, 35,* 246–301.

Graesser, A. C., & Kreuz, R. J. (1993). A theory of inference generation during text comprehension. *Discourse Processes, 16,* 145–160.

Graesser, A. C., León, J. A., & Otero, J. C. (2002). Introduction to the psychology of science text comprehension. In J. C. Otero, J. A. León, & A. C. Graesser (Eds.), *The psychology of science text comprehension* (pp. 1–15). Mahwah, NJ: Lawrence Erlbaum Associates.

Graesser, A. C., Singer, M., & Trabasso, T. (1994). Constructing inferences during narrative text comprehension. *Psychological Review, 101,* 371–395.

Graesser, A. C., & Zwaan, R. A. (1995). Inference generation and the construction of situation models. In C. Weaver, S. Mannes, & C. R. Fletcher (Eds.), *Discourse comprehension: Strategies and processes revisited. Essays in honor of Walter Kintsch* (pp. 117–139). Hillsdale, NJ: Lawrence Erlbaum Associates.

Guéraud, S., I., & O'Brien, E. J. (2005). Components of comprehension: A convergence between memory-based processes and explanation-based processes. [Special issue]. *Discourse Processes, 39* (2&3).

Haberlandt, K. F., & Graesser, A. C. (1985). Component processes in text comprehension and some of their interactions. *Journal of Experimental Psychology: General, 114,* 357–374.

Haviland, S. E., & Clark, H. H. (1974). What's new? Acquiring new information as a process in comprehension. *Journal of Verbal Learning and Verbal Behavior, 13,* 512–521.

Johnson, M. K., Bransford, J. D., & Solomon, S. K. (1973). Memory for tacit implications of sentences. *Journal of Experimental Psychology, 98,* 203–205.

Johnson-Laird, P. N. (1983). A computational analysis of consciousness. *Cognition and Brain Theory, 6,* 499–508.

Keenan, J. M., Baillet, S. D., & Brown, P. (1984). The effects of causal cohesion on comprehension and memory. *Journal of Verbal Learning and Verbal Behavior, 23,* 115–126.

Kintsch, W. (1972). Notes on structure of semantic memory. In E. Tulving & W. Donaldson (Eds.), *Organization of memory*. New York: Academic Press.

Kintsch, W. (1988). The role of knowledge in discourse comprehension: A construction-integration model. *Psychological Review, 95,* 163–182.

Kintsch, W. (1998). *Comprehension*. New York: Cambridge University Press.

Kintsch, W., & Keenan, J. (1973). Reading rate and retention as a function of the number of propositions in the base structure of sentences. *Cognitive Psychology, 5,* 257–274.

Kintsch, W., Kozminsky, E., Streby, W. J., McKoon, G., & Keenan, J. M. (1975). Comprehension and recall of text as a function of context variable. *Journal of Verbal Learning and Verbal Behavior, 14,* 158–169.

Kintsch, W., & van Dijk, T. A. (1978). Toward a model of text comprehension and production. *Psychological Review, 85*, 363–394.

Koriat, A., Goldsmith, M., & Pansky, A. (2000). Toward a psychology of memory accuracy. *Annual Review of Psychology, 51*, 481–537.

Lemke, J. L. (1990). *Talking science: Language, learning, and values*. Norwood, NJ: Ablex.

León, J. A., & Peñalba, G. E. (2002). Understanding causality and temporal sequence in scientific discourse. In J. C. Otero, J. A. León, & A. C. Graesser (Eds.), *The psychology of science text comprehension* (pp. 155–178). Mahwah, NJ: Lawrence Erlbaum Associates.

Loftus, E. F. (1975). Leading questions and the eyewitness report. *Cognitive Psychology, 7*, 560–572.

Long, D. L., Seely, M. R., & Oppy, B. J. (1996). The availability of causal information during reading. *Discourse Processes, 22*, 145–170.

Lorch, R. F., & van den Broek, P. (1997). Understanding reading comprehension: Current and future contributions of cognitive science. *Contemporary Educational Psychology, 22*, 213–246.

Lucas, M. M., Tanenhaus, M. K., & Carlson, G. N. (1990). Levels of representation in the interpretation of anaphoric reference and instrument inference. *Memory & Cognition, 18*, 611–631.

Madden, C. J., & Zwaan, R. A. (2003). How does verb aspect constrain event representations? *Memory & Cognition, 31*, 663–672.

Magliano, J. P., & Graesser, A. C. (1991). A three-pronged method for studying inference generation in literary texts. *Poetics, 20*, 193–232.

Magliano, J. P., & Schleich, M. C. (2000). Verb aspect and situation models. *Discourse Processes, 29*, 83–112.

McClelland, J. L. (1991). Can connectionist models discover the structure of natural language? In R. Morelli, D. Anselmi, M. Brown, K. Haberlandt, & D. Lloyd (Eds.), *Minds, brains, and computers: Perspectives in cognitive science and artificial intelligence*. Norwood, NJ: Ablex.

McKeown, M. G., Beck, I. L., Sinatra, G. M., & Loxterman, J. A. (1992). The contribution of prior knowledge and coherent text to comprehension. *Reading Research Quarterly, 27*, 78–93.

McKoon, G., & Ratcliff, R. (1980). Priming in item recognition: The organization of propositions in memory for text. *Journal of Verbal Learning and Verbal Behavior, 19*, 369–386.

McKoon, G., & Ratcliff, R. (1986). Inferences about predictable events. *Journal of Experimental Psychology: Learning, Memory, and Cognition, 12*, 82–91.

McKoon, G., & Ratcliff, R. (1988). Contextually relevant aspects of meaning. *Journal of Experimental Psychology: Learning, Memory, and Cognition, 14*, 331–343.

McKoon, G., & Ratcliff, R. (1992). Inference during reading. *Psychological Review, 99*, 440–466.

McKoon, G., & Ratcliff, R. (1998). Memory-based language processing: Psycholinguistic research in the 1990s. *Annual Review of Psychology, 49*, 25–42.

Means, M. L., & Voss, J. (1985). Star Wars: A developmental study of expert-novice knowledge structures. *Journal of Memory and Language, 24*, 746–757.

Miller, J. R. (1985). A knowledge-based model of prose comprehension: Applications to expository texts. In B. K. Britton & J. B. Black (Eds.), *Understanding expository text: A theoretical and practical handbook for analyzing explanatory text* (pp. 199–226). Hillsdale, NJ: Lawrence Erlbaum Associates.

Morrow, D. G., Greenspan, S. L., & Bower, G. H. (1987). Accessibility and situation models in narrative comprehension. *Journal of Memory and Language, 2*, 165–187.

Myers, J. L., Shinjo, M., & Duffy, S. A. (1987). Degree of causal relatedness and memory. *Journal of Verbal Learning and Verbal Behavior, 26*, 453–465.

O'Brien, E. J., & Albrecht, J. E. (1992). Comprehension strategies in the development of a mental model. *Journal of Experimental Psychology: Learning, Memory, and Cognition, 18*, 777–784.

O'Brien, E. J., Shank, D. M., Myers, J. L., & Rayner, K. (1988). Elaborative inferences during reading: Do they occur on-line? *Journal of Experimental Psychology: Learning, Memory, and Cognition, 14*, 410–420.

Otero, J. C., León, J. A., & Graesser, A. C. (Eds.) (2002). *The psychology of science text comprehension*. Mahwah, NJ: Lawrence Erlbaum Associates.

Potts, G. R. (1972). Information-processing strategies used in the encoding of linear orders. *Journal of Verbal Learning and Verbal Behavior, 11*, 727–740.

Potts, G. R., Keenan, J. M., & Golding, J. M. (1988). Assessing the occurrence of elaborative inferences: Lexical decision versus naming. *Journal of Memory and Language, 27*, 399–415.

Radvansky, G. A., & Copeland, D. E. (2000). Functionality and spatial relations in memory and language. *Memory & Cognition, 28*, 987–992.

Ratcliff, R., & McKoon, G. (1978). Priming in item recognition. *Journal of Verbal Learning and Verbal Behavior, 17*, 403–417.

Reder, L. M. (1982). Plausibility judgments versus fact retrieval: Alternative strategies for sentence verification. *Psychological Review, 89*, 250–280.

Rinck, M., Hahnel, A., & Becker, G. (2001). Using temporal information to construct, update, and retrieval situation models of narratives. *Journal of Experimental Psychology: Learning, Memory, and Cognition, 27*, 67–80.

Rinck, M., Hahnel, A., Bower, G. H., & Glowalla, U. (1997). The metrics of spatial situation models. *Journal of Experimental Psychology: Learning, Memory, and Cognition, 23*, 622–637.

Roediger, H. L. (1990). Implicit memory: Retention without remembering. *American Psychologist, 45*, 1043–1056.

Sachs, J. D. (1967). Recognition memory for syntactic and semantic aspects of connected discourse. *Perception and Psychophysics, 2*, 437–442.

Sanford, A. J., & Garrod, S. (1998). The role of scenario mapping in text comprehension. *Discourse Processes, 26*, 159–190.

Schank, R. C. (1972). Conceptual dependency: A theory of natural language understanding. *Cognitive Psychology, 3*, 552–631.

Schank, R. C. (1999). *Dynamic memory revisited*. New York: Cambridge University Press.

Schmalhofer, F., McDaniel, M. A., & Keefe, D. E. (2002). A unified model for predictive and bridging inferences. *Discourse Processes, 33*, 105–132.

Singer, M. (1980). The role of case-filling inferences in the coherence of brief passages. *Discourse Processes, 3*, 185–201.

Singer, M., & Ferreira, F. (1983). Inferring consequences in story comprehension. *Journal of Verbal Learning and Verbal Behavior, 22*, 437–448.

Singer, M., Graesser, A. C., & Trabasso, T. (1994). Minimal or global inference during reading. *Journal of Memory and Language, 33*, 421–441.

Singer, M., & Halldorson, M. (1996). Constructing and validating motive bridging inferences. *Cognitive Psychology, 30*, 1–38.

Stanfield, R. A., & Zwaan, R. A. (2001). The effect of implied orientation derived from verbal context on picture recognition. *Psychological Science, 12*, 153–156.

Suh, S., & Trabasso, T. (1993). Inferences during reading: Converging evidence from discourse analysis, talk-aloud protocols and recognition priming. *Journal of Memory and Language, 32*, 279–300.

Trabasso, T., & Sperry, L. L. (1985). Causal relatedness and importance of story events. *Journal of Memory and Language, 24*, 595–611.

Trabasso, T., & van den Broek, P. (1985). Causal thinking and the representation of narrative events. *Journal of Memory and Language, 24*, 612–630.

Trabasso, T., van den Broek, P., & Suh, S. Y. (1989). Logical necessity and transitivity of causal relations in stories. *Discourse Processes, 12*, 1–25.

van den Broek, P. (1990). Causal inferences and the comprehension of narrative texts. In A. Graesser & G. Bower (Eds.), *The psychology of learning and motivation* (Vol. 25, pp. 175–196). New York: Academic Press.

van den Broek, P., & Lorch, Jr., R. F. (1993). Network representations of causal relations in memory for narrative texts: Evidence from primed recognition. *Discourse Processes, 16*, 75–98.

van Dijk, T. A., & Kintsch, W. (1983). *Strategies of discourse comprehension*. New York: Academic Press.

Weisberg, R. A. (1969). Sentence processing assessed through intrasentence word associations. *Journal of Experimental Psychology, 82*, 332–338.

Wilson, S. G., Rinck, M., McNamara, T. P., Bower, G. H., & Morrow, D. G. (1993). Mental models and narrative comprehension: Some qualifications. *Journal of Memory and Language, 32*, 141–154.

Winograd, T. (1972). *Understanding natural language*. Oxford: Academic Press.

Yore, L. D. (1991). Secondary science teacher's attitudes toward and beliefs about science reading and science textbooks. *Journal of Research in Science Teaching, 28*, 55–72.

Zwaan, R. A., Langston, M. C., & Graesser, A. C. (1995). The construction of situation models in narrative comprehension: An event-indexing model. *Psychological Science, 6*, 292–297.

Zwaan, R. A., & Madden, C. J. (2004). Updating situation models. *Journal of Experimental Psychology: Learning, Memory, and Cognition, 30*, 283–288.

Zwaan, R. A., Madden, C. J., & Stanfield, R. A. (2001). Time in narrative comprehension. In D. H. Schram & G. J. Steen (Eds.), *Psychology and sociology of literature*. Amsterdam: John Benjamins.

Zwaan, R. A., Magliano, J. P., & Graesser, A. C. (1995) Dimensions of situation-model construction in narrative comprehension. *Journal of Experimental Psychology: Learning, Memory, and Cognition, 21*, 386–397.

Zwaan, R. A., & Radvansky, G. A. (1998). Situation models in language comprehension and memory. *Psychological Bulletin, 123*, 162–185.

Zwaan, R. A., Radvansky, G. A., Hilliard, A. E., & Curiel, J. M. (1998). Constructing multidimensional situation models during reading. *Scientific Studies of Reading, 2*, 199–220.

Zwaan, R. A., Stanfield, R. A., & Yaxley, R. H. (2002). Language comprehenders mentally represent the shapes of objects. *Psychological Science, 13*, 168–171.

Zwaan, R. A., & van Oostendorp, H. (1993). Do readers construct spatial representations in naturalistic story comprehension. *Discourse Processes, 16*, 125–143.

3

Why Are Computational Models of Text Comprehension Useful?

Susan R. Goldman
University of Illinois at Chicago

Richard M. Golden
University of Texas at Dallas

Paul van den Broek
University of Minnesota

Text comprehension is a complicated process. Phenomena such as word perception, syntactical analysis, semantic analysis, and inference making are essential components of the text comprehension process. Not surprisingly, most empirical research and theories encompass only a subset of the phenomena and processes that constitute a complete account of text comprehension. Indeed, the component phenomena are themselves quite complicated, and there are multiple competing theoretical accounts of them. Theoretical accounts of text comprehension are further complicated by the need to consider production of text. This is so because a large body of research assesses text comprehension via text that the comprehender produces, usually from memory. In the face of such complexity, many theories of text comprehension focus on a subset of the phenomena and attempt to create psychological process models that can account for behavioral data.

For the purposes of this chapter, the term *model* refers specifically to a representation of the psychological processes that comprise a component or set of components involved in human text comprehension. *Computational models* refer to representations that are expressed in forms that can be run, providing simulated data that can be compared with data obtained from real people. Often computational models contain learning algorithms (e.g., the back-propagation rule) and mathematical formalisms (e.g., global memory-matching; see Gillund & Shiffrin, 1984) that have been found to provide reasonably robust accounts of other learning and memory phenomena. Models of text comprehension, more so than models of simpler psychological phenomena, have benefited from the use of computers to run simulations because of the sheer computational power needed to capture the psychological complexity of text comprehension.

It is important to emphasize that a model is not equivalent to a theory. A *theory* is typically more comprehensive than any specific model and consists of a set of explicit assumptions about mechanisms and parameters, and logical arguments about the relations among them. Theories, especially of text comprehension, often permit the derivation of multiple models that differ in terms of the specific mechanisms and parameter values that they represent. Thus, multiple models might represent acceptable instantiations of the same theory. The process of generating multiple models and testing them is critical to the process of advancing theoretical accounts of text comprehension.

In this chapter we argue that computational models in particular have played an important role in the process of unraveling and understanding the psychological complexity of text comprehension. They have done so for three major reasons. First, the process of transforming verbally described theories of text comprehension (conceptual theories) into computational models of text comprehension promotes the development and evolution of the conceptual theories by showing where the models accord with behavioral data and where they do not. Agreements with behavioral data are evidence supporting the assumptions giving rise to the model, whereas disagreements point out areas where the computational model, the theory, or both need further development. Tests of alternative computational models further expand the usefulness of the enterprise for theory development. Second, computational models can be applied to behavioral data to better understand and test alternative explanatory constructs, especially in cases where patterns of behavioral data are not as expected *a priori.* In such cases, researchers provide post hoc explanations, many of which are quite reasonable. Computational models can provide a way to test or enact such explanations. Because computational models make specific and, sometimes, non-obvious predictions, we can test alternative models against one another, and the results can help us distinguish among competing conceptual theories. Finally, and partly as a result of the first two benefits, computational models promote communication among researchers within and across research areas. They promote consolidation and integration of theories and empirical findings about text comprehension, highlight areas where further theoretical development is needed, and integrate with other areas of research by showing where mechanisms important to text comprehension may also be important in understanding other phenomena. These claims are further developed and illustrated in the remainder of this chapter.

COMPUTATIONAL MODELS STIMULATE THEORY DEVELOPMENT

As discussed earlier, describing the psychological processes involved in text comprehension is complicated because a large number of cognitive systems are involved. Current theories of text comprehension acknowledge this complexity in assumptions about complex interactions among various levels and systems of language (e.g., words, sentences; syntax, semantics), especially in the face of limited attentional and verbal memory capacity resources (e.g., Gernsbacher, 1990; Goldman & Varma, 1995; Graesser, Singer, & Trabasso, 1994; Just & Carpenter, 1992; Kintsch, 1998; McKoon & Ratcliff, 1992; Myers & O'Brien, 1998; van Dijk & Kintsch, 1983; van den Broek, 1990). Advances in text comprehension theory have come about through efforts to translate theoretical formulations that posited such variables in tractable computational models. In showing what could and could not be accounted for, the computational efforts have spurred the evolution of text comprehension theories. We develop this position by first describing the work of Walter Kintsch and colleagues, because they developed a very influential text comprehension theory in which computational modeling has played a major role. We then outline two other computational approaches that evolved from Kintsch's work.

Evolving Theories of Text Comprehension

The roots of a major class of current text comprehension theories can be traced to two seminal publications by Walter Kintsch, *The Representation of Meaning in Memory* (Kintsch, 1974) and a *Psychological Review* paper published in 1978 (Kintsch & van Dijk, 1978). In the former, Kintsch laid the groundwork for psychological theories of text processing and memory by documenting the linguistic and empirical research motivating the assumption that the proposition rather than the word or sentence is the appropriate unit for representing meaning. He showed systematic relations between propositions, reading time, and memory, using mathematical models of memory processes to account for data obtained when people read and recalled or recognized information from texts constructed to have specific characteristics. For example, three- or four-sentence paragraphs were written to contain the same number of words but different numbers of propositions. Propositional characteristics, such as the number of propositions in a sentence, were shown to predict behavioral data to a greater degree than did word characteristics, such as the number of words in a sentence (Kintsch, 1974).

Kintsch and van Dijk (1978) proposed a theory of text processing that worked with propositional representations of the input text. In doing so, they consciously put aside issues of how people processed sentences to derive propositions. Rather, they focused their theory on how propositions from successive sentences in a text were processed to produce connected and hierarchically organized sets of propositions. The 1978 theory was foundational for interactive models of comprehension and learning from text because it laid out a clear representational format for the text input; a processing model; and mechanisms for incorporating prior knowledge, comprehension goals, and strategies. It "located" comprehension in the interaction of the text, the reader, and the task, although at that time attention was primarily focused on the text.

Interactive theories of text comprehension (e.g., Gernsbacher, 1990; Goldman & Varma, 1995; Just & Carpenter, 1992; Kintsch, 1998; Myers & O'Brien, 1998; van Dijk & Kintsch, 1983; van den Broek, 1990) continue to dominate other classes of text comprehension models (e.g., letter-by-letter or word-by-word models such as that proposed by Gough [1972]). An important commonality among interactive models is that the online text comprehension process is assumed to proceed in a series of sequential cycles in which the reader processes a small group of propositions in each cycle, making connections among the new input and propositions from previous cycles. Details of the operation of cyclical processing differ somewhat among models. We use Kintsch and van Dijk's work (Kintsch & van Dijk, 1978) to illustrate the prototype and discuss how it evolved in response to results from both behavioral and computational modeling studies.

In the 1978 Kintsch and van Dijk model, the number of propositions processed on each cycle is a parameter, assumed to be equivalent to the number of chunks that can be held in working memory, typically 7 plus or minus 2. Note that the contents of a chunk are flexible and often vary across researchers and content domains. Connection making is subject to constraints imposed by a limited-capacity verbal working memory, so that not all previously processed propositions are typically available to connect with the new input. The number of propositions that are available from prior processing cycles when the next input is processed is termed the buffer size, represented as a parameter *s*. When new input fails to connect to available prior input, the reader reactivates previously processed propositions and/or makes connecting inferences based on prior knowledge. The results of the processing create an explicit text base representation (the set of propositions that were in the input) and an implicit textbase representation (the explicit textbase plus the propositions added through inference making during processing). The Kintsch and van Dijk (1978) theory posited that people often substitute a single proposition for several propositions, called a macroproprosition, but it was not until 1983 that the assumptions about the rules for generating macropropositions were laid out (van Dijk & Kintsch, 1983).

In the 1978 and 1983 versions of the theory, connection making is a critical process in achieving comprehension because it allows the propositional representation to reflect the semantic coherence across the sentences in the text. Coherence across sequential sentences is precisely what differentiates the processing of text as connected discourse from processing of lists of sentences. Although the 1978 theory discussed the importance of readers' goals and the task in relation to efforts to create coherence, little attention was given to how they might influence cyclical processing and connection making.

The Kintsch and van Dijk (1978) model was the basis for a computational model developed by Miller and Kintsch (1980). The Miller and Kintsch (1980) model consisted of two components: a chunking program and a microstructure coherence program. In limiting their model to these two components, the Miller and Kintsch model focused on the subset of the Kintsch and van Dijk processing theory that was concerned with local (cycle to cycle, proposition to proposition) coherence and strategies for resolving breaks in local coherence.

The *chunking program* operated by reading one word at a time from the text, identifying the proposition or propositions associated with the word, and then deciding whether the current proposition under consideration should be added to the current "chunk of propositions." The minimum number of words per chunk was specified by the *input size parameter I*.

The *microstructure coherence program* operated by processing a chunk of propositions on each processing cycle. One proposition was designated to be the superordinate proposition and was placed at the top of a hierarchical *working memory coherence graph*. The designation of the superordinate proposition had to be done "outside" the computational model by a human modeler and often relied on sophisticated use of that individual's prior knowledge. In the working-memory coherence graph, propositions that were semantically similar to the superordinate proposition were located at levels "higher" in the hierarchy. Semantic similarity was determined by the presence of overlap in the arguments (nouns) in the propositions. The *buffer-size parameter s* determined the number of propositions that were kept active during processing of the next cycle of propositions. When the number of propositions in working memory at the end of a cycle was greater than *s*, priority for being held over was based on the level in the coherence graph hierarchy and recency of processing, a form of the Kintsch and van Dijk (1978) "leading edge" strategy.

In addition to the working-memory coherence graph, a *long-term memory coherence* graph was constructed. It differed from the working memory graph in that all propositions that were processed on any cycle were represented. When a new input could not be connected to a proposition in the working memory graph, a reinstatement search of the long-term memory graph ensued. Propositions that provided links to "dangling" new propositions were incorporated back into the current working-memory coherence graph. Failure of the reinstatement search to provide a linking proposition resulted in a coherence break. Coherence breaks were remedied by making inferences that brought in information from prior knowledge, but this process was not part of the computational model developed by Miller and Kintsch (1980). What was computationally modeled was that when a coherence break occurred, a new working-memory coherence graph was created, with a new superordinate node (determined outside of the computational model). The probability that a proposition would be recalled was computed by the formula $1 - (1 - p)^n$, where n is the number of processing cycles for which a proposition was maintained in the working memory buffer and p is a free parameter that corresponds to the probability that a proposition will be recalled if it was entered in only one ($n \nabla 1$) processing cycle in working memory. Thus, p is a "base" recall probability, and all propositions start out at that level once they are processed in a cycle. With each additional working memory cycle in which a proposition is processed, the likelihood of recall increased.

Miller and Kintsch (1980) evaluated the computational model against data from 120 participants who had each read and recalled 20 paragraph-length texts of varying complexity. They used the computational model to predict the expected recall frequency of particular propositions in each of the 20 texts. They found a positive correlation of .6 between observed and predicted recall frequencies. This correlation was considerably less than Kintsch and van Dijk (1978) and other researchers (e.g., Spilich et al., 1979) had obtained when they constructed working- and long-term memory coherence graphs by hand and tested alternative values of the parameter *s*. Miller and Kintsch (1980) attributed the lower performance of their model to the lack of a component that generated macropropositions and the macrostructure of the text that resulted from application of the hierarchical organization rules that applied to micropropositions. Thus, the apparent limitations of a computational model that did not exploit macropropositions led to further development of this aspect of the text comprehension theory, treated at length in the 1983 book *Strategies of Discourse Comprehension* (van Dijk & Kintsch, 1983).

The text comprehension theory detailed in van Dijk & Kintsch (1983) devoted a large amount of attention to how comprehenders translate lengthy, detailed texts into more summary-like representations that rely on frequent and judicious application of rules for substituting a single macroproposition for groups of micropropositions. They also developed the theory of representations and moved from explicit and implicit textbase to a three-level theory of representation. Specifically, van Dijk and Kintsch (1983) postulated that mental representations of text had multiple layers that captured different aspects of text, including the surface form (the specific words, sentences, layout of the text), the meaning of the text itself (textbase), and the interpretation or model of the world referred to by the text (mental or situation model) (van Dijk & Kintsch, 1983). The textbase captures the referential and intra- and inter-sentential relations among the words in the text. The textbase representation maps most clearly onto the earlier local coherence graph. The situation model reflects the integration of prior knowledge with the information explicitly "in" the text. The claim was that situation model construction increased the likelihood that the information could be used in new situations. There were a number of behavioral demonstrations of the validity of both the layers of representations and the importance of macroproposition and macrostructure creation (e.g., Fletcher, 1994; E. Kintsch, 1990; Kintsch et al., 1993; McNamara, Kintsch, Songer, & Kintsch, 1996; Perrig & Kintsch, 1985; Schmalhofer & Glavanov, 1986). However, efforts to formalize the 1983 version of the theory and develop computational models of it proved elusive, largely because of the importance of strategic and prior knowledge in generating macropropositions and situation models. There seemed no *a priori* computational techniques suitable for modeling the strategic management of prior knowledge.

In the face of the computational intractability of the 1983 text comprehension theory, Kintsch proposed a radically different form of text comprehension theory (Kintsch, 1988) that "managed" prior knowledge through nonstrategic, associative processes. The model, called the Construction-Integration (CI) model (Kintsch, 1988), is another interesting example of how the *failure* to formulate a computational model of the theory provided impetus for the formulation of a radically different theoretical proposal.

Conceptually, CI is a two-phase, constraint-satisfaction process model (Kintsch, 1988, 1998) in which there is no reliance on strategic processing mechanisms and macrostructure construction. Kintsch (1988) described it as a "dumb" model. The *construction* phase is a text-based, bottom-up process that results in an initial and frequently incoherent representation of the concepts and ideas in the text plus those elements of prior knowledge that are activated by the concepts and ideas/propositions from the text. Concepts and propositions are represented by nodes in a semantic-network-like representation. Links among nodes reflect sentence and text-level semantic and logical connections among the nodes. During the *integration* phase, activation is distributed among the nodes and links according to a connectionist algorithm that has the effect of strengthening the nodes that have a lot of connections and are therefore central to the meaning and situation and neglecting those with few connections. Nodes with few connections are often associates to an individual concept but irrelevant to the meaning in the context of the developing network, or are inconsistent with the core meaning. In effect, concepts and ideas that are compatible mutually enhance one another, and ones that are incompatible or irrelevant are "ignored." Thus, during integration relevant knowledge becomes more strongly connected to ideas from the text, and gaps among ideas are filled in with prior knowledge that is activated through associative memory processes that are consistent with contemporary theories of memory storage and retrieval (e.g., Diller, Noble, & Shiffrin, 2001; Gillund & Shiffrin, 1984; Hintzman, 1988; McClelland & Rumelhart, 1985; Murdock, 1982; Raajmakers & Shiffrin, 1981; Shiffrin & Steyvers, 1997).

Computationally, Kintsch (1988, 1998) modeled CI as a connectionist network (e.g., Rumelhart, Hinton, & McClelland, 1986) of nodes and links among them, arrayed as a matrix in which nodes are the row and column headers and nonzero entries in the cells of the matrix indicate a relation or link between the header nodes for that cell. Each node and link has associated with it an initial, numerical *activation* value. The construction phase builds the matrix and fills in the nonzero cell values, resulting in the *coherence* matrix (Kintsch, 1988). The integration phase then takes over and iteratively applies an activation updating rule. Specifically, all nodes are typically initially activated, and then each node updates its activation by computing a weighted sum of the links entering the node and the activation levels of the other nodes in the network attached to the node via those links. All nodes in the network simultaneously update their activation levels, and then the activation levels of all nodes are reduced by a fixed amount to prevent activation levels from growing without bounds. Under general conditions, the activations, when updated in this manner, eventually tend to stop changing (Guha & Rossi, 2001).

When the change in activation levels across the nodes becomes minimal across iterations, the integration phase ends and the resulting activation values of the nodes and links are "saved" in a long-term memory matrix of connection strengths, with the use of a version of the Hebbian learning rule as described by Kintsch (1988). These connection strengths (or equivalently "links") among nodes are additively updated if the link participates in additional processing cycles. Typically, when a sentence is processed, it produces a matrix in which each noun is a concept node, and the verb generates a predicate proposition node that references the concept nodes. Thus the cells in the matrix capture the intersection of the concept nodes with themselves and the intersection of the concept nodes with the predicate proposition (in a drawing of a network, nonzero entries in the cells correspond to links between nodes). Assuming a constant activation parameter, the predicate proposition receives greater initial activation than the concept nodes it relates. When successive sentences in a text are processed, the CI model adopts the assumption of cycles of input in a limited working memory environment that was part of the 1978 and 1983 versions of Kintsch and van Dijk's theory. Across cycles of the construction process, links between predicate propositions are formed if they are present during the same construction cycle and if there is overlap between them. A frequently made assumption is that the nodes most active at the end of a cycle are carried into the next input cycle (Kintsch, 1988, 1998). Although 2 is the number frequently used for this "carryover" parameter, modelers have manipulated this value, sometimes finding better fits of the model for larger values and sometimes not (e.g., Tapiero & Denhière, 1995).

Simulations of behavioral data based on the CI model (Kintsch, 1988, 1998) have resulted in moderate to good correlations between the model's performance and human performance across a range of comprehension and learning tasks (Kintsch, 1998; Kintsch & Greeno, 1985; Singer & Kintsch, 2001; Wolfe & Goldman, 2003), although the predictions have typically been better for memory tasks than for online processing tasks. Furthermore, in the implementation of the CI model, there are—quite understandably—many places where modelers must make decisions about various parameters (e.g., the number of propositions to bring in on a cycle; the number and which propositions to carry over to the next cycle; initial activation values, weighting of different kinds of relationships among nodes; how much and what prior knowledge to include in the construction phase; what the relations are among nodes across textbase and situation model levels of the representation, and so on). As a result, the CI model has prompted the development of a number of additional computational models that bear a family resemblance to CI but which make different assumptions about one or more of the components or parameters of the computational processing model, including the operation of working memory and the carryover parameter (Goldman & Varma, 1995; Goldman, Varma, & Coté, 1996; Langston & Trabasso, 1999; Tapiero & Denhière, 1995), the learning algorithm (Goldman, et al., 1996; van den Broek, Risden, Fletcher, & Thurlow, 1996; van den Broek, Young, Tzeng, & Linderholm, 1998), and the basis of establishing connections among nodes in the coherence matrix (Langston & Trabasso, 1999; van den Broek et al., 1998).

All of these computational modeling efforts have helped define important yet unresolved issues in text comprehension or have presented convincing evidence for the utility of the particular computational model that was tested. In so doing these computational modeling efforts have spurred the development of text comprehension theory. In the present context we highlight two modeling efforts in the CI family. The first, a relatively close relative to CI, is the Capacity-Constrained Construction Integration (3CI) model (Goldman & Varma, 1995; Goldman et al., 1996). It examined an alternative conception of working memory processes but otherwise remained faithful to the assumptions of the CI model. The second case, Landscape theory (van den Broek et al., 1996; van den Broek et al., 1998), is a more distant cousin to CI and makes different assumptions about a number of process mechanisms.

The Capacity-Constrained Construction Integration Model

The 3CI model altered the working memory mechanism of the CI model. Goldman and Varma (1995; Goldman et al., 1996) used the computational architecture of the Just and Carpenter Collaborative Activation-base Production system model (3CAPS) so that they could substitute a dynamic working memory process for the fixed working memory parameter *s* in the CI model. The critical feature of 3CAPS for the Goldman and Varma (1995) 3CI model is the assumption that elements active in working memory compete with one another for activation in a limited or capacity-constrained working memory. Elements gain and lose activation dynamically. Processing in the 3CI model operates on a cycle-to-cycle basis. The more activation an element starts a processing cycle with, the more likely it is to accrue activation on that cycle, as is true in the CI model. Different from the CI model is that there is no forced removal (or decision to "hold over" some propositions and delete others) of specific propositions for processing with the next cycle of input. Rather, as elements decrease in activation, they become less available for connection with other elements, eventually falling to such low levels that they are effectively no longer "present" in working memory. As in the CI model, at the conclusion of each processing cycle, activation levels of elements and links among them are updated in a long-term memory matrix. Strengths in this matrix are the basis for predicting the likelihood of inclusion in recall.

Goldman and Varma (1995) applied the 3CI and the CI model to the same sets of recall data to examine the differences in the predictions made by the alternative models. The behavioral data had been obtained from adults and from children who had read short, informational passages (250–300 word) that had a hierarchical global structure. The 3CI model produced a pattern of activation levels across the passage sentences that mimicked the global structure of the passage, whereas the CI model produced activation patterns that were sensitive only to the local, sentence-to-sentence structure. That is, the 3CI model produced higher activations for topic sentences relative to the detail sentences of each paragraph in the passage, corresponding to the hierarchical content structure of the passage. Recall predictions that were derived from the 3CI model significantly correlated with behavioral recall data from adults. As a group, the adults' recall patterns showed sensitivity to the global structure of the passage in that they recalled main ideas more frequently than they did the details that elaborated them. However, among the children the distinction between main ideas and details was far less obvious. The two models were equally good at predicting the children's data when the students did written recall. When children orally recalled what they had read, CI correlated with recall performance better than 3CI did.

The comparative predictive ability of 3CI versus CI was tested further by examination of the ability of each model to predict recall for informational passages that had content structures that were different from those of the passages examined in the initial comparison (Goldman et al., 1996). Two findings are particularly relevant to the current point. In a detailed analysis of the sentences for which the computational models underpredicted (i.e., the sentence was recalled more frequently than predicted by the computational models), behavioral recall data indicated that these tended to be of two types. First, sentences in which the information was highly familiar to readers, for example, *Dentists have to fix cavities*, were underpredicted by both 3CI and CI. This is understandable because neither model had been implemented with a mechanism for incorporating prior knowledge into the construction process. This underprediction led Goldman and colleagues to argue for the need to include situation-model nodes as well as a principled means of introducing prior knowledge into the construction and integration phases of text processing.

The other kind of sentence that was underpredicted was those that had high overlap with prior sentences and were important to the content structure but which came late in the passage. The underprediction of these turns out to be the result of a property of an evolving network of propositions in which new and old propositions compete for available activation. As the network becomes larger and more stable, it essentially feeds itself, and it is more difficult for a new proposition to accrue sufficient activation to "break into" the network. To deal with this problem, Goldman and colleagues modified the way in which the integration process operated in the 3CI model. They incorporated a "top-end" activation threshold: Once a proposition exceeded this threshold, it no longer competed with other propositions for activation, allowing new input to have a greater chance of accruing activation. This threshold cap embodied the notion that some ideas are so prevalent in a passage that once they reach a certain strength (the threshold), they will be remembered regardless of what else comes in. The top-end threshold essentially substituted a sigmoidal for a linear activation function.

Interestingly, neither CI nor 3CI was able to account for the online processing of the passages. Reading time data were not predicted by the number of cycles needed for the network to settle, a measure derived from the integration phase of the modeling. Thus, the 3CI effort advanced the theory in the area of working memory processes but did not shed light on the predictions of reading time. This should not be surprising, because a large amount of the variance in reading time is predicted by many characteristics of the surface, input text (Haberlandt & Graesser, 1985). Both CI and 3CI operate on propositional input rather than surface text sentences. The lack of prediction of processing time and its relation to characteristics of the surface text of passages underline the importance of developing ways to parse the input language of the text, a significant computational challenge. New theories of parsing and syntactic analysis are emerging, however. Some of these appear promising for use in computational models of text comprehension (e.g., Dennis, 2004; Durbin et al., 2000). For example, Golden and his colleagues (Durbin et al., 2000; Ghiasinejad & Golden, 2002) are developing a computational model for automatically identifying the presence of propositions in free response data. The essential idea of the computational model is that representative free response data are first semantically annotated with the use of a semantic annotation system embodied within a user-friendly software interface. The computational model then learns statistical regularities between subsequences of words in the free response data and the semantic annotations by interacting with an experienced human coder. Specifically, the percentage of times that a word is used to express a particular word-concept, and the percentage of times that one word-concept follows another when expressing a particular proposition is recorded during the learning process. Eventually the system (in relatively constrained task domains) is capable of automatic identification of propositions in free response data.

The Landscape Theory and Computational Model

The second example we elaborate is the Landscape theory, developed by van den Broek and colleagues (van den Broek et al., 1996, 1998). As indicated in a prior section of the chapter, Landscape theory shares features with CI theory but differs in several important ways. First, Landscape theory posits a dynamic and reciprocal interaction between online processes and the gradually emerging offline product of reading. Second, readers' goals and judgments of coherence are integral to the architecture of the Landscape model, and their relation to reading processes is explicit. Third, Landscape theory treats coherence as arising from multiple representational dimensions and their interactions (see also Zwaan, Magliano, & Graesser, 1995) and connects these dimensions to the readers' standards of coherence in that situation. This contrasts with other theories that typically focus on a single dimension of coherence.

The Landscape theory captures both online comprehension processes and memory performance after reading is completed. In this theory reading is conceived as a cyclical process, in which propositions (or other units of text) fluctuate in their activation from one cycle to the next. There are several major sources of activation at each cycle: the current input cycle, the preceding cycle (through carryover), the memory representation of the text as constructed in the preceding processing cycles, and background knowledge. The last two—memory for the text read so far and background knowledge—can be accessed through a spread of activation process (called *cohort activation*) or through strategic (re)instatement. Together with working memory or attentional limitations, these sources result in an *activation vector* that forms the basis for updating the episodic memory representation for the text. In the computational implementation of the Landscape model, at each cycle the representational node strength of a proposition increases as a function of the amount of activation it receives. In addition, a connection is established (or, in the case of an existing connection, strengthened) between co-activated propositions, as a function of the amount of activation each receives. A central component of the computational model is that the activations vectors and the developing memory representation interact dynamically: with each reading cycle the memory representation is updated, and, in turn, the updated memory representation strongly influences subsequent activation vectors. Another central component of Landscape theory is that in each reading situation a reader applies a particular set of *standards of coherence* (van den Broek, Risden, & Husebye-Hartman, 1995; see also Goldman et al., 1996). At each individual reading cycle, these standards determine whether the information activated through cohort activation is adequate to satisfy the reader or whether strategic processes are required. Standards of coherence differ across readers and across reading situations, depending on reading goal, task demands, textual properties, and so on, but in most cases they include at least standards of referential and causal coherence. From a computational standpoint, standards of coherence set a threshold value. If the threshold is met or exceeded, the reader proceeds to the next input cycle; otherwise, processing of the current cycle continues.

To keep track of the many components and their interactions, van den Broek and colleagues implemented the theory in a computational model (van den Broek et al., 1996, 1998; Linderholm, Virtue, van den Broek, & Tzeng, 2004). Tests of the computational model showed that it did a good job predicting behavioral data. The model's predictions for online activations and frequency of offline recall correlated between .55 and .65 with readers' data.

Furthermore, the change in activation vector from one cycle to the next (called the *activation gradient*) predicted reading times for the second cycle. As a final example, the model does a good job postdicting the inconsistency detection data reported by O'Brien and Albrecht (1992) and the effects of reading goal on inference generation reported by van den Broek, Lorch, Linderholm, and Gustafson (2001).

Development of the computational model allowed initial testing of Landscape theory and showed that it captures a wide array of phenomena observed in the reading process and representation construction. Equally important for our current purpose, however, is that the process of creating the computational model led to considerable development of Landscape theory. For example, to implement computationally the notion that the activation vectors result in (or update an existing) memory representation, it was necessary to provide an explicit "mini" theory of exactly *how* such construction/updating occurs. Such a "mini" theory had to address a number of questions in order to specify the precise manner in which co-activation leads to connection construction:

- Is the connection strength that results from an activation vector all or none (i.e., if two propositions are co-activated a connection is forged regardless of their actual activation values), additive (i.e., the connection strength is the sum or each of their activations or if one allows negative activations, the sum of the absolute values of their activations), or multiplicative (i.e., the connections strength is a function of the product of the two activations)?
- Do subsequent co-activations change the strength of an existing connection in a linear or a nonlinear (e.g., asymptotic) fashion?

Findings in prior research in memory and in connectionist models formed the basis for a theoretical component that made the translation from activation vector to memory representation explicit. With regard to the examples above, the mini-theory assumes that the change in connection strength is a multiplicative function and that updating follows an asymptotic curve.

A second contribution to the development of theory concerns the fact that both the episodic memory representation and semantic background knowledge are presumed to be accessed via cohort activation. When it came to deciding on parameters to describe such spread of activation, a choice had to be made whether the parameter settings would be identical for the sources of activation. By allowing the parameters to differ, it is possible to consider differential "weights" for the two sources. Thus, the translation of the Landscape theory into a computational model stimulated the development of further theoretical notions as well as the precise specification of the existing theory.

Summary

The evolution of Kintsch's comprehension theory, along with examples of additional computational models of text comprehension, has been used to illustrate ways in which building computational models from theoretical formulations of text comprehension has resulted in advances in text comprehension theory. In the process we have reported some of the behavioral data that modelers have attempted to explain. Computational models are often used to help formalize relationships in behavior data. In the process they are sometimes able to help make sense of both expected and unexpected patterns in behavioral data.

COMPUTATIONAL MODELS ASSIST IN MAKING SENSE OF SURPRISING BEHAVIORAL DATA

In addition to providing impetus for the development of theory, computational modeling can help provide and/or test post hoc explanations of behavioral data whose patterns differ from *a priori* predictions, are surprising, or seem contradictory. For example, the features of the computational Landscape model led to unexpected—and theoretically important—predictions. For example, with the addition of input cycles that were "empty" (i.e., zero-vector that did not contain activation for any propositions), the patterns of activation in the final activation vector and the connection matrix that constitutes the final memory representation were altered in structural ways. By comparing the two sets of predictions (before and after the empty cycles) with human data, van den Broek and colleagues noticed that the first set (before empty cycles) predicted immediate recall well but was much poorer at predicting delayed recall; the pattern for the second set (after empty cycles were added) was the reverse: there were much better predictions for delayed than for immediate recall. These observations suggested that a major difference between immediate and delayed recall consists of a period of no new activation and thereby of additional weeding out of transient activations from the activation vectors as well as memory representation. In addition, they suggested that immediate recall is a function of both the memory representation and the activation vector for the final reading cycle, whereas delayed recall is determined just by the (now further updated) memory representation. These findings and speculations allowed the two types of memory to be included in a single architecture.

A second example involving the Landscape model pertains to the adoption, described above, of an asymptotic learning curve. In the architecture of the Landscape model the asymptotic learning curve resulted in the prediction that the memory representation connection from proposition A to proposition B might differ in strength from proposition B to proposition A. In other words, the connections between propositions were predicted to be *asymmet-*

ric. Although this predictive effect was unintended, similar effects have been extensively documented in the research literature on semantic memory and, on occasion, in the literature on discourse processing (Lutz & Radvansky, 1997; Trabasso, Secco, & van den Broek, 1984).

Applications of Computational Modeling to Inferences. Inference making is one area of text-processing research that has generated conflicting theories, models, behavioral data, and attendant controversy (cf. Graesser et al., 1994; McKoon & Ratcliff, 1992, 1995). Computational modeling of various inference tasks and behavioral data is leading to better understanding of some of the issues. In this section we discuss two of these applications, one dealing with the time course of recognition and retrieval memory for inferences as compared with explicitly presented text (Singer & Kintsch, 2001) and the other dealing with different types of inferences (Schmalhofer, McDaniel, & Keefe, 2002).

Recognition and Retrieval of Inferences. Singer and Kintsch (2001) combined the C-I framework with the Gillund and Shiffrin global memory-matching model (Gillund & Shiffrin, 1984) in an effort to account for a complex pattern in inference memory data collected by Zimny (1987; also reported in Kintsch, Welsch, Schmalhofer, & Zimny, 1990). Zimny tested memory for probe words at three delays, using a recognition memory task and a sentence verification task. Probe words were related to explicit, paraphrased, or inferred text information or were related to distractors. Of particular interest here are the different patterns that Zimny (1987) reported in the two tasks. In both tasks and across the three delay conditions, probes related to explicit information were always recognized the best and at high levels (70–80% in recognition; 85–95% in verification). However, the pattern for inferences was different, depending on the task. In the recognition task, memory for probe words related to inferences grew stronger over time: At immediate test, only 20% of the participants said the probe word had been presented (a false recognition), whereas at the long delay almost 60% said it had been presented. In contrast, in the sentence verification task, participants verified that probe words related to inferences had occurred in the text as often as they said that probes related to explicit information had been presented in the text. In other words, in the sentence verification task, memory for inference-related words was as strong as memory for explicit information at each delay, whereas on the recognition task, memory for inference-related words became stronger over time.

Singer and Kintsch (2001; also see Kintsch et al., 1990) found that they could account for this complex pattern of results by using a version of the CI model to characterize the dynamical changes to the reader's working memory connection matrix by specifying how sentence nodes, proposition nodes, and macrostructure proposition nodes are interconnected. Singer and Kintsch (2001) then used a modified version of the Gillund and Shiffrin (1984) theory of recognition memory to make predictions regarding performance on sentence recognition memory and sentence verification tasks. Specifically, they calculated the familiarity of a probe based on its connection strength over the whole coherence matrix, consistent with the global memory-match retrieval mechanism of Gillund and Shiffrin (1984). Furthermore, familiarity calculations were done with the Gillund and Shiffrin (1984) multiplicative combining rule rather than a linear one. Finally, they used response decision rules from signal detection theory and determined different response thresholds for recognition memory and sentence verification tasks. This three-part process produced simulation data that were consistent with the previously obtained behavioral data. Singer and Kintsch (2001) noted that the three parts of the simulation needed to operate together to produce the particular observed qualitative (and quantitative) pattern of predictions. Each was necessary but not sufficient; all three were essential for the model to make the correct qualitative pattern of predictions. Space does not permit us to treat this model in all of its complexity and detail; the interested reader is referred to Singer and Kintsch (2001) for a full explication of the derivation and arguments for it.

Simulating Bridging and Predictive Inferences. Schmalhofer et al. (2002) pointed out that there are a number of explanations and theories about when and why different kinds of inferences are made. For example, they indicate that inferences that fill in gaps among bits of information that have already been processed (backward or bridging inferences) are made with high probability. In contrast, inferences that predict what will happen next (forward inferences) are made with much less frequency. Their goal was to use the CI model to provide a unifying account of both kinds of inferences. Using materials that Keefe and McDaniel (1993) used to examine bridging and forward inferences, Schmalhofer et al. (2002) constructed connectivity matrices for three levels of representation (surface text, propositional, and situational) as well as the connectivity between levels. Thus, concepts explicitly presented in the text would have multiple levels at which to accrue activation, whereas nodes generated from prior knowledge would be represented at the situation level and perhaps at the propositional level. Key to understanding their argument is that nodes accrue activation on the basis of within- and between-level connectivity. As processing proceeds, new input provides reason to continue to activate specific nodes at all levels; if there is not input that connects to an activated node on a particular cycle, it will lose activation and be less likely to show priming effects.

Connectivity is the unifying principle in the Schmalhofer account. Nodes that are more highly connected to other nodes, especially if this is sustained over multiple processing cycles, would show an increased likelihood of a priming effect, regardless of whether the node represents a bridging or predictive inference. CI simulations based on the derivation of the connectivity matrices, paying close attention to within- and across-level connectivity, yielded both qualitative and quantitative predictions that were consistent with the data of Keefe and McDaniel (1993). Schmalhofer and colleagues were thus able to account for the time course of activation of predictive and bridging inferences.

The use of computational models to account for patterns of behavioral data, expected as well as unexpected, helps to integrate and unify empirical findings and support theory development. In developing these models, researchers are forced to be quite explicit regarding the mechanisms, processes, and relations among them. This characteristic of computational models enables better communication.

COMPUTATIONAL MODELS SUPPORT COMMUNICATION

The precise specification required to enact computational models facilitates communication among researchers working in similar areas as well as those working in seemingly unrelated areas. First, we discuss the issue of automated coding of free response data. Second, we discuss how computational models are useful for integrating comprehension and memory, areas that are typically seen as quite related. Our final example illustrates the communication role of computational models through the use of a text comprehension model to account for decision-making data.

Reliable and Documented Coding of Free Response Data

A typical procedure for coding protocol data involves having two experienced human coders work together in the analysis of a portion of the protocol data. Critical propositions and methodologies for identifying such propositions in an objective manner where possible are then developed by the coders. The remaining portion of the protocol data is then coded independently by the two coders for the purposes of computing a measure of intercoder reliability. Typically, in text comprehension research, agreement measures in the 95% range with Cohen Kappa (Cohen, 1960; Carletta, 1966) scores in the 70% range are considered to establish acceptable and reliable coding procedures.

This widely used methodology for coding verbal protocol data, however, suffers from a variety of serious intrinsic problems. First, despite the best of efforts, explicit details governing all aspects of how free response data are mapped into a propositional representation can never be provided by the above procedure. There will always be a subjective component to the above process. Second, even if all details of the coding procedure could be explicitly documented, there is no guarantee that the resulting coding procedure would always be applied in a consistent manner by human coders. Third, efficient unambiguous communication of complex ideas is an essential component of science. Even if all details of the coding process could be explicitly documented and then always consistently implemented without error, the resulting coding process (as typically implemented in the current scientific literature) would probably be highly complex and difficult to efficiently communicate to other scientists. If the efficiency of such communications could be improved, then the measurement of detailed methodological coding issues upon experimental behavioral findings would be facilitated. In addition, replications of experimental findings across research labs could be improved as well. Finally, detailed semantic coding of protocol data tends to be time consuming and effort-intensive. If the costs of data analysis could be reduced, then protocol data could be analyzed more rapidly, which would ultimately increase the overall rate of scientific progress in the area of discourse processes. Ericsson and Simon (1984) provide a further discussion of these issues.

These concerns suggest that an important challenge for text comprehension research in the next century will be to aggressively incorporate tools from artificial intelligence to facilitate the automatic coding (or at least support manual coding) of free response data. Some important steps in this direction have already been taken, but more work needs to be done. Examples of progress in this area include the string theory approach of Dennis (2004; also see Dennis & Kintsch, this volume), the Hidden Markov Model approach of Ghiasinejad and Golden (2002; also see Durbin, Earwood, & Golden, 2000), Latent Semantic Analysis methodologies (Dunn et al., 2002; Foltz et al., 1998; Landauer & Dumais, 1997), and the probabilistic automated semantic role-labeling methodology of Gildea and Jurafsky (2002).

Integrating Text Comprehension and Memory

Earlier in the chapter we discussed examples of the integration of memory models with text comprehension theories and resulting improvements in model fits to behavioral data (e.g., Goldman & Varma, 1995; Singer & Kintsch, 2001; Schmalhofer et al., 2002). Other examples include the work of Fletcher, van den Broek, and Arthur (1996), who used an alternative modification of the Gillund and Shiffrin (1984) model to develop a theory of text recall based upon local coherence strategies. Fletcher et al. (1996) found that the resulting model provided good predictions of what propositions were recalled by participants as well as the order in which the propositions were recalled.

There are also efforts being made to integrate models of prior knowledge with text comprehension. Kintsch (1998) has incorporated Latent Semantic Analysis (LSA; Landauer & Dumais, 1997) as the engine for generating prior knowledge elements during the construction phase of CI. Briefly, LSA is a computational approach to word meaning that is based on co-occurrences of words in printed text from which semantic spaces that reflect meaning relationships among words are derived. In the context of text comprehension, concepts are added to the situation-level representation based on their similarity of meaning with the words in the text. The integration process then operates, and only those nodes that are relevant in the context tend to receive higher activation and become part of the situation-level representation. In a further elaboration of the use of LSA in comprehension, Kintsch (2001) has proposed a predication model that enables computational modeling of metaphor comprehension.

In a somewhat different vein, computational modeling has been useful in efforts to understand the resonance theory account of the "distance effect" (Myers & O'Brien, 1998). O'Brien, Plewes, & Albrecht (1990) identified the distance effect in their research on situations involving two potential referential antecedents for a referent in an incoming target sentence. The referential antecedents were positioned in the text so that they would normally not be strongly activated in working memory when the target sentence was read. Given this situation, O'Brien et al. (1990) found that the referential antecedent that is closest to the target sentence will be more strongly activated in working memory relative to the antecedent that is farthest from the target sentence. Myers and O'Brien (1998) interpreted these results as supporting a resonance memory theory that asserts that information in both working memory and long-term memory is available for reactivation in working memory, given appropriate retrieval cues.

However, based on previously published accounts of the resonance model, Lutz and Radvansky (1997) concluded that the resonance model would always predict a "distance effect" (i.e., increasing the amount of intervening text between a referential or causal antecedent and its target sentence would tend to decrease the activation of the antecedent in working memory when the target sentence is processed). Myers and O'Brien (1998), however, emphasized that in the resonance model the presence or absence of a distance effect is not merely a function of the number of intervening statements between the antecedent, but is also a complex function of the propositional content of the text passage. To illustrate their point, they proposed a two-parameter model that could simultaneously capture the presence of a distance effect for experimental texts from studies in which the behavioral effect was observed, as well as the absence of such a distance effect for texts where no distance effect was observed in the behavioral data (e.g., Lutz & Radvansky, 1997). By expressing their theory as a computational model, Myers and O'Brien (1998) provided a medium for the communication and evaluation of the structural properties and implications of a particular explicit model of reading comprehension processes.

Integrating Text Comprehension Mechanisms with Decision Making

Support for a number of phenomena in social psychology and decision making relies on the use of vignettes or short texts about people and situations in which they find themselves. For example, Kahneman and Tversky (1982) had participants read a story about a Mr. Jones who left his office, did not drive home by his regular route, stopped at a light, and then was killed by a speeding truck at an intersection. According to "norm theory" in the decision-making literature (Kahneman & Miller, 1986), it is easier for decision makers to construct typical alternatives to typical events rather than atypical alternatives to typical events. Thus, norm theory would predict that decision makers (upon encountering this story) have a tendency to focus upon the unusual causal antecedent, inasmuch as the statement of the unusual event tends to evoke normal alternatives. Thus, the unusual antecedent is usually viewed by participants reading the text as the reason for the traffic accident.

Trabasso and Bartolone (2003) provided an explanation for the "unusual antecedent" phenomenon based on text comprehension processes and the use of the resulting representation to make decisions about possible causes of the accident. They used the discourse analysis techniques of Trabasso, Secco, and van den Broek (1984) to create a causal network of clauses and causal links among them. Integration of the network occurs via a connectionist model (Langston & Trabasso, 1999) to produce connection strengths for the various clauses. The connection strengths index accessibility of various clauses as explanations for specific events. Trabasso and Bartolone's (2003) analysis showed that in the story with the unusual route, there were more events explaining why that route had been taken than there were explanatory events for the typical route in the typical-route story. They hypothesized that the explanatory focus on the unusual event might make it more accessible as a cause for the accident. Trabasso and Bartolone (2003) tested this hypothesis by constructing a series of variations of the Mr. Jones text that systematically and independently manipulated the typicality and explanation variables. They constructed the causal networks for each and integrated them, using their connectionist simulation model. The causal network construction showed different patterns of connections for the different versions of the stories and hence differential connection strength and accessibility values resulting from integration, using the Langston and Trabasso model (1999; also see Langston, Trabasso, & Magliano, 1999). Indeed, the connection strengths that resulted from the simulations showed that explanation but not typicality was the essential variable in readers' decisions about what caused the accident.

The discourse analysis and computational modeling conducted by Trabasso and Bartolone (2003) show that causal explanation plays a powerful role in both text comprehension and decision making. Both the detailed analysis of the connections among the events and the computational modeling of those connections in terms of strength and accessibility were necessary to make a forceful and convincing argument regarding the centrality of explanation in both comprehension and decision making.

SUMMARY AND CONCLUSIONS

We have provided three answers to the question *Why are computational models of text comprehension useful?* First, we illustrated the role of computational models in the evolution of theories of text comprehension. Both success and failures of computational models were shown to be informative for theory development. Second, the computational models were shown to be useful for testing explanatory constructs and accounting for unexpected findings. The use of computational models allows for the explication of the mechanisms involved in performing specific text comprehension tasks. Creating models of these mechanisms and tasks that are then successful at replicating qualitative patterns in behavioral data adds plausibility to explanatory constructs and may shed light on unifying constructs. Third, we provided a discussion of the role of computational models in enabling and enhancing communication with and across areas of work in psychology. Although we used different examples to illustrate each of these contributions of computational models, all computational models have the potential for increasing communication, and most contribute, albeit indirectly, to theory development.

Our examples were necessarily limited, drawing on just a subset of the computational models that have contributed to the advancement of text comprehension. The other chapters in this volume bring to the reader cutting-edge work on new and emerging computational approaches that are increasingly multidisciplinary. In a multidisciplinary context precise communication is even more important than among researchers from the same discipline. As researchers in the fields of computer science, neuroscience, and cognitive psychology attempt to reconcile their findings and theories, the communicative value of computational models takes on even greater importance than it has had until now. Specification sufficient for computational modeling will serve to clarify the intentions of the models and make the outcomes and implications easier to evaluate and interpret. With this level of clarity, multidisciplinary discussions can benefit from and build on the cumulative knowledge base resulting from theoretical and empirical advancements in text comprehension research.

REFERENCES

Carletta, J. (1996). Assessing agreement on classification tasks: The kappa statistic. *Computational Linguistics, 22,* 250–254.

Cohen, J. (1960). A coefficient of agreement for nominal scales. *Educational and Psychological Measurements, 20,* 20, 37–46.

Dennis, S. (2004). An unsupervised method for the extraction of propositional information from text. *Proceedings of the National Academy of Sciences, 101,* 5206–5213.

Dennis, S., & Kintsch, W. (2007). The Text Mapping and Inference Rule Generation Problems in Text Comprehension: Evaluating a Memory-Based Account. In

F. Schmalhofer & C. A. Perfetti (Eds.), *Higher Level Language Processes in the Brain: Inference and Comprehension Processes* (pp. 105–132). Mahwah, NJ: LEA.

Diller, D. E., Nobel, P. A., & Shiffrin, R. M. (2001). An ARC-REM model for accuracy and response time in recognition and recall. *Journal of Experimental Psychology: Learning, Memory, and Cognition, 27*, 414–435.

Dunn, J. C., Almeida, O. P., Barclay, L., Waterreus, A., & Flicker, L. (2002). Latent semantic analysis: A new method to measure prose recall. *Journal of Clinical and Experimental Neuropsychology*, 24(1), 26–35.

Durbin, M. A., Earwood, J., & Golden, R. M. (2000). Hidden Markov models for coding story recall data. In *Proceedings of the 22nd Annual Cognitive Science Society Conference* (pp. 113–118). Mahwah, NJ: Lawrence Erlbaum Associates.

Ericsson, K. A., & Simon, H. A. (1984). *Protocol analysis: Verbal reports as data*. Cambridge, MA: MIT Press.

Fletcher, C. R. (1994). Levels of representation in memory for discourse. In M. A. Gernsbacher (Ed), *Handbook of psycholinguistics* (pp. 589–607). San Diego: Academic.

Fletcher, C. R., van den Broek, P., & Arthur, E. J. (1996). A model of narrative comprehension and recall. In B. K. Britton and A. C. Graesser (Eds.), *Models of understanding text* (pp. 141–163). Mahwah, NJ: Lawrence Erlbaum Associates.

Foltz, P. W., Kintsch, W., & Landauer, T. K. (1998). The measurement of textual Coherence with Latent Semantic Analysis. *Discourse Processes, 25*, 285–307.

Gernsbacher, M. A. (1990). *Language comprehension as structure building*. Hillsdale, NJ: Lawrence Erlbaum Associates.

Ghiasinejad, S., & Golden, R. M. (2002, June). *An empirical evaluation of the AUTOCODER system for automatic semantic coding of children summarization data.* Poster presented at the 12th Annual Meeting of the Society for Text and Discourse. Palmer House Hilton, Chicago, IL.

Gildea, D., & Jurafsky, D. (2002). Automatic labeling of semantic roles. *Computational Linguistics, 28*, 245–288.

Gillund, G., & Shiffrin, R. M. (1984). A retrieval model for both recognition and recall. *Psychological Review, 91*, 1–67.

Goldman, S. R., & Varma, S. (1995). CAPping the construction-integration model of discourse comprehension. In C. A. Weaver, S. Mannes, & C. R. Fletcher (Eds.), *Discourse comprehension: Essays in honor of Walter Kintsch* (pp. 337–358). Mahwah, NJ: Lawrence Erlbaum Associates.

Goldman, S. R., Varma, S., & Coté, N. (1996). Extending capacity-constrained construction integration: Toward "smarter" and flexible models of text comprehension. In B. K. Britton & A. C. Graesser (Eds.), *Models of text comprehension* (pp. 73–113). Hillsdale, NJ: Lawrence Erlbaum Associates.

Goldman, S., & Varnhagen, C. (1986). Memory for embedded and sequential story structures. *Journal of Memory and Language, 25*, 401–418.

Gough, P. (1972). One second of reading. In J. F. Kavanaugh & I. G. Mattingly (Eds.), *Language by ear and by eye: The relationships between speech and reading* (pp. 331–358). Cambridge, MA: MIT Press.

Graesser, A. C., Singer, M., & Trabasso, T. (1994). Constructing inferences during narrative text comprehension. *Psychological Review, 95*, 163–182.

Guha, A., & Rossi, J. P. (2001). Convergence of the integration dynamics of the construction-integration model. *Journal of Mathematical Psychology, 45*, 355–369.

Haberlandt, K., & Graesser, A. C. (1985). Component processes in text comprehension and some of their interations. *Journal of Experimental Psychology: General, 114,* 357–374.

Hintzman, D. L. (1988). Judgments of frequency and recognition memory in a multiple-trace memory model. *Psychological Review, 95,* 528–551.

Just, M. A., & Carpenter, P. A. (1992). A capacity theory of comprehension: Individual differences in working memory. *Psychological Review, 99,* 122–149.

Kahneman, D., & Miller, D. T. (1986). Norm theory: Comparing reality to its alternatives. *Psychological Review, 93,* 136–153.

Kahneman, D., & Tversky, A. (1982). The simulation heuristic. In D. Kahneman, P. Slovic, & A. Tversky (Eds.), *Judgment under uncertainty: Heuristics and biases* (pp. 201–208). New York: Cambridge University Press.

Keefe, D. E., & McDaniel, M. A. (1993). The time course and durability of predictive inferences. *Journal of Memory and Language, 32,* 446–463.

Kintsch, E. (1990). Macroprocesses and microprocesses in the development of summarization skill. *Cognition and Instruction, 7,* 161–195.

Kintsch, W. (1974). *The representation of meaning in memory.* Hillsdale, NJ: Lawrence Erlbaum Associates.

Kintsch, W. (1988). The role of knowledge in discourse comprehension: A construction-integration model. *Psychological Review, 95,* 163–182.

Kintsch, W. (1998). The use of knowledge in discourse processing: A construction-integration model. *Psychological Review, 95,* 163–182.

Kintsch, W. (2001). Predication. *Cognitive Science, 25,* 173–202.

Kintsch, W., Britton, B. B., Fletcher, C. R., Kintsch, E., Mannes, S. M., and Nathan, M. J. (1993). A comprehension-based approach to learning and understanding. In D. Medin (Ed.), *The psychology of learning and motivation* (Vol. 30, pp. 165–214). New York: Academic Press.

Kintsch, W., & Greeno, J. (1985). Understanding and solving word arithmetic problems. *Psychological Review, 92,* 109–129.

Kintsch, W., & van Dijk, T. A. (1978). Toward a model of text comprehension and production. *Psychological Review, 85,* 363–394.

Kintsch, W., & Welsch, D. M. (1991). The construction-integration model: A framework for studying memory for text. In. W. Hockley & S. Lewandowsky (Eds.), *Relating theory and data: Essays on human memory in honor of Bennet B. Murdock* (pp. 367–386). Hillsdale, NJ: Lawrence Erlbaum Associates.

Kintsch, W., Welsch, D. M., Schmalhofer, F., & Zimny, S. (1990). Sentence memory: Theoretical analysis. *Journal of Memory and Language, 29,* 133–159.

Landauer, T. K., Dumais, S. T. (1997). A solution to Plato's problem: The Latent Semantic Analysis theory of acquisition, induction and representation of knowledge. *Psychological Review, 104,* 211–240.

Langston, M., & Trabasso, T. (1999). Modeling causal integration and availability of information during comprehension of narrative texts. In H. van Oostendorp & S. R. Goldman (Eds.), *The construction of mental representations during reading* (pp. 29–69). Mahwah, NJ: Lawrence Erlbaum Associates.

Langston, M. C., Trabasso, T., & Magliano, J. P. (1999). Modeling on-line comprehension. In A. Ram and K. Moorman (Eds.), *Understanding language understanding: Computational models of reading* (pp. 181–225). Cambridge, MA: MIT Press.

Linderholm, T., Virtue, S., Tzeng, Y., & van den Broek, P. (2004). Fluctuations in the availability of information during reading: Capturing cognitive processes using the landscape model. *Discourse Processes, 37*(2), 165–186.

Lutz, M. F., & Radvansky, G. A. (1997). The fate of completed goal information in narrative comprehension. *Journal of Memory and Language, 29*, 469–492.

McClelland, J. L., & Rumelhart, D. E. (1985). Distributed memory and the representation of general and specific information. *Journal of Experimental Psychology: General, 114*, 159–188.

McKoon, G., & Ratcliff, R. (1992). Inference during reading. *Psychological Review, 99*, 440–466.

McKoon, G., & Ratcliff, R. (1995). The minimalist hypothesis: Directions for research. In In C. A. Weaver, S. Mannes, & C. R. Fletcher (Eds.), *Discourse comprehension: Essays in honor of Walter Kintsch* (pp. 97–116). Mahwah, NJ: Lawrence Erlbaum Associates.

McNamara, D. S., Kintsch, E., Songer, N. B., & Kintsch, W. (1996). Are good texts always better? Text coherence, background knowledge, and levels of understanding in learning from text. *Cognition and Instruction, 14*, 1–43.

Miller, J. R., & Kintsch, W. (1980). Readability and recall of short prose passages: A theoretical analysis. *Journal of Experimental Psychology: Learning, Memory, and Cognition, 6*, 335–354.

Murdock, B. B. (1982). A theory for the storage and retrieval of item and associative information. *Psychological Review, 89*, 609–626.

Myers, J. L., & O'Brien, E. J. (1998). Accessing the discourse representation during reading. *Discourse Processes, 26*, 131–157.

O'Brien, E. J., & Albrecht, J. E. (1992). Comprehension strategies in the development of a mental model. *Journal of Experimental Psychology: Learning, Memory, and Cognition, 18*, 777–784.

O'Brien, E. J., Plewes, S., & Albrecht, J. E. (1990). Antecedent retrieval processes. *Journal of Experimental Psychology: Learning, Memory, and Cognition, 12*, 346–352.

Perrig, W., & Kintsch, W. (1985). Propositional and situational representations of text. *Journal of Memory and Language, 24*, 503–519.

Raajmakers, J. G. W., & Shiffrin, R. M. (1981). Search of associative memory. *Psychological Review, 88*, 93–134.

Rumelhart, D. E., Hinton, G. E., & McClelland, J. L. (1986). A general framework for parallel distributed processing. In D. E. Rumelhart, J. L. McClelland, & the PDP Research Group (Eds.), *Parallel distributed processing: Explorations in the microstructure of cognition: Vol. 1. Foundations* (pp. 45–76). Cambridge, MA: MIT Press.

Schmalhofer, F., & Glavanov, D. (1986). Three components of understanding a programmer's manual: Verbatim, propositional, and situation representations. *Journal of Memory and Language, 25*, 279–294.

Schmalhofer, F., McDaniel, M. A., & Keefe, D. (2002). A unified model of predictive and bridging inferences. *Discourse Processes, 33*, 105–132.

Shiffrin, R. M., & Steyvers, M. (1997). A model for recognition memory: REM: Retrieving effectively from memory. *Psychonomic Bulletin and Review, 4*(2), 145–166.

Singer, M., & Kintsch, W. (2001). Text retrieval: A theoretical exploration. *Discourse Processes, 31*, 27–59.

Spilich, G. J., Vesonder, G. T., Chiesi, H. L., & Voss, J. F. (1979). Text processing of domain-related information for individuals with high and low domain knowledge. *Journal of Verbal Learning and Verbal Behavior, 18,* 275–290.

Tapiero, I., & Denhière, G. (1995). Simulating recall and recognition by using Kintsch's construction-integration model. In C. A. Weaver, S. Mannes, & C. R. Fletcher (Eds.), *Discourse comprehension: Essays in honor of Walter Kintsch* (pp. 211–232). Mahwah, NJ: Lawrence Erlbaum Associates.

Trabasso, T., & Bartolone, J. (2003). Story understanding and counterfactual reasoning. *Journal of Experimental Psychology: Learning, Memory, and Cognition, 29,* 904–923.

Trabasso, T., Secco, T., & van den Broek, P. (1984). Causal cohesion and story coherence. In H. Mandl, N. L. Stein, & T. Trabasso (Eds.), *Learning and comprehension of text* (pp. 83–111).

van den Broek, P. (1990). The causal inference maker: Towards a process model of inference generation in text comprehension. In D. A. Balota, G. B. d'Arcais, & K. Rayner (Eds.), *Comprehension processes in reading* (pp. 423–445). Hillsdale, NJ: Lawrence Erlbaum Associates.

van den Broek, P., Lorch, R. F., Jr., Linderholm, T., & Gustafson, M. (2001). The effects of readers' goals on inference generation and memory for texts. *Memory and Cognition, 29,* 1081–1087.

van den Broek, P, Risden, K., Fletcher, C. R., & Thurlow, R. (1996). A "landscape" view of reading: Fluctuating patterns of activations and the construction of a stable memory representation. In. B. K. Britton & A. C. Graesser (Eds.), *Models of understanding text* (pp. 165–187). Mahwah, NJ: Lawrence Erlbaum Associates.

van den Broek, P., Risden, K., & Husebye-Hartman, E. (1995). The role of readers' standards for coherence in the generation of inferences during reading. In R. F. Lorch, Jr., & E. J. O'Brien (Eds.), *Sources of coherence in text comprehension* (pp. 353–373). Hillsdale, NJ: Lawrence Erlbaum Associates.

van den Broek, P., Young, M., Tzeng, Y., & Linderholm, T. (1998). The landscape model of reading: Inferences and the on-line construction of a memory representation. In H. van Oostendorp & S. R. Goldman (Eds.), *The construction of mental representations during reading* (pp. 71–98). Mahwah, NJ: Lawrence Erlbaum Associates.

van Dijk, T., & Kintsch, W. (1983). *Strategies of discourse comprehension.* New York: Academic Press.

Vuong, Q. H. (1989). Likelihood ratio tests for model selection and nonnested hypotheses. *Econometrica, 57,* 307–333.

Wolfe, M. B. W., & Goldman, S. R. (2003). Use of latent semantic analysis for predicting psychological phenomena: Two issues and proposed solutions. *Behavior Research Methods, Instruments, & Computers, 35*(1), 22–32.

Zimny, S. T. (1987). *Recognition memory for sentence from a discourse.* Unpublished doctoral dissertation, University of Colorado, Boulder.

Zwaan, R. A., Magliano, J. P., & Graesser, A. C. (1995). Dimensions of situation-model construction in narrative comprehension. *Journal of Experimental Psychology: Learning, Memory, and Cognition, 21,* 386–397.

4

The Functional Neuroanatomy of Text Comprehension: What's the Story So Far?

Evelyn C. Ferstl
University of Leipzig, Germany

In the last decade, positron emission tomography and functional magnetic resonance tomography have evolved into widely used brain-imaging techniques supplementing behavioral methods from traditional experimental psychology. One of the most fundamental higher-level cognitive processes is text comprehension and, more generally, the use of language in a communicative setting. Only recently, however, have there been attempts to apply the conceptual and methodological advances of psychological theories of text comprehension to the design and evaluation of neuroimaging studies of language use. The goal of the present chapter is to provide a summary of findings relevant for the question of how neuroimaging can inform psychological theories of comprehension.

The difference from previous reviews including some of this work (Mar, 2004; Gernsbacher & Kaschak, 2003; Bookheimer, 2002) is that I concentrate on the still limited number of studies relevant for text comprehension theories. Experimental findings on syntactic, lexical, and semantic processes are mentioned only when they add to the understanding of text-level experiments. Studies on language production are not considered. Most importantly, the point of view adopted is that of an experimental psychologist interested in text comprehension, more than that of a neuroscientist interested in language.

In the first part of the introduction, I sketch a text comprehension framework in which to embed the variety of neuroimaging experiments and I summarize the most important research questions from the psycholinguistic literature. These introductory remarks might be superfluous in a book in which each of these issues receives more extensive treatment in other chapters (see also Goldman, Golden, & van den Broek, this volume). However, they provide a common terminology for the subsequent review. The second part has a slight tutorial touch. Without going into too much detail, I summarize neuropsychological theories of text comprehension, outline the applications of neuroimaging, and introduce some methodological considerations. After the review, which forms the core of the chapter, I discuss the findings first in light of neuroanatomical mappings and then return to the psycholinguistic questions posed at the outset.

A FRAMEWORK OF COMPREHENSION

As the general framework, I adopt the psycholinguistic theory of text comprehension put forward by Kintsch and van Dijk (1978; van Dijk & Kintsch, 1983; Kintsch, 1988, 1998). Text comprehension is conceptualized as the cognitive process of mapping the linguistic input onto a mental model of the text contents, called the situation model (Ferstl & Kintsch, 1999; Ferstl, 2001; Gernsbacher, 1990; van Dijk & Kintsch, 1983; Zwaan & Radvansky, 1998). This global representation of "what the text is about" contains an integration of the text information with the reader's or listener's background knowledge. Thus, the situation model goes beyond the explicit information and includes elaborations and interpretations. Pragmatic interpretations and figurative language are special cases of situation model building in this framework. Although these aspects of language interpretation are not comprehensively included in the text comprehension framework, there are attempts, for instance, to account for metaphor comprehension (e.g., Kintsch, 2000).

To be able to develop the situation model, two lower-level representations are required. First, the surface structure encodes the verbatim form of the text information. This representation of the exact wording preserves subtle differences in the syntactic structure or the specific choice of vocabulary. Building a surface structure is a requirement for higher-level memory representations, but the specific component processes (e.g., parsing or lexical access) are not actually part of the text comprehension framework. The second level, the so-called text base, is a semantic representation of the text. In a propositional format, this level represents content units that are independent of the exact wording but still true to the specific information given. The text base is augmented by implicit information necessary for establishing local coherence, that is, for sensibly connecting subsequent sentences to the discourse context.

One account of how the text base is derived is the construction-integration model (Kintsch, 1988). In this model, two basic mechanisms are combined to form a coherent propositional network. In the construction phase, associations to the text propositions are retrieved from the recipient's background knowledge and linked with the text propositions. Second, a constraint-satisfaction process integrates the loosely associated content units and deactivates those that are not contextually appropriate. Thus, the construction phase proposes a large number of possible interpretations and inferences, whereas the integration phase yields a coherent and plausible representation by an inhibitory process.

Importantly, Kintsch (1998) argues for the domain independence of this comprehension model. Although it was developed specifically to describe the process sequence of language understanding in context, its constraint-satisfaction mechanism has also proved useful for modeling conceptual retrieval of categories and scripts and the comprehension of computer programming commands and problem solving processes (Doane, McNamara, Kintsch, Polson, & Clawson, 1992; Kintsch, 1998; Mannes & Kintsch, 1991).

This account has long been the driving force of much of text comprehension research. Although there are many overviews available (Graesser, Millis, & Zwaan, 1997; Gernsbacher, 1994; Graesser, Gernsbacher, & Goldman, 2003; chapters in this volume), it seems useful to once more summarize the most important issues. The first general question concerns the influence of text properties, that is, the interface between word- and sentence-level features and the resulting interpretation. In particular, there is overlap with psycholinguistic parsing theories that are concerned with the issue of how the sequence of incoming words is translated into a correct propositional representation, that is, how phrases are put together (cf. Mitchell, 1994). On the text-base level, lexical and other linguistic features have been shown to influence the coherence of text representations or the marking of macropropositions (e.g., Gernsbacher, 1990).

The second main research question concerns the process of inferencing. It has been a matter of debate which inference types are mandatory and drawn automatically online, during comprehension. In the minimalist approach, only briding inferences required for local coherence between successive utterances and inferences based on immediately available knowledge were considered automatic (McKoon & Ratcliff, 1992). In contrast, the particular importance of causal and goal-related inferences for the comprehension of narrative text has been stressed (Singer, 1994; Singer, Graesser, & Trabasso, 1994; Trabasso & van den Broek, 1985; van den Broek, 1990). Moreover, it has been proposed that text structures might be based on these causal relationships rather than on the propositional coherence of text, as initially proposed by Kintsch and van Dijk (1978).

The third research domain concerns the use of discourse context and background knowledge during comprehension. Although it is clear that without the relevant context comprehension cannot succeed, there is debate about how and when the appropriate knowledge is integrated into the concurrent representation. And how is it decided which knowledge units are contextually appropriate and relevant? A related issue is the way in which different types of external knowledge, for instance, pictorial representations (Gyselinck & Tardiau, 1999), advance organizers, or domain-specific factual knowledge, facilitate text comprehension and subsequent learning (Ferstl, 2001).

Most importantly, the notion of the situation model has received considerable attention. The initially vague formulation of a mental model has been fleshed out with the use of empirical data. For narrative text, Zwaan, Magliano, and Graesser (1995; Zwaan, Langston, & Graesser, 1995) put forward the event-indexing model postulating that comprehenders track information about dimensions such as the temporal sequence, the spatial properties, or the status of the protagonist's goals. Furthermore, considerable effort was spent on characterizing the representational format of the situation model, which is not necessarily verbal or propositional, but can also include nonverbal aspects such as spatial or emotional information. Recently this proposal has been taken further to suggest that comprehension might go directly from the language input to an experientally grounded representation, without the need for an intermediate, propositional text-base representation (cf. Glenberg & Kaschak, 2002; Glenberg, Havas, Becker, & Rinck, 2005). For instance, a phrase such as *the eagle in the sky* immediately primes an image of a flying bird with spread wings. Thus, Zwaan (2004) postulates an immediate link from surface-level comprehension to perceptual representations. A similar approach, abandoning the distinction between a linguistic, literal reading and pragmatic interpretation, has been suggested for the comprehension of figurative language (Gibbs, 1994).

Empirical knowledge of these and many related issues has been accumulated in the last quarter-century, and the experimental paradigms have been fine-tuned to answer ever more specific questions about the comprehension process. Text researchers know how to design stimulus materials controlling for word- and sentence-level features; they utilize subtle timing differences to separate online activation from the final integrated representation, and a variety of distinct tasks are available for assessing specific subprocesses of comprehension. Last but not least, as shown in this volume, computational models have been developed for testing of the resulting theoretical conclusions.

WHAT CAN NEUROSCIENCE CONTRIBUTE?

For a neuroscientist, the answer to the question of what neuroscience can contribute to a theoretical understanding of these issues is self-evident. Neuroimaging provides a window into the brain, and neuropsychological lesion studies help to elucidate the circumstances under which a particular function is lost or impaired. The research endeavor concerns a careful analysis of the functional properties of specific brain regions. An introduction to the different methodologies, their advantages, and restrictions is beyond the scope of this chapter. An excellent introduction is provided by Rugg (1999), who also details the goals and fallacies of neuroscientific methods (see also Cabeza & Kingstone, 2001; Silbersweig & Stern, 2001).

From a cognitive psychology point of view, neuroscientific methods become useful only if they can provide information going beyond the behavioral results. The most important distinction between data such as response times and performance measures on one hand, and results from positron emission tomography (PET), functional magnetic resonance imaging (fMRI), magneto-encephalography (MEG), and evoked brain potentials (ERP) on the other, is the multidimensionality of the latter. In addition to the presence or absence of an effect, we obtain information about the localization, polarity, or time course of reflections of cognitive processes. One of the most convincing examples of how these qualitative differences can be used to dissociate cognitive processes comes from ERP research (see McNamara et al., this volume; Perfetti & Schmalhofer, this volume). In their seminal study on semantic predictability, Kutas and Hillyard (1980) showed that an unexpected word in a sentence context does not elicit the P300 effect (a positive deflection of the EEG signal with a peak at about 300 ms) previously found for so-called oddballs, but a clearly distinct N400 effect (with a negative polarity peaking slightly later). These results were taken as evidence for semantic integration as a language-specific process, and they were subsequently supplemented by the detection of disssociable components elicited by syntactic anomalies (e.g., Osterhout & Holcomb, 1992). Such qualitative dissociations are difficult if not impossible to obtain with the use of behavioral measures alone. In fMRI and PET, the multidimensionality of the spatial information obtained provides similar tools for qualitative rather than quantitative differentiation.

WHAT ARE THE PROBLEMS WITH NEUROIMAGING?

Interestingly, there is still much scepticism concerning neuroimaging methods in the traditional world of experimental psychology. Some of the scepticism stems from the fact that both experimentation and theorizing in cognitive psychology are considered more sophisticated than in neuroimaging. And indeed, because for many topics there is no or very little prior work, it seemed necessary to start with the "big effects"—for an evaluation of the methods' sensitivity. Some studies were and still are deliberately exploratory, using relatively coarse comparisons, and others might not take the requirements for operationalizing a cognitive process too seriously. Even in theoretically based, well-designed studies, empirical restrictions necessitate an adaptation of the experimental paradigms. For instance, because of the lower signal-to-noise ratio a large number of trials are needed, which often prevents researchers from using an acceptable proportion of filler trials. The temporal resolution is in the range of seconds, so that detecting subtle differences due to, let's say, a manipulation of the interstimulus interval seems futile. As a consequence, the psycholinguistic paradigms need to be simplified and methodological compromises are unavoidable. Such a deviation from empirical standards is most dramatically indicated in studies that had to use blocked presentation in which trials of the same condition are bundled one right after another.

The second reason for some behavioral researchers remaining somewhat unsatisfied is the discussions and interpretations of neuroimaging results. Many interpretations seem relatively vague and post hoc—at least when compared with the elaborate weighing of a wealth of behavioral data in light of specific psycholinguistic or cognitive theories. This is due—in part—to the lack of empirical differentiation, and—in part—to the fact that the brain keeps surprising us. Even in studies based on neuropsychological knowledge or prior hypotheses, unpredicted activations might pop up, so that the well-planned line of argumentation needs to be abandoned or extended. And because scanner time is still valuable, it is usually not an option to just test a post hoc explanation by conducting a further, minimally altered neuroimaging experiment.

These criticisms have merit, undoubtedly. Some restrictions, such as the low temporal resolution, will be difficult to tackle (however, see Ruge, Brass, Lohmann, & von Cramon, 2003, for a promising approach). As already apparent in the most recent studies, other drawbacks are not principled at all, but they can and will be overcome when the still very young field develops further. In the meantime, we take a detour into the neuropsychological literature to gather ideas about theoretical proposals on the functional neuranatomy of text comprehension.

NEUROPSYCHOLOGICAL ACCOUNTS OF TEXT COMPREHENSION

In the neuropsychological and neurolinguistic literature, the dominant view is that text comprehension and pragmatics are realized in the right hemisphere (e.g., Bookheimer, 2002). Apparently, this RH hypothesis is supported by a wealth of empirical data (see Brownell & Martino, 1998; Chiarello & Beeman, 1998; McDonald, 1993, 2000; Nicholas & Brookshire, 1995). Patients with RH lesions have been shown to exhibit difficulties with all aspects of higher-level comprehension, including inferencing, the derivation of a story's theme, the revision of erroneous interpretations, the comprehension of metaphors, and many more. However, despite this overwhelming evidence, less attention has been paid to delineating the functional properties of the RH contribution to language (McDonald, 2000). I will briefly summarize four important, disparate, but not necessarily mutually exclusive, theories.

The most general account rests on the fact that RH damage often compromises visuospatial functions and, in particular, the synthesis of visuospatial constructions (Corbalis, 1997). For visual perception, it has been proposed that the left hemisphere processes local features, whereas the right hemisphere integrates global features (cf. Springer & Deutsch, 1997). LH processes are seen as analytic, RH processes as holistic. Consequently, as McDonald (2000) summarizes, the ability to derive mental models should suffer (e.g., Benowitz, Moya, & Levine, 1990). Applied to higher-level language comprehension, the subprocess singled out by this theory is situation model building or, more generally, "language synthesis," as formulated by McDonald (2000). In our terminology then, we would obtain a simple dichotomy between surface structure and text-base representations being built with the use of LH functions, and situation model building being realized by RH functions.

A second, rather general account is resource theory (Navon, 1984). The classic idea of limited cognitive resources has been applied to account for aphasic language deficits (Murray, 1999), but also as an explanation for interhemispheric cross-talk (Weissman & Banich, 2000). Monetta and Joanette (2003) suggested that the right hemisphere comes into play during complex and demanding language tasks (cf. Meyer, Friederici, & von Cramon, 2000; Ferstl & von Cramon, 2001a). Based on the intuition that many text comprehension tasks are more difficult than comprehension on the word or sentence level, this theory accounts for a number of studies on RH language deficits. However, the terms *complex* and *demanding* do not readily map onto the discourse comprehension framework. For instance, setting up a situation model is often less effortful than paying attention to the exact wording. Thus, rather than a differential involvement of the RH on the text level versus the word or sentence level, the resource account predicts a continuous increase of RH involvement with increasing task difficulty.

Through a very different explanation, higher-level language deficits in RH patients have been attributed to underlying problems with social, pragmatic, and affective aspects of communication. This proposal is related to the observation that in some RH patients the perception or evaluation of emotional prosody or facial expressions is impaired (Borod, 1993). In the domain of language processing, Brownell and Martino (1998) point to RH patients' problems with understanding indirect requests, verbal humor, or metaphors. And in fact, in many studies on RH language deficits, the materials do not allow for a separation of these "hot" aspects of communication from the cognitive, or "cold" aspects (Lehmann & Tompkins, 2000). It is important to note that this theory does not make any predictions about the functional realization of the "cold" subprocesses of comprehension outlined above.

The most specific proposal to account for RH language deficits was formulated by Beeman (1993, 1998). Based on the results of patient and priming studies using semifield presentation (reviewed in Chiarello & Beeman, 1998), Beeman (1993) postulated a particular role for the RH during the activation of loosely structured semantic fields. Through the finding of overlapping contents, disparate utterances might be connected—a process accounting for inferencing, but also for the comprehension of metaphors or some nonliteral meanings. This so-called coarse coding hypothesis nicely maps onto the construction-integration model (Kintsch, 1988). Following Beeman (1993), the construction phase, which consists of an unselective, overboarding activation of potentially useful associations, is predicted to require RH contributions, whereas the integration phase should involve left hemispheric inhibition or selection processes.

But is the picture of the RH as the text comprehender so clear-cut? Of course not. The description of language deficits of closed-head injury patients, whose impairment often concerns frontal lobe (FL) functions, overlaps a great deal with that of RH patients. Moreover, in many studies on RH language, some patients' lesions reached into the frontal lobes (McDonald, 1995; cf. Martin & McDonald, 2003), so that no specific attribution of deficits to either brain region ensues. And in fact, when listing cognitive processes required during text comprehension, such as sequencing, structuring, goal-directed reading, inferencing, integration, or monitoring, it can be seen that all of them fall in the category of what neuropsychologists call "executive functions." The view that nonaphasic communication deficits are closely related to executive dysfunction (cf. Novoa & Ardila, 1987) is confirmed by the observation of left frontal contributions to aspects of text comprehension (Channon & Crawford, 2000; Ferstl, Guthke, & von Cramon, 1999, 2002; Kaczmarek, 1984; Novoa & Ardila, 1987; Prigatano, Roueche, & Fordyce, 1986; Sirigu et al., 1998; Zalla, Phipps, & Grafman, 2002). Despite this relation, it is not yet clear whether communication deficits are secondary to basic executive deficits, or whether they make an independent contribution to the syndrome of executive dysfunction (e.g., Ettlin, Beckson, Gaggiotti, Rauchfleisch, & Benson, 2000).

The RH and frontal lobe attributions of discourse comprehension deficits are by no means mutually exclusive. They cover different aspects of the comprehension process, and the neuroanatomical specification is relatively imprecise. Thus, a coexistence of separable processes in different subregions is possible and likely. It also seems that the available psycholinguistic models of text comprehension are more detailed than the corresponding neuropsychological proposals. However, many of the neuroimaging studies on text comprehension refer to one of these theories. Keeping their respective predictions in mind enables a better evaluation of empirical findings.

THE BRAIN PRIMER

For readers not as familiar with concepts from neuroanatomy, it might be useful to take a short detour into the ways of talking about the brain. There are various alternative taxonomies for naming and describing brain regions (see Kolb & Wishaw, 1996, for a good introduction). One possibility is to use the macrostructure of the brain for labeling the relevant locations. Most of these labels refer to the gyrification, that is, the structure of its cortical folding (e.g., fusiform gyrus, central sulcus), whereas others use the location with respect to a landmark (e.g., retrosplenial cortex). An alternative is to use the cytoarchitectonic fields as listed and delineated by Brodmann (1909) based on the postmortem analysis of one brain. Cytoarchitecture describes the distribution of cell types across the six cortical layers, which is related to functional properties. A third, supplementary type of information is the extent within a standard space (Talairach atlas: Talairach & Tournoux, 1988; MNI atlas: Mazziotta et al., 1995). The size of each brain is adjusted to fit into a comparison brain, and the coordinates in the resulting three-dimensional space provide the exact localization of specific regions. This method is very useful because it allows for a direct comparison of results across participants and across laboratories. However, the objectivity comes at the cost of neglecting interindividual anatomical differences. Finally, there are taxonomies based on functional attributions (e.g., secondary auditory cortex, supplementary motor area), historical descriptions (e.g., Wernicke's area, Exner's writing area), or classifications based on theoretical distinctions (e.g., dorsolateral vs. ventrolateral prefrontal cortex). Although these latter classifications are the most tangible ones, it is important to note that there is a lack of agreement with respect to the exact localization and extent of the regions. Furthermore, the labels often go beyond the description and already imply an interpretation that might not always be agreed upon.

As an example, consider the inferior frontal gyrus (IFG; see Fig. 4–1), which is clearly part of the ventrolateral prefrontal cortex. On a macroscopic level, this cortical fold is divided—from anterior to posterior—into the orbital, the triangular, and the opercular parts, roughly corresponding to the cytoarchitectonic Brodmann areas BA 47, BA 45, and BA 44. There is no doubt that in the left hemisphere the IFG is crucial for language comprehension and production, but the label "Broca's area" implies language specificity. Moreover, different researchers disagree about its extent and have thus used this label for any or all of the IFG's parts (Uylings, Malofeeva, Bogolepova, et al., 1999).

For consistency within this review, I focus on a number of cortical regions of interest, most of which are in the frontal or temporal lobes. The regions' labels, the corresponding Brodmann areas, and descriptions of their extent are provided in Figs. 4–1 and 4–2. Where necessary, a further specification within these regions is provided in the text. Activations not overlapping with these regions of interest I describe as needed, but occipital, subcortical, and cerebellar activations are not considered.

THE REVIEW

In the following review, I discuss the growing number of published neuroimaging studies (PET and fMRI) on language comprehension in context. The studies are selected for their specific relevance to text comprehension issues. Studies on the word level are not considered, studies on the sentence level only if they speak to contextual integration or to the interpretation of specific brain regions. The main interest lies in those studies that used text beyond the sentence. To facilitate discussion of the findings, I use the terminology of the text comprehension framework outlined above, aiming for a careful analysis of both materials and tasks.

In neuroimaging studies, a crucial component is the choice of the baseline task. Most experiments are built on a subtraction approach in which the brain

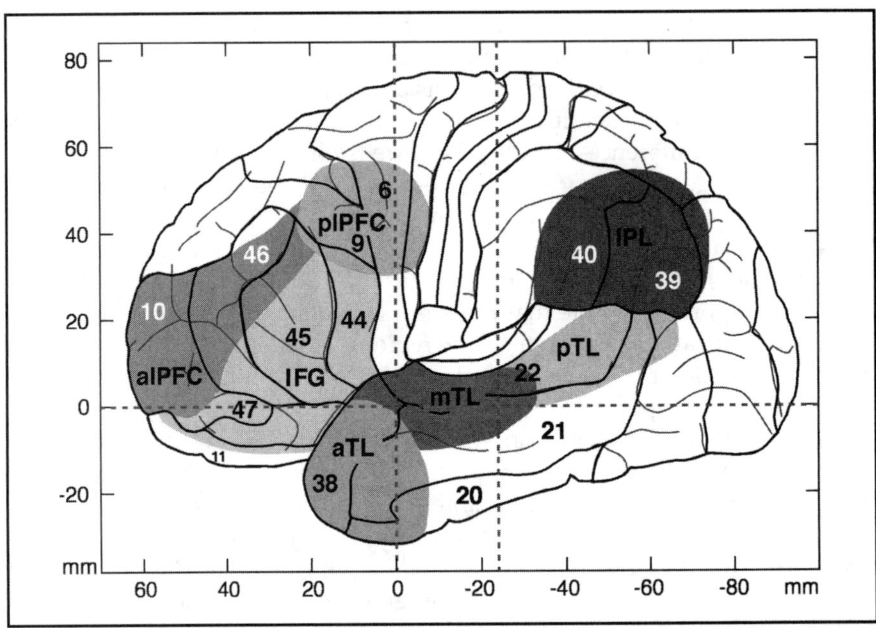

FIGURE 4–1. A view of the medial surface of the brain adopted from Talairach and Tournoux (1988), displaying the regions of interest as considered in the present review. A ruler is shown as well, so that the approximate Talairach coordinates can be determined. In the frontal lobe, we first distinguish the middle and inferior frontal gyri (MFG and IFG). The anterior parts of the MFG (BA 46/10), including polar aspects, are referred to as anterior lateral prefrontal cortex (alPFC). The posterior part of the MFG and its neighboring region around the junction of the inferior frontal sulcus and the precentral sulcus (BA 6/9/44), is labelled posterior lateral prefrontal cortex (plPFC). The third frontal region, the inferior frontal gyrus (IFG), is further subdivided into the opercular part (BA 44), the triangular part (BA 45/47), and the orbital part (BA 47/11). In the temporal lobe, the lateral areas in the superior and middle temporal gyri (STG and MTG) are further subdivided along the anterior-posterior dimension. The most anterior region, including the temporal pole (BA 38/21) is referred to as anterior temporal lobe (aTL). Note that medial aspects, near the amygdala or the hippocampal formation are not included in this region. The middle portions of the superior temporal and middle temporal gyri (STG and MTG) are abbreviated mTL (BA 21/22), and the posterior portion, corresponding to the classical Wernicke's area pTL (BA 21/22). This division does not map onto Brodmann's cytoarchitectonic one. A further distinction of superior and middle temporal regions does not seem necessary, because many activations have their focus in the superior temporal sulcus (STS). Finally, the adjacent region, including the supramarginal and angular gyri (BA 39/40), is labelled inferior parietal lobe (IPL).

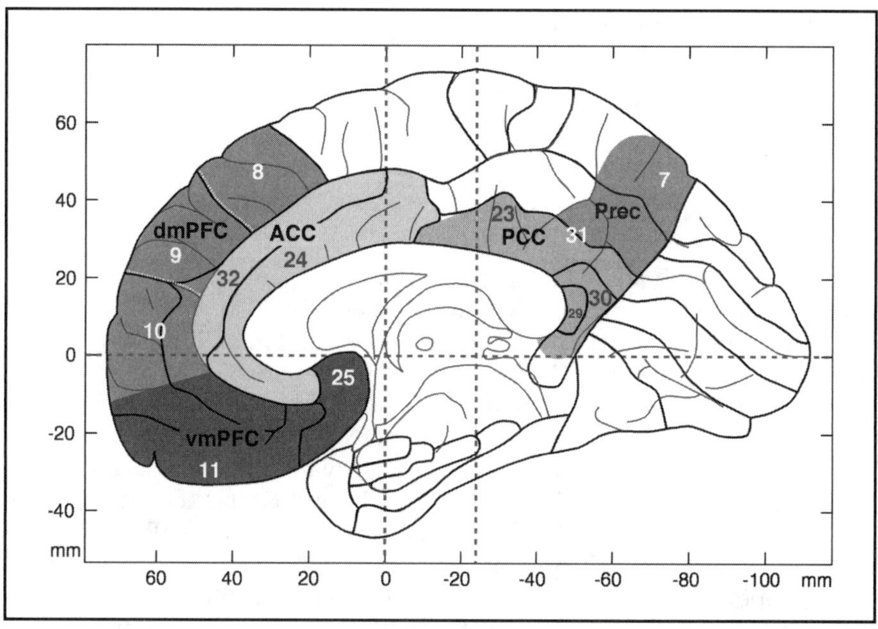

FIGURE 4–2. A view of the medial surface of the brain adopted from Talairach and Tournoux (1988). The numbers refer to the cytoarchitectonic classification of the Brodmann areas (BA). The shading indicates the regions of interest as considered in the present review. The cingulate gyrus extending along the corpus callosum is referred to as anterior cingulate cortex (ACC, BA 24/32) or posterior cingulate cortex (PCC, BA23/31), respectively. The most posterior part (BA 29/30) is also called the retrosplenial cortex. The gyrus extending from the PCC to the edge is the precuneus (BA 31/7). Frontally, we distinguish the dorso-medial and the ventro-medial prefrontal cortices. The vmPFC encompasses BAs 11, 25 and 33, including the subcallosal area. The dmPFC consists of the medial aspects of BAs 8, 9 and 10. This part of the superior frontal gyrus is also referred to as the fronto-medial gyrus. Note once more, that these divisions and labels are arbitrary conventions only. The labels and the definitions of the regions vary across laboratories.

activation elicited by two more or less similar tasks is directly compared. The organization of the review proceeds from relatively coarse comparisons—which are nevertheless informative—to very specific ones. First, I identify regions involved during language comprehension compared with a resting baseline or with a nonlanguage baseline in which perceptual processes are factored out. Second, studies using a language baseline of words or unrelated sentences are considered. These experiments speak to the issue of contextual integration across the sentence boundary and, in particular, inference processes. A further section is concerned with degrees of coherence and the resulting variation in inference demands. The next section reviews studies on how background knowledge and discourse context influence narrative situation model building. A section on pragmatic aspects of language use, in particular the comprehension of metaphors and jokes, concludes the review.

ALL PLAYERS: CONNECTED TEXT AGAINST REST OR A NONLANGUAGE BASELINE

A first step in studying the neuroanatomy of text comprehension is to identify all brain regions involved during reading of or listening to connected text. The seminal study used PET to compare a number of different language conditions (Mazoyer et al., 1993). Employing an anatomically based region-of-interest analysis, the authors reported bilateral superior temporal gyrus activation (mTL), reflecting the auditory perception of the stimuli. In addition, story comprehension elicited bilateral activation in the aTLs, including the temporal poles. Even in these bilateral regions, the activations were clearly left-dominant. The MTG (mTL and/or pTL) and the IFG were only active in the left hemisphere. Most importantly, there was a contribution of the left superior frontal gyrus (BA 8), possibly reaching into dmPFC. No activations were reported however, in other prefrontal regions, in medial parietal regions (PCC/prec) or in temporoparietal regions, such as the supramarginal or angular gyri (IPL) (cf. Tzourio, Crivello, Mellet, Nkanga-Ngila, & Mazoyer, 1998; Papathanassiou et al., 2000, for replications).

Very similar results have been obtained during passive listening tasks (Ozawa et al., 2000; Müller et al., 1997; Humphries, Willard, Buchsbaum, & Hickok, 2001) and with more demanding comprehension tasks (Caplan & Dapretto, 2002; Dapretto & Bookheimer, 1999; Friederici, Rüschemeyer, Hahne, & Fiebach, 2003). Because all of these studies used auditory presentation, the core regions were always the superior temporal lobes. The variations mainly concerned the extent and the lateralization of this activation. In addition, the presence of lateral and medial prefrontal activations is of interest. Left IFG activation, reflecting phonological, syntactic, or semantic processes, was present in most studies. In contrast, an increase in more anterior or more dorsal lateral PFC probably depends on explicit task demands. In particular, the posterior lateral PFC, including an area related to task set management and executive functions (inferior frontal junction area; Derrfuss, Brass, & von Cramon, 2004) and the middle frontal gyrus (alPFC), including areas related to working memory processes and medial or superior frontal activations (dmPFC), have been reported.

With the subtraction of a perceptual baseline, the patterns change surprisingly little. Perani, Dehaene, Grassi, et al. (1996) and Dehaene, Dupoux, Mehler, et al. (1997) compared story comprehension with a foreign language unknown to the participants. There was still superior temporal activation, but it fell now more clearly into the superior temporal sulcus, rather than extending along the superior temporal gyrus. Moreover, the activation split up into a focus in the anterior (aTL) and one in the posterior (pTL) superior temporal sulcus, whereas the mTL area was subtracted out by the perceptual baseline. Crinion, Lambon-Ralph, Warburton, et al. (2003), in a study comparing story comprehension with the same story played backward, recently replicated these results. Activation was restricted to these temporal regions, with the left aTL activation reaching into the inferiormost IFG. Despite their rather conservative analysis criteria, the authors attribute the lack of more dorsal prefrontal activation to the absence of task demands.

To evaluate the modality specificity of this general language network, we now turn to studies using visual presentation. Bavelier et al. (1997) used fMRI to compare reading of sentences with reading of consonant strings. To ensure comprehension, a sentence recognition task followed each imaging run. Extensive frontotemporal activation was reported in the left hemisphere. It is important that the temporal activation extended into the most anterior portion, near the temporal poles (aTL). The superior frontal gyrus (dmPFC) was not considered in the region of interest analysis. In contrast to the findings of Mazoyer et al. (1993), there was additional activation in the prefrontal cortex (alPFC and plPFC). Moreover, the superior temporal activation extended into the supramarginal and angular gyri (IPL). Although these inferior parietal regions are known for their role in reading (see Benson & Ardila, 1996), they are usually not active in studies of single word processing (cf. Turkeltaub, Guinevere, Jones, & Zeffiro, 2002; Chee, O'Craven, Bergida, Rosen, & Savoy, 1999). The prefrontal activations, in contrast, are most likely caused by task-related increases in encoding and working memory demands due to the recognition task. All activations were left-lateralized, except for a small activation in the right middle superior temporal sulcus (mTL).

An interesting analysis of the time course of activation suggests that the extended left-sided network can be separated into functionally distinct subnetworks. In the prefrontal cortex, activation started in IFG regions related to word-level processes and proceeded through the plPFC, an area related to the task management, into the anterior inferior frontal sulcus (alPFC), an area most likely related to working memory processes. Similarly, in the temporal lobe, activation first appeared in the posterior language region (mTL/pTL), then extended along the superior temporal sulcus more anteriorly (aTL) as well as more posteriorly (pTL). The final pattern—possibly related to successful comprehension—involves the temporal pole (aTL) and the supramarginal gyrus (IPL), suggesting that the function of these two regions has to do with the end product of successful comprehension.

Corroborating evidence for this latter interpretation comes from a study on semantic integration within a sentence context. Baumgärtner, Weiller, and Büchel (2002) used a lexical decision task in which a target word was expected, unexpected, or anomalous. In a comparison of the activation of all words to pseudowords, activation was found in left aTL and the supramarginal gyrus

(IPL). Both of these regions showed larger signal change when the resulting interpretation was felicitous, independent of the cloze probability. In contrast, a region in the posterior middle temporal gyrus (pTL) was equally engaged during the processing of all words, suggesting a role for lexical processing.

Once more, other studies confirm this general pattern. Vandenberghe, Nobre, and Price (2002) used a nonword baseline and a less demanding monitoring task and found left temporal activations, and no prefrontal contribution, except for the frontal operculum (IFG/BA 44). In one of our own studies we used short two sentence texts and a baseline consisting of nonwords (Ferstl & von Cramon, 2001a). In addition to bilateral aTL activations and a pTL focus on the left, there was left-dominant but bilateral involvement of the triangular part of the IFG and the plPFC. Similar to the results of Mazoyer et al. (1993), we also found activation in the left dmPFC, now coupled with an activation in PCC. Finally, Robertson et al. (2000) used a baseline made up of nonletter characters. Reading of sentences elicited left-dominant activation along the entire superior temporal sulcus. Comprehension was tested with a sentence recognition task, leading to extensive lateral prefrontal contributions. In addition, Robertson et al. (2000) reported activity in the lingual and fusiform gyri, probably related to the reading process (cf. Chee et al., 1999; Price, Indefrey, & Turennout, 1999).

Summary

From the studies in which the relatively coarse comparison of language processing against rest or a nonlanguage baseline was reported, a very clear picture emerges. The first result is that in the absence of an overt, demanding comprehension task, language processing in context proceeds with surprisingly little brain power. The highly overlearned task of listening to sentences or text requires contributions from left anterior and posterior STS and the opercular and/or triangular parts of the left IFG. There is no doubt that the right hemispheric homologues are also involved, and the aTL is most likely to be activated. Second, when additional task demands are introduced, these core regions are supplemented by any or all of their neighbors. A typical pattern is additional activation in temporoparietal and inferior parietal areas, in the triangular and opercular parts of the IFG, and in the plPFC, near the inferior frontal junction area. Most importantly, some studies also involve dmPFC and PCC. A third finding is that the patterns of activation in sentence processing studies are not in any way different from studies on connected text. We find aTL activations in both (e.g., Vandenberghe et al., 2002; Crinion et al., 2003), and we find the presence or absence of plPFC activations in both. As a quick, preliminary test of the RH hypothesis, finally, we can evaluate whether the lateralization patterns distinguish language processing in context from sentence-level comprehension. This is not the case. In most studies on the sentence level, activation in anterior and midtemporal regions is bilateral (e.g.,

Friederici et al., 2003; Müller et al., 1997; Humphries et al., 2001, Bavelier et al., 1997; Dapretto & Bookheimer, 1999). Conversely, most bilateral activation patterns reported in studies on the text level are clearly left dominant (e.g., Mazoyer et al., 1993; Crinion et al., 2003; Ferstl & von Cramon, 2001a,b).

Before going on to more specific comparisons, it is necessary to mention a slight caveat. The extended, common network described is not in any way specific to contextual language comprehension. Very similar results were reported for semantic decision tasks on the word level (Scott, Leff, & Wise, 2003; Binder, Frost, Hammeke, et al., 1997), involving an internally guided, knowledge-based categorization (*Can this word refer to a person? Is the lion a domestic animal?*). And even during rest, in the absence of any stimulation, a comparable pattern was found when compared with activation during a simple task capturing the participants' attention (Binder, Frost, Hammeke, et al., 1999). Thus, it seems that at least part of the language comprehension network is continually at work, even when there is no external task demand.

THE DISCOURSE CREW: CONNECTED TEXT AGAINST A LANGUAGE BASELINE

In order to narrow down the network to those regions that are specifically important for language comprehension in context, we now turn to studies in which not only the perceptual features of the stimuli, but also word- and/or sentence-level features are factored out. The control task now contains stimuli related to the comprehender's native language, such as pseudowords, jabberwocky sentences, or word lists.

Let's start once more with the seminal study by Mazoyer et al. (1993). In addition to the story and rest conditions, they also presented word lists, syntactic prose (i.e., jabberwocky sentences), and pseudoword sentences. The results show that the superior prefrontal region (BA 8/ dmPFC) was the only area specifically activated in the story condition, whereas the temporal poles (aTL) also appear in both sentence conditions. Word lists without syntactic structure did not engage the aTL regions. The conclusion, consistent with the results of Bavelier et al. (1997), is that the aTLs play a role during the propositionalization, or during the derivation of the text base—a process that even in the pseudoword sentences might be attempted to a limited extent if the syntactic structure is intact.

Bottini et al. (1994), in a study on metaphor comprehension, compared a sentence-based plausibility judgment with a lexical decision task. There was extensive activation predominantly in the left hemisphere, including the entire extent of the superior and middle temporal lobe, the PFC, including the IFG, as well as the more dorsal plPFC region. The aTL and the IFG were also activated in the right hemisphere. In addition, medial activations were seen in the dmPFC as well as the PCC/prec. Despite the use of sentences rather than longer texts, and despite the lexical decision task factoring out perceptual and word-level processes, the plausibility judgment task elicited an extensive network related to language comprehension in context.

The auditory version of our experiment described in the previous section (Ferstl & von Cramon, 2001a) required a pronounceable baseline rather than nonwords. Thus, the language trials were compared with pseudoword sentences, some of which contained function words (jabberwocky sentences). To match the decision components of the task, the baseline condition required participants to indicate whether the two pseudosentences belonged to the same "artificial" language. When the language trials were compared with this baseline containing phonological and syntactic information, there was activation along the left STS, with the anteriormost focus also active in the right hemisphere (Ferstl & von Cramon, 2001b). Furthermore, the temporal activation reached into the temporoparietal junction and the angular gyrus (IPL). In lateral PFC, the activation depended on the specific condition. Most importantly, there was extensive activation in the superior frontal gyrus, reaching into the dmPFC, and an associated region in the PCC/prec.

Thus, both visual and auditory presentation yielded extended networks of frontotemporal regions to be involved during language processing in context. Given the restricted bilateral temporal activations reported in some of the studies with resting baseline, this seems somewhat unexpected. However, as we have seen, a "resting" condition alone might also activate a similar network (Binder et al., 1999), probably caused by self-guided thought. Consequently, the subtraction of a resting baseline, while uncovering regions related to the perceptual subprocesses of reading or listening, might cancel out activity in those brain regions most likely to play a role in integrative text comprehension processes.

THE INFERENCE MACHINE: TEXT VS. UNRELATED SENTENCES

The most basic but specific process of text comprehension is to link successive utterances across the sentence boundary, that is, to establish local coherence. On a more global level, understanding requires setting up a globally coherent representation of the contents. For both of these coherence-building processes, inferences are needed that take into account the prior discourse context as well as the recipient's general world knowledge. To separate coherence building from syntactic, lexical, and semantic processes, I now turn to studies comparing connected text with a baseline of unrelated sentences (cf. Mar, 2004).

Fletcher et al. (1995) conducted a PET experiment to study the functional neuroanatomy of so-called Theory-of-Mind (ToM) processes. Theory of Mind refers to the appreciation of other peoples' motivations, goals, and feelings as a driving force for their behavior (Frith & Frith, 1999, 2003). Using story materials developed for the assessment of ToM abilities (Happé, 1994), Fletcher et al. (1995) compared the reading of stories with or without a ToM component with that of unrelated sentences. The comparison of unrelated sentences with the stories yielded bilateral activation in the middle frontal gyrus (alPFC) and the dorsal precuneus, indicating increased demands on memory and attention (cf. Brass, Zysset, & von Cramon, 2001; Fink et al., 1997). Behavioral data confirmed that encoding for subsequent comprehension questions was more difficult when the sentences were unrelated. In the reverse comparison, stories elicited activation in the aTL bilaterally and the left temporoparietal junction (pTL), as well as an area in the PCC (cf. Ferstl & von Cramon, 2002). Partly consistent with the results of Mazoyer et al. (1993), the dmPFC (BA 8) was also active—but only in those stories that contained a ToM component.

Using the same materials, supplemented by an additional story condition, Vogeley et al. (2001) report very different patterns of activation. In their comparison of stories with unrelated sentences, all significant regions were in the right hemisphere, and they included regions most likely reflecting response requirements (e.g., the motor cortex), rather than parts of the previously identified extended language network. The only result resembling those of Fletcher et al. (1995) was an activation in the dmPFC for three of the four story conditions. However, in addition to being right lateralized, this region was more anterior and ventral (BA 10). Although the former study used PET and the latter fMRI, the use of identical procedures and materials should have led to a closer correspondence of results.

Ferstl and von Cramon (2001a) used event-related fMRI to study inference processes in the context of simple two sentence stories. In the coherent condition, sentence pairs were presented that required a bridging inference that was not directly based on propositional or associative overlap. An example is the sentence pair: *The lights have been on since last night. The car doesn't start.* To control for word- and sentence-level features, they created the incoherent condition by switching context sentences of two trials, but leaving the target sentences identical (e.g., *Sometimes a truck drives by the house. The car doesn't start.*). The participants' task was to judge whether the sentences were related (cf. Ferstl, 2006). In comparison of the coherent with the incoherent trials, activation was found once more in the dmPFC and the PCC. In contrast to Fletcher et al. (1995), the aTLs were not sensitive to coherence, but were equally activated in both conditions. An auditory replication uncovered the same activations (Ferstl & von Cramon, 2001b). When the authors increased the power of the analysis by analyzing the visual and auditory versions together, additional activation appeared in the right mTL and in IPL bilaterally. To exclude the possibility that the frontomedial activation might have been due to concurrent ToM processes (cf. Fletcher et al., 1995), Ferstl and von Cramon (2002; Experiment A) replicated the finding once more. All sentence pairs that mentioned people were excluded, so that the coherence judgment was less likely to be based on a ToM evaluation. Because of the reasoning instruction used for this version of the experiment, left prefrontal (IFG, BA 45/47) and bilateral posterior parietal cortices were now active. Most importantly, the coherent sentence pairs elicited even stronger and more extended activation in both dmPFC and PCC/prec.

THE COHERENCE BUILDER: JUST A MATTER OF DEGREE?

Coherence is never all or none. In everyday language, unrelated sentences are a rare occurrence. A coherence gap is an indication of comprehension difficulties, and readers or listeners intentionally attempt to resolve it. When in an experimental setting participants are explicitly alerted to the fact that incoherent text materials might appear, their inferencing activities might be curtailed. Closer to a natural setting, several studies investigated the degree of coherence, rather than its presence in an all-or-none fashion. In these experiments coherent texts were compared directly with each other, but the closeness or type of the relation was varied.

In a study very similar to that of Ferstl and von Cramon (2001a), Caplan and Dapretto (2001) used spoken dialogues in two conditions. In the reasoning condition, they asked participants to judge the logical validity of question-answer pairs such as: *Do you like having fun? Yes/No, because it makes me happy.* In the topic condition, participants were asked to indicate a switch of topics. A coherent example is *Do you believe in angels? Yes, I have my own special angel.* The incoherent pairs introduced a new topic, such as *Yes, I like to go to camp.* The latter sentence pair thus resembles the incoherent condition of Ferstl and von Cramon (2001a).

The comparison of reasoning blocks with topic maintenance blocks yielded activation in left IFG and left STS (pTL). This pattern might be interpreted as reflecting language processing on the word level, possibly related to the comprehension of the connective *yes* or *no* at the beginning of the target sentences. The reverse comparison, topic maintenance versus reasoning, which in our terminology requires more inferencing and the use of general world knowledge, activated an extended network of frontotemporal regions in both hemispheres, including the right IFG.

Although the tasks and some sentence pairs in Ferstl and von Cramon (2001a) and Caplan and Dapretto (2001) are so similar, a direct comparison of the studies is difficult. Caplan and Dapretto (2001) did not analyze coherent and incoherent (i.e., switch vs. no-switch) trials separately. Moreover, they used the activation from the baseline comparison for masking the specific contrasts. Thus, we cannot evaluate the prediction that coherent and incoherent sentence pairs in the topic switch condition might engage the dmPFC to different degrees.

Robertson et al. (2000) used a surface structure variation to manipulate coherence. *Lexical cohesion* refers to the connection between sentences or utterances that is directly indicated by lexical items, such as pronouns, repetitions, or conjunctions (Halliday & Hasan, 1976). Robertson et al. (2000) took advantage of the observation that definite articles serve as cohesive ties and thus increase the likelihood that comprehenders will set up a coherent situation model. Consider the sentence pair *The child played in the backyard. The mother talked on the telephone.* The reader immediately infers a common scenario in which it is the child's mother who is close by. When the definite articles are replaced by indefinite ones, cohesion suffers and the comprehender is more likely to assume unrelated events. Comprehension was tested in a sentence recognition task, focusing the reader on the surface and text-base levels.

Reading of the less coherent texts with the indefinite article elicited activation in the left ACC and the left IFG (more specifically, the frontal operculum). The reverse comparison, in which a coherent scenario was more likely to be derived, yielded activation in the right IFG (BA 44/6). The authors concluded that the process of mapping during comprehension, that is, setting up a coherent representation of the verbal input (cf. Gernsbacher, 1990), requires the contribution of the right inferior frontal lobe.

The relationship between cohesion and coherence was also investigated in the aforementioned study by Ferstl and von Cramon (2001a). Half of the sentence pairs contained cohesive ties, and half did not. In the coherent trials, the cohesive marker (for instance, a conjunction) aided the judgment by explicitly signaling the connection. In the incoherent trials, the cohesive marker rendered the sentence pairs odd and more difficult—as confirmed by behavioral data. In this latter condition (e.g., *The lights were on since last night. That's why the dishes start to rattle.*), additional activation was seen in the left plPFC. More specifically, we interpreted this activation anteriorly adjacent to the junction of the inferior frontal sulcus and the precentral sulcus to be related to a pragmatic garden-path effect. Based on the findings of similar regions being engaged during dual-task demands, Stroop tasks, or inhibitory tasks (Dove et al., 2001; Zysset, Müller, Lohmann, & von Cramon, 2001; Brass, Zysset, & von Cramon, 2001), we concluded that the activation reflected the difficulty of reconciling the lexical with the pragmatic information. There were no other interactions between cohesion and coherence.

The degree of coherence can also depend on the distance of the resulting inference chain. Mason and Just (2004; see Reichle & Mason, this volume) adopted a paradigm in which, in reference to a given target sentence (e.g., *The next day his body was covered in bruises*), three context sentences were considered (cf. Keenan, Baillet, & Brown, 1984; Myers, Shinjo, & Duffy, 1987). In closely related sentences the causal connection was immediately obvious (e.g., *Joey's brother punched him*); in moderately related ones, the connection required an additional causal step (*Joey's mother got angry at him*); and in distantly related ones (*Joey went to a friend's house*), a number of alternative inferences could be drawn (e.g., Joey was hit, Joey had a car accident on his way, Joey fell off a tree, etc.), but they were not directly implied. Behavioral data show that the reading times increase with causal distance, but that memorability for the generated inference is superior for the moderately related sentences (Myers et al., 1987). The fMRI results were analyzed in very large regions of interest. Mason and Just (2004) found that activation in their prefrontal region (including our alPFC and plPFC) increased slightly but nonsignificantly with a decrease in coherence. Right frontotemporal regions were most active during processing of the moderately related sentences. Thus, the authors concluded that the lateral PFC activation was related to the difficulty or effort of drawing an inference, and that the right hemispheric activation was related to the memory encoding of the resulting bridge. Despite the parallel to the recall data, it might be more parsimonious to attempt an interpretation of this latter result based on the coarse coding hypothesis. A specific function for the right temporal lobe during verbal memory tasks seems unlikely. For a more detailed account of these data, see Reichle and Mason (this volume).

In an inspection of the sentence examples, it can be seen that the distantly related sentences contain cohesive markers. Thus, the finding of increased involvement of the lateral PFC seems consistent with the activation for the cohesive, incoherent condition in our study (Ferstl & von Cramon, 2001a). Moreover, the coherent condition in our study is probably most similar to the moderately related sentence pairs of Mason and Just (2004). Thus, our comparison of coherent with incoherent trials is similar to the comparison of moderately with distantly related sentences used by Mason and Just (2004). Although we did not find RH activation in the original study, there was some evidence for right mTL activation when the data were combined with that of an auditory replication (Ferstl & von Cramon, 2001b). For a more specific comparison of these data, a more fine-grained differentiation within the rather large regions of interest used by Mason and Just (2004) would be desirable.

Unfortunately, medial regions were not included in the region of interest analysis reported by Mason and Just (2004). In order to investigate the specific properties of the coherence-building processes reflected by the dmPFC activation, Siebörger, Ferstl, and von Cramon (2003) instructed participants to initiate an intentional search for coherence, even when an apparently incoherent sentence pair was presented. The hypothesis was that these instructions would induce dmPFC activation independent of the predefined stimulus properties. Using the same materials as Ferstl & von Cramon (2001a,b, 2002; Ferstl, Guthke, and von Cramon, 2002; Ferstl, 2003), we asked the participants to rate on a scale from 1 to 4 how closely related the sentences were. The 25% coherent sentence pairs were mostly categorized as very closely related (Category 1). Confirming that the instructions indeed changed the comprehenders' effort in linking the sentences was the finding that among the 75% incoherent sentence pairs more than 60% were categorized as at least somewhat related (Category 2 or 3). Pretests had shown that the resulting inferences were plausible elaborations. The fMRI results were based on the individual ratings. Thus, as in Mason and Just (2004), three levels of coherence (from 1 to 3) resulted, and they could be compared with an additional incoherent condition. However, in contrast to experimenter defined levels, we used the participants' individual categories. In the fMRI analysis, the direct comparison of trials classified in category 1 with all others, similar to the previous comparison of coherent with incoherent trials, included dmPFC activation. Given the assumption that the inference process leading to a category 2 or 3 rating should have been more extended, this result was suprising. When the time course of the BOLD response was inspected, however, it became apparent that the signal indeed increased in dmPFC in all four conditions. The peak amplitude was comparable, but the delay reflected the rather variable response times. At an early point the signal elicited by the most closely related sentence pairs had increased already, whereas in the other three categories the dmPFC response had not yet unfolded. These results suggest that the dmPFC activation is related to the result of the coherence decision and that it is not stimulus-dependent, but varies with the listener's intentions and goals.

Further evidence for a fronto-medial contribution to inferencing comes from a recent study by Schmalhofer, Raabe, Friese, Pietruska, and Rutschmann (2004) on predictive inferences. They presented passages in which an outcome was explicitly mentioned or highly likely. An example is a scenario on an airplane, in which a glass of wine is being served and then turbulences start. In the explicit condition, it is mentioned that the wine spills, and the paraphrase condition presents a reworded phrase (. . . *emptied the glass*). The inference condition strongly implies the same outcome (. . . *and began shaking badly*). The question of interest was whether fMRI scanning would yield evidence for comprehenders' drawing the predictive inference (cf. Schmalhofer, McDaniel, & Keefe, 2002; Schmalhofer, this volume). During reading of the inference statement, compared with the explicit condition, activation was observed in the dmPFC (BA 9). This result is particularly important because it was obtained during self-guided reading, in the absence of an explicit coherence judgment task. Later, during the verification of the inference statement (wine spilled), additional activation for the inference condition was observed in left IFG, among others. This activation suggests additional effort at test, indicating that the inference was not encoded during reading. The verification of the test item in the paraphrase condition activated the PCC, suggesting an integration with the discourse context. Once more, there was no evidence for right hemisphere contributions.

Summary

The studies on inferencing yielded clear evidence for a contribution of the dmPFC to coherence building (Ferstl & von Cramon, 2001a,b; Fletcher et al., 1995; Schmalhofer et al., 2004), in particular when it was knowledge based and goal directed (Siebörger et al., 2003). However, the exact locations differed (e.g., right BA 10 for Vogeley et al., 2001; left BA 8 for Fletcher et al., 1995), and dmPFC activation did not appear in all studies. In contrast, other studies provided evidence for right lateral frontotemporal activations when the inference demands were higher (Caplan & Dapretto, 2001; Ferstl, 2001b; Mason & Just, 2004; Robertson et al., 2000).

THE SITUATION MODEL: KNOWING AND FEELING

The studies summarized in the previous section were concerned with the influence of levels of coherence on brain activity. However, in all studies except for one (Schmalhofer et al., 2004), the properties of the situation model are also greatly affected by the differences in coherence. In this section, three studies explicitly concerned with situation model building are reviewed. It is important to keep in mind that a convergence of the results with those of the coherence studies in the previous section is expected.

Early convincing demonstrations of the psychological reality of the situation model were the studies by Bransford and colleagues (Bransford & Johnson, 1972; Bransford & Franks, 1972). In these experiments, it was shown that comprehension fails when the reader or listener does not know what the text is about. When either a title or a picture (Dooling & Lachman, 1971) provided the necessary background knowledge, a situation model for the loosely structured and semantically vague texts could be derived. In two imaging studies this paradigm was adopted to test the influence of background knowledge on brain activation during comprehension.

St. George, Kutas, Martinez, and Sereno (1999) used the version in which a title provides the necessary link for hooking up the incoming sentences to the necessary background knowledge. For instance, a description of doing laundry is formulated so vaguely (e.g., *you have to sort everything according to colors*) that the topic is usually not inferrable, and the sentences remain globally incoherent. In a previous ERP study, St. George, Mannes, and Hoffmann (1994) had found reduced N400 amplitudes for content words when the title was provided, a result suggesting facilitated semantic integration during comprehensible passages. In their fMRI study, St. George et al. (1999) used the same materials. An advantage of this paradigm is that the text materials are identical across conditions. Thus, lexical, semantic, and syntactic features are perfectly controlled. The passages were presented visually, and no comprehension task was employed.

The results were analyzed in regions of interest, covering the anterior and middle temporal lobe (aTL and mTL) and the inferiormost IFG. However, the temporal regions of interest were differentiated according to the dorsal-ventral dimension, not according to the anterior-posterior dimension used here. Both conditions elicited frontotemporal activation. In the titled, coherent condition, this network was left-lateralized, whereas in the untitled condition, the pattern of activation was clearly bilateral. Consequently, there were interactions between title condition and hemisphere, in particular in right middle and inferior temporal regions. Because no whole-brain analysis was presented, the exact location of the differences cannot be evaluated. Moreover, there is no information on possible contributions of the dmPFC or lateral prefrontal regions.

The right temporal activation is consistent with the proposal of increased semantic integration demands in the untitled condition (cf. Beeman, 1993). It is important to note, once more, that the data could also be accommodated with a resource explanation. For comprehensible, easy language material, the pattern of activations was clearly left lateralized, whereas increased processing demands in the untitled paragraphs might have led to additional recruitment of the right hemispheric homologues. At first sight, the data seem consistent with the study by Robertson et al. (2000), who also reported that the RH was sensitive to coherence and situation model building. However, the activations in this study were in right lPFC rather than in the temporal lobe, and, most importantly, they were found when comprehension succeeded, that is, during the coherent trials. In contrast, St. George et al. (1999) found the right temporal lobe to be more engaged in the untitled condition, that is, when the situation model was difficult to construct. Because of the region of interest analysis, it cannot be evaluated whether the attempt to do so might have led to increases in executive areas, such as the plPFC.

Maguire, Frith, and Morris (1999) used the picture version of this paradigm to study three different factors influencing the ease of situation model building. Based on Dooling and Lachman (1971), descriptive texts were used that are globally incoherent unless a pictorial depiction of the scene provides the necessary background knowledge. In addition to comparing comprehension of unusual texts with and without a relevant picture, they also compared the unusual texts with so-called standard stories that were easily comprehensible and had a complete story structure. And finally, the authors argued, the comprehenders might devise a situation model of their own even for the unusual texts, so that a comparison between the first and a second presentation of the same story could also shed light on situation model building.

The results identified four brain regions differentially sensitive to comprehensibility and coherence, closely resembling the pattern described by Fletcher et al. (1995). The PCC was most sensitive to successful situation model building: It was more active during the second presentation as compared with the first, it was more active when a picture aided comprehension compared with an incoherent story, and its activation correlated with the comprehensibility ratings given by individual subjects. The second region directly involved in story comprehension was the left aTL. This activation was reported for standard versus unusual stories during the first presentation, in the absence of any relevant pictures. Note, however, that in this contrast, different stories were compared. The left aTL was also involved during the second presentation when a previously incoherent story was made comprehensible by the relevant picture. Left fronto-polar activation (alPFC) was found during the second presentation, and it correlated with recall performance, lending support to its interpretation as being related to memory processes. Finally, activation in a small vmPFC region (BA 11) correlated with comprehensibility and was active in the direct contrast comparing standard stories with nonstandard stories. Although this activation is considerably more ventral than the coherence region found in Ferstl and von Cramon (2001a), it might be consistent with the proposal of dmPFC playing an important role during coherence building (but see the next section for an alternative account).

Although these results replicate and extend those of Fletcher et al. (1995), there is no overlap with the results of St. George et al. (1999). Why is this the case? For successful situation model building it should not play a role in how the relevant background was acquired. In terms of its effect on comprehensibility, there should be no difference between pictorial or verbal presentation. Of course, there are a number of methodological differences. Not only the imaging technique (PET vs. fMRI) and the analysis method (whole brain vs. region of interest), but also the presentation modality (auditory vs. visual), the task (recall vs. passive reading), and the story contents differed. Nevertheless, the divergence of the results is somewhat puzzling.

In both studies, the design necessitated that text materials were included that left the comprehender confused. Thus, comprehensibility had a large effect, as Maguire et al. (1999) confirmed in their correlation analyses. As a more specific test of the text contents on situation model updating, we recently conducted an event-related fMRI study, using coherent, comprehensible stories only (Ferstl, Rinck, & von Cramon, 2005). Two issues were of interest. First, we wanted to identify the linguistic processes needed for detecting and integrating a global inconsistency. And second, based on the event-indexing model (Zwaan, Langston, & Graesser, 1995), we were curious about whether different information aspects would influence this updating process. Taking advantage of the previous research on situation model building using an inconsistency paradigm (Rinck, this volume; Rinck, Hähnel, & Becker, 2001; Rinck & Weber, 2003; Otero & Kintsch, 1992), we selected stories varying emotional and temporal situation model aspects. Emotional inconsistencies were created by contradicting the inferred affective status of the protagonist, and chronological inconsistencies were created by reversing the order of two events. In all cases, the consistent and inconsistent versions differed by one or a few words only.

The results were analyzed in two time windows. First, we evaluated the immediate processing of the target word (inconsistent vs. consistent). Detection of an inconsistent word elicited activation in the right aTL. The left aTL was equally active in the two conditions. The difference between emotional and chronological stories confirmed that the information aspect elicits qualitative differences in processing. Emotional information led to activation in the vmPFC and the extended amygdala complex, a pattern clearly consistent with the interpretation that merely listening to a story with emotional content already involves brain areas directly engaged during emotion processing (Davidson & Irwin, 1999; Luan Phan, Wager, Taylor, & Liberzon, 2002; Kringelbach & Rolls, 2004). In contrast, temporal or chronological information activated an extended frontoparietal network. We interpreted parts of this network as reflecting the reinstatement search needed for reaccessing the relevant context information (Kintsch & van Dijk, 1978; cf. Rinck, Gamez, Diaz, & de Vega, 2003, for converging eye movement data). In addition, there was activation in the right temporoparietal junction, an area implicated for the processing of magnitude, spatial relations, and—most importantly—temporal information (Walsh, 2003). These results clearly confirm that the specific story information leads to qualitatively different patterns of brain activation.

In a more extended window starting at the target word, but also including the remainder of the stories, we found systematic differences related to the type of available integration processes. In the temporal stories, the target sentence needed to be integrated with context information mentioned several sentences earlier. Thus, the processing following the target information engaged the precuneus and—when it was inconsistent—the orbital part of the IFG (BA 47/11), an area implicated for memory-based decisions. In contrast, in the emotional stories the relevant context information had to be integrated across a number of sentences throughout the previous story, and a further inference could possibly reconcile the inconsistency with the previous context. For instance, when the description of a cheerful party is followed by the statement that the host feels sad, comprehenders can easily construct an elaborative explanation for why this might be the case. Consequently, processing of the information following the inconsistent target information was reflected in increased involvement of the left dmPFC.

Summary

The three studies on situation model building once more left the issue of the right hemisphere involvement undecided. Whereas St. George et al. (1999), using a region of interest analysis, reported a lateralization difference for temporal regions, Maguire et al. (1999) found components of the extended language network to be engaged during a similar experiment (vmPFC, aTL, and PCC/prec). In one of our own studies, we seem to have disentangled different subprocesses of situation model building, suggesting that various brain regions are concurrently engaged during situation model building. Although we found right temporal activation for inconsistent information, dmPFC and executive frontotemporal regions were engaged during the updating and integration of the siutation model (Ferstl et al., 2005). This latter study demonstrates that fMRI is sufficiently sensitive for testing rather specific text-linguistic issues. Two distinct situation model aspects elicited qualitatively different patterns of activation—both during detection and integration—although in behavioral studies both types of inconsistencies lead to increases in reading times or question answering times. In particular, the vmPFC activation related to emotional processes clearly shows that story comprehension immediately engages the listener's affective system, a finding lending support to the idea of language comprehension eliciting an immediate immersion in the experiential world (Zwaan, 2004; Glenberg & Kaschak, 2002).

PRAGMATIC LANGUAGE, METAPHORS, AND JOKES

The description of the comprehension process as building a cognitive representation leaves out the important aspect of social and contextual factors. Without pragmatic interpretations of language, however, the richness of communication would be lost. Diplomatic negotiations, the appreciation of literature, or the enjoyment of comedy crucially depends on interpretations beyond the literal meaning of utterances.

It has long been taken for granted that the right hemisphere is responsible for this type of language use (e.g., Brownell & Martino, 1998). And, in fact, many of the studies on inference deficits in RH patients can be accounted for by affective or "hot" components of the language materials (Lehmann & Tompkins, 2000). Except for Ferstl et al. (2005), the imaging studies summarized so far have not separated the hot from the cold aspects of comprehension. When we look at the text materials, however, there are plenty of hints that these latter factors played a role in some of the studies. For example, Tzourio, Nkanga-Ngila, and Mazoyer (1998) mention that their stories were exciting police reports (see Mazoyer et al., 1993; Papathanassiou et al., 2000). The pictures used by Maguire et al. (1999) for rendering unusual stories coherent are pretty funny, and the "topic maintenance" condition employed by Caplan and Dapretto (2002) (*. . . yes, I have my own special angel*) definitely contains a metaphoric or even esoteric element.

Imaging evidence from the two classic PET studies on this issue also points to the role of the right hemisphere for pragmatic language processes. Bottini et al. (1994) used a plausibility judgment task to compare the processing of metaphorical to literal sentences. In the left hemisphere, literal sentences, such as *The hunter used the tiger as a rug*, elicited activation in the superior frontal sulcus (BA 8), lateral prefrontal activation in the middle frontal gyrus (alPFC), and a region in the central cingulate cortex. Because performance on the literal sentence task was better, the left alPFC activation is unlikely to be due to task or memory demands. Consistent with the hypotheses, metaphorical sentences (e.g., *Paul has the sense of a goose*) engaged the right hemisphere more. In particular, activation in the alPFC was consistent with the authors' account of metaphor comprehension applying the coarse coding hypothesis. Connecting *sense* with *goose* requires evaluation of the overlap of distant semantic fields. However, as we have seen, in other studies using the same explanation, the activations were right temporal rather than right prefrontal. A replication of this study with matched difficulty level of the plausibility judgment task could answer the question of whether the right hemisphere played a role in nonliteral interpretation or whether it was involved merely because of increased task demands (cf. Bookheimer, 2002; Monetta & Joanette, 2003).

Recently, Rapp, Leube, Erb, Grodd, and Kircher (2004) attempted this replication. Using event-related fMRI, they sought converging evidence for the finding that the RH is crucial for metaphor comprehension. The materials included correct, plausible sentences only. The participants' task was to judge the sentence's affective valence, which was manipulated independently of the metaphoricity (e.g., *The lover's words are lies,* negative connotation, literal meaning; *the lover's words are harp sounds,* positive connotation, metaphor). In contrast to Bottini et al. (1994), Rapp et al. (2004) found no right hemispheric activation. When comparing metaphoric sentences directly to literal interpretations, three left-sided foci in IFG (BA 45/47), aTL, and the inferior temporal lobe emerged. The discrepancy could be accounted for by methodological differences between the studies, most notably the differences in task instructions and the difficulty level of the sentence materials. However, the authors argue that both the neuropsychological literature as well as theories of metaphor comprehension (e.g., Glucksberg, 2003; Gibbs, 1994) are consistent with their pattern of results, indicating a mostly semantic process.

The second classic and often-cited study on pragmatics used Aesop's fables to elicit processes related to various levels of text comprehension (Nichelli et al., 1995). The crucial comparison was between the semantic task, monitoring for a specified feature (e.g., *Is the main character an animal with scales?*), and the moral task, deciding whether the character shared a specified moral. In the terminology of our framework, only the moral task requires an elaborate situation model in which the contents of the fable are integrated with the comprehender's background knowledge. In contrast, the semantic task is based on the textbase level, with inferences needed only for identification of the main characters and semantic evaluation of the animals' features.

In the direct comparison of the moral with the semantic task, Nichelli et al. (1995) report right-sided activation in IFG (BA 47/12) and the aTL. From inspection of the figures, there seems to be additional posterior temporal activation (pTL) in the vicinity of the area reported by Bottini et al. (1994). Once more, these activations are interpreted to be consistent with the coarse coding hypothesis. However, moral judgment cannot be as easily explained by semantic activation as the metaphorical processing described by Bottini et al. (1994). Given the findings on the role of the dmPFC for inference and evaluation processes, we would have predicted frontomedial involvement during the judgment task. In fact, recent studies on moral judgment (Heekeren,

Wartenburger, Schmidt, Schwintowski, & Villringer, 2003; Moll et al., 2002; see also Greene, Sommerville, Nystrom, Darley, & Cohen, 2001) implicated the bilateral "extended language network," particularly the dmPFC during verbally stimulated moral judgment. Thus, the special contribution of the right hemisphere is still an open question.

A third aspect of pragmatic communication is the appreciation of humor, which has also been attributed to right hemisphere processes (Brownell & Martino, 1998; Brownell, Michel, Powelson, & Gardner, 1983). The first neuroimaging study on this topic used three different text genres, including a joke condition (Ozawa et al., 2000). However, there were no direct comparisons with the other two text genres, newspaper articles and philosophical texts, and, most importantly, comprehensibility and funniness were confounded. Therefore, the hint for the funny story eliciting stronger activations in the lateral prefrontal cortex bilaterally cannot yet be interpreted as reflecting the affective component of joke comprehension.

In a more controlled study, Goel and Dolan (2001) used two different types of jokes, consisting of question-answer pairs. The jokes they labeled "phonological" were based on a pun, such as: *Why does the golfer wear two pairs of pants? Because he's got a hole in one*. The punchline becomes funny because of the ambiguity of *hole in one*, either idiomatically referring to the golfer's play, or literally to the golfer's pants. Comprehension of this joke requires semantic integration in addition to the revision of an initially infelicitous interpretation. The second type of joke, the so-called semantic joke (e.g., *What do engineers use for birth control? Their personalities*), was based on pragmatic knowledge about the world, such as prejudices and social conventions.

From a text-linguistic point of view, these materials have the following properties: The nonfunny control condition uses expected, immediately coherent continuations, semantically primed by the questions. In contrast, the jokes use unexpected responses that at first sight comprise pragmatic violations. Only a subsequent reinterpretation process renders the jokes coherent. As we have seen, pragmatic violations in a sentence context elicit activation in a frontotemporal network related to lexico-semantic processing (Baumgärtner, Weiller, & Büchel, 2002). Consistent with these results, Goel and Dolan (2001) report activation in the left IFG and bilateral posterior inferior and middle temporal cortex (pTL) for reading jokes compared with nonfunny continuations (e.g., *Because it's cold; The pill*). The frontal activation was more pronounced in the "phonological" conditions, whereas the temporal activation was more apparent in the "semantic" condition.

Contrary to the neuropsychological evidence, this imaging study did not support the prediction of an independent right hemispheric contribution to joke comprehension, attributable either to the revision or to the affective component. As a reflection of humor, activation in vmPFC emerged, but only for comparing within the jokes the funny ones against the unfunny ones. In addition, this region's involvement proved to be correlated with the off-line funniness ratings the subjects provided. The vmPFC is more generally related to emotional processing. Goel and Dolan (2004) recently reported the same region to be more active for reasoning about emotionally salient syllogisms as compared with solving neutral ones. Similarly, the emotional aspects of situation model representations were reflected in this region (Ferstl et al., 2005). Thus, the fact that comprehensibility ratings reported by Maguire et al. (1999) correlated with activation in the vmPFC might have been a side effect of some of the stories' affective content or funniness.

A recent study in our own laboratory was designed to separate hot and cold aspects of joke comprehension within one experiment (Siebörger, Ferstl, & von Cramon, 2005). Many jokes are based on a surprise effect and the subsequent reinterpretation of a piece of information. Such a revision of an erroneus interpretation seems necessary but not sufficient for verbal humor. Both reinterpretation and the affective appreciation of humor have been attributed to the right hemisphere, however. To deconfound these two components, we contrasted jokes with stories that required a revision, but were not funny, as confirmed in rating studies. An example of a revision story is: The cook to his wife: "The soup is too salty!" She: "Sorry, darling, I'll pay more attention next time." In this story, the initial assumption of the cook having prepared dinner has to be revised in the second sentence. An example of a joke is: The new employee asks her supervisor: "How many people work in this department?" He: "About half of them, I guess." Control conditions were incoherent continuations and straightforward, coherent continuations without the need for revision. In order to avoid confounds on the lexical or sentence levels, the context sentences were varied across conditions, but the target sentences (punch line) were identical.

Although the materials were decidedly different from those of the prior coherence studies, the comparison of all coherent (joke/revision/straightforward) against the incoherent trials nicely replicated the findings of activation in the dmPFC and the PCC/prec as an indication of successful coherence building. When a linguistic revision was required, that is, when an active integration with the discourse context was needed, the PCC/prec was more engaged than when the continuation was straightforward. At a low threshold, the direct comparison between jokes and revision uncovered activation in the vmPFC, very close to the region reported by Goel and Dolan (2001). Corroborating this finding were a parametric analysis, in which individual funniness ratings for each joke predicted vmPFC engagement, and a second-level correlation analysis that showed more activation in this region for those participants whose funniness ratings distinguished more clearly between jokes and revision stories. Based on this converging evidence, we concluded that the vmPFC played a role for the humorous or affective component of joke comprehension, rather than being related to the intrinsic reward value of successful comprehension (cf. Kringelbach & Rolls, 2004).

Summary

The short review on the pragmatic components of language comprehension has again produced mixed results. While there were clear indications for a RH contribution (Nichelli et al., 1995; Bottini et al., 1994; Caplan & Dapretto, 2001), there was also evidence for a role of frontomedial areas during processing of nonliteral meanings. Most notably, the vmPFC seems to indicate the "hot" aspects of pragmatic comprehension, particularly the affective component of humor (Goel & Dolan, 2001; Siebörger et al., 2005).

WHAT HAVE WE LEARNED?

The review of studies on text comprehension and pragmatics confirms the intuition that language processing in context is a highly complex endeavor that requires an intricate interplay of linguistic and cognitive processes. Besides the perisylvian language areas, reflecting word- and sentence-level processes (cf. Bookheimer, 2002; Brown & Hagoort, 1999; Caplan, 1992; Gernsbacher & Kaschak, 2003), there was evidence of a contribution of areas related to working memory, emotion processing, attention, and many more.

Ideally, a functional interpretation would map these regions directly onto subprocesses postulated in the text comprehension framework, based on a careful task analysis. As was seen in the review, however, these postulated subprocesses, such as situation model building and inferencing, often overlap. In addition, these processes might be further broken down into lower-level components, for example, association, inhibition, knowledge activation, or integration. Because there are too few studies on specific issues that are directly comparable, a functional attribution based on the text comprehension findings alone cannot succeed. Thus it is necessary to draw on knowledge about the functional neuroanatomy of the contributors derived from studies investigating more basic cognitive processes.

Although the results do not yet converge with respect to specific issues, several brain regions emerged as consistently involved during a variety of text comprehension tasks. The somewhat selective discussion of this *extended language network* is divided into four sections. The first two sections relate back to the neuropsychological theories of text comprehension. The evidence on the right hemisphere hypothesis is discussed first. The hypothesis of executive functions being crucial is evaluated in a section on the lateral prefrontal cortex. Subsequently, I speculate on the role of the anterior temporal lobe and of the frontomedial cortex. These two regions appear to be most specific to language processing in context and thus most relevant in light of the comprehension framework outlined in the introduction. In conclusion, I return to the research questions posed at the outset and evaluate whether the neuroimaging data provide hints for the further development of text comprehension theories.

TEXT COMPREHENSION: A RIGHT HEMISPHERE FUNCTION?

The role of the right hemisphere during language processing in context is still a mystery. There is no doubt about a considerable contribution of the right hemisphere, but many studies, even those testing complex language comprehension, report left-lateralized or left-dominant activation. Although other studies provided evidence for right hemisphere contributions, these were by no means specific to text comprehension, but appeared during sentence processing as well. Furthermore, in some studies, bilateral networks including homolog areas in the left and right hemispheres were found (e.g., Caplan & Dapretto, 2001). When evaluating findings on specific issues, we saw no consistency either. For each issue there seems to be a study showing RH involvement, and one that does not: inferencing (RH: Mason & Just, 2004; no RH: Ferstl & von Cramon, 2001), predictability in context (RH: Ferstl, Rinck, & von Cramon, 2005; no RH: Baumgärtner, Weiller, & Büchel, 2002), situation model and comprehensibility (RH: St. George et al., 1999; no RH: Maguire et al., 1999), situation model and theory of mind (RH: Vogeley et al., 2001; little or no RH: Fletcher et al., 1995), or metaphors (RH: Bottini et al., 1994; no RH: Rapp et al., 2004). Based on these mixed results, the global and somewhat simplifying claim that higher-level text comprehension is a right hemisphere function seems premature (cf. Bookheimer, 2002; Mar, 2004).

The reason for these seemingly discrepant results might be methodological. It is always difficult to argue based on null results. A failure to find RH involvement might be due to the choice of regions of interest (e.g., Baumgärtner, Weiller, & Büchel, 2002), to interindividual lateralization differences, or merely to a lack of experimental power (cf. Ferstl & von Cramon, 2001b). Furthermore, there is more interindividual anatomical variability in the RH compared with the LH. Thus, averaging across participants might not yield an overlapping region of activation. And in fact, many studies reporting clear evidence for an RH involvement used a region-of-interest analysis that does not require the same interindividual comparability as an averaging procedure (e.g., Mason & Just, 2004; St. George et al., 1999).

A more productive explanation for the divergence of results is that the various experiments elicit qualitatively different processes. As pointed out in the introduction, a wide variety of very distinct theories on the source of right hemisphere language deficits are available. These sources (e.g., capacity limitation, affective processing, semantic activation) need to be mapped onto distinct brain regions within the right hemisphere. Furthermore, the theories make differential predictions for specific tasks and materials. For instance, an emotion- or pragmatics-based theory would certainly predict RH involvement for reading jokes as compared with revision stories. In contrast, resource theory would not, because in our experiment jokes were easier to comprehend than revision stories (Siebörger et al., 2005). This example shows that it is necessary to specify the cognitive processes thought to be realized in the right hemisphere, to specify subregions within the RH, and to design experiments tailored to distinguishing between competing theories. Until we have a broader empirical data base, the role of the right hemisphere during text comprehension remains elusive.

HIGHER LEVEL COGNITION: A FUNCTION OF THE LATERAL PREFRONTAL CORTEX?

Before conducting any neuroimaging studies, everyone would have agreed on the clear-cut prediction of the lateral prefrontal cortex being crucial for language comprehension, and even more so for comprehension in context. Broca's area, within the inferior prefrontal cortex, is involved during phonological and syntactic processes on the sentence level, and understanding connected text requires working memory and executive functions, such as inhibition, monitoring, selection, or sequencing—all functions of the frontal lobes. For a mapping of these candidate processes onto specific brain regions, a finer partition of the frontal lobes is surely necessary. It goes way beyond the scope of this article to elaborate on the different proposals and the respective functional attributions (the interested reader is referred to Fuster, 1997; Miller & Cummings, 1999; Stuss & Knight, 2002).

When the imaging results are inspected, the picture becomes fuzzier. Consider as an example the study by Crinion et al. (2003), who reported activation only in temporal regions, when comparing story listening with a perceptual baseline. The authors explained this result by the absence of a comprehension task. If this account holds true, however, the conclusion must surely be that the processes realized in frontal regions are not automatic, not mandatory, and not necessary for passive comprehension, but that they come into play only if the particular situation asks for more thorough treatment of the language input.

Such an account is hard to reconcile with a syntax function of the inferior frontal gyrus, or more specifically its opercular part (BA 44). In contrast, for applications to text comprehension theories, this assumption provides the basis for an analysis of the materials and the task, guided by the brain's response. An alternative explanation for the failure to find prefrontal activations is that the baseline or comparison tasks engage the prefrontal regions to a degree similar to that of the experimental conditions. For instance, in the auditory versions of the coherence judgment task (Ferstl & von Cramon, 2001b) the control condition required increased phonological processing, leading to less prefrontal activation in the comparison with the language trials than in the visual version (Ferstl & von Cramon, 2001a). An interpretation of prefrontal activation always requires a thorough task analysis, and I would suggest that lateral prefrontal activation is often an indication of increased task demands. Based on the specific localization and laterality, it becomes feasible to attribute these demands to distinct causes.

What are the specific functions needed for comprehension in context? First, phonological, syntactic, and semantic analysis is carried out. These processes are likely to engage the inferior frontal gyrus (see Bookheimer, 2002, for a review). In particular, when semantic selection or semantic integration with the context is required, the triangular part of the IFG is implicated (e.g., Baumgärtner, Weiller, & Büchel, 2002; Rapp et al., 2004; Thompson-Schill, d'Esposito, & Kan, 1999). When the information is unexpected or a decision based on recent memory is required, this activation reaches into the orbital part (BA 47/11; Ferstl, Rinck, & von Cramon, 2005; cf. Petrides, Alivisatos, & Frey, 2002; Nobre, Coull, Frith, & Mesulam, 1999, for studies using nonverbal materials). Second, executive processes are required for the application of task rules (cf. Derrfuss, Brass, & von Cramon, 2004), for inhibition of task irrelevant information (Dove et al., 2001; Zysset, Müller, Lohmann, & von Cramon, 2001), for sequencing (Crozier et al., 1999; Sirigu et al., 1998; cf. Mar, 2004), or for the integration of inconsistent information in light of the task requirements (Ferstl & von Cramon, 2001). These processes are likely to engage the posterior lateral prefrontal cortex. Finally, working memory and attentional processes are needed. These processes are likely to enage the anterior parts of the middle frontal gyrus (Gruber, 2001; Ferstl et al., 2005). Of course, for all of these regions, these functional attributions are somewhat simplified. However, in the context of text comprehension experiments as reviewed here, they provide the basis for a differential attribution of activations to qualitatively distinct subprocesses.

COMPREHENSION IN A SENTENCE CONTEXT: THE ANTERIOR TEMPORAL LOBES

Closely linked to the inferiormost frontal lobe is the temporal pole (BA 38). And in fact, some activations cannot unambiguously be located within either the frontal operculum or the temporal pole. The anterior temporal region considered in this chapter was larger and encompassed the anteriormost parts of the superior, middle, and inferior temporal gyri. In addition, in some studies on anterior temporal functions, in particular lesion studies, medial temporal regions related to the hippocampal formation and the amygdala are included. The most important proposals for anterior temporal lobe functionality include memory functions, in particular for autobiographical and emotional, episodic memory, and semantic processes, in particular category-specific retrieval of proper names or animate entities (e.g., Damasio, Grabowski, Tranel, Hichwa, & Damasio, 1996; Leveroni et al., 2000; Maratos, Dolan, Morris, Henson, & Rugg, 2001; Martin & Chao, 2001).

The anterior temporal lobes were activated in studies both on the text and the sentence level when the integration of incoming words into a semantically based representation was needed. In our own studies, the specific location was at the anteriormost end of the superior temporal sulcus, reaching into the superior and middle temporal gyri, but was slightly more posterior than the temporal pole. For this lateral region, we might postulate a function related to the propositionalization process (Kintsch & van Dijk, 1978). It is important to note that this notion does not necessarily hinge on a verbal or abstract representation (cf. Zwaan, 2004), but that it might also refer to a chunking process in which phrases are identified and combined into content units. However, Humphries et al. (2001) provided evidence for the language specificity of the left aTL activation. When temporally extended auditory events (e.g., a gunshot followed by steps fading into the distance) were to be integrated into a meaningful representation, the aTLs were less active than when a verbal description was presented. Such a language-specific role at least of the left aTL is also consistent with the findings of Long and Baynes (2002; Long, this volume), whose hemifield priming studies povided evidence for left lateralized effects of the propositional structure, compared with bilateral effects of the situation model.

A role during propositionalization, that is, during the construction phase (Kintsch, 1988), clearly predicts aTL activation during sentence integration (cf. Baumgärtner, Weiller, & Büchel, 2002) but can also be reconciled—somewhat counterintuitively—with studies implicating the aTL for syntactic processes. The combination of single words into proposition-like content units requires lexico-semantic and syntactic information, so that both information types affect the ease or success of propositionalization. For instance, Friederici, Rüschemeyer, Hahne, and Fiebach (2003) report superior aTL activation for syntactically anomalous sentences such as *The shirt was on ironed*, in which the noun completing the prepositional phrase was missing. This error renders both the syntactic phrase structure as well as the semantic integration infelicitous. Similarly, Vandenberghe, Nobre, and Price (2002) found aTL activation for sentences containing syntactic structure, independent of the meaning. Even in scrambled sentences, the aTL was engaged. However, inspection of the examples shows that many sentences started with a full noun phrase, which probably elicited propositional integration. In support of this interpretation, Stowe et al. (1998), in a study on syntactic complexity, found bilateral aTL activation for all conditions except for the scrambled sentences, in which the absence of phrasal units was explicitly controlled.

If the aTL function is propositionalization on the sentence level, we would not expect specific activation on the text level, a finding reported by Mazoyer et al. (1993) and Ferstl and von Cramon (2001), among others. In contrast, the left aTL was prominently engaged in the study on situation model building by Maguire et al. (1999), when standard stories were compared with unusual stories. Similarly, Fletcher et al. (1995) reported bilateral aTL activation when comparing stories with unrelated sentences, and Ferstl, Rinck, & von Cramon (1995) found the right aTL to be sensitive to the local detection of inconsistencies, an early process also related to the text base level. Thus, the aTL activation in these cases might reflect the successful construction of a propositional network across the sentence boundary. A careful analysis of the materials in these studies is needed to provide hypotheses on the conditions under which additional aTL involvement across the sentence boundary is likely.

MAKING SENSE OF WHAT HAPPENS: THE DORSOMEDIAL PREFRONTAL CORTEX

One of the most interesting results of recent text comprehension studies is the importance of the dorsomedial prefrontal cortex (dmPFC) (Ferstl & von Cramon, 2001a, 2001b, 2002; Ferstl, Rinck, & von Cramon, 2005; Fletcher et al., 1995; Mazoyer et al., 1993; Schmalhofer et al., 2004; Siebörger et al., 2003, 2005; Vogeley et al., 2001). Distinct from the slightly more dorsal region in BA6/8, which was recently associated with processing under uncertainty and error related processing (Volz, Schubotz, & von Cramon, 2003; Ullsperger & von Cramon, 2001), the dmPFC (BA 8/9/10) seems to be the most likely candidate as an inference region. In addition to our own results from studies using a coherence judgment task, this conclusion is supported by findings from reasoning experiments and studies on evaluative judgments (Goel, Gold, Kapur, & Houle, 1997; Zysset et al., 2002, 2003). However, there are a variety of other proposals for the function of the anterior dmPFC, including reflections of a default state in the absence of stimulation (Gusnard, Akbudak, Shulman, & Raichle, 2001), self-referential processes (Northoff & Bermpohl, 2004), emotion (Greene, Sommerville, Nystrom, Darley, & Cohen, 2001), or moral judgments (Moll, de Oliveira-Souza, Eslinger, et al., 2002).

The most prominent account relates the dmPFC to theory of mind processes (Frith & Frith, 2003; Saxe, Carey, & Kanwisher, 2004). Theory of mind or mentalizing refers to the ability to attribute other people's actions and intentions to their beliefs, motivations, and goals. And in fact, communication and theory of mind are so closely intertwined that it might be impossible to separate these two driving forces of behavior. On one hand, complex reasoning about other people's beliefs and motivations, for instance in the context of a deception task, is facilitated by language (Saxe, Carey, & Kanwisher, 2004). On the other hand, comprehending narrative text involves the protagonists' state of mind, including their goals and emotions (e.g., van den Broek, 1994). Even when faced with expository texts, an implicit interaction between the speaker or the writer and the recipient takes place. Thus, Frith and Frith (2003) argue that the findings of dmPFC activation might reflect concurrent ToM processes rather than particular inferencing activities during communication. More specifically, Gallagher and Frith (2003) postulated that the dmPFC function during ToM processing concerns the decoupling of information from reality. In contrast, the anterior temporal lobes, which are also often engaged during ToM tasks, are seen to play a role in the retrieval of personal or episodic memories that enable a "simulation" of the other's state of mind (cf. Vogeley et al., 2001).

It is difficult to argue against this proposal, and it might be that text comprehension theories need to be extended to include this aspect of communication. However, when adopting this point of view, it is a challenge to make predictions concerning the circumstances under which the dmPFC should be particularly involved. Why is it more active during the processing of coherent as compared with incoherent trials? Based on the results of a study successfully separating inference processes from ToM processes (Ferstl & von Cramon, 2002), we postulated a more general process encompassing both ToM components and inferencing. This account makes use of the observation of patients with lesions in this area to have problems with drive and motivation (Marin, 1991). Thus, we argued, the function of the dmPFC is related to an integration of the inner world with the external stimulation (Ferstl & von Cramon, 2002). This function is closely related to the comprehender's self (cf. Northoff & Bermpohl, 2004) and is consequently involved in a wide variety of tasks, not only those using self-referential stimuli (cf. Siebörger et al., 2005). What is important in the context of text comprehension studies, however, is that dmPFC activation is observed when the task's time frame allows for hypothesis formation, when there is no right or wrong answer, but an ideosyncratic response criterion needs to be established, and when prior knowledge or contextual information plays a role.

This latter component, the integration of novel information with the prior discourse context or background knowledge (cf. Northoff & Bermpohl, 2004; Zysset, Huber, Ferstl, & von Cramon, 2002; Zysset, Huber, Samson, Ferstl, & von Cramon, 2003), is often reflected in activation in the posterior cingulate cortex (PCC/prec). And in fact, consistent with a number of findings reviewed here (Schmalhofer et al., 2004; Siebörger et al., 2005; Ferstl et al., 2005; Ferstl & von Cramon, 2001a, 2002; see also Kuperberg et al., 2000), the PCC has been interpreted as related to situation model updating (Maguire et al., 1999). Given the close link to the dmPFC via pericallosal connections, we interpret the pairwise activation of the fronto- and parietomedial regions to reflect different components of the same domain-independent process.

IMPLICATIONS FOR TEXT COMPREHENSION THEORIES

At the outset of this chapter, the most influential research issues in the text comprehension literature were summarized. I would now like to return to these issues, summarize the relevant neuroimaging findings, and sketch ideas about further research and theory development.

The first question posed was concerned with the interface between the surface level and higher-level representations. How do linguistic differences propagate to a conceptual or situational understanding? Relevant to this question are, of course, studies on syntactic parsing (see Kaan & Swaab, 2002; Friederici, 2002; Hagoort, Brown, & Osterhout, 1999, for reviews). The main interest of many of these studies, however, is how a correct reading is obtained, rather than how subtle differences in wording influence the quality or the content of the resulting conceptual representations. Two studies were included in this review that directly manipulated surface level features in a text comprehension experiment. The difficulty of reconciling a cohesive marker with an implausible pragmatic interpretation led to activation in the left prefrontal cortex (Ferstl & von Cramon, 2001a). Robertson et al. (2000) showed that connecting sentences with definite articles activated the right prefrontal cortex, compared with a less coherent version using indefinite articles. These results clearly show that neuroimaging methods are sufficiently sensitive for capturing subtle effects caused by linguistic variation.

This finding leads directly to the question of the psychological relevance of the text base. It has been proposed that this intermediate, propositional level is circumvented by a direct experiential link between the surface level and the situation model (Zwaan, 2004). Such an account still requires hypotheses on how the specific language input gives rise to the appropriate perceptual representation. Which perceptual features are selected as contextually relevant? For instance, in the example *The ranger saw the eagle in the sky*, an image of an eagle with spread wings pops up. However, the syntactic ambiguity requires attaching the prepositional phrase to the noun *eagle*, rather than to the verb *saw* (cf. Ferstl & Flores-d'Arcais, 1999). No such ambiguity is present in the sentence *The eagle in the sky was seen by the ranger*. The resulting situation model representations are predicted to be equal, but the propositionalization, or phrasal packaging, is more difficult in the ambiguous sentence. If the hypothesis is that the anterior temporal lobe has a role during this packaging of content units, activation differences would be expected. A further example illustrating the importance of the lower representations is the study on verbal humor by Goel and Dolan (2001). Although both joke conditions elicited vmPFC activation indicating the affective component, that is, an aspect of the resulting situation model, the comprehension-related frontotemporal activation varied with the lexical and semantic features of the jokes. Finally, Schmalhofer et al. (2004) reported differences in PCC activation for a verification task caused by surface-level features, even if the meaning on the text-base level was comparable. More direct tests of the psychological reality of the text base include adopting experimental paradigms from the behavioral literature for neuroimaging applications (cf. Long & Baynes, 2002; Long, this volume).

The second question concerned the status of qualitatively different inference types. The evidence seems strong that the frontomedial cortex plays a role in inference processes (Ferstl & von Cramon, 2001, 2002; Schmalhofer et al., 2004). On the other hand, there is evidence that right-hemisphere regions, particularly the right temporal lobe, are also related to inferencing

(Mason & Just, 2004; St. George et al., 1999). A speculative account consistent with both findings is based on a qualitative distinction between different inference types. In line with the coarse coding hypothesis, those inferences might be realized in the RH, which can be drawn by associative activation of distant semantic fields and subsequent integration into a common representation. In contrast, knowledge-based inferences requiring the use of background and discourse information as well as a deliberate plausibility judgment might engage the fronto- and parietomedial cortices. Unfortunately, no direct within-subject comparison of different inference types has been attempted yet. The findings of dissociable integration processes in our study on situation model building (Ferstl, Rinck, & von Cramon, 2005) are preliminary evidence for such an interpretation, but the materials were not sufficiently controlled to exclude alternative explanations. If a qualitative distinction of, for instance, neuroanatomical sequels of elaborative and bridging inferences could be confirmed empirically, neuroimaging would provide a useful tool for separating inference types by analyzing their realizations in the frontomedial or right temporal brain regions, respectively.

The third question concerned the use of knowledge and context during comprehension. The two studies on situation model building that directly adopt the knowledge paradigm (Maguire et al., 1999; St. George et al., 1999) did not converge in their results. As pointed out, there are too many differences between the studies to pinpoint a likely reason for this discrepancy. In particular, medial structures were not included in the region-of-interest analysis conducted by St. George et al. (1999). A speculative explanation, based on the type of integration, takes into account the complexity of the adjunct information. For the Dooling and Lachman (1971) stories, the background information consisted of a depiction of a rather complex and unusual scene. In the Bransford example, highly familiar topics were used that can be labeled with one word or phrase (*doing laundry*). Thus, linking the text information to the latter background knowledge might just consist of associatively relating the input to the title or label. In contrast, the more complex pictorial representation needs to be encoded and integrated with the incoming sentences, leading to activation in the PCC/prec area. Further neuroimaging research might investigate the effects of expertise in the text domain or differences due to the modality of adjunct information matched with respect to complexity and familiarity.

The fourth question concerned the representation of situation models. The review of pragmatics as well as situation model processing clearly showed that qualitative differences in information aspects have a direct reflection in brain activation. Ventromedial prefrontal activation was observed for emotional information and for jokes (Goel & Dolan, 2001, 2004; Ferstl et al., 2005; Sieborger et al., 2005), whereas parietal activation was observed during the processing of chronological information (Ferstl et al., 2005). Thus, neuroimaging facilitates a qualitative dissociation of different situation model aspects (cf. Perfetti, 1999). Behavioral research has identified a multitude of variables influencing situation model building (Zwaan & Radvansky, 1998).

Spatial or visual situation models have been studied most extensively, but so far, no neuroimaging data on this information aspect are available (but see Ruff, Knauff, Fangmeier, & Spreer, 2003, for a related reasoning experiment). Further valuable research topics are causal mental models elicited by expository texts. In addition, these results are promising because they prove the sensitivity of the imaging methods for capturing subtle differences caused by language variations. Thus, text materials can be used to study variables known for influencing emotional processing, such as the affective valence or the level of arousal.

FURTHER RESEARCH ISSUES

In addition to these main research questions, a number of other promising areas for further study emerged from the review of neuroimaging experiments. I will briefly mention three examples. One issue central to the comprehension of longer texts is the reinstatement search (Kintsch & van Dijk, 1978) or, more specifically, the reaccess of relevant discourse context during comprehension of subsequent sentences. When discussing the results of our experiment on situation model building (Ferstl, Rinck, & von Cramon, 2005), I argued that the activation patterns observed for the chronological stories contained components indicating an attentional shift from local to global representations and components indicating memory functions. These hypotheses can easily be tested in experiments varying the distance between the context and the target information. The results might aid particularly in shaping ideas on the influence of attentional factors on text comprehension, an issue that has not received much treatment yet (cf. Gaddy, van den Broek, & Sung, 2001).

Many of the explanations of activation patterns drew on task differences. Thus, a systematic differentiation of how the patterns change as a function of the specific paradigm can shed light, for instance, on whether the contribution of working memory processes is due to comprehension per se or whether it is due to a subsequent recognition or recall task. In some experiments, task manipulations were used for eliciting text-level versus word-level processing (e.g., Nichelli et al., 1994), but in others differences in materials were confounded with task differences (e.g., Caplan & Dapretto, 2001; Ferstl & von Cramon, 2002). In further research, manipulations of the comprehension tasks on the same text materials can shift processing from the surface level to the situation model level, depending on whether wording or a deeper understanding is targeted.

A further issue not yet addressed is individual differences in reading skill or working memory capacity (cf. McNamara, this volume; Daneman & Carpenter, 1980; Gernsbacher, 1990). Statistical methods have only recently become available for comparing brain activation patterns of subgroups, or for parametrically including a between-subjects variable. In addition, stable and predictable result patterns are required before useful group comparisons can be attempted. For instance, when the role of the frontomedial cortex in inferencing is further cemented by additional replications, a trade-off between lateral prefrontal and frontomedial activations might be used as an indication of comprehension skill or effort. Currently, we are conducting fMRI studies of patients with brain lesions for investigating how language processing in context proceeds when one of the key regions is lesioned. First results suggest that patients with left aTL lesion require a larger contribution of the posterior lateral PFC, a result consistent with the recruitment of compensation strategies.

CONCLUSIONS

In recent years, a still small but growing literature on the functional neuroanatomy of text comprehension has been accumulated. The promise of neuroimaging methods lies in a more detailed description of the concert of cognitive processes contributing to comprehension in context. Rather than identifying single brain regions specific to subprocesses of comprehension, the task of the future will be a delineation of the relative contributions of components of the extended language network. To facilitate theoretical conclusions on the functional role of the various players, it is necessary to draw on the results of neuroimaging studies on more basic cognitive processes. Furthermore, a specific and detailed analysis of the tasks and materials used in neuroimaging studies is needed so that the sometimes puzzling divergence of results can be uniquely attributed to experimental, methodological, or strategic differences. The thorough understanding of text comprehension processes as it has been achieved within the last 25 years provides the framework for this enterprise.

ACKNOWLEDGMENTS

During the work on this chapter, I was supported by a grant from the Deutsche Forschungsgemeinschaft. I greatly appreciate the helpful comments on a draft of this chapter by D. Yves von Cramon and Florian Siebörger. Heike Schmidt-Duderstedt drew the figures. Last but not least, I thank Franz Schmalhofer and Chuck Perfetti for their editorial support and for giving me the opportunity to contribute to this volume.

REFERENCES

Baumgärtner, A. , Weiller, C., & Büchel, C. (2002). Event-related fMRI reveals cortical sites involved in contextual sentence integration. *NeuroImage, 16*, 736–745.

Bavelier, D., Corina, D., Jezzard, P., Padmanabhan, S., Clark, V. P., Karni, A., et al. (1997). Sentence reading—a functional MRI study at 4 Tesla. *Journal of Cognitive Neuroscience, 9*, 664–686.

Bechara, A., Tranel, D., & Damasio, H. (2000). Characterization of the decision-making deficit of patients with ventromedial PFC lesions. *Brain, 123,* 2189–2202.

Beeman, M. (1993). Semantic processing in the right hemisphere may contribute to drawing inferences from discourse. *Brain and Language, 44,* 80–120.

Beeman, M. (1998). Coarse semantic coding and discourse comprehension. In M. Beeman & C. Chiarello (Eds.), *Right hemisphere language comprehension: Perspectives from cognitive neuroscience* (pp. 255–284). Mahwah, NJ: Lawrence Erlbaum Associates.

Benowitz, L. I., Moya, K. L, & Levine, D. N. (1990). Impaired verbal reasoning and constructional apraxia in subjects with right hemisphere damage. *Neuropsychologia, 28,* 231–241.

Bihrle, A. M., Brownell, H. H., Powelson, J. A., & Gardner, H. (1986). Comprehension of humorous and nonhumorous materials by left and right brain-damaged patients. *Brain and Cognition, 5,* 399–411.

Binder, J. R., Frost, J. A., Hammeke, T. A., Bellgowan, P. S. F., Rao, S. M., & Cox, R. W. (1999). Conceptual processing during the conscious resting state: A functional MRI study. *Journal of Cognitive Neuroscience, 11,* 80–93.

Binder, J. R., Frost, J. A., Hammeke, T. A., Cox, R. W., Rao, S. M., & Prieto, T. (1997). Human brain language areas identified by functional magnetic resonance imaging. *The Journal of Neuroscience, 171,* 353–362.

Binder, J. R., & Rao, S. M. (1994). Human brain mapping with functional magnetic resonance imaging. In A. Kertesz (Ed.), *Localization and neuroimaging in neuropsychology* (pp. 185–212). San Diego: Academic Press.

Bookheimer, S. (2002). Functional MRI of language: New approaches to understanding the cortical organization of semantic processing. *Annual Review of Neuroscience, 25,* 151–188.

Borod, J. C. (1993). Cerebral mechanisms underlying facial, prosodic, and lexical emotional expression: A review of neuropsychological studies and methodological issues. *Neuropsychology, 7,* 445–463.

Bottini, G., Corcoran, R., Sterzi, R., Paulesu, E., Schenone, P., Scarpa, P., et al. (1994). The role of the right hemisphere in the interpretation of figurative aspects of language: A positron emission tomography activation study. *Brain, 117,* 1241–1253.

Bransford, J. D., & Franks, J. J. (1972). The abstraction of linguistic ideas: A review. *Cognition, 1,* 211–249.

Bransford, J. D., & Johnson, M. K. (1972). Contextual prerequisites for understanding: Some investigations of comprehension and recall. *Journal of Verbal Learning and Verbal Behavior, 11,* 717–726.

Brass, M., Zysset, S., & von Cramon, D. Y. (2001). The inhibition of imitative response tendencies. *NeuroImage, 14,* 1416–1423.

Brodmann, K. (1909). *Vergleichende Lokalisationslehre der Großhirnrinde in ihren Prinzipien dargestellt auf Grund des Zellenbaues.* [Comparative localization of the cortex based on its zytoarchitecture] Leipzig: J. A. Barth.

Brownell, H. H., Gardner, H., Prather, P., & Martino, G. (1995). Language, communication and the right hemisphere. In H. S. Kirshner (Ed.), *Handbook of neurological speech and language disorders* (pp. 325–349), New York: Marcel Dekker.

Brownell, H. H., & Martino, G. (1998). Deficits in inference and social cognition: The effects of right hemisphere brain damage on discourse. In M. Beeman and C. Chiarello (Eds.), *Right hemisphere language comprehension: Perspectives from cognitive neuroscience* (pp. 309–328). Mahwah, NJ: Lawrence Erlbaum Associates.

Brownell, H. H., Michel, D., Powelson, J. A., & Gardner, H. (1983). Surprise but not coherence: Sensitivity to verbal humor in right-hemisphere patients. *Brain and Language, 18*, 20–27.

Brownell, H. H., Potter, H. H., Bihrle, A. M., & Gardner, H. (1986). Inference deficits in right brain-damaged patients. *Brain and Language, 27*, 310–321.

Cabeza, R., & Kingstone, A. (Eds.). (2001). *Handbook of functional neuroimaging of cognition*. Cambridge, MA: MIT Press.

Caplan, D. (1992). *Language: Structure, processing, and disorders*. Cambridge, MA: MIT Press.

Caplan, R., & Dapretto, M. (2002). Making sense during conversation: An fMRI study. *NeuroReport, 12*, 3625–3632.

Channon, S., & Crawford, S. (2000). The effects of anterior lesions on performance of a story comprehension test: left anterior impairment on a theory of mind-type task. *Neuropsychologia, 38*, 1006–1017.

Chee, M. W. L., O'Craven, K. M., Bergida, R., Rosen, B. R., & Savoy, R. L. (1999). Auditory and visual word processing studied with fMRI. *Human Brain Mapping, 7*, 15–28.

Corbalis, M. C. (1997). Mental rotation and the right hemisphere. *Brain and Language, 57*, 100–121.

Crinion, J. T., Lambon-Ralph, A., Warburton, E. A., Howard, D., & Wise, R. J. S. (2003). Temporal lobe regions engaged during normal speech comprehension. *Brain, 126*, 1193–1201.

Crozier, S., Sirigu, A., Lehéricy, S., Moortele, P. F. van de, Pillon, B., Grafman, J., et al. (1999). Distinct prefrontal activations in processing sequence at the sentence and script level: An fMRI study. *Neuropsychologia, 37*, 1469–1476.

Damasio, H., Grabowski, T. J., Tranel, D., Hichwa, R. D., & Damasio, A. R. (1996). A neural basis for lexical retrieval. *Nature, 380*, 499–505.

Danemann, M., & Carpenter, P. A. (1980). Individual differences in working memory and reading. *Journal of Verbal Learning and Verbal Behavior, 19*, 450–466.

Dapretto, M., & Bookheimer, S. Y. (1999). Form and content: dissociating syntax and semantics in sentence comprehension. *Neuron, 24*, 427–432.

Davidson, R. J., & Irwin, W. (1999). The functional neuroanatomy of emotion and affective style. *Trends in Cognitive Sciences, 3*, 11–21.

Dehaene, S., Dupoux, E., Mehler, J., Cohen, L., Paulesu, E., Perani, D., et al. (1997). Anatomical variability in the cortical representation of first and second language. *Neuroreport, 8*, 3809–3815.

Derrfuss, J., Brass, M., & von Cramon, D. Y. (2004). Cognitive control in the posterior frontolateral cortex: Evidence from common activations in task coordination, interference control, and working memory. *NeuroImage, 23*, 604–612.

Doane, S. M., McNamara, D. S., Kintsch, W., Polson, P. G., & Clawson, D. (1992). Prompt comprehension in UNIX command production. *Memory & Cognition, 20*, 327–343.

Dolan, R. J. (2002). Emotion, cognition and behavior. *Science, 298*, 1191–1194.

Dooling, D. J., & Lachman, R. (1971). Effects of comprehension on retention of prose. *Journal of Experimental Psychology, 88*, 216–222.

Dove, A., Pollmann, S., Schubert, T., Wiggins, C. J., & von Cramon, D. Y. (2000). Prefrontal cortex activation in task switching: An event-related fMRI study. *Cognitive Brain Research, 9*, 103–109.

Ettlin, T. M., Beckson, M., Gaggiotti, M., Rauchfleisch, U., & Benson, D. F. (2000). The frontal lobe score: Part I: Construction of a mental status of frontal systems. *Clinical Rehabilitation, 14,* 260–271.

Ferstl, E. C. (2001). Learning from text. In N. J. Smelser & P. B. Baltes (Eds.), *International encyclopedia of the social & behavioral sciences: Vol. 3.13. Cognitive psychology and cognitive science* (W. Kintsch, Ed.). Amsterdam: Elsevier.

Ferstl, E. C. (2006). Text comprehension in middle aged adults: Is there anything wrong? *Aging, Neuropsychology and Cognition, 13,* 62–85.

Ferstl, E. C., & Flores d'Arcais, G. B. (1999). The reading of words and sentences. In A. D. Friederici (Eds.), *Language comprehension: A biological perspective* (2nd ed., pp. 175–210). Berlin: Springer.

Ferstl, E. C., Guthke, T., & von Cramon, D. Y. (1999). Change of perspective in discourse comprehension: Encoding and retrieval processes after brain injury. *Brain and Language, 70,* 385–420.

Ferstl, E. C., Guthke, T., & von Cramon, D. Y. (2002). Text comprehension after brain injury: Left prefrontal lesions affect inference processes. *Neuropsychology, 16,* 292–308.

Ferstl, E. C., & Kintsch, W. (1999). Learning from text: Structural knowledge assessment in the study of discourse comprehension. In H. Oostendorp &. S. Goldman (Eds.), *The construction of mental models during reading* (pp. 247–277). Mahwah, NJ: Lawrence Erlbaum Associates.

Ferstl, E. C., Rinck, M., & von Cramon, D. Y. (2005). Emotional and temporal aspects of situation model processing during text comprehension: An event-related fMRI study. *Journal of Cognitive Neuroscience.* 17, 724–739.

Ferstl, E. C., & von Cramon, D. Y. (2001a). The role of coherence and cohesion in text comprehension: An event-related fMRI study. *Cognitive Brain Research, 11,* 325–340.

Ferstl, E. C., & von Cramon, D. Y. (2001b). Inference processes during text comprehension: Is it the left hemisphere after all? *Journal of Cognitive Neuroscience (Supplement),* 128.

Ferstl, E. C., & von Cramon, D. Y. (2002). What does the fronto-medial cortex contribute to language processing: Coherence or theory of mind? *NeuroImage, 17,* 1599–1612.

Fink, G. R., Halligan, P. W., Marshall, J. C., Frith, C. D., Frackowiak, R. S. J., & Dolan, R. J. (1997). Neural mechanisms involved in the processing of global and local aspects of hierarchically organized visual stimuli. *Brain, 120,* 1779–1791.

Fletcher, P. C., Happe, F., Frith, U., Baker, S. C., Dolan, R. J., Frackowiak, R. S. J., et al. (1995). Other minds in the brain: A functional imaging study of "theory of mind" in story comprehension. *Cognition, 57,* 109–128.

Friederici, A. D. (2002). Towards a neural basis of auditory sentence processing. *Trends in Cognitive Sciences, 6,* 78–84.

Friederici, A. F., Rüschemeyer, S.-A., Hahne, A., & Fiebach, C. J. (2003). The role of left inferior frontal and superior temporal cortex in sentence comprehension: Localizing syntactic and semantic processes. *Cerebral Cortex, 13,* 170–177.

Frith, C. D., & Frith, U. (1999). Interacting minds—A biological basis. *Science, 286,* 1692–1695.

Frith, U., & Frith, C. D. (2003). Development and neurophysiology of mentalizing. *Philosophical Transactions of the Royal Society of London, 358,* 459–473.

Fuster, J. M. (1997). *The prefrontal cortex: Anatomy, physiology, and neuropsychology of the frontal lobe.* Philadelphia: Lippincott-Raven.

Gaddy, M. L., van den Broek, P., & Sung, Y.-C. (2001). The influence of text cues on the allocation of attention during reading. In T. Sanders, J. Schilperoord, W. Spooren, & W. (Eds.), *Text representation: Linguistic and psycholinguistic aspects* (pp. 89–110). Amsterdam: John Benjamins.

Gallagher, H. L., & Frith, C. D. (2003). Functional imaging of "theory of mind." *Trends in Cognititve Sciences, 7,* 77–83.

Gallagher, H. L., Happé, F., Brunswick, N., Fletcher, P. C., Frith, U., & Frith, C. D. (2000). Reading the mind in cartoons and stories: An fMRI study of "theory of mind" in verbal and nonverbal tasks. *Neuropsychologia, 38,* 11–21.

Gernsbacher, M. A. (1990). *Language comprehension as structure building.* Hillsdale, NJ: Lawrence Erlbaum Associates.

Gernsbacher, M. A. (Ed.). (1994). *Handbook of psycholinguistics.* San Diego: Academic Press.

Gernsbacher, M. A., & Kaschak, M. P. (2003). Neuroimaging studies of language production and comprehension. *Annual Review of Psychology, 54,* 16.1–16.24.

Gibbs, R. W., Jr. (1994). Figurative thought and figurative language. In M. A. Gernsbacher (Ed.), *Handbook of psycholinguistics* (pp. 411–446). San Diego: Academic Press.

Glenberg, A. M., Havas, D., Becker, R., & Rinck, M. (2005). Grounding language in bodily states: The case for emotion. In R. Zwaan and D. Pecher (Eds.), *The grounding of cognition: The role of perception and action in memory, language, and thinking.* (pp. 115–118). Cambridge: Cambridge University Press.

Glenberg, A. M., & Kaschak, M. P. (2002). Grounding language in action. *Psychonomic Bulletin & Review, 9,* 558–565.

Glucksberg, S. (2003). The psycholingustics of metaphor. *Trends in Cognitive Sciences, 7,* 92–96.

Goel, V., & Dolan, R. J. (2001). The functional anatomy of humor: Segregating cognitive and affective components. *Nature Neuroscience, 4*(3), 237–261.

Goel, V., & Dolan, R. J. (2004). Reciprocal neural response within lateral and ventral medial prefrontal cortex during hot and cold reasoning. *NeuroImage, 20,* 2314–2321.

Goel, V., Gold, B., Kapur, S., & Houle, S. (1997). The seats of reason? An imaging study of deductive and inductive reasoning. *Neuro Report, 8,* 1305–1310.

Graesser, A. C., Gernsbacher, M. A., & Goldman, S. R. (Eds.). (2003). *Handbook of discourse processes.* Mahwah, NJ: Lawrence Erlbaum Associates.

Graesser, A. C., Millis, K. K., & Zwaan, R. A. (1997). Discourse comprehension. *Annual Review of Psychology, 48,* 163–189.

Graesser, A. C., Singer, M., & Trabasso, T. (1994). Constructing inferences during narrative text comprehension. *Psychological Review, 101,* 371–395.

Greene, J. D., Sommerville, R. B., Nystrom, L. E., Darley, J. M., & Cohen, J. D. (2001). An fMRI investigation of emotional engagement in moral judgment. *Science, 293,* 2105–2108.

Gruber, O. (2001). Effects of domain-specific interference on brain activation associated with verbal working memory task performance. *Cerebral Cortex, 2001,* 1047–1055.

Gusnard, D. A., Akbudak, E., Shulman, G. L., & Raichle, M. E. (2001). Medial prefrontal cortex and self-referential mental activity: relation to a default mode of brain function. *Proceedings of the National Academy of the Sciences, 98,* 4259–4264.

Gyselinck, V., & Tardieu, H. (1999). The role of illustrations in text comprehension: what, when, for whom, and why? In H. Oostendorp &. S. Goldman (Eds.), *The construction of mental models during reading* (pp. 195–218). Mahwah, NJ: Lawrence Erlbaum Associates.

Hagoort, P., Brown, C. M., & Osterhout, L. (1999). The neurocognition of syntactic processing. In C. M. Brown, & P. Hagoort (Eds.), *The neurocognition of language* (pp. 273–316). Oxford: Oxford University Press.

Halliday , M. A. K., & Hasan, R. (1976). *Cohesion in English*. London: Longman.

Happe, F. (1994). An advanced test of theory of mind: Understanding of story characters' thoughts and feelings by able autistics, mentally handicapped and normal children and adults. *Journal of Autism and Developmental Disorders, 24*, 129–154.

Hartley, L. L., & Levin, H. S. (1990). Linguistic deficits after closed head injury: A current appraisal. *Aphasiology, 4*, 353–370.

Heekeren, H. R., Wartenburger, I., Schmidt, H., Schwintowski, H.-P., & Villringer, A. (2003). An fMRI study of simple ethical decision-making. *NeuroReport, 14*, 1215–1219.

Humphries, C., Willard, K., Buchsbaum, B., & Hickok, G. (2001). Role of anterior temporal cortex in auditory sentence comprehension: An fMRI study. *Neuroreport, 12*, 1749–1752.

Kaan, E., & Swaab, T. Y. (2002). The brain circuitry of syntactic comprehension. *Trends in Cognitive Sciences, 6*, 350–356.

Kaczmarek, B. L. J. (1984). Neurolinguistic analysis of verbal utterances in patients with focal lesions of frontal lobes. *Brain and Language, 21*, 52–58.

Keenan, J. M, Baillet, S. D., & Brown, P. (1984). The effects of causal cohesion on comprehension and memory. *Journal of Verbal Learning and Verbal Behavior, 23*, 115–126.

Kintsch, W. (1988). The use of knowledge in discourse processing: A construction-integration model. *Psychological Review, 95*, 163–182.

Kintsch, W. (1998). *Comprehension: A paradigm for cognition*. Cambridge: Cambridge University Press.

Kintsch, W. (2000). Metaphor comprehension: A computational theory. *Psychonomic Bulletin & Review, 7*, 257–266.

Kintsch, W., & van Dijk, T. A. (1978). Toward a model of text comprehension and production. *Psychological Review, 85*, 363–394.

Kircher, T. T. J., Brammer, M., Andreu, N. T., Williams, S. C. R., & McGuire, P. K. (2001). Engagement of right temporal cortex during processing of linguistic context. *Neuropsychologia, 39*, 798–809.

Kolb, B., & Wishaw, I. Q. (1996). *Fundamentals of human neuropsychology*. New York: Freeman.

Kringelbach, M. L., & Rolls, E. T. (2004). The functional neuroanatomy of the human orbitofrontal cortex: Evidence from neuroimaging and neuropsychology. *Progress in Neurobiology, 72*, 341–372.

Kuperberg, G. R., McGuire, P. K., Bullmore, E. T., Brammer, M. J., Rabe-Hesketh, S., Wright, I. C., et al. (2000). Common and distinct neural substrates for pragmatic, semantic, and syntactic processing of spoken sentences: An fMRI study. *Journal of Cognitive Neuroscience, 12*, 321–341.

Kutas, M., & Hillyard, S. A. (1980). Reading senseless sentences: Brain potentials reflect semantic incongruity. *Science, 207*, 203–205.

Lehmann, M. T., & Tompkins, C. A. (2000). Inferencing in adults with right hemisphere brain damage: An analysis of conflicting results. *Aphasiology, 14*(5/6), 485–499.

Leveroni, C. L., Seidenberg, M., Mayer, A. R., Mead, L. A., Binder, J. R., & Rao, S. M. (2000). Neural systems underlying the recognition of familiar and newly learned faces. *Journal of Neuroscience, 20*, 878–886.

Long, D. L., & Baynes, K. (2002). Discourse representation in the two cerebral hemispheres. *Journal of Cognitive Neuroscience, 14*, 228–242.

Luan Phan, K., Wager, T., Taylor, S. F., & Liberzon, I. (2002). Functional neuroanatomy of emotion: A meta-analysis of emotion activation studies in PET and fMRI. *NeuroImage, 16*, 331–348.

Maguire, E. A., Frith, C. D., & Morris, R. G. M. (1999). The functional neuroanatomy of comprehension and memory: The importance of prior knowledge. *Brain, 122*, 1839–1850.

Mannes, S. M., & Kintsch, W. (1991). Planning routine computing tasks: Understanding what to do. *Cognitive Science, 15*, 305–342.

Mar, R. A. (2004). The neuropsychology of narrative: Story comprehension, story production and their interrelation. *Neuropsychologia, 42*, 1414–1434.

Maratos, E. J., Dolan, R. J., Morris, J. S., Henson, R. N. A., & Rugg, M. D. (2001). Neural activity associated with episodic memory for emotional context. *Neuropsychologia, 29*, 910–920.

Marin, R.W. (1991). Apathy: A neuropsychiatric syndrome. *Journal of Neuropsychiatry and Clinical Neuroscience, 3*, 243–254.

Martin, A., & Chao, L. L. (2001). Semantic memory and the brain: Structure and processes. *Current Opinion in Neurobiology, 11*, 194–201.

Martin, I., & McDonald, S. (2003). Weak coherence, no theory of mind, or executive dysfunction? Solving the puzzle of pragmatic language disorders. *Brain and Language, 85*, 451–466.

Martin, R. C. (2003). Language processing: Functional organization and neuroanatomical basis. *Annual Review of Psychology, 54*, 15.1–15.35.

Mason, R. A., & Just, M. A. (2004). How the brain processes causal inferences in text: A theoretical account of generation and integration component processes utilizing both cerebral hemispheres. *Psychological Science, 15*, 1–7.

Mazoyer, B. M., Tzourio, N., Frak, V., Syrota, A., Murayama, N., Levrier, O., et al. (1993). The cortical representation of speech. *Journal of Cognitive Neuroscience, 5*, 467–479.

Mazziotta, J. C., Toga, A. W., Evans, A., Fox, P., & Lancaster, J. (1995). A probabilistic atlas of the human brain: Theory and rationale for its development. *NeuroImage, 2*, 89–101.

McDonald, S. (1993). Viewing the brain sideways? Frontal versus right hemisphere explanation of non-aphasic language disorders. *Aphasiology, 7*, 535–549.

McDonald, S. (2000). Exploring the cognitive basis of right-hemisphere pragmatic language disorders. *Brain and Language, 75*, 82–107.

McDonald, S., Togher, L., & Code, C. (Eds.). (1999). *Communication disorders following traumatic brain injury*. Hove, UK: Psychology Press.

McKoon, G., & Ratcliff, R. (1992). Inference during reading. *Psychological Review, 99*, 440–466.

Meyer, M., Friederici, A. D., & von Cramon, D. Y. (2000). Neurocognition of auditory sentence comprehension: Event related fMRI reveals sensitivity to syntactic violations and task demands. *Cognitive Brain Research, 9*, 19–33.

Miller, B. L., & Cummings, J. L. (Eds.). (1999). *The human frontal lobes: Functions and disorders*. New York: Guilford Press.

Mitchell, D. C. (1994). Sentence parsing. In M. A. Gernsbacher (Ed.), *Handbook of psycholinguistics* (pp. 375–410). San Diego: Academic Press.

Moll, J., de Oliveira-Souza, R., Eslinger, P. J., Bramati, I. E., Mourao-Miranda, J., Andreiuolo, P. A. et al. (2002). The neural correlates of moral sensitivity: A functional magnetic resonance imaging investigation of basic and moral emotions. *The Journal of Neuroscience, 22*, 2730–2736.

Monetta, L., & Joanette, Y. (2003). Specificity of the right hemsiphere's contribution to verbal communication: The cognitive resources hypothesis. *Journal of Medical Speech-Language Pathology, 11*, 203–211.

Müller, R.-A., Rothermel, R. D., Behen, M. E., Muzick, O., Mangner, T. J., & Chugani, H. T. (1997). Receptive and expressive language activations for sentences: A PET study. *Neuroreport, 8*, 3767–3770.

Murray, L. L. (1999). Attention and aphasia: Theory, research and clinical implications. *Aphasiology, 13*, 91–111.

Myers, J. L., Shinjo, M., & Duffy, S. A. (1987). Degree of causal relatedness and memory. *Journal of Memory and Language, 26*, 453–465.

Navon, D. (1984). Resources: A theoretical soup stone? *Psychological Review, 91*, 206–234.

Nichelli, P., Grafman, J., Pietrini, P., Clark, K., Lee, K. Y., & Miletich, R. (1995). Where the brain appreciates the moral of a story. *NeuroReport, 6*, 2309–2313.

Nicholas, L. E., & Brookshire, R. H. (1995). Comprehension of spoken narrative discourse by adults with aphasia, right-hemisphere brain damage, or traumatic brain injury. *American Journal of Speech-Language Pathology, 4*, 69–81.

Nobre, A. C., Coull, J. T., Frith, C. D., & Mesulam, M. M. (1999). Orbitofrontal cortex is activated during breaches of expectation in tasks of visual attention. *Nature Neuroscience, 2*, 11–12.

Northoff, G., & Bermpohl, F. (2004). Cortical midline structures and the self. *Trends in Cognitive Sciences, 8*, 102–107.

Novoa, O. P., & Ardila, A. (1987). Linguistic abilities in patients with pre-frontal damage. *Brain & Language, 30*, 206–225.

Osterhout, L., & Holcomb, P. (1992). Event-related brain potentials elicited by syntactic anomaly. *Journal of Memory and Language, 31*, 785–806.

Otero, J., & Kintsch, W. (1992). Failures to detect contradictions in text: What readers believe versus what they read. *Psychological Science, 3*, 229–235.

Ozawa, F., Matsuo, K., Kato, C., Nakai, T., Isoda, H., Takehara, Y., et al. (2000). The effects of listening comprehension of various genres of literature on response in the linguistic area: an fMRI study. *Neuroreport, 11*, 1141–1143.

Papathanassiou, D., Etard, O., Mellet, E., Zago, L., Mazoyer, B., & Tzourio-Mazoyer, N. (2000). A common language network for comprehension and production: A contribution to the definition of language epicenters with PET. *NeuroImage, 11*, 347–357.

Perani, D., Dehaene, S., Grassi, F., Cohen, L., Cappa, F., Dupoux, E., et al. (1996). Brain processing of native and foreign languages. *Neuroreport, 7*, 2439–2444.

Perfetti, C. A. (1999). Comprehending written language: A blueprint of the reader. In C. M. Brown & P. Hagoort (Eds.), *The neurocognition of language* (pp. 167–208). Oxford: Oxford University Press.

Petrides, M., Alivisatos, B., & Frey, S. (2002). Differential activation of the human orbital, mid-ventrolateral, and mid-dorsolateral PFC during the processing of visual stimuli. *Proceedings of the National Academy of the Sciences, 99*, 5649–5654.

Price, C., Indefrey, P., & van Turennout, M. (1999). The neural archtiecture underlying the processing of written and spoken word forms. In C. M. Brown & P. Hagoort (Eds.), *The neurocognition of language* (pp. 211–240). Oxford: Oxford University Press.

Prigatano, G. P., Roueche, J. R., & Fordyce, D. J. (1986). Nonaphasic language disturbances after brain injury. In G. P. Prigatano, D. J. Fordyce, H. K. Zeiner, J. R. Roueche, M. Pepping, & B. C. Wood (Eds.), *Neuropsychological rehabilitation after brain injury* (pp. 18–28). Baltimore: John Hopkins University Press.

Rapp, A. M., Leube, D. T., Erb, M., Grodd, W., & Kircher, T. T. J. (2004). Neural correlates of metaphor processing. *Cognitive Brain Research, 20*, 395–402.

Rinck, M., Gámez, E., Díaz, J. M., & de Vega, M. (2003). Processing of temporal information: Evidence from eye movements. *Memory & Cognition, 31*, 77–86.

Rinck, M., Hähnel, A., & Becker, G. (2001). Using temporal information to construct, update, and retrieve situation models of narratives. *Journal of Experimental Psychology: Learning, Memory, and Cognition, 27*, 67–80.

Rinck, M., & Weber, U. (2003). Who, when, where: An experimental test of the event-indexing model. *Memory & Cognition, 31*, 1284–1292.

Robertson, D. A., Gernsbacher, M. A., Guidotti, S. J., Robertson, R. R. W., Irwin, W., Mock, B. J., et al. (2000). Functional neuroanatomy of the cognitive process of mapping during discourse comprehension. *Psychological Science, 11*, 255–260.

Ruff, C. C., Knauff, M., Fangmeier, T., & Spreer, J. (2003). Reasoning and working memory: common and distinct neuronal processes. *Neuropsychologia, 41*, 1241–1253.

Ruge, H., Brass, M., Lohmann, G., & von Cramon, D. Y. (2003). Event-related analysis for event types of fixed order and restricted spacing by temporal quantification of trial-averaged fMRI time courses. *Journal of Magnetic Resonance Imaging, 18*, 599–607.

Rugg, M. D. (1999). Functional neuroimaging in cognitive neuroscience. In C. M. Brown & P. Hagoort (Eds.), *The neurocognition of language* (pp. 15–36). Oxford: Oxford University Press.

Saxe, R., Carey, S., & Kanwisher, N. (2004). Understanding other minds: Linking developmental psychology and functional neuroimaging. *Annual Review of Psychology, 55*, 87–124.

Schmalhofer, F., & Glavanov, D. (1986). Three components of understanding a programmer's manual: Verbatim, propositional, and situational representations. *Journal of Memory and Language, 25*, 279–294.

Schmalhofer, F., McDaniel, M. A., & Keefe, D. (2002). A unified model for predictive and bridging inferences. *Discourse Processes, 33*, 105–132.

Schmalhofer, F., Raabe, M., Friese, U., Pietruska, K., & Rutschmann, R. (2004). Evidence from an fMRI experiment for the minimal encoding and subsequent substantiation of predictive inferences. *Proceedings of the ?? Meeting of the Cognitive Science Society.*

Scott, S. K., Leff, A. P., & Wise, R. J. S. (2003). Going beyond the information given: A neural system supporting semantic interpretation. *NeuroImage, 19*, 870–876.

Siebörger, F. Th. (2005). *Funktionelle Neuroanatomie des Textverstehens: Kohärenzbildung bei Witzen und anderen ungewöhnlichen Texten [Functional neuroanatomy of text comprehension: Coherence building in jokes and other unusual texts]*. Unpublished dissertation, University of Leipzig.

Siebörger, F. Th., Ferstl, E. C., Volkmann, B., & von Cramon, D. Y. (2004). Spass beiseite! Eine fMRI-Studie und eine behaviorale Patientenstudie zu verbalem Humor und sprachlicher Revision. [All joking aside! An fMRI study and a behavioral patient study on verbal humour and linguistic revision]. *Zeitschrift für Neuropsychologie, 15.*

Silbersweig, D., & Stern, E. (Eds.). (2001). Functional neuroimaging and neuropsychology fundamentals and practice: Convergence, advances and new directions. Special issue of *Journal of Clinical and Experimental Neuropsychology*. Lisse: Swets & Zeitlinger.

Singer, M. (1994). Discourse inference processes. In M. A. Gernsbacher (Ed.), *Handbook of psycholinguistics* (pp. 479–515). San Diego: Academic Press.

Singer, M., Graesser, A. C., & Trabasso, T. (1994). Minimal or global inference during reading. *Journal of Memory & Language, 33*, 421–441.

Sirigu, A., Cohen, L., Zalla, T., Pradat-Diehl, P., van Eeckhout, P., Grafman, J., et al. (1998). Distinct frontal regions for processing sentence syntax and story grammar. *Cortex, 34*, 771–778.

Springer, S. P., & Deutsch, G. (1997). *Left brain, right brain*. New York: Freeman.

St. George, M., Kutas, M., Martinez, A., & Sereno, M. I. (1999). Semantic integration in reading: Engagement of the right hemisphere during discourse processing. *Brain, 122*, 1317–1325.

St. George, M., Mannes, S., & Hoffman, J. E. (1994). Global semantic expectancy and language comprehension. *Journal of Cognitive Neuroscience, 6*, 70–83.

Stowe, L. A., Broere, C. A. J., Paans, A. M. J., Wijers, A. A., Mulder, G., Vaalburg, W., et al. (1998). Localizing components of a complex task—Sentence processing and working memory. *Neuroreport, 9*, 2995–2999.

Stuss, D. T., & Knight, R. T. (Eds.). (2002). *Principles of frontal lobe function*. Oxford, UK: Oxford University Press.

Talairach, J., & Tournoux, P. (1988). *Coplanar stereotaxic atlas of the human brain*. New York: Thieme.

Thompson-Schill, S. L., D'Esposito, M., & Kan, I. P. (1999). Effects of repetition and competition on activity in left prefrontal cortex during word generation. *Neuron, 23*, 513–522.

Trabasso, T., & van den Broek, P. (1985). Causal thinking and the representation of narrative events. *Journal of Memory and Language, 24*, 612–630.

Turkeltaub, P. E., Guinevere, F. E., Jones, K. M., & Zeffiro, T. A. (2002). Meta-analysis of the functional neuroanatomy of single-word reading: method and validation. *Neuroimage, 16*, 765–780.

Tzourio, N., Crivello, F., Mellet, E., Nkanga-Ngila, B., & Mazoyer, B. (1998). Functional anatomy of dominance for speech comprehension in left handers vs. right handers. *Neuroimaging, 8*, 1–16.

Tzourio, N., Nkanga-Ngila, B., & Mazoyer, B. (1998). Left planum temporale surface correlates with functional dominance during story listening. *Neuroreport, 9*, 829–833.

Ullsperger, M., & von Cramon, D. Y. (2001). Subprocesses of performance monitoring: A dissociation of error processing and response competition revealed by event-related fMRI and ERPs. *NeuroImage, 14*, 1387–1401.

Uylings, H. B. M., Malofeeva, L. I., Bogolepova, I. N., Amunts, K., & Zilles, K. (1999). Broca's language area from a neuroanatomical and developmental perspective. In C. M. Brown & P. Hagoort (Eds.), *The neurocognition of language* (pp. 319–336). Oxford: Oxford University Press.

van den Broek, P. (1990). Causal inferences and the comprehension of narrative texts. In A. C. Graesser & G. H. Bower (Eds.), *The psychology of learning and motivation: Inferences and text comprehension*. San Diego: Academic Press.

van den Broek, P. (1994). Comprehension and memory of narrative texts: Inferences and coherence. In M. A. Gernsbacher (Ed.), *Handbook of psycholinguistics* (pp. 536–588). San Diego: Academic Press.

van Dijk, T. A., & Kintsch, W. (1983). *Strategies of discourse comprehension*. New York: Academic Press.

Vandenberghe, R., Nobre, A. C., & Price, C. J. (2002). The response of left temporal cortex to sentences. *Journal of Cognitive Neuroscience, 14*, 550–560.

Vogeley, K., Bussfeld, P., Newen, A., Herrmann, S., Happé, F., Falkai, P., et al. (2001). Mind reading: Neural mechanisms of Theory of Mind and self-perspective. *NeuroImage, 14*, 170–181.

Volz, K. G., Schubotz, R. I., & von Cramon, D. Y. (2003). Predicting events of varying probability: Uncertainty investigated by fMRI. *NeuroImage, 19*, 271–280.

Walsh, V. (2003). A theory of magnitude: Common cortical metrics of time, space and quantity. *Trends in Cognitive Sciences, 7*, 483–488.

Weissman, D., & Banich, M. T. (2000). The cerebral hemispheres cooperate to perform complex but not simple tasks. *Neuropsychology, 14*, 41–59.

Whalen, P. J., Bush, G., McNally, R. J., Wilhelm, S., McInerney, S. C., Jenike, M. A., et al. (1998). The emotional counting Stroop paradigm: A functional magnetic resonance imaging probe of the anterior cingulate affective division. *Biological Psychiatry, 44*, 1219–1228.

Zalla, T., Phipps, M., & Grafman, J. (2002). Story processing in patients with damage to the prefrontal cortex. *Cortex, 38*, 215–231.

Zwaan, R. A. (2004). The immersed experiencer: Toward an embodied theory of language comprehension. In B. H. Ross (Ed.), *The psychology of learning and motivation* (Vol. 44, pp. 35–62). Amsterdam: Elsevier.

Zwaan, R. A., Langston, M. C., & Graesser, A. C. (1995). The construction of situation models in narrative comprehension: An event-indexing model. *Psychological Science, 6*, 292–297.

Zwaan, R. A., Magliano, J. P., & Graesser, A. C. (1995). Dimensions of situation model construction in narrative comprehension. *Journal of Experimental Psychology: Learning, Memory, and Cognition, 21*, 386–397.

Zwaan, R. A., & Radvansky, G. A. (1998). Situation models in language comprehension and memory. *Psychological Bulletin, 123*, 162–185.

Zysset, S., Huber, O., Ferstl, E. C., & von Cramon, D. Y. (2002). The anterior dmPFC and evaluative judgment: An fMRI study. *NeuroImage, 15*, 983–991.

Zysset, S., Huber, O., Samson, A., Ferstl, E. C., & von Cramon, D. Y. (2003). Functional specialization wihtin the anterior medial PFC: A functional magnetic resonance imaging study with human subjects. *Neuroscience Letters, 335*, 183–186.

Zysset, S., Müller K., Lohmann, G., & von Cramon D. Y. (2001). Color-word matching stroop task: Separating interference and response conflict. *Neuroimage, 13*, 29–36.

II

COMPUTATIONAL MODELS

5

The Text Mapping and Inference Rule Generation Problems in Text Comprehension: Evaluating a Memory-Based Account

Simon Dennis and Walter Kintsch
University of Colorado

Words and concepts are obviously useful units for the analysis of language. A number of representational mechanisms have been proposed to capture their meaning, such as feature systems (Katz & Fodor, 1963; E. E. Smith, Shoben, & Rips, 1974) or semantic networks (Collins & Quillian, 1969). There are, however, other levels of analysis that have proved useful in the study of language, both finer grained units (such as syllables or phonemes) and coarser grained ones. A particularly important level of analysis has been the propositional level. The term derives from logic but has been widely used in linguistics and psychology to designate units consisting of one or more concepts that function as arguments (with specific semantic roles) and a relational term. In one form or another such units played an important role in the work of linguists like Fillmore (1968), Bierwisch (1969), or van Dijk (1972). Psychologists, too, felt a need for units of this kind, either talking informally about "idea units," or using propositional analysis, following the lead of linguists (e.g., Kintsch, 1974). Indeed, the addition of propositional analysis to the toolbox of psychologists played a major role in their efforts to understand discourse comprehension and to model it.

The problem of how to map texts into propositional structures has never been solved adequately, however. What is needed is a formal way of mapping a text into a propositional structure that represents the meaning of the text, not only what is explicitly stated in the text but also the knowledge activated by the text and the inferences involved in constructing a situation model for the text. Twenty years ago, many researchers were confident that such a system could soon be designed. In the meantime, a certain amount of progress could be made by hand coding texts into propositions (e.g., Kintsch, 1974, 1998). For the purpose of constructing experimental materials for discourse studies, hand coding proved to be adequate, as long as the texts were short and ambiguities could be avoided. But it is certainly not a satisfactory solution, and an algorithm for deriving propositions and inferences from texts in an automatic and fully principled way has yet to be devised. There has been some partial progress along these lines (e.g., Blaheta & Charniak, 2000; Durbin, Earwood, & Golden, 2000; Gildea & Jurafsky, 2002; Lin, 1998; and see next section), but the problem has not been solved and is beginning to appear to be intractable.

Propositions, in the sense used here (e.g., Kintsch, 1998), not the original logical meaning, are the product of the analysis of language as practiced by philosophers and linguists over a long period of time. The concept is clearly defined and well motivated—but it is just one possible product of linguistic analysis, and there may be other ways to arrive at workable multiword units that function much like propositions. Propositions have proved their usefulness in discourse studies, and there are strong arguments that some such unit at a level higher than the word is needed for the study of language comprehension (see Kintsch, 1998, Section 2.2, for a summary of those arguments), but the failure so far to solve the mapping problem for propositions makes imperative the search for alternatives. Are there higher-order units that are not defined in the same way as propositions, but that could do the same work in discourse models that propositions do? What we need is some way to tell that the words in *Sampras outgunned Agassi* belong together, and to represent the relationship of this unit to other units in complex sentences, such as *Sampras outgunned an injured Agassi in a five-set struggle.*

In this chapter we investigate the Syntagmatic Paradigmatic model (SP; Dennis, S., 2005; Dennis, S., 2004) as a candidate mechanism for solving the text-mapping problem. The SP model is a memory-based approach that generates structured knowledge representations automatically from a large text corpus. Although these representations have some properties that are similar to those of propositions, they are also different in important respects. One of the objectives of this chapter is to examine the extent to which they are capable of supporting and extending the role that propositions play in existing accounts of text comprehension.

The relational representations provided by the SP model function much like propositions, but have some important advantages over propositional representations: texts can be mapped into these units automatically and on a large scale. The model achieves this by shifting from an intentional semantics representation to an extensional representation.

INTENTIONAL VERSUS EXTENSIONAL SEMANTICS

In systems that employ intentional semantics, such as propositional analysis, the meanings of representations are defined by their intended use and have no inherent substructure. For instance, the statement *Sampras outguns Agassi* might be represented propositionally as OUTGUN(SAMPRASS, AGASSI), where the relation OUTGUN is specified between the two arguments SAMPRAS and AGASSI, which have specific semantic roles:

Sampras: *Winner*
Agassi: *Loser*

However, the names of the roles are completely arbitrary (often they are called *Agent* and *Patient* instead, or even arg0 and arg1) and carry representational content only by virtue of the inference system in which they are embedded.

Now contrast the above situation with an alternative *extensional* representation of *Sampras outguns Agassi*, in which roles are defined by enumerating exemplars, as follows:

Sampras: Kuerten, Hewitt
Agassi: Roddick, Costa

The winner role is represented by the distributed pattern of Kuerten and Hewitt, words that have been chosen because they are the names of people who have filled the *X* slot in a sentence like *X outguns Y* within the experience of the system. Similarly, *Roddick* and *Costa* are the names of people who have filled the *Y* slot in such a sentence and form a distributed representation of the loser role. Note that the issue is not just a matter of distributed versus symbolic representation. The tensor product representation employed in the STAR model (Halford et al., 1994) of analogical reasoning uses distributed representations of the fillers, but assigns a unique rank to each role and thus forms an intentional scheme. By contrast, the temporal binding mechanism proposed by Hummel and Holyoak (1997) allows for both distributed filler and role vectors and hence could implement extensional semantics.

The use of extensional semantics of this kind has a number of advantages. First, defining a mapping from raw sentences to extensional meaning representations is much easier than defining a mapping to intentional representations because it is now only necessary to align sentence exemplars from a corpus with the target sentence. The difficult task of either defining or inducing semantic roles is avoided.

Second, because the role is now represented by a distributed pattern it is possible for a single role vector to simultaneously represent roles at different levels of granularity. The pattern {Kuerten, Hewitt} could be thought of as a proto-agent, an agent, a winner, and a winner of a tennis match simultaneously. The role vectors can be determined from a corpus during processing, and no commitment to an a priori level of role description is necessary.

Third, extensional representations carry content by virtue of the other locations in the experience of the system where those symbols have occurred. That is, the systematic history of the comprehender grounds the representation. For instance, we might expect systematic overlap between the winner role and person-who-is-wealthy role because some subset of {Kuerten, Hewitt} may also have occurred in an utterance such as *X is wealthy*. These contingencies occur as a natural consequence of the causality being described by the corpus. We will call this type of implicit inference, *inference by coincidence*, and as we will see in subsequent sections, the performance of the model is due in large part to this emergent property.

INSTANCE-BASED MODELS OF COGNITION

The SP model is a model of memory; with appropriate elaborations that allow it to deal with the complexity of language. The SP model belongs to the class of models that assume that the memory system stores traces that are representative of the instances that an organism has experienced. Instance-based models of memory were introduced in response to data showing that people retain a surprising amount of detail during memory experiments (Hintzman, 1984). For instance, Tulving and Thompson (1973) demonstrated that even when subjects were unable to recognize an item as having appeared on a list, they were nevertheless able to recall it when given appropriate cues. This indicates that the fallibility of human memory cannot be taken as direct evidence of what is stored. Rather, factors such interference and cue reinstatement play pivotal roles in performance. Furthermore, Hintzman (1988) showed that people were able to identify not only the frequency with which items appeared in memory, but also the approximate locations of each of the occasions on which they were presented, something that would be impossible unless they retained some information about specific instances. As a consequence of this and a large body of additional data that has been collected in the last two decades, many of the most influential models in memory (Shiffrin & Steyvers, 1997), learning (Logan, 1988), decision-making (Dougherty, 1999), phonology (Nakisa & Plunkett, 1998), lexical access (Goldinger, 1998), and categorization (Nosofsky, 1986), are instance-based.

In our case, because the SP model is concerned with sentence comprehension and memory, the assumption is that sentence memory consists of a large sample of the sentences a person has encountered. Although instance-based models have not to date played a significant role in psychological models of sentence processing, they have become popular in the computational linguistics literature (Daelemans, 1999). Thus, an instance model of sentence comprehension like the SP model cannot be rejected a priori as irrelevant psychologically but needs to be evaluated, like any model, by the success and range of the predictions it generates.

In this chapter we first outline existing systems for semantic role assignment and propositional analysis. Then we sketch the SP model and describe how it addresses the text-mapping and inference generation problems.

SYSTEMS FOR SEMANTIC ROLE ASSIGNMENT AND PROPOSITIONAL ANALYSIS

We would like to make a distinction at the outset between methods designed to extract semantic role assignments and those designed to extract propositional units. Although these endeavors are closely related, semantic role assignment involves assigning roles to constituents relative to a given verb. No attempt is made to resolve the referent of a constituent or to determine when different constituents might be referring to similar entities. Computational linguistics has tended to focus on the semantic role assignment task, whereas work in the text comprehension literature has focused on propositional assignment.[1]

In this section, we briefly discuss two classes of extraction methods that have been investigated in the computational linguistics literature—supervised semantic parsers and dependency parsers and one model for propositional analysis (Durbin et al., 2000) that has been developed in the text comprehension literature.

Supervised Semantic Parsing

The task addressed by supervised semantic parsers is to take a sentence and assign role labels to the relevant constituents for each of the predicates in the sentence (Blaheta & Charniak, 2000; Gildea & Jurafsky, 2002; O'Hara & Wiebe, 2002; Palmer, Rosenzweig, & Cotton, 2001).

For instance, given the sentence:

Sampras outguns Agassi in US Open Final

these systems might produce an intentional annotation, such as

[$_{Winner}$ Sampras] outguns [$_{Loser}$ Agassi] [$_{Location}$ in US Open Final]

This work has been driven, at least in part, by the availability of semantically labeled corpora such as Propbank (Kingsbury, Palmer, & Marcus, 2002) and FrameNet (Fillmore, Wooters, & Baker, 2001), which provide the relevant training data.

Perhaps the most appropriate of these systems for use in text comprehension is that of Gildea and Jurafsky (2002) as they attempt to label all roles available in a sentence (cf. Blaheta & Charniak, 2000). In their system, a classifier is trained with the use of features such as voice, constituent grammatical type, the path between predicate and the constituent, the lexical head of the constituent, and the predicate. To label a new sentence, the system first uses a statistical parser (such as Collins, 1999) to extract the features and then applies the classifier. As a consequence, errors can arise both because of parse errors resulting in improperly identified constituents and because of role mislabeling. Although the sys-

---

[1]We thank Richard Golden for raising this distinction.

tem achieves 82% accuracy in labeling, performance drops to 65% precision and 61% recall when it must also find the constituents.

Whether the system would be sufficient for text comprehension research is an open question. Although the precision and recall figures may seem low, some of the difficulty arises because of differences in the parsing formalism between the Collins parser and the identification of constituents in the FrameNet corpus on which it is trained. For instance, in FrameNet relative pronouns are included with their antecedents in constituents. For instance, consider the sentence

In its rough state he showed it to [$_{Agt}$ the Professor, who] bent [$_{BPrt}$ his grey beard] [$_{Path}$ over the neat script] and read for some time in silence.

Notice that "who" has been included in the agent constituent, a consistent property of the FrameNet corpus that the Collins parser does not replicate (Gildea & Jurafsky, 2002).

One important limitation of supervised semantic parsers is that they rely on the accuracy, coverage, and labeling scheme of their training set. In particular, the semantic roles employed by the systems are those defined by the corpus annotators. However, deciding upon a best set of semantic roles has proved extremely difficult. There are a great many schemes that have been proposed, ranging in granularity from very broad, such as the two macrorole proposal of Van Valin (1993), through theories that propose nine or ten roles, such as Fillmore (1971), to much more specific schemes that contain domain-specific slots such as ORIG_CITY, DEST_CITY or DEPART_TIME that are used in practical dialogue understanding systems (Stallard, 2000). In any given experimental context then, it is necessary to consider how specific the role labels must be in order to demonstrate the phenomena of interest.

Dependency Parsers

Dependency parsers are another mechanism that provides relational information from open sentences. The purpose of a dependency parser is to annotate a sentence with links that specify the dependencies in a sentence. For instance, in the sentence *the large cat sat on the mat*, the Minipar dependency parser (Lin, 1993, 1994, 1998) generates the following labeled arcs:

sit:s:cat

cat:det:the

cat:mod:large

sit:subj:cat

sit:mod:on

on:pcomp-n:mat

mat:det:the

which can be visualized as in Fig. 5–1.

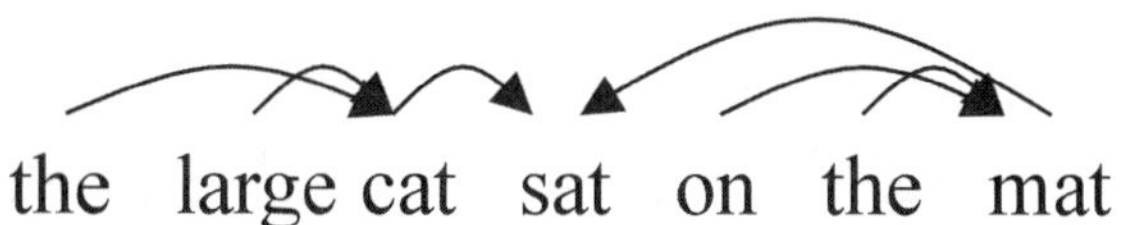

FIGURE 5–1. Example of Minipar dependency parse for the sentence "The large cat sat on the mat."

Although dependency parsers do not give role-filler bindings per se, they do enumerate relationships and they have the advantage of much better performance than existing semantic parsers. For instance, Lin (1998) reported 79% recall and 89% precision on the SUZANNE corpus.

Furthermore, dependency parsers have been shown to be useful for extracting inference rules from text. Lin and Patel (2001) used Minipar to extract simple inference rules such as if "X solves Y" then "X deals with Y." Although the rules extracted in this case are mainly surface form transformations, given the inference by coincidence results reported in this paper, it seems likely that Minipar could be used to extract deeper relationships as well.

AUTOCODER

The final system we will review in this section is the AUTOCODER model (Durbin et. al. 2000). Unlike the systems outlined previously, AUTOCODER is designed to take text, usually in the form of recall transcripts, and indicate which of a predefined set of propositions each text fragment might be expressing—the job of the human coder in typical text comprehension experiments. In this system, different surface forms for the same entity (e.g., *life savings, gold, money*) are resolved to the same underlying concept, so the system is performing propositional analysis, not just semantic role assignment.

To train AUTOCODER, a set of concepts, a set of propositions, and a set of mappings of words (or word phrases) into concepts and propositions is provided. Then a separate Markov model is constructed for each of the complex propositions in the reference text to account for the sequence of concepts in each of the text fragments corresponding to that proposition and the words that these concepts map into. To classify a fragment at test, an information theoretic measure is calculated for each of the models. The proposition corresponding to the minimal information (most probable) model is then chosen.

Table 5–1 shows three examples (taken from Durbin et al., 2000) of test fragments and the corresponding propositions selected by AUTOCODER.

Durbin et al. (2000) showed that they were able to achieve near-human reliabilities on this task, which makes the system potentially useful in experimental settings, as it provides a reliable mechanism for coding texts.

TABLE 5–1.
Examples of Novel Text Fragments and the Propositions to Which They Were Assigned by AUTOCODER (Durbin, et. al. 2000)

Human Recall Data	*Proposition Selected by AUTOCODER*
"and he went over every day to look at where the money was where the lump of gold was"	ATTEND AGENT: MISER OBJECT: GOLD
"and a bystander tells the miser to take a rock and bury it in the ground"	TELLS-INFO FROM: NEIGHBOR TO: MISER INFO: BURY(STONE)
"and the bystander says well all you ever did was look at the ground anyway"	TELLS-INFO FROM: NEIGHBOR TO: MISER INFO: ATTEND(MISER, GROUND)

Note. A simple story entitled "Miser" was the reference text in this case.

As a model of how people encode texts, each of the systems outlined above leaves some questions unanswered. Dependency parsers do not provide complete semantic analysis, and so although they may be an interesting starting point, they are not a complete solution. Semantic parsers can be used for assigning semantic roles, but they do not resolve reference in any sense and are dependent on the specification of an a priori set of roles. The AUTO CODER system attempts the entire task of propositional analysis but relies on both the relevant concepts and propositions and the mappings between text fragments and propositions to be provided by an annotator. In addition, none of these models provide any specific insights into how inference rules are learned (although simple inference rule generation systems have been built on dependency parsers). In the next section, we outline the syntagmatic paradigmatic model and describe how it addresses these issues.

THE SYNTAGMATIC PARADIGMATIC MODEL

The SP model has been designed as a model of verbal cognition. It has been used to account for a number of phenomena, including long-term grammatical dependencies and systematicity (Dennis, 2005), the extraction of statistical lexical information (syntactic, semantic, and associative) from corpora (Dennis, 2003b), sentence priming (Harrington & Dennis, 2003), verbal categorization and property judgment tasks (Dennis, 2005), serial recall (Dennis, 2003a), and relational extraction and inference (Dennis, 2005, 2004). In this section, we give a brief overview of the SP model. More complete descriptions, including the mathematical foundations, are provided by Dennis (2005; 2004).

In the SP model, sentence processing is characterized as the retrieval of associative constraints from sequential and relational long-term memory and the resolution of these constraints in working memory. Sequential long-term memory contains the sentences from a corpus. Relational long-term memory contains the extensional representations of the same sentences (see Fig. 5–2).

Creating an interpretation of a sentence/utterance involves the following steps.

Sequential Retrieval. The current sequence of input words is used to probe sequential memory for traces containing similar sequences of words. In the example, traces four and five, *Who did Kuerten beat? Roddick* and *Who did Hewitt beat? Costa,* are the closest matches to the target sentence, *Who did Sampras beat?* # and are assigned high probabilities.

Sequential Resolution. The retrieved sequences are then aligned with the target sentence to determine the appropriate set of substitutions for each word. Note that the slot adjacent to the # symbol aligns with the pattern {Costa, Roddick}. This pattern represents the role that the answer to the question must fill (i.e., the answer is the loser).

Relational Retrieval. The bindings of input words to their corresponding role vectors (the relational representation of the target sentence) are then used to probe relational long-term memory. In this case, trace one is favored, as it

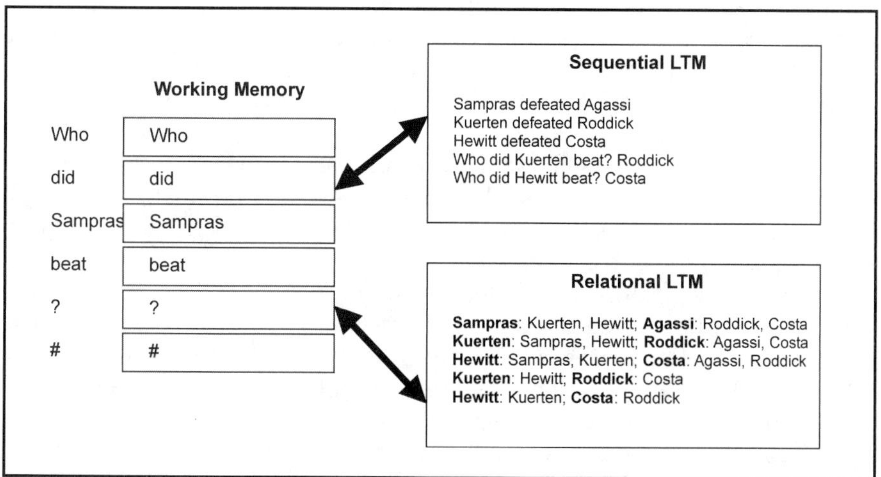

FIGURE 5–2. The Syntagmatic Paradigmatic (SP) architecture. The # symbol indicates an empty slot. Ultimately, it will contain the answer to the question.

involves similar role filler bindings. That is, it contains a binding of Sampras onto the {Kuerten, Hewitt} pattern, and it contains the {Roddick, Costa} pattern. Despite the fact that *Sampras defeated Agassi* has a different surface form than *Who did Sampras beat ? #*, it contains similar relational information and consequently has a high retrieval probability.

Relational Resolution. Finally, the paradigmatic associations in the retrieved relational traces are used to update working memory. In the relational trace for *Sampras defeated Agassi, Agassi* is bound to the {Roddick, Costa} pattern. Consequently, there is a strong probability that *Agassi* should align with the # symbol, which as a consequence of sequential retrieval is also aligned with the {Roddick, Costa} pattern. Note that the model has now answered the question—it was Agassi who was beaten by Sampras.

A common misconception about the model, which may be driven by transformational grammar notions, is that relational similarity is determined with the use of string edit theory, as is the case with sequential similarity. Rather relational similarity is determined by overlap in the role filler bindings generated separately by each of the sentences. In the example, it is not the string edit distance between *Sampras defeated Agassi* and *Who did Sampras beat?* that determines relational similarity; it is the fact that *Sampras* is bound to similar role vectors in the two cases and that the role vector {Roddick, Costa} appears in both relational traces.

Another common question that arises is whether the SP mechanism would be undermined if questions of the form *Who beat Sampras?* were also part of sequential memory. The intuition is that such a question should match the target question *Who did Sampras beat?* quite well and as a consequence the role vectors associated with *Sampras* and the answer slot would contain both winners and losers. This is a valid concern, and its impact is determined by the number of traces in memory that are of the same form as the target question *Who did Sampras beat?* These questions match more accurately than the distractor question *Who beat Sampras?* so provided there are enough of these types of exemplars, they will dominate the probability mass and the impact of the distractors will be negligible. However, in sparsely populated sequential memories (e.g., those used to model second language learners; see Harrington & Dennis 2003) some role confusion may occur.

Although the instance-based mechanisms employed in the SP model were originally inspired by episodic memory models such as Minerva II (Hintzman 1984) and Retrieving Effectively from Memory (Shiffrin & Steyvers 1997), sequential and relational memory do not align naturally with traditional notions of episodic and semantic memory. Rather, it is assumed that the traces in either sequential or relational memory may or may not contain specific kinds of contextual information. Episodic memory is not a separate system, but refers to the subset of traces that contain the kind of contextual information present in the retrieval cue.

That completes the description of the basic model. An outstanding question, however, is how one decides how similar two strings of words are and how they should align during sequential retrieval and resolution. Fortunately, there is a significant literature on this problem, known as String Edit Theory (SET). In the next section, we give a brief outline of SET.

INTRODUCTION TO STRING EDIT THEORY

String Edit Theory (SET) was popularized in a book by Sankoff and Kruskal (1983) titled *Time Warps, String Edits and Macromolecules* and has been developed in both the fields of computer science and molecular biology (Allison, Wallace, & Yee, 1992; Levenshtein, 1965; Needleman & Wunsch, 1970; Sellers, 1974). As the name suggests, the purpose of string edit theory is to describe how one string, which could be composed of words, letters, amino acids, etc., can be edited to form a second string. That is, what components must be inserted, deleted, or changed to turn one string into another. As indicated above, in the SP model, SET is used to decide which sentences from a corpus are most like the target sentence and which tokens within these sentences should align.

As an example, suppose we are trying to align the sentences *Sampras defeated Agassi* and *Kuerten defeated Roddick*. The most obvious alignment is that which maps the two sentences to each other in a one-to-one fashion:

Sampras	defeated	Agassi	
|	|	|	A1
Kuerten	defeated	Roddick	

In this alignment, we have three edit operations. There is a **change** of *Sampras* for *Kuerten,* a **match** of *defeated* and a **change** of *Agassi* for *Roddick.* In fact, this alignment can also be expressed as a sequence of edit operations:

<Sampras, Kuerten>

<defeated, defeated>

<Agassi, Roddick>

In SET, sentences do not have to be of the same length in order to be aligned. If we add *Pete* to the first sentence, we can use a **delete** to describe one way in which the resulting sentences could be aligned:

Pete	Sampras	defeated	Agassi	
|	|	|	|	A2
–	Kuerten	defeated	Roddick	

A dash is used to fill the slot left by a deletion (or an insertion) and can be thought of as the empty word. The corresponding edit operation is denoted by <Sampras, ->. Although these alignments may be the most obvious ones, there are many other options.

For instance, in aligning *Sampras defeated Agassi* and *Kuerten defeated Roddick*, we could start by deleting *Sampras*:

Sampras	defeated	Agassi	–	A3
|	|	|		
–	Kuerten	defeated	Roddick	

Note that *Roddick* is now inserted at the end of the alignment (denoted <-, Roddick>).

Alternatively, we could have deleted *Sampras* and then inserted *Kuerten* to give:

Sampras	–	defeated	Agassi	A4
|	|	|		
–	Kuerten	defeated	Roddick	

There are a total of 63 ways in which *Sampras defeated Agassi* can be aligned with *Kuerten defeated Roddick*, but not all of these alignments are equally likely. Intuitively, alignment A4 seems better than A3 because the word *defeated* is matched. However, this alignment still seems worse than A1 because it requires *Sampras* to be deleted and *Kuerten* to be inserted. A mechanism that produces alignments of sentences should favor those that have many matches and should penalize those that require many insertions and deletions. To capture these intuitions, edit operations are assigned probabilities. Typically, match probabilities are higher than change probabilities, which are higher than insertion or deletion probabilities. Assuming conditional independence of the edit operations, the probability of an alignment is the multiplication of the probabilities of the edit operations of which it is composed. Each alignment is an exclusive hypothesis about how the two strings might be aligned, and so the probability that the strings are aligned in one of these ways is the addition of the probabilities of the alignments. Given that there are an exponential number of alignments between strings, one may be concerned that any algorithm based on SET would be infeasible. However, there are efficient dynamic programming algorithms that have $O(nm)$ time and space complexity, where n and m are the lengths of the two strings (Needleman & Wunsch, 1970).

Only a cursory explanation of SET has been possible in this chapter. Interested readers are referred to Sankoff and Kruskal (1983) and Allison, Wallace, and Yee (1992). In addition, Dennis (1995) provides a more complete mathematical treatment in the context of the SP model, including an explanation of how the edit model can be trained so that it does not rely on direct word overlap, as is the case in the examples above.

TEXT MAPPING IN THE SP MODEL

In order for the relational representations generated by the SP model to play the same role as propositions in text comprehension theory, the basic requirements are that they be capable of encapsulating information at something like the idea unit level and that they be able to bind fillers to something like roles that participate systematically across different sentence instances. For instance, when presented with the sentence *Sampras outguns Agassi*, the model must be capable of realizing that this is an idea unit, capturing the fact that Sampras and Agassi are not equivalent within this sentence and, furthermore, of generalizing that realization across utterances with potentially very different structures, such as *Who won the match between Sampras and Agassi?* In this section, we describe a simulation experiment designed to investigate these issues. We start by outlining the domain that was used to test the model.

The Tennis News Domain

There were a number of criteria that were used to select the domain on which to test the model. First, the domain was required to be one for which naturally occurring text was available, as it is important that the model be capable of dealing robustly with the variety of sentences that are typically found in real text. Also, in real corpora there are many sentences that do not refer to the facts of interest at all, and the model should be capable of isolating the relevant ones.

Second, we wished to test the model's ability to extract relational information from sentences. Many question-answering systems employ type heuristics rather than engage in relational analysis. For instance, they might determine the date of the running of the Melbourne Cup by looking for sentences containing the term *Melbourne Cup* and returning any date within these sentences regardless of the role this date might fill. Although such heuristics are often very successful in practice, there are some questions for which a relational analysis is necessary.

Finally, we were interested in testing the model's ability to take advantage of inference by coincidence and so chose a domain in which the opportunities for such inferences are abundant.

Sixty-nine articles were taken from the Association of Tennis Professionals (ATP) website at http://www.atptennis.com/. The articles were written between September 2002 and December 2002 and ranged in length from 134 to 701 words. In total there were 21,212 words in the corpus. The documents

TABLE 5-2.
Example of Articles From the Association of Tennis Professionals (ATP) Website

US OPEN Sep. 08, 2002
Sampras Outguns Agassi in US Open Final
Sampras claims 14th Grand Slam title
Pete Sampras captured his 14th Grand Slam title—and fifth US Open—with a 6–3, 6–4, 5–7, 6–4 victory over Andre Agassi in the final at Flushing Meadows. Sampras, who had gone 33 tournaments without lifting a trophy since last winning Wimbledon in 2000, defeated his long-time rival Agassi for the 20th time in 34 meetings. With the win, Sampras joins Jimmy Connors as the only five-time US Open winners in the Open era, and at 31 years, 28 days, becomes the oldest since Ken Rosewall in 1970 (35 years, 10 months). The victory also marked Sampras' 71st match win at the US Open, which ties Bill Tilden in fourth place on the all-time singles list at the tournament, and also takes Sampras to 12th position in the ATP Champions Race 2002. Agassi moves to second behind Lleyton Hewitt. . . .

were manually divided into sentences; the mean sentence length was 23.7 words. Table 5–2 provides an example article.

The tennis domain fulfills the criteria outlined above. Naturally occurring text is available, and there were many nontarget sentences that the model was required to reject in its search for relevant information. Choosing the winner of a tennis match cannot be solved by appealing to simple type heuristics, as relevant source sentences often contain the names of both the winner and the loser, so that the correct answer must be selected from items of the same type. Finally, in sports reporting of this kind there are often multiple cues, many of which are indirect, that allow the disambiguation of key facts—like who the winner of a match was.

Then 377 questions of the form *Who won the match between X and Y? X* were created. Any result that could be deduced from the article text was included. So, for instance, results that required the resolution of an anaphoric reference from other sentences in the same document were retained. Also, the winner was alternated between the first and second name positions, so that the model could not simply repeat the name in the first slot in order to answer the question.

Results and Discussion

To test the model, each question was presented with the final answer slot vacant (e.g., *Who won the match between Sampras and Agassi? #*). The SP model was invoked to complete the pattern. During sequential retrieval the model was allowed to retrieve any sentence or question from the entire corpus. During relational retrieval, however, only facts derived from the sentences were allowed as retrieval candidates—that is, the factual knowledge embodied by the questions was not permitted to influence the results.

The token with the highest probability in the # slot was assumed to be the answer returned by the model. Figure 5–3 shows a breakdown of the number of results in each category after sequential resolution and after relational resolution. Following relational processing, on about 67% of occasions the model correctly returned the winner of the match; 26% of the time it incorrectly produced the loser of the match; 5% of the time it responded with a player other than either the winner or loser of the match; and on 3% of occasions it committed a type error, responding with a word or punctuation symbol that was not a player's name.

There are a number of ways in which one might seek to establish an appropriate baseline against which to compare these results. Because the model is developed in a pattern completion framework it is possible for any symbol in the vocabulary to be returned. There were 2,522 distinct tokens in the corpus, so nominally the chance rate is less than 1%. However, one might also argue that the chance rate should be related to the number of elements of the appropriate type for a response—that is, the number of names of players. There were 142 distinct players' names, and so by this analysis the baseline would also be below 1%. A further type distinction would be between winners and losers. There were 85 distinct winners, which results in a baseline of just over 1%. Note that in any of these cases, the model is performing well above chance.

Note that the SP model is only given a pattern to complete and so is not only answering the question, but is also extracting the relevant schema

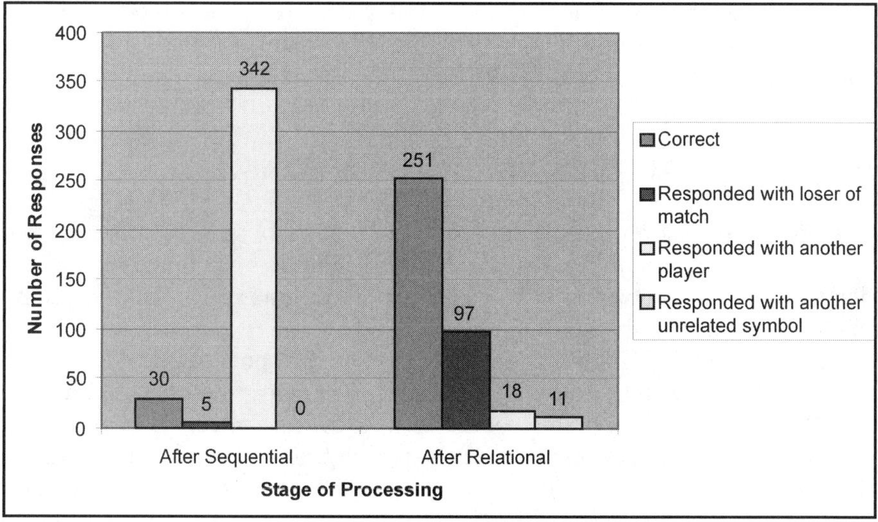

FIGURE 5–3. Breakdown of result types after sequential processing and after relational processing.

within which the question must be answered. In addition, when the SP model is run without relational retrieval or resolution, performance drops from 67% to 8% correct (see Fig. 5–3)—so relational processing was critical. Given that the questions were not included in relational memory, performance must have been driven by the statistics of the articles rather than by the statistics of the questions—the model was not simply looking up the answer in sequential memory.

Issues That Compromised Performance

In examining the types of errors committed by the model, we found a number of recurring types. As mentioned earlier, the use of anaphora is quite common in this corpus. The current model has no mechanism for the resolution of anaphora, which undermines both its ability to isolate the sentences containing the appropriate relational information and its ability to select the correct answer token. In addition, a mechanism for isolating appropriate context is necessary. On seven occasions in the current data set there are sets of players for whom the questions are ambiguous without the use of context to isolate the correct match. In addition, inference by coincidence can sometimes induce an incorrect response. For instance, the model induces that Schalken won the match against Pete Sampras, in part on the basis of the sentence *Schalken, from the Netherlands, made his best-ever grand slam showing at the US open last month . . .* However, although having a best-ever showing is indicative of winning, in this case it is misleading, as it was in fact Sampras who defeated him in the semifinals. Finally, the model's lack of sensitivity to sublexical structure creates difficulties, particularly in deriving relational match when possessives are employed. There are then many avenues by which one could look to improve performance.

INFERENCE IN THE SP MODEL

Inference generation presents even more serious problems to propositional systems than text mapping. The mental representation of a text that comprehenders construct consists not only of the information explicitly expressed by the text, but also of the knowledge activated by the text and the inferences generated that fill in gaps in the text and link prior knowledge to new information. Currently, the process of formulating inference rules relies even more heavily on the intuition of the theorist, and assessing the adequacy of a modeling effort often hinges on the extent to which these intuitions are shared in the research community. Not only do inference rules need to be formal and fully automatic; they should also be an inherent component of the comprehension system, not some sort of add-on. There are important distinctions to be made between the mental representation of the text itself (text base) and the situation model, which incorporates the comprehender's goals, interests, and prior knowledge, but a process model of comprehension must account for both.

The dominant questions about inferences in the literature on discourse comprehension have focused on which inferences are made and when they are made, during comprehension or on demand at some later time. Inferences have been classified along the dimensions of automatic versus controlled and retrieval versus generation (Kintsch, 1998), and a great deal of discussion has been devoted to the question of when inferences are made (Graesser, Singer, & Trabasso, 1994; McKoon & Ratcliff, 1992). The SP model suggests a different approach to the study of inferences based on inference mechanisms that cuts across these distinctions and complements them. Specifically, the SP model addresses the following inference mechanisms:

1. Inference by coincidence. This is not a process per se. Rather, the inference occurs as an emergent property of the model as the consequences of role-filler overlap between proposition-like traces.
2. Linguistic pattern completion. A person follows a specific linguistic pattern by filling in the values of variables. This is what typically happens in formal logic, but it can also happen in much less formal ways as well, such as when the rule *I before E except after* C requires the pattern to be instantiated in either inner or outer speech.
3. Inference by relational retrieval (analogical inference). Borrowing from the STAR model of analogical reasoning (Halford et al., 1994), the SP model proposes that analogical inference occurs as a consequence of doing retrieval over structured (proposition-like) units.

For completeness we note two additional inference mechanisms not considered here:

4. Associative inference, which links causally or temporally connected propositions by means of constraint satisfaction (e.g., Golden & Rumelhart, 1993; Frank, Koppen, Noordman, & Vonk, 2003).
5. Perceptual simulation, which generates a visual or auditory image of a situation. This process allows the constraints embodied in that system (e.g., spatial or form constraints) to act, forming a coherent image from which the facts of interest can be read off.

In the following sections, we outline how the SP model accounts for inference by coincidence, linguistic pattern completion, and inference by relational retrieval, before demonstrating inference by coincidence in the tennis news domain.

Inference by Coincidence

In production system models of inferencing, commonsense knowledge is encoded in the form of if-then rules. For instance, most people know that if X sold the Y to Z then it is also the case that Z bought the Y from X. Furthermore, it is the case that Z now has the Y and X does not have the Y.

In production system parlance this might be expressed as
if SOLD(X, Z, Y) then

BOUGHT(Z, X, Y)
POSSESS(Z, Y)
NOT POSSESS(X, Y)

When attempting to establish whether John owns a camera, the inferencing system might be asked to verify that POSSESS(John, camera), in which case it would activate the above rule and search memory to determine whether John had ever been sold a camera (i.e., SOLD(X, John, camera)). This process, known as backward chaining, has two major disadvantages. First, successful inference relies on all relevant common sense being appropriately coded in production system rules. Second, even inferences that people would find trivial can be computationally expensive, because there may be many such rules that must be consulted in order to establish the truth value of the predicate. In this example, John may possess a camera because he was given it, or because he found it, or because he stole it, etc. All of these possibilities must be considered as new predicates, which in turn may rely upon additional rules and so forth.

The SP model provides a mechanism that exploits corpus statistics to avoid the necessity of explicit inferencing of this kind. To illustrate, suppose the model had been exposed to the following corpus:

1. IBM sold the widget to Microsoft.
2. Microsoft bought the widget from IBM.
3. SPSS sold the software to SAS.
4. SAS bought the software from SPSS.
5. Liverpool sold the player to Manchester.
6. Manchester bought the player from Liverpool.

Table 5–3 shows the most probable alignments for the sentences *Charlie bought the lemonade from Lucy* and *Lucy sold the lemonade to Charlie*. As the order of bindings in relational traces is irrelevant, these sentences have very similar representations. In both cases, Charlie is bound to {Microsoft, SAS, Manchester}, lemonade is bound to {widget, software, player}, and Lucy is bound to {IBM, SPSS, Liverpool}. That is, if we know that Charlie bought the

TABLE 5–3.
Most Probable Alignments for *Charlie Bought the Lemonade From Lucy* and *Lucy Sold the Lemonade to Charlie*

Charlie	*bought*	*the*	*lemonade*	*from*	*Lucy*
Microsoft	bought	the	widget	from	IBM
SAS	bought	the	software	from	SPSS
Manchester	bought	the	player	from	Liverpool

Lucy	*sold*	*the*	*lemonade*	*to*	*Charlie*
IBM	sold	the	widget	to	Microsoft
SPSS	sold	the	software	to	SAS
Liverpool	sold	the	player	to	Manchester

Note here that we show just the most probable alignments for ease of exposition. The model, however, always computes the sum of all possible alignments probability weighted.

lemonade from Lucy, we automatically also know that Lucy sold the lemonade to Charlie without ever explicitly extracting or applying a rule to effect the transformation. Furthermore, if we consider the pattern {Microsoft, SAS, Manchester} as an owner role, then the model also automatically "knows" that Charlie owns the lemonade.

By this account, the process that allows us to implicitly form simple inferences and the process that allows us to generalize over different surface forms of a sentence are identical. It is the existence of a critical subset of sequential traces that allows the inference to occur. This type of inference provides a plausible account of how the human cognitive system is able to acquire the wealth of commonsense knowledge that it appears to (cf. Lenat, 1995), despite never being explicitly exposed to this information. In a way reminiscent of Latent Semantic Analysis (Landauer & Dumais, 1997), factual knowledge is accumulated implicitly via the statistics of the corpus. Note, however, that unlike LSA, the SP model assumes that this knowledge becomes available as a consequence of simple retrieval mechanisms operating over a large set of memory traces, rather than proposing comprehensive induction processes.

Linguistic Pattern Completion (Logical Inference)

Although inference by coincidence may be responsible for the majority of automatic inference making that takes place during text comprehension, people are also able to engage in more controlled forms of inference. For instance, people are able to follow rules such as *if X sold the Y to Z then it is also the case that Z bought the Y from X*, even in the absence of examples illustrating this principle. To show how this type of inference can be addressed, suppose that the SP model had been exposed to the following corpus:

1. if X sold the Y to Z
2. then Z bought the Y from X
3. if Lucy sold the lemonade to Charlie

Note that traces one and two provide the linguistic fragments necessary to define the abstract rule, whereas trace three is a specific example, which the model will be required to use to infer that Charlie bought the lemonade from Lucy. Processing now proceeds as in the previous example, with Lucy bound to {X}, lemonade to {Y}, and Charlie to {Z}. Then in a second step, trace two is used to infer that Charlie bought the lemonade from Lucy.

Unlike in the previous example, no specific examples are available to make the connection between buying and selling in the way that they did in the previous section. Rather, the abstract rule is used in a two-stage process. Note, however, that the use of an abstract rule in this way does not lead to the rich set of bindings that were generated in the previous section. For instance, *Lucy* will be bound to {X} with the explicit rule, whereas in the previous example *Lucy* was bound to {IBM, SPSS, Liverpool}, all symbols that have a grounded meaning and hence are liable to be used systematically within the systems experience. The symbol X, on the other hand, may be used to mean many different things in different circumstances and consequently is not a useful symbol for making additional inferences, such as inferring possession. So although explicit reasoning is useful in domains where direct experience is limited, matching explicit rules may interfere with the process of acquiring richly interwoven knowledge structures when direct experience can be made available.

Also note that implicit inference made the relevant information immediately available in relational memory, whereas explicit inference relies on the application of a rule that must be retrieved from sequential memory, resolved, retrieved from relational memory, and resolved before the relational trace is entered into relational memory. This difference may explain why explicit inference takes more time and is more prone to dual task interference and why the process of explicit inference can be available for report.

In this example, the inference was made by the application of a logical rule. However, some controlled inference may be made not by the application of a rule, but rather by analogy to a separate domain. The next section addresses this kind of analogical inference.

Inference by Relational Retrieval (Analogical Inference)

There is now a well-developed literature on analogical reasoning with a long history of well-specified computational models (Kokinov, B. & French, R. M. 2003). A prerequisite for all of these models is a propositional representation of the relevant facts in the base and target domains. In some models these propositional representations are symbolic (ANALOGY: Evans, 1964; SMT: Falkenhainer, Forbus, & Gentner, 1989; Gentner, 1983; ACME: Holyoak & Thagard, 1989), whereas other models employ distributed representations (STAR: Halford et al., 1994; LISA: Hummel & Holyoak, 1997; Wilson, Halford, Gray, & Phillips, 2001). In either case, however, the practice has been to hand code the relevant facts in the appropriate representational format. Although there has been considerable work on representation creation mechanisms (COPYCAT: French, 1995; Hofstadter, 1995; Mitchell, 1993), the focus in this work has been on allowing different aspects of an analogical mapping problem to be highlighted by dynamically changing the representational scheme rather than on extracting the relevant information from naturalistic corpora (e.g., text corpora). As in the text comprehension domain, the inability to solve the text mapping problem has been an important limitation in assessing the viability of analogical reasoning models and has prevented them from scaling to realistic size knowledge bases. The SP model has the potential to solve this dilemma, as it provides a mechanism by which a propositional knowledge base can be extracted automatically from a large corpus.

In addition, however, the basic mechanisms of the SP model implement a form of analogical inference. To illustrate we will use the model to solve a simple proportional analogy such as MAN:HOUSE::DOG:?.

Suppose the model has been exposed to the following corpus:

1. a mother is to a daughter
2. a father is to a son
3. CC a man is to a house

Table 5–4 shows the most probable alignment for *a dog is to a #*. The input word *dog* has been aligned with {man}, and the empty slot at the end of the sentence is aligned with {house}.

Now, the relational trace for *a kennel is where a dog lives* also has a binding of *dog* onto {man} (see Table 5–4) and hence is selected in relational retrieval. In the selected trace *kennel* is bound to {house}, so during relational retrieval the empty slot is now filled with the correct answer.

TABLE 5–4.
Most Probable Alignments of *A Dog Is to a #* and *A Kennel Is Where a Dog Lives*

a	*dog*	*is*	*to*	*a*	*#*	
a	man	is	to	a	house	
a	*kennel*	*is*	*where*	*a*	*dog*	*lives*
a	house	is	where	a	man	lives

Although the simple mechanisms proposed in the SP model are clearly insufficient to model the broad spectrum of analogical reasoning results, they may prove useful in describing the sort of analogical inference that happens routinely during the normal course of text comprehension.

In this section, three types of inference that can be implemented by the SP model have been demonstrated. Inference by coincidence, linguistic pattern completion, and inference by relational retrieval all occur as a consequence of the basic processing assumptions of the model with minimal requirements on the content of the input corpus. In particular, the distinction between automatic and controlled inference is explained by the fact that automatic inference is not a process at all, but rather a coincidence of relational representation that embodies an inference.

Of the three inference processes outlined here, it is inference by coincidence that one would expect to be ubiquitous. The question then arises: To what extent were the results of the tennis news simulation study a consequence of inference by coincidence? We address this question in the next section.

Demonstration of Inference by Coincidence

To assess the contribution that inference by coincidence made to the performance of the model in the tennis news task, the sentence with maximum retrieval probability for each query was classified into one of three categories.

The literal category contained those sentences where there was an explicit statement of the result—even if it required some interpretation. For example, in the processing of the question *Who won the match between Ulihrach and Vicente? Ulihrach*, the highest probability relational trace was *Vicente bounced by Ulihrach*, which literally states the result (even if it is necessary for one to interpret *bounced* in this context).

The inference category contained those sentences that did not contain a literal statement of the result, but which provided some evidence (not necessarily conclusive) for what the result may have been (see Table 5–5 for examples). For instance, in the processing of the question *Who won the match between Portas and Sampras? Sampras,* the relational trace with the highest retrieval probability was *Sampras claims 14th Grand Slam title*. Although this sentence does not explicitly state the result of this match, one can infer that if Sampras won the title, then it is likely that he won this match. Note that this inference does not always follow, as the writer may have made reference to a result from a different tournament, or the question may have come from a different article. However, the fact that Sampras won the title does provide evidence in favor of his having won this match. Unlike a traditional inference system, however, the SP model is making the inference by virtue of the fact that the names of people that appear in statements of the form *X claims— title* also tend to appear in the winner slot at the end of the questions.

TABLE 5-5.
Examples of Inference by Coincidence in the Tennis News Domain

Who won the match between Carlsen and Kiefer? Carlsen
Kafelnikov now meets Kenneth Carlsen of Denmark in the second round.

Who won the match between Kiefer and Safin? Safin
Safin, Kafelnikov surge toward hometown showdown

Who won the match between Ljubicic and Kutsenko? Ljubicic
Sixth seed Davide Sanguinetti of Italy and eighth seed Ivan Ljubicic of Croatia took different paths to their opening-round wins at the president's cup in Tashkent.

Who won the match between Voltchkov and Haas? Voltchkov
According to Haas, the injury first arose during Wednesday's match against Sargis Sargsian, and became progressively worse during practice and then the match against Voltchkov.

Who won the match between Srichaphan and Lapentti? Srichaphan
Srichaphan has now won two titles in four finals this year.

Note: Each example shows the question and the sentence that generated the most probable relational trace.

Finally, the other category included all remaining cases. These included traces in which both players were mentioned, but the sentence could not have been used to conclude who the winner may have been. For example, when the question *Who won the match between Acasuso and Pavel? Acasuso* was presented, the most probable relational trace was *Pavel and Acasuso to clash in Bucharest semis*. In addition, this category contains sentences that contradict the correct result. For example, the question *Who won the match between Pavel and Srichaphan? Pavel* produced the relational trace *Pavel, now 38–22 on the year, has reached two semifinals in 2002 Chennai l. to Srichaphan and Bucharest l. to Acasuso*. This situation occurs when a player revenges an earlier loss. In addition, the other category was assigned when the sentence was unrelated to the question. For instance, when the model was presented with the question *Who won the match between Meligeni and Etlis? Etlis*, it returned *Kiefer quickly overcame Gaston Etlis of Argentina 6–2, 6–4 on Monday to qualify for the main draw of the Kremlin cup*. Figure 5–4 shows the number of most probable relational traces in each category.

To get an indication of the contribution that inference by coincidence is making to correct responding, consider those correct responses that can be attributed to either literal or inference traces. On 59% of occasions the model was inferring the answer rather than relying on literal retrieval. Given that in each case a literal statement of the results existed in the corpus, it is significant that inference by coincidence seems to be playing such a crucial role in the performance of the model.

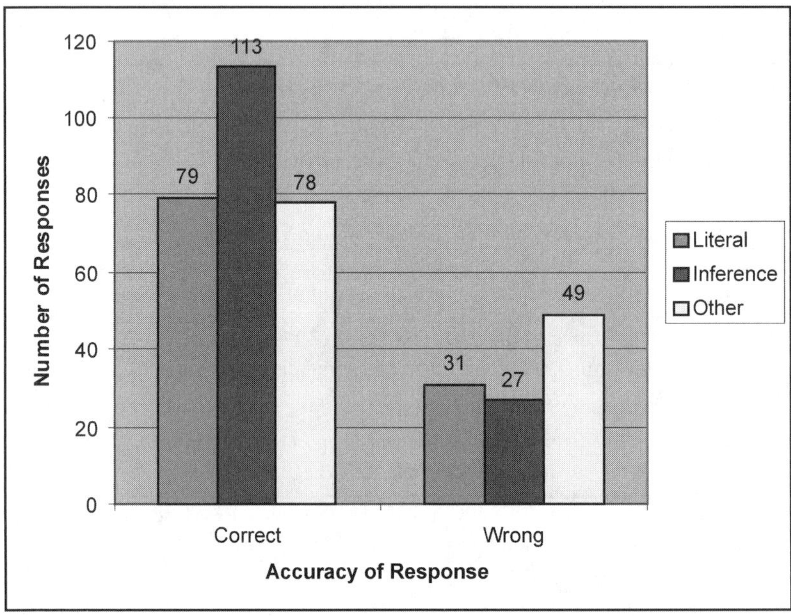

FIGURE 5–4. Breakdown of responses based on the accuracy of the response and the type of the most probable relational trace according to the model. *Literal* refers to traces in which the answer was stated explicitly. *Inference* refers to traces in which the answer was not stated, but from which it could be inferred. *Other* refers to traces from which the answer was not derivable. Note that these statistics are for the most probable trace only. The model, however, accumulates information from multiple traces, so that it is still possible for it to answer correctly, even if the most probable trace does not contain the relevant information.

CONCLUSIONS

The purpose of this chapter was to assess the ability of the Syntagmatic Paradigmatic model to address the text mapping and inference generation problems in text comprehension. The extent to which the relational representations generated by the SP model are capable of playing the role that propositions have previously done was critical.

On three important criteria they seem to be adequate. First, they are capable of encapsulating something equivalent to an idea unit. Second, they are able to maintain filler–role bindings. Finally, they are capable of doing this in a systematic way across sentence instances with different surface structures. Unlike propositions, however, relational representations can be generated directly from text and do not require a grammar or semantic roles to be specified in advance. They are deduced in an unsupervised fashion from the corpus.

In addition, the SP model offers a new inference mechanism. Inference by coincidence provides an explanation of how people are able to acquire a large database of inference rules without being exposed to them explicitly or even seeing antecedents and consequences in a contingent relationship. Furthermore, unlike previous notions of inference, inference by coincidence is not a process. Rather, it is an emergent property that occurs as a direct consequence of retrieval. Inference by coincidence rules have no explicit instantiation and exist only as potentialities until they are used.

Despite the success of the model in the demonstrations outlined in this chapter, there remain a number of issues to be resolved. First, the model has no real sense of a constituent. In the tennis news domain as outlined above, the answer was always a single word. In general, however, it will be necessary to accommodate multiword fillers and to do so in a way that respects linguistic structure.

Second, although inference by coincidence seems to be robust, it has yet to be demonstrated that the types of sentence necessary to support inference by linguistic pattern completion and inference by relational retrieval occur in real corpora. Indeed, it may well be the case that written text is unsuitable and that it will be necessary to turn to child-directed speech corpora to find the relevant linguistic fragments. Although the model does not currently address the sort of inference induced by contingent events, the fact that it is based on an episodic memory model suggests that this deficiency can be overcome. What is likely to be more difficult is addressing inference by perceptual simulation, as this would seem to require the inclusion of an adequate model of the perceptual processing apparatus.

ACKNOWLEDGMENTS

This research was supported by Australian Research Council grant A00106012, U.S. National Science Foundation grant EIA—0121201, and U.S. Department of Education grant R305G020027. We thank Richard Golden and an unnamed reviewer for helpful comments on an earlier version of this chapter.

REFERENCES

Allison, L., Wallace, C. S., & Yee, C. N. (1992). Finite-state models in the alignment of macromolecules. *Journal of Molecular Evolution, 35*(1), 77–89.

Bierwisch, M. (1969). On certain problems of semantic representation. *Foundations of language, 5*, 153–184.

Blaheta, D., & Charniak, E. (2000). *Assigning function tags to parsed text.* Paper presented at the Proceedings of the First Annual Meeting the North American Chapter of the ACL (NAACL), Seattle, Washington.

Collins, M. (1999). *Head-driven statistical models for natural language parsing*. University of Pennsylvania, Philadelphia.

Collins, M., & Quillian, M. R. (1969). Retrieval from semantic memory. *Journal of Verbal Learning and Verbal Behavior, 8*, 240–247.

Daelemans, W. (1999). Introduction to the special issue on memory-based language processing. *Journal of Experimental and Theoretical Artificial Intelligence, 11*, 369–390.

Dennis, S. (2003a). *An alignment-based account of serial recall*. Paper presented at the 25th Conference of the Cognitive Science Society.

Dennis, S. (2003b). *A comparison of statistical models for the extraction of lexical information from text corpora*. Paper presented at the 25th Conference of the Cognitive Science Society.

Dennis, S. (1995). A memory-based theory of verbal cognition. *Cognitive Science. 29*(2). 145–193.

Dennis, S. (1994). An unsupervised method for the extraction of propositional information from text. *Proceedings of the National Academy of Sciences. 101*, 5206–5213.

Dougherty, M. R. P. (1999). MINERVA-DM: A memory processes model for judgements of likelihood. *Psychological Review, 106*(1), 180–209.

Durbin, M. A., Earwood, J., & Golden, R. M. (2000). *Hidden Markov Models for coding story recall data*. Paper presented at the Proceedings of the 22nd Annual Cognitive Science Society Conference.

Evans, T. (1964). A Heuristic Program to Solve Geometric-Analogy Problems. In: Spring Joint Computer Conference, vol. 25. Reprinted in: M. Fischler & O. Firschein (eds.) Readings in Computer Vision. Morgan Kaufman Publ., 1987.

Falkenhainer, B., Forbus, K. D., & Gentner, D. (1989). The structure-mapping engine: Algorithm and examples. *Artificial intelligence, 41*, 1–63.

Fillmore, C. J. (1968). The case for case. In E. Black & R. T. Harms (Eds.), *Universals of linguistic theory*. New York: Holt, Rinehart & Winston.

Fillmore, C. J. (1971). Some problems for case grammar. In R. J. O'Brien (Ed.), *22nd round table. Linguistics: delopments of the sixties—Viewpoints of the seventies* (Vol. 24, pp. 35–56). Washington, DC: Georgetown University Press.

Fillmore, C. J., Wooters, C., & Baker, C. F. (2001). *Building a large lexical databank which provides deep semantics*. Paper presented at the Proceedings of the Pacific Asian Conference on Language, Information and Computation, Hong Kong.

Frank, S. L., Koppen, M., Noordman, L. G. M., & Vonk, W. (2003). Modeling knowledge-based inferences in story comprehension. *Cognitive Science, 27*(6), 807–950.

French, R. M. (1995). *The subtlety of sameness: A theory and computer model of analogy-making*. Cambridge, MA: MIT Press.

Gentner, D. (1983). Structure-mapping—A theoretical framework for analogy. *Cognitive Science, 7*(2), 155–170.

Gildea, D., & Jurafsky, D. (2002). Automatic labeling of semantic roles. *Computational Linguistics, 28*(3), 245–288.

Golden, R. M., & Rumelhart, D. E. (1993). A parallel distributed processing model of story comprehension and recall. *Discourse processes, 16*, 203–207.

Goldinger, S. D. (1998). Echoes of echoes? An episodic theory of lexical access. *Psychological Review, 105*(2), 251–279.

Graesser, A. C., Singer, M., & Trabasso, T. (1994). Constructing inferences during narrative text comprehension. *Psychological Review, 101*, 375–395.

Halford, G., Wilson, W., Guo, K., Gayler, R., Wiles, J., & Stewart, J. (1994). Connectionist implications for processing capacity limitations in analogies. In K. J. Holyoak & J. Barnden (Eds.), *Analogical connections* (Vol. 2, pp. 363–415). Norwood: Ablex.

Harrington, M., & Dennis, S. (2003). *Structural priming in sentence comprehension.* Paper presented at the 25th Conference of the Cognitive Science Society.

Hintzman, D. L. (1984). Minerva–2—A simulation-model of human memory. *Behavior Research Methods Instruments & Computers, 16*(2), 96–101.

Hintzman, D. L. (1988). Judgments of frequency and recognition memory in a multiple-trace memory model. *Psychological Review, 95*(4), 528–551.

Hofstadter, D. (1995). *Fluid concepts and creative analogies: Computer models of fundamental mechanisms of thought*. New York: Basic Books.

Holyoak, K. J., & Thagard, P. (1989). Analogical mapping by constraint satisfaction. *Cognitive Science, 13*(3), 295–355.

Hummel, J., & Holyoak, K. J. (1997). Distributed representations of structure: A theory of analogical access and mapping. *Psychological Review, 104*, 427–466.

Katz, J. J., & Fodor, J. A. (1963). The structure of semantic theory. *Language, 39*, 170–210.

Kingsbury, P., Palmer, M., & Marcus, M. (2002). *Adding semantic annotation to the Penn TreeBank.* Paper presented at the Proceedings of the Human Language Technology Conference, San Diego.

Kintsch, W. (1974). *The representation of meaning in memory*. New York: Wiley.

Kintsch, W. (1998). *Comprehension: A paradigm for cognition*. Cambridge, UK: Cambridge University Press.

Kokinov, B., & French, R. M. (2003). Computational models of Snalogy-making. In Nadel, L. (Ed.) *Encyclopedia of the Cognitive Science. Vol. 1, pp. 113–118.* London: Nature Publishing Group.

Landauer, T. K., & Dumais, S. T. (1997). A solution to Plato's problem: The Latent Semantic Analysis theory of the acquisition, induction, and representation of knowledge. *Psychological Review, 104*, 211–240.

Lenat, D. B. (1995). CYC: A large-scale investment in knowledge infrastructure. *Communications of the ACM, 38*(1).

Levenshtein, V. I. (1965). Binary codes capable of correcting deletions, insertions and reversals. *Dokl. Akad. Nauk. SSSR, 163*, 845–848.

Lin, D. (1993). *Principle-based parsing without overgeneralization.* Paper presented at the Proceedings of ACL–93, Columbus, OH.

Lin, D. (1994). *Principar—An efficient, broad-coverage, principle-based parser.* Paper presented at the Proceedings of COLING–94, Kyoto, Japan.

Lin, D. (1998). *Dependency-based evaluation of MINIPAR.* Paper presented at the Workshop on the Evaluation of Parsing Systems, Granada, Spain.

Lin, D., & Pantel, P. (2001). Discovery of inference rules for question answering. *Natural Language Engineering, 7*(4), 343–360.

Logan, G. D. (1988). Towards an instance theory of automatization. *Psychological Review, 95*, 492–527.

McKoon, G., & Ratcliff, R. (1992). Inference during reading. *Psychological Review, 99*, 440–466.

Mitchell, M. (1993). *Analogy-making as perception: A computer model*. Cambridge, MA: MIT Press.

Moldovan, D., Harabagiu, S., Girju, R., Morarescu, P., Lacatusu, F., Novischi, A., et al. (2002). *LCC tools for question answering*. Paper presented at the Eleventh Text Retrieval Conference (TREC 2002).

Nakisa, R. C., & Plunkett, K. (1998). Evolution for rapidly learned representations for speech. *Language and Cognitive Processes, 13*(2/3), 105–127.

Needleman, S. B., & Wunsch, C. D. (1970). A general method applicable to the search for similarities in the amino acid sequence of two proteins. *Journal of Molecular Biology, 48*, 443–453.

Nosofsky, R. (1986). Attention, similarity and the identification-categorization relationship. *Journal of Experimental psychology: General, 115*, 39–57.

O'Hara, T., Wiebe, J. (2003). Preposition semantic classification via treebank and framenet. In: Proc. of the 7th Conference on Natural Language Learning (CoNLL-2003), Edmonton, Canada.

Palmer, M., Rosenzweig, J., & Cotton, S. (2001). *Automatic predicate arguemnt analysis of the Penn TreeBank*. Paper presented at the Proceedings of HLT 2001, First International Conference on Human Language Technology Research, San Francisco.

Sankoff, D. & Kruskal, J. B. (1983). *Time warps, string edits, and macromolecules: The theory and practice of sequence comparison*. Reading, MA: Addison-Wesley Publishing Company.

Sellers, P. H. (1974). An algorithm for the distance between two finite sequences. *Journal of Combinatorial Theory, 16*, 253–258.

Shiffrin, R. M., & Steyvers, M. (1997). Model for recognition memory: REM—Retrieving effectively from memory. *Psychonomic Bulletin & Review, 4*(2), 145–166.

Smith, E. E., Shoben, E. J., & Rips, L. J. (1974). Structure and process in semantic memory: A feature model for semantic decision. *Psychological Review, 81*, 214–241.

Soubbotin, M. M., & Soubbotin, S. M. (2002). *Use of patterns for detection of answer strings: A systematic approach*. Paper presented at the Eleventh Text Retrieval Conference (TREC 2002).

Stallard, D. (2000). *Talk'n'travel: A conversational system for air travel planning*. Paper presented at the Proceedings of the 6th Applied Natural Language Processing Conference (ANLP'00).

Tulving, E., & Thompson, D. M. (1973). Encoding spcificity and retireval processes in episodic memory. *Psychological Review, 80*, 352–373.

van Dijk, T. A. (1972). *Some aspects of text grammars*. The Hague: Mouton.

Van Valin, R. D. (1993). A synopsis of role and reference grammar. In R. D. Van Valin (Ed.), *Advances in role and reference grammar*. Amsterdam: John Benjamins.

Wilson, W., Halford, G., Gray, B., & Phillips, S. (2001). The STAR–2 model for mapping hierarchially structured analogs. In D. Gentner, K. J. Holyoak, & B. Kokinov (Eds.), *The analogical mind*. Cambridge, MA: MIT Press.

6

Modeling Multiple Levels of Text Representation

Stefan L. Frank
Tilburg University and University of Nijmegen, The Netherlands

Mathieu Koppen and Wietsk Vonk
University of Nijmegen, The Netherlands

Leo G. M. Noordman
Tilburg University, The Netherlands

A broad model of text comprehension should not only simulate how information is extracted from the text itself, but also how this information is interpreted in light of the reader's knowledge. This distinction is related to the distinction among three levels of discourse representation whose existence has been assumed ever since it was proposed by Kintsch and Van Dijk (1978; see also Van Dijk & Kintsch, 1983). The first level is the *surface representation*, consisting of the text's literal wording. This representation gives rise to the second level, called the *textbase*, where the meaning of the text is represented as a network of concepts and propositions from the text (Kintsch, 1988, 1998). Items in this network are generally assumed to be connected to each other if they have some structural feature in common (e.g., two propositions sharing an argument) or if a connective in the text signals that they are connected: "connection relations between propositions in a coherent text base are typically expressed by connectives such as 'and,' 'but,' 'because,' 'although,' 'yet,' 'then,' 'next,' and so on" (Kintsch & Van Dijk, 1978, p. 390).

When textbase elements are combined with elements from the reader's general knowledge, the third level of representation arises. In this *situation model*, relations among items no longer depend on their structural features. Whereas Zwaan (1999) has argued for the importance of perceptual information to the situation model, Kintsch and Van Dijk (1978) claim that relations among items of the situation model (or "facts," as they call them) depend on the effect the items have on one another's probability of occurring: "relations between facts in some possible world . . . are typically of a conditional nature, where the conditional relation may range from possibility, compatibility, or enablement via probability to various kinds of necessity" (p. 390).

Several researchers have attempted to show that Kintsch and Van Dijk's three levels are present in the mental representation of discourse (see, e.g., Kintsch, Welsch, Schmalhofer, & Zimny, 1990). Compelling evidence comes from a series of experiments by Fletcher and Chrysler (1990). They had subjects read short stories, each describing a linear ordering among five objects. For instance, one of the stories read:

> George likes to flaunt his wealth by purchasing rare art treasures. He has a Persian rug worth as much as my car and it's the cheapest thing he owns. Last week he bought a French oil painting for $12,000 and an Indian necklace for $13,500. George says his wife was angry when she found out that the necklace cost more than the carpet. His most expensive "treasures" are a Ming vase and a Greek statue. The statue is the only thing he ever spent more than $50,000 for. It's hard to believe that the statue cost George more than five times what he paid for the beautiful Persian carpet. (Fletcher & Chrysler, 1990, Table 1).

In this example, five art treasures can be ordered by price: rug/carpet, painting, necklace, vase, and statue. After reading ten such stories, subjects were given from each story one sentence without its final word. Their task was to choose which of two words was the last of the sentence. For the story above, the test sentence was *George says his wife was angry when she found out that the necklace cost more than the* . . . and subjects might have to recognize either *carpet* or *rug* as the actual last word of this sentence in the story they read. Since *carpet* and *rug* are synonyms, the difference between them appears at the surface-text level only. If subjects score better than chance on this decision, they must have had some kind of mental representation of the surface text.

Alternatively, the choice might be between *carpet* and *painting*. Because these are not synonyms, this comes down to a choice between different propositions: One states that the necklace costs more than the carpet, whereas according to the other the necklace costs more than the painting. Scoring better on this choice than on the choice between *carpet* and *rug* shows the existence of a level of representation beyond the surface text.

In fact, the necklace cost more than both the carpet and the painting. Subjects who erroneously choose *painting* over *carpet* do not violate the situation model, because their choice will still result in a statement that is true in the story. However, if the choice is between *carpet* and *vase*, different choices correspond to different situation models. If subjects score better on this choice than on the choice between *carpet* and *painting*, they must have developed a situation-level representation.

Indeed, Fletcher and Chrysler (1990) did find a better than chance score on the choice between synonyms, an even higher score on the choice between propositions, and the highest score on the choice between situation models.

This result strongly supports the existence of at least three levels of representation. Nevertheless, most models of discourse comprehension restrict themselves to only one level. For instance, the Resonance model (Myers & O'Brien, 1998) includes only concepts and propositions that originate from the text, and the connections between them are based on argument overlap. No part of the reader's knowledge is included in the model's text representation, so it remains at the textbase level. Other models are concerned with the situation level only. The units of representation in the models by Langston and Trabasso (1999; Langston, Trabasso, & Magliano, 1999) and by Golden and Rumelhart (1993; Golden, Rumelhart, Strickland, & Ting, 1994), which correspond to story events, are connected to each other only if there is a causal relation between the represented events. Because this causal information originates from the reader's knowledge, and not from the text, these models represent texts at a situational level.

There are models that combine information from text and the reader's knowledge and can therefore be said to implement two levels of representation. However, such models are still mainly textbase-oriented. For example, the episodic memory structures computed by the Landscape model (Van den Broek, Risden, Fletcher, & Thurlow, 1996; Van den Broek, Young, Tzeng, & Linderholm, 1999) consist mainly of concepts originating from the text. Inferred concepts can be added, but they need to be given in advance by the modeler. The model cannot explain why or how these knowledge-based concepts are inferred and added to the text representation.

Kintsch's (1988, 1998) Construction-Integration model does include a process for the integration of knowledge items into the textbase representation. However, this model, too, is mainly concerned with the textbase. Kintsch's (1988) referring to the combination of text and knowledge items as the "enriched textbase" (p. 166) is a case in point. This enriched textbase does contain a few items from the reader's general knowledge, but most of its structure comes directly from text items.

The model by Schmalhofer, McDaniel, and Keefe (2002) is especially noteworthy because it includes all three levels of representation. In contrast to the models mentioned above, its situational level is not a simple extension of the textbase, but a script-based, independently developed representation.

In short, discourse comprehension models, with the exception of that of Schmalhofer et al., either implement only one level of representation or model the situational level as identical to the textbase plus only a few added items. In this chapter, we work the other way around. First, we present a purely situational model of knowledge-based inferences for story comprehension. In this Distributed Situation Space model (DSS; Frank, Koppen, Noordman, & Vonk, 2003), the representation of a story completely overlaps with the model's representation of knowledge and is not derived from the textual formulation of the story. Next, it is shown how surface texts can give rise to the DSS model's situational representations. The textbase, we argue, is of less importance, only playing a role in the transformation of text into a situational representation by providing an intermediate representation that is useful for this process.

REPRESENTING SITUATIONS: THE DSS MODEL

The Distributed Situation Space model simulates how knowledge-based inferences are made during story comprehension. Its main concern is therefore the implementation and use of the reader's world knowledge and not the representation of a story text. Using world knowledge in a computational model is problematic because the amount of knowledge readers have is simply too large to implement any significant part of. The DSS model avoids this problem by restricting itself to a microworld, all knowledge of which is implemented in the model. Because this microworld is quite restrictive, only very simple stories can take place in it. Nevertheless, it is complex enough to allow for the evaluation of the model's properties.

The Microworld

In our microworld, there are two story characters, called Bob and Jilly. Table 6–1 lists the 14 *basic events*[1] describing Bob and Jilly's possible activities and states. Any story taking place in the microworld can be constructed from these events. Note that they do not have a propositional predicate-argument structure. The DSS model is only concerned with units of meaning to which a truth value can be assigned. There is no such thing as a predicate, argument, or concept in the DSS model, because these cannot carry truth values.

Events in the microworld are assumed to follow one another in discrete *story time steps*. At each time step, some events occur and others do not. The combination of all events that occur and all events that do not occur at the same moment in story time is called the *situation* at that time step.

Of course, some situations are more likely to occur than others. For instance, Bob and Jilly are more likely to be outside than inside when the sun shines, and the reverse is true during rain. There also exist impossible situations, such as situations in which soccer is played inside or a computer game outside, or both Bob and Jilly win. Also note that soccer and hide-and-seek are always played by Bob and Jilly together (this is why there are no basic events, 'Jilly plays soccer' or 'Bob plays hide-and-seek'), whereas they can play a computer game or play with the dog individually. Apart from constraints among events within a time step, there are constraints on how situa-

---

[1]Basic events were called "basic propositions" in Frank et al.'s (2003) paper.

TABLE 6-1.
Fourteen Basic Microworld Events and Their Intended Meanings

Event	*Meaning*
SUN	The sun shines.
RAIN	It rains.
B OUTSIDE	Bob is outside.
J OUTSIDE	Jilly is outside.
SOCCER	Bob and Jilly play soccer.
HIDE-AND-SEEK	Bob and Jilly play hide-and-seek.
B COMPUTER	Bob plays a computer game.
J COMPUTER	Jilly plays a computer game.
B DOG	Bob plays with the dog.
J DOG	Jilly plays with the dog.
B TIRED	Bob is tired.
J TIRED	Jilly is tired.
B WINS	Bob wins.
J WINS	Jilly wins.

tions follow each other in story time. For instance, someone who is tired is less likely to win at the following moment in story time.

Microworld knowledge about these regularities within and between situations is not directly implemented. Instead, a realistic sequence of 250 consecutive example situations is constructed, and the world knowledge needed by the model is extracted from this sequence. The representations of basic events follow from their co-occurrence in these example situations, as explained in more detail below. Contingencies between consecutive situations form the basis for the implementation of microworld knowledge about temporal relations.

Representing Basic Events

The DSS model uses distributed representations of events, which means that there is no one-to-one mapping between the represented events and the model's processing elements. Instead, each event is represented by several elements, and each element forms part of the representation of several events. A mathematically equivalent (and often easier) way to think of distributed representations is to view each representation as a vector in a high-dimensional space. The relations among these vectors mirror the relations among the events they represent.

A well-known example of a distributed representation is Latent Semantic Analysis (LSA; Landauer & Dumais, 1997). In this model, each vector stands for a word, and the distance between two vectors is a measure of the semantic relatedness of the represented words. The high-dimensional space the vectors reside in is therefore called a *semantic space*. In the DSS model, the vector representations stand for microworld situations and therefore reside in a *situation space*. This is, of course, how the model gets its name.

For the DSS vectors to represent situations, the relations among vectors should reflect relations among the represented situations. But what are situational relations? According to Kintsch and Van Dijk (1978), as quoted in the introduction to this chapter, facts in the situation model are related by the effect they have on one another's probability. Therefore, a distributed situational representation should consist of vectors that reflect the relations among probabilities of the situations they represent. Below it is explained how precisely such a representation is developed for use in the DSS model. It is also shown how both the conditional and unconditional subjective probabilities of events can be directly computed from their vectors.

Each of the 250 microworld example situations can be denoted by a 14-dimensional binary vector containing a 0 for each basic event of Table 6–1 that does not occur and a 1 for each basic event that does. These 250 vectors serve as input to a Self-Organizing Map (SOM; Kohonen, 1995), consisting of hexagonal cells forming a 10×15 grid. Each of the 150 cells is associated with a 14-dimensional weight vector, which is adapted to regularities in the 250 input vectors during an unsupervised training process (see Frank et al., 2003, for details). As a result, each of the 14 values in a cell's weight vector indicates the extent to which the cell belongs to the representation of one of the 14 basic events. Each basic event is thereby represented as a pattern of values, between 0 and 1, over all SOM cells. After training the SOM, the value of element p of the weight vector of cell i, denoted $\mu_i(p)$, is the extent to which cell i is part of the representation of basic event p. Figure 6–1 shows these so-called membership values for each basic event of our microworld.

We have talked about distributed representations as vectors in a high-dimensional space, but the SOM representations in Fig. 6–1 are two-dimensional areas. However, the two are mathematically equivalent. Each SOM cell can be viewed as one dimension of the 150-dimensional state space $[0,1]^{150}$. A SOM area, defined by membership values $\nleq_i(p)$ for all cells i, is thereby equivalent to the vector $\nleq(p) \nabla (\nleq_1(p), \nleq_2(p), \ldots, \nleq_{150}(p))$ in the state space.

Belief Values

The representation of basic events discussed above has some interesting and useful properties. Most importantly, the representations are not arbitrary, but are closely linked to the probabilities of, and probabilistic relations among, the events. This is what makes them truly situational representations.

Given the vector representation $\nleq(p)$ of any event p, it is possible to compute the subjective unconditional probability that p occurs in the microworld. This value, denoted $\tau(p)$, is called the *belief value* of p because it indicates the

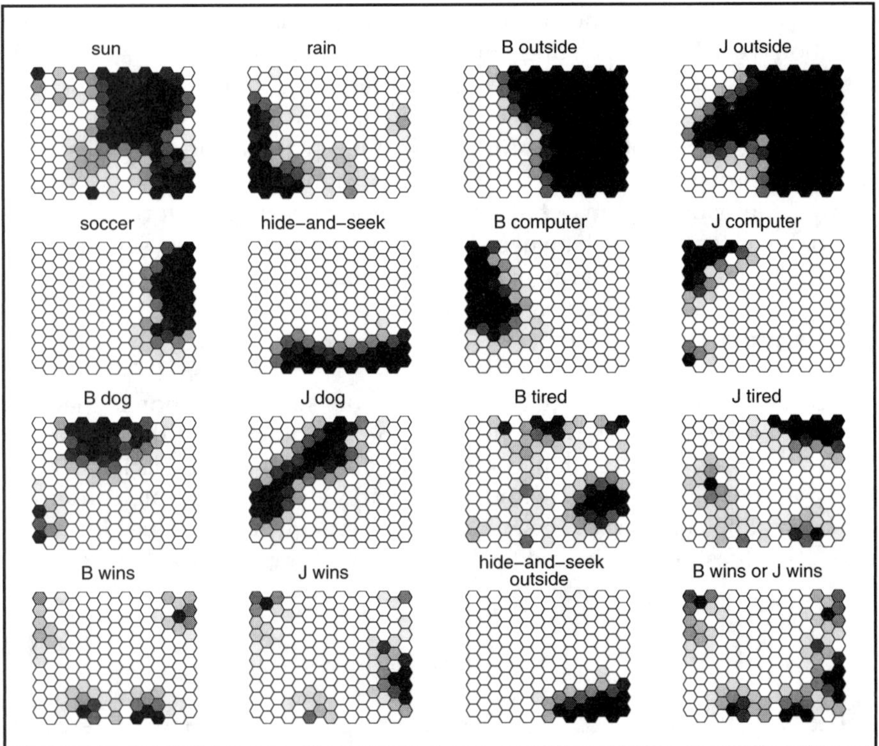

FIGURE 6–1. Self-organized mappings of basic events. A cell's membership value for an event is indicated by the cell's darkness. Two examples of complex events are shown in two rightmost mappings of the bottom row: HIDE-AND-SEEK 'B OUTSIDE' J OUTSIDE (Bob and Jilly play hide-and-seek outside), and B WINS J WINS (Bob or Jilly wins). Copyright 2003 by the Cognitive Science Society. Reprinted with permission.

extent to which a reader may believe *p* to occur at a particular moment in the story. Formally, the belief value of *p* is computed by

$$\tau(p) 5 \frac{1}{150} \sum_{i} \mu_{i}(p) \tag{1}$$

Also, it is possible to compute the subjective probability that event *p* occurs in the microworld, given that *q* occurs at the same moment in story time:

$$\tau(p \mid q) 5 \frac{\sum_{i} \mu_{i}(p) \mu_{i}(q)}{\sum_{i} \mu_{i}(q)} \tag{2}$$

This value is used to determine the meaning of situation vectors. If some situation (vector) X, which does not need to correspond to any basic event, is given, belief values $\tau(p \mid X)$ for any event p can be computed, giving an indication of what is (not) likely to occur in situation X.

The subjective probabilities (or belief values) correspond very closely to the actual probabilities in the microworld, as Frank et al. (2003) have shown. Using belief values, Frank et al. (2003) define measures of story coherence and of the extent to which an event fits in the story, which are useful for validating the model's results against empirical data.

Representing Complex Events

A second important property of the DSS model's representation is that it is productive, in the sense that events can be combined with the use of the Boolean operators of negation, conjunction, and disjunction. This means that the representation of any microworld situation can be computed from the representations of basic events. Given a cell's membership values for p and for q, its values for "not p" and for "p and q" are computed by

$$\begin{aligned} &\mu_i(-p) = 1 - \mu_i\ (p) \\ &\mu_i(p \wedge q) 5 \mu\ _i(P)\mu_i(q) \end{aligned} \tag{3}$$

Because all connectives in propositional logic can be defined in terms of negation and conjunction, any story situation can be represented with the use of the representations of basic events and the two rules in Equation 3. Figure 6–1 (bottom right) shows two examples of such complex events.

Temporal Knowledge and the Inference Process

The DSS model's implementation of temporal knowledge and its inference process are of less importance to this chapter, so we discuss these only briefly here. Microworld knowledge about constraints among events *within* a story time step is implemented in the distributed representations of the events sketched above. Knowledge concerning constraints *between* consecutive time steps is also extracted from the sequence of 250 microworld example situations discussed here and implemented distributively. The model uses this temporal microworld knowledge to infer what is likely (not) to be the case in a story, apart from the facts already mentioned by the story text.

A story is represented as a temporal sequence of story situation vectors, which enter the model one by one. From the model's mathematical basis, it follows precisely how the situation vectors should be transformed to result in the situation sequence that is most likely, given temporal microworld knowledge and the constraints put by the story, and thereby increasing the story's coherence (see Frank et al., 2003, for details). During this process, the change in belief values of events can be obtained to ascertain whether they are inferred to occur or not to occur.

Immediately after a new situation vector enters the model, much can still be inferred, resulting in a high rate of change in the story situations. As model processing time passes, the rate of change in situation vectors decreases until it drops below a threshold level, which is controlled by a depth-of-processing parameter. At that moment, the new story situation is said to be processed sufficiently, and the next situation enters the model. The amount of model processing time that was needed to process the situation is taken as a measure of sentence reading time.

This implementation is in accordance with the hypothesis that whether or not an inference is made does not directly depend on the type of inference, but on the availability of relevant knowledge, the extent to which the inference contributes to the story's coherence and the reader's goals. Noordman, Vonk, and Kempff (1992), as well as Vonk and Noordman (1990), present empirical evidence supporting this view.

Evaluation of the DSS Model

Frank et al. (2003) show that the model indeed infers events that can be expected to occur in the story. In the model, the inference process is not driven by a search for coherence but does result in increased story coherence because the story representation is adjusted to be in closer correspondence with world knowledge. Moreover, the model predicts a fair amount of empirical data. It simulates how processing a story situation that is less related to the previous statement results in more inferences and longer processing times, which is in accordance with data obtained by Myers, Shinjo, and Duffy (1987); Sanders and Noordman (2000); and Vonk and Noordman (1990). Increased amounts of inference and processing time also result from increasing the value of the depth-of-processing parameter. This, too, has been found empirically (Noordman et al., 1992; Stewart, Pickering, & Sanford, 2000). The model has been shown to be easily extended to simulate several other processes. A model for story retention, based on DSS, simulates how events that contribute least to the story's coherence are the first to be forgotten. Moreover, it correctly predicts that less is recalled as retention time grows, that events are more likely to be recalled if they fit better in the story, that intrusion (i.e., false recall) is more likely for events that fit better in the story, and that these latter two effects increase over retention time. All of these effects have also been found empirically (Bower, Black, & Turner, 1979; Goldman & Varnhagen, 1986; Luftig, 1982; Varnhagen, Morrison, & Everall, 1994).

An extension for pronoun resolution has been shown to simulate how the initial interpretation of an ambiguous pronoun depends on focus, but can be overridden by context information that is inconsistent with the focus (Frank, Koppen, Noordman, & Vonk, in press). Experimentally, Arnold, Eisenband,

Brown-Schmidt, and Trueswell (2000) found a similar time course of pronoun resolution. Moreover, the model can account for empirical data by Leonard, Waters, and Caplan (1997) and Stewart et al. (2000) regarding reading times and error rates and can explain how these are affected by focus, context informativeness, and depth of processing.

The DSS model presents a picture of discourse comprehension that is quite different from the view that has been prevalent since Kintsch and Van Dijk's (1978) influential paper. Like Golden and Rumelhart (1993), we have focused on the situation model and its relation to the reader's knowledge, instead of the propositional textbase and its relation to the text. The model does not deal with propositional structures, but explains how general microworld knowledge shapes the interpretation of incoming facts. Consequently, the model lacks any realistic, textual input. The following section makes a beginning at solving this limitation.

REPRESENTING SENTENCES

The stories processed by the DSS model are represented at a situational level, while the text from which these situations originate is ignored. In this section a first step is made toward extending the model with a more textual level of representation. This is accomplished by training of a simple recurrent neural network (Elman, 1990) to take as input sentences (i.e., word sequences) describing microworld situations and to transform them into the DSS-vector representations of these situations.

This task is quite similar to the one performed by St. John and McClelland's (1990, 1992) Sentence Gestalt model. One important difference between that model and ours is that the Sentence Gestalt model does not produce a complete representation of the sentence's meaning, but only answers questions about the contents of the sentence. Also, the output representation of the Sentence Gestalt model is localist, whereas ours is distributed.

A model developed by Desai (2002) to simulate language learning by children also consists of a recurrent network that transforms sentences into representations of their meaning. Contrary to the Sentence Gestalt model, these output representations do contain all of the information in the sentence. They are, however, still localist. A model even more similar to ours is the Connectionist Sentence Comprehension and Production (CSCP) model by Rohde (2002). It consists of a neural network that, like ours, learns to transform sentences into independently developed, distributed output representations. However, unlike our DSS vectors, the distributed output vectors of the CSCP model were not designed to represent statements at a situational level but only to encode and decode propositional structures. The relations between those vectors do not reflect probabilistic relations between the world events they represent.

The most important respect in which all three of the models mentioned above differ from the one presented in this section is that we look at the network's internal representation that develops during training, whereas the above models are mainly concerned with the training process itself and with the generated output. This internal representation, we argue, provides a different view of the traditional surface/textbase/situation-distinction in levels of text representation.

The Microlanguage

The sentences the network learns to process are composed of 15 different "word" units, most of which are words in English: *Bob, Jilly, and, play, be, win, lose, soccer, hide-and-seek, a_computer_game, with_the_dog, outside, inside, tired, awake*. To simplify the already simple language, both *a_computer_game* and *with_the_dog* are considered one word. For further simplification, verbs are not inflected. Note that the microlanguage vocabulary lacks the word *not* and other negations. Kaup and Zwaan (2003) argue that processing a negation involves first constructing the situation model of the corresponding non-negated statement and then directing attention away from it. Such a two-step process is beyond the network's capabilities.

The 15 words can be combined into sentences by following the grammar of Table 6–2. In total, the microlanguage consists of 328 different sentences. Thirty-eight of these, shown in Table 6–3, are put aside as a test set. Because the network is not trained on these, it is not shown any sentences in which

- hide-and-seek is played outside (Group 1);
- anyone plays with the dog inside (Group 2);
- *Bob and Jilly* (in this order) play soccer (Group 3);
- *Jilly and Bob* (in this order) play a computer game (Group 4).

TABLE 6–2.
Grammar of Bob and Jilly's Microlanguage

S	→	NP VP
NP	→	*Bob* ∣ *Jilly* ∣ *Bob and Jilly* ∣ *Jilly and Bob*
VP	→	*play* Game [Place ∣ *and be* State ∣ *and* Result]
	→	*be* Place [*and play* Game ∣ *and* State ∣ *and* Result]
	→	*be* State [*and play* Game ∣ *and* Place ∣ *and* Result]
	→	Result [*and play* Game ∣ Place ∣ *and be* State]
Game	→	*soccer* ∣ *hide-and-seek* ∣ *a_computer_game* ∣ *with_the_dog*
Place	→	*outside* ∣ *inside*
State	→	*tired* ∣ *awake*
Result	→	*win* ∣ *lose*

TABLE 6–3.
Thirty-Eight Sentences Used as a Test Set

Group	*Sentence*
1	Bob play hide-and-seek outside
	Bob be outside and play hide-and-seek
	Jilly play hide-and-seek outside
	Jilly be outside and play hide-and-seek
	Bob and Jilly play hide-and-seek outside
	Bob and Jilly be outside and play hide-and-seek
	Jilly and Bob play hide-and-seek outside
	Jilly and Bob be outside and play hide-and-seek
2	Bob play with_the_dog inside
	Bob be inside and play with_the_dog
	Jilly play with_the_dog inside
	Jilly be inside and play with_the_dog
	Bob and Jilly play with_the_dog inside
	Bob and Jilly be inside and play with_the_dog
	Jilly and Bob play with_the_dog inside
	Jilly and Bob be inside and play with_the_dog
3	Bob and Jilly play soccer
	Bob and Jilly play soccer outside
	Bob and Jilly play soccer inside
	Bob and Jilly play soccer and be tired
	Bob and Jilly play soccer and be awake
	Bob and Jilly play soccer and win
	Bob and Jilly play soccer and lose
4	Jilly and Bob play a_computer_game
	Jilly and Bob play a_computer_game outside
	Jilly and Bob play a_computer_game inside
	Jilly and Bob play a_computer_game and be tired
	Jilly and Bob play a_computer_game and be awake
	Jilly and Bob play a_computer_game and win
	Jilly and Bob play a_computer_game and lose
5	Bob be tired and play soccer
	Bob be outside and tired
	Bob play hide-and-seek and be awake
	Bob be awake and win
	Jilly play a_computer_game and be tired
	Jilly be tired and inside
	Jilly be awake and play with_the_dog
	Jilly lose and be awake

Moreover, some conjunctions only appear in one of the two possible orders (Group 5). For instance, the network is trained on *Bob play soccer and be tired*, but not on *Bob be tired and play soccer*. Note that the first two groups of test sentences describe situations not mentioned by any of the training sentences, and the last three groups consist of alternative descriptions of situations also present in the training set.

Training the Network

Figure 6–2 shows the architecture of the recurrent neural network that learns to transform microlanguage sentences into the corresponding microworld situation vectors. The words of a sentence enter the network one by one. Each word is represented locally, by activation of one of 15 input units. This activation is fed to the hidden layer, consisting of six units, which also receives its own previous activation state. As a result, the pattern of activation over the six units of the hidden layer forms a representation of the sentence read so far. When the last word of the sentence is processed, the activation pattern over the 150 output units should be the 150-dimensional DSS vector representing the situation described by the sentence, which can be used as input to the DSS model. The activation pattern of the hidden layer after processing of a complete sentence is called the *intermediate representation* of the sentence,

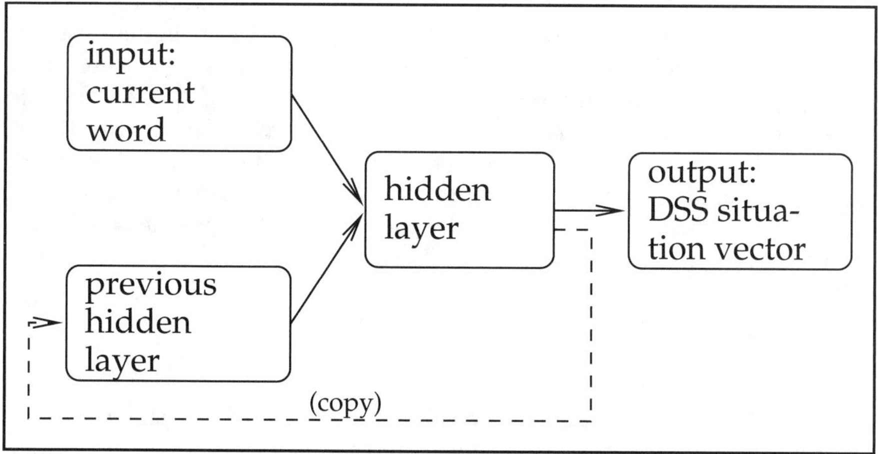

FIGURE 6–2. Architecture of the network used to develop intermediate representations of microlanguage sentences. The input layer has 15 units, one for each word. The hidden layer, consisting of six units, receives activation from the input layer and a copy of its own previous state. The output layer has 150 units, one for each situation-space dimension. A solid arrow between two layers indicates that the first layer is fully connected to the second. The dashed arrow indicates that the activations of the hidden layer are copied to the previous hidden layer.

because it lies between the network's word-level input and its situation-level output.

Of course, the network has to be trained to produce the correct situation vector for each input sentence. During training, the output activations are compared with the correct situation vector whenever the complete sentence has been processed. For example, the network is shown the word sequence *Bob play soccer* and produces an output, which is compared with the situation vector μ(SOCCER).[2] Next, the error in the output is back-propagated to update the connection weights. The set of 290 training sentences was presented to the network 220 times, each time in a different random order. The network is trained seven times, with different random initial weight settings on each occasion. All results presented below are averaged over the results for these seven training sessions.

Amount of Comprehension

To investigate whether the network learned to produce the correct situation vector for each training input, the produced and correct output vectors are compared. This could be done by computation of the mean squared error of vector values, but a more easily interpreted measure is available from the use of belief values. Assume the input sentence describes event p and the network's output is the vector $X(p)$. If the network has not learned anything, we may expect $\tau(p \mid X(p))$, the belief value of event p in the situation represented by situation vector $X(p)$, to equal the a priori belief value $\tau(p)$. In that case, the network's "amount of comprehension" of the sentence is 0. If belief value $\tau(p \mid X(p))$ is larger than $\tau(p)$, the sentence can be said to be "understood" to some extent. In the ideal case, when $X(p) \nabla \mu(p)$ so $\tau(p \mid X(p)) \nabla \tau(p \mid p)$,[3] the amount of comprehension is defined to equal 1. If, on the other hand, $\tau(p \mid X(p))$ is smaller than $\tau(p)$, the sentence is misunderstood and the amount of comprehension is negative. Formally, the amount of comprehension of the sentence by the network equals

$$compr\ (p) = \frac{\tau(p \mid \tau(p)) - \tau(p)}{\tau(p \mid p) - \tau(p)} \tag{4}$$

Most microlanguage sentences form a conjunction of two statements. In that case, the comprehension measure of Equation 4 can be somewhat mis-

[2]The network's output to the sentence *Bob play soccer* cannot be compared with the situation vector μ(B SOCCER), because the basic event B SOCCER does not exist. The sentence describes the situation in which both Bob and Jilly play soccer, because they always play this game *together*.

[3]Note that $\tau(p \mid p)$ can be somewhat less than 1; that is, even a given statement may not be fully believed to be the case.

leading. For instance, if the sentence *Jilly play hide-and-seek outside* results in an output vector that is identical to μ(J OUTSIDE), the network has not understood that Jilly plays hide-and-seek, but only that she is outside. Nevertheless, the amount of comprehension will be positive because the belief value of HIDE-AND-SEEK ^ J OUTSIDE is larger given J OUTSIDE than a priori. Therefore, for sentences describing a conjunction $p \wedge q$, the amount of comprehension is also computed for p and q separately. Note that the amount of comprehension for the individual statements is computed after processing of the complete sentence, that is, the conjunction $p \wedge q$.

RESULTS

Learning and Generalization

Table 6–4 shows the average amounts of comprehension for the sentences in the training and test sets, for the complete sentence as well as for the first and second statements separately. All values are significantly positive, indicating that the network does learn to comprehend the training sentences above chance level and generalizes this skill to test sentences. However, first statement comprehension is quite poor, especially for the test sentences. The second statement often seems to overwrite the information in the first.

It is also informative to look at the percentages of misunderstood sentences (i.e., resulting in a negative amount of comprehension). The error rates closely follow the amounts of comprehension. Again, first statements are often processed poorly: The error percentages for training sentences are 25.2% and 0.8% for the first and second statements, respectively. For test sentences, almost half of the first statements are misunderstood, as can be seen from Table 6–5. However, these errors are not divided evenly over the 38 test sentences. The network seems to have particular difficulty learning to process sentences that describe new situations (Groups 1 and 2). The first statement of such sentences seems to be completely overwritten by the second. In comparison, the network had more success learning that the connective *AND* is

TABLE 6–4.
Amounts of Comprehension, Averaged Over n Values, and 95% Confidence Interval for Training and Test Sentences, Both for the Complete Statement and Separately for the First and Second Statements of a Sentence Describing a Conjunction

		Statement		
Set	*n*	*Complete*	*First*	*Second*
Training	2030	.28 ± .01	.18 ± .02	.56 ± .01
Test	266	.20 ± .03	.06 ± .04	.62 ± .03

TABLE 6–5.
Error Percentages and Amounts of Comprehension, Averaged Over *n* Values, for Test Sentences, Both for the First and Second Statement of a Sentence Describing a Conjunction, per Test Sentence Group and Averaged Over All Test Sentences

		Statement			
		First		*Second*	
Group	*n*	*% errors*	*Compr.*	*% errors*	*Compr*
1	56	64.3	–.15	0.0	.78
2	56	75.0	–.05	0.0	.68
3	49	31.0	.31	0.0	.50
4	49	16.7	.16	2.4	.44
5	56	35.7	.10	1.8	.62
All	266	46.8	.06	0.8	.62

Group numbers refer to Table 6.3.

commutative (Groups 3 to 5), so novel descriptions of previously trained situations are processed reasonably well.

The surprisingly large first statement error rates and negative comprehension scores for Group 2 test sentences can be explained by the microworld situations these sentences refer to. They are all about playing with the dog inside, but Bob and Jilly are more likely to play with their dog *outside*: The a priori belief value of Bob and Jilly being inside is $\tau(\neg(\text{B OUTSIDE}) \wedge \neg(\text{J OUTSIDE})) \nabla .26$, whereas the belief value given that they play with the dog is only $\tau(\neg(\text{B OUTSIDE}) \wedge \neg(\text{J OUTSIDE}) \mid \text{B DOG} \wedge \text{J DOG}) \nabla .12$. This means that understanding only half of a sentence in which Bob and Jilly play with the dog outside will reduce the belief value (and thereby the amount of comprehension) of the other half. Similarly, the large first statement error rates for test sentences in Group 1 are caused by the fact that hide-and-seek is more likely to be played inside, contrary to what these sentences state. Given that they play hide-and-seek, the belief value of Bob and Jilly being inside increases to $\tau(\neg(\text{B OUTSIDE}) \wedge \neg(\text{J OUTSIDE}) \mid \text{HIDE-AND-SEEK}) \nabla .36$.

The Intermediate Representation

Recall from the introduction the experiment by Fletcher and Chrysler (1990), from which they concluded that there are three distinct levels of discourse representation: the surface text, the textbase, and the situation model. In this experiment, subjects more often confused two sentences that differed only at the surface-text level than two sentences that differed also at the textbase level. A similar distinction can be made with sentences in our microlanguage. The sentences *Bob and Jilly play soccer* and *Jilly and Bob play soccer* differ at the surface level but, supposedly, not at the propositional level, because the commutative property of AND makes AND(BOB,JILLY) the same proposition as AND(JILLY,BOB). Contrary to this, the sentences *Bob play soccer* and *Jilly play soccer* differ both as surface texts and as propositions. They describe the same situation, however, because soccer is always played by both Bob and Jilly.

Eight pairs of sentences about *Bob and Jilly* and their *Jilly and Bob* counterparts form the so-called surface different set of sentence pairs, shown in Table 6–6. The two sentences of each of these pairs differ only at the surface text level. The 10 "textbase different" sentence pairs, also shown in Table 6–6, describe different propositions but identical situations.

Fletcher and Chrysler's subjects were also more likely to confuse two sentences that differed only at the surface text and textbase levels than two sentences that differed at the situational level as well. Again, this distinction can be made in our microlanguage. The sentences *Bob play soccer* and *Jilly play soccer,* like those of all other pairs in the "textbase different" set, differ propositionally but not situationally. The sentences *Bob play with_the_dog* and *Jilly play with_the_dog,* on the other hand, differ at both the textbase and situational levels. Ten of such sentence pairs, given in Table 6–6, form the "situation different" set.

Directly modeling Fletcher and Chrysler's experiment would require the implementation of some kind of word recognition process. We propose that this difficulty can be circumvented by taking the sentences' intermediate vector representations and assuming that similar vectors are more difficult to tell apart than dissimilar ones. This implies that similarity in the intermediate representations corresponds to confusability of the sentences.

As a measure of dissimilarity of two vectors, the euclidean distance between them is used. For each of the seven trained networks, the distances between the 328 vectors for all microlanguage sentences are normalized to an average of 1. Figure 6–3 shows the normalized distances between the vector representations of sentence pairs from the three different sets, averaged over seven repetitions of eight distances for the "textbase different" set and of ten distances for the other two sets. The distances follow the percentages of correct responses found by Fletcher and Chrysler: Sentences that differ only in surface text are more similar to one another than sentences that differ also propositionally but not situationally ($t_{124} \nabla 9.38$; $p < .001$), which in turn are more similar to one another than sentences that do differ situationally ($t_{138} \nabla 2.05$; $p < .05$).

This effect cannot be explained by a difference in the amount of comprehension among the three sets. Although there is an effect of sentence set on the amount of comprehension, this does not follow the same pattern as the effect on distances between intermediate representations. The average amount of comprehension of sentences in the "textbase different" set (compr ∇ .67) was significantly larger than for both the "surface different" set (compr ∇ .58; $t_{250} \nabla 3.75$; $p < .001$) and the "situation different" set (compr ∇ .56; $t_{278} \nabla 4.88$; $p < .001$). The comprehension difference between the "surface different" and "situation different" sets was not significant ($t_{250} \nabla .60$; $p > .4$).

TABLE 6–6.
Three Sets of Sentence Pairs

Surface different	
Bob and Jilly play soccer	Jilly and Bob play soccer
Bob and Jilly play soccer outside	Jilly and Bob play soccer outside
Bob and Jilly play hide-and-seek	Jilly and Bob play hide-and-seek
Bob and Jilly play hide-and-seek inside	Jilly and Bob play hide-and-seek inside
Bob and Jilly play a_computer_game	Jilly and Bob play a_computer_game
Bob and Jilly play a_computer_game inside	Jilly and Bob play a_computer_game inside
Bob and Jilly play with_the_dog	Jilly and Bob play with_the_dog
Bob and Jilly play with_the_dog outside	Jilly and Bob play with_the_dog outside
Textbase different	
Bob play soccer	Jilly play soccer
Bob play hide-and-seek	Jilly play hide-and-seek
Bob play soccer	Bob play soccer outside
Jilly play soccer	Jilly play soccer outside
Bob play a_computer_game	Bob play a_computer_game inside
Jilly play a_computer_game	Jilly play a_computer_game inside
Bob and Jilly play soccer	Bob and Jilly play soccer outside
Jilly and Bob play soccer	Jilly and Bob play soccer outside
Bob and Jilly play a_computer_game	Bob and Jilly play a_computer_game inside
Jilly and Bob play a_computer_game	Jilly and Bob play a_computer_game inside
Situation different	
Bob play a_computer_game	Jilly play a_computer_game
Bob play with_the_dog	Jilly play with_the_dog
Bob play hide-and-seek	Bob play hide-and-seek inside
Jilly play hide-and-seek	Jilly play hide-and-seek inside
Bob play with_the_dog	Bob play with_the_dog outside
Jilly play with_the_dog	Jilly play with_the_dog outside
Bob and Jilly play hide-and-seek	Bob and Jilly play hide-and-seek inside
Jilly and Bob play hide-and-seek	Jilly and Bob play hide-and-seek inside
Bob and Jilly play with_the_dog	Bob and Jilly play with_the_dog outside
Jilly and Bob play with_the_dog	Jilly and Bob play with_the_dog outside

Two sentences of a pair from the "surface different" set differ only in surface text and not propositionally. Sentences of a pair from the "textbase different" set differ propositionally but describe identical situations. Sentences of a pair from the "situation different" set differ both propositionally and situationally.

DISCUSSION

Although the network's performance was far from impressive, it did learn to comprehend both training and test sentences significantly above chance level, with the exception of the first statement of sentences describing situa-

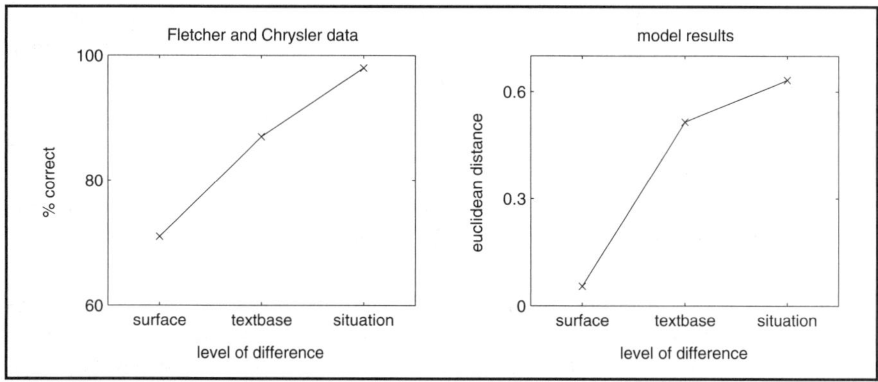

FIGURE 6–3. Left: experimental results by Fletcher and Chrysler (1990). Right: distances between vectors representations in the network's hidden layer, for sentences that differ only at the surface level, sentences that differ only at the surface and textbase levels, and sentences that differ also at the situational level.

tions not mentioned in the training set (test sentence Groups 1 and 2). Future research will have to show how generalization performance can be improved. For now, however, we are mainly concerned with the intermediate representation that developed during training.

The intermediate vector representation is neither fully based on surface text nor purely situational. Any difference between two sentences increases the distance between the corresponding vectors, regardless of whether the difference is one of surface text, proposition, or situation. Two sentences that describe different situations necessarily also form different propositions, so they will be at least as different from each other as two sentences that differ only propositionally. Likewise, two sentences that differ propositionally must also differ in surface form, so they will be at least as different from each other as two sentences that differ only in surface form. Because any difference between sentences adds to the distance between the corresponding intermediate vector representations, vectors are less similar to one another if the sentences they represent differ at a higher level. This indicates that a *single* representation can encode information about the surface text, the proposition, and the situation. Interestingly, such a representation can predict Fletcher and Chrysler's (1990) findings, even though they took their results as providing "strong converging evidence for the psychological reality of van Dijk and Kintsch's (1983) distinction among surface memory, the propositional textbase, and the situation model" (p. 177).

We do not claim that only one level of representation exists. In fact, a purely situational representation was needed to train the network and develop the intermediate representation. It is clear, however, that Fletcher and Chrysler's result does not require three levels of representation to be present at the same time. One property of distributed representations is that they can simultaneously encode different aspects of the represented item. Therefore, a single sentence vector can represent, to some extent, surface text, proposition, and situation.

It is interesting to speculate whether these vectors could account for other experimental data dealing with different levels of text representation. For instance, Schmalhofer and Glavanov (1986) and McDaniel, Schmalhofer, and Keefe (2001) found that reading goal affects the mental representation of text. Unlike the DSS model's story interpretations, the intermediate sentence representations do not depend on the value of a parameter controlling processing depth or reading goal. Each sentence has only one intermediate representation, meaning that the effect of reading goal on this representation cannot be simulated.

Zimny (1987; reported in Kintsch et al., 1990) showed that textual, propositional, and situational information decays from a text's memory trace at different rates. Although this seems to indicate that there are distinct levels of representation, Zimny's results might be accounted for by a single intermediate vector representation. The sentence vector S can be thought of as a location in six-dimensional state space, each dimension of which corresponds to one of the six units in the recurrent network's hidden layer. Surrounding this location is a region, all points of which are closer to S than to the representation of any other sentence. We call this the *text region* of S. Also surrounding S is the *proposition region* of S, consisting of all text regions of sentences propositionally identical to S. Because different sentences can correspond to the same proposition, but different propositions cannot be described with a single sentence, all of S's text region must lie within its proposition region. Likewise, S's proposition region is part of a larger *situation region* consisting of the text regions of all sentences describing the same situation as S. Outside this situation region, only sentences describing a situation different from S are represented.

During retention of S in memory, its representation decays. This can be modeled by the addition of random noise, changing S into a vector we denote by S'. More random noise is added as retention time increases, meaning that S' moves randomly through the state space. As long as it stays within S's text region, the literal sentence is remembered. However, sooner or later S' will move out of the text region, which means that the surface text of S is forgotten. As long as S' remains in the proposition region of S, however, the proposition described by S is known. In other words, the surface text is forgotten more quickly than the textbase. Likewise, when S' leaves the proposition region, but is still within the situation region, only the described situation is remembered. This shows that the model may be able to account for data other than Fletcher and Chrysler's (1990).

Of course, all of these findings are tentative. The network only processes single sentences, whereas a textbase should be able to include several sentences. Also, our microworld and microlanguage are extremely simple, so research is needed with worlds and languages of more realistic size. It is in fact not unlikely that this will increase the textbase-like character of the intermediate representations, since it may be the need to comprehend complex language about relations in a complex world that drives the development of representations that, in some sense, can be regarded propositional. For example, Dennis and Kintsch (this volume) present a system that analyzes natural language texts about a microworld in which different kinds of relations among many entities are of major importance. To answer questions about these texts, the system develops representations that function similarly to propositions, although they do not have predicate-argument structures.

CONCLUSION

The Distributed Situation Space model shows how inferences arise from application of world knowledge to story statements, affecting the interpretation of these statements. In this chapter, we have made a first attempt to extend the model with a simple recurrent network to simulate word-by-word reading. However, much work remains to be done before it can be considered a model for the incremental transformation of word sequences into an interpretation of the story. For instance, the current model cannot predict word reading times, nor does it handle textual processing cues such as connectives and pronouns. Nevertheless, it is able to show how multiple levels of discourse representation can automatically arise from learning the task of transforming a textual representation of a sentence into a situational one.

Traditionally, constructing a textbase is viewed as one of the main goals of text comprehension. Such a textbase is assumed to consist of propositional structures. Our simple recurrent network challenges both of these views. First, in our view, understanding a text comes down to constructing a situational representation. Levels of representation prior to the situation model exist only because they are necessary, or at least useful, for transforming a text into a situation model. Second, although the units of meaning at which the text is represented may be proposition-like at the intermediate level, there is no need for propositional predicate-argument structures. A vector that represents a sentence at the hidden layer of our recurrent network does not have such a structure.

Where does this leave empirical evidence of the existence of propositions in the mental representation of a text? Goetz, Anderson, and Schallert (1981) found that subjects often recall all of a proposition or none of it. This has been interpreted as evidence for the cognitive reality of propositions (e.g., Fletcher, 1994; Kintsch, 1998, chap. 3.1; Van Dijk & Kintsch, 1983, chap. 2.2), but it only shows that the units of a text's mental representation may correspond to propositional units. All-or-nothing recall of such propositional units can in fact be interpreted as evidence *against* the existence of propositional *structures*. If subjects never recall part of a proposition, it is very possible that it does not have any parts. In that case, propositions are represented holistically and not as a collection of related concepts.[4]

Ratcliff and McKoon (1978) performed an experiment designed to show that propositional structures are part of a text's mental representation. They had subjects read sentences such as *The mausoleum that enshrined the tzar overlooked the square,* which consists of two propositions: ENSHRINED (MAUSOLEUM,TZAR) and OVERLOOKED(MAUSOLEUM,SQUARE). If the mental representation of the sentence also contained these propositional structures, so they hypothesized, the words *square* and *mausoleum,* which share a proposition, should prime each other more strongly in a recognition task than the words *square* and *tzar* do, even though the words of this latter pair are closer together in the sentence. Indeed, they did find stronger priming between words that share a proposition than they did between words that do not and concluded that propositional structures are cognitively real. However, as suggested by the above example, they seem not to have taken into account the possibility that readers form a mental image of the events in the text instead of a propositional structure. As noted by Zwaan (1999), the effect on priming might have occurred because, in this mental image, the square and the mausoleum are closer together than the square and the tzar, or even because the tzar, being inside the mausoleum, is not visible from the square.

The same problem occurs in the texts used as experimental stimuli by Dell, McKoon, and Ratcliff (1983). One of these reads: "A burglar surveyed the garage set back from the street. Several milk bottles were piled at the curb. The banker and her husband were on vacation. The criminal slipped away from the streetlamp" (Dell, McKoon, & Ratcliff, 1983, Table 1).

After reading of the word *criminal* in the last sentence, recognition of *garage* was found to be faster than after reading of a similar text in which *criminal* was replaced by *cat*. This effect was explained by the assumption of a propositional representation. The text's first sentence gives rise to the proposition SURVEYED(BURGLAR,GARAGE). The anaphor *criminal* in the last sentence refers to the burglar and therefore activates BURGLAR in the reader's mental representation. This results in activation of the concept GARAGE because BURGLAR and GARAGE share the proposition coming from the first sentence.

Such within-proposition activation between concepts can be taken as evidence that the story's mental representation does consist of propositional structures. As in Ratcliff and McKoon's (1978) experiment, however, the stimuli do not seem to have been controlled for the mental image they might evoke in a reader. Experimental findings by Zwaan, Stanfield, and Yaxley

---

[4]This does not exclude the possibility that predicates and arguments can somehow be extracted from the intermediate representations, that is, that these are functionally compositional in the sense of Van Gelder (1990).

(2002) support the hypothesis that the reader of a text constructs a mental image of the scene described by the text. Concepts from the same proposition tend to be close together physically in this scene. In the above example, the burglar is probably very close to the garage in order to survey it. Therefore, focusing attention on the burglar in the mental image of this scene will also highlight the garage.

To conclude, although propositional structures are often assumed, their status in the human cognitive system may not be that well established. Our model shows that a recurrent neural network can learn to transform a string of words into a representation of the story situation described by the words, without needing to first extract any propositional structure from the sentence. The intermediate representation that develops during training of the network may be considered a textbase-level representation, but it does not contain propositional structures. Instead, textual, propositional, and situational aspects can be detected simultaneously in this intermediate representation.

ACKNOWLEDGMENTS

The research presented here was supported by grant 575-21-007 of the Netherlands Organization for Scientific Research (NWO).

REFERENCES

Arnold, J. E., Eisenband, J. G., Brown-Schmidt, S., & Trueswell, J. C. (2000). The rapid use of gender information: Evidence of the time course of pronoun resolution from eyetracking. *Cognition, 76*, B13–B26.

Bower, G. H., Black, J. B., & Turner, T. J. (1979). Scripts in memory for text. *Cognitive Psychology, 11*, 177–220.

Dell, G. S., McKoon, G., & Ratcliff, R. (1983). The activation of antecedent information during the processing of anaphoric reference in reading. *Journal of Verbal Learning and Verbal Behavior, 22*, 121–132.

Desai, R. (2002). *Modeling interaction of syntax and semantics in language acquisition.* Unpublished doctoral dissertation, Indiana University, Bloomington, IN.

Elman, J. L. (1990). Finding structure in time. *Cognitive Science, 14*, 179–211.

Fletcher, C. R. (1994). Levels of representation in memory for discourse. In M. A. Gernsbacher (Ed.), *Handbook of psycholinguistics* (pp. 589–607). San Diego: Academic Press.

Fletcher, C. R., & Chrysler, S. T. (1990). Surface forms, textbases, and situation models: Recognition memory for three types of textual information. *Discourse Processes, 13*, 175–190.

Frank, S. L., Koppen, M., Noordman, L. G. M., & Vonk, W. (2003). Modeling knowledge-based inferences in story comprehension. *Cognitive Science, 27*, 875–910.

Frank, S. L., Koppen, M., Noordman, L. G. M., & Vonk, W. (in press). *A computational model.*

Goetz, E. T., Anderson, R. C., & Schallert, D. L. (1981). The representation of sentences in memory. *Journal of Verbal Learning and Verbal Behavior, 20,* 369–385.

Golden, R. M., & Rumelhart, D. E. (1993). A parallel distributed processing model of story comprehension and recall. *Discourse Processes, 16,* 203–237.

Golden, R. M., Rumelhart, D. E., Strickland, J., & Ting, A. (1994). Markov random fields for text comprehension. In D. S. Levine & M. Aparicio (Eds.), *Neural networks for knowledge representation and inference* (pp. 283–309). Hillsdale, NJ: Lawrence Erlbaum Associates.

Goldman, S. R., & Varnhagen, C. K. (1986). Memory for embedded and sequential story structures. *Journal of Memory and Language, 25,* 401–418.

Hinton, G. E., McClelland, J. L., & Rumelhart, D. E. (1986). Distributed representations. In D. E. Rumelhart & J. L. McClelland (Eds.), *Parallel distributed processing: Vol. 1. Foundations* (pp. 77–109). Cambridge, MA: MIT Press.

Kaup, B., & Zwaan, R. A. (2003). Effects of negation and situational presence on the accessibility of text information. *Journal of Experimental Psychology: Learning, Memory, and Cognition, 29,* 439–446.

Kintsch, W. (1988). The role of knowledge in discourse comprehension: A construction-integration model. *Psychological Review, 95,* 163–182.

Kintsch, W. (1998). *Comprehension: A paradigm for cognition.* Cambridge, UK: Cambridge University Press.

Kintsch, W., & Van Dijk, T. A. (1978). Toward a model of text comprehension and production. *Psychological Review, 85,* 363–394.

Kintsch, W., & Welsch, D. M., Schmalhofer, F., & Zimny, S. (1990). Sentence memory: A theoretical analysis. *Journal of Memory and Language, 29,* 133–159.

Kohonen, T. (1995). *Self-organizing maps.* Berlin: Springer-Verlag.

Landauer, T. K., & Dumais, S. T. (1997). A solution to Plato's problem: The latent semantic analysis theory of acquisition, induction, and representation of knowledge. *Psychological Review, 104,* 211–240.

Langston, M. C., & Trabasso, T. (1999). Modeling causal integration and availability of information during comprehension of narrative texts. In H. van Oostendorp & S. R. Goldman (Eds.), *The construction of mental representations during reading* (pp. 29–69). Mahwah, NJ: Lawrence Erlbaum Associates.

Langston, M. C., Trabasso, T., & Magliano, J. P. (1999). A connectionist model of narrative comprehension. In A. Ram & K. Moorman (Eds.), *Understanding language understanding: Computational models of reading* (pp. 181–226). Cambridge, MA: MIT Press.

Leonard, C. L., Waters, G. S., & Caplan, D. (1997). The influence of contextual information on the resolution of ambiguous pronouns by younger and older adults. *Applied Psycholinguistics, 18,* 293–317.

Luftig, R. L. (1982). Effects of paraphrase and schema on intrusions, normalizations, and recall of thematic prose. *Journal of Psycholinguistic Research, 11,* 369–380.

McDaniel, M. A., Schmalhofer, D., & Keefe, D. E. (2001). What is minimal about predictive inferences? *Psychonomic Bulletin & Review, 8,* 840–860.

Myers, J. L., & O'Brien, E. J. (1998). Accessing the discourse representation during reading. *Discourse Processes, 26,* 131–157.

Myers, J. L., Shinjo, M., & Duffy, S. A. (1987). Degree of causal relatedness and memory. *Journal of Memory and Language, 26,* 453–465.

Noordman, L. G. M., Vonk, W., & Kempff, H. J. (1992). Causal inferences during the reading of expository texts. *Journal of Memory and Language, 31,* 573–590.

Ratcliff, R., & McKoon, G. (1978). Priming in item recognition: evidence for the propositional structure of sentences. *Journal of Verbal Learning and Verbal Behavior, 17*, 403–417.

Rohde, D. L. T. (2002). *A connectionist model of sentence comprehension and production.* Unpublished doctoral dissertation, Carnegie Mellon University, Pittsburgh.

Sanders, T. J. M., & Noordman, L. G. M. (2000). The role of coherence relations and their linguistic markers in text processing. *Discourse Processes, 29*, 37–60.

Schmalhofer, F., & Glavanov, D. (1986). Three components of understanding a programmer's manual: Verbatim, propositional, and situational representations. *Journal of Memory and Language, 25*, 279–294.

Schmalhofer, F., McDaniel, M. A., & Keefe, D. (2002). A unified model for predictive and bridging inferences. *Discourse Processes, 33*, 105–132.

Stewart, A. J., Pickering, M. J., & Sanford, A. J. (2000). The time course of the influence of implicit causality information: Focusing versus integration accounts. *Journal of Memory and Language, 42*, 423–443.

St. John, M. F., & McClelland, J. L. (1990). Learning and applying contextual constraints in sentence comprehension. *Artificial Intelligence, 46*, 217–257.

St. John, M. F., & McClelland, J. L. (1992). Parallel constraint satisfaction as a comprehension mechanism. In R. G. Reilly & N. E. Sharkey (Eds.), *Connectionist approaches to natural language processing* (pp. 97–136). Hove, UK: Lawrence Erlbaum Associates.

Van den Broek, P., Risden, K., Fletcher, C. R., & Thurlow, R. (1996). A "landscape" view of reading: Fluctuating patterns of activation and the construction of a stable memory representation. In B. K. Britton & A. C. Graesser (Eds.), *Models of understanding text* (pp. 165–187). Mahwah, NJ: Lawrence Erlbaum Associates.

Van den Broek, P., Young, M., Tzeng, Y., & Linderholm, T. (1999). The landscape model of reading: Inferences and the online construction of a memory representation. In H. van Oostendorp & S. R. Goldman (Eds.), *The construction of mental representations during reading* (pp. 71–98). Mahwah, NJ: Lawrence Erlbaum Associates.

Van Dijk, T. A., & Kintsch, W. (1983). *Strategies of discourse comprehension.* New York: Academic Press.

Van Gelder, T. (1990). Compositionality: a connectionist variation on a classical theme. *Cognitive Science, 14*, 355–384.

Varnhagen, C. K., Morrison, F. J., & Everall, R. (1994). Age and schooling effects in story recall and story production. *Developmental Psychology, 30*, 969–979.

Vonk, W., & Noordman, L. G. M. (1990). On the control of inferences in text understanding. In D. A. Balota, G. B. Flores d'Arcais, & K. Rayner (Eds.), *Comprehension processes in reading* (pp. 447–464). Hillsdale, NJ: Lawrence Erlbaum Associates.

Zimny, S. T. (1987). *Recognition memory for sentences from a discourse.* Unpublished doctoral dissertation. University of Colorado, Boulder.

Zwaan, R. A. (1999). Embodied cognition, perceptual symbols, and situation models. *Discourse Processes, 28*, 81–88.

Zwaan, R. A., Stanfield, R. A., & Yaxley, R. H. (2002). Language comprehenders mentally represent the shapes of objects. *Psychological Science, 13*, 168–171.

III

INTEGRATIVE PROCESSES IN TEXT COMPREHENSION

7

Neural and Behavioral Indicators of Integration Processes across Sentence Boundaries

Franz Schmalhofer
University of Osnabrück

Charles A. Perfetti
University of Pittsburgh

A fundamental characteristic of a text is that its sentences are not unrelated but cohere. To understand a text, a reader must therefore cognitively establish specific relations between a new statement and the previously read text. The coherence between sentences can be established by different kinds of integration processes: anaphora resolution, memory processes that resonate for words with related meanings (O'Brien, Rizzella, Albrecht, & Halleran, 1998), and more effortful inference processes that are driven by a search for meaning (Graesser, Singer, & Trabasso, 1994). These processes may work at different levels of a text representation (cf. van Dijk & Kintsch, 1983; Fletcher, 1994). Anaphora resolution may occur at a linguistic level creating argument overlap (Kintsch & van Dijk, 1978), resonance processes may be strongly memory-based, and the more effortful inference processes may occur at the situational level, as suggested by Schmalhofer, McDaniel, and Keefe (2002).

Readers process a text sequentially word by word. We can thus investigate how the proposed integration processes unfold at one word or another or at two subsequent words (e.g., a noun followed by a verb) that reference a proposition. Such two-word combinations may also be employed in verification tasks (cf. Griesel, Friese, & Schmalhofer, 2003).

So far, research on word-level effects across sentence boundaries is relatively sparse. In one example of "on-line" word comprehension research, Van Berkum, Zwitserlood, Haagort, and Brown (2003) investigated when and how listeners bring the knowledge from the prior discourse to bear on the processing of the final word in a new sentence. They presented sentences like *Jane told the brother that he was exceptionally slow* and measured ERPs on the word *slow*, when the preceding two sentences had established that her brother was indeed fast. In a second experimental condition, the previous sentence context had established that her brother was indeed slow. The discourse-anomalous words (e.g., the word *slow* after sentences had established that the brother was indeed fast) elicited an N400 effect that started 150–200 ms after the acoustic word onset.

In similar experiments, van Berkum, Hagoort, and Brown (1999) investigated how the presence of one or two possible referents in a preceding sentence would influence the processing of a noun phrase in the middle of the next sentence. In their ERP experiment, the waveforms showed that within 280 ms after the onset of the critical noun, the brain was already differentially influenced by whether the noun phrase had a unique referent in the earlier discourse. Their results show that the discourse context from preceding sentences can affect the comprehension of a word quite rapidly. van Berkum et al. (2003) thus concluded that the contact between a preceding discourse and the unfolding of the visual or acoustic signal of the newly presented word occurs quite early during the processing of a word in sentence-medial and sentence-final positions.

Integration across sentence boundaries has been most prominently discussed in the literature on inference processes in text comprehension (McKoon & Ratcliff, 1992; Graesser et al., 1994; Graesser et al., this volume). Automatic and memory-based processes (McKoon & Ratcliff, 1992; Gerrig & O'Brien, 2005), as well as explanation-based or "search after meaning" related processes (Long & Lea, 2005), have been explored by numerous experimental studies for almost two decades. The results of these behavioral experiments show that both types of processes may occur in establishing coherence across sentence boundaries.

In this chapter, we explore whether ERP and brain imaging (fMRI) studies can contribute any additional knowledge to our understanding of inference and integration processes in text comprehension that has not already been unraveled by behavioral experiments on inferencing and integration processes in text comprehension. It is sometimes argued that ERP and brain imaging data would provide no more than additional correlates for the systematic effects in human behavior without enhancing our scientific understanding of human cognition and comprehension processes.

We thus proceed as follows. First, we focus on a set of experiments that—at least for some time—had attained pivotal significance in the inferencing literature concerning memory-based and explanation-based processes in online inferencing. We then review three experiments that used essentially the same experimental materials, and similar procedures and tasks. The first experiment was intended to replicate a previously established experimental finding so that the particular procedures would also be well suited for an ERP as well as an fMRI experiment. In other words, we designed the behavioral experiment so that we would get a maximum of overlap in materials, independent variables, and experimental procedures among the behavioral, EEG, and fMRI experiments. The experiments, of course, differ in what they measure. The behavioral experiments measure response latencies, the EEG experiments measure voltage shift components (N400; P300), and the fMRI experiment records the brain areas that become differentially activated (as indicated by the bold signal).

EXPERIMENTS ON WORD-TO-TEXT INTEGRATION AND INFERENCE PROCESSES

Our general question is how prior contexts affect the processing of a single or a few words at the beginning of a new linguistic processing unit (e.g., the beginning of a sentence) or when a statement has to be verified with respect to a previously read text. Across the three experiments that address this question, materials and procedures were very similar, with only a few modifications needed to obtain the necessary sensitivity in the dependent measures. These modifications concerned the task instructions and some minor differences in the analyzed stimulus segments.

Experimental Conditions

There were four different conditions in which the preceding context was manipulated. In the *explicit repetition condition,* the first content word at the beginning of the second sentence had appeared toward the end of the first sentence. (More specifically, what was repeated was the word's morphological stem, with inflectional variations counting as explicit repetition.) In the three other conditions, the beginning of the second sentence was also identical to the explicit repetition condition, but the first sentence was slightly modified. In the *repetition by paraphrase* condition, a synonym or paraphrase of the critical word was used in the first sentence. In the *implicitly primed condition,* the first sentence was modified so that the critical event might be inferred by a predictive inference. The critical event was thus not explicitly mentioned. Finally, in the *novelty condition,* the first sentence was again slightly modified so that it neither contained the critical word that began the second sentence nor implied any referential link to it. In short, we will refer to the four conditions as 1) *explicit,* 2) *paraphrase,* 3) *implicit,* and 4) *novelty* conditions. Table 7–1 shows example materials for the four conditions. (Yang et al. (under review) labeled the last two conditions as inference and baseline, respectively.)

The presentation of the texts in the three experiments was as follows. Each word was presented for 300 ms, with an inter-word interval also of 300 ms. In the ERP experiment, an additional blank interval of 300 ms was added at the end of the first sentence. In the behavioral and fMRI experiments, a somewhat longer interval of 1.7 sec was used so that the bold signal from reading

TABLE 7–1.
Example Materials for the Four Experimental Conditions (Explicit, Paraphrase, Implicit and Novelty) and the Two Additional Conditions That Were Used in Experiment 2 and 3 (Filler and Pseudoword)

Phases	*Words*	*Explicit*	*Paraphrase*	*Implicit*	*Novelty*	*Filler*	*Pseudoword*
Header	1	Garden	Garden	Garden	Garden	The	Euwi
	2	work	work	work	wok	Dog	qaszo
Reading phase	3	Steve	Steve	Steve	With	Michael	With
	4	saw	saw	saw	the	committed	anbyv
	5	that	that	that	turn	to	Naa
	6	the	the	the	of	take	kentragle
	7	grass	grass	grass	the	care	Uode
	8	was	was	was	seasons,	of	Uv
	9	dry,	dry,	dry,	Steve	the	God
	10	went	went	went	went	neighbours'	II
	11	outside	outside	outside	outside,	dog	lizle
	12	to	and	to	across	during	im
	13	turn	turned	turn	the	their	heene
	14	on	on	on	dry	holidays.	od
	15	the	the	the	grass,	He	wonuxe
	16	hose	hose	hose,	and	fed	rusq
	17	and	and	which	brought	him	uob
	18	watered	sprinkled	was	in	twice	risy
	19	the	the	quite	the	a	hiw
	20	lawn.	lawn.	long.	hose.	day.	nez
Verification task *(exp. 2 and 3)*	21	Lawn	Lawn	Lawn	Lawn	Holiday	hiw nez
	22	watered	watered	watered	watered	postponed	
Continued reading (exp. 1)	The water was ...	The water was ...	The water was ...	The water was ...	The water was ...		

Note. Experiment 1 employed the continued reading task and collected the ERP signals on the critical ward of the second sentence (e.g. "water"). The headers and the filler and pseudoword conditions were only used in Experiment 2 and 3. Instead of continued reading, Experiments 2 and 3 employed the verification task where the statement "lawn watered" indicated the statement "The lawn was watered." In Experiment 3, the BOLD response was analyzed for the 1.8 second time period during which a statement was typically processed.

the sentence would have more time to settle before the processing of the critical words of the statement verification task.

There were also differences in the particular task the subjects had to perform and in the dependent measure. In the first experiment, EEG signals were recorded when subjects read the critical word (e.g., *water*) of the second sentence (see Table 7–1). In the second experiment, two words (e.g., *lawn watered*) were presented, but now the task became to verify whether the statement that was implied by these words (i.e., *the lawn was watered*) was true or false. This verification was to be performed with respect to the situation that has been described by the preceding sentence (see Table 7–1). The response and its latency were recorded as dependent measures. Verification explicitly requires integration, and reading requires integration implicitly, because readers usually relate a newly read statement to the previous context (Singer, 2004; van Berkum, Brown, Zwitserlood, Kooijman, & Hagoort, 2005). The third experiment was an fMRI experiment and was identical to the second one, except that the participants were now lying in a scanner so that the BOLD-signal could be recorded as an additional dependent measure.

Combining the Experiments to Draw Conclusions

We thus report the three experiments (with behavioral data, ERP, and BOLD responses collected), which uniformly employed 1) explicit repetition, 2) repetition by synonym, 3) implicitly primed, and 4) novelty as the crucial independent manipulation. We expected that the differences among experimental conditions would signify the relative duration and results (Experiment 1), the critical timing (Experiment 2), and the location (Experiment 3) of the effects of these conditions on the specific instantiation of the cognitive integration process across a sentence boundary.

EXPERIMENT 1

For the four experimental conditions, the participants' responses as well as the latencies of the responses were recorded as the dependent measures. A filler condition and a pseudo-word condition, for which the participants performed a recognition rather than a verification task, were also included.

Participants

Forty students (19 women and 21 men) from the University of Osnabrück between 19 and 29 years of age (average 21 years) participated in the experiment for course credit. The design and experimental procedure were completely identical to the subsequently reported fMRI experiment.

Results

The left side of Table 7–2 shows the proportion of correct responses in the four experimental conditions together with the pseudo-word condition and the mean latencies for the correct responses. There was a significant difference in the mean latencies among these five conditions ($F(4,156) \nabla 19.7$, $p <$

TABLE 7–2.
Mean Response Latencies and Response Frequencies From Experiment 2 and Experiment 3.

	Behavioral Study N = 40 (Experiment 2)			*fMRI-Experiment N = 13 (Experiment 3)*		
Condition	**Response freq. (SE)*	*Response time in ms (SE)*	*t-test (Response time difference)*	**Response freq. (SE)*	*Response time in ms (SE)*	*t-test (Response time difference)*
Pseudo-word	.94 (.02)	826 (43)	$t(39) = .62$, $p > .05$	1 (.00)	828 (37)	$t(12) = 3.01$, $p < .01$
Explicit	.99 (.00)	850 (28)	$t(39) = 3.45$, $p < .01$	.99 (.01)	961 (54)	$t(12) = 1.19$, $p > .05$
Para-phrase	.98 (.01)	886 (29)	$t(39) = 4.59$, $p < .01$	.98 (.01)	999 (57)	$t(12) = 2.45$, $p < .05$
Implicit	.89 (.02)	994 (45)	$t(39) = 2.04$, $p < .05$	.89 (.04)	1085 (61)	$t(12) = 2.56$, $p < .05$
Novelty	.93 (.01)	1058 (38)		.90 (.02)	1207 (65)	

* Response frequencies denote the relative frequency of correct responses (hits and correct rejections) in the pseudoword conditon and the relative frequency of "yes"-responses in the explicit, paraphrase and implicit conditions. In the novelty condition the proportion of "no" responses is indicated.

This behavioral experiment clearly indicated latency differences between various conditions. It thus becomes a quite interesting question whether different ERP-components can be found for those conditions and whether such results would then be contradictory or consistent to the latency differences of the behavioral experiment.

.001). Pairwise *t*-tests furthermore showed that the latencies of explicit, paraphrase, implicit, and novelty conditions were all significantly different from each other (see Table 7–1). The latencies increased monotonically from the explicit condition to the paraphrase, implicit, and novelty conditions, which showed the longest latency. The largest latency difference of 108 ms between adjacent experimental conditions occurred between the paraphrase and the implicit conditions. This condition difference was also most reliable with the highest *t*-score. The latency difference between the explicit and the paraphrase conditions, on the other hand, was only 36 ms, and the difference between the inference and the novelty condition was 66 ms.

EXPERIMENT 2

In the experiment by Yang, Perfetti, and Schmalhofer (submitted), 16 native English-speaking students from the University of Pittsburgh read 120 two-sentence texts, ranging between 13 and 43 words, with an average of 28 words. Each of these passages occurred in one of the four different conditions, as is shown in Table 7–1. The experimental manipulations were counterbalanced across 4 groups of 4 subjects each and the four sets of materials by a Latin-square. Each participant read about each setting and event only once while contributing 30 trials to each of the four experimental conditions. Participants were individually tested in a series of two experimental blocks which lasted between 60 and 90 minutes. The 120 trials were presented in a random order.

Instruction and visual stimuli were presented on a 15-inch CRT monitor. The experimental trials were controlled by experimental software that presented the trials and recorded relevant trial information and sent event information to the electroencephalogram (EEG) recording system (Net Station, Electrical Geodesics Inc., Eugene, Oregon). The EEG was recorded using the 128 Electrical Geodesics system (Tucker, 1993) consisting of Geodesic Sensor Net electrodes, Netamps and Netstation software running on an Apple Macintosh 1000MHz computer. The data were recomputed off-line against the average reference, the vertex (Lehmann & Skrandies, 1980). Impedances were maintained below 50 kΩ, an acceptable level for the electrodes and amplifier used (Ferree, Luu, Russell, & Tucker, 2001; Tucker, 1993). The EEG was amplified and analog filtered with .1 Hz to 100 Hz bandpass filters, referenced to the vertex, and a 60 Hz notch filters then digitized at 250 Hz. Six eye channels were used to monitor the trials with eye movement and blinks. The EEG signals were recorded continuously at 250 Hz by the Net Station with a 12 bit A/D converter. The EGI Net Station also recorded all event onset times, and accuracy for later analysis.

To orient a participant's visual attention, a fixation mark was presented at the center of the computer screen at the beginning of each trial. After a subject started a trial by pressing the space-bar, a text passage was then presented one word at a time in the center of the screen. Each word was presented for 300 msec with an additional 300 ms blank interval before the next word. A comprehension question was presented intermittently, approximately every fourth trial. After answering the two alternative forced choice questions, the subjects were informed of whether or not their answer was correct.

Yang et al. segmented the EEG data into 900 ms epochs spanning 200 ms pre-stimulus to 700 ms post-stimulus for the critical word (e.g. "water"). There were a total number of 30 possible trials per participant per condition. Preprocessing and filtering procedures for eliminating noise were applied in a standard manner. The 200 ms pre-stimulus period was used for baseline correction. The ERP-data were also re-referenced to an average reference frame so that a possible topographic bias that can result from selecting a specific reference site was removed.

Results

Three different types of analyses were performed. A temporal PCA analysis was performed to identify the number and types of significant components which are present in the EEG-data of processing the critical word. Such a PCA analysis resembles a factor analysis in that it determines how many orthogonal components or factors are needed to account for the statistically reliable variation in the data. A PCA analysis is therefore suited to determine which and how many components there are in the data, without specifying in which condition these components have occurred. Each factor can be considered to represent a particular pattern of neural activity over time associated with the cognitive process of integrating across a sentence boundary. More specifically, when we observe a difference between two experimental conditions, this difference would be attributed to differences in how the preceding context affect the processing of the critical word. In other words, differences among the experimental conditions may be attributed to the differences in the cognitive processes of immediate integration across sentence boundaries.

The results from the PCA-analysis are shown in Figure 7–1. The PCA extracted 4 significant factors that accounted for 85% of the total variance from the 325 sampling points corresponding to each 2 ms ERP time frame. The components C1, C2 and C3, together explained 82% of the total variance. The component C4 is an exogenous component (3% additional variance) and thus an artifact with respect to our interest of analyzing brain waves. It was therefore excluded from the analysis. On the basis of their profiles, the C1, C2 and C3 components can be described as N400, P300 and N200.

Furthermore, analyses of Variance (ANOVAs) were performed on the component scores of the three temporal factors (C1, C2, and C3). Thereby, the three midline electrodes (Fz, Cz, and Pz) were used to assess the medial areas.

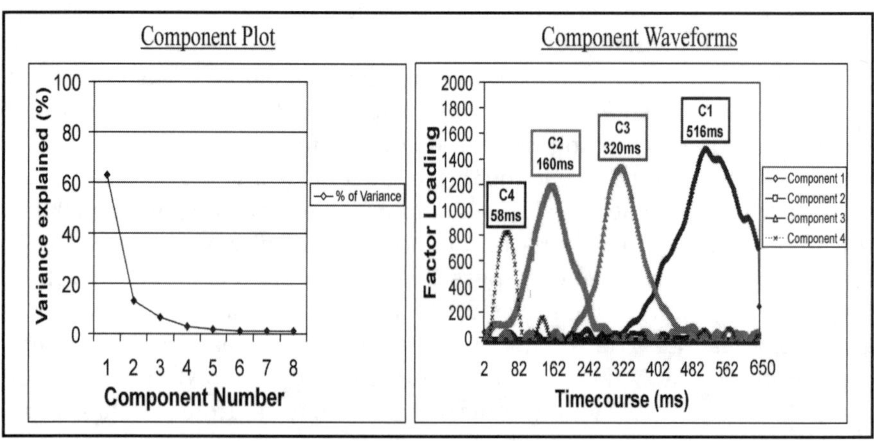

FIGURE 7–1. (Caption ?)

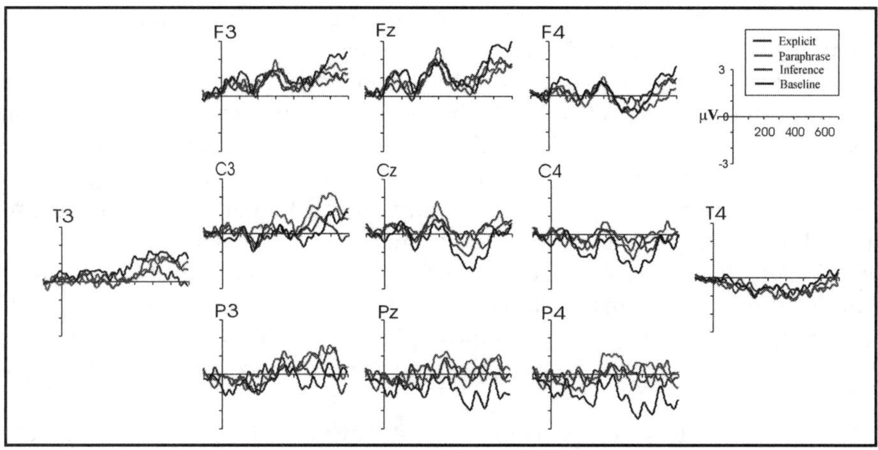

FIGURE 7–2. (Caption ?)

The lateral areas were assessed by four pairs of bilateral electrodes (F3–F4, C3–C4, P3–P4, and T3–T4). Figure 7–2 shows the grand average ERPs for the four different experimental conditions during the processing of the critical target word. The recording sensors that correspond to the international 10/20 system are shown.

The analysis of the midline area revealed significant differences among the four experimental conditions for the N400 component (*F*(3,45) ∇ 5.14; *p* ∇ 0.004 and the P300 component (*F*(3,45) ∇ 4,03; *p* ∇ 0.015). For both of these components, there were also significant differences among the electrodes but no significant interaction between the electrodes and the experimental conditions. The N200 component did not show any significant differences in this analysis.

The analysis of the lateral areas did not show any significant main effect among the experimental conditions for the three components (all Fs < 1). For the P300 component there was a significant effect for the electrodes (*F*(3,45) ∇ 7,73, *p* ∇ 0.001). For the N200 component, the experimental conditions interacted significantly with the electrodes (*F*(9,135) ∇ 2.03, *p* ∇ 0.040), possibly due to a significant difference between the hemispheres (*F*(1,15) ∇ 8,70, *p* ∇ 0.010). Finally, for the N200 component, there was also a significant electrodes by hemisphere interaction *F*(3,45) ∇ 3,84; *p* ∇ 0.035. None of the other comparisons yielded significant differences.

In sum, the most convincing differences were observed in the analyses of the medial locations where main effects of the experimental conditions occurred for the P300 and the N400 component but not for the N200 component. Although Yang et al have performed more detailed analyses for the N200 component which yielded some significant interaction effects, in reporting the pair-wise comparisons, we will restrict our attention to those components which showed a main effect among the experimental conditions, namely the P300 and the N400 components.

Pair-wise comparisons of the P300 component showed that the paraphrase condition yielded a significantly higher amplitude than the novelty condition ($t(15)$ ∇ 3,13; $p < 0.01$), while the difference between paraphrase vs. explicit condition was only marginal ($t(15)$ ∇ 2,01; p ∇ 0.06). The average of the explicit condition and the paraphrase condition was higher than the mean amplitude of the implicit and the novelty conditions, but this difference was not significant ($t(15)$ ∇ 1,84, p ∇ 0.08). The paraphrase condition had a significantly larger amplitude than the average of the implicit and the novelty condition ($t(15)$ ∇ 2,52, $p < 0.05$), but the explicit condition was not significantly higher than the average of the implicit and the novelty condition ($t(15)$ ∇ 0.33, p ∇ 0.75).

In summary, these comparisons suggest that at about 300 ms, a paraphrase word attracts additional processing relative to all other conditions. Although we specifically targeted the N400 as the indicator of integration, we may need to consider the P300 component as part of the cognitive integration process across a sentence boundary. Such early integration processes may not occur in the implicit and the novelty conditions because the informational prerequisites for such processing are not present in the respective stimulus materials. An early integration process at around three hundred milliseconds may only occur when there is a direct conceptual match with a preceding sentence.

In case these prerequisites are not satisfied, as in the implicit and the novelty conditions, the cognitive processes that achieve the integration occur somewhat later and possibly in a different manner. If so, a prediction is that an N400 effect should be observed only for those conditions that did not produce early effects in the ERPs, namely the implicit and the novelty conditions. Indeed, this prediction was actually confirmed.

For the N400 component (300–550 ms time window), both the implicit and the novelty conditions produced larger amplitudes than the explicit and the paraphrase conditions. The pair-wise comparisons showed significant differences between the explicit and the implicit conditions ($t(15)$ ∇ 11,35, $p < 0.001$), between the explicit and the novelty conditions ($t(15)$ ∇ 6.96, $p < 0.001$, and between the paraphrase and the novelty conditions $t(15)$ ∇ 12.05, $p < 0.001$. Neither the differences between explicit and paraphrase conditions nor between implicit and novelty conditions were significant.

These ERP results can thus be summarized in a concise way. When there is an explicit or a conceptual match between a word at the beginning of a sentence and the contents of a preceding sentence, integration across a sentence boundary may occur as early as 200 or 300 ms after the onset of the word. When there is only an implicit overlap or a concept is newly introduced, the integration processes may occur later because the informational prerequisites for an early integration are not given under these circumstances.

These ERP results thus hint at a differentiation of the integration process into two episodes and early one (around 200–300 ms) and a later one (around 300–550 ms). The four experimental conditions were clearly separated by these two episodes. The paraphrase (as well as the explicit) conditions were associated with the early episode and the implicit and the novelty condition were associated with the late episode.

Discussion

These results indicate that one can differentiate between early and late components. The early components were observed for the explicit and the paraphrase conditions and the late component for the implicit and the novelty condition For interpreting the results more fully, it will be useful to specify the cognitive processes which may occur when the first sentence is read as well as the subsequent processes which occur during the processing of the first content word of the following sentence.

In the novelty condition, a referent must be established and integrated into the previously established situation model. The integration processes across sentence boundaries can thus be subdivided into two components. One component may indicate the construal of the new referent associated with the newly read word. A second component may indicate the relational processes which are necessary to integrate this referent into the situation specified by the previous sentence. The substantial amplitude of the N400 component in the novelty condition may indicate that both of these processes are performed in the novelty conditions or, alternatively, that referent construction and discourse integration are so tightly interwoven that one may consider this to be only one immediate integration process.

The implicit condition is somewhat different. In order to achieve an integration a new referent must at least be partially constructed for the given situational context, when a predictive inference was not fully constructed in the preceding sentence (McKoon & Ratcliff, 1992, McDaniel, Schmalhofer & Keefe, 2001). To the extent that the predictive inferences were fully drawn, the implicit condition would be similar to the explicit and paraphrase conditions.

In the explicit condition, a referent has already been mentioned and situationally established by the preceding sentence. Therefore no construction processes but only memory maintenance and immediate integration processes would be required. Such processes should occur much earlier in processing time.

Paraphrases may also allow for a rather effortless integration, but a more coarse grained memory maintenance and integration would be required as compared to the repetition by of a lexical root in the explicit condition. An integration could thus be achieved via an episodic memory trace to the referent that was established by the preceding sentence. In comparison to the explicit condition such an episodic memory match would require a more coarsely grained rather than a fine grained match. The P300 effect could indicate this process.

The ERP results converge with the results of Experiment 1, despite the differences in tasks and measures. The ERP results, moreover, go beyond what can be obtained in the response times, by exposing both early and later components associated with integration, and further suggesting that differences in response latencies between conditions (e.g. between paraphrase and implicit conditions) may reflect neural processes that are temporally differentiated during the reading of the word.

EXPERIMENT 3

The third experiment was conducted with exactly the same materials as experiment 2 while the BOLD-signal was recorded by fMRI, which can provide a good spatial resolution of the physiological correlates of neural processing. In this fMRI-experiment, we can further corroborate the differences in the integration processes across sentence boundaries between the paraphrase condition and the implicit condition. If, in the paraphrase condition, the integration occurs by retrieving, activating and modifying a episodic memory trace, we should find brain areas active that are involved in memory processes. On the other hand, if the implicit condition requires more constructive processes at a situational level, we should find different areas active, in particular areas in the prefrontal brain.

Method

Participants. Thirteen right handed students with a mean age of 22.8 years, all native speakers of German (7 women, 6 men) participated and received course credit.

Procedure. All subjects received written instructions as well as a training session outside the scanner to become familiar with the type of stimuli and the corresponding tasks. Participants were instructed to press the YES key when the test statement was true with regard to the situation described by the just read sentence and the NO key otherwise. For the pseudo-word condition (see Table 7–1), they were told to press the YES key when the pseudo-words of the test statement were identical to the last two presented letter stings of the pseudo-word reading phase and the NO key otherwise.

After a training session in the scanner, participants were presented with the three functional scanning sessions. Each session took 16 min 12 sec. The participants were allowed to rest up to three minutes between sessions.

For each trial, the words of a sentence were displayed by a rapid serial visual presentation (RSVP) technique. All MR-images were acquired in a 1.5 T Siemens Sonata whole body MRT equipped with an 8-channel head coil (MRI-devices). Data analyses were performed by applying the customary analysis steps with SPM2 (for more details on these steps see Schmalhofer et al., 2005). A general linear model was applied to the individual data. For each condition, the processing of the title, the sentence and the test task were modeled. The modeling of sentence presentation was split into 3 blocks of equal length covering the entire sentence presentation to account for differences in sentence encoding before the verification.

The verification process was modeled by a block, beginning with the onset of the presentation of the test task. The length of the block was selected to coincide with the average response time in the inference condition of the slowest participant (1.8 seconds). *t*-test contrasts were calculated between test tasks in the inference, explicit, paraphrase, and control conditions. For statistical analyses, a Random Effects Model was used bringing the appropriate individual contrast measures into a simple *t*-test on 2nd level. Statistical maps were thresholded with $t \nabla 3.93$ (uncorrected $p \nabla .001$) and clusters surpassing a corrected *p* value of .05 on cluster level (approx. 110 voxels) are reported as significantly activated.

Results

Behavioral Results. The response latencies to the test statements showed again an increase from the explicit to the paraphrase and the inference conditions. The mean latency was longest in the novelty condition. While the difference between explicit and paraphrase was not significant, all other differences were (see Table 7–2). This pattern of results is in good agreement with the results from Experiment 1. Two differences may be worth noticing. The latency difference between the implicit and the novelty condition is somewhat larger in this experiment than in Experiment 1. Secondly, the latencies are overall somewhat longer than in Experiment 1, possibly due to the fact that the participants were lying in the scanner rather than sitting at a desk. But all structural aspects of the latency and response data are identical.

In previous research (Perrig & Kintsch, 1985; Schmalhofer & Glavanov, 1986; Fletcher, 1992), such results have been employed to determine the memory strengths of verbatim, propositional and situational representations in a level theory of representation (Kintsch, 1998). According to such reasoning, it was assumed that there are different representations which are jointly processed to determine a true or false response in the verification task. Potentially, the fMRI-data allow us to identify the neural sources of the processes that correspond to the levels of representation differences that were established in behavioral experiments. The contrast paraphrase—explicit of the BOLD signal would thus indicate those processes that operate only on a

TABLE 7–3.
Brain Regions, Cluster Size and Their Activation Level Which Were Found With a Lower Threshold.

Contrast / Area	*Side*	*Size*	P_{corr}	*Z-Max*	*X*	*Y*	*Z*
TEST							
paraphrase > explicit (*T* = 2.5)							
cuneus - BA 18/19							
temporal lobe - BA 22/21							
parietal lobe - BA 7/37/39	L	734	.019	3.21	−58	−62	10
cuneus - BA 17/18/19							
posterior cingulate - BA 29/30/31/23	L/R	659	.033	3.92	10	−60	8
inference > paraphrase (*T* = 2.5)							
IFG, MFG - BA 10/13/44/45/47							
temoral lobe - BA 38	L	777	.049	3.25	−52	34	−10
anterior cingulate - BA 24/32							
SFG, MFG - 6/8/9/10	L/R	3989	.00	4.9	−2	46	46
control > inference (*T* = 2.0)							
precuneus - BA7							
posterior cingulate = BA 29/30/31/23							
cuneus = BA 18/19	R/L	1484	.036	4.02	0	−66	38

match at the semantic/propositional level rather than specific lexical level. The contrast implicit—paraphrase indicates the processing that occurs when there is no match at a semantic/propositional level but only at the situational level. The contrast novelty—implicit indicates the processes that occur when more extensive situational constructions and elaborations are needed, compared with the straightforward mapping of the implicit condition. Finally, the explicit—pseudoword contrast of the verification task indicates those processes that are relevant for a lexical match (as opposed to a match of stings). We will therefore report the fMRI contrasts in this order and subsequently inform about other significant differences.

FMRI Results. Table 7–3 and Figure 7–3 show the different clusters that indicate the significant processing differences in the various contrasts.

The comparison *Paraphrase > Explicit* showed one significant cluster in the right posterior cingulate gyrus. The posterior cingulate gyrus has been consistently found in successful episodic memory retrieval (Cabeza & Nyberg, 2000; Wheeler & Bucker, 2004). Fletcher et al. (1995) attributed posterior cingulate regions to be involved in visual imagery and possibly the

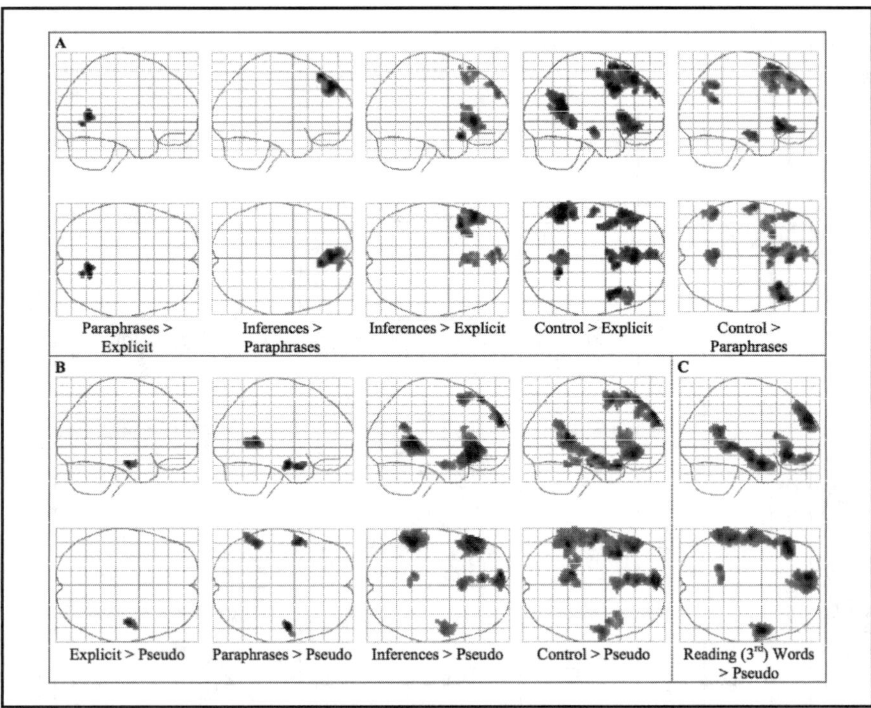

FIGURE 7–3. Statistical activation maps showing significant clusters in the statement verification task of the four experimental conditions

incorporation of information into an evolving discourse structure. Posterior cingulate and neighboring cuneal and precuneal regions are also activated when picture stories are processed (Gernsbacher & Kaschak, 2003). These areas may thus reflect either memory retrieval or mental imagery processes (or both) that occur in story comprehension (Maquire et al., 1999).

When the contrast Paraphrase > Explicit is calculated with the more relaxed criterion of $T \nabla 2.5$, the already identified area becomes somewhat larger (see Table 7–4). In addition, a second cluster emerges. This second cluster is left lateralized and covers cuneal and pre-cuneal regions (BA 19, 39) extending into the posterior temporal lobe (BA 22, 21, 37). These regions of the posterior middle and superior temporal gyrus are associated with phonological, semantic and lexical processes involved in sentence reading (Bavelier, Corina, Jezzard, Padmanabhan, Clark, Karni et al., 1997). Using lists of unrelated words and a recognition task instead of a verification task, Wheeler and Buckner (2003) found that parietal areas were involved in successfully remembering and perceiving of the oldness of an item. In particular, they found that BA 40/39

TABLE 7–4.
Brain Regions, Cluster Size and Their Activation Level of the Significant Clusters.

Region	*BA*		*Cluster size*	p_{corr}	*z-max*	*X*	*Y*	*Z*
Paraphrase > Explicit								
posterior cingulate gyrus	30	R	179	0.010	4.03	12	−62	6
Inference > Paraphrase								
SFG & MFG	8/9/6	R/L	733	0.000	4.68	−2	46	46
Inference > Explicit								
IFG	45	L	754	0.000	4.81	−50	32	0
SFG & MFG	8	R/L	269	0.001	3.62	2	22	52
SFG & MFG	8/9	L	160	0.015	3.87	−10	60	32
Control > Explicit								
SFG & MFG	6/8/9	R/L	1225	0.000	4.70	0	34	50
MTG, STG & supramarginal gyrus	21/22/39/40	L	1096	0.000	4.62	−60	−52	18
IFG	45/47	L	736	0.000	4.28	−54	24	4
MFG	6	L	410	0.000	4.13	−44	12	38
posterior cingulate gyrus	23/29/30	R/L	366	0.000	4.49	16	−56	14
MFG & precentral gyrus	9	R	356	0.000	4.74	40	14	40
IFG	47	R	154	0.013	3.51	42	22	−8
Control > Paraphrase								
SFG & MFG	6/8/9	R/L	1097	0.000	4.35	4	36	52
IFG	47	R	430	0.000	4.91	52	28	−8
Precuneus	7	R/L	270	0.001	4.14	0	−54	42
MFG	6/8	L	261	0.002	3.98	−46	16	46
STG, angular gyrus & supramarginal gyrus	39/40	L	250	0.002	4.13	−50	−56	24
IFG	47	L	239	0.000	3.88	−46	32	−10
MFG & precentral gyrus	8/9	R	181	0.011	3.92	40	18	40
ITG & MTG	21	L	171	0.015	4.10	−60	−6	−18

Note: IFG = inferior frontal gyrus; SFG = superior frontal gyrus; MFG = middle frontal gyrus; ITG = inferior temporal gyrus; MTG = middle temporal gyrus; STG = superior temporal gyrus.

increased activity when participants decided that items were old, regardless of whether the items were actually old or new. An important difference of the current findings to the results from Wheeler and Buckner concerns hemispheric differences. Whereas Wheeler and Buckner found activation in the left parietal areas, the current results show most activation in right parietal regions.

This difference may be explained by the lateralization of coarse and fine semantic comparisons. Beeman (1998) has proposed that coarse semantic comparisons would be predominantly performed in the right hemisphere and fine semantic comparisons would be performed in the left hemisphere. Whereas Wheeler and Buckner presented exactly the same word as during the study phase, the contrast paraphrase > explicit reveals the areas that are especially involved when a synonym of a previously presented word is recognized as denoting the same object, thus producing a successful memory retrieval or memory resonance. If this is true one would then expect that word repetitions would be processed more to the left hemisphere (cf. Wheeler & Buckner, 2004) and a repetition by synonym would resonate more in the right hemisphere, as it was observed in this experiment.

The comparison *implicit > paraphrase* showed a large cluster in the medial portion of the left and right superior and middle frontal gyri. Such middle frontal activations have been attributed to theory of mind inferences and more generally, inferences that are needed to establish a coherent conceptual representation as it is established in situation models (Ferstl & von Cramon, 2001, 2002; Fletcher et al. 1995; Mazoyer, Tzourio, Frak, & Syrota, 1993). Fronto-median activations have also been implicated for the generation of plans and internally guided force in general (Vaillancourt, Thulborn & Corcos, 2003). These areas exceed the functions that are unique to memory and language processes and may in particular be relevant for constructing a particular situation to act in it. Ferstl and von Cramon (2002) have succinctly described the function of this area as being related to an integration of an inner world with the external stimulation. This function is also closely related to the comprehender's self and when an idiosyncratic response criterion needs to be established on the basis of prior knowledge and contextual information (Ferstl, this volume).

With a threshold of *T* ∇ 2,5, the *implicit > paraphrase* contrast additionally showed activation in the left inferior prefrontal cortex (LI-PFC) and superior temporal pole (BA 47, 45, 10, 13, 38). As can be seen from Table 7–4, almost the same LI-PFC cluster was also found in the implicit–explicit contrast with the conservative threshold. The inferior frontal gyrus has been implicated for semantic integration (Ferstl, this volume) and the larger area of the inferior temporal cortex has been termed the prefrontal reasoning network by Mason and Just (2004).

The *novelty > implicit* contrast did not yield any significant clusters when a conservative criterion was used. With the liberal criterion of *T* ∇ 2.0, an area extending from the precuneus (BA7), posterior cingulate (BA 29/30/31/23) and cuneus (BA 18/19) was shown as active (see Table 7–4). These areas show the closest overlap to the areas that were found in the paraphrase > explicit contrast and may thus indicate that for the novelty condition memory processes might play a larger role than in the implicit condition, where the reader is better prepared to process the specific statement than in the novelty condition.

The comparison *implicit > explicit* showed in addition to the significant results of the *implicit > paraphrase* contrast, a large area in the left inferior frontal gyrus overlapping with Broca's areas 45 and 47.

The comparison *Novelty > Explicit* showed once more the middle frontal gyri and the left inferior frontal gyrus to a somewhat larger extent and with higher activations than in the *implicit > explicit* comparison. In addition to these areas, a region at the junction of the left temporal and parietal lobes, covering parts of the middle and superior temporal gyri and the supra-marginal gyrus was significant. Furthermore clusters in the posterior cingulate gyri bilaterally, in the right middle frontal and pre-central gyri, as well as an area in the right inferior frontal gyrus were found. With a lower threshold this comparison yielded the same areas but with much larger extensions, possibly including right posterior areas as well.

The comparison *Novelty > Paraphrase* yielded similar results as the comparison of *Novelty > Explicit*. The regions most prominently activated were in the middle frontal gyri and the right inferior frontal gyrus. A posterior midline activation was found in the pre-cuneus. Further clusters in the left inferior frontal gyrus, the middle frontal gyrus, the left temporo-parietal junction, the right middle frontal and pre-central gyri as well as an area in the inferior and middle temporal gyri also showed significant activation.

When the contrasts were calculated in the opposite directions (e.g. explicit > paraphrase), no significant clusters were found with a high threshold. To provide a complete analysis of the data, we calculated all tests consecutively in the opposite direction (explicit < paraphrase < implicit < novelty) with a lower threshold as well. With the exception of the explicit > implicit contrast which yielded one cluster (post-central gyrus—BA2/3 extending to the inferior parietal lobule—BA 40) with a criterion of $T \nabla 2.5$, no significant results were found in these comparisons either. These results thus clearly demonstrate that the processing demands do indeed increase from integrating an explicit statement to integrating a statement that requires an inference or even a more substantial adjustment in the representation of the referred situation as was the case in the novelty condition.

Finally, differences in the error variances and differences in the power of the respective tests may have caused activation differences in some areas to fall short of statistical reliability. For example, the cluster in the left inferior frontal gyrus that emerges in the implicit > explicit contrast, could also be present in the implicit > paraphrase contrast, and indeed a lower threshold showed such activation difference.

Discussion

The results of the fMRI experiment showed that at least four areas are implicated when a statement is to be integrated with a preceding discourse in a verification task. (1) Parietal areas showed differences most distinctly in the paraphrase > explicit condition, but also and to a larger extent (probably due to the larger power of the comparison) in the novelty > explicit comparison. (2) An area in the medial prefrontal cortex was most clearly seen in the implicit > paraphrase comparison, but also in the novelty > explicit and novelty > paraphrase comparisons. (3) An area of inferior prefrontal cortex produced differences in the novelty > explicit and also in the novelty > paraphrase conditions. (4) The middle and superior temporal gyri extending into the angular and supramarginal gyri showed differences in the novelty > explicit contrasts and the novelty > paraphrase contrasts.

Each of these areas may participate in support of higher level comprehension. In fact, Ferstle (this volume; also Ferstl & von Cramon, 2001; 2002) suggests that they all play an important role in establishing and maintaining coherence. The dorsal medial prefrontal cortex (BA 8/9/10) seems to be crucially involved in inferences, supporting the construction of a situation model from the reader's personal knowledge in interaction with the text (Ferstl & von Cramon, 2002; Ferstl, this volume). The posterior cingulate cortex may be important in situation model updating (Maquire et al., 1999; Ferstl, this volume). Generally, frontal regions may support strategic processes that could serve text comprehension (Ferstl, this volume, Crinion et al. 2003). Specifically, the lateral prefrontal cortex has been implicated in semantic analysis and semantic integration with a given context, and integration demands may also recruit the triangular part of the inferior frontal gyrus. Finally, the anterior temporal lobe may have specific higher level language functions when an integration of incoming words into a semantically based representation is needed (Ferstl, this volume). In the following paragraphs, we examine this "text comprehension network" further in terms of comprehension functions identified in text research.

Updating a Situation Model: Construction and Resonance

Fletcher et al. (1995) argued that the posterior cingulate regions were involved in visual imagery and possibly the incorporation of information into an evolving discourse structure. Posterior cingulate and neighboring cuneal and precuneal regions are also activated when picture stories are processed (Gernsbacher & Kaschak, 2003). These areas may thus also reflect mental imagery processes in story comprehension (Maquire et al., 1999). Memory retrieval, which has to be part of updating, may depend upon an interaction between posterior parietal association areas, prefrontal areas and mid temporal lobe structures: The medial temporal lobe retrieves information from memory and parietal regions maintain representations of the remembered information.

The prefrontal cortex modulates activated memory representations in the parietal lobe as well as less active memories in the temporoparietal regions. It sets up a retrieval mode, initiates the retrieval attempt in temporal regions and monitors and selects activated memory representations. Temporal and parietal regions are strongly interlinked to frontal regions via the arcuate fasciculus and the uncinate fasciculus. Particularly the retrosplenial cingulate (BA 30)—see the paraphrase > explicit contrast—next to its links to the mid temporal lobe and the thalamus, has connections to regions in the dorsolateral prefrontal cortex (BA9, BA9/46, BA46) and adjacent parietal regions (BA19) and may play a role in working memory processes (Morris et al., 1999).

Updating is not a strictly constructive process. It also makes use of a rapid and more passive resonance-like memory processes (O'Brien et al., 1998). For such processes, the posterior cingulate gyrus, rather than the midline prefrontal areas, may be a supporting structure. It has not been associated with effortful cognitive control and conscious reasoning. In our results, the observed posterior cingulate activation in the paraphrase minus explicit contrast could indicate this kind of a fast acting passive memory resonance process.

Reasoning with a Situation Model. (Mental analogies for moving objects, others, self and force exertion). A more general process of mental simulations characterizes cognitive activity such as visualizing and planning. Frontal midline activations have been associated with general non-linguistic inferences that help establish a coherent situational representation (Ferstl & von Cramon, 2001, 2002; Fletcher et al. 1995; Mazoyer, Tzourio, Frak, & Syrota, 1993) and with generating plans and mentally making comparisons between imagined forces (Vaillancourt, Thulborn & Corcos, 2003). These frontal areas may support internally guided (as opposed to stimulus-driven) situation model manipulation, including constructed inferences. (See Schmalhofer, McDaniel & Keefe, 2002).

Conceptual and Syntactic Structures. A large cluster of activation was found in the left inferior prefrontal cortex (LI-PFC) (BA 13, 46, 47, 45, 44), which reached slightly into anterior superior parts of the temporal pole (BA 38). Fletcher et al. (1995) hypothesized the temporal pole region to be involved maintaining coherence in narratives through linking text propositions. Studies by Maguire, Frith and Morris (1999) and Mazoyer et al. (1993) confirm temporal pole involvement in higher level language processes.

The linking of propositional information is a function that requires procedural knowledge about grammar to establish structural relations, as well as a declarative memory system that provides the entities that these grammatical procedures act upon. A procedural role of the temporal pole was suggested by Ullman (2004) who argued that this region in combination with the anterior superior temporal sulcus acts "as a storage repository of procedural knowledge" (Ullman, 2004, p. 243). Nearby regions in the left ventrolateral-prefrontal cortex (BA 44, 45, 47) may support similar functions in procedural and declarative memory systems. Broca's area (BA 44), which is strongly interconnected with the superior temporal sulcus (Rizolatti, Fogassi, & Gallese, 2001), is engaged in a range of sequential processes (Gelfand & Bookheimer, 2003), including those that operate on abstract, hierarchical information (Conway & Christiansen, 2001), phonological information in working memory (Smith & Jonides, 1999), and in mental rotation tasks (Jordan, Heinze, Lutz, Kanowski, & Jancke, 2001). These functions assign Broca's area a key role in implementing the syntactic, combinatorial work required to conceptually interlink the words of a sentence.

The left inferior prefrontal cortex (LI-PFC) is not limited to procedural memory functions. Research has suggested Broca's Area (BA 44) and the LI-PFC support general working memory functions by selecting and maintaining information that is currently activated in parietal lobes (Petrides, 1996; Ullman, 2004). Furthermore, this region links working memory to long term memory by retrieving and acting upon information which is stored in temporal and temporo-parietal regions (Ruchkin, Grafman, Cameron, & Berndt, 2003; Petrides, Alivisatos, & Evans, 1995). Particularly Ruchkin et al. (2003) as well as Sakai (2003) argue that the prefrontal working memory system corresponds to a "retention space" for activated long term memories in parietal regions.

Especially relevant for comprehension is the likelihood that left inferior prefrontal cortex (LI-PFC) has a role in encoding and semantic analysis of verbal information that goes beyond task difficulty (Demb, Desmond, Wagner, Vaidya, Glover, & Gabrieli, 1995). The activation of the LI-PFC in conditions that require semantic encoding predicts subsequent superior memory performance in recognizing the presented verbal information (Fujii et al., 2002; Otten et al., 2001). A study by Kohler, Paus, Buckner and Milner (2004), which applied transcranial magnetic stimulation (rTMS) in combination with fMRI, even suggests a causal connection between LI-PFC activation and successful verbal episodic encoding. A basis for this link is that increased LI-PFC activation during semantic processing of linguistic input leads to an enhanced item distinctiveness and firmer integration into long term memory.

Finally, text comprehension requires some degree of controlled processing, as the reader attends to words and considers their meaning in relation to the text. The controlled processing function of LI-PFC has been identified in memory research by Wheeler and Buckner (2003), who found that two left frontal regions (BA 45/47) and BA 44 showed increased activity during the retrieval of only minimally studied words in comparison to repeatedly studied words. They attributed this additional activity to an increased demand for controlled processing during the retrieval of weakly established memories. In text processing, we should expect this kind of controlled process to be involved when integration processes requires a weakly established word or referent memory to be retrieved.

The functions attributed to the left inferior prefrontal region and the temporal pole are well suited to implement the conceptual and syntactic encoding of a sentence. In our study, the implicit condition produced only a weakly established conceptual representation. Encountering a word across a sentence boundary that might be related to this weak representation approximates a condition of novel word. The implicit condition therefore requires more semantic analysis and conceptual coding of the verbal information than the explicit condition. The activation in the left inferior prefrontal cortex in combination with the temporal pole appears to reflect such processes.

CONCLUSIONS

Until recently, integration processes across sentence boundaries have been studied primarily with behavioral measures, e.g., when and how bridging inferences are built between sentences. As explained in the chapter by Singer and Leon (this volume) a sentence is processed faster when it contains a noun that was already introduced by the previous sentence. The sentence "The beer is warm," is thus more quickly read after the sentence "We got the beer out of the trunk" than after the sentence "We got the picnic supplies out of the trunk" (Haviland & Clark, 1974). Similarly, for sentences that are causally related, less processing time is required when a causal consequence has already been expressed by the preceding sentence rather than being only implicated. A statement that the lawn was watered is therefore verified faster after a sentence is read which states that Steve saw that the grass was dry, went outside to turn on the hose and watered the lawn, in relation to a sentence which only implies that the lawn was watered (e.g. Griesel et al., 2003; experiment 2).

The Processing of Explicit, Paraphrased, Implicit and Novel Statements

It is quite interesting to compare the results of the same experimental manipulations across the three different experiments and thus associate the ERP with the behavioral data and the fMRI-results. In the ERP and fMRI experiments, novelty and implicit conditions yielded similar results. In particular, there was no significant difference between the two conditions in either experiment. Differences did, however, occur, in both experiments between the paraphrase and the explicit conditions (P300 in experiment 1; posterior cingulate in experiment 3) as well as between the implicit and the paraphrase (N400 in experiment 1; dorsomedial prefrontal areas in experiment 3) in combination with other but less prominent differences. The behavioral experiment showed that the largest latency gap occurred between the paraphrase and the implicit conditions when adjacent experimental conditions (explicit $<$ paraphrase $<$ implicit $<$ novelty) are compared.

The immediate integration hypothesis suggests that integration processes across sentence boundaries occur immediately, i.e., at the earliest possible time during processing. When a word at the beginning of a sentence repeats the morpheme of a word in a previous sentence, early perceptual encoding and related memory processes could determine this earliest possible time for building a connection. Propositions that were only implied or are completely new on the other hand (as in the implicit and the novelty conditions) would require additional analysis and a later point in time when the integration can be performed.

In accordance with this prediction, the ERP experiment showed that for the explicit and paraphrase conditions an early positivity between—around 150–200 ms, which was salient at the bilateral posterior regions with right-hemisphere prominence distinguished the explicit and paraphrase conditions from the other two conditions. Further supporting this finding, the fMRI experiment indicated that a right parietal area was clearly involved in the paraphrase as compared to the explicit condition.

Because, for the implicit and novelty conditions, the integration across a sentence boundary can not occur within this early time frame, the ERP experiment should show an indication of an additional processing effort at some later time for the implicit and novelty conditions. This prediction was clearly confirmed. There was an N400 effect, at the central electrode for the implicit as well as for the novelty condition. The fMRI results showed that for the implicit condition, the integration processes occurred mostly in the medial frontal cortex and in the left inferior frontal cortex. For the novelty condition, the integration processes furthermore included the right inferior prefrontal areas (compare the contrasts implicit > explicit and novelty > explicit in Table 7–4 and Figure 7–3).

The fMRI results thus showed that the integration and verification of a statement in relation to a previously read sentence may occur in posterior and frontal areas of the brain. As in the ERP-experiment there was a clear separation between the experimental conditions. In addition, the separation between the experimental conditions coincided between the fMRI and the ERP experiment. The paraphrase condition showed a P300 effect in the ERP experiment and an activation in the posterior cingulate gyrus in the fMRI experiment. The implicit and the novelty condition, on the other hand, showed an N400 effect and activations in medial frontal areas, in combination with other frontal, temporal and parietal areas.

For language and memory tasks (cf. Ullman, 2004), posterior and prefrontal regions form an interdependent network. The posterior cingulate's connections to prefrontal regions (Morris, Petrides & Pandya, 1999) show its link to a more integrative, structure-building region of the brain. Memory retrieval may depend on an interaction between posterior cingulate, posterior parietal association areas, prefrontal areas and mid temporal lobe structures. The medial temporal lobe supports the retrieval of information from memory and parietal regions maintain representations of remembered information. The prefrontal cortex exerts an important role concerning activated memory representations in the parietal lobe as well as offline memories in temporoparietal regions. It sets up retrieval mode, initiates the retrieval attempt in temporal regions and monitors and selects upon activated memory representations. The extensive connections between those regions would indeed allow for a coordinated interplay. Such an interdependency between automatic and strategic components in inferencing and integration has recently also been demonstrated in behavioral experiments as well (Calvo et al. in press).

The fMRI experiment showed which brain areas become differentially involved in relating one and the same statement to variations of a previously read text. The posterior cingulate gyrus, supposedly signifying routine processes, was found to be active when an integration is achieved via a paraphrase. The medial frontal gyrus, supposedly indicating more effortful and strategic construction processes, becomes involved when an additional coherence link needs to be established.

The constructive processes of the *novelty condition* require more extensive memory retrievals involving the posterior cingulate gyrus and the left STG. In addition, coarse semantic relations may become activated in the right hemisphere (e.g. the right IFG; cf. Mason & Just, 2004). The activated situational knowledge may then become integrated in the left IFG (cf. Hagoort et al. 2004). This hypothesis is empirically supported by the *Novelty > Explicit* and *Novelty > Paraphrase* contrasts which show these specific brain areas. In the explicit and paraphrase conditions such construction processes are not required because of the autonomous memory resonance process which achieves the linkage in a more economic way.

Overall, the current results provide a means for differentiating the role of a more passive process of inferencing and integration (O'Brien et al., 1998) and a more active construction process (Graesser et al., 1994) in relating a statement to a previously read text. The passive process could be termed memory resonance because it establishes a relation more or less automatically. This process may peak earlier (about 200–300 ms after the onset of the word) than the more effortful strategic process (400–500 ms). Thus, we can suggest that there are indeed two different processes that support inferences and meaning-based text integration processes generally. A more active meaning search process (e.g. Graesser, Singer & Trabasso, 1992) is slower and perhaps less robust; a more passive memory resonance process (O'Brien et al., 1998) is faster, more robust, but perhaps insufficient for complete coherence under some conditions, which then require the slower more active process. Both are important for establishing coherence in texts in terms of their neural correlates. Quite surprisingly and re-assuring for the behavioral results, the timing and location of these processes in the brain coincide very well with the theoretical conclusions derived from the behavioral experiments. Integration processes across sentences boundaries may therefore occur at the earliest opportunity that is afforded by the preceding context and the specific word which has to become integrated into the emerging discourse structure.

REFERENCES

Bavelier, D., Corina, D., Jezzard, P., Padmanabhan, S., Clark, V. P., Karni, A., et al. (1997). Sentence reading: A functional MRI study at 4 Tesla. *Journal of Cognitive Neuroscience, 9*(5), 664–686.

Cabeza, R., & Nyberg, L. (2000). Imaging cognition II: An empirical review of 275 PET and fMRI studies. *Journal of Cognitive Neuroscience, 12*(1), 1–47.

Calvo, M. G., Castillo, M. D., & Schmalhofer, F. (in press). Strategic influence on the time course of predictive inferences in reading. *Memory and Cognition.*

Conway, C. M., & Christiansen, M. H. (2001). Sequential learning in non-human primates. *Trends in Cognitive Sciences, 5*(12), 539–546.

Crinion, J. T., Lambon-Ralph, A., Warburton, E. A., Howard, D., & Wise, R. J. S. (2003). Temporal lobe regions engaged during normal speech comprehension. *Brain, 126,* 1193–1201.

Demb, J. B., Desmond, J. E., Wagner, A. D., Vaidya, C. J., Glover, G. H., & Gabrieli, J. D. (1995). Semantic encoding and retrieval in the left inferior prefrontal cortex: A functional MRI study of task difficulty and process specificity. *Journal of Neuroscience, 15,* 5870–5878.

Ferree, T. C., Luu, P., Russell, G. S., & Tucker, D. M. (2001). Scalp electrode impedance, infection risk, and EEG data quality. *Journal of Clinical Neurophysiology, 112*(3), 536–544.

Ferstl, E. C., & Cramon, D. Y. V. (2001). The role of coherence and cohesion in text comprehension: An event-related fMRI study. *Cognitive Brain Research, 11,* 325–340.

Ferstl, E. C., Guthke, T., & von Cramon, D. Y. (2002). Text comprehension after brain injury: Left prefrontal lesions affect inference processes. *Neuropsychology, 16*(3), 292–308.

Fletcher, P. C., Happe, F., Frith, U., & Baker, S. C. (1995). Other minds in the brain: A functional imaging study of "theory of mind" in story comprehension. *Cognition, 57*(2), 109–128.

Frazier, L., & Rayner, K. (1982). Making and correcting errors in the analysis of structurally ambiguous sentences. *Cognitive Psychology, 14,* 178–210.

Fujii, T., Okuda, J., Tsukiura, T., Ohtake, H., Suzuki, M., Kawashima, R., et al. (2002). Encoding-related brain activity during deep processing of verbal materials: A PET study. *Neuroscience Research, 44*(4), 429–438.

Gabrieli, J. D. E., Desmond, J. E., Demb, J. B., & Wagner, A. D. (1996). Functional magnetic resonance imaging of semantic memory processes in the frontal lobes. *Psychological Science, 7*(5), 278–283.

Gelfand, J. R., & Bookheimer, S. Y. (2003). Dissociating neural mechanisms of temporal sequencing and processing phonemes. *Neuron, 38*(5), 831–842.

Gernsbacher, M. A., & Kaschak, M. P. (2003). Neuroimaging studies of language production and comprehension. *Annual Review of Psychology, 54,* 91–114.

Graesser, A. C., Singer, M., & Trabasso, T. (1994). Constructing inferences during narrative text comprehension. *Psychological Review, 101*(3), 371–395.

Griesel, C., Friese, U., & Schmalhofer, F. (2003). What are the differences in the cognitive representations of predictive and bridging inferences? In F. Schmalhofer, R.

Young, & G. Katz (Eds.), *Proceedings of EuroCogSci03* (pp. 145–150). Mahwah, NJ: Lawrence Erlbaum Associates.

Hagoort, P., Hald, L., Bastiaansen, M., & Petersson, K. M. (2004). Integration of word meaning and world knowledge in language comprehension. *Science, 304*, 438–441.

Haviland, S. E., & Clark, H. H. (1974). What's new? Acquiring new information as a process in comprehension. *Journal of Verbal Learning and Verbal Behavior, 13*, 512–521.

Jarvella, R. J. (1971). Syntactic processing of connected speech. *Journal of Verbal Learning and Verbal Behavior, 10*, 409–416.

Jordan, K., Heinze, H-J., Lutz, K., Kanowski, M., & Jancke, L. (2001). Cortical activations during the mental rotation of different visual objects. *NeuroImage, 13*(1), 143–152.

Kintsch, W. (1998). *Comprehension: A paradigm for cognition*. Cambridge: Cambridge University Press.

Kohler, E., Keysers, C., Umilta, M. A., Fogassi, L., Gallese, V., & Rizzolatti, G. (2002). Hearing sounds, understanding actions: Action representation in mirror neurons. *Science, 297*(5582), 846–848.

Kutas, M., & Hillyard, S. A. (1980). Reading senseless sentences: Brain potentials reflect semantic incongruity. *Science, 207*, 203–205.

Lehmann, D., & Skrandies, W. (1980). Reference-free identification of components of checkerboard-evoked multi-channels potential fields. *Electroencephalography and Clinical Neurophysiology, 48*, 609–621.

Maguire, E. A., Frith, C. D., & Morris, R. G. M. (1999). The functional neuroanatomy of comprehension and memory: The importance of prior knowledge. *Brain, 122*(10), 1839–1850.

Mason, R. A., & Just, M. A. (2004). How the brain processes causal inferences in text. *Psychological Science, 15*(1), 1–7.

Mazoyer, B. M., Tzourio, N., Frak, V., Syrota, A., Murayama, N., Levrier, O., et al. (1993). The cortical representation of speech. *Journal of Cognitive Neuroscience, 5*(4), 467–479.

McDaniel, M. A., Schmalhofer, F., & Keefe, D. E. (2001). What is minimal about predictive inferences? *Psychonomic Bulletin & Review, 8*(4), 840–846.

McKoon, G., & Ratcliff, R. (1986). Inferences about predictable events. *Journal of Experimental Psychology: Learning, Memory, & Cognition, 12*, 82–91.

McKoon, G., & Ratcliff, R. (1992). Inference during reading. *Psychological Review, 99*(3), 440–466.

Morris, R., Petrides, M., & Pandya, D. N. (1999). Architecture and connections of retrosplenial area 30 in the rhesus monkey (*Macaca mulatta*). *European Journal of Neuroscience, 11*(7), 2506–2518.

Newell, A. (1973) You can't play 20 questions with nature and win. In W. G. Chase (Ed.), *Visual information processing* (pp. 283–310). New York: Academic Press.

O'Brien, E. J., Rizzella, M. L., Albrecht, J. E., & Halleran, J. G. (1998). Updating a situation model: A memory-based text processing view. *Journal of Experimental Psychology: Learning, Memory, & Cognition, 24*(5), 1200–1210.

Otten, L. J., Henson, R. N., & Rugg, M. D. (2001). Depth of processing effects on neural correlates of memory encoding: Relationship between findings from across- and within-task comparisons. *Brain, 124*(Pt 2), 399–412.

Petrides, M. (1996). Specialized systems for the processing of mnemonic information within the primate frontal cortex. *Philosophical Transactions of the Royal Society of London, Series B, Biological Sciences, 351*(1346), 1455–1461; discussion 1461–1452.

Petrides, M., Alivisatos, B., & Evans, A. (1995). Functional activation of the human ventrolateral frontal cortex during mnemonic retrieval of verbal information. *Proceedings of the National Academy of Sciences USA, 92*(13), 5803–5807.

Pickering, M. J. & Taxler, M. J. (1998). Plausibility and recovery from garden paths: An eye-tracking study. *Journal of Experimental Psychology: Learning, Memory and Cognition, 24*, 949–961.

Raichle, M. E., Fiez, J. A., Videen, T. O., MacLeod, A. M., Pardo, J. V., Fox, P. T., et al. (1994). Practice-related changes in human brain functional anatomy during nonmotor learning. *Cerebral Cortex, 4*(1), 8–26.

Rayner, K., Warren, T., Juhasz, B. J., & Liversedge, S. P. (2004) Effects of plausibility on eye-movements. *Journal of Experimental Psychology: Learning, Memory, and Cognition, 30, 6, 000–000.*

Rizolatti, G., Fogassi, L., & Gallese, V. (2001). Neurophysiological mechanisms underlying the understanding and imitation of action. *Nature Review Neuroscience, 2*(9), 661–670.

Ruchkin, D. S., Grafman, J., Cameron, K., & Berndt, R. S. (2003). Working memory retention systems: a state of activated long-term memory. *Behavioral Brain Science, 26*(6), 709–28; discussion 728–777.

Schmalhofer, F. (1997). Zur Bedeutung von integrativen Theorien für die experimentelle Kognitionspsychologie. In H. Mandl (Ed.), *Bericht über den 40. Kongress der Deutschen Gesellschaft für Psychologie in München: Schwerpunktthema Wissen und Handeln* (pp. 864–869). Göttingen: Hogrefe Verlag.

Schmalhofer, F. (2001). Will dreams come true? A review of John R. Anderson & Christian Lebiere: The atomic components of thought. *Journal of Mathematical Psychology, 45*, 917–923.

Schmalhofer, F., Friese, U., Pietruska, K., Raabe, M., & Rutschmann, R. M. (2005). Brain processes of relating a statement to a previously read text: Memory resonance and situational constructions. In B. B. Bara, L. Barsalou, M. Bucciarelli (Eds.), *Proceedings of the XVII Conference of the Cognitive Science Society* (pp. 1949–1954). Mahwah, NJ: Lawrence Erlbaum Associates.

Schmalhofer, F., McDaniel, M. A., & Keefe, D. (2002). A unified model for predictive and bridging inferences. *Discourse Processes, 33*(2), 105–32.

Singer, M. (2004). *Tacit verification in text comprehension: Memory-based and pragmatic influences.* Paper presented at the 45th Annual Meeting of the Psychonomic Society. Minneapolis, Minnesota, Nov. 18–21, 2004.

Smith, E. E., & Jonides, J. (1999). Storage and executive processes in the frontal lobes. *Science, 283*(5408), 1657–1661.

Tucker, D. M. (1993). Spatial sampling of head electrical fields: The geodesic sensor net. *Electroencephalography and Clinical Neurophysiology, 87*, 154–163.

Ullman, M. T. (2004). Contributions of memory circuits to language: The declarative/procedural model. *Cognition, 92*(1–2), 231–70.

Vaillancourt, D. E., Thulborn, K. R., & Corcos, D. M. (2003). Neural basis for the processes that underlie visually guided and internally guided force control in humans. *Journal of Neurophysiology, 90*, 3330–3340.

van Berkum, J. J. A., Brown, C. M., Zwitserlood, P., Kooijman, V., & Hagoort, P. (2005). Anticipating upcoming words in discourse: Evidence from ERPs and reading times. *Journal of Experimental Psychology: Learning, Memory and Cognition*.

van Berkum, J. J. A., Hagoort, P., & Brown, C. M. (1999). Semantic integration in sentences and discourse: Evidence from the N400. *Journal of Cognitive Neuroscience, 11*(6), 657–671.

van Berkum, J. J. A., Zwitserlood, P., Brown, C. M., & Hagoort, P. (2003). When and how do listeners relate a sentence to the wider discourse? Evidence from the N400 effect. *Cognitive Brain Research, 17*, 701–718.

Wheeler, M. E., & Buckner, R. L. (2003). Functional dissociation among components of remembering: control, perceived oldness, and content. *Journal of Neuroscience, 23*(9), 3869–3880.

Wheeler, M. E., & Buckner, R. L. (2004). Functional-anatomic correlates of remembering and knowing. *Neuroimage, 21*(4), 1337–1349.

Yang, Ch-L., Perfetti, Ch. A., & Schmalhofer, F. (under review). ERPs expose integration processes in text comprehension.

8

Retrieval of Explicit and Implicit Text Ideas: Processing Profiles

Murray Singer
University of Manitoba

Gilbert Remillard
Morehead State University

Two central goals of the information processing approach to discourse comprehension have been (a) the identification of the mental processes of deriving meaning from verbal messages and (b) the characterization of the resulting representations. In this chapter we describe research designed to evaluate the quality of the processes of retrieving previously encountered text ideas and to thereby assess representations from which the retrieved ideas were derived. More specifically, we set out to measure the relative contributions of recollection and familiarity to text retrieval, as diagnosed by the process dissociation procedure (Jacoby, 1991; see also Mandler, 1980). The intention was to compare the retrieval profiles for explicit text ideas, bridging inferences, and elaborative inferences. These comparisons were considered to bear on the representation of those idea classes.

The remainder of this *introduction* comprises three parts. First, we identify a discrepancy between the theoretical analyses of explicit versus implicit text ideas on the one hand and certain behavioral evidence on the other. Second, we briefly review contemporary treatments of the automaticity of text-inference processing. Then we outline how the process dissociation method may shed light on both of these issues.

Subsequent sections of the chapter then describe our previous research and a new experiment that apply process dissociation to the retrieval of (a) elaborative inferences and (b) bridging inferences. Then (c) we consider some of the theoretical issues pertinent to the pursuit of the present approach.

REPRESENTATION OF EXPLICIT AND IMPLICIT TEXT IDEAS

Relatively early in the modern investigation of language comprehension, inference was interpreted to lie at the center of human communication (Schank,

1976). In subsequent inference processing research, the distinction between bridging and elaborative inferences emerged as an important one. Bridging inferences enhance coherence by connecting discourse ideas with reference to unstated concepts or relations (Haviland & Clark, 1974). Elaborative inferences, in contrast, represent plausible extrapolations from discourse but do not particularly contribute to message coherence. Consider example (1) (Singer, 1980):

(1) a. The dentist pulled the tooth painlessly. The patient liked the new method. (explicit)
  b. The tooth was pulled painlessly. The dentist used a new method. (bridging inference)
  c. The tooth was pulled painlessly. The patient liked the new method. (elaborative inference)

Sequence (1a) explicitly states that a dentist pulled the tooth. Sequence (1b) would be incoherent if the understander did not infer that it was the dentist who pulled the tooth. For sequence (1c), it is a sensible but not coherence-preserving elaboration that the tooth was pulled by a dentist. Both bridging and elaborative inferences are generally viewed as deriving from the understander's world knowledge rather than from computations in a formal domain such as logic (cf. Lea, O'Brien, Fisch, Noveck, & Braine, 1990).

A variety of methods have indicated that bridging inferences are robustly encoded by the understander, whereas elaborative inferences are either not routinely encoded or are more weakly encoded (Keenan, Baillet, & Brown, 1984; McKoon & Ratcliff, 1986; Myers, Shinjo, & Duffy, 1987; Potts, Keenan, & Golding, 1988; Singer & Ferreira, 1983). These findings are consistent with the dependence of text coherence upon bridging inferences.

Many theorists (e.g., Graesser, Singer, & Trabasso, 1994; Kintsch, 1988; Raney, 2003; Schmalhofer & Glavanov, 1986) have addressed inference processing in terms of the multilevel analysis of discourse representation (van Dijk & Kintsch, 1983). According to the multilevel view, text representations comprise the surface features of the text (specific wording, grammatical constructions), a *textbase* network consisting mainly of the propositions explicitly conveyed by the text, and a multidimensional model of the situation to which the text refers. The situation model constitutes an integration of discourse ideas and world knowledge. The understander's inferences are frequently characterized as residing in the situation model (Kintsch, 1992), although the textbase is sometimes proposed to capture certain inferences (Singer, 1994; Singer & Kintsch, 2001).

Recently, Schmalhofer, McDaniel, and Keefe (2002) incisively distinguished among different categories of text-related ideas, using the multilevel analysis. Singer and Leon (this volume) described that treatment as follows:

> (Schmalhofer et al.) proposed that whereas explicit text ideas are encoded at surface, propositional, and situational levels of representation, inferences are

> initially constructed primarily or exclusively in the situation model. According to the construction-integration model (Kintsch, 1988), encoded elements at any representational level will endure only if they receive relatively high degrees of activation, which in turn depends on their degree of interconnection with other elements. Bridging inferences generally exceed elaborative inferences in their connections to other text ideas and pertinent knowledge. However, high constraint . . . can augment the interconnections of elaborative inferences. In this circumstance, elaborative inferences may become an enduring part of the text representation. (pp.10–11)

This analysis identifies a research problem: In particular, there are fundamental differences between the explicit ideas and the bridging inferences of text (e.g., only the explicit ideas are subject to perceptual encoding), but several behavioral measures tend to equate the two (Keefe & McDaniel, 1993; Potts et al., 1988; Singer, 1980). A central goal of the present research was to refine the behavioral distinction between the explicit ideas and inferences encoded from text.

AUTOMATICITY OF TEXT INFERENCE PROCESSES

An important text comprehension controversy has been whether text inference processes are controlled or automatic. The reliable encoding of bridging inferences in particular has promoted the tendency to view them as automatic. However, the equivocal status of the automaticity of text inference processes was considered by Singer, Graesser, and Trabasso (1994). They noted that bridging inferences are supported by *fast* resonance processes of which the reader is *unaware* (e.g., Albrecht & Myers, 1995; O'Brien & Albrecht, 1991; O'Brien, Albrecht, Hakala, & Rizzella, 1995), indices of automatic processes (Logan, 1988; Posner & Snyder, 1975; Schneider & Shiffrin, 1977). On the other hand, bridging computations are taxing of cognitive resources (Daneman & Carpenter, 1980; Singer, Andrusiak, Reisdorf, & Halldorson, 1992). Bridging processes are also, overall, quite slow; they are more time-consuming than (a) the detection of direct connections among text ideas (Haviland & Clark, 1974), (b) reinstating antecedent ideas to working memory (Kintsch & van Dijk, 1978; Lesgold, Roth, & Curtis, 1979), and even (c) mentally reorganizing referentially incongruent sequences of sentences (Yekovich, Walker, & Blackman, 1979). A comparable analysis emerged from Singer et al.'s (1994) inspection of anaphoric resolution, a simple form of bridging.

Thus, evidence concerning the automaticity of text inference processing is equivocal. To the extent that process dissociation patterns, a central focus of this study, bear on the automaticity *of the original encoding* of a stimulus as well as its retrieval, they might have the capacity to clarify the automaticity of deriving inferences from discourse.

PROCESS DISSOCIATION AND TEXT COMPREHENSION

The Process Dissociation Analysis

According to the process dissociation analysis, the recognition of a test probe is supported by the *familiarity* of the probe and one's *recollective* experience relating the probe to the context in which it was encountered (Jacoby, 1991; Mandler, 1980). In ordinary experience, encountering a slightly known acquaintance in an unexpected setting, such as seeing the pharmacist at the movie theatre, may produce a sense of familiarity *in the absence of* recollection.

Two dissociations between familiarity and recollection (Yonelinas, 2002) are particularly relevant for the present purposes: (a) Familiarity is sensitive to both perceptual manipulations (e.g., maintenance rehearsal of words; Gardiner, Gawlick, & Richardson-Klavehn, 1994) and conceptual manipulations (e.g., deep versus shallow semantic processing; Dehn & Engelkamp, 1997; Jacoby, Lindsay, & Toth, 1992). Recollection, in contrast, reflects only conceptual factors but is more sensitive to such manipulations than is familiarity. (b) Familiarity bears the signature of an automatic process, whereas recollection is controlled (Yonelinas, 2002).

Process dissociation blends the latter theoretical analysis with both empirical and computational procedures. The empirical method sets recollection and familiarity in opposition to one another. In a word recognition experiment, for example (Jacoby, 1991, Experiment 3), subjects encountered anagrams to solve and words to read in an initial study phase. Next, they recited a different list of words as they heard them. In a subsequent recognition test, so-called *inclusion* subjects were instructed to label a word old if it had occurred either in the initial study phase or in the heard list. *Exclusion* subjects, in contrast, answered "old" only if a word appeared in the heard list. According to the exclusion instruction, subjects ought to report recognizing an anagram/read word only if it seems *familiar*, but they are unable to *recollect* it as originating in the anagram/read list. Using R for recollection and F for familiarity, the probabilities of labelling a probe as old in inclusion (O_i) and exclusion (O_e) are expressed as follows (Jacoby, 1991):

$$O_i \nabla R \lesssim F - RF \nabla R \lesssim (1 \quad R)F \qquad (8.1)$$

$$O_e \nabla \qquad (1 \quad R)F \qquad (8.2)$$

Subtraction of Eq. (8.2) from Eq. (8.1) reveals that recollection can be estimated as $R \nabla O_i \quad O_e$. Substituting that expression in Eq. (8.2) then reveals that $F \nabla O_e/(1 \quad (O_i \quad O_e))$. Using this analysis, Jacoby (1991) showed that anagram words considerably exceeded phase-1 read words in degree of recollection, but not in familiarity.

It is noteworthy that it is controversial whether memory retrieval is supported by two processes or by a single, activation-based familiarity process (Gillund & Shiffrin, 1984; Hintzman, 1988; Ratcliff, van Zandt, & McKoon, 1995). However, the contribution of a second process, such as the influence in recognition of a controlled recall process, is often at least tacitly acknowledged by one-process theorists (Gillund & Shiffrin, 1984; Hintzman & Curran, 1994; see also Clark & Gronlund, 1996; Yonelinas, 2002).

Two Influences in Text Retrieval

We assumed that dual-process principles apply to text retrieval as well as other memory phenomena. To assume otherwise would require a memory theory unique to discourse, certainly an unparsimonious approach (Singer & Kintsch, 2001). Equally importantly, there is empirical evidence that both familiarity and recollection contribute to text retrieval. First, *the influence of familiarity* is reflected by the fact that reading time is faster for a story that repeats, in new words, the theme of a prior text than it is for unrelated stories and for stories that repeat words but present a novel theme (Levy, Campsall, & Browne, 1995; Masson, 1993). Because ordinary reading is not an explicit memory task, the enhancement of comprehension fluency is more likely to be due to the familiarity of the text ideas than to an experience of recollection (see also Reder, 1987). Second, *the contribution of recollection* to text memory tends to be supported by people's ability to confidently associate retrieved ideas with antecedent texts (Hasher & Griffin, 1978; Reder, 1982).

Indeed, a small number of studies have already used variants of process dissociation to distinguish the contributions of familiarity and recollection in text retrieval and related domains. In the retrieval of *Star Trek* stories, for example, Long and Prat (2002) examined the impact of readers' knowledge on the quality of text memory. Readers high or low in *Star Trek* knowledge read either a pair of *Star Trek* stories or a pair of psychology chapters. In inclusion, the subjects were instructed to label a test sentence old if they remembered that it originated in the first text or if it seemed familiar but they could not remember from which text it came. The exclusion subjects, in contrast, used the old label only for sentences that derived from the second text. The results dissociated familiarity and recollection in the domain of the readers' expertise. Specifically, readers' knowledge affected recollection and not familiarity in the recognition of *Star Trek* test sentences, but affected neither recollection nor familiarity in memory for psychology material, of which the *Star Trek* experts had no distinctive knowledge.

Likewise, Caldwell and Masson (2001) presented evidence that, in memory for the location of objects, familiarity is the same for old and young adults, but recollection is greater for young adults. Caldwell and Masson's stimuli were memorized spatial arrangements rather than texts. However, their study of spatial situations converges closely with language-based studies of spatial situation models (e.g., Morrow, Greenspan, & Bower, 1987).

Potential of Process Dissociation in This Realm

It is likely that the process dissociation analysis has the capacity to clarify central problems of text and discourse processing. One example is that memory theorists have proposed that people's experience of remembering distractor stimuli that are *related* to previously studied stimuli is supported by a process of misrecollection that is distinct from ordinary recollection (Brainerd, Wright, Reyna, & Mojardin, 2001). Because text inferences fit the definition of related distractor, this proposal carries useful implications about memory for such inferences. Second, process dissociation may be able to distinguish between multiprocess (e.g., recollection, familiarity) and multirepresentation analyses of text retrieval (Mandler, 1980). Third, process dissociation explicitly addresses the automaticity of retrieval processes, but it may likewise pertain to the automaticity of encoding (Jacoby, 1991). Clarifying the automaticity of discourse encoding would offer an important advance to the field. These ramifications of the process dissociation framework are considered in more detail in the General Discussion.

Conclusion

The scientific evaluation of whether certain inferences accompany text comprehension is frequently achieved through the use of various behavioral measures to compare those inferences with (a) control statements, (b) statements representing other inference categories, and, perhaps most stringently, (c) explicit text statements. Such investigations have sometimes revealed the indistinguishability of inferences and explicit text ideas (e.g., Potts et al., 1988). On the other hand, the physical absence of the inference from the message, coupled with the multilevel analysis of text representation (Schmalhofer et al., 2002; van Dijk & Kintsch, 1983), tends to deny that inferences and explicit ideas will be encoded in an identical manner.

Process dissociation offers the opportunity to clarify these issues, in the form of an integrated theoretical, empirical, and computational framework for the analysis of memory phenomena. The present research applied process dissociation to the encoding differences between explicit and implicit text ideas and, more speculatively, to the automaticity of text inferences processes. The next section documents our empirical investigations of these issues. First, it considers Singer and Remillard's (2004) contrast of explicit text ideas versus elaborative inferences, along with evidence stemming from a new experiment. Then it presents a comparable experiment about bridging inferences.

FAMILIARITY AND RECOLLECTION IN THE RETRIEVAL OF TEXT IDEAS

Elaborative Inferences: Deep Versus Shallow Processing

Experiment 1 of Singer and Remillard (2004; henceforth SR) focused on elaborative inferences about high-probability case-filling elements. For example, *The letter was delivered in the rain* implies the involvement of the agent, mailman (Singer, 1980). Several hypotheses were of concern. First, the physical appearance in text of the words corresponding to explicit ideas but not inferences suggests that there will be fundamental differences in their encoding (e.g., Schmalhofer et al., 2002). Therefore, we predicted that the process dissociation patterns of explicit text statements and elaborative inferences would differ. Second and furthermore, the absence of the opportunity to perceptually process the words corresponding to an elaborative inference tends to suggest a lower familiarity component for inferences than explicit ideas, because familiarity in part reflects perceptual processing. However, because familiarity is also sensitive to conceptual processing, the distinct qualities of the conceptual processing of elaborative inferences (e.g., they are generated by the reader) might complicate the interpretation of the familiarity component. Third, because recollection reflects only conceptual processes, we predicted a stronger recollective contribution to explicit ideas than to elaborative inferences.

The subjects of SR's Experiment 1 rated the activity conveyed by each stimulus sentence. In a new experiment, we replaced that semantic orienting task with a shallow task. Consistent with prior findings in the process dissociation literature, we predicted that *both* recollection and familiarity would be weaker in shallow than in deep processing (e.g., Dehn & Engelkamp, 1997; Komatsu, Graf, & Uttl, 1995; Toth, 1996), because weaker conceptual representations are derived from shallow processing, and both recollection and familiarity are supported by conceptual representations. We also advanced the stronger hypothesis that shallow processing would reduce recollection more than familiarity (e.g., Yonelinas, 2002, Figure 2).

More generally, these experiments served to validate the application of process dissociation to language processes. Violations of the assumptions of process dissociation result in anomalous result patterns, such as a particular manipulation yielding a decrease in recollection but an increase in familiarity (Jacoby, 1998). We scrutinized the results for anomalies of this sort. We also monitored the data for familiar patterns, such as the aforementioned detrimental impact of shallow processing on both recollection and familiarity.

Method. In Experiment 1 of SR, the critical materials were 24 sentences that included an explicit high-probability case-filling element (e.g., *mailman* in 2a) and an implicit counterpart (e.g., 2b):

(2) a. The mailman delivered the letter in the rain.
b. The letter was delivered in the rain.

The experiment used the three phases of Jacoby's (1991) classic procedure. During phase 1, the subjects used four keyboard keys to rate, on a four-point scale, the activity level conveyed by the explicit and implicit sentences. The sentences were viewed on computer monitors. In phase 2, the subjects read unrelated words aloud from the screen. In phase 3, they recognized test words stemming from explicit and implicit sentences of phase 1 and phase 2 words, plus distractor words.

Inclusion subjects were instructed to label a phase 3 test word as old if it had appeared among either the phase 1 or phase 2 stimuli. Exclusion subjects, in contrast, were instructed to restrict the reply *old* to those words that had appeared in phase 2. The exclusion instructions specified that if the subject remembered that a test word originated in a phase-1 sentence, it could be confidently labeled *no*, because no word appeared in both phases 1 and 2.

In the first of four counterbalanced phase-1 lists, sentence frames like set (2) were randomly assigned to the explicit and implicit conditions plus an absent condition in the respective proportions of .25 (namely, six frames), .25, and .50. Absent passages simply did not appear in phase 1. However, their critical words (e.g., *mailman*) were still presented in the phase-3 recognition test. Accordingly, the target words functioned as their own controls across the three conditions. In the remaining three lists, the sentences sets were cycled across condition following a Latin-square scheme, resulting in their assignment once each to the explicit and implicit conditions and twice to the absent condition.

The procedure of the new, shallow-processing experiment was identical, except that, during phase 1, the subjects used four keys to indicate how many words in the stimulus sentence began with a vowel (0 to 3). The deep and shallow processing experiments had 154 and 64 subjects, respectively, all of whom were students of introductory psychology.

Data Analyses. The descriptive data were the proportions of acceptance (i.e., old responses) across conditions. Recollection and familiarity were derived from the acceptance rates with the use of the *extended* process dissociation computations of Buchner, Erdfelder, and Vaterrodt-Plunnecke (1995; see also Jacoby, 1998). The distinct features of Buchner et al.'s approach are that it (a) avoids the sometimes problematic assumption that recollection and familiarity are independent processes (Jacoby, 1991; Joordens & Merikle, 1993), (b) includes distinct guessing parameters for inclusion and exclusion, and (c) uses multinomial tree processing computations to estimate recollection and familiarity. Within this framework, hypotheses are tested with the use of the chi-square goodness-of-fit statistic, G^2. This is accomplished by subtraction of the G^2 value for the full extended process dissociation model from that for the submodel constrained by a particular null hypothesis. Consider, for example,

TABLE 8–1.
Elaborative Inferences: Acceptance Rate as a Function of Relation, Instruction, and Task Relation

Task	*Instruction*	*Explicit*	*Implicit*	*Absent*
Deep	Inclusion	.57	.34	.23
	Exclusion	.15	.10	.10
Shallow	Inclusion	.32	.30	.19
	Exclusion	.08	.06	.07

Source: Deep Task data adapted from Singer and Remillard (2004, Table 1), *Memory & Cognition*. Copyright 2004, Psychonomic Society. Adapted by permission.

the hypothesis that familiarity makes no contribution to recognition in the implicit condition (i.e., familiarity ∇ 0). This hypothesis entails a model with one less free parameter than the full model (i.e., familiarity is not free to vary). The resulting difference of G^2 statistics also has the chi-square distribution.

Results. The mean acceptance rates as a function of relation (explicit, implicit, absent), instruction (inclusion, exclusion), and task are shown in Table 8–1. Analyses of variance (ANOVA) applied separately to the deep (activity) and shallow (vowel-counting) data revealed main effects of both relation and instruction. In addition, the Relation χ Instruction interaction was significant for the activity task and marginally so for the counting task; in both cases, this reflected a stronger effect of relation under the inclusion than the exclusion instruction. All effects were significant according to both subjects-random and items-random ANOVAs. Finally, tests of simple main effects within the absent condition revealed significantly higher acceptance rates for inclusion than exclusion, for both the deep and shallow tasks. These were the false alarm rates.

Of greatest interest were the parameters derived from the extended process dissociation analysis, shown in Table 8–2. We tested a limited number of hypotheses to evaluate the recollection (*R*) and familiarity (*F*) parameters.[1] In the deep processing task, *R* was greater in the explicit than the implicit condition, which in turn significantly exceeded 0. *F* was likewise greater for the explicit than the implicit condition, but the latter value was approximately 0. In the *vowel counting* task, in contrast, neither *R* nor *F* differed significantly between the explicit and implicit conditions, and only the *R* values were statistically distinguishable from 0.

[1]Singer and Remillard (2004) used the symbols *c* and *u* (conscious and unconscious processing) rather than *R* and *F*, respectively, following the conventions of Buchner et al. However, consensus in the field is converging on the terms *recollection* and *familiarity*.

TABLE 8–2.
Parameter Estimates in Retrieval of Explicit Text Ideas Versus Elaborative Inferences

Task	*Parameter*	*Explicit*	*Implicit*
Deep	Recollection	.34[a]	.13[b]
	Familiarity	.15[a]	.02
Shallow	Recollection	.13	.13[b]
	Familiarity	*.03*	*.00*

[a]Explicit statistically higher than implicit.
[b]Implicit statistically higher than 0.
Alpha was set to .05 throughout.
Source: Adapted from Singer and Remillard (in press, Table 2), *Memory & Cognition*. Copyright 2004, Psychonomic Society. Adapted by permission.

Comparisons were also made between the corresponding parameters of the deep and shallow tasks. For explicit targets, both *R* and *F* were greater for deep than for shallow processing ($G^2(1)$'s ∇ 12.68, 9.86, respectively), whereas in the implicit condition there were no such differences.

Discussion. We highlight several features of the results. Consider first the *deep task*: (a) The implicit condition exhibited weaker recollection than the explicit condition, and no support of familiarity at all. This suggests that explicit and implicit text ideas are encoded differently, consistent with our prediction. (b) Near-zero familiarity in the implicit condition is generally consistent with the irrelevance of perceptual processes (e.g., word recognition) to implied text ideas. Furthermore, it tends to demonstrate conceptual representations strong enough to support recollection but not familiarity for implied text ideas, because familiarity reflects conceptual as well as perceptual processes (Yonelinas, 2002). Had the conceptual representations of the implicit ideas been stronger, familiarity as well as recollection would have significantly exceeded 0 in the implicit condition. (c) Greater recollection in the explicit than in the implicit condition signifies richer conceptual representations for the former, because recollection is supported exclusively by conceptual representations.

The main *shallow task* results were as follows: (a) Whereas both *R* and *F* were greater in the explicit than the implicit condition for the deep task, *neither* of them was in the shallow task. This shows that vowel counting, a surface orienting task, so impairs semantic processing that robust effects distinguishing explicit and implicit stimuli are abolished (see also Singer & Halldorson, 1996, Experiment 4). (b) Both *R* and *F* were significantly lower in the explicit condition of the shallow than in the deep task. This is consistent with the reduction in both parameters in a shallow processing task, as discussed earlier (Yonelinas, 2002). Lower values of *F* in shallow than in deep orienting tasks constitute one basis for associating conceptual as well as perceptual processes with that parameter (Toth, 1996). If *F* reflected only perceptual processes, then there would be no reason for that value to diminish when people perform a semantically shallow task. Finally, we were not able to evaluate our strong hypothesis that shallow processing would reduce recollection more than familiarity, because the amount of reduction of familiarity may have been limited by a floor effect ($F \nabla .03$). (c) Harder to explain is why *R* in the implicit condition was *not* lower in the shallow than in the deep task. This might indicate that *R* reflects two types of recollection—recollection of specific *target* words and recollection of gist. Gist recollection might be about equal in the explicit and implicit conditions, whereas target recollection should be greater in the explicit condition. With respect to the deep/shallow manipulation, because the sentences were short, subjects in the counting condition may have read the sentences before counting vowels, thus extracting the gist. Subsequent counting may have interfered with the ability to recollect the target but not the gist. This would explain why counting, relative to activity judgment, reduced *R* in the explicit but not the implicit condition. According to this account, recognition only in the explicit condition partly reflects recollection of the specific target word.

The latter proposal is speculative in nature. However, the phantom recognition analysis of Brainerd et al. (2001) addresses the gist-based recollection of related distractor items such as text inferences. The phantom recollection framework offers the conceptual and computational tools to evaluate hypotheses of this sort.

We note that SR (Experiment 1) examined an additional variable involving the inspection of sentence frames such as (3):

(3) a. The poet broke the television with the brick.
 b. The television was broken with the brick.

Mailman is a highly predictable agent for delivering a letter, whereas *poet* is a low-probability agent for (3b). Most important for the present purposes is that neither *R* nor *F* significantly differed from 0 in the low-probability implicit condition. Insofar as there is little reason to incorrectly recognize *poet* having read (3b), this outcome tended to validate the application of process dissociation to the domain of language processes.

Other features of the results likewise tend to validate process dissociation for the present purposes. First, the substance of the parametric profiles was sensible and interpretable. Second, we detected certain familiar process dissociation patterns, such as the aforementioned reduction of both recollection and familiarity in a shallow processing task. Third, completely absent were anomalous signatures that appear when crucial process dissociation assumptions are violated (Jacoby, 1998).

We assume that the higher acceptance rate in inclusion than exclusion reflects the higher ratio of officially correct old to new responses in inclusion. This results in a higher tendency to guess old in inclusion, an outcome detected by other investigators (e.g., Graf & Komatsu, 1994) but contrary to an assumption of process dissociation (Jacoby, 1991).

In conclusion, these experiments yielded different process dissociation profiles for explicit text ideas and elaborative inferences. Those idea categories have likewise been distinguished on some behavioral measures, so these findings tend to support the application of the process dissociation framework to the text processing domain. We considered process dissociation to have the potential to yield new insights concerning the representation of bridging inferences, which a number of measures tend not to distinguish from explicit ideas. We turn next to an experiment designed to address this issue.

Bridging Inferences

In this section, we review SR's (Experiment 2) examination of bridging inferences. Applying the process dissociation analysis to bridging inferences is especially useful, because, as discussed earlier, (a) bridging inferences preserve text coherence and (b) empirical evidence suggests that they frequently accompany comprehension. One might accordingly posit equivalent retrieval profiles for explicit ideas and bridging inferences. Nonetheless, like for elaborative inferences, we predicted (a) different process dissociation profiles for explicit ideas and bridging inferences and (b) anticipated lower familiarity estimates in the bridging than in the explicit condition. These predictions particularly rested on the absence from the text of the bridging-inference words (Schmalhofer et al., 2002). (c) The relatively reliable encoding of bridging inferences might suggest that the contributing processes are automatic. Insofar as familiarity is the more automatic of the retrieval influences, familiarity for bridging inferences might significantly exceed 0 (while simultaneously being lower than for explicit ideas), in contrast with our observations for elaborative inferences.

Method. The method was highly similar to that of the elaborative inference experiments, discussed earlier. The focus was on motive-inference materials, such as set (4) (Singer & Halldorson, 1996):

(4) a. The comedian delivered the punch line. The audience howled with amusement at the JOKE. (explicit)

b. The comedian delivered the punch line. The audience howled with amusement. (implicit)

c. The comedian forgot the punch line. The audience howled with amusement. (control)

Sentence (4a) explicitly refers to a critical concept, joke. The coherence of (4b) is promoted by a bridging inference about a joke. Sequence (4c) uses wording similar to that of (4b) but implies the involvement of a joke more weakly than (4b).

The sessions again comprised Jacoby's (1991) three process-dissociation phases. The phase 1 materials were derived from 16 sets like (4). In each of four counterbalanced lists, the passages were randomly assigned in equal numbers to the explicit, implicit, and control conditions, plus an absent condition.

Phase 1 also included eight buffer passages. This large volume of text prompted us to conduct the sessions in four process dissociation miniblocks. In each block, the subject rated the activity conveyed by each of one buffer, three experimental, and then another buffer passage (phase 1); read 11 words comparable to the target words from the screen (phase 2); and then made recognition judgments about phase 1 and 2 words and distractors. The subjects were 136 naive individuals from the same pool that was used for the other experiments.

Results. The mean recognition rates are shown in Table 8–3 and the process dissociation parameters appear in Table 8–4. ANOVA applied to the acceptance rates revealed significant effects of relation, instruction, and Relation χ Instruction. The interaction reflected a stronger effect of relation under the inclusion instruction than it did under exclusion. The acceptance rates in the absent condition were again higher in inclusion (.16) than exclusion (.05).

The extended process dissociation analysis revealed that *R* (recollection) for the explicit condition exceeded that of the bridging condition, which was greater than the control condition, which did not significantly exceed 0. *F* (familiarity) was greater in the explicit condition than both the bridging and control conditions. The latter conditions did not differ significantly. However, *F* in the control condition significantly exceeded 0.

Discussion. Differences were detected between the process dissociation profiles of the explicit and implicit conditions: Namely, (a) both recollection and familiarity were greater in the explicit than in the implicit condition, and (b) recollection significantly exceeded 0 in the implicit condition but familiarity did not. These results carry several implications. First, the recognition

TABLE 8–3
Bridging Inferences: Acceptance Rate as a Function of Relation and Instruction

	Relation			
Instruction	*Explicit*	*Implicit*	*Control*	*Absent*
Inclusion	.57	.34	.24	.16
Exclusion	.13	.06	.10	.05

Source: Adapted from Singer and Remillard (2004, Table 3), *Memory & Cognition*. Copyright 2004, Psychonomic Society. Adapted by permission.

TABLE 8–4
Parameter Estimates in Retrieval of Explicit Text Ideas Versus Elaborative Inferences

	Relation		
Parameter	*Explicit*	*Implicit*	*Control*
Recollection	.39[a]	.20[b]	.05
Familiarity	.16[a]	.02	.06[c]

Source: Adapted from Singer and Remillard (2004, Table 4), *Memory & Cognition*. Copyright 2004, Psychonomic Society. Adapted by permission.

[a]Explicit statistically higher than implicit.

[b]Implicit statistically higher than 0.

[c]Control statistically higher than 0.

of bridging concepts after reading appears to receive no support from perceptual processes (if it did, then *F* would exceed 0). We also cautiously note that the negligible contribution of familiarity to the recognition of implicit probes might deny the automaticity of the encoding of bridging inferences. We pursue this issue in the General Discussion.

Second, several features of the results suggest that the conceptual representation of bridging inferences must, in some respect, be weaker than for explicit ideas: (a) Recollection was lower in the implicit than the explicit condition. (b) There was a significant recollective component in the bridging condition but familiarity was approximately zero. Because familiarity, like recollection, reflects conceptual representations, those representations must have been relatively weak to simultaneously permit *R* to exceed 0 and *F* to approximately equal 0.

Two parametric features of the *control condition* were noteworthy. First, recollection was greater in the bridging than in the control condition, confirming the more robust conceptual representation of the bridging concepts in the former condition. This feature of the results (e.g., Singer & Halldorson, 1996) is critical to discounting the possibility that the mere wording of the stimulus sentences might, by association, promote the recognition of the bridging words. Second, SR proposed that the modest familiarity component ($F \nabla .06$) of the control condition might reflect the convergence upon the target concept of excitation from transiently activated word meanings (Swinney, 1979; Till, Mross, & Kintsch, 1988). This result has been replicated (SR, Experiment 3) but requires more direct scrutiny.

The process dissociation profile differences between the explicit and bridging inferences resembled those detected for elaborative inferences under deep processing, as considered earlier. This might raise questions about the privileged status of bridging inferences. Instead, we interpret this similarity to constitute a dissociation from the patterns generated by timed judgments of text inferences. Like other dissociations in the evaluation of cognitive constructs (e.g., Jacoby, 1983), we propose that this one has the capacity to discriminate among subtly different theoretical analyses.

GENERAL DISCUSSION

The main focus of this research was the evaluation of the quality of the processes of text retrieval. Simultaneously, however, we validated the application of process dissociation and its variants to this domain. Validation was necessary because the process dissociation analysis entails several stringent assumptions (e.g., Buchner et al., 1995; Joordens & Merikle, 1993; Jacoby, 1991), which, if violated, result in the appearance of uninterpretable findings (Jacoby, 1998, addresses the latter issue). The orderly comparisons among experimental conditions provided convincing evidence that process dissociation has the capacity to illuminate text representation and retrieval. For example, both recollection and familiarity approximated zero for low-probability case-filling elements (e.g., *poet* with reference to *The television was broken with the brick*), just as one would expect; and both recollection and familiarity diminished in shallow processing relative to deep processing. These patterns mesh with findings from the few other studies that have used process dissociation to study language processes (Long & Prat, 2002).

Equally importantly, the experiments distinguished among the representation of different categories of text ideas, including explicit statements, elaborative and bridging inferences, and appropriate control statements. The most robust result was that both recollection and familiarity were greater in the explicit condition than they were in the implicit conditions. This outcome is consistent both with the obvious difference that explicit but not implicit ideas find direct expression in a message and with theoretical explorations of encoding differences between explicit ideas and inferences (Schmalhofer et al., 2002). However, some features of the results were surprising or challenging, such as the findings of qualitative similarity between the bridging- and elaborative-inference retrieval profiles and of the failure of familiarity to support the acceptance of implied ideas.

These findings create an agenda for further investigation. The following theoretical issues provide a framework for our ongoing research.

Inference Recollection—Or Misrecollection

Although the recognition of an implied text concept is technically an error, it is well known that experimental subjects recognize (a) several categories of associates of learned items (Underwood, 1965), (b) concepts that capture the semantic convergence among learned items (Deese, 1959; Roediger & McDermott, 1995), and (c) discourse inferences (Johnson, Bransford, & Solomon, 1973). The tendency to recognize related distractors may reflect the representation, during learning, either of a prototype of a learned item or of a cohort of its associates (Underwood, 1965; Clark & Gronlund, 1996). The tendency may also result simply from the detection, during retrieval, of an adequate degree of semantic similarity between a related distractor and previously learned items (Yonelinas, 2002).

People's propensity to recognize implied ideas raises the possibility that a misrecollective process, distinct from recollection and familiarity, contributes to memory retrieval. In this regard, Brainerd et al. (2001) presented evidence that people's recognition within the critical-lure paradigm (Roediger & McDermott, 1995) was fit better by a three-process model than a two-process model. Also consistent with Brainerd et al.'s analysis was the conclusion that phantom recollection (their third process) made stronger contributions to the recognition of related distractors than did recollection. The phantom recollection model maps well onto the retrieval of explicit and implicit text retrieval and merits future scrutiny.

Multiple Processes or Multiple Representations?

An alternative theoretical analysis emphasizes the contribution of multiple representations to the recognition of the test probe rather than that of multiple processes. According to the conjoint recognition hypothesis (Brainerd, Reyna, & Mojardin, 1999; see also Clark & Gronlund, 1996; Mandler, 1980), for example, recognition receives support both from surface (e.g., verbatim details) and gist representations of the antecedent stimuli. Brainerd et al. (1999) proposed that recognition targets constitute superior retrieval cues for surface representations, whereas distractors, whether outright foils or implied or associated concepts, tend to cue gist representations.

Multirepresentation analyses correspond convincingly with the view that discourse comprehension results in surface, textbase, and situational representations. They also generate predictions that have the capacity to clarify the fundamentals of text retrieval. For example, if the implicit test cue *dentist* specifically reminded the subject that the original passage stated *The tooth was pulled painlessly*, then that cue ought to be *rejected* rather than accepted. This outcome, labeled recognition to reject, plays an important role in the evaluation of competing theoretical analyses (Brainerd et al., 1999, 2001). It will also be important to relate surface versus gist analyses with the alternative multirepresentation view that text retrieval invokes episodic versus world knowledge representations (Reder, 1987; Singer, 1991).

Automaticity During Retrieval—Or Encoding?

The main thrust of process dissociation is to distinguish the contributions of controlled and automatic processes to *retrieval*. However, Jacoby's (1991) treatment suggests that there may be a systematic relationship between process dissociation retrieval patterns and the antecedent *encoding* processes. He proposed, for example, that superficial processing during encoding would restrict the subsequent contribution of recollection to recognition decisions (Jacoby, 1991, p. 530). Consistent with this claim, recollection is reduced or even eliminated (Jacoby, Toth, & Yonelinas, 1993) when encoding is performed (a) under divided rather than full attention (Jacoby et al., 1992, 1993), (b) in a superficial rather than semantic manner (Dehn & Engelkamp, 1997; Komatsu et al., 1995; Toth, 1996), (c) by elderly rather than young subjects (Caldwell & Masson, 2001; Jennings & Jacoby, 1993; Titov & Knight, 1997; see also Craik & Byrd, 1981), and (d) by amnesic patients rather than healthy individuals (Verfaellie & Treadwell, 1993). The former member of each of these dichotomies is associated with the reduction or exclusion of controlled *encoding*. The corresponding process dissociation patterns are ones of reduced contributions to *retrieval* of recollection. Thus, the controlled retrieval process of recollection may be diagnostic of controlled encoding.

Such an association between the processing profiles of retrieval and encoding is relevant to the controversial question of the automaticity of inference encoding. It was discussed in the introduction that although text inference processes rely at least in part on automatic resonance processes and are not open to awareness, they apparently fit the controlled-process criteria of being resource-demanding and quite slow. Characterizing the computation of text inferences as a controlled process meshes with the view that automaticity requires invariance between task and performance (Bock, 1982; Logan, 1988). For example, the appearance of a written word permits, by the application of certain perceptual processes, the reliable identification of that word. Even more complex language functions, including parsing and regularization rules (e.g., pluralization, past tense) may exemplify such invariance (Bock, 1982). Perfetti (1989) proposed that the latter processes meet some criteria of automaticity; such as speed and immunity from interference by other ongoing processes. However, according to his analysis, the output of these processes is highly specific to their input stimuli and, as such, is sparse in its inferential content. The automaticity of these processes ensures the availability of cognitive resources for other, strategic components of comprehension. Strategic processing might be needed to encode an unfamiliar word, to decipher an ambiguous syntactic construction, or to draw certain inferences.

Such an analysis accommodates certain features of our results. First, inference processes are controlled (reflected here by the negligible contribution of familiarity, an automatic process; Yonelinas, 2002) because they do not represent an invariance between task and performance. Rather, the highly productive nature of language ensures that most text inferences are novel. This novelty does not stem from the relevance of, for example, mailmen to the letter-delivery context. Rather, it results from the fact that a text that implies the role of a mailman implies numerous competing ideas (depending on contextual subtleties; Kintsch, 1988) and, conversely, that many subtly different texts imply the role of a mailman. Second, as discussed earlier, the automatic influence detected in the explicit conditions largely reflects the operation of processes such as word identification.

These proposals are speculative, and there are some caveats to consider. First, in one instance, Singer and Remillard (2004, Experiment 3) measured a small but statistically significant contribution of familiarity to the recognition of bridging concepts. Like for the control condition of our bridging-inference experiment, this may result from the passive convergence upon the target concept of activation from the words in the stimulus sentence. Second, test items comprising phrases (e.g., *howled with amusement at the joke*) rather than single words (*joke*) might more effectively reinstate the perceptual operations of encoding than single word targets, thereby permitting the appearance of familiarity support for recognition.

CONCLUSION

This research offers convincing evidence that the process dissociation framework can be fruitfully applied to problems of language processing. The experiments indicate that there are measurable differences between people's representation of explicit and implicit text ideas. They also map out a considerable agenda of future research. It will be necessary to clarify the distinction between the recollection and misrecollection of text inferences, compare the efficacy of multiprocess versus multirepresentation theories, and clarify the relation between the automaticity of retrieval as opposed to the antecedent encoding processes.

REFERENCES

Albrecht, J. E., & Myers, J. L. (1995). The role of context in accessing distant information during reading. *Journal of Experimental Psychology: Learning, Memory, and Cognition, 21*, 1459–1468.

Bock, J. K. (1982). Toward a cognitive psychology of syntax: Information processing contributions to sentence formation. *Psychological Review, 89*, 1–47.

Brainerd, C. J., Reyna, V. F., & Mojardin, A. H. (1999). Conjoint recognition. *Psychological Review, 106*, 160–179.

Brainerd, C. J., Wright, R., Reyna, V. F., & Mojardin, A. H. (2001). Conjoint recognition and phantom recollection. *Journal of Experimental Psychology: Learning, Memory, and Cognition, 27*(2), 307–327.

Buchner, A., Erdfelder, E., & Vaterrodt-Plunnecke, B. (1995). Toward unbiased measurement of conscious and unconscious memory processes within the process dissociation framework. *Journal of Experimental Psychology: General, 124*, 137–160.

Caldwell, J. L., & Masson, M. E. J. (2001). Conscious and unconscious influences of memory for object location. *Memory & Cognition, 29*, 254–266.

Clark, S. E., & Gronlund, S. D. (1996). Global matching models of recognition memory: How the models match the data. *Psychonomic Bulletin & Review, 3*, 37–60.

Corbett, A. (1984). Prenominal adjectives and the disambiguation of anaphoric nouns. *Journal of Verbal Learning and Verbal Behavior, 23*, 683–695.

Craik, F. I. M., & Byrd, M. (1981). Aging and cognitive deficits: The role of attentional processes. In F. Craik & S. Trehub (Eds.), *Aging and cognitive processes*. New York: Plenum.

Daneman, M., & Carpenter, P. A. (1980). Individual differences in working memory and reading. *Journal of Verbal Learning and Verbal Behavior, 19*, 450–466.

Deese, J. (1959). On the prediction of occurrence of particular verbal intrusions in immediate recall. *Journal of Experimental Psychology, 58*, 17–22.

Dehn, D. M., & Engelkamp, J. (1997). Process dissociation procedure: Double dissociations following divided attention and speeded responding. *Quarterly Journal of Experimental Psychology, 50A*, 318–336.

Dell, G. S., McKoon, G., & Ratcliff, R. (1983). The activation of antecedent information during the processing of anaphoric reference in reading. *Journal of Verbal Learning and Verbal Behavior, 22*, 121–132.

Gardiner, J. M., Gawlick, B., & Richardson-Klavehn, A. (1994). Maintenance rehearsal affects knowing, not remembering; elaborative rehearsal affects remembering, not knowing. *Psychonomic Bulletin & Review, 1*, 107–110.

Gillund, G., & Shiffrin, R. M. (1984). A retrieval model for both recognition and recall. *Psychological Review, 91*, 1–67.

Graesser, A. C., Singer, M., & Trabasso, T. (1994). Constructing inferences during narrative text comprehension. *Psychological Review, 101*, 371–395.

Graf, P., & Komatsu, S. (1994). Process dissociation procedure: Handle with caution! *European Journal of Cognitive Psychology, 6*, 113–129.

Hasher, L., & Griffin, M. (1978). Reconstructive and reproductive processes in memory. *Journal of Experimental Psychology: Human Learning and Memory, 4*, 318–330.

Haviland, S. E., & Clark, H. H. (1974). What's new? Acquiring new information as a process in comprehension. *Journal of Verbal Learning and Verbal Behavior, 13*, 512–521.

Hintzman, D. L. (1988). Judgments of frequency and recognition memory in a multiple-trace memory model. *Psychological Review, 95*, 528–551.

Hintzman, D. L., & Curran, T. (1994). Retrieval dynamics of recognition and frequency judgments: Evidence for separate processes of familiarity and recall. *Journal of Memory and Language, 33*, 1–18.

Jacoby, L. L. (1983). Perceptual enhancement. Persistent effects of an experience. *Journal of Experimental Psychology: Learning, Memory, and Cognition, 9*, 21–38.

Jacoby, L. L. (1991). A process dissociation framework: Separating automatic from intentional uses of memory. *Journal of Memory and Language, 30*, 513–541.

Jacoby. L. L. (1998). Invariance in automatic influences of memory: Toward a user's guide for the process dissociation procedure. *Journal of Experimental Psychology: Learning, Memory, and Cognition, 24*, 3–26.

Jacoby, L. L., Lindsay, D. S., & Toth, J. P. (1992). Unconscious influences revealed. *American Psychologist, 47*, 802–809.

Jacoby, L. L., Toth, J. P., & Yonelinas, A. P. (1993). Separating conscious and unconscious influences of memory: Measuring recollection. *Journal of Experimental Psychology: General, 122*, 139–154.

Jennings, J. M., & Jacoby, L. L. (1993). Automatic versus intentional uses of memory: Aging, attention, and control. *Psychology and Aging, 8*, 283–293.

Johnson, M. K., Bransford, J. D., & Solomon, S. K. (1973). Memory for tacit implications of sentences. *Journal of Experimental Psychology, 98*, 203–205.

Joordens, S., & Merikle, P. M. (1993). Independence or redundancy. Two models of conscious and unconscious influences. *Journal of Experimental Psychology: General, 122*, 462–467.

Keefe, D. E., & McDaniel, M. A. (1993). The time course and durability of predictive inferences. *Journal of Memory and Language, 32*, 446–463.

Keenan, J. M., Baillet, S. D., & Brown, P. (1984). The effects of causal cohesion on comprehension and memory. *Journal of Verbal Learning and Verbal Behavior, 23*, 115–126.

Kintsch, W. (1988). The role of knowledge in discourse comprehension: A construction-integration model. *Psychological Review, 95*, 163–182.

Kintsch, W. (1992). How readers construct situation models for stories: The role of syntactic cues and causal inferences. In A. Healy, S. Kosslyn, & R. Shiffrin (Eds.), *From learning processes to cognitive processes: Essays in honor of William K. Estes* (Vol. 2, pp. 261–278). Hillsdale, NJ: Lawrence Erlbaum Associates.

Kintsch, W. (1998). *Comprehension*. New York: Cambridge University Press.

Kintsch, W., & van Dijk, T. A. (1978). Toward a model of text comprehension and production. *Psychological Review, 85*, 363–394.

Komatsu, S., Graf, P., & Uttl, B. (1995). Process dissociation procedure: Core assumptions fail, sometimes. *European Journal of Cognitive Psychology, 7*, 19–40.

Lea, R. B., O'Brien, D. P., Fisch, M., Noveck, I. A., & Braine, M. D. S. (1990). Predicting propositional logic inferences in text comprehension. *Journal of Memory and Language, 29*, 361–387.

Lesgold, A. M., Roth, S. F., & Curtis, M. E. (1979). Foregrounding effects in discourse comprehension. *Journal of Verbal Learning and Verbal Behavior, 18*, 291–308.

Levy, B. H., Campsall, J., Browne, J., Cooper, D., Waterhouse, C., & Wilson, C. (1995). Reading fluency: Episodic integration across tests. *Journal of Experimental Psychology: Learning, Memory, and Cognition, 21*, 1169–1185.

Logan, G. (1988). Toward an instance theory of automatization. *Psychological Review, 95*, 492–527.

Long, D. L., & Prat, C. S. (2002). Memory for *Star Trek*: The role of prior knowledge in recognition revisited. *Journal of Experimental Psychology: Learning, Memory and Cognition, 28*, 1073–1082.

Mandler, G. (1980). Recognizing: The judgment of previous occurrence. *Psychological Review, 87*, 252–271.

Masson, M. E. (1993). Episodically enhanced comprehension fluency. *Canadian Journal of Experimental Psychology, 47*, 428–465.

McKoon, G., & Ratcliff, R. (1986). Inferences about predictable events. *Journal of Experimental Psychology: Learning, Memory, and Cognition, 12*, 82–91.

McKoon, G., & Ratcliff, R. (1992). Inference during reading. *Psychological Review, 99*, 440–466.

Moray, N. (1959). Attention in dichotic listening: Affective cues and the influence of instructions. *Quarterly Journal of Experimental Psychology, 9*, 56–90.

Morrow, D. G., Greenspan, S. L., & Bower, G. H. (1987). Accessibility and situation models in narrative comprehension. *Journal of Memory and Language, 2*, 165–187.

Myers, J. L., Shinjo, M., & Duffy, S. A. (1987). Degree of causal relatedness and memory. *Journal of Memory and Language, 26*, 453–465.

O'Brien, E. J., & Albrecht, J. E. (1991). The role of context in accessing antecedents in text. *Journal of Experimental Psychology: Learning, Memory, and Cognition, 17*, 94–102.

O'Brien, E. J., Albrecht, J. E., Hakala, C. M., & Rizzella, M. L. (1995). Activation and suppression of antecedents during reinstatement. *Journal of Experimental Psychology: Learning, Memory, and Cognition, 21*, 626–634.

O'Brien, E. J., Plewes, P. S., & Albrecht, J. E. (1990). Antecedent retrieval processes. *Journal of Experimental Psychology: Learning, Memory, and Cognition, 16*, 241–249.

Perfetti, C. A. (1989). There are generalized abilities and one of them is reading. In L. Resnick (Ed.), *Knowing and learning: Issues for a cognitive science of instruction* (pp. 307–335). Hillsdale, NJ: Lawrence Erlbaum Associates.

Posner, M. I., & Snyder, C. R. R. (1975). Attention and cognitive control. In R. Solso (Ed.), *Information processing and cognition: The Loyola symposium* (pp. 55–85). Hillsdale, NJ: Lawrence Erlbaum Associates.

Potts, G. R., Keenan, J. M., & Golding, J. M. (1988). Assessing the occurrence of elaborative inferences: Lexical decision versus naming. *Journal of Memory and Language, 27*, 399–415.

Raney, G. E. (2003). A context-dependent representation model for explaining text repetition effects. *Psychonomic Bulletin & Review, 10*, 15–28.

Ratcliff, R., van Zandt, T., & McKoon, G. (1995). Process dissociation, single process theories, and recognition memory. *Journal of Experimental Psychology: General, 124*, 352–374.

Reder, L. M. (1982). Plausibility judgements versus fact retrieval: Alternative strategies for sentence verification. *Psychological Review, 89*, 250–280.

Reder, L. M. (1987). Strategy-selection in question answering. *Cognitive Psychology, 19*, 90–134.

Roediger, H. L., III, & McDermott, K. B. (1995). Creating false memories: Remembering words not presented in lists. *Journal of Experimental Psychology: Learning, Memory, and Cognition, 21*, 803–814.

Schank, R. C. (1976). The role of memory in language processing. In C. Cofer (Ed.), *The nature of human memory*. San Francisco: W. H. Freeman Press.

Schmalhofer, F., & Glavanov, D. (1986). Three components of understanding a programmer's manual: Verbatim, propositional, and situation representations. *Journal of Memory and Language, 25*, 279–294.

Schmalhofer, F., McDaniel, M. A., & Keefe, D. E. (2002). A unified model for predictive and bridging inferences. *Discourse Processes, 33*, 105–132.

Schneider, W., & Shiffrin, R. M. (1977). Controlled and automatic human information processing: I. Detection, search, and attention. *Psychological Review, 84*, 1–66.

Singer, M. (1980). The role of case-filling inferences in the coherence of brief passages. *Discourse Processes, 3*, 185–201.

Singer, M. (1991). Independence of question answering strategy and searched representation. *Memory & Cognition, 19*, 189–196.

Singer, M. (1994). Discourse inference processes. In M. Gernsbacher (Ed.), *Handbook of psycholinguistics*. San Diego: Academic Press.

Singer, M., Andrusiak, P., Reisdorf, P., & Black, N. (1992). Individual differences in bridging inference processes. *Memory & Cognition, 20*, 538–548.

Singer, M., & Ferreira, F. (1983). Inferring consequences in story comprehension. *Journal of Verbal Learning and Verbal Behavior, 22*, 437–448.

Singer, M., Graesser, A. C., & Trabasso, T. (1994). Minimal or global inference during reading. *Journal of Memory and Language, 33,* 421–441.

Singer, M., & Halldorson, M. (1996). Constructing and validating motive bridging inferences. *Cognitive Psychology, 30,* 1–38.

Singer, M., & Kintsch, W. (2001). Text retrieval: A theoretical exploration. *Discourse Processes, 31,* 27–59.

Singer, M. & Remillard, G. (2004). Controlled and automatic influences in text retrieval. *Memory & Cognition,* 32, 1223–1237.

Swinney, D. A. (1979). Lexical access during sentence comprehension: (Re)consideration of context effects. *Journal of Verbal Learning and Verbal Behavior, 18,* 545–569.

Till, R. E., Mross, E. F., & Kintsch, W. (1988). Time course of priming for associate and inference words in a discourse context. *Memory & Cognition, 16,* 283–298.

Titov, N., & Knight, R. G. (1997). Adult age differences in controlled and automatic memory processing. *Psychology and Aging, 12,* 565–573.

Toth, J. P. (1996). Conceptual automaticity in recognition memory: Levels-of-processing effects on familiarity. *Canadian Journal of Experimental Psychology, 50,* 123–138.

Underwood, B. J. (1965). False recognition produced by implicit verbal responses. *Journal of Experimental Psychology, 70,* 122–129.

van Dijk, T. A., & Kintsch, W. (1983). *Strategies of discourse comprehension.* New York: Academic Press.

Verfaellie, M., & Treadwell, J. R. (1993). Status of recognition memory in amnesia. *Neuropsychology, 7,* 5–13.

Yekovich, F. R., Walker, C. H., & Blackman, H. S. (1979). The role of presupposed and focal information in integrating sentences. *Journal of Verbal Learning and Verbal Behavior, 18,* 535–548.

Yonelinas, A. P. (2002). The nature of recollection and familiarity: A review of 30 years of research. *Journal of Memory and Language, 46,* 441–517.

9

The Neural Signatures of Causal Inferences: A Preliminary Computational Account of Brain-Imaging and Behavioral Data

Erik D. Reichle
University of Pittsburgh

Robert A. Mason
Carnegie Mellon University

What does it mean to make an inference during reading? Consider the following pair of sentences:

> *Ann was falling behind in her schoolwork.*
> *She decided to study harder.*

To really understand the full meaning of these two sentences, one has to first infer that Ann decided to study harder because she had fallen behind in her schoolwork. To make such a *causal inference,* one must first do whatever language processing is necessary to understand the actions that are described in each of the sentences, and then use knowledge that is already stored in long-term memory to "connect" the sentences, so that the action that is described in the second sentence can be interpreted as being a consequence of the first (Grasser, Singer, & Trabasso, 1994; McKoon & Ratcliff, 1982).[1] The fact that readers can usually make such causal inferences so rapidly and effortlessly belies the fact that the cognitive processes that allow readers to make inferences are actually quite complex and—for the most part—remain poorly understood. Because of this, many of the most basic questions about how readers make causal inferences remain largely unanswered. For example, how are readers able to so rapidly and accurately re-

[1]Of course, to understand the sentences in this example, it is also first necessary to make a *referential inference* to connect the pronoun "*she*" at the beginning of the second sentence to its antecedent "*Ann*" in the first.

trieve only the contextually relevant information that allows correct inferences to be made? And how do readers even know that the information contained in a pair of sentences is insufficient to support the full (intended) meaning of the sentences, and that a causal inference is therefore warranted? Finally, is the information that is generated by making a causal inference the same as the information that is explicitly contained in the text, or is it somehow different?

In this chapter, we address each of these questions in an attempt to offer some preliminary—and admittedly very tentative—answers. To do this, we first describe a recent brain-imaging experiment (Mason & Just, 2004) that used *functional magnetic resonance imaging* (fMRI) to examine the cortical areas that are active when readers make causal inferences. We believe that the results of this experiment (and the other brain-imaging studies that are reviewed in this chapter) are invaluable because they provide an additional set of constraints to evaluate theories of how readers make inferences and—more generally—theories of how readers understand text. To show why we believe that brain-imaging experiments are useful in this capacity, we describe four simple computational principles that are sufficient to explain the patterns of cortical activation that were observed in the Mason and Just experiment. Although these principles are at best both incomplete and a gross oversimplification of the cognitive and neural processes that allow readers to make causal inferences, we believe the exercise of developing these principles is a useful one because they provide a conceptual framework for thinking about the relationship between cognitive processing and its behavioral consequences, on one hand, and the location and activity of those cortical systems that mediate cognition and behavior, on the other. As such, the principles that we describe are very general (e.g., working memory has a limited capacity), have been widely used in existing theories of text processing (Frank, Koppen, Noordman, & Vonk, 2003; Golden & Rumelhart, 1993; Goldman & Varma, 1995; Kintsch, 1988; Kintsch & van Dijk, 1978; Langston & Trabasso, 1999; Myers & O'Brien, 1998; Schmalhofer, McDaniel, & Keefe, 2002; Van den Broek, Risden, Fletcher, & Thurlow, 1996; Van den Broek, Young, Tzeng, & Linderholm, 1999), and are also sufficient to explain certain key behavioral results (e.g., sentence reading times) that have been observed in experiments in which readers make causal inferences (Keenan et al., 1984; Myers, Shinjo, & Duffy, 1987). The principles are thus meant to provide an example of how one might go about integrating the results of brain-imaging experiments with the results of traditional behavioral experiments so as to gain additional insight into both the functional roles that are played by different cortical areas and the way in which inherent properties of these cortical areas provide constraints on cognition and behavior (for a recent example of this type of more integrative modeling approach, see Anderson, Qin, Sohn, Stenger, & Carter, 2003).

BEHAVIORAL AND BRAIN-IMAGING STUDIES OF CAUSAL INFERENCES

Mason and Just (2004) recently reported an fMRI experiment that was designed to examine the cortical areas that are involved in making inferences during reading. This experiment was similar to two earlier experiments by Keenan et al. (1984) and Myers et al. (1987) in which participants read pairs of sentences that varied in terms of their degree of causal relatedness (see also Kim, Morales, & Reichle, 2004; and Myers & Duffy, 1990). For example, an "outcome" sentence (e.g., *The next day his body was covered with bruises.*) was preceded by one of four sentences (equated for overall length and number of propositions) that described an antecedent situation that varied with respect to how well it could be interpreted as causing the consequence described in the outcome sentence. Examples of the antecedent sentences (with Level 1 being the most highly related to the outcome and Level 4 for being the least related to the outcome) include the following:

Level 1: *Joey's big brother punched him again and again.*
Level 2: *Racing down the hill, Joey fell off his bike.*
Level 3: *Joey's crazy mother became furiously angry with him.*
Level 4: *Joey went to a neighbor's house to play.*

In the experiments, participants were instructed to read the sentences at their own pace and to judge the degree of semantic relatedness between the sentences (using a 7-point Likert scale, with 7 indicating that the sentences were highly related) or to recall either the first or second sentence (using cued recall, with either the first sentence being used as a cue to recall the second, or vice versa). The underlying logic of the experiments was to examine the effect of causal relatedness on the propensity to generate and remember causal inferences, under the assumption that participants would be more likely to generate inferences (which would slow down sentence reading time and perhaps improve memory for the sentences) with sentence pairs that were less related (Level 4) than they would be with pairs that were more related (Level 1).

As expected, the Keenan et al. (1984) and Myers et al. (1987) experiments demonstrated three important facts about the role of relatedness in making causal inferences. The first was simply a validation that participants who were asked to rate the degree of causal relatedness between the various antecedent-outcome sentence pairs provided reliably different ratings to describe the differing degree of causal relatedness among the sentence pairs (the mean ratings for Levels 1–4 were 6.25, 5.00, 3.34, and 2.05, respectively). The second finding was that the self-paced reading times on the outcome sentences increased as the degree of causal relatedness between the antecedent and outcome sentences decreased; that is, the participants' reading times on the second sentence increased from the Level 1 (highly related) to the Level 4 (unrelated) sentence pairs. This result was interpreted as evidence that participants were more likely to read more slowly so as to make more causal inferences when the sentence pairs were less related. Finally, participants' memory for the two-sentence passages followed an inverted-U-shaped function, with sentences in the Level 2 condition being remembered better than those in either the Level 1 or Level 3 conditions, and sentences in the Level 4 condition being the least well remembered. This third result is somewhat paradoxical because it indicates that the participants' memory for the sentences was not a simple monotonic function of either the time that was needed to read the sentences or the degree of causal relatedness between the two sentences. This result was instead taken as evidence that, with moderately related (Level 2) sentence pairs, participants were most likely to both generate inferences and successfully integrate those inferences into long-term memory; in contrast, with the highly related (Level 1) sentence pairs, participants were less likely to generate inferences by virtue of the fact that the sentences could easily be understood with such inferences, while the most distantly related sentence pairs may have been so unrelated as to make it difficult for participants to generate meaningful inferences that could then be integrated into memory and subsequently remembered. By this account, only the moderately related sentence pairs were unrelated enough that participants would need to generate inferences, but related enough that the participants would be likely to both successfully generate and then remember those inferences.

In an fMRI variant of the Keenan et al. (1984) and Myers et al. (1987) experiments, Mason and Just (2004) instructed their participants to read and answer comprehension questions about sentence pairs that were similar to those that were described above, but which varied in only three degrees of causal relatedness (i.e., distantly related vs. moderately related vs. highly related). The results of this experiment revealed three main foci of fMRI measured cortical activation (see Fig. 9–1). Although there was a considerable amount of activation (as measured by the number of activated *voxels*, i.e., volumetric units of cortical tissue) in the left-hemisphere language areas, the volume of activation in these areas did not vary across the three relatedness conditions. Our discussion therefore focuses on the other two sets of areas (see Fig. 9–2).

The amount of activation that was observed in the bilateral dorsolateral prefrontal cortices (DLPFC) did not differ reliably across the three relatedness conditions; however, there was a trend such that the DLFPC activation volume exhibited a tendency to increase going from the highly to moderately to distantly related conditions. In the right-hemisphere homologues of the left-hemisphere language areas, the activation volume was actually more pronounced in the moderately related condition than in the other two condi-

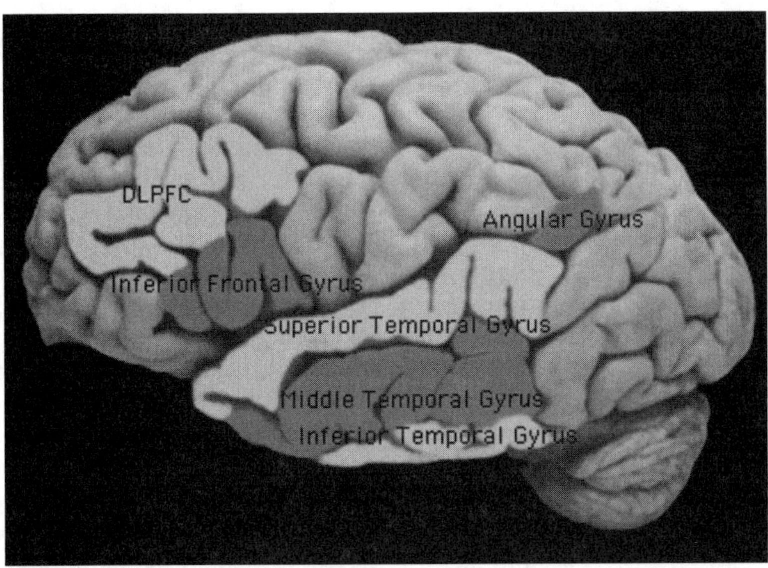

FIGURE 9–1. Active cortical areas of readers making causal inferences (Mason & Just, 2004). The figure shows only the left hemisphere; the DLPFC region consists of the left and right DLPFC; the right-hemisphere language areas consist of the homologues of the left-hemisphere language areas.

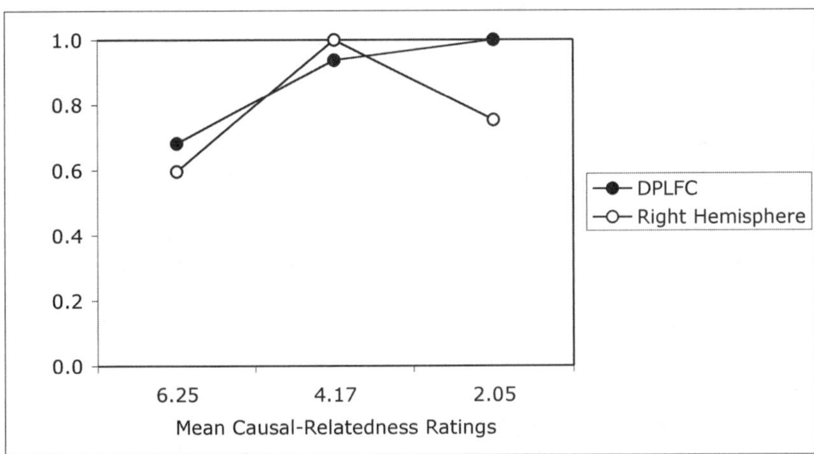

FIGURE 9–2. Volume of fMRI-measured cortical activation (mean number of above-threshold voxels) as a function of degree of causal relatedness (distantly vs. moderately vs. highly related) in the right-hemisphere areas (inferior frontal gyrus; superior, middle, and inferior frontal gyri; and angular gyrus) and bilateral DLPFC (Mason & Just, 2004).

tions. The pattern of fMRI results can thus be summarized as follows: Whereas the left-hemisphere language areas were equally active in all three of the relatedness conditions, the DLPFC tended to become more active as the sentence pairs became less causally related, and the right-hemisphere homologues of the language areas were most active when the sentence pairs were only moderately related.

Mason and Just (2004) maintained that their fMRI results were compatible with the earlier behavioral results that were reported by both Keenan et al. (1984) and Myers et al. (1987). In fact, Mason and Just explained their fMRI findings by building upon the earlier accounts that were offered by Myers et al. (1987) to explain their behavioral results, predicating their account on a theoretical distinction between the process of generating inferences, on one hand, and a subsequent process of integrating those inferences into long-term memory, on the other. Mason and Just extended this distinction and posited that different cortical areas mediate these two processes: Whereas the DLPFC is responsible for generating inferences during reading, the right-hemisphere "language" areas are responsible for integrating those inferences into memory.

According to this account, in all three of the relatedness conditions, participants are required to do the same amount of basic linguistic processing (e.g., lexical access, syntactic parsing, etc.) to interpret the meanings of each sentence, resulting in equivalent amounts of cortical activation across the three relatedness conditions in the left-hemisphere language areas. However, as the sentences become more distantly related, participants are more likely to generate causal inferences so that the second sentence can be understood in the context of the first. If the DLPFC plays a role in monitoring comprehension and/or generating the causal inferences, it then follows that the DLPFC activity should increase as the sentences become more distantly related, thereby causing an increase in the DLFPC activation volume going from the highly related to distantly related conditions (see Fig. 9–2). Finally, those inferences that actually allow the reader to "connect" and make sense of the antecedent and outcome sentences are integrated into memory; this is done in the right hemisphere, and the fact that more inferences are successfully integrated in the moderately related condition than the other two conditions causes the right-hemisphere areas to be most active in the moderately related condition, resulting in the inverted U-shaped pattern of activation that was observed in this region (see Fig. 9–2).

Although Mason and Just's (2004) account is congruent with both the behavioral and brain-imaging data already discussed, it is only a verbal description of the cognitive and neural processes that are thought to mediate causal inferences. Their account thus lacks the precision that would be necessary to make quantitative predictions about the outcomes of future experiments. It also fails to address many basic questions, such as whether or not their explanation is consistent with principles that are instantiated by existing computational models of inference making (Langston & Trabasso, 1999;

Schmalhofer et al., 2002) and text processing (Frank et al., 2003; Golden & Rumelhart, 1993; Goldman & Varma, 1995; Kintsch, 1988; Kintsch & van Dijk, 1978; Langston & Trabasso, 1999; Myers & O'Brien, 1998; Van den Broek et al., 1996, 1999). In the next section of this chapter, we attempt to deal with some of these limitations by describing four computational principles that are congruent with prior theories of text processing and that we believe provide a more accurate and precise description of the processes involved in making causal inferences. These principles provide a framework for describing the behavioral and brain-imaging data that were discussed in this section, and thereby show how one might go about developing a single, integrated account of the cognitive and neural processes that allow readers to make causal inferences.

A PRELIMINARY ACCOUNT OF SOME BRAIN-IMAGING AND BEHAVIORAL DATA

It is clear that many simple inferences (e.g., referential inferences that connect pronouns to their antecedents; see Footnote 1) are necessary to understanding what is being read and are probably generated automatically, with little or no cognitive effort (McKoon & Ratcliff, 1992). Although the extent to which readers automatically make more elaborative inferences (such as causal inferences) is more equivocal (see Graesser, Singer, & Trabasso, 1994), we sidestep this issue and simply assume that, in the context of the sentences used by Mason and Just (2004), the probability with which a reader will make an inference is directly proportional to how necessary such inferences are to understanding the overall meaning of the two sentences—that is, how necessary such inferences are to interpreting the content of the second, outcome sentence as being a consequence of the first, antecedent sentence. Although this assumption may sound circular, "how necessary" can be operationally defined by asking participants to judge how related the two sentences are. Indeed, as has already been discussed, Myers et al. (1987) did this by instructing their participants to rate the degree of causal relatedness of their sentence pairs and found that the perceived relatedness between the antecedent and outcome sentences did vary in a reliable and systematic fashion across the four levels of relatedness. Although Myers et al. did not speculate about what cognitive processes were used to make their relatedness judgments, it is clear that such decisions were not based on overall sentence length or the number of propositions per sentence, because these variables were controlled.[2]

[2]The mean numbers of syllables in the first (antecedent) sentences were 11.68, 11.50, 11.43, and 11.49 for the highly related (Level 1) to distantly related (Level 4) conditions, respectively. The mean numbers of syllables in the second (outcome) sentences was 11.68. The mean numbers of propositions in the first sentences were 2.47, 2.39, 2.38, and 2.45 for Levels 1–4, respectively. The mean number of propositions in the outcome sentences was 2.42.

It is important that we are explicit about the fact that we are not claiming to know how readers go about assessing the degree to which two sentences are meaningfully related. Our starting point will instead be what Myers et al. demonstrated—that the perceived degree of causal relatedness between the antecedent and outcome sentences decreases continuously from the highly related (Level 1) to the distantly related (Level 4) conditions, and that the likelihood that participants will make causal inferences seems to vary in a monotonic fashion with this perceived relatedness. In the remainder of this chapter, we refer to the variable that underlies the perceived degree of causal relatedness as *relatedness*. In the framework presented in this chapter, we simply assume that the probability of generating a causal inference is linearly related to the perceived relatedness of two sentences, as measured by the relatedness norms that were collected by Myers et al. (1987). To convert these relatedness ratings from the 7-point Likert scale to probabilities of making causal inferences, we use the following linear transformation:

$$p(\text{generating inference}) \nabla 1.167 \quad (.167 * \text{relatedness}) \tag{1}$$

Although the relationship between the perceived degree of causal relatedness (or more specifically, the participants' ratings of perceived causal relatedness) and the probability of generating an inference is undoubtedly much more complicated than our simple function suggests (e.g., the rating scale is probably not linearly related to the probability of generating an inference across the full range of values), the transform nevertheless ensures that the relatedness-judgment ratings have the potential to be converted into probabilities that span the entire range of values (i.e., relatedness ratings of 7 and 1 correspond to probabilities of 0 to 1, respectively). Moreover, the assumption that readers will be increasingly likely to generate causal inferences as two sentences become more distantly related is broadly consistent with Kintsch and van Dijk's (1978, p. 367) proposal that, if the reader notices gaps in text coherence, then "inference processes are initiated to close them; specifically, one or more propositions will be added to the text base that make it coherent." In the case of the causal inference experiments, these "gaps in text coherence" are simply those occasions in which the participant fails to "connect" the two sentences, so that the outcome sentence can be interpreted as being a consequence of the antecedent sentence; to the degree that this happens, participants are more likely to (on average) generate a causal inference to connect the two sentences.

Our second assumption is that text processing requires working memory (Frank et al., 2003; Golden & Rumelhart, 1993; Goldman & Varma, 1995; Kintsch, 1988; Kintsch & van Dijk, 1978; Langston & Trabasso, 1999; Myers & O'Brien, 1998; Schmalhofer et al., 2002; Van den Broek et al., 1996, 1999), which has a limited capacity, *S*. Again, following precedent (e.g., Kintsch, 1988), we will assume that during text processing working memory can at any given time hold five propositions, and that the amount of information carried over from one time step to the next decreases by some fixed proportion ($\alpha \nabla .5$). At any given time t, the amount of information (i.e., the mean number of propositions derived from the text-base and maintained in working memory, N_p) is given by the following equation, in which N_t is the mean number of propositions that are derived from the text-base at time t, and m is an index of the number of consecutive time steps that a particular proposition has been held in working memory:

$$N_p = \begin{cases} N_t & \text{if } t = 1 \\ N_t + \sum_{m=1}^{t-1} N_{t-m}\alpha^m & \text{if } t > 1 \text{ and } \sum_{m=1}^{t-1} N_{t-m}\alpha^m \leq S - N_t \\ S & \text{if } t > 1 \text{ and } \sum_{m=1}^{t-1} N_{t-m}\alpha^m > S - N_t \end{cases} \tag{2}$$

Because the paradigms discussed in this chapter only required participants to read two sentences, the paradigm can be conceptualized as comprising exactly two time steps: reading the first sentence and reading the second. The mean number of propositions that are held in working memory during the second time step is therefore equal to the number of propositions contained in the second sentence plus exactly half of the propositions carried over from the previous time step. Also note that working memory capacity is enforced (in the bottom two branches of Eq. 2) by scaling back the information from previous time steps; for example, if two sentences each contain four propositions, then at time step $t \nabla 2$, $N_p \nabla 5$ (i.e., the four propositions from the second sentence plus one proposition from the first sentence).[3]

Two other points about Eq. 2 should be explicitly mentioned. The first is that the equation describes what happens *on average* across both participants and trials. A more precise formulation of the relationship between working memory capacity and the amount of information that is maintained therein would need to specify how *units* of information (i.e., whole propositions) are maintained or forgotten across time. The second point that needs to be mentioned is that Eq. 2 is agnostic regarding the question of whether information

[3]In this chapter, we ignore what happens with sentences containing more than five propositions (i.e., $N_t \geqslant 5$) because such materials were not used in the experiments that are being considered (i.e., Mason & Just, 2004; Myers et al., 1987). However, if these materials had included sentences containing more than five propositions, then the amount of information held in working memory at any given time would still be limited by working memory capacity (i.e., S). For example, with an antecedent sentence containing more than five propositions, $N_p \nabla 5$ (because $S \nabla 5$).

in working memory is forgotten because of interference or decay. The assumptions that (a) current information is maintained at the expense of older information and (b) older information is on average lost at a rate that is proportional to how long it has already been maintained in working memory are both roughly consistent with how other researchers have modeled how information is lost from working memory (e.g., Gillund & Shiffrin, 1984; Raaijmakers & Shiffrin, 1981).

Our third assumption is that the mean number of inferences, N_i, that are actually generated by a group of participants in a given condition is directly proportional to the mean probability of generating an inference (as given by Eq. 1) as scaled by a free parameter (β ∇ 1.7). This parameter reflects both how motivated the reader is to make inferences (which undoubtedly also reflects the goals in reading; van den Broek, Lorch, Linderholm, & Gustafson, 2001) and the reader's ability to make inferences (e.g., as limited by the reader's background knowledge about a particular topic). This relationship between the mean number of generated inferences and the mean probability of generating an inference is given by

$$N_i = \begin{cases} \beta * p(\text{generating inference}) & \text{if } N_i + N_p \leq S \\ S - N_p & \text{if } N_i + N_p > S \end{cases} \tag{3}$$

Again, because Eq. 3 describes the number of inferences that are expected to be generated *on average* across both participants and trials, the quantity that is given by the equation may not be an integer. A more precise formulation would therefore need to specify how *units* of information (i.e., whole propositions) are generated for individual subjects and trials so that this information can be used in an attempt to "connect" the antecedent and outcome sentences. Whether or not the information allows for a successful inference would then be dependent upon how well the propositions that were retrieved from long-term memory allow the reader to interpret the actions that are described by the propositions of the second sentence as being a consequence of the actions described by the propositions of the first sentence *and* the propositions that were generated by the inference. Finally, the total number of propositions that can be generated via inference making is limited by the capacity of working memory; inferred propositions can be generated only if there is a sufficient amount of working memory resources available to do so. In other words, the total number of propositions that are being held in working memory from either text or via making inferences cannot exceed working memory capacity (i.e., $N_p \lesssim N_i \nless S$).

These three assumptions (Eqs. 1–3) provide one basis for explaining the patterns of reading time data that have been reported in experiments where participants make causal inferences (Keenan et al., 1984; Kim et al., 2004;

Myers & Duffy, 1990; Myers et al., 1987). To account for these data, one only has to assume that reading times on the outcome sentences reflect the relative difficulty (i.e., the computational demands placed on working memory) in each of the respective conditions. Reading difficulty can thus be approximated by simply assuming that it is directly proportional to the mean number of propositions that are being maintained in working memory in each condition (i.e., $N_p \lesseqgtr N_i$) and then normalizing these values by dividing each one by the maximum value. (When the values are normalized in this way, the reading times are converted into an arbitrary scale that extends from 0 to 1, with 1 representing the maximum time that is needed to read one of the sentences and lesser values indicating the proportion of this time that was needed to read the sentences in each of the other conditions.) The predicted reading times for each of the four conditions used by Myers et al. are shown in Fig. 9–3. Notice that, as Myers et al. observed, the reading times increase as the degree of causal relatedness between the antecedent and outcome sentences decreases.

The inverted-U-shaped recall curves that have been reported (Keenan et al., 1984; Myers et al., 1987) emerged from two assumptions. The first is that how well the sentences are remembered is directly proportional to how well they and/or the inferences that may be generated to "connect" them are integrated with each other and with information that is already in long-term memory. The second is that how well the sentences and inferences are integrated depends upon the amount of working memory resources that are available and can be allocated to encoding. The first of these assumptions is based on the fact that items (e.g., the propositions that represent the meaning

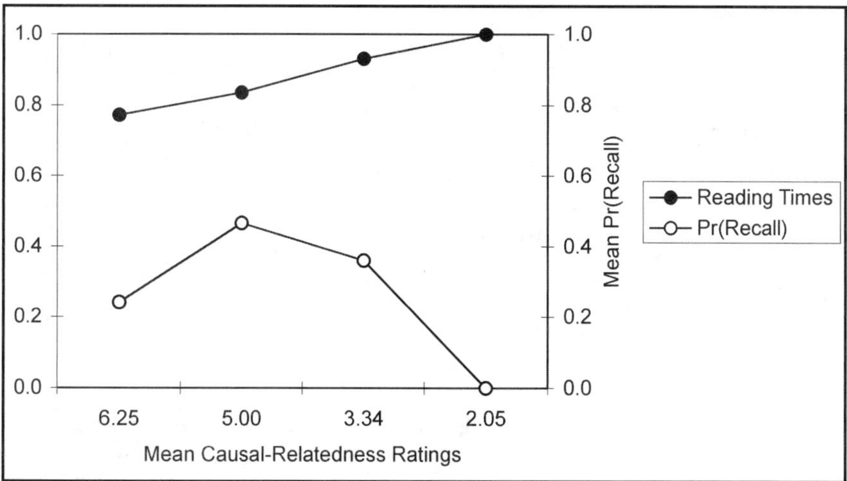

FIGURE 9–3. Simulated (normalized) reading times and probabilities of recalling the second sentence as a function of degree of causal relatedness.

of the sentences and any inferences) that are associated with many retrieval cues are easier to retrieve from memory than are items that are associated with fewer cues (e.g., Gillund & Shiffrin, 1984; Raaijmakers & Shiffrin, 1981). The second of these assumptions is also consistent with existing models of both text processing (e.g., Kintsch & van Dijk, 1978; Kintsch, 1988) and episodic memory (e.g., Gillund & Shiffrin, 1984; Raaijmakers & Shiffrin, 1981), because, in such models, the associative strength between an item and its cues is typically assumed to increase with the amount of time that the items and its cues are concurrently maintained in working memory.

Thus, to make predictions about the mean probabilities of successfully recalling the sentences in each of the four relatedness conditions, we assume that the mean probability of successfully integrating the meanings of the sentences and any inferences that are generated during reading is a multiplicative function of both the number of generated inferences and the number of unused working memory resources that are available for encoding the information into long-term memory. One way to represent this quantitatively is given by the following equation, in which the probability of recall of the sentences, p(recall), is the product of the number of generated inferences, N_i, and the number of available working memory resources (as specified by the right-hand term of the equation):

$$p(\text{recall}) \nabla N_i * [S - (N_p \lesseqgtr N_i)] \tag{4}$$

Equation 4 is consistent with the simple fact that there is an inherent limit on how much cognitive processing can be done per unit of time (Just & Carpenter, 1992; Just, Carpenter, Keller, Eddy, & Thulborn, 1996; Reichle, Carpenter, & Just, 2000). In the context of text processing, this limit means that, to the degree that working memory resources are being used to process the text and generate inferences, those resources will not be available for integrating those inferences into long-term memory.

Figure 9–3 also shows the predicted probabilities for successfully recalling the sentences in each of the four relatedness conditions used by Myers et al. (1987). The most salient thing about the predicted values is that they exhibit the same inverted-U shape that was observed by Myers et al., with the highest probability of recalling the sentences occurring with the moderately related (Level 2) sentence pairs.

The assumptions that are described by Eqs. 1–4 are thus sufficient to capture the overall pattern of the behavioral data that have been observed in the causal-inference paradigm that was used by Mason and Just (2004). To account for the patterns of fMRI-measured cortical activation that were observed by Mason and Just, it is only necessary to add the assumptions that the left-hemisphere language areas play an active but equal role in all four relatedness conditions, that bilateral DLPFC plays some type of active role in generating inferences, and the right-hemisphere areas play some type of active role in integrating whatever inferences are generated into long-term memory. (These assumptions are consistent with Mason and Just's verbal explanation of their data.)

Figure 9–4 shows the mean predicted volumes of cortical activation for the bilateral DLPFC and right-hemisphere areas. (We will ignore the predictions for the left-hemisphere areas because they do not vary across the different conditions and hence are not very diagnostic for attempting to understand the cognitive and neural processes that mediate inference making.) To generate these predictions, we assumed (as did Mason & Just, 2004) that the DLFPC activation volume reflects the amount of effort expended in generating causal inferences in the four conditions (i.e., N_i, as given by Eq. 3) and that right-hemisphere activation volume reflects the amount of effort extended in integrating those inferences into long-term memory (i.e., as indexed by Eq. 4). Also, because the experiment by Mason and Just included only three levels of causal relatedness (rather than the four used by both Keenan et al., 1984, and Myers et al., 1987), we used the mean relatedness-judgment value from the Level 2 and Level 3 conditions ($M \nabla 4.17$) to generate predictions for the moderately related condition. Figure 9–4 shows the predicted activation volume in these two sets of areas after the values are converted into an arbitrary (normalized) scale; within each area, each of the predicted values was divided by the maximum value, so that all of the values would be in the interval 0 to 1, with 1 representing the maximum amount of

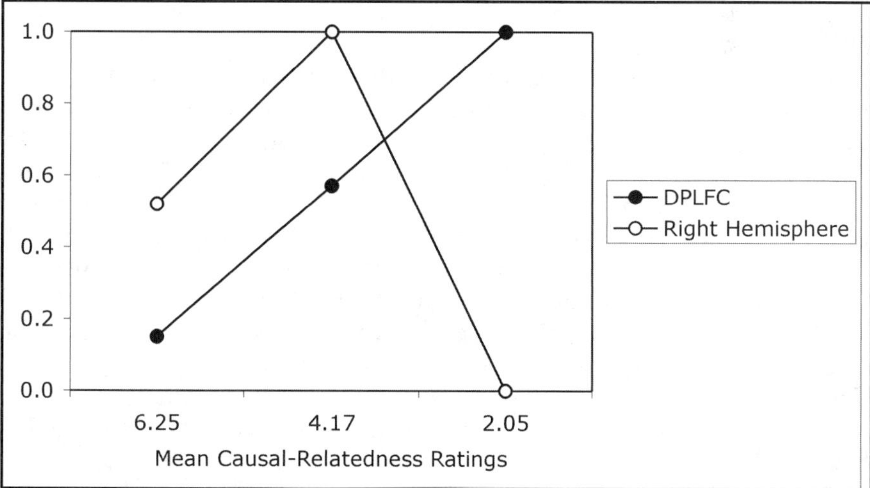

FIGURE 9–4. Simulated (normalized) volumes of cortical activation in bilateral DLPFC and the right-hemisphere language area homologues as a function of degree of causal relatedness.

activation in an area and lesser values indicating the proportion of this activation that was predicted in this area in each of the other three relatedness conditions. Notice that there is close qualitative agreement between the observed and predicted patterns of cortical activation in these two sets of areas (cf. Figs. 9–2 and 9–4).

SOME SPECULATION ABOUT NEURAL IMPLEMENTATION

Our account of the Mason and Just (2004) brain-imaging results is largely a functional one; it describes how the perceived degree of causal relatedness between two sentences affects the probability with which the reader will successfully generate a causal inference to better understand the sentences, as well as how this affects the time that is needed to read the sentence and the probability that the inference will be successfully integrated into long-term memory so that it can subsequently be remembered. Apart from specifying which cortical areas mediate these processes, our account is largely agnostic with respect to its underlying neural implementation. In this section, we briefly sketch how the principles that comprise our functional account might be instantiated in the brain. Of course, it goes without saying that this "sketch" is both tentative and incomplete. Because our focus has been on the Mason and Just (2004) results and the cortical areas that were implicated as being involved in generating and integrating causal inferences during reading, we will continue to focus on those areas (see Fig. 9–1): (1) the left-hemisphere language areas; (2) their right-hemisphere homologues; and (3) bilateral DLPFC.

The left hemisphere contains several areas that have been shown to play important roles in language processing. For example, the inferior frontal gyrus (roughly corresponding to Broca's area) is thought to mediate articulation and/or syntactic processing, whereas the temporal gyri (roughly corresponding to Wernicke's area) and angular gyrus are thought to mediate lexical and semantic processing (Mesulam, 1990, 1998). This view of the left-hemisphere language network is consistent with ours; the left hemisphere does all the lexical, syntactic, and semantic processing that is necessary to understand the literal meaning of the text. This processing includes making available whatever arguments are needed to fill the roles of the propositions. This is depicted in the top panel of Fig. 9–5, where the various arguments of a pair of sentences are shown as foci of activated cortical tissue in the left hemisphere.

Although the right hemisphere includes homologues of the left-hemisphere language areas, its functional role(s) remains more equivocal. One possibility is that the right hemisphere performs the same linguistic functions as its left-hemisphere counterpart, but that it does so when the language task is

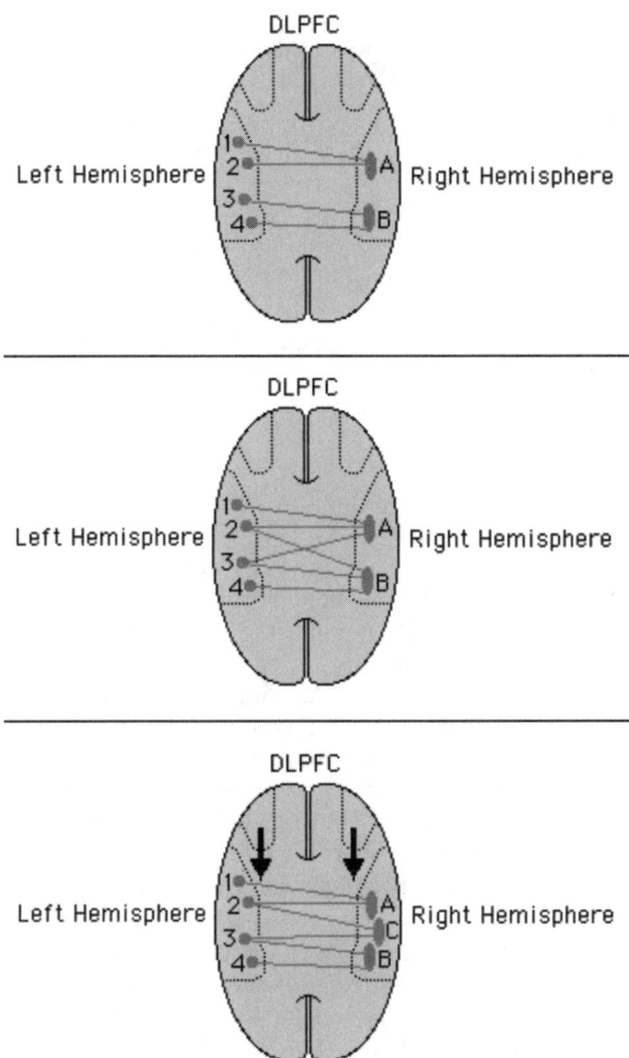

FIGURE 9–5. A schematic diagram of how the computational principles that are described by Eqs. 1–4 might be instantiated in the left-hemisphere language areas, their right-hemisphere homologues, and bilateral DLPFC. The top panel illustrates how linguistic arguments (which are represented in the left hemisphere) are "bound" to propositions (which are represented in the right hemisphere): The two propositions (A and B) share no arguments. The middle panel shows two propositions (A and B) that share two arguments (2 and 3). The bottom panel shows how a new proposition (C) can be generated to coreference two arguments (2 and 3) of two existing propositions (A and B).

difficult and requires additional working memory resources (which are thought to be supplied by the right hemisphere; Just et al., 1996).

Another possibility is that the right hemisphere performs one or more unique functions. This latter conjecture is supported by the neuropsychological literature. For example, patients with lesions of the right hemisphere often have trouble drawing inferences in order to integrate sentences and maintain coherence (Beeman, 1993; Brownell, Potter, Bihrle, & Gardner, 1986). And in contrast to normal readers, these patients fail to confuse the content of text that they are reading with inferences that (with normal readers) are likely to be drawn from the text, presumably because the patients make few such inferences while reading (Grafman, Salazar, Vance, Weingartner, & Amin, 1987). Given this evidence, it is not a question of *if* the right hemisphere plays an important role in making inferences, but is instead one of trying to understand *what* this role is.

One possibility is suggested by Beeman's (1998) *coarse-coding hypothesis*. According to Beeman, word meanings are represented differently in the two cerebral hemispheres. In the left hemisphere, word meanings are represented by localized semantic fields so that their core meanings can be rapidly and reliably accessed. In the right hemisphere, word meanings are represented by more distributed (and possibly overlapping) semantic fields; the less rapid activation of these fields presumably allows more than one sense of a word's meanings to be accessed, so that the meanings can be used figuratively (e.g., as is necessary to understand metaphors, puns, etc.). Several empirical results are consistent with this conceptualization of the right hemisphere. For example, several weakly associated words will prime a concept word (e.g., *space*, *ground*, and *shuttle* together prime *launch*) when these words are displayed to the left visual field/right hemisphere (LVF/RH), but not when these words are displayed to the RVF/LH (Beeman et al., 1994). Similarly, distantly related concepts will prime each other (e.g., *deer* primes *pony*) over longer time intervals in the LVF/RH than in the RVF/LH (Beeman et al, 1994; Chiarello, Burgess, Richards, & Pollock, 1990; Nakagawa, 1991). This indicates that peripheral aspects of a word's meaning are available longer in the right hemisphere than in the left.

How could coarse coding be related to inference making during reading? The hypothesized, broadly distributed fields in the right hemisphere might be ideally suited for allowing the cortical activation from several distantly related and/or weakly activated concepts to accrue and converge, and thereby "connect" whatever semantic information happens to be represented in their fields. These overlapping semantic fields in the right hemisphere might have two important functions: First, the overlap might be important for linking or "binding" the linguistic arguments that are represented in the left hemisphere into configurations in the right hemisphere that correspond to propositions; second, it might allow new propositions (configurations of arguments) to be generated. The former function is illustrated in Fig. 9–5 (top), which shows the representations of linguistic arguments (1–4) in the left hemisphere bound to propositions in the right hemisphere (A and B). The coarse-coding properties of the right hemisphere can thus be viewed as neural mechanisms underlying structure-building capability.

The second function (generating inferences) can happen in two ways. The first is illustrated in the center panel of Fig. 9–5. Here, an inference is automatically made wherever the argument overlap between two propositions is sufficient to maintain coreference. For example, if two propositions (A and B) share two overlapping arguments (2 and 3), the propositions may be coreferenced by their arguments. This would allow, for instance, a pronoun to unambiguously refer to its antecedent in the case of referential inferences.

The second way of generating inferences is illustrated in the bottom of Fig. 9–5. Here, a new proposition is generated to link the arguments of two existing propositions. For example, if two propositions (A and B) are bound to nonoverlapping arguments (A ∇ 1 and 2; B ∇ 3 and 4), then a third proposition (C ∇ 2 and 3) can be generated. This new proposition does not require any new arguments, but is instead bound to existing arguments. One implication of this is that texts that necessitate many inferences may not require the reader to maintain any more linguistic arguments than texts that require few inferences. This suggests why highly, moderately, and distantly related sentence pairs produce equivalent left-hemisphere cortical activation: The sentences in each condition will on average contain approximately the same number of arguments; only the number of propositions (which are represented in the right hemisphere) increase with the number of inferences being made. Of course, to predict the inverted U-shaped function observed by Mason and Just (2004), it is also necessary to assume that the cortical activation that was observed in the right hemisphere *largely* reflects the process of integrating—rather than generating—the causal inferences.

Finally, the DLPFC has been implicated in a variety of executive processes, such as maintaining information in an active state, planning and evaluating sequences of behaviors, and inhibiting contextually inappropriate responses (Cohen et al., 1997; Mesulam, 1998; Pennington, 1997). Given the sophisticated level of functionality that is ascribed to this area, one might argue that it has to perform only a fairly modest role in the service of making inferences—assessing whether or not a text has been understood and, in cases where it has not, prompting the right-hemisphere regions to continue generating inferences. Thus, the DPFLC may play an active role in both monitoring text coherence and signaling the inference-making system to continuing to generate inferences in an attempt to make sense of the material that is being read. We believe that by performing these actions, the DLPFC causes the inference-making process to continue until the information that is contained in the text is understood. This account is consistent with the observation that the amount of cortical activation that was observed in this region increases as the degree of causal relatedness between the two sentences decreases; with distantly related sentence pairs, the DLPFC will (on average) be more engaged in generating inferences to connect the outcome sentences to their antecedents in a causally meaningful way. Notice, however, that this account differs from the one given by Mason and Just (2004). They suggest that the "bilateral DLPFC is involved whenever the generation of an inference is necessary to maintain coherence in the text" and that "if an inference is successfully generated, the right-hemisphere language areas play an active role in integrating that inference" (p. 6). In contrast, our account suggests that both cortical regions are involved in generating inferences, but that only the right-hemisphere areas are involved in integrating inferences into long-term memory.

CONCLUSION

During the last decade, the many claims that brain-imaging methods are finally going to illuminate our understanding of the human mind have become so commonplace that they are almost blasé. Nevertheless, we believe that brain imaging—especially when combined with sound behavioral experiments and computational modeling—will provide exciting new ways of evaluating and developing theories of text processing. In this chapter, we have tried to demonstrate how the results of one fMRI experiment (Mason & Just, 2004) can advance our understanding of the cognitive processes that allow readers to make causal inferences during reading. By considering the patterns of fMRI-measured activation that were observed in various cortical areas when participants read sentences and made causal inferences, and then considering the different functional roles that have been ascribed to these areas, we were able to develop a small number of simple computational principles that are precise enough to be useful in making predictions about the outcomes of both brain-imaging and behavioral experiments (Keenan et al., 1984; Myers et al., 1987).

Although we acknowledge that many of our assumptions are speculative and that the principles that we have put forward are incomplete, we hasten to point out that the principles are broadly consistent with assumptions of existing text-processing models (e.g., the *Construction-Integration model*; Kintsch, 1988). Moreover, our attempt to explain both fMRI and behavioral results is also notable because brain imaging has only recently been used to address questions related to how people make causal inferences during reading. The principles that we discussed in this chapter therefore represent the first attempt—at least that we know of—to use fMRI results to evaluate the adequacy of several assumptions (which are included in many text-processing models) to simultaneously account for patterns of results obtained from both brain-imaging and behavioral experiments. This effort to develop a set of principles that can be used to describe both types of results reflects our belief that brain-imaging methods will ultimately provide data that are as important to theory development as the behavioral data that have been collected during the last 30 years have been. But of course, this is just an inference on our part.

ACKNOWLEDGMENTS

We thank Charles Perfetti and Franz Schmalhofer for helpful discussions about the contents of this paper. We also thank Patryk Laurent, Jessica Nelson, Tessa Warren, and two anonymous reviewers for their suggestions for improving an early version of this chapter.

REFERENCES

Anderson, J. R., Qin, Y., Sohn, M.-H., Stenger, V. A., & Carter, C. S. (2003). An information-processing model of the BOLD response in symbol manipulation tasks. *Psychological Review, 10*, 241–261.

Beeman, M. (1993). Semantic processing in the right hemisphere may contribute to drawing inferences during comprehension. *Brain and Language, 44*, 80–120.

Beeman, M. (1998). Coarse semantic coding and discourse comprehension. In M. Beeman & C. Chiarello (Eds.), *Getting it right: The cognitive neuroscience of right hemisphere language comprehension* (pp. 225–284). Mahwah, NJ: Lawrence Erlbaum Associates.

Beeman, M., Friedman, R. B., Grafman, J., Perez, E., Diamond, S., & Lindsay, M. B. (1994). Summation priming and coarse coding in the right hemisphere. *Journal of Cognitive Neuroscience, 6*, 26–45.

Brownell, H. H., Potter, H. H., Bihrle, A. M., & Gardner, H. (1986). Inference deficits in right brain-damaged patients. *Brain and Language, 29*, 310–321.

Chiarello, C., Burgess, C., Richards, L., & Pollock, A. (1990). Semantic and associative priming in the cerebral hemispheres: Some words do, some don't sometimes, some places. *Brain and Language, 38*, 75–104.

Cohen, J. D., Petit, L., Maisog, J. M., Ungerleider, L. G., & Haxby, J. V. (1997). An area specialized for spatial working memory in human frontal cortex. *Science, 279*, 1347–1351.

Ferstl, E. C., Guthke, T., & von Cramon, D. Y. (2002). Text comprehension after brain injury: Left prefrontal lesions affect inference processes. *Neuropsychology, 16*, 292–308.

Ferstl, E. C., & von Cramon, D. Y. (2001). The role of coherence and cohesion in text comprehension: An event-related fMRI study. *Cognitive Brain Research, 11*, 325–340.

Frank, S. L., Koppen, M., Noordman, L. G. M., & Wietske, V. (2003). Modeling knowledge-based inferences in story comprehension. *Cognitive Science, 27*, 875–910.

Gillund, G., & Shiffrin, R. M. (1984). A retrieval model of both recognition and recall. *Psychological Review, 91*, 1–67.

Golden, R., & Rumelhart, D. E. (1993). A parallel distributed processing model of story comprehension and recall. *Discourse Processes, 16*, 203–237.

Goldman, S. R., & Varma, S. (1995). CAPping the construction-integration model of discourse comprehension. In C. A. Weaver, S. Mannes, & C. R. Fletcher (Eds.), *Discourse comprehension: Essays in honor of Walter Kintsch* (pp. 337–358). Hillsdale, NJ: Lawrence Erlbaum Associates.

Graesser, A. C., Singer, M., & Trabasso, T. (1994). Constructing inferences during narrative text comprehension. *Psychological Review, 101*, 371–395.

Grafman, J., Salazar, A. M., Vance, S. C., Weingartner, H., & Amin, D. (1987). Immediate memory for story discourse in Vietnam veterans with penetrating brain wounds. *Journal of Clinical and Experimental Neuropsychology, 9*, 23–34.

Just, M. A., & Carpenter, P. A. (1992). A capacity theory of comprehension: Individual differences in working memory. *Psychological Review, 99*, 122–149.

Just, M. A., Carpenter, P. A., Keller, T. A., Eddy, W. F., & Thulborn, K. R. (1996). Brain activation modulated by sentence comprehension. *Science, 274*, 114–116.

Keenan, J. M., Baillet, S. D., & Brown, P. (1984). The effects of causal cohesion on comprehension and memory. *Journal of Verbal Learning and Verbal Behavior, 23*, 115–126.

Kim, S. Y., Morales, F. J., & Reichle, E. D. (2004). Exploring the bases of causal inferences. Poster presented at the 26th Annual Meeting of the Cognitive Science Society, Chicago.

Kintsch, W. (1988). The role of knowledge in discourse comprehension: A construction-integration model. *Psychological Review, 95*, 163–182.

Kintsch, W., & van Dijk, T. A. (1978). Towards a model of text comprehension and production. *Psychological Review, 85*, 363–394.

Langston, M., & Trabasso, T. (1999). Modeling causal integration and availability of information during comprehension of narrative texts. In H. van Oostendorp & S. R. Goldman (Eds.), *The construction of mental representations during reading* (pp. 29–69). Mahwah, NJ: Lawrence Erlbaum Associates.

Mason, R. A., & Just, M. A. (2004). How the brain processes causal inferences in text: A theoretical account of generation and integration component processes utilizing both cerebral hemispheres. *Psychological Science, 15*, 1–7.

McKoon, G., & Ratcliff, R. (1992). Inference during reading. *Psychological Review, 99*, 440–466.

Mesulam, M.-M. (1990). Large-scale neurocognitive networks and distributed processing for attention, language and memory. *Annals of Neurology, 28*, 597–613.

Mesulam, M.-M. (1998). From sensation to cognition. *Brain, 121*, 1013–1052.

Myers, J. L., & Duffy, S. A. (1990). Causal inferences and text memory. *The Psychology of Learning and Motivation, 25*, 159–173.

Myers, J. L., & O'Brien, E. J. (1998). Accessing the discourse representation during reading. *Discourse Processes, 26*, 131–157.

Myers, J. L., Shinjo, M., & Duffy, S. A. (1987). Degree of causal relatedness and memory. *Journal of Memory and Language, 26*, 453–465.

Nakagawa, A. (1991). Role of the anterior and posterior attention networks in hemispheric asymmetries during lexical decisions. *Journal of Cognitive Neuroscience, 3*, 315–321.

Pennington, B. F. (1997). Dimensions of executive functions in normal and abnormal development. In N. A. Krasnegor, G. R. Lyon, & P. S. Goldman-Rakic (Eds.), *Development of the prefrontal cortex: Evolution, neurobiology, and behavior* (pp. 265–281). Baltimore: Brookes.

Raaijmakers, J. G. W., & Shiffrin, R. M. (1981). Search of associative memory. *Psychological Review, 88*, 93–134.

Reichle, E. D., Carpenter, P. A., & Just, M. A. (2000). The neural bases of strategy and skill in sentence-picture verification. *Cognitive Psychology, 40*, 261–295.

Schmalhofer, F., McDaniel, M. A., & Keefe, D. (2002). A unified model for predictive and bridging inferences. *Discourse Processes, 33*, 105–132.

Van den Broek, P., Lorch, R. F., Linderholm, T., & Gustafson, M. (2001). The effects of readers' goals on inference generation and memory for texts. *Memory & Cognition, 29*, 1081–1087.

Van den Broek, P., Risden, K., Fletcher, C. R., & Thurlow, R. (1996). A "landscape" view of reading: Fluctuating patterns of activation and the construction of a stable memory representation. In B. K. Britton & A. C. Graesser (Eds.), *Models of understanding text* (pp. 165–187). Mahwah, NJ: Lawrence Erlbaum Associates.

Van den Broek, P., Young, M., Tzeng, Y., & Linderholm, T. (1999). The landscape model of reading: Inferences and the online construction of a memory representation. In H. van Oostendorp & S. R. Goldman (Eds.), *The construction of mental representations during reading* (pp. 71–98). Mahwah, NJ: Lawrence Erlbaum Associates.

10

Comprehension Skill, Inference Making, and the Role of Knowledge

Danielle S. McNamara and Tenaha O'Reilly
University of Memphis

Manuel de Vega
Universidad de la Laguna

Texts and other forms of written media are frequent means of transmitting information. Thus, the ability to comprehend written material is a critical skill for successfully functioning in modern society. Consequently, one important goal for many reading researchers is to identify the differences between skilled and less skilled readers in terms of cognitive aptitudes and processes engaged during reading. Developing a better understanding of these differences contributes both to theoretical explanations of the reading process and to interventions designed to improve reading ability.

Many researchers are concerned with the initial stages of reading when the reader is essentially acquiring lexical and syntactic decoding skills. Such researchers have found for example that the more successful novice readers have had greater exposure to print (Stanovich, West, Cunningham, Cipielewski, & Siddequi, 1996) and have greater phonological awareness (Hulme & Snowling, 1992). Other research has shown that lower level processes such as lexical quality can distinguish between skilled and less skilled readers (Perfetti, 1985; Perfetti & Hart, 2001). According to this view, readers vary in terms of their processing efficiency and lexical knowledge. Comprehension difficulty arises from inefficient lower level processes required for the identification of words. Indeed, one important factor that can affect word identification is the quality of the lexical representation. For example, Perfetti and Hart (2001) found that the quality of the reader's representation affects not only the speed of word retrieval but also the selection of sense (meaning) of ambiguous words. Based on these findings, the authors formulated the Lexical Quality Hypothesis to account for difference in sense selection between skilled and less skilled readers.

According to the Lexical Quality Hypothesis, word quality can vary on three dimensions (constituents): orthographic, phonetic, and semantic. The orthographic code specifies the word's spelling, the phonetic code specifies the pronunciation, and the semantic code provides the meaning. If one or more constituents of the word code are deficient, then the quality of the representation decreases. When the representation is of low quality, retrieval may be hampered in terms of the time needed to retrieve the word (i.e., efficiency) or whether the intended word is retrieved at all (i.e., accuracy).

Moreover, the lexical quality hypothesis asserts that skilled and less skilled readers differ in two ways. First, skilled readers have more resources to repair or embellish impoverished representations. These resources may include more effective decoding, spelling, and grammatical skills. However, the key characteristic that distinguishes skilled from less skilled readers is the number of high-quality word representations. Skilled readers are more efficient and accurate at retrieving words because the majority of their word representations are complete. This allows for fast and efficient retrieval of orthographic, phonemic, and semantic information. However, even skilled readers have low-quality representations for some words, such as low-frequency words.

Although the quality of a word representation and decoding ability have an impact on word identification and low-level comprehension, the focus of this chapter, in contrast, is on readers' higher level comprehension skills. Comprehension refers to the construction of meaning of the words and phrases, such as recognizing the interrelationships within the text, making inferences using prior knowledge, and integrating the text with existing knowledge structures. Although decoding and comprehension processes are tightly interwoven, they are nevertheless separate processes. For example, a dyslexic reader can comprehend, but not decode; and a hyperlexic reader can decode, but not comprehend. Of course, word decoding difficulties are correlated with and may ultimately result in reading comprehension deficits (e.g., Perfetti, 1985; Schankweiller et al., 1999). However, research also indicates that there are many poor comprehenders who do not have deficits at the level of word decoding or syntactic decomposition (Cain, 1996; Hoover & Gough, 1990; Stothard & Hulme, 1996; Cornoldi et al., 1996). These readers may read fluently and with apparent ease and yet still perform poorly when answering questions.

How do these readers, who can decode words and syntax without difficulties but struggle to comprehend the deeper meaning of the text, differ from those who more successfully comprehend text? Behavioral studies of individual differences in comprehension have shown that good and poor readers differ in terms of inference processes such as solving anaphoric reference, selecting the meaning of homographs, processing garden-path sentences, making appropriate inferences on-line, integrating text structures, and so on (e.g., Long & Golding, 1993; Long, Oppy, & Seely, 1994; Oakhill, 1983, 1984; Singer, Andrusiak, Reisdorf, & Black, 1992; Singer & Ritchot, 1996;

Whitney, Ritchie, & Clark, 1991; Yuill & Oakhill, 1988). Skilled readers are more likely to generate inferences that repair conceptual gaps between clauses, sentences, and paragraphs (e.g., Long, Oppy, & Seely, 1994; Magliano & Millis, 2003; Magliano, Wiemer-Hastings, Millis, Muñoz, & McNamara, 2002; Oakhill, 1984; Oakhill & Yuill, 1996). In contrast, less skilled readers tend to ignore gaps and fail to make the inferences necessary to fill in the gaps (e.g., Garnham, Oakhill, & Johnson-Laird, 1982; Oakhill, Yuill, & Donaldson, 1990; Yuill, Oakhill, & Parkin, 1989). In sum, one of the clearest distinctions between skilled and less skilled comprehenders is their ability to make inferences while reading.

Less skilled readers perform poorly on tasks that require inferential reasoning. They are less likely to generate topic-related inferences on-line or to integrate incoming information with preceding discourse (Long, Oppy, & Seely, 1994). In particular, skilled readers are more likely to process the separate relations between sentences and paragraphs; that is, they are more likely to make bridging inferences. For example, skilled readers perform better on questions that address both text-based and implicit inferences, even when the text is made available during questioning (Oakhill, 1984). However, less skilled readers' performance on non-inference questions is the same as skilled readers' when the text is present. Oakhill (1982) also found that skilled readers made more recognition errors with foils that were congruent with the story theme but not explicitly mentioned in the text. Skilled readers are more likely to construct an integrated representation of related sentences that are organized around the main purpose or theme of the text. Thus, skilled readers' inferencing ability allows them to relate ideas in text to one another and to their existing knowledge.

Whereas the differences found between good and poor readers in a variety of linguistic tasks are generally robust and replicable, the theoretical explanations are more questionable. The most popular explanatory theory of these differences is that comprehension skills are determined by differences in working memory capacity, generally measured by various versions of the reading span task (e.g., Daneman & Carpenter, 1980; Just & Carpenter, 1992). This account holds that skilled readers are better able to make inferences while reading because they have greater working memory capacity and are able to hold in working memory more information from the text or discourse. A second explanation proposes that poor readers have difficulty suppressing "noisy" information, such as contextually irrelevant meanings of homographs. One such theory proposes that less skilled readers lack a suppression mechanism and thus perform frequent structure "shifts," whereas good readers continue mapping information into an ongoing structure (e.g., Gernsbacher, 1990). As such, the successful comprehender is better able to suppress or inhibit irrelevant information, leaving more resources for relevant information (e.g., Rosen & Engle, 1998). Recently, a third class of explanations has emerged that emphasizes skilled comprehenders' more active and efficient use of knowledge and strategies (e.g., Bereiter & Bird, 1985; Ericsson & Kintsch, 1995; McNamara, 1997; McNamara & McDaniel, 2004; McNamara & Scott, 2001; Schmalhofer, 1998; MacDonald & Christiansen, 2002; Paris & Jacobs, 1984; Pressley & Afflerbach, 1995; Snow, Burns, & Griffin, 1998; see also Zwaan & Kaup, this volume). Accordingly, skilled readers activate and use knowledge more than less skilled readers, either because they know and use more metacognitive reading strategies (e.g., McNamara & Scott, 2001) or because they have more prior knowledge about the text topic (e.g., McNamara & McDaniel, 2004). Below, we review evidence supporting the knowledge-based explanation of reading skill.

KNOWLEDGE-BASED ACCOUNT OF COMPREHENSION SKILL

The knowledge-based account of reading comprehension skill asserts that better readers more actively and efficiently use prior knowledge to comprehend text (Bereiter & Bird, 1985; Ericsson & Kintsch, 1995; McNamara, 1997; McNamara & McDaniel, 2004; McNamara, & Scott, 2001; MacDonald & Christiansen, 2002; Paris & Jacobs, 1984; Pressley & Afflerbach, 1995; Snow, Burns, & Griffin, 1998). This knowledge use may arise because they have more prior knowledge about the text topic (e.g., McNamara & McDaniel, 2004) or because they know and use more metacognitive reading strategies (e.g., McNamara & Scott, 2001). However, the underlying assumption of these theories is that it is greater activation and use of knowledge that drives comprehension skill, rather than working memory capacity or suppression mechanisms.

There is ample evidence that readers who have more knowledge about the topic of a text better understand the written material (e.g., Chiesi, Spilich, & Voss, 1979; Bransford & Johnson, 1972; Haenggi & Perfetti, 1994). Readers with greater prior knowledge are also better able to comprehend texts that require numerous inferences (McNamara, Kintsch, Songer, & Kintsch, 1996; McNamara & Kintsch, 1996; O'Reilly & McNamara, 2007). This latter research demonstrated that the comprehension differences between high- and low-knowledge readers were most exaggerated for texts with more conceptual gaps (low-coherence texts). Moreover, high-knowledge readers show a reversed-cohesion effect. They benefit from reading low-coherence texts, assumedly because they induce the reader to generate more inferences while reading. Other studies have similarly demonstrated advantages for text-induced active processing (e.g., Einstein, McDaniel, Owen, & Cote, 1990; Mannes & Kintsch, 1987; McDaniel, Einstein, Dunay, & Cobb, 1986; O'Brien & Myers, 1985; Rauenbusch & Bereiter, 1991). Essentially, comprehension is enhanced when readers are induced by the text to generate inferences and these inferences are successful.

McNamara (2001) provided further evidence that the reversed-cohesion effect found for high-knowledge readers was the result of active processing induced by a low-cohesion text. In this study, adult participants read both high and low versions of a text about cell mitosis. Comprehension was enhanced only for participants who read the low-cohesion version, followed by the high-cohesion version. This result showed that the low-cohesion text induced gap-filling inferences while the participant was reading the text, and it was this on-line active processing that enhanced comprehension. When the reader was exposed to the high-cohesion version first and thus was not induced to generate the inferences, these benefits did not appear. These results further demonstrated that the amount of material read is not a factor that can explain the reversed cohesion effect. That is, the readers were all exposed to the same information and thus the same amount of information—only the order of presentation differed.

According to the Construction-Integration model of text comprehension (Kintsch, 1988; 1998), text-based and knowledge-based inferences result in more links between concepts and thus a more cohesive mental structure. Thus, activation of prior knowledge helps the reader form a more coherent mental representation of the text. Readers with more knowledge of the text domain (e.g., science or history) show better comprehension when they use their prior knowledge to comprehend and learn, particularly on measures that assess deeper levels of understanding (e.g., bridging-inference and problem-solving questions, rating and sorting tasks).

Along the same lines, Ericsson and Kintsch (1995) proposed that skilled performance (such as reading skill) is due to the use of *long-term working memory* (LTWM), which is a more efficient WM with faster access to LTM than normal WM. Typical WM retrievals from LTM require 1 to 2 seconds, whereas LTWM retrievals require approximately 400 milliseconds (e.g., McNamara & Kintsch, 1996b). More efficient LTM access results from using cues in STM to activate retrieval structures. LTWM bypasses STM processing limitations because experience within a particular domain leads to enriched knowledge structures and information retrieval strategies.

McNamara and Scott (2001) proposed that LTWM retrieval structures and strategies may be particularly important to WM task performance because of the need to switch attention repeatedly between processing and storage tasks. LTWM allows an individual to more efficiently re-access the words from LTM that were no longer available in STM. Hence, a person using strategies would appear to have greater WM capacity. Other researchers have similarly proposed that WM constraints are not caused by limits in the amount of WM activation, but instead by how efficiently that capacity or activation is used (e.g., Case, Kurland, & Goldberg, 1982; Cowan, 1988; Daneman & Carpenter, 1980; Engle & Marshall, 1983; Shiffrin & Schneider, 1977). McNamara and Scott demonstrated that participants who reported using more effective memory strategies such as imagery when completing STM tasks also performed better on the WM span task. Moreover, participants who received training in the use of a chaining strategy (i.e., creating sentences to link the words) during STM tasks showed substantial improvement on WM tasks.

These results collectively show that participants can and do use strategies during WM tasks, and these strategies improve WM performance.

McNamara and Scott (2001) reasoned that if WM task performance depended at least partially on strategy use, that factor may contribute to correlations between reading skill and WM capacity. Accordingly, high-capacity individuals and skilled readers are more strategic across a variety of tasks. In this sense, skilled readers make more inferences because they are strategic, they know how to make the inferences, and they know when the inferences are necessary. This explanation is further supported by research showing that skilled readers have more metacognitive knowledge (Baker, 1982; Wong, 1985) and are more likely to use reading strategies (e.g., Baker, 1994; Garner, 1987; Long & Golding, 1993; Long et al., 1994; Oakhill, 1982, 1983).

As mentioned earlier, another critical difference between skilled and less skilled readers is their ability to resolve anaphors, especially when the referent is distant (Oakhill & Yuill, 1986; Yuill & Oakhill, 1988). Anaphor resolution is problematic for younger and less skilled readers, particularly with one type of anaphor, personal pronouns. This difficulty persists even when there is a gender cue and when the clause containing the referent is available to the reader (Oakhill & Yuill, 1986). Moreover, skilled and less skilled readers seem to have a different method of resolving anaphoric relations. Less skilled readers seem to search the preceding sentence for an appropriate syntactic form, whereas the high-skilled readers tend to resolve anaphors by relying on their model of the story and integrating this into existing knowledge (Yuill & Oakhill, 1988; see also Noordman, Vonk, & Frank, this volume). Thus, skilled readers are more likely to make the inferences to resolve anaphors, and they do so using information from the text and their background knowledge.

As mentioned earlier, skilled readers are also more likely to make elaborative and bridging inferences. Results showing that the advantage of a skilled reader's performance on inference questions persists even when the text is made available to the readers (Oakhill, 1983, 1984) shed doubt on a working memory or capacity account. The reader's memory resources should be at least partially relieved if the text is made available when the reader answers the inference questions. In contrast, these results indicate that inferencing ability requires knowledge and that relating different parts of the text is necessary for successful comprehension.

One of the strongest sources of evidence in favor of knowledge-based accounts is that interventions that target more active or strategic use of knowledge improve reading skill and comprehension (e.g., Bereiter & Bird; 1985; Chi, de Leeuw, Chiu, & LaVancher, 1994; Cornoldi & Oakhill, 1996; Dewitz, Carr, & Patberg, 1987; Hansen & Pearson; 1983; Kucan & Beck, 1997; McNamara, 2004; McNamara & Scott, 1999; Palincsar & Brown, 1984; Paris, Cross, & Lipson, 1984; Yuill & Oakhill, 1988). Such studies demonstrate that simply knowing how and when to make inferences dramatically improves reading comprehension. This large body of research shows that when readers learn strategies to more effectively use their knowledge while reading, their reading comprehension improves.

Whereas there is a large body of evidence that comprehension skill is critically tied to readers' ability to activate and use knowledge, there is another body of literature indicating that inhibiting or suppressing irrelevant knowledge is linked to comprehension ability (e.g., Gernsbacher, 1990; Rosen & Engle). However, McNamara (1997) proposed that suppression could be explained in terms of greater elaboration of sentences. Within the framework of the Construction-Integration model of comprehension (Kintsch, 1988), she demonstrated that the results reported by Gernsbacher and colleagues (e.g., Gernsbacher et al., 1991) could be explained more parsimoniously in terms of enhancement of relevant information via elaborative inferences, rather than inhibition of irrelevant information. According to the Construction-Integration model, incoming information and associated knowledge are represented as an associative network of nodes (concepts, ideas, or propositions) and links (relations or actions). Concepts that are compatible with the overall context generally have more links, whereas irrelevant concepts tend to have fewer links. Because the model relies on connectionist principles of constraint satisfaction, concepts with more links increase in activation, whereas concepts with fewer links gradually lose activation.

McNamara (1997) proposed that if more knowledge associated with the context provided in the sentence were activated during comprehension, then more links to the relevant meaning of the ambiguous word would be created and the irrelevant meaning would quickly lose activation. In support of that hypothesis, she demonstrated within a computational simulation that the number of activated associations to the relevant meaning predicted the rate of activation loss for the irrelevant meaning. In this knowledge-based model, skilled comprehenders were assumed to more actively process the information provided in the sentence, which in turn activated more relevant knowledge. These links essentially fed activation to the relevant meaning of the ambiguous word and led to a rapid deactivation of the irrelevant meaning. To simulate less skilled comprehenders, less associated knowledge was activated. The relevant meaning was rapidly activated to threshold, leading to an accurate understanding of the sentence, but the irrelevant meaning retained enough below-threshold activation to interfere with processing when it was presented in the decision task.

McNamara (1997) showed that the differences between skilled and less skilled comprehenders in her simulation emerged primarily from interference from the irrelevant meaning (for less skilled comprehenders), and not because of differences in facilitation. That is, the increase in associations with the appropriate meaning (for skilled comprehenders) had minimal effects on the time for the correct response to reach threshold. However, the increased associations in the skilled comprehender simulation essentially took over the network such that the irrelevant meanings essentially died out. In contrast, in the less skilled comprehender simulation, the lack of competition for resources between relevant links and irrelevant links resulted in residual activation for the irrelevant meaning of the ambiguous word. Accordingly, less skilled comprehenders do not use resources effectively, whereas skilled comprehenders' maximal use of resources drives out irrelevant information.

It is important to note that suppression can be simulated with the use of the Construction-Integration model with either inhibition mechanisms or enhancement processes (cf. Kintsch, 1998). McNamara (1997), however, showed that enhancement (i.e., elaborative inferences) provides a more parsimonious explanation because a decline in activation simply falls out of the model for information with fewer links. In addition, the Construction-Integration model has been used similarly to account for declining activation associated with other kinds of comprehension processes, such as predictive inferences (McDaniel, Schmalhofer, & Keefe, 2001; Schmalhofer, McDaniel, & Keefe, 2002).

More recently, McNamara and McDaniel (2004) provided empirical evidence for McNamara's (1997) model by showing that greater domain or general knowledge produced effects similar to those obtained for skilled comprehenders. Specifically, participants with greater general knowledge showed a reduction of the ambiguity effect after a delay, whereas the interference persisted for those with less general knowledge. In addition, participants with more knowledge of baseball showed an ambiguity effect with baseball sentences at the immediate test and the absence of an effect after a delay. In contrast, participants with less knowledge of baseball maintained a reliable ambiguity effect after a delay. These results support the theoretical framework that individual differences in ambiguity resolution can depend on dynamics associated with knowledge activation during comprehension.

NEUROLOGICAL RESEARCH

Neuropsychological studies can shed some light on the issue of individual differences in comprehension. In this section, we review some of these studies. As far as we know, PET or fMRI has not been applied yet in this field, probably because the number of participants in such studies is usually very small. Nevertheless, there are several well-designed studies using event-related potential (ERP) that show how poor and good readers differ in their brain activity while they perform comprehension tasks.

The Study of Language with ERP

ERP consists of forming averages from the EEG of many individual trials, time-locked to the triggering event (e.g., a word). The assumption behind this approach is that transient activity that is not directly associated with the triggering event is random and will average out over the course of many repetitions. By contrast, an ERP signal will emerge for the specific activity associated with the time-locked events.

The ERP data are becoming a standard dependent measure in psycholinguistic experiments, having some clear advantages over more traditional behavioral measures (see also Perfetti & Schmalhofer, this volume). Some of these advantages include high temporal resolution and a continuous picture of brain (and cognitive) activity; and it is less intrusive than other techniques. Most of the ERP components associated with language processes are fast, transient responses triggered by individual words (e.g., N280, N400, P300, LAN, P600, etc). There is also a slower activity in very low-frequency bands of the ERP (less than 1 Hz) that is much less used in language research, although it is quite appropriate for analyzing processes that occur in longer linguistic units such as whole clauses or sentences. For the present purpose of exploring individual differences in comprehension, we will focus on some of the fast components generated by individual words (mainly the N400), but also on slow potentials generated by whole sentences.

Individual Differences in Fast-Response Components of ERP

In the investigations we are going to review, participants perform a comprehension task while their EEG is recorded, and ERPs for good and poor readers are calculated separately. Typically, the comprehension task involves reading sentences, presented automatically word by word. Sentence reading tasks are sufficient to explore cohesion and coherence processes at the local level. This provides the means to study the processing of inferences, cohesion marks, anaphor resolution, and interclausal integration processes.

The overarching idea behind the studies described here is that good readers' ERPs responses are generally much more sensitive to manipulations in the reading tasks, showing a more extensive brain activity for more difficult versions of sentences. By contrast, poor readers' responses remain relatively insensitive to manipulations of the reading task.

Among the transitory components of ERP, N400 and P600 have been especially informative in revealing language processes at the sentence level. N400 is a negative-going wave between 200 and 600 ms, peaking around 400 ms, with a somewhat posterior, slightly right-hemisphere amplitude maximum. The N400 is obtained both with isolated words and with words embedded in linguistic contexts. It is sensitive to lexical parameters such as word frequency, or word concreteness, but is also sensitive to the sentence and the discourse context in which the words appear. In particular, N400 amplitude increases when a word is semantically anomalous within a sentence (e.g., Kutas & Hillyard, 1980). P600 is a positive-going wave starting 500 ms after stimulus onset, reaching the maximum amplitude at about 600 ms, which is usually observed at posterior sites. It is sensitive to morpho-syntactic violation in sentences and corresponds to sentence re-processing, of both syntactic and semantic natures (Friederici, 2002).

One research question is whether individual differences in the comprehension of sentences arise at the lexical associative level or at a more thematic level (cf. Long et al., 1994). Van Petten et al. (1997) asked individuals with high, medium, and low working memory capacity (as measured by Daneman & Carpenter's span test) to read sentences that included two critical associated words or non-associated words, and the context was manipulated to produce congruent and anomalous sentences. Examples of the four resulting experimental conditions follow:

Congruent-associated

When the **moon** is full it is hard to see many **stars** or the Milky Way.

Congruent-unassociated

When the **insurance** investigators found that he'd been drinking they **refused** to pay the claim.

Anomalous-associated

When the **moon** is rusted it is available to buy many **stars** or the Santa Ana.

Anomalous-unassociated

When the **insurance** supplies explained that he'd been complaining they **refused** to speak the keys.

Thus, the lexical association factors and the sentence congruence factors were dissociated experimentally. The results suggested that all subjects were sensitive to the lexical association of words. Thus, when anomalous-associated and anomalous-unassociated sentences were contrasted, all readers showed the same increase in N400 for the non-associated critical word. However, when congruent-unassociated and anomalous-unassociated sentences were compared, only the high and medium working memory capacity groups showed a larger N400 for the anomalous-unassociated sentences. Interestingly, the contextual effect for high and medium span groups continued in the next temporal window of 500 to 700 ms after the word onset, suggesting that these readers tried to solve the semantic incongruence for almost one second.

These results concur with behavioral studies and fit quite well with the knowledge-based account of individual differences. Poor readers efficiently activate basic word-based associations, which help them to build the sentence meaning. However, poor readers fail to activate deeper background knowledge necessary for understanding sentence-level thematic relations (see, e.g., Cantor & Engle, 1993) when lexical associations are not available in the text. In contrast, more skillful readers activate a rich network of background knowledge, even when they try to understand anomalous-unassociated sentences.

More specific comprehension skills have been explored in a jokes comprehension task by Coulson and Kutas (2001). They recorded participants' EEG while the participants read sentences that ended either as jokes involving a frame-shifting or had equally surprising non-joke endings. For instance, "She read so much about the bad effects of smoking she decided she'd have to give up reading/the habit." The ERPs were averaged for the critical final word, and the participants were split into good and poor joke comprehenders, depending on their responses to control questions about the meaning of the jokes. The pattern of ERP was considerably more complex for good joke comprehenders, who elicited a left-lateralized sustained negativity for all jokes (N400) combined with a frontal and posterior positivity (P600). By contrast, poor joke comprehenders showed only a right frontal negativity to jokes that continued beyond the N400 temporal window. The N400 obtained by all participants indicates that all of them are sensitive to the contextually unexpected critical word. But the later positivity, only observed in good joke comprehenders, suggests that they engaged in an additional frame-shifting process. Namely, they initially activated a schema or frame-based expectation, but when they read the critical joke word they successfully shifted to another frame. Poor readers, instead, are unable to manage schematic information efficiently enough to produce a frame shift.

Other studies analyzed ERP in good and poor readers when they read relative sentences (Mueller, King, & Kutas, 1997; Vos & Friederici, 2003). Relative sentences provide a controlled way to study different factors in sentence processing because they differ in complexity despite a close similarity in structure. Some studies on relative clause comprehension developed in German demonstrated that good comprehenders produce a much clearer ERP pattern than poor comprehenders. For instance, Vos and Friederici (2003) used subject-first (e.g., *He found out that it was the actress who distracted the producers*) and object-first (*He found out that it was the actress who the producers distracted*) relative sentences. They found that skilled readers showed a larger late positivity (P600) for disambiguating words in the object-first than in the subject-first relative clauses. In contrast, poor readers' ERP was not sensitive to the relative clause manipulation. Vos and Friederici (2003) proposed that skilled readers' P600 reflected their syntactic re-analysis of the disambiguating information, after they had followed a garden path. By contrast, poor readers would not garden-path because of their lack of working memory resources. However, P600, even when triggered by a syntactic garden path, occurs too late to exclusively reflect a syntactic process. Actually, P600 is also sensitive to semantic factors and could reflect an interaction between syntactic and semantic processes (Friederici, 2002). Moreover, P600 increases for target words that are incoherent with a previous text, even though the target words are embedded in syntactically appropriate sentences (e.g., Bartholow, Fabiani, Gratton, & Bettencourt, 2001; Díaz, León, & de Vega, 2003). Consequently, individual differences in the P600 component could reflect in part that skilled readers more efficiently mobilize background knowledge to integrate syntactic and semantic information in the object-first clauses.

Finally, individual differences in inference generation have also been explored by St. George, Mannes, and Hoffman (1997). They gave high-span and low-span participants different types of paragraphs that were intended to produce either bridging inferences (necessary to establish the local coherence of discourse) or elaborative inferences (invited by the context, but not required for local coherence). In addition, there were two control conditions: word-based priming paragraphs and non-inference paragraphs. Examples of the materials follow:

Bridging:

Pam set the dinning room table

She forgot about the turkey in the oven

The guests were disappointed with the ruined meal.

It was too bad the turkey burned.

Elaborative:

Pam set the dinning room table

She forgot about the turkey in the oven

Pan was disappointed when the argumentative guests ruined the meal.

It was too bad the turkey burned.

Word-based priming:

Pam set the dinning room table

She put the turkey in the oven

Pan was disappointed when the argumentative guests ruined the meal.

It was too bad the turkey burned.

No inference:

Pam set the dinning room table

She put the turkey in the oven

The guests were outside playing badminton

It was too bad the turkey burned.

A reduction in the amplitude of N400 for the final sentence words in bridging or elaborative paragraphs (in comparison with the control conditions) could be considered evidence that an inference was generated. All participants showed a N400 reduction in the final sentence of bridging paragraphs. However, poor readers also showed the same amount of N400 reduction for word-based priming paragraphs, which means that their bridging inferences could be based on lexical associations rather than broader general knowledge background (see similar results in the aforementioned study by van Petten et al., 1997). The ERP pattern considerably differs in skilled readers. They showed a significant N400 reduction for bridging and elaborative paragraphs, but not for word-based priming, suggesting that they mobilize broader nets of pre-stored knowledge (not just lexical associations) to support both necessary and optional inferences.

Individual Differences in Sentence-Level Slow Potentials

The most striking picture of individual differences in comprehension emerges when ERP slow potentials are explored. Slow potentials are obtained in sentence reading when the ordinary, more transient potentials produced by words are low-pass filtered. The resulting signals are positively or negatively drifting potentials along the whole sentence, with a very distinctive distribution throughout the scalp. Slow potentials are particularly appropriate to exploration of more global language processes beyond lexical factors, because they offer a picture of unfolding sentence processing and are presumably sensitive to the mobilization of knowledge and integrative processes.

In an exploratory experiment, Kutas and King (1996) recorded slow potentials for six-word clauses (e.g., *The secretary answered the phone because . . .*) without any specific manipulation of variables, and the data from poor and good readers (categorized according to their recall of the sentences in the experiment) were analyzed separately. The results showed a more left-hemisphere lateralized frontal positivity for the good than the poor comprehenders. By contrast, poor comprehenders showed a larger and more left-hemisphere positivity at occipital electrode sites. These results strongly suggest that poor comprehenders devote more cognitive resources to the encoding of words' visual features (more occipital activity), having fewer resources available for sentence integration processes (less frontal activity). By contrast, good readers devote much more resources to the whole sentence integrative processes, as evidenced by more frontal activity (see also Münte, Schiltz, & Kutas, 1998).

CONCLUSIONS

Event-related potentials have proved to provide a useful tool for exploring individual differences in comprehension skills. Despite the apparent complexity of the ERP data, good and poor readers produced clearly different electrophysiological patterns in most experiments. Good readers produced responses that were more sensitive to manipulations in the reading task, showing a more extensive and discriminative brain activity to the most difficult, or less normative, versions of the sentences, such as syntactic garden-path, non-normative role assignment, joke comprehension, or elaborative inferences. In most cases the good readers' ERP pattern could be interpreted as a more extensive knowledge-based processing of less normative sentences. By contrast, poor readers' responses remain relatively insensitive to sentence-level manipulations in the reading task, because they tend to rely on a more superficial processing of discourse. They devote more cognitive resources to the visual encoding of sentences and to the lexical-associative processes, and they do not manage efficiently deeper background knowledge, such as schematic or situation model information.

These neurological results concur with behavioral studies showing that poor comprehenders fail to generate sentence-based and knowledge-based inferences (even when the text is present), but do not have difficulties processing at the word or syntactic levels. Moreover, teaching readers to generate inferences successfully improves comprehension.

As has happened regarding so many cognitive phenomena, we imagine that, in the end, the most viable account of skilled comprehension will be a "Multifactor" account. We can easily imagine that working memory capacity, suppression, and metacognitive processes work together in a complex, interdependent fashion. However, the knowledge-based account is useful in the sense that it provides a direction of remediation for students and educators. Knowing that a less skilled reader's working memory capacity may be low, or that he or she may lack the ability to suppress irrelevant information hardly provides hope that the comprehension gap will be bridged. In contrast, the focus on metacognitive reading strategies has led to a host of reading skill remediation techniques. And these techniques have successfully improved both text comprehension and academic performance.

REFERENCES

Baker, L. (1982). An evaluation of the role of metacognitive deficits in learning disabilities. *Topic in Leaning and Learning Disabilities, 2,* 27–35.

Baker, L. (1994). Fostering metacognitive development. In H. Reese (Ed.), *Advances in child development and behavior* (Vol. 25, pp. 201–239). San Diego: Academic Press.

Bartholow, B. D., Fabiani, M., Gratton, G., & Bettencourt, B. A. (2001). A psychophysiological examination of cognitive processing of affective responses to social expectancy violations. *Psychological Sciences, 12,* 197–204.

Bereiter, C., & Bird, M. (1985). Use of thinking aloud in identification and teaching of reading comprehension strategies. *Cognition and Instruction, 2,* 131–156.

Bransford, J. D., & Johnson, M. K. (1972). Contextual prerequisites for understanding: Some investigations of comprehension and recall. *Journal of Verbal Learning and Verbal Behavior, 11,* 717–726.

Cain, K. (1996). Story knowledge and comprehension skill. In C. Cornoldi & J. Oakhill (Eds.), *Reading comprehension difficulties* (pp. 167–192). Mahwah, NJ: Lawrence Erlbaum Associates.

Cantor, J., & Engle, R. (1993). Working memory capacity as long term memory activation: An individual-differences approach. *Journal of Experimental Psychology: Leaning, Memory, and Cognition, 19,* 1101–1114.

Case, R., Kurland, D., & Goldberg, J. (1982). Operational efficiency and the growth of short-term memory span. *Journal of Experimental Child Psychology, 33,* 384–404.

Chi, M. T. H., De Leeuw, N., Chiu, M., & LaVancher, C. (1994). Eliciting self-explanations improves understanding. *Cognitive Science, 18,* 439–477.

Chiesi, H. L., Spilich, G. J., & Voss, J. F. (1979). Acquisition of domain-related information in relation to high and low domain knowledge. *Journal of Verbal Learning and Verbal Behavior, 18,* 257–273.

Conway A., & Engle, R. (1994). Working memory and retrieval: A resource-dependent inhibition model. *Journal of Experimental Psychology: General, 123,* 354–373.

Cornoldi, C., & Oakhill, J. (1996). In C. Cornoldi and J. Oakhill (Eds.), *Reading comprehension difficulties.* Mahwah, NJ: Lawrence Erlbaum Associates.

Coulson, S., & Kutas, M. (2001). Getting it: Human event-related brain response to jokes in good and poor comprehenders. *Neuroscience Letters, 316,* 71–74.

Cowan, N. (1988). Evolving conceptions of memory storage, selective attention, and their mutual constraints within the human information system. *Psychological Bulletin, 104,* 163–191.

Daneman, M., & Carpenter, P. (1980). Individual differences in working memory and reading. *Journal of Verbal Learning and Verbal Behavior, 19,* 450–466.

Daneman, M., & Carpenter, P. (1983). Individual differences in integrating information between and within sentences. *Journal of Experimental Psychology: Learning, Memory, and Cognition, 9,* 561–584.

Daneman, M., & Merikle, P. (1996). Working memory and language comprehension: A meta-analysis. *Psychonomic-Bulletin-and-Review, 3,* 422–433.

Daneman, M., & Tardif, T. (1987). Working memory and reading skill re-examined. M. Coltheart (Ed.), *Attention and performance 12: The psychology of reading.* (pp. 491–508). Hillsdale, NJ: Lawrence Erlbaum Associates.

Dewitz, P., Carr, E., & Patberg, J. (1987). Effects of interference training on comprehension and comprehension monitoring. *Reading Research Quarterly, 22,* 99–121.

Díaz, J. M., León, I., & de Vega, M. (2003). Brain potentials during the reading of emotionally incongruent texts. *Thirteenth Annual Meeting of the Society for Text and Discourse,* June, Madrid.

Dixon, P., LeFevre, J. A., & Twilley, L. C. (1988). Word knowledge and working memory as predictors of reading skill. *Journal of Educational Psychology, 80,* 465–472.

Einstein, G. O., McDaniel, M. A., Owen, P. D., & Cote, N. C. (1990). Encoding and recall of texts: The importance of material appropriate processing. *Journal of Memory and Language, 29,* 566–581.

Engle, R. (1996). Working memory and retrieval: An inhibition-resource approach. In *Working memory and human cognition.* New York: Oxford University Press.

Engle, R., & Marshall, K. (1983). Do developmental changes in digit span result from acquisition strategies? *Journal of Experimental Child Psychology, 36,* 429–436.

Ericsson, K. A., & Kintch, W. (1995). Long-term working memory. *Psychological Review, 102,* 211–245.

Friederici, A. D. (2002). Towards a neural basis of auditory sentence processing. *Trends in Cognitive Sciences, 6,* 78–84.

Garner, R. (1987). *Metacognition and reading comprehension.* Norwood, NJ: Ablex.

Garnham, A., Oakhill, J., & Johnson-Laird, P. (1982). Referential continuity and the coherence of discourse. *Cognition, 11,* 29–46.

Gernsbacher, M. A. (1990). *Language comprehension as structure building.* Hillsdale, NJ: Lawrence Erlbaum Associates.

Gernsbacher, M. A., & Faust, M. (1991). The mechanism of suppression: A component of general comprehension skill. *Journal of Experimental Psychology: Learning, Memory, and Cognition, 17,* 245–262.

Gernsbacher, M. A., Varner, K. R., & Faust, M. (1990). Investigating differences in general comprehension skill. *Journal of Experimental Psychology: Learning, Memory, and Cognition, 16,* 430–445.

Haenggi, D., & Perfetti, C. (1994). Processing components of college-level reading comprehension. *Discourse Processes, 17,* 83–104.

Hansen, J., & Pearson, P. (1983). An instructional study: Improving the inferential comprehension of good and poor fourth-grade readers. *Journal of Educational Psychology, 75,* 821–829.

Hoover, W., & Gough, P. (1990). The simple view of reading. *Reading and Writing, 2,* 127–160.

Hulme, C., & Snowling, M. (1992). Phonological deficits in dyslexia: A "sound" reppraisal of the verbal deficit hypothesis. In N. Singh & I. Beale (Eds.), *Current perspectives in learning disabilities* (pp. 270–301). New York: Springer.

Just, M. A., & Carpenter, P. A. (1992). A capacity theory of comprehension: Individual differences in working memory. *Psychological Review, 99,* 122–149.

Kintsch, W. (1988). The use of knowledge in discourse processing: A construction-integration model. *Psychological Review, 95,* 163–182.

Kintsch, W. (1998). *Comprehension: A paradigm for cognition.* Cambridge, UK: Cambridge University Press.

Kucan, L., & Beck, I. (1997). Thinking aloud and reading comprehension research: Inquiry, instruction and social interaction. *Review of Educational Research, 67,* 271–299.

Kutas, M., & Hillyard, S. (1980). Event-related brain potentials to semantically inappropriate and surprisingly large words. *Biological Psychology, 11,* 99–116.

Kutas, M., & King, J. W (1996). The potentials for basic sentence processing: Differentiating integrative processes. In I. Ikeda & J. L. McClelland (Eds.), *Attention and Performance* (Vol. 16, pp. 501–46). Cambridge, MA: MIT Press.

Kutas, M., & Van Petten, C. (1994). Psycholinguistics electrified. In M. A. Gernsbacher (Ed.), *Handbook of psycholinguistics* (pp. 83–143). San Diego: Academic Press.

Long, D., & Golding, J. (1993). Superordinate goal inferences: Are they automatically generated during comprehension? *Discourse Processes, 16,* 55–74.

Long, D. L., Oppy, B. J., & Seely, M. R. (1994). Individual differences in the time course of inferential processing. *Journal of Experimental Psychology: Learning, Memory, and Cognition, 20,* 1456–1470.

MacDonald, M. C., & Christiansen, M. H. (2002). Reassessing working memory: Comment on Just and Carpenter (1992) and Waters and Caplan (1996). *Psychological Review, 109,* 35–54.

Magliano, J. P., & Millis, K. K. (2003). Assessing reading skill with a think-aloud procedure. *Cognition and Instruction, 21,* 251–283.

Magliano, J. P., Wiemer-Hastings, K., Millis, K. K., Muñoz, B. D., & McNamara, D. S. (2002). Using latent semantic analysis to assess reader strategies. *Behavior Research Methods, Instruments, and Computers, 34,* 181–188.

Mannes, S., & Kintsch, W. (1987). Knowledge organization and text organization. *Cognition and Instruction, 4,* 91–115.

McDaniel, M. A., Einstein, G. O., Dunay, P. K., & Cobb, R. (1986). Encoding difficulty and memory: Toward a unifying theory. *Journal of Memory and Language, 25,* 645–656.

McDaniel, M. A., Finstad, K. A., & McNamara, D. S. (2003). The suppression effect: Effects of word-level elaboration. Unpublished manuscript, University of New Mexico, Albuquerque.

McDaniel, M. A., Schmalhofer, F., & Keefe, D. (2001). What is minimal about predictive inferences? *Psychonomic Bulletin & Review, 8,* 840–846.

McNamara, D. S. (1997). Comprehension skill: A Knowledge-based account. In *Proceedings of Nineteenth Annual Meeting of the Cognitive Science Society* (pp. 508–513). Mahwah, NJ: Lawrence Erlbaum Associates.

McNamara, D. S. (2001). Reading both high-coherence and low-coherence texts: Effects of text sequence and prior knowledge. *Canadian Journal of Experimental Psychology, 55,* 51–62.

McNamara, D. S. (2004). SERT: Self-explanation reading training. *Discourse Processes, 38,* 1–30.

McNamara, D. S., & Kintsch, W. (1996). Learning from texts: Effects of prior knowledge and text coherence. *Discourse Processes, 22,* 247–288.

McNamara, D. S., Kintsch, E., Songer, N., & Kintsch, W. (1996). Are good texts always better? Interactions of text coherence, background knowledge, and levels of understanding in learning from text. *Cognition and Instruction, 14,* 1–43.

McNamara, D. S., & McDaniel, M. A. (2004). Suppressing irrelevant information: Knowledge activation or inhibition. *Journal of Experimental Psychology: Learning, Memory and Cognition, 30,* 465–482.

McNamara, D. S., & Scott, J. L. (1999). Training reading strategies. In M. Hahn & S. C. Stoness (Eds.), *Proceedings of the Twenty-first Annual Meeting of the Cognitive Science Society* (pp. 387–392). Mahwah, NJ: Lawrence Erlbaum Associates.

McNamara, D. S., & Scott, J. L. (2001). Working memory capacity and strategy use. *Memory & Cognition, 29,* 10–17.

Mueller, H. M., King, J. W., & Kutas, M. (1997). Event-related potentials to relative clause processing in spoken sentences. *Cognitive Brain Research, 5,* 193–203.

Münte, T. F., Schiltz, K., & Kutas, M. (1998). When temporal terms belie conceptual order. *Nature,* 395, 71–73.

Oakhill, J. (1982). Constructive processes in skilled and less skilled comprehenders' memory for sentences. *British Journal of Psychology, 73,* 13–20.

Oakhill, J. (1983). Instantiation in skilled and less skilled comprehenders. *Quarterly Journal of Experimental Psychology, 35,* 441–450.

Oakhill, J. (1984). Inferential and memory skills in children's comprehension of stories. *British Journal of Educational Psychology, 54,* 31–39.

Oakhill, J., & Yuill, N. (1986). Pronoun resolution in skilled and less skilled comprehenders: Effects of memory load and inferential complexity. *Language and speech, 29,* 25–37.

Oakhill, J., & Yuill, N. (1996). Higher order factors in comprehension disability: Processes and remediation. In C. Cornaldi & J. Oakhill (Eds.), *Reading comprehension difficulties: Processes and Intervention.* Mahwah, NJ: Lawrence Erlbaum Associates.

Oakhill, J., Yuill, N., & Donaldson, M. (1990). Understanding of causal expressions in skilled and less skilled text comprehenders. *British Journal of Developmental Psychology, 8,* 401–410.

Oakhill, J., Yuill, N., & Parkin, A. (1988). Memory and inference in skilled and less skilled comprehenders. In M. M. Gruneberg, P. E. Morris, and R. N. Sykes (Eds.), *Practical aspects of memory* 2 (pp. 315–320). Chichester: Wiley.

O'Brien, E. J., & Myers, J. L. (1985). When comprehension difficulty improves memory for text. *Journal of Experimental Psychology: Learning, Memory and Cognition, 11,* 12–21.

O'Reilly, T., & McNamara, D. S. (2007). Reversing the Reverse Cohesion Effect: Good Texts Can be Better for Strategic, High-Knowledge Readers. *Discourse Processes, 43*(2), 121–152.

Palincsar, A. S., & Brown, A. L. (1984). Reciprocal teaching of comprehension-fostering and monitoring activities. *Cognition and Instruction, 2,* 117–175.

Paris, S., Cross, D., & Lipson, M. (1984). Informed strategies for learning: A program to improve children's reading awareness and comprehension. *Journal of Educational Psychology, 76,* 1239–1252.

Paris, S., & Jacobs, J. (1984). The benefits of informed instruction for children's reading awareness and comprehension skills. *Child Development, 55,* 2083–2093.

Perfetti, C. (1985). *Reading ability*. New York: Oxford University Press.

Perfetti, C. (1989). There are generalized abilities and one of them is reading. In L. B. Resnick (Ed.), *Knowing, learning, and instruction: Essays in honor of Robert Glaser* (pp. 307–336). Hillsdale, NJ: Lawrence Erlbaum Associates.

Perfetti, C. A., & Hart, L. (2001). The lexical bases of comprehension skill. In David Gorfien (Ed.), *On the consequences of meaning selection* (pp. 67–86). Washington, DC: American Psychological Association.

Pressley, M., & Afflerbach, P. (1995). Verbal protocols of reading: *The nature of constructively responsive reading*. Hillsdale, NJ: Lawrence Erlbaum Associates.

Rauenbusch, F., & Bereiter, C. (1991). Making reading more difficult: A degraded text microworld for teaching reading comprehension strategies. *Cognition and Instruction, 8,* 181–206.

Rosen, V., & Engle, R. (1997). The role of working memory capacity in retrieval. *Journal of Experimental Psychology: General, 126,* 211–227.

Rosen, V., & Engle, R. (1998). Working memory capacity and suppression. *Journal of Memory and Language, 39,* 418–436.

Schmalhofer, F. (1998). Constructive knowledge acquisition: A computational model and experimental evaluation. Mahwah, NJ: Lawrence Erlbaum Associates.

Schmalhofer, F., McDaniel, M. A., & Keefe, D. (2002). A unified model for predictive and bridging inferences. *Discourse Processes, 33,* 105–132.

Shankweiler, D., Lundquist, E., Katz, L., Stuebing, K., Fletcher, J., Brady, S., et al., (1999). Comprehension and decoding: Patterns of association in children with reading difficulties. *Scientific Studies of Reading, 3,* 69–94.

Shiffrin, R., & Schneider, W. (1977). Controlled and automatic human information processing: II. Perceptual learning, automatic attending, and a general theory. *Psychological Review, 84,* 127–190.

Singer, M., Andrusiak, P., Reisdorf, P., & Black, N. (1992). Individual differences in bridging inference processes. *Memory & Cognition, 20,* 539–548.

Singer, M., & Ritchot, K. (1996). The role of working memory capacity and knowledge access in text inference processing. *Memory & Cognition, 24,* 733–743.

Snow, C. E., Burns, M., & Griffin, P. (1998). *Preventing reading difficulties in young children*. Washigton, DC: National Academy Press.

St. George, M., Mannes, S., & Hoffman, J. E. (1997). Individual differences in inference generation: An ERP analysis. *Journal of Cognitive Neuroscience, 9*, 776–787.

Stanovich, K., West, R., Cunningham, A., Cipielewski, J., & Siddequi, S. (1996). In C. C. Cornoldi & J. Oakhill (Eds.), *Reading comprehension difficulties: Processes and intervention*. Mahwah, NJ: Lawrence Erlbaum Associates.

Stothard, S. E., & Hulme, C. (1996). A comparison of reading comprehension and decoding difficulties in children. In C. Cornoldi and J. Oakhill (Eds.), *Reading comprehension difficulties* (pp. 93–112). Mahwah, NJ: Lawrence Erlbaum Associates.

Turner, M., & Engle, R. (1989). Is working memory capacity task dependent? *Journal of Memory and Language, 28*, 127–154.

Van Petten, C., Weckerly, J., McIsaac, H. K., & Kutas, M. *(1997).* Working memory capacity dissociates lexical and sentential context effects. *Psychological Science, 8*, 238–242.

Vos, S. H., & Friederici, A. D. (2003). Intersentential syntactic context effects on comprehension: the role of working memory. *Cognitive Brain Research, 16*, 111–122.

Whitney, P., Ritchie, B., & Clark, M. (1991). Working memory capacity and the use of elaborative inferences in text comprehension. *Discourse Processes, 14*, 133–145.

Wong, B. (1985). Metacognition and learning disabilities. In D. Forrest-Pressley, G. MacKinnon, & T. Waller (Eds.), *Metacognition, cognition, and human performance* (Vol. 2, pp. 137–180). New York: Academic Press.

Yuill, N., & Oakhill, J. (1988). Understanding of anaphoric relations in skilled and less skilled comprehenders. *British Journal of Psychology, 79*, 173–186.

Yuill, N., & Oakhill, J. (1991). *Children's problems in text comprehension: An experimental investigation*. Cambridge monographs and texts in applied psycholinguistics. New York: Cambridge University Press.

Yuill, N., Oakhill, J., & Parkin, A. (1989). Working memory, comprehension ability and the resolution of text anomaly. *British Journal of Psychology, 80*, 351–361.

IV

COGNITIVE REPRESENTATIONS

11

The Experiential View of Language Comprehension: How Is Negation Represented?

Barbara Kaup and Jana Lüdtke
Technical University of Berlin

Rolf A. Zwaan
Florida State University

Consider the following anecdote: *A young boy is separated from his mother on an afternoon visit to a very busy fair. After a while he starts questioning the passers-by: "Have you seen a lady who is without a young boy who looks a little like me?"* What is odd about the boy's question? Describing his mother in terms of what is missing might seem natural to the boy, but to the listener, who is facing the task of identifying the boy's mother from a group of many potential referents, it most likely constitutes a rather useless description of the target entity. After all, what does a woman look like, who is without a particular boy, who may be wearing a green jacket? Doesn't she, at least without further knowledge, look exactly like a woman who went to the fair without her five-year-old daughter who happened to be wearing a blue sweatshirt that day, or for that matter like any other woman of appropriate age who went to the fair by herself? To the listener, the problem must therefore seem nearly unsolvable. The boy's description simply does not allow for construction of a specific mental representation of the target referent, which could then be compared with the previously formed perceptual representations of the various female visitors to the fair.

The difficulty of creating a specific mental representation of the boy's mother seems to spring from the fact that, apart from specifying the target entity as being female, the boy's description concerns only properties of an entity whose presence is explicitly negated. What the anecdote illustrates is that the information conveyed by negative assertions of this type is not useful when it comes to creating a visual representation. However, does this imply that negated information is not represented in a nonlinguistic fashion?

There is growing evidence in the literature that the creation of nonlinguistic representations is an important component of language comprehension. Considering that negation is an important and frequently used linguistic operator, it seems unlikely that negative information would simply not be included in nonlinguistic representations. Instead, our cognitive apparatus is probably more flexible and provides some kind of mechanism by which negative information can be represented—even when the representations in question are nonlinguistic in nature and therefore do not allow an explicit representation of negation. This prompts the question of how negation is represented in a nonlinguistic format.

The present chapter addresses this question. The first section briefly outlines the experiential view of language comprehension. This view conceptualizes comprehension as the construction of an experiential simulation of the described situation. This simulation can be thought of as a vicarious experience of the described situation. The second section provides an overview of empirical findings relevant to the question of how negation is represented in language comprehension. The third section introduces a hypothesis of how negation might be implicitly represented in experiential simulations. The fourth section addresses the question of whether the findings reported in the second section are consistent with this hypothesis. The fifth section reports the results of a series of experiments that directly tested our hypothesis regarding the nonlinguistic representation of negation. Finally, the sixth section summarizes our main conclusions.

THE EXPERIENTIAL VIEW OF LANGUAGE COMPREHENSION

There is growing evidence in the literature that comprehending a text should be conceived of as the construction of a so-called *situation model* or *mental model*, a mental representation of the described state of affairs (Glenberg, Meyer, & Lindem, 1987; Graesser, Millis, & Zwaan, 1997; Johnson Laird, 1983; Morrow, Bower, & Greenspan, 1990; van Dijk & Kintsch, 1983; Zwaan & Radvansky, 1998). Situation models are nonlinguistic representations, as their components are not propositions about particular aspects of the described state of affairs, but tokens standing for the entities and properties that make up this state of affairs.

Recently, the notion that situation models are of a representational format that is the same as that utilized in other nonlinguistic cognitive processes (e.g., perception, action, imagery) has been gaining in importance in text comprehension research (e.g., Barsalou, 1999; Glenberg, 1997; Glenberg & Kaschak, 2002; Glenberg & Robertson, 2000; Kelter, 2003; Kelter, Kaup, & Claus, 2004; MacWhinney, 1999; Stanfield & Zwaan, 2001; Zwaan, 2004; Zwaan & Madden, 2005; see also Johnson-Laird, 1983). Proponents of this notion of situation models believe that comprehenders construct mental simulations of the states of affairs described in the text. These mental simulations are considered to be experiential in nature, as they are assumed to be grounded in perception and action. Accordingly, as Johnson Laird put it already in 1983, "A major function of language is thus to enable us to experience the world by proxy" (p. 471).

There is already some empirical evidence for the experiential view of language comprehension (for an overview see Zwaan, 2004, and the contributions in Pecher & Zwaan, 2005). On the one hand there are neuroscience studies that directly show a considerable overlap between the mental subsystems in which linguistically conveyed situational information is represented and those that are involved when these situations are directly perceived or enacted (e.g., Pulvermüller, 2002; Pulvermüller, Härle, & Hummel, 2000). On the other hand, behavioral data suggest that language comprehension leads to the creation of representations in those mental subsystems that are utilized in other nonlinguistic cognitive processes such as action planning, perception, or imagery. Two different types of findings can be distinguished.

The first type of finding indicates that the representations constructed in language comprehension have properties in common with representations constructed in nonlinguistic cognition. These kinds of equivalence effects have been demonstrated in a number of studies—for instance, with respect to the representations' spatial extendedness, which provides a basis for mental scanning processes (e.g., Glenberg et al., 1987; Morrow et al., 1990; Rinck & Bower, 1995), with respect to the size-resolution trade-off principle (Kaup, Kelter, & Habel, 1999), and with respect to the representations' dynamic nature (Kelter et al., 2004; Zwaan, Madden, Yaxley, & Aveyard, 2004; Kaschak et al., 2005). All of these are well-documented properties of representations constructed in visual-spatial imagery (mental scanning and size-resolution trade-off: e.g., Baddeley, 1986; Kosslyn, 1994; dynamic nature: e.g., Freyd, 1987, 1993). Equivalence effects have also been shown with respect to processing costs associated with switching between the different modalities. In perceptual tasks, processing a stimulus in an unexpected modality leads to prolonged response times (Spence, Nicholls, & Driver, 2001). In a semantic priming study, Pecher, Zeelenberg, and Barsalou (2003) obtained the same pattern of results when participants were presented with noun-adjective pairs and evaluated whether the corresponding property held for the object under consideration. Response times were shorter when the evaluated property of an object was from the same modality as the property of the previous pair compared with when it was from a different modality. Finally, recent eye-tracking studies indicate that participants listening to the description of a complex scene tend to make eye movements that mimic the kinds of eye movements that would be made if they were viewing that actual scene (e.g., Spivey, Tyler, Richardson, & Young, 2000).

The second type of finding concerns facilitation or interference effects due to similarities or dissimilarities between the experimental task on the one hand and the content of the described state of affairs on the other hand. For instance, Glenberg and Kaschak (2002) found that responses to a sentence-sensibility judgment task, involving sentences such as *He closed a drawer*, were faster when the hand movement required for correctly responding to the task matched the movement implied by the sentence (e.g., movement toward the comprehender) compared with when there was a mismatch (e.g., movement away from the comprehender; see also Klatzky, Pellegrino, McCloskey, & Doherty, 1989). Similarly, Zwaan and colleagues (e.g., Stanfield & Zwaan, 2001; Zwaan, Stanfield, & Yaxley, 2002) demonstrated in a series of experiments that responding to a depicted object (e.g., an eagle) after reading of a sentence mentioning this object (e.g., *The ranger saw an eagle in the sky*) was easier when the depicted shape or orientation of the object matched the shape or orientation implied by the sentence (e.g., the depicted eagle has its wings outstretched) compared with when there was a mismatch (e.g., the depicted eagle has folded wings). Match/mismatch effects were also found when participants were presented with individual words instead of sentences. More specifically, Zwaan and Yaxley (2003a, 2003b) presented pairs of words (e.g., *attic–basement*) on a computer screen, with one word appearing below the other. Participants were faster in judging the semantic relatedness of the words when their spatial relation on the computer screen matched their spatial relation in the world (i.e., *attic* on top) than when the relations mismatched (i.e., *basement* on top).

Interference has also been demonstrated in studies that investigated the impact of spatial or visuospatial secondary tasks on the success of constructing nonlinguistic representations during text comprehension. Fincher-Kiefer (2001), for instance, presented readers of short stories with either a visuospatial or a verbal memory load and found that situation-model construction was significantly impaired with the former but not with the latter secondary task. The results of a study by Kaup et al. (1999) suggest that spatial aspects of a described situation are easier to represent when the corresponding narrative was presented auditorily than when it was presented visually. The disadvantage in the visual condition can be attributed to the fact that reading but not listening requires the control of eye movements, which in turn can be considered a spatial task that may cause interference with creating a nonlinguistic spatial representation (cf. Baddeley, 1986).

To summarize, research conducted in the context of the experiential view of language comprehension has produced a number of findings suggesting that comprehenders mentally simulate the state of affairs described by the linguistic input in a way that is similar to directly experiencing or reexperiencing this state of affairs. These findings therefore illustrate that language comprehension is in important ways equivalent to creating representations in the same mental subsystems as those used in other sensorimotor processes. As such, these findings support the experiential view of language comprehension.

The linguistic materials used in these studies were mostly simple descriptions of concrete situations, making it relatively straightforward to hypothesize about experiential representations to which they would give rise. It has been proposed that abstract concepts are grounded in perception and action via the process of metaphorical extension (Lakoff, 1987; Lakoff & Johnson, 1980; however, see Barsalou & Wiemer-Hastings, 2005, for an alternative account). Recent studies have demonstrated experiential effects with abstract concepts. For instance, Glenberg and Kaschak (2002) presented subjects with sentences such as *He told me the story* or *I told him the story*, describing states of affairs in which—metaphorically speaking—information moves toward or away from the comprehender. These sentences produced action-compatibility effects similar to those of the more concrete sentences (e.g., *He opened the drawer*; see also Boroditsky, 2000; Boroditsky & Ramscar, 2002).

However, a potentially even bigger hurdle for experiential theories is produced by the existence of linguistic operators, such as negation or disjunction, for which there does not seem to be a direct equivalence in experience. Obviously this hurdle needs to be cleared if the experiential view is meant to hold for language processing in general. With respect to negation, the experiential view faces two challenges. First, the experiential view needs to clarify how negated text information can be captured in a representation that does not allow for the explicit representation of negation. Second, the experiential view needs to account for existing empirical findings pertaining to the representation of negation in language comprehension. Before outlining a hypothesis regarding the representation of negation in experiential representations, we provide an overview of empirical findings concerning negation in language comprehension.

EMPIRICAL FINDINGS RELATED TO THE REPRESENTATION OF NEGATION

The Impact of Negation on Processing Difficulty

A considerable amount of research into the processing of negation was conducted in the 1960s and 1970s. In numerous studies employing a variety of different methods and materials, participants were presented with sentences or sentence fragments that either did or did not contain negative particles. Most of these studies employed sentence-verification tasks in which the sentences were to be verified either against background knowledge (e.g., Arroyo, 1982; Eiferman, 1961; Wales & Grieve, 1969; Wason, 1961; Wason & Jones, 1963) or against a picture that was presented before or after the corresponding sentence (e.g., Carpenter & Just, 1975; Clark & Chase, 1972; Gough, 1965, 1966; Just & Carpenter, 1971; Trabasso, Rollins, & Shaughnessy, 1971). Other studies employed sentence completion tasks (e.g., Donaldson,

1970; de Villiers & Tager Flusberg, 1975; Wason, 1959, 1961, 1965). Yet other studies investigated the impact of negation more indirectly, for instance by measuring the number of inferences that were drawn from negative sentences compared with the number of inferences drawn from affirmative sentences (e.g., Just & Clark, 1973), by measuring how well negative instructions are followed (e.g., Jones, 1966, 1968), or by investigating the impact of a negative object description in object-selection tasks (Donaldson, 1970). In all of these studies, negative sentences were harder to process than affirmative sentences, as evidenced by longer processing times and/or higher error rates for negative sentences compared with affirmative sentences. A negation effect was observed across a variety of different experimental paradigms and with a variety of different negative sentences. A negation effect was not only observed with explicit negation (e.g., 1a, 2a), but also with implicit negation (e.g., 1b, 2b) or when explicit negative particles were replaced with artificial syllables with equivalent function (e.g., Trabasso et al., 1971; Wason & Jones, 1963). A negation effect was observed for regular sentence negation (e.g., 3a), but also when the sentence was embedded in an *It is true . . .* phrase (e.g., 3b), which forces a reading in which the negation operator applies specifically to the predicate of the sentence. Moreover, the negation effect seems to be independent of the negation operator's position in the sentence as long as the operator's semantic scope is not affected (e.g., 4a and 4b). Finally, negative sentences are harder to process not only when they are less specific than their affirmative counterparts (e.g., 5a and 5b), but also when affirmative sentences with the same truth conditions can be inferred either because the sentences contain complementary terms (6b follows from 6a) or because the experiment employs only two different contrary predicates (e.g., 7b "follows" from 7a):

(1) a: The circle is not present.
    b: The circle is absent. (Chase & Clark, 1971)
(2) a: None of the dots are red.
    b: Few of the dots are red. (Just & Carpenter, 1971)
(3) a: The dots are not red.
    b: It is true that the dots are not red. (Carpenter & Just, 1975)
(4) a: That the dots are red is not true.
    b: It is not true that the dots are red. (Carpenter & Just, 1975)
(5) a: There is both green and yellow.
    b: There is not both green and yellow. (Wason, 1959)
(6) a: Seven is not an even number.
    b: Seven is an odd number. (Wason, 1961)
(7) a: The dots are not red.
    b: The dots are black. (Just & Carpenter, 1971)

Various explanations have been proposed to account for the difference in processing difficulty between affirmative and negative sentences. An obvious explanation is that negative sentences necessarily contain an extra syllable compared with the corresponding affirmative sentences. However, the reading time differences that are due to this extra syllable can at best account for a small part of the processing differences between affirmative and negative sentences (Clark & Chase, 1972). First, the time needed to process the extra syllable is estimated to be between 25 and 90 ms (cf. Clark & Chase, 1972) but the negation effect is of a magnitude of several hundred milliseconds. Second, in sentence-picture verification tasks, negative sentences are significantly harder to verify than affirmative sentences, even when the picture is not presented until 3 seconds after the end of the sentence read (Gough, 1966). A related explanatory attempt was based on Chomsky's (1957) transformational grammar. Negative sentences are assumed to be harder to process than affirmative sentences, because the former presumably involve a greater number of grammatical transformations than the latter. However, this explanation has proved to be untenable for theoretical (cf. Jackendoff, 1969; Partee, 1970) as well as empirical (cf. Gough, 1965; 1966; Slobin, 1966) reasons.

Another explanatory attempt is related to connotation. Participants often report that negative sentences have an unpleasant connotation because of their association with prohibition (cf. Wason & Johnson-Laird, 1972). Studies that addressed this hypothesis directly mostly produced ambiguous results (Eiferman, 1961; Wason & Jones, 1963; for a discussion see Clark, 1974).

The most convincing explanation for the processing difficulty associated with negative sentences is a pragmatic one, which was first put forward by Wason (1965). Outside of the laboratory, negative sentences are typically not uttered unless the proposition being negated was explicitly mentioned by one of the discourse partners (A: *I was told you went to Paris last year*. B: *No, I did not.*) or could plausibly be inferred from the discourse context (*My train was not late this morning,* uttered in a context in which the speaker's train is usually late; Wason, 1972; see also Clark, 1974, p. 1312; Givon, 1978). In a majority of the studies that produced a main effect of negation, the negative sentences were presented without a context that would have pragmatically legitimized the negation. Negative sentences may therefore have been particularly difficult to process because participants needed to infer such a legitimizing context retrospectively. In accordance with this pragmatic hypothesis, the negation effect is considerably diminished when negative sentences are presented within an adequate context (Wason, 1965; Glenberg, Robertson, Jansen, & Johnson-Glenberg, 1999; see also Arroyo, 1982; Cornish, 1971; Greene, 1970; de Villiers & Tager Flusberg, 1975). It should be noted, however, that even in pragmatically felicitous contexts, negative sentences are often still harder to process than the corresponding affirmative sentences. Thus, the negation effect may only be partially explained by the pragmatic hypothesis.

The Impact of the Sentence's Truth Value

As mentioned earlier, most of the studies discussed above employed a sentence-verification task. Thus, these studies provided information not only with respect to the affirmation/negation manipulation, but also with respect to the truth value of the sentence that was being verified. Although very stable results were obtained with respect to the impact of the negation operator, the various studies do not allow definite conclusions about the impact of the sentence's truth value. In some studies, false sentences were generally harder to process than true sentences, independent of whether or not they contained a negation operator (Arroyo, 1982; Eiferman, 1961; Gough, 1965; Trabasso et al., 1971; see also Wason, 1959, 1961). The majority of the studies, however, have produced a negation by truth value interaction. Whereas true affirmative sentences [e.g., (8)] are easier to evaluate than false affirmative sentences [e.g., (9)], the opposite holds for negative sentences; here, true sentences [e.g., (11)] are more difficult to process than false ones [e.g., (10)].

(8) The star is above the plus. (true affirmative)
(9) The plus is above the star. (false affirmative)
(10) The star is not above the plus. (false negative)
(11) The plus is not above the star. (true negative)

Processing Strategies

To account for the two patterns of verification latencies, it was suggested that comprehenders encode the pictures, just like the sentences, in a propositional format. The two representations are then compared constituent by constituent, with the comparison process being easier when the two constituents are congruent than when they are incongruent (for a detailed description of the model, see Carpenter & Just, 1975; Clark & Chase, 1972). Two strategies can be distinguished that produce the two observed response time patterns (main effect of truth value vs. truth value by negation interaction).

The negation by truth value interaction arises when participants are using the original sentence representation for the comparison process. For true affirmative sentences [e.g., (8)], the predicate in the sentence representation matches the predicate in the picture representation [both: above (star, plus)], whereas for false affirmatives [e.g., (9)] the two predicates mismatch [sentence: above (plus, star); picture: above (star, plus)]. This explains why false affirmatives take longer to verify than true affirmatives. In contrast, for negatives, it is the false case in which the predicates match [e.g., (10); sentence: not(above(star,plus)); picture: above(star,plus))], and the true case where there is a mismatch [e.g., (11); sentence: not(above(plus, star)); picture: above(star, plus))]. This explains why true negatives take longer to verify than false negatives. Thus, the negation by truth value interaction can be accounted for by these assumptions. The main effect of negation is explained similarly. For negative sentences, the sentence representation contains a negation marker that mismatches with the affirmative picture representation. Accordingly, negative sentences take longer to verify than affirmative sentences.

The strategy producing a main effect of truth value differs from the preceding strategy in that participants convert the negative sentence into an affirmative one with the same truth conditions before starting the comparison process [e.g., (10) is converted into (9) and (11) into (8)]. After this conversion, true sentences imply a match and false sentence imply a mismatch, which explains the main effect of truth value. The main effect of negation is attributed to the fact that converting a negative sentence into an affirmative sentence takes time.

Despite the many studies in which negation and truth value were being manipulated, there are still no definite criteria for when participants employ one or the other strategy. However, all in all, the conditions that produced a main effect of truth value are more or less consistent with the conversion assumption. A main effect of truth value has mainly been observed under conditions in which conversion is possible and plausible, namely (1) when the experimental task was extensively practiced (e.g., Carpenter & Just, 1975), (2) when the sentence was presented prior to the picture (e.g., Trabasso et al., 1971), (3) when there was a delay between presenting the sentence and presenting the picture (e.g., Carpenter & Just, 1975), (4) when the predicates were complementary (*odd* and *even*) or when the experiment employed only two contrary predicates (*red* and *black*) (e.g., Trabasso et al., 1971; Wason, 1961; Wason & Jones, 1963; see also Mayo, Schul, & Burnstein, 2004; Kroll & Corrigan, 1981), (5) when participants were instructed accordingly (cf. Clark, 1974), and (6) when participants were adults as opposed to children (Slobin, 1966).

Some researchers have pointed out that a main effect of truth value is consistent with a pictorial strategy in which participants encode the sentence pictorially and then directly compare this representation to the representation of the picture. In a study by MacLeod, Hunt, and Mathews (1978), the group of participants who produced a main effect of truth value was found to have higher spatial abilities than the group of participants who produced a truth value by negation interaction, whereas the two groups did not differ in linguistic abilities. Also, for the former group sentence verification times were correlated with spatial abilities, whereas for the latter group they were correlated with linguistic abilities (see also Mathews, Hunt, & MacLeod, 1980). This finding is usually taken as positive evidence for the claim that the truth value main effect reflects a pictorial rather than a recoding strategy. However, some authors have noted that it is problematic to divide the participants into different strategy groups on the basis of their performance on the experimental task alone, because the same response time patterns may reflect very different strategies (Marquer & Pereira, 1990). It has also been argued that diagnosed high spatial or verbal abilities do not allow the researcher to deduce that a particular subject is using a pictorial or verbal strategy (Roberts, Wood, & Gilmore, 1994). Other studies have explicitly instructed participants to use one or the other strategy, and the similarity of the results to the respective response time patterns in the "free choice" condition is again taken as evidence for the claim that pictorial strategies are being used (e.g., Mathews et al., 1980; Reichle, Carpenter, & Just, 2000; Richards & Frensch, 1987). However, as before, it seems questionable that the mere similarity of the response time patterns affords the inference that the same strategies were being employed.

To summarize, in the context of sentence-verification studies, most authors believe that sentences are by default encoded in a propositional format in which negation is explicitly represented and takes a whole proposition into its scope. Different response time patterns are attributed to different modification processes that operate on these propositional representations. Strategies involving other kinds of representations (i.e., spatial representations) are considered special cases that (at best) are exhibited under conditions in which participants are specifically instructed.

Negation and Accessibility

More recent studies have been concerned with more local effects of negation, namely with the question of whether negation has an impact on the accessibility of information mentioned within its scope. For instance, in a study by MacDonald and Just (1989), participants were presented with sentences such as (12), and immediately afterward the accessibility of the relevant concepts was measured by means of a probe-recognition or word-naming task. Probe words that had been mentioned in the negated phrase (*cookies*) yielded significantly longer response times than probe words mentioned in the nonnegated phrase (*bread*) (for a similar effect with inferred concepts, see Lea & Mulligan, 2002). MacDonald and Just took their results as support for the hypothesis that readers construct a propositional representation in which the negation operator encapsulates the information mentioned in its scope and thereby specifically reduces the accessibility of this information.

(12) Almost every weekend Mary bakes some bread but no cookies for the children.

A study by Kuschert (1999) similarly showed that resolving a pronominal anaphor takes more time if the referent is introduced in the context of a double negation [e.g., (13)] than when it is introduced within an affirmative phrase [e.g., (14)]. The same results were not obtained for entities outside of the negation's scope (e.g., *I had met him in the mall this morning.*), which rules out that the effect is due to a general increase in processing times for material that follows a negated sentence.

(13) I contradicted Jim's report that Oliver does not have a big sister. I had met her in the mall this morning.

(14) I confirmed Jim's report that Oliver has a big sister. I had met her in the mall this morning.

An accessibility-reducing effect of negation is not obtained, however, when instead of explicitly mentioned concepts, associates of these concepts are being probed. More specifically, MacDonald and Just did not find evidence for the hypothesis that reading a sentence containing a negative such as *no bread* also reduces the accessibility of a word associated with the negated noun (e.g., *butter*). In line with this latter finding, Giora, Balaban, Fein, and Alkabets (2004) found that associates (e.g., *piercing*) were activated independently of whether the activating concept (e.g., *sharp*) was or was not negated in the sentence (e.g., *This instrument is sharp* versus *This instrument is not sharp*). Similarly, in an evaluative priming study by Deutsch (2002), priming effects were independent of whether the primes were modified by an affirmative or negative determiner (e.g., prime: *a party* versus *no party*; see also Draine, 1997). These latter findings may of course reflect a fast-acting surface-level priming component of language processing (cf. Albrecht & Myers, 1998; Kintsch, 1988; McKoon & Ratcliff, 1998). In other words, different priming results may emerge with longer SOAs.

To summarize, there is considerable evidence that negation has an accessibility-reducing effect in language comprehension, the effect being restricted to concepts explicitly mentioned within the negation operator's scope. Most authors take this finding as indirect evidence for the view that comprehenders construct a propositional representation of the linguistic input in which negation is being explicitly encoded. Let us now turn to an alternative view, according to which negation is not explicitly but only implicitly encoded during language comprehension.

HOW IS NEGATION REPRESENTED IN EXPERIENTIAL SIMULATIONS?

The experiential view conceptualizes language comprehension as the performance of a sensorimotor simulation of the described sequence of events. Negation, being a linguistic operator, cannot be assumed to be represented explicitly in these nonlinguistic experiential simulations. This prompts the question of how negated text information can be captured in terms of a sensorimotor simulation. In some cases, negative statements allow inference of affirmative propositions with equivalent truth conditions. In these cases, it seems possible that negative text information is represented via representation of the affirmative inference. Thus, for instance, for (15), the comprehender would represent a female surgeon:

(15) Ann entered the office and was surprised to find out that the surgeon was not male.

However, first, there are aspects of meaning other than those related to the truth conditions (e.g., pragmatic aspects), and these typically go missing when a negative statement is transformed into an affirmative statement with the same truth conditions. Second, and more important, in most cases, the sentence or text does not allow inference of an affirmative statement with the same truth conditions. Take for instance text (16):

(16) Charles had been very lucky to get hold of tickets for a concert by the Berlin Philharmonic Orchestra for tonight. He was now sitting in the fifth row of the concert hall, from where he had a real good view of the stage. Finally, the musicians entered the hall. Charles knew that the concert would begin any minute now. Then, he suddenly realized that the conductor was not present.

Here the presence of the conductor is explicitly negated, and intuitively, the experiential simulation constructed for (16) therefore does not contain a representation of the conductor. Yet, if this were the case, then the simulation would not allow the comprehender to determine what the text was about. More specifically, on the basis of the experiential simulation alone, the comprehender would not be able to tell whether the text specified the conductor as being absent, or whether there just had not been any information regarding the conductor. Moreover, the experiential simulation would be exactly the same, independently of the particular entity mentioned in the fifth sentence of the text. Thus, the experiential representation would not even allow the comprehender to rule out that, for instance, Elvis Presley had been mentioned as not being present.

It does not seem plausible to assume that negated text information is absent from the experiential representations constructed in language comprehension. If the experiential view is intended to hold for language comprehension in general, then there must be a mechanism by which negated text information can be captured in these representations. One possibility suggests itself when the pragmatics of negation is taken into account.

As mentioned earlier, the contexts in which negative utterances occur are rather limited. Typically, negative statements are uttered when the negated proposition was either explicitly mentioned before by one of the discourse partners or at least constitutes a plausible assumption in the respective context. Thus, negation is used to communicate deviations from expectations (Givón, 1978; Glenberg et al., 1999; Wason, 1965; see also Arroyo, 1982; Cornish, 1971; Greene, 1970; de Villiers & Tager Flusberg, 1975). Applied to the example text in (16), this implies that a sentence such as *The conductor was not present* should only be produced in a context where a conductor's presence can be presupposed. Assuming that comprehenders not only represent explicitly stated information, but also infer information that is highly likely in the current context (see Singer, 1994, for an overview on inferencing), a conductor representation should be present in the mental simulation that is available prior to encountering the sentence containing the negation. If so, the negation would give rise to the deletion of this representation and the new mental simulation would deviate from the expected mental simulation by not containing a conductor representation. A comparison of the two simulations would allow the comprehender to determine what the text was about. The new simulation implicitly contains the information that a conductor was not present.

However, it is not warranted to assume that the mental simulation prompted by a negative sentence necessarily contains the exact information that the sentence negates. For instance in (17), the negation seems pragmatically felicitous, but the expectation regarding the presence of a teacher's aid is presumably not strong enough to insert a respective token into the simulation during processing of the first part of the text.

(17) Mr. Brigham works as a high school teacher. Tonight was open house. He entered the meeting room at 8 pm and quickly scanned the room to see whose parents were present. Lots of parents had come, but Mrs. Simonis, the teacher's aid, was missing.

Yet this does not mean that the mental simulation could not implicitly contain the information about the aid's absence. Given the assumptions about the pragmatic licensing conditions for negative sentences, it is possible to assume that negative sentences convey information not only about the actual state of affairs (the teacher's aid is absent), but also about the expected state of affairs (the teacher's aid is present), with this latter information constituting the presupposition that is being denied in the sentence (cf. Clark, 1986; Horn, 1989; Wason, 1965; see also Moxey, Sanford, & Dawydiak, 2001). Thus, the negative sentence in (17) presumably introduces or activates the expectation that a teacher's aid is present at a high school open house. As a consequence, a simulation of the expected state of affairs most likely contains a representation of a teacher's aid. Comparing this simulation to the mental simulation for the actual state of affairs allows the comprehender to determine that the teacher's aid was absent from the meeting.

In view of these considerations, we hypothesize that negative text information is implicitly encoded in the deviation between the mental simulations of the actual and the expected state of affairs. Two cases are to be distinguished. The first case is where the negated text information is already represented in the mental simulation that is available prior to encountering the negation (cf. Kaup, 1999). In this case, all the comprehender needs to do is create a mental simulation of the actual state of affairs, which deviates from the prior simulation with regard to the negated information. The second case is where the negated information is not represented in the model that is available upon encountering the negation, be it because the negative sentence was presented out of context, or because the respective expectation was not strong enough to trigger forward inferences of the required type. For this case, we assume that the comprehender does two things: first, construct a mental simulation of the expected state of affairs, which corresponds to the state of affairs that is being negated in the sentence, and second, construct a mental simulation of the actual state of affairs (cf. Fauconnier, 1985; Langacker, 1991). Thus, for instance, when processing an isolated sentence such as *The conductor was not present in the concert hall*, the comprehender first simulates a concert hall with a conductor and then a concert hall without a conductor. We will call this the *two-step simulation hypothesis of negation*.

Negative sentences often do not specify the actual situation with respect to the dimension that was affected by the negation. For instance, the sentence *Susan's dress was not red* does not specify the actual color of Susan's dress. In cases such as these, the actual simulation leaves unspecified the dimension of the negated property; it only contains the affirmative information (if any) that the negative sentence conveys. Thus, for the given example, the actual simulation would contain Susan with a dress of an unspecified color. Experiential simulations are radically different in this sense from pictorial representations. They are much less restricted with respect to what can be left unspecified. For instance, whereas a picture cannot contain the information that a particular entity A is next to an entity B without specifying whether A is to the left or to the right of B, an experiential representation does not need to specify spatial relations in this manner (cf. Barsalou, 1999, section 2.2.4). Thus, in processing a sentence such as *The star is not above the plus*, the simulation of the actual state of affairs would contain a star and a plus while leaving the spatial relation between the two unspecified. After all, the star could be next to the plus, on the right or left, or below it, or at a range of oblique angles. Of course, the comprehender could under certain conditions make an inference about the actual property on the negated dimension. For instance, if the star can be either above or below a plus, a sentence like *The star is not above the plus* most likely prompts the inference that the star must be below the plus. If so, the actual simulation would be specified with respect to the negated dimension. Sentences with complementary negation (e.g., *The surgeon was not male*) provide an interesting case in point. On the one hand they do not explicitly specify the actual situation with respect to the negated dimension, but on the other hand they provide enough information that the actual property can be inferred with 100% certainty. Again, whether the actual simulation is specified with respect to the negated dimension (i.e., surgeon's gender) depends on whether the comprehender made the respective inference. Complementary negation differs from the previous cases only in the likelihood that such an inference is actually made.

ACCOUNTING FOR THE FINDINGS IN SECTION 2

General Processing Difficulty

The *two-step simulation hypothesis* of negation can readily account for the elevated processing times and high error rates associated with negative sentences. Processing a negative sentence typically involves the manipulation of two simulations, whereas processing an affirmative sentence normally involves only one. This additional step required for negative sentences compared with affirmative sentences provides a likely explanation for the difference in processing cost. The fact that this difference in processing cost between affirmative and negative sentences is attenuated when the negative sentences are presented in a pragmatically adequate context is predicted by the hypothesis. In a pragmatically appropriate context, the negated information had already been simulated when the negation was encountered, or at least fits particularly well with contextually appropriate background knowledge. Thus, the first step of the two-step process either has already been performed or should be fairly easy to perform, resulting in shorter overall response times compared with a condition without an adequate context.

Truth Value

The two-step simulation hypothesis can also account for the two different patterns that were observed in sentence-verification studies with respect to the impact of the sentence's truth value on processing times. A negation by truth value interaction comes about when response times are faster for false negatives than they are for true negatives. Responses are fast when the picture matches the *negated* situation. In contrast, a main effect of truth value is observed when true negatives lead to shorter response times than false ones. Response times are short when the picture matches the *actual* situation. *The two-step simulation hypothesis* posits that two simulations are involved in the processing of a negated sentence, a simulation of the expected (negated) situation and a simulation of the actual situation. This predicts match effects for both simulations.

The interesting question is whether the conditions under which one or the other match effect is observed correspond to the predictions of the *two-step simulation hypothesis*. Directly in line with this hypothesis is the finding that inserting a delay between the end of the sentence and the presentation of the picture enhances the probability of finding a main effect of truth value (e.g.,

Carpenter & Just, 1975). With no delay, comprehenders are likely still simulating the negated state of affairs. From a certain delay on, however, they have presumably started simulating the actual situation. As a consequence, responses after a certain delay depend on the match or mismatch with the actual situation, not with the negated situation. Similarly, the reason that extensive practice (e.g., Carpenter & Just, 1975) and high spatial ability (e.g., MacLeod et al., 1978) led to a main effect of truth value suggests that practiced and high-spatial ability comprehenders arrive at the second stage at an earlier point in time than other comprehenders, which should enhance the probability of a match effect with respect to the actual situation. A similar account explains the fact that a main effect of truth value was found only for adults, but not for children (e.g., Slobin, 1966). Finally, the *two-step hypothesis* explains why a main effect of truth value has mainly been found in experiments using two complementary predicates or the same contrary predicates throughout (e.g., Trabasso et al., 1971; Wason, 1961). Only in these conditions is it possible to specify the actual situation when given the negated aspect. In all other conditions, the negative sentences simply do not provide enough information about this aspect of the actual situation. Why a main effect of truth value has primarily been observed in studies in which the sentence was presented prior to the picture (e.g., Trabasso et al., 1971) remains unclear from the perspective of the two-step simulation hypothesis.

To be sure, these considerations are only post hoc speculations, which cannot be taken as direct support for the two-step simulation hypothesis. It is plausible that a sentence verification task engenders strategic processes on the part of the comprehender. It is also possible that the different response time patterns are indeed due to a variety of different strategies. This is particularly likely when participants were explicitly instructed to use one or the other strategy (e.g., Mathews et al., 1980; Reichle et al., 2000; Richards & Frensch, 1987). These considerations show, however, that there is an alternative to the view that sentences per default are encoded in an amodal propositional representation (which in the case of a picture sentence-verification task is then compared with a propositional representation of the picture). Similar response time patterns are expected when comprehenders mentally simulate the described state of affairs in the way specified by the two-step simulation hypothesis. For a recent study conducted in our lab that provides evidence for an interpretation of the results in terms of the two-step simulation hypothesis, see Kaup, Lüdtke, and Zwaan, 2005.

It should be noted that Clark and Chase (1972) explicitly discussed the possibility that the sentences are encoded in the form of mental images. They ruled out this possibility for logical as well as empirical reasons. The logical problem that these authors addressed springs from the view that negative sentences cannot be encoded by mental images because they are typically consistent with a variety of different states of affairs, rendering impossible the construction of a single model that encodes the state of affairs described by the sentence. However, as noted earlier, uncertainty about the actual situation does not appear to pose a problem for the two-step simulation hypothesis. Negation is implicitly encoded in the sequencing of two different mental simulations. Even in cases where it is unclear what the actual situation is like, this representational mechanism still allows one to encode what the sentence is about. In an extreme case, the actual simulation is empty, and the expected simulation contains the negated state of affairs, that is, the representation contains only the information that a particular state of affairs does not hold, without specifying what holds instead.

The empirical counterargument against visual imagery models was based on the finding that differential effects were obtained with the prepositions *above* and *below* (cf. Clark & Chase, 1972). The argument was based on the assumption that visual images do not include a point of reference, such that two sentences with the same truth conditions, such as *The star is above the plus* and *The plus is below the star,* lead to the same representation (Clark & Chase, 1972, p. 499). However, these assumptions do not hold for the experiential simulations proposed here. These simulations do not convey an objective state of affairs, but a specific interpretation of a particular state of affairs, a construal (Langacker, 1987)—simulations are separated into figure and ground and do have foregrounded regions. Thus, the experiential simulations constructed for *The star is above the plus* and *The plus is below the star* are not equivalent, but differ with respect to which of the two entities is foregrounded (e.g., Langacker, 1987). The differential behavior of the two prepositions therefore poses no problem for the experiential view of language comprehension.

Accessibility

The accessibility-reducing effect of negation that was observed by MacDonald and Just (1989) for sentences such as *Almost every weekend Mary bakes some bread but no cookies for the children* is easily explained by the two-step simulation hypothesis. There is bread present but no cookie. Accordingly, the mental simulation of the actual state of affairs involves an experiential trace for bread but not for cookie, which may well be the reason why *bread* leads to faster response times than *cookies*. In fact, the results of earlier studies (Kaup, 1997, 2001; Kaup & Zwaan, 2003) confirm the hypothesis that the putative negation effect is due at least in part to the fact that in sentences of this type, the negated entity is absent from the actual situation. Admittedly, it may seem a little arbitrary to assume that here the simulation of the *actual* situation (containing only bread) is decisive, whereas in most of the sentence-verification studies it was the simulation of the negated situation that was considered to be decisive. However, the sentences used by MacDonald and Just (1989), unlike the sentences used in most of the sentence-verification studies, *explicitly* specified the actual situation (i.e., bread is being baked). When the sentence explicitly specifies the actual situation, the comprehender possibly first simulates the actual situation and then updates his or her expected simulation according to the presupposition of the negated sentence. If so, it would be of no surprise that response times measured immediately after the end of the sentence reflected the content of the actual and not the content of the negated situation.

Kuschert (1999) found that resolving an anaphor takes more time when the antecedent was mentioned in a double negative construction compared with the case where the introductory construction was affirmative. This finding can be explained by the fact that a discourse entity that was introduced within a double negative construction (*I disconfirmed his supposition that Carl does not have a sister*) is present in the actual situation but absent in what we have called the expected situation. Assuming that the comprehender may still be engaged in simulating the expected situation when encountering the anaphor in the subsequent sentence, resolving the anaphor should lead to difficulties compared with the versions in which the target entity was introduced within an affirmative phrase. It should be noted that in contrast to the materials employed by MacDonald and Just (1989), the negative versions employed by Kuschert (1999) did not provide explicit information regarding the actual situation, but only allowed inference of the target entity's existence.

Giora et al. (2004) found that a sentence containing an explicit property negation (*not sharp*) shows the same priming effects as the corresponding affirmative sentence (*sharp*). This finding is consistent with the two-step simulation hypothesis, in that the two sentences initially give rise to the exact same simulation processes. To summarize, the two-step hypothesis can account for the extant empirical findings on negation. Comprehenders mentally simulate the negated as well as the actual situation when processing a negative sentence. In the next section we report a series of experiments that directly addressed this hypothesis.

AN EMPIRICAL STUDY EVALUATING THE TWO-STEP SIMULATION HYPOTHESIS OF NEGATION

The first three experiments reported in this section focus on the first part of the two-step simulation hypothesis, the claim that negative sentences, when presented without a context in which the negated state of affairs is highly available, are a cue to the comprehender to construct a mental simulation of the negated state of affairs. We asked the question: "Are negated states of affairs initially present in comprehenders' simulations?" The fourth experiment addresses the second part of the two-step simulation hypothesis, the claim that negative sentences eventually lead to a simulation of the actual state of affairs. All experiments used the paradigm developed by Zwaan et al. (2002) for testing the experiential view with affirmative sentences (see Kaup, Yaxley, Madden, Zwaan, & Lüdtke, in press, for details on Experiments 2 and 3, and Kaup, Lüdtke, & Zwaan, 2006, for details on Experiment 4).

In the study by Zwaan et al., participants were presented with sentences such as *The ranger saw an eagle in the sky* or *The ranger saw an eagle in the nest*, and afterward saw a picture of the object mentioned in the verb phrase of the sentences. Participants judged as quickly as possible whether the object in the picture was mentioned in the sentence. For experimental trials, the correct response was always yes, but the picture either matched the implied shape of the object (outstretched wings for . . . *in the sky*; folded wings for . . . *in the nest*) or not (folded wings for . . . *in the sky*; outstretched wings for . . . *in the nest*). Zwaan et al. found a strong match/mismatch effect. Response latencies were significantly shorter when there was a match between the sentence and the picture with respect to the object's shape than when there was a mismatch. This finding suggests that comprehenders routinely infer the implied shapes of objects mentioned in a sentence, which in turn can be considered positive evidence for the idea that the processing of affirmative sentences of the type investigated by Zwaan et al. triggers experiential simulations of the referent situations.

What can be predicted about negated sentences in this paradigm? If it is true that comprehending an isolated negative sentence in a first step requires the construction of an experiential simulation of the negated states of affairs, then the negated sentences should initially yield effects similar to those of the affirmative sentences. Thus, if comprehending a sentence such as *There was no eagle in the sky* requires a simulation of an eagle in the sky, then this should be reflected in the response latencies elicited by pictures of an eagle with outstretched or folded wings, respectively. Latencies should be shorter if the picture matches the negated state of affairs (i.e., outstretched wings) than when the picture matches some other state of affairs (i.e., folded wings). Conversely, *There was no eagle in the nest* should lead to the reversed latency pattern. In this case, latencies should be shorter for a picture with folded wings than for a picture with outstretched wings. In short, a response-time pattern should be obtained that is analogous to the pattern observed with affirmative sentences. This prediction was investigated in Experiments 1 through 3, in which the picture was presented with a delay of only 250 ms after the end of the sentence. Differential response time patterns should be observed later in the comprehension process, when comprehenders begin simulating the actual state of affairs. In Experiment 4 we therefore presented the picture with longer delays, 750 ms and 1500 ms.

In Experiment 1, participants were presented with 28 experimental sentences of the form *There was no X in/on the Y* and 56 filler sentences (14 negative and 42 affirmative). There were two versions of each experimental sentence that differed only with respect to the noun that was used in the locational phrase (e.g., *There was no eagle in the sky/There was no eagle in the nest*). The sentence pairs were constructed such that the corresponding affirmative sentences (*There was an X in/on the Y*) implied a different shape of the same object. For instance, *There was an eagle in the sky* implies that the eagle has its wings outstretched, whereas *There was an eagle in the nest* implies that the eagle has its wings folded. A picture followed each sentence. Subjects indicated whether the depicted object had been mentioned in the sentence. For the experimental sentences, the correct answer was always yes, but the picture either matched the shape of the object in the negated situation (outstretched wings for *There was no eagle in the sky*; folded wings for *There was no eagle in the nest*) or not (folded wings for . . . *in the sky*; outstretched wings for . . . *in the nest*; see Fig. 11–1).

As predicted, participants responded significantly faster to a picture that matched the negated state of affairs than to a picture that matched a different state of affairs (the means in the two conditions are shown in Fig. 11–1). Apparently, comprehenders represented the shape that the object had in the negated state of affairs. In fact, the similarity between the present results and the results obtained for affirmative sentences (Zwaan et al., 2002) suggests, as was hypothesized, that the processing of negative sentences triggers (at first) the same simulations as the processing of the corresponding affirmative sentences does.

However, the similarity between the results for the two sentence types also presents a challenge for a coherent interpretation of the findings. The experimental task did not require participants to pay attention to the polarity of the sentence (affirmative vs. negative). They only needed to decide whether a particular object had been named in the sentence. Maybe par-

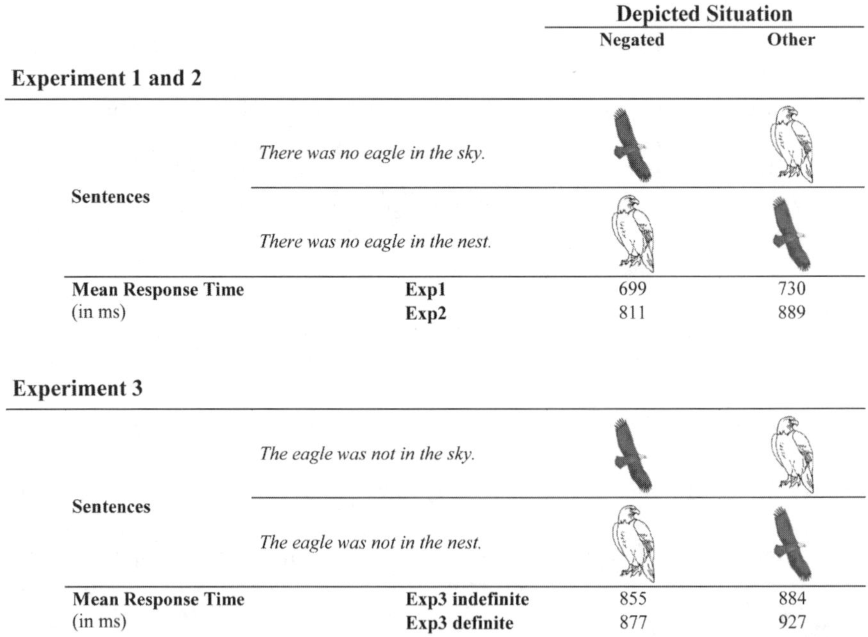

		Depicted Situation	
		Negated	Other
Experiment 1 and 2			
Sentences	*There was no eagle in the sky.*		
	There was no eagle in the nest.		
Mean Response Time (in ms)	**Exp1**	699	730
	Exp2	811	889
Experiment 3			
Sentences	*The eagle was not in the sky.*		
	The eagle was not in the nest.		
Mean Response Time (in ms)	**Exp3 indefinite**	855	884
	Exp3 definite	877	927

Note: The negated condition is the condition in which the picture matches the negated situation.

FIGURE 11–1. Sample sentence-picture pairs used in Experiments 1 through 3, and mean recognition times as a function of the depicted state of affairs.

ticipants simply ignored the negation markers in the sentences and processed the sentences as if they had been affirmative. This alternative hypothesis seems all the more plausible, considering that paying attention to the meaning of the negative sentences might lead to interference with the experimental task. After all, participants had to respond with "yes" to a picture of an object that was mentioned within the scope of the negation operator in the sentence. If it is true that participants ignored the negation operators in the experimental sentences of this experiment, then finding shorter response times in the negated condition would not be surprising and would not constitute support for the hypothesis that the first step in processing a negated sentence is to simulate the negated situation. The result would merely constitute further evidence for the experiential simulation view of language comprehension.

Experiment 2 was designed to address this concern. We presented participants with comprehension questions after some of the filler sentences. The questions were designed so that a correct answer indicated that the participant had not only attended to the polarity of the sentence, but had also understood the meaning of the corresponding sentence. For instance, a sentence such as *There was no light bulb in the lamp* was followed by *Was the lamp useless for illuminating the room?*, and a sentence such as *There was a flower in the vase* was followed by *Was the vase empty?* We reasoned that this modification would (a) prevent participants from adopting the potential strategy to ignore the negation operator in the experimental sentences, and (b) allow us to exclude post hoc those participants who nevertheless seemed to have adopted this strategy (as indicated by a relative high occurrence of incorrect answers to questions after negative sentences in particular).

The results again supported the predictions. As in Experiment 1, there was a significant effect of the depicted state of affairs with shorter latencies in the negated than in the "other" condition, and analyses of the comprehension question indicate that this effect cannot be due to participants strategically ignoring the negative particles: The mean comprehension accuracy for affirmative sentences was not higher than that for negative sentences (77%; SD ∇ .16 and 80%; SD ∇ .17, respectively). Furthermore, a significant effect of the depicted state of affairs was observed even when particular subgroups of the total set of participants were analyzed, namely the group of participants who had a mean accuracy of at least 83% (i.e., at least 20 out of 24 correct responses; *N* ∇ 20), or the group of participants (*N* ∇ 25) who made fewer than two mistakes with the overall 12 negative questions. For both subgroups, the accuracy scores indicate that they could not have adopted the ignoring strategy. That they nevertheless showed a significant effect therefore rules out that this effect reflects this particular strategy. These results thus provide further evidence for the hypothesis that the processing of negated sentences involves mentally simulating the negated states of affairs.

The goal of a third experiment was to investigate whether the effect of the depicted state of affairs would generalize to other kinds of negated sentences.

In addition to the negative sentences of the form *There was no X in/on the Y*, we presented participants with negative sentences of the form *The X was not in/on the Y*. Thus, we compared the indefinite negations from the previous experiments with definite negations. These two types of negations differ with respect to the scope of the negation operator. In the indefinite negative sentences (*There was no X in/on the Y*), the negation operator has wide scope—the only affirmative information in the sentence is the presupposition that there is a particular unambiguously identifiable Y. Thus, a sentence of this kind does not provide much information about the actual state of affairs. In contrast, the definite negative sentences (*The X was not in/on the Y*) carry the additional presupposition about the existence of a particular X. Moreover, this is the subject of the sentence and therefore suggests an agent for a simulation of the actual state of affairs. Therefore, a negative sentence of this kind provides the comprehender with more specific information about the actual state of affairs than does the corresponding indefinite negative sentence. If indefinite but not the definite negations produced a significant effect of the depicted state of affairs, then this would suggest that our two-step simulation hypothesis holds only for very specific cases of negation, namely cases in which the negative sentence is so nonspecific that it provides nearly no information about the actual state of affairs. In other words, such a result would indicate that comprehenders construct an experiential simulation of the negated state of affairs only if there is nothing else to simulate. Obviously this would reduce the scope of our account dramatically. However, the results of this experiment speak against this view: The effect of the depicted state of affairs did not interact with definiteness but proved significant for both types of negations (see Fig. 11–1). That response times were not faster in the definite than in the indefinite conditions speaks against the interpretation that comprehenders simulate the negated *and* the actual state of affairs in parallel right from the beginning. As was mentioned earlier, the definite negations carry a presupposition about the existence of the critical entity (the eagle), which provides an agent for the simulation of the actual state of affairs, whereas the indefinite negations do not. Accordingly, it can be assumed that in the definite conditions, the actual state of affairs contains an eagle, whereas in the indefinite conditions it does not. Hence, had comprehenders had available a simulation of the actual state of affairs as early as 250 ms after processing the negative sentence, this should have been reflected in shorter response latencies in the definite than in the indefinite conditions (for details see Kaup et al., in press).

Experiment 4 was designed to examine whether the processing of negative sentences would eventually result in a simulation of the actual state of affairs. To this end, we prolonged the delay with which the picture was being presented after the sentences from 250 ms to 750 ms and 1500 ms in Experiment 4 (for details see Kaup et al., 2006). Because we were interested in detecting effects based on simulations of the actual state of affairs, we used negative sentences that left little ambiguity about the actual state of affairs. Negative sentences with contradictory predicates (e.g., *The umbrella was not open / The umbrella was not closed.*) satisfy this condition. Also, we used a picture-naming task instead of a recognition task in this experiment. Furthermore, to allow a direct comparison between the effects obtained with negative sentences and those obtained with affirmative sentences, we presented the set of participants not only with the two negative versions of the sentences, but also with the two corresponding affirmative versions (e.g., *The umbrella was open / The umbrella was closed*). Thus, on a given trial, the image could depict the actual state of affairs of the preceding negative or affirmative sentence, or the image could depict the respective "other" state of affairs (which corresponds to the negated state of affairs for negative sentences; see Fig. 11–2). If comprehending a negative sentence does indeed result in a simulation of the actual state of affairs, there should be a main effect of the depicted state of affairs, with shorter response times in conditions where the picture matches the actual state of affairs than in conditions where the picture matches the negated or other state of affairs. No clear-cut predictions can be made with respect to the

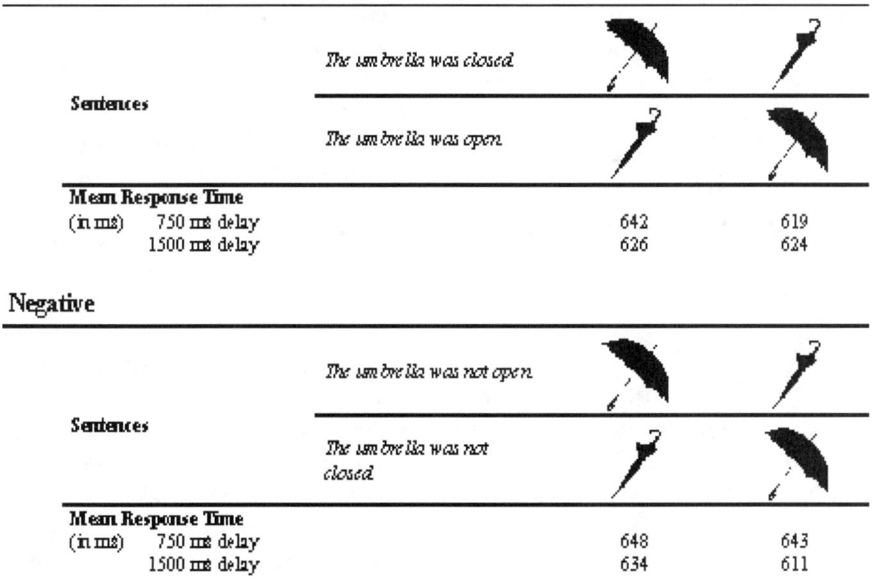

Sentences	The umbrella was closed		
	The umbrella was open		
Mean Response Time (in ms) 750 ms delay		642	619
1500 ms delay		626	624

Negative

Sentences	The umbrella was not open		
	The umbrella was not closed		
Mean Response Time (in ms) 750 ms delay		648	643
1500 ms delay		634	611

Note: The negated/other condition is the condition in which the picture matches the negated situation for negative sentences and a situation other than the actual situation for the affirmative sentences. The actual condition is the condition in which the picture matches the actual situation.

FIGURE 11–2. Sample sentence-picture pairs used in Experiment 4 and mean picture-naming latencies as a function of sentence polarity and the depicted state of affairs.

delay manipulation, because we do not know in advance the time in the comprehension process at which participants will switch from simulating the negated state of affairs to simulating the actual state of affairs when processing negative sentences. If the facilitation effect for the actual state of affairs turns out to be stronger for the 1500-ms delay condition than for the 750-ms delay condition, this would indicate that some participants in some conditions were still engaged in simulating the negated state of affairs 750 ms after reading the negative sentences. In summary, participants were presented with 40 experimental sentence-picture pairs in one of eight versions intermixed with 40 filler sentences (20 affirmative, 20 negative).

In accordance with the hypotheses, there was a main effect of the depicted state of affairs with shorter response times in the conditions where the depicted state of affairs matched the actual state of affairs than in the conditions where it matched the negated or other state of affairs. However, there was also a significant three-way interaction of delay, sentence polarity, and depicted state of affairs. With a 750-ms delay, the advantage of the actual state of affairs was due to the affirmative versions of the sentences, whereas with a 1500-ms delay it was due to the negative versions of the sentences. In other words, with a 750-ms delay, responses were faster when an affirmative sentence was followed by a picture that matched the actual state of affairs compared with a picture that mismatched this state of affairs, but no such difference was found for the negative versions. In contrast, with a 1500-ms delay, responses were faster when a negative sentence was followed by a picture that matched the actual state of affairs compared with a picture that mismatched this state of affairs, but no such difference was found for the affirmative versions.

The overall main effect of the depicted state of affairs, with shorter response times for actual than for negated/other, suggests that comprehenders eventually simulated the actual state of affairs when processing affirmative and negative sentences. Moreover, the fact that there was no two-way interaction of depicted state of affairs and sentence polarity indicates that this simulation was similar for the affirmative and the negative versions of the sentences. In other words, as far as the resulting simulation is concerned, a sentence such as *The door was not open* is equivalent to *The door was closed*, and a sentence such as *The door was not closed* is equivalent to *The door was open*. The former two sentences lead to a simulation of a closed door, and the latter two lead to a simulation of an open door. In this respect the results support the idea that comprehending a negative sentence results in a simulation of the actual state of affairs. The finding that the main effect of the depicted state of affairs was qualified by an interaction of depicted state of affairs, delay, and sentence polarity indicates that affirmative and negative sentences *do* differ with respect to temporal characteristics of the simulation process. For negative sentences, an advantage of the actual state of affairs was found with a 1500-ms delay but not with a 750-ms delay. This supports the view that for negative sentences the actual state of affairs is not simulated right away, but only after the negated state of affairs has been simulated. In contrast, for affirmative sentences, an advantage of the actual state of affairs already occurred at 750 ms, supporting the view that the actual state of affairs is simulated right away for affirmative sentences. The absence of an advantage effect with affirmative sentences at 1500 ms was not predicted, but is not surprising. Obviously, comprehenders will not keep their simulations accessible indefinitely. Considering that affirmative sentences presumably involve only one simulation step, it seems plausible that comprehenders were long finished with their simulations and had turned their attention elsewhere 1500 ms after self-paced reading of an affirmative sentence.

It could be argued that the differences in results obtained in the experiments with the short and long delays are not due to the differences in the delays but rather to properties of the predicates in the experimental sentences. In Experiments 1 through 3, in which the pictures were presented after a 250-ms delay, the predicates were locational specifications (e.g., to be in the nest / to be in the sky), the negation of which usually does not provide specific information about the actual location of the target entity. In contrast, in Experiment 4, in which the pictures were presented with longer delays (750 ms and 1500 ms), the predicates were contradictory state descriptions (to be open / to be closed), the negation of which does provide specific information about the actual state of the critical entity. At first sight, this seems to suggest that participants represent the negated state of affairs for sentences with predicates of the first type, and the actual state of affairs for sentences with predicates of the second type. Such a view comes close to assumptions made by Mayo et al. (2004). These authors propose that negative sentences with unipolar adjectives (e.g., *He is not responsible*) lead to *schema-plus-tag* representations, in which a core supposition is combined with a negation tag, whereas sentences with bipolar adjectives (e.g., *He is not warm*) lead to *fusion* representations, in which the core proposition and the negation are integrated into one meaning unit. There are two main reasons for why we do not believe in an account based solely on the type of predicate. First, the two delay conditions examined in Experiment 4 employed the exact same contradictory predicates but still produced different results. When the picture was presented with a 750-ms delay, there was an advantage of the actual state of affairs in the affirmative conditions but not in the negative conditions. When the picture was presented with a 1500-ms delay, the affirmative conditions produced a null result, whereas the negative conditions produced an advantage of the actual state of affairs. These findings indicate that delay does have an effect on the response latencies. In addition, they suggest that there is a point in the comprehension process at which participants switch from simulating the negated state of affairs to simulating the actual state of affairs. Around this point in time, the negated state of affairs should still be more available than the actual state of affairs in some cases, and the actual state of affairs should already be more available than the negated state of affairs in others. Overall, this should produce a null result. Thus, although the two-step simulation hypothesis does not predict the null result specifically for the 750-ms delay condition, the null result is predicted for some intermediate delay condition. An account based solely on the type of predicate does not predict these results in any way. We conclude therefore that participants do not simulate the actual state of affairs right away with contradictory predicates. Rather, the results of Experiment 4 suggest that they first simulate the negated and then the actual state of affairs, just as with any other negative sentence. This interpretation is also supported by the results of a recent study by Hasson & Glucksberg (2006): Participants were presented with a lexical-decision task after reading affirmative and negative metaphors (e.g., *My lawyer is / is not a shark*). When presented after a 1000-ms delay, probes related to the affirmative version of the metaphor (e.g., *vicious*) led to faster response times after affirmative than after negative metaphors, whereas probes related to the negative version of the metaphor (e.g., *gentle*) led to faster response times after negative than after affirmative metaphors. After shorter delays (150 ms and 500 ms) this prime-by-target interaction was not significant. Under these conditions, probes related to the affirmative version of the metaphor seemed to be facilitated after both the negative and the affirmative version of the metaphor.

The second reason we do not believe in an account based solely on the type of predicate is a theoretical one. If negative sentences with contradictory predicates (e.g., *The door was not open.*) would lead to a simulation of the actual state of affairs right away, then the simulation processes conducted for these sentences would be indistinguishable from those conducted for the affirmative sentences with the same truth conditions (e.g., *The door was closed.*). But if this is so, why would the speaker use a negative sentence in the first place? If all the hearer does is translate it back into the affirmative form, the speaker could have used this easier affirmative form in the first place. It is more plausible to assume that the subtle (pragmatic) differences between *The door was not open* and *The door was closed* that prompt the speaker to use one or the other form in a particular communicative situation are also reflected in the hearer's mental representations of the communicated content.

CONCLUSIONS

We focused on the question of how negation is captured in experiential representations in language comprehension. In contrast to linguistic representations, experiential representations do not allow negation to be represented explicitly. Taking into account the pragmatic licensing conditions of negative utterances, we hypothesized that negation is implicitly encoded in the sequencing of two mental simulations: The simulation of the actual state of affairs, as the sentence or text describes it, and the simulation of the expected state of affairs. We distinguished two cases. The first case is where the negated state of affairs was already present in the discourse representation prior to encountering the negative sentence. In this case, processing the negative statement consists of correcting the expectation by simulating the actual state of affairs according to the negative sentence. The second case is where the negated state of affairs was not included in the discourse representation prior to encountering the negative sentence. In such a case, the comprehender first constructs a mental simulation of the negated state of affairs and then turns toward simulating the actual state of affairs.

In arguing for the two-step simulation hypothesis, we first reexamined empirical findings reported in the literature that are relevant to the question of how negation is represented in language comprehension. We examined three findings in particular: the impact that negation has on processing difficulty, the impact that the truth value of a negative sentence has on sentence-verification latencies, and the impact that negation has on the accessibility of text information. All three classes of findings are usually explicitly or implicitly interpreted as positive evidence for the claim that comprehenders construct a propositional representation in which negation is explicitly represented. A reevaluation of the findings showed that the majority of the findings can be accounted for by the two-step simulation hypothesis. Of course, this accounting is post hoc and should not be taken as positive evidence for the two-step simulation hypothesis. However, it does suggest that there is an alternative account for these findings, meaning that they cannot be taken as positive evidence for propositional representations either.

We also reported four experiments that directly addressed the two-step simulation hypothesis. Their results support the predictions. Shortly after reading a sentence that denied that a particular kind of target entity (e.g., an eagle) was in a particular location (e.g., the sky / the nest), participants were faster to respond to a picture of the target entity if the depicted shape matched the shape that the target entity would have had in the negated situation compared with when the depicted shape did not match the negated shape. Thus, at this point in the comprehension process (namely 250 ms after reading the sentences) comprehenders' response time patterns obtained with negative sentences (*There was no eagle in the sky / nest*) were equivalent to the response time patterns obtained in previous experiments employing the corresponding sentences without negation (*There was an eagle in the sky / nest*). This equivalence supports the assumption that negative sentences at first lead to exactly the same simulation processes as the corresponding sentences without negation. The results obtained with longer delays (750 ms, 1500 ms) suggest that comprehenders from a certain point in time on are simulating the actual state of affairs. One and a half seconds after reading negative sentences that denied that a particular target entity (e.g., door) was in a particular state (e.g., open / closed), participants were faster to respond to a picture of the target entity when the depicted state corresponded to the actual state of the target entity compared with when this was not the case. In fact, at this point in the comprehension process, the effects obtained with negative sentences (e.g., *The door was not closed*) resembled the effects obtained with affirmative sentences (e.g., *The door was open*), except that in the affirmative case, the effects come to light earlier in the comprehension process (namely, by 750 ms instead of by 1500 ms). Thus, in summary, the results of the four experiments are in line with the two-step hypothesis.

In conclusion, we would like to note that the two-step simulation hypothesis of negation also accords well with findings from outside of the psychology of language. We briefly mention three different findings. First, in social and pedagogical psychology, it is well known that negations, when used in explicit behavior-controlling instructions, are counterproductive in that they often cause the opposite of what the instructor intended (e.g., Brehm & Brehm, 1981). Children at a certain age, when explicitly told not to do something, almost certainly will go ahead with the forbidden action. It seems as if the action is even more likely after an explicit negation than without an explicit instruction altogether. It is therefore usually recommended not to tell a child what he or she is not supposed to be doing but to state what he or she is supposed to be doing instead. There are different explanations for this counterproductive effect of negation. One of the most prominent ones is based on Brehm's reactance theory (Brehm, 1966), according to which forbidden behavior becomes particularly attractive. Another explanation can be based on propositional theories of comprehension: In a propositional representation the negation operator is applied to a complete proposition. Thus in case the negation operator is lost, a proposition remains that corresponds to the negated state of affairs. The two-step simulation hypothesis points to another reason that may contribute to the counterproductive effect of negative instructions. In order to understand the negation, the child needs to mentally simulate the negated state of affairs before turning to the question of what action should be done instead. It seems likely that children are less able than adults to mentally simulate states of affairs and accordingly often overtly act out the to-be-simulated state of affairs by accident. Consistent with this idea, counterproductive effects of negation also have been observed in conditions for which reactance is not a likely explanation. In a study by Wegner, Ansfield, and Pilloff (1998), one group of participants was instructed to prevent a pendulum from swinging along a particular axis that was marked on a piece of paper in front of them, whereas the other group did not receive such an explicit instruction. Participants in a condition in which they were being distracted by having to solve a secondary task showed more swinging along the particular "forbidden" axis than a group that did not receive such an instruction.

Second, research on mental control has shown that counterproductive effects of negation also occur when mental processes are being targeted by explicit instruction instead of overt behavior. Participants who are being explicitly told not to think about a particular concept are usually unable to effectively suppress the corresponding thoughts (Wegner & Erber, 1992; Wegner, Schneider, Carter, & White, 1987). Obviously, the two-step simulation hypothesis would predict these problems in thought suppression, because according to this hypothesis, understanding the explicit instruction that a particular concept is not to be thought of requires simulating this concept.

Third, research on social judgment has shown that media audiences are influenced by information they are explicitly told is not true (e.g., Fiedler, Armbruster, Nickel, Walther, & Asbeck, 1996; Wegner, Wenzlaff, Kerker, & Beattie, 1981). Thus, the reputation of a person can be severely damaged simply by spreading the news that a particular undesirable attribute does not hold for the person in question (e.g., *Mr. Smith did not sell drugs to minors*!). Again, there are different explanations for this *incrimination by innuendo* effect. The most convincing explanation is that this type of negation pragmatically suggests that there was reason to believe that the undesirable attribute did in fact hold for the person in question, which in and of itself may be reputation-damaging. The two-step simulation hypothesis is based on these pragmatic aspects of negation, but goes one step further in explaining the effect. When processing the news, a simulation is run in which the undesirable attribute is in fact actively applied to the person in question. As a result, the connection between the person and the attribute may seem even more plausible.

In conclusion, we have introduced a mechanism by which a linguistic operator such as negation is implicitly represented in the experiential simulations created during language comprehension. Such a mechanism is a necessary ingredient of the experiential view of language comprehension if this view is intended to hold for language processing in general. The specific mechanism we propose is grounded in assumptions concerning the pragmatic licensing conditions of negative sentences and appears to be in accordance not only with the extant empirical findings on negation in the literature but also with the results of the four experiments that we reported in this chapter.

ACKNOWLEDGMENTS

Preparation of this chapter was supported in part by grants KA1389/2-1 and 2-2 (Deutsche Forschungs Gemeinschaft) to Barbara Kaup and grant MH-63972 to Rolf. A. Zwaan (National Institutes of Health). We thank Berry Claus for helpful comments on an earlier draft of this manuscript, and Lennart Schalk, Rebecca Schindele, and Manuela Zirngibl for their help with data collection. We also thank Burchard Kaup for bringing the anecdote mentioned in the introduction to our attention.

REFERENCES

Albrecht, J. E., & Myers, J. L (1998). Accessing distant text information during reading: Effects of contextual cues. *Discourse Processes, 26*, 87–107.

Arroyo, F. V. (1982). Negatives in context. *Journal of Verbal Learning and Verbal Behavior, 21*, 118–126.

Baddeley, A. (1986). *Working memory*. Oxford: Clarendon Press.

Barsalou, L. W. (1999). Perceptual symbol system. *Behavioral and Brain Sciences, 22,* 577–660.

Barsalou, L. W., & Wiemer-Hastings, K. (2005). Situating abstract concepts. In D. Pecher & R. Zwaan (Eds.), *Grounding cognition: The role of perception and action in memory, language, and thinking* (pp. 129–163). New York: Cambridge University Press.

Boroditsky, L. (2000). Metaphoric structuring: Understanding time through spatial metaphors. *Cognition, 75,* 1–28.

Boroditsky, L., & Ramscar, M. (2002). The roles of body and mind in abstract thought. *Psychological Science, 13,* 185–188.

Brehm, J. W. (1966). *A theory of psychological reactance*. New York: Academic Press.

Brehm, S. S., & Brehm, J. W. (1981). *Psychological reactance: A theory of freedom and control*. New York: Academic Press.

Carpenter, P. A., & Just, M. A. (1975). Sentence comprehension: A psycholinguistic processing model of verification. *Psychological Review, 82,* 45–73.

Chase, W. G., & Clark, H. H. (1971). Semantics in the perception of verticality. *British Journal of Psychology, 62,* 311–326.

Chomsky, N. (1957). *Syntactic structures*. The Hague: Mouton.

Clark, H. H. (1974). Semantics and comprehension. In T. A. Sebeok (Ed.), *Current trends in linguistics* (pp. 1291–1428). The Haag: Mouton

Clark, H. H. (1986). *Semantics and comprehension*. The Hague: Mouton.

Clark, H. H., & Chase, W. G. (1972). On the process of comparing sentences against pictures. *Cognitive Psychology, 3,* 472–517.

Clark, H. H., & Chase, W. G. (1974). Perceptual coding strategies in the formation and verification of descriptions. *Memory & Cognition,* 2(1A), 101–111.

Cornish, E. R. (1971). Pragmatic aspects of negation in sentence evaluation and completion task. *British Journal of Psychology, 62,* 505–511.

Deutsch, R. (2002). *What does it take to negate? How processing negated information affects cognition and behavior*. Unpublished doctoral dissertation, University of Würzburg, Germany.

de Villiers, J. G., & Tager Flusberg, H. (1975). Some facts one simply cannot deny. *Journal of Child Language, 2,* 279–286.

Donaldson, M. (1970). Developmental aspects of performance with negatives. In G. B. Flores d`Arcais & W. M. Levelt (Eds.), *Advances in psycholinguistics* (pp. 369–412), Amsterdam: North-Holland.

Draine, S. (1997). *Analytic limitations of unconscious language processing*. Unpublished doctoral dissertation, University of Washington.

Eiferman, R. R. (1961). Negation, a linguistic variable. *Acta Psychologica, 18,* 258–273.

Fauconnier, G. (1985). *Mental spaces: Aspects of meaning construction in natural language*. Cambridge, MA: MIT Press.

Fiedler, K., Armbruster, T., Nickel, S., Walther, E., & Asbeck, J. (1996). Constructive memory and social judgment: Experiments in the self-verification of question contents. *Journal of Personality and Social Psychology, 71,* 861–873.

Fincher-Kiefer, R. (2001). Perceptual components of situation models. *Memory & Cognition, 29,* 336–343.

Freyd, J. J. (1987). Dynamic mental representations. *Psychological Review, 94,* 427–438.

Freyd, J. J. (1993). Five hunches about perceptual processes and dynamic representations. In D. E. Meyer & S. Kornblum (Eds.), *Attention and performance XIV. Syn-*

ergies in experimental psychology, artificial intelligence, and cognitive neuroscience (pp. 99–119). Cambridge, MA: MIT Press.

Giora, R., Balaban, N., Fein, O., & Alkabets, I. (2004). Negation as positivity in disguise. In H. L. Colston & A. Katz (Eds.), *Figurative language comprehension: Social and cultural influences* (pp. 233–258), Mahwah, NJ: Lawrence Erlbaum Associates.

Givon, T. (1978). Negation in language: Pragmatics, function, ontology. In P. Cole (Ed.), *Syntax and semantics* (pp. 69–112). New York: Academic Press.

Glenberg, A. M. (1997). What memory is for. *Behavioral and Brain Science, 20,* 1–41.

Glenberg, A. M., & Kaschak, M. P. (2002). Grounding language in action. *Psychonomic Bulletin & Review, 9,* 558–565.

Glenberg, A. M., Meyer, M., & Lindem, K. (1987). Mental models contribute to foregrounding during text comprehension. *Journal of Memory and Language, 26,* 69–83.

Glenberg, A. M., & Robertson, D. A. (1999). Indexical understanding of instructions. *Discourse Processes, 28,* 1–26.

Glenberg, A. M., Robertson, D. A., Jansen, J. L., & Johnson-Glenberg, M. C. (1999). Not propositions. *Journal of Cognitive Systems Research, 1,* 19–33.

Gough, P. B. (1965). Grammatical transformations and speed of understanding. *Journal of Verbal Learning and Verbal Behavior, 4,* 107–111.

Gough, P. B. (1966). The verification of sentences: The effects of delay of evidence and sentence length. *Journal of Verbal Learning and Verbal Behavior, 5,* 492–496.

Graesser, A. C., Millis, K. K., & Zwaan, R. A. (1997). Discourse comprehension. *Annual Review of Psychology, 48,* 163–189.

Greene, J. M. (1970). The semantic function of negatives and passives. *British Journal of Psychology, 61,* 17–22.

Hasson, U., & Glucksberg, S. (2006). Does understanding negation entail affirmation? *Journal of Pragmatics, 38,* 1015–1032.

Horn, L. (1989). *A natural history of negation*. Chicago: University of Chicago Press.

Jackendoff, R. S. (1969). An interpretive theory of negation. *Foundations of Language, 5,* 218–241.

Johnson Laird, P. N. (1983). *Mental models*. Cambridge, MA: Harvard University Press.

Jones, S. (1966). The effect of a negative qualifier in an instruction. *Journal of Verbal Learning and Verbal Behavior,* 5, 497–501.

Jones, S. (1968). Instructions, self-instructions and performance. *Quarterly Journal of Experimental Psychology, 20,* 74–781.

Just, M. A., & Carpenter, P. A. (1971). Comprehension of negation with quantification, *Journal of Verbal Learning and Verbal Behavior, 10,* 244–253.

Just, M. A., & Clark, H. H. (1973). Drawing inferences from the presuppositions and implications of affirmative and negative sentences. *Journal of Verbal Learning and Verbal Behavior, 12,* 21–31.

Kaschak, M. P., Madden, C. J., Therriault, D. J., Yaxley, R. H., Aveyard, M. E., Blanchard, A. A., et al. (2005). Perception of motion affects language processing. *Cognition, 94,* B79–B89.

Kaup, B. (1997). The processing of negatives during discourse comprehension. In M. G. Shafto & P. Langley (Eds.), *Proceedings of the Nineteenth Conference of the Cognitive Science Society* (pp. 370–375). Mahwah, NJ: Lawrence Erlbaum Associates.

Kaup, B. (1999). *Zur verarbeitung und repräsentation von negation bei der textrezeption*. Unpublished dissertation, Technical University Berlin.

Kaup, B. (2001). Negation and its impact on the accessibility of text information. *Memory & Cognition, 20,* 960–967.

Kaup, B., Kelter, S., & Habel, Ch. (1999). Taking the functional aspect of mental models as a starting point for studying discourse comprehension. In G. Rickheit & C. H. Habel (Eds.), *Mental models in discourse processing and reasoning* (pp. 93–112). Amsterdam: North-Holland.

Kaup, B., Lüdtke, J., & Zwaan, R. A. (2005). Effects of negation, truth value, and delay on picture recognition after reading affirmative and negative sentences. In B. G. Bara, L. Barsalou, & M. Bucciarelli (Eds.), *Proceedings of the 27th Annual Conference of the Cognitive Science Society* (pp. 1114–1119). Mahwah, NJ: Lawrence Erlbaum.

Kaup, B., Yaxley, R. H., Madden, C. M., Zwaan, R. A., & Lüdtke, J. (in press). Perceptual simulation of negated text information. *Quarterly Journal of Experimental Psychology.*

Kaup, B., & Zwaan, R. A. (2003). Effects of negation and situational presence on the accessibility of text information. *Journal of Experimental Psychology: Learning, Memory and Cognition, 29*, 439–446.

Kaup, B., Lüdtke, J., & Zwaan, R. A. (2006). Processing negated sentences with contradictory predicates: Is a door that is not open mentally closed? *Journal of Pragmatics, 38*, 1033–1050.

Kelter, S. (2003). Mentale modelle. In G. Rickheit, T. Herrmann, & W. Deutsch (Eds.), *Psycholinguistik—Psycholinguistics* (pp. 505–517). Berlin: de Gruyter.

Kelter, S., Kaup, B., & Claus, B. (2004). Representing a described sequence of events: A dynamic view of narrative comprehension. *Journal of Experimental Psychology: Learning, Memory, and Cognition, 30*, 451–464.

Kintsch, W. (1988). The use of knowledge in discourse processing: A construction-integration model. *Psychological Review, 95*, 163–182.

Klatzky, R. L., Pellegrino, J. W., McCloskey, B. P., & Doherty, S. (1989). Can you squeeze a tomato? The role of motor representations in semantic sensibility judgments. *Journal of Memory and Language, 28*, 56–77.

Kosslyn, S. M. (1994). *Image and brain*. Cambridge, MA: MIT Press.

Kroll, J. F., & Corrigan, A. (1981). Strategies in sentence-picture verification: The effect of an unexpected picture. *Journal of Verbal Learning and Verbal Behavior, 20*, 515–531.

Kuschert, S. (1999). *Dynamic meaning and accommodation*. Unpublished dissertation, Saarland University.

Lakoff, G. (1987). *Woman, fire, and dangerous things. What categories reveal about the mind.* Chicago: University of Chicago Press.

Lakoff, G., & Johnson, M. (1980). *Metaphors we live by.* Chicago: University of Chicago Press.

Langacker, R. L. (1987). *Foundations of cognitive grammar* (Vol. 1). Stanford, CA: Stanford University Press.

Langacker, R. L. (1991). *Foundations of cognitive grammar* (Vol. 2). Stanford, CA: Stanford University Press.

Lea, R. B., & Mulligan, E. J. (2002). The effect of negation on deductive interferences. *Journal of Experimental Psychology: Learning, Memory, and Cognition, 28*, 303–317.

MacDonald, M. C., & Just, M. A. (1989). Changes in activation levels with negation. *Journal of Experimental Psychology: Learning, Memory, and Cognition, 15*, 633–642.

MacLeod, C. M., Hunt, E. B., & Mathews, N. N. (1978). Individual differences in the verification of sentence-picture relationships. *Journal of Verbal Learning and Verbal Behavior, 17*, 493–507.

MacWhinney, B. (1999). The emergence of language from embodiment. In B. MacWhinney (Ed.), *Emergence of language* (pp. 213–256). Mahwah, NJ: Lawrence Erlbaum Associates.

Marquer, J. M., & Pereira, M. (1990). Reaction times in the study of strategies in sentence-picture verification: A reconsideration. Quarterly *Journal of Experimental Psychology, 42A,* 147–168.

Mathews, N. N., Hunt, E. B., & MacLeod, C M. (1980). Strategy choice and strategy training in sentence-picture verification. *Journal of Verbal Learning and Verbal Behavior, 19,* 531–548.

Mayo, R., Schul, Y., & Burnstein, E. (2004). "I am not guilty" vs "I am innocent": Successful negation may depend on the schema used for its encoding. *Journal of Experimental Social Psychology, 40,* 443–449

McKoon, G., & Ratcliff, R. (1998). Memory-based language processing: Psycholinguistic research in the 1990s. *Annual Review of Psychology, 49,* 25–42.

Morrow, D. G., Bower, G. H., & Greenspan, S. L. (1990). Situation-based inferences during narrative comprehension. In A. C. Graesser & G. H. Bower (Eds.), *The psychology of learning and motivation: inferences and text comprehension* (pp. 123–135). New York: Academic Press.

Moxey, L. M., Sanford, A. J., & Dawydiak, E. J. (2001). Denials as controllers of negative quantifier focus. *Journal of Memory and Language, 44,* 427–442.

Partee, B. H. (1970). Negation, conjunction, and quantifiers: Syntax vs. semantics. *Foundations of Language, 6,* 153–165.

Pecher, D., Zeelenberg, R., & Barsalou, L. W. (2003). Verifying properties from different modalities for concepts produces switching costs. *Psychological Science, 14,* 119–124.

Pecher, D., & Zwaan, R. A. (2005). Introduction to grounding cognition. In D. Pecher & R. A. Zwaan (Eds.). *Grounding cognition: The role of perception and action in memory, language, and thinking* (pp. 1–7). Cambridge, UK: Cambridge University Press.

Pulvermüller, F. A. (2002). Brain perspective on language mechanisms: From discrete neuronal ensembles to serial order. *Progress in Neurobiology, 67,* 85–111.

Pulvermüller, F., Härle, M., & Hummel, F. (2000). Neurophysiological distinction of semantic verb categories. *NeuroReport, 11,* 2789–2793.

Reichle, E. D., Carpenter, P. A., & Just, M. A. (2000). The neural bases of strategy and skill in sentences-picture verification. *Cognitive Psychology, 40,* 261–295.

Richards, A., & Frensch, C. C. (1987). The effects of independently validated strategies on visual hemifield asymmetry. *British Journal of Psychology, 78,* 163–181.

Rinck, M., & Bower, G. H. (1995). Anaphora resolution and the focus of attention in situation models. *Journal of Memory and Language, 34,* 110–131.

Roberts, M., Wood, D. J., & Gilmore, D. J. (1994). The sentence-picture verification task: Methodological and theoretical difficulties. *British Journal of Psychology, 85,* 413–432.

Singer, M. (1994). Discourse inference processes. In M. A. Gernsbacher (Ed.), *Handbook of psycholinguistics* (pp. 479–515). San Diego: Academic Press.

Slobin, D. I. (1966). Grammatical transformations and sentence comprehension in childhood and adulthood. *Journal of Verbal Learning and Verbal Behavior, 5,* 219–227.

Spence, C. J., Nicholls, M. E. R., & Driver, J. (2001). The cost of expecting events in the wrong sensory modality. *Perception & Psychophysics, 63,* 330–336.

Spivey, M., Tyler, M., Richardson, D., & Young, E. (2000). Eye movements during comprehension of spoken scene descriptions. In *Proceedings of the 22nd Annual*

Conference of the Cognitive Science Society (pp. 487–492). Mahwah, NJ: Lawrence Erlbaum Associates.

Stanfield, R. A., & Zwaan, R. A. (2001). The effect of implied orientation derived from verbal context on picture recognition. *Psychological Science, 16*, 153–298.

Trabasso, T., Rollins, H., & Shaughnessy, E. (1971). Storage and verification stages in processing concepts. *Cognitive Psychology, 2*, 239–289.

van Dijk, T. A., & Kintsch, W. (1983). *Strategies of discourse comprehension*. New York: Academic Press.

Wales, R. J., & Grieve, R. (1969). What is so difficult about negation? *Perception and Psychophysics, 6*, 327–332.

Wason, P. C. (1959). The processing of positive and negative information. *Quarterly Journal of Experimental Psychology, 11*, 92–107.

Wason, P. C. (1961). Response to affirmative and negative binary statements. *British Journal of Psychology, 52*, 133–142.

Wason, P. C. (1965), The contexts of plausible denial. *Journal of Verbal Learning and Verbal Behavior, 4*, 7–11.

Wason, P. C. (1972). In real life, negatives are false. *Logique et Analyse, 57–58*, 19–38.

Wason, P. C., & Johnson-Laird, P. N. (1972). *Psychology of reasoning*. London: Batsford.

Wason, P. C., & Jones, S. (1963). Negatives: Denotation and connotation. *British Journal of Psychology, 54*, 299–307.

Wegner, D. M., Ansfield, M. E., & Pilloff, D. (1998). The putt and the pendulum: Ironic effects of the mental control of action. *Psychological Science, 9*, 196–199.

Wegner, D. M., & Erber, R. (1992) The hyperaccessibility of suppressed thoughts. *Journal of Personality and Social Psychology, 63*, 903–912.

Wegner, D. M., Schneider, D. J., Carter, S., & White, L. (1987) Paradoxical effects of thought suppression. *Journal of Personality and Social Psychology, 58*, 409–418.

Wegner, D. M., Wenzlaff, R., Kerker, R. M., & Beattie, A. E. (1981). Incrimination through innuendo: Can media questions become public answers? *Journal of Personality and Social Psychology, 40*, 822–832.

Zwaan, R. A. (2004). The immersed experiencer: Toward an embodied theory of language comprehension. In B. H. Ross (Ed.), *The psychology of learning and motivation* (Vol. 44, pp. 35–62). New York: Academic Press.

Zwaan, R. A., & Madden, C. J. (2005). Embodied sentence comprehension. In D. Pecher & R. A. Zwaan (Eds.), *Grounding cognition: The role of perception and action in memory, language, and thinking* (pp. 224–245). Cambridge, UK: Cambridge University Press.

Zwaan, R. A., Madden, C. J., Yaxley, R. H., & Aveyard, M. E. (2004). Moving words: Dynamic mental representations in language comprehension. *Cognitive Science, 28*, 611–619.

Zwaan, R. A., & Radvansky, G. A. (1998). Situation models in language comprehension and memory. *Psychological Bulletin, 123*, 162–185.

Zwaan, R. A., Stanfield, R. A., & Yaxley, R. H. (2002). Language comprehenders mentally represent the shapes of objects. *Psychological Science, 13*, 168–171.

Zwaan, R. A., & Yaxley, R. H. (2003a). Hemispheric differences in semantic-relatedness judgments. *Cognition, 87*, B79–B86.

Zwaan, R. A., & Yaxley, R. H. (2003b). Spatial iconicity affects semantic-relatedness judgments. *Psychonomic Bulletin & Review, 10*, 945–958.

12

Inference Generation and Cohesion in the Construction of Situation Models: Some Connections with Computational Linguistics

Arthur C. Graesser, Max M. Louwerse, Danielle S. McNamara, Andrew Olney, Zhiqiang Cai, and Heather H. Mitchell
The University of Memphis

It is widely accepted in discourse psychology that readers construct situation models (mental models) as they attempt to comprehend text (Graesser, Millis, & Zwaan, 1997; Kintsch, 1998; Zwaan & Radvansky, 1998). When the text is in the narrative genre, such as a simple story, the situation model is a mental microworld of events and actions, with characters performing actions in the pursuit of goals, events that present obstacles to the goals, conflicts between characters, methods of resolving conflicts, and emotional reactions to the events and conflicts. If the reader has sufficient time and motivation, the mental microworld can have quite vivid elaborations that flesh out details of the spatial setting, the style and procedure of actions, and the properties of objects that characters use. There may also be content that refers to mental states of characters (what they believe, know, perceive, and want). Mental models are created from information in the text as well as knowledge of the reader.

It is comparatively easy for adults to construct situation models for narrative texts because the microworlds have a close correspondence to everyday experiences. In contrast, it is more difficult to construct a situation model for informational texts, such as an expository text on a scientific mechanism. Ideally, the reader would be able to construct a mental model of the components, causal chains, and processes that capture a scientific mechanism. However, this is very difficult or impossible when the reader has little world knowledge to furnish the content needed to construct the mental model.

Discourse psychologists also widely acknowledge that the explicit text does not sufficiently constrain or determine what information is constructed in the situation model. Instead, the content in the situation model is the result of complex interactions among (a) explicit features in the text, (b) capacities of the reader (such as background world knowledge, generic reading skills, cognitive limitations), and (c) the task or goals the reader is attempting to achieve while reading the text (Kintsch, 1998; McNamara, Kintsch, Songer, & Kintsch, 1996; Snow, 2002). Thus, it is appropriate to view comprehension as a complex function or mechanism that considers Representation-Text-Reader-Goal interactions. An explanatory account of situation model construction has required cognitive models that are far more sophisticated and detailed than a handful of general laws or principles. Prominent examples of these cognitive models in discourse psychology include the construction integration model (Kintsch, 1988, 1998; Schmalhofer, McDaniel, & Keefe, 2002; Singer & Kintsch, 2001), the constructionist theory (Graesser, Singer, & Trabasso, 1994; Singer, Graesser, & Trabasso, 1994), the structure building framework (Gernsbacher, 1997), the event indexing model (Zwaan, Langston, & Graesser, 1995; Zwaan & Radvansky, 1998), memory-based resonance models (Lorch, 1998; O'Brien, Rizzella, Albrecht, & Halleran, 1998), and the landscape model (van den Broek, Everson, Virtue, Sung, & Tzeng, 2002).

Research on discourse comprehension will presumably grow in sophistication (and hopefully not confusion or obfuscation) to the extent that there is more analytical detail and a more multidisciplinary perspective in specifying the representations and processes. A scientific understanding of deeper levels of comprehension has benefited from several fields that offer enriched analytical detail, as history has proved (Graesser, Gernsbacher, & Goldman, 2003). In the 1970s, the fields of linguistics and text linguistics identified the constituents of explicit sentences and text (van Dijk, 1972); the field of artificial intelligence identified the representational formats and structures of different types of world knowledge (Schank & Abelson, 1977; Winograd, 1972); and cognitive psychology identified the processes that access, use, and manipulate text representations (Bower, Black, & Turner, 1979; Kintsch, 1974). In the 1980s and 1990s, there was shift to more complex and dynamic processing architectures that dominated the fields of cognitive science, such as production systems (Just & Carpenter, 1992) and neural networks (Kintsch, 1988; St. John, 1992). *Handbook of Discourse Processes* (Graesser, 2003) forecasted that the next generation of discourse psychologists will substantially benefit from contributions in corpus linguistics, computational linguistics, and neuroscience.

In this chapter, we hope to achieve two objectives. The first objective is to briefly identify a landscape of inferences and cohesion relations. Researchers in discourse psychology are encouraged to consider these if they want a comprehensive vision of comprehension. Such an approach will prevent researchers from overly concentrating on a small set of inferences and relations, at the expense of ignoring a large chuck of the terrain. A portion of this landscape of inferences and cohesion relations has already been investigated by discourse psychologists who collect behavioral data, but there still are regions that have been neglected.

A second objective of this chapter is to briefly identify some advances in computational linguistics that offer promising ideas and tools for discourse psychology and cognitive neuroscience. In these advances, researchers have managed to automate aspects of language and comprehension modules, which is no small engineering feat. For example, as we discuss in this chapter, we have made some headway in our development of *Coh-Metrix* (Graesser, McNamara, Louwerse, & Cai, 2004). Coh-Metrix analyzes texts on several dozens of measures of cohesion and language. One version of Coh-Metrix under development takes into consideration the reader's reading skills and prior knowledge. The contributions of computational linguistics, computational discourse, and Coh-Metrix extend beyond engineering and into science to the extent that the representations and processing modules have correspondences to the components in our theories of cognition and neuroscience. Whether these correspondences succeed or fail very much remains an open question.

INFERENCES

Table 12–1 lists and describes 13 classes of inferences that are potentially constructed during text comprehension. This classification was adopted from Graesser, Singer, and Trabasso (1994). The classification scheme covers a diverse set of inferences, although one might question whether this list is exhaustive and whether the grain size and categorical distinctions are optimal for conducting a program of research. All of these classes of inferences require world knowledge to construct. These knowledge-based inferences are constructed by activating and recruiting world knowledge in an effort to make sense out of the text. They are not constructed by logical truth tables, predicate calculus, propositional calculus, Bayes' theorem, and statistical algorithms that many researchers and scholars have traditionally associated with inferences (Kahneman, Slovic, & Tversky, 1982; Rips, 1983; Russell & Whitehead, 1925).

It is beyond the scope of this chapter to define these inference classes precisely and to review the empirical research that assesses the extent to which they are generated during comprehension. However, we can offer a few observations. The classes of inferences differ according to the span of text that is needed to generate the inferences. Classes 1–3 are normally triggered by single words, classes 4–9 by clauses or sentences, and classes 12–13 by lengthy stretches of text, if not the entire composition. It is easiest, methodologically, to investigate inferences that are triggered by shorter spans of text because the researcher can readily designate the points in the text where the inferences are supposed to be made. Most of the available research on on-line comprehension has been conducted on inference classes 1, 4, 5, 6, 7, 8, and 11, whereas there has been a modest amount of research on classes 2, 3, 9, and 10

TABLE 12–1.
Landscape of Inferences

Type of Inference	*Brief Description*
1. Referential	A word or phrase refers to previous element or constituent in the text.
2. Case structure role assignment	An explicit noun-phrase is assigned to a particular case structure rule, e.g., agent, recipient, object, location, time.
3. Instantiation of a noun category	The inference is a subcategory or exemplar that instantiates an explicit noun, e.g., *president* is inferentially instantiated with *George Bush.*
4. Superordinate goal	The inference is a goal that motivates an agent's intentional action.
5. Subordinate goal or action	The inference is a goal, plan, or action that specifies how an agent's action is achieved.
6. Instrument	The inference is an object, part of the body, or resource that is used when an agent executes an intentional action.
7. Causal antecedent	The inference is on a causal chain that bridges the current explicit action, event, or state to the previous passage context.
8. Causal consequence	The inference is on a forecasted causal chain, including physical events, psychological events, and new goals, plans, and actions of agents. Classes 4 and 9 are excluded.
9. Character emotional reaction	The inference is an emotion experienced by an agent, immediately caused by or in response to an event or action.
10. Emotion of reader	The inference is an emotion the reader experiences, or is intended to experience, while reading a text.
11. State	The inference is an ongoing state, from the standpoint of the text, that is not causally related to the story plot. The states include agent's traits, knowledge, and beliefs; the properties of objects and concepts; and the spatial location of entities.
12. Themes	This is a main point or moral of the text.
13. Author's intent	The inference is the author's attitude or motive in writing the text.

and very little research on classes 12 and 13. When evaluating the status of an inference with respect to on-line processing, researchers have used a variety of behavioral measures and methods: self-paced reading times for words or sentences, gaze durations in eye tracking studies, latencies of word naming and lexical decision judgments for test words that periodically occur during reading of text, speeded recognition judgments for test words or sentences, and so on (Haberlandt, 1994). There recently have been a number of studies that have used methods in neuroscience, such as evoked potentials and fMRI (Beeman, Bowden, & Gernsbacher, 2000; Griesel, Friese, & Schmalhofer, 2003; Reichle, Carpenter, & Just, 2000; Wharton et al., 2000).

The classes of inferences presumably differ in how readily they are generated on line. For the sake of the present chapter, the processing status of an inference may be viewed as being in one of a handful of categories. Inferences are *automatic* if they are generated reliably and very quickly (i.e., within a half a second, approximately, of the onset of an inference triggering word), with very little cognitive effort and processing resources. Inferences are *routine* if they require more cognitive effort, but are made reliably and moderately quickly (within a second or less). Inferences are *strategic* if their construction is sensitive to the reader's goals and comprehension strategies, but otherwise are generated moderately quickly. Inferences are *off-line* if they can only be made after comprehension of the text and ordinarily with considerable time, effort, and perhaps extended study and reflection. If we had to place our bets, examples of automatic, routine, strategic, and off-line inferences would be classes 2, 4, 11, and 13, respectively. That is, an example of an automatic inference is the case structure role assignment, where the reader automatically infers the functional role of each explicit noun phrase or prepositional phrase (e.g., agent, recipient, object, time, location). Routine inferences are less automatic, as in the case of superordinate goal inferences. The reader needs some additional time to access knowledge structures from long-term memory that help reconstruct the inferred goals of explicit intentional actions. An example of a strategic inference is a state that specifies the location of an agent or object in a spatial layout. Details about spatial location of entities are not normally constructed on-line unless there is an explicit goal to monitor spatiality and there is enough time to construct such detail. The author's intention is an example of an inference that ordinarily is constructed off-line, after some reflection.

Although this classification of inferences provides a reasonably accurate overview of inferences during comprehension, there are some important caveats. In any test of this classification, it is essential that the sample of readers has the prerequisite amount of world knowledge and reading skill when a fair test of the processing status of an inference is offered. All bets are off if the readers lack critical world knowledge. As a second caveat, it is important that the composition of the text is sufficiently well formed when a fair test of the processing status of an inference is offered. All bets are off if the text is pointless, incoherent, haphazardly assembled, or otherwise "inconsiderate." For example, it would be inappropriate to conclude that theme inferences are not made if the text in a study had a scrambled sequence of experimenter-generated sentences. These two caveats provide important lessons for discourse psychology, computational linguistics, and cognitive neuroscience. Researchers must consider the background knowledge and reading skills of the reader before firm conclusions can be made about the processing status of inferences. Although experimenter-manipulated texts allow for control over potential extraneous variables, they introduce a set of confounding variables that accrue from unnaturalness. Without some assessment of a phenomenon on a natural text, the validity of the phenomenon is fundamentally threatened.

The classification scheme in Table 12–1 was proposed when the constructionist theory was introduced by Graesser et al. (1994). Among other things, the constructionist theory attempted to predict and explain what classes of inferences are routinely made during comprehension and what classes are not. There were two distinctive assumptions of the constructionist theory: the coherence assumption and explanation assumption. The *coherence assumption* states that readers attempt to construct a meaning representation that is coherent at both local and global levels. Local coherence refers to the content, structures, and processes that organize elements, referents, and constituents of adjacent clauses or short sequences of clauses. Global coherence is established when these local chunks of information are organized and interrelated into higher order chunks. The *explanation assumption* states that readers attempt to explain ***why*** actions, events, and states are mentioned in a text. The explanations normally include naïve theories of physical and psychological causality, but the content would have scientific integrity to the extent that the reader has more background knowledge in science.

The other assumptions of the constructionist theory are less distinctive in the sense that they are frequently adopted by other theories of comprehension. For example, the reader goal assumption states that readers construct inferences that address their comprehension goals and the task that they are attempting to achieve. Other uncontroversial components and assumptions stipulated that there are multiple information sources, different levels of representation (surface code, textbase, situation model), multiple memory stores (short-term, long-term, and working memory), a discourse focus, the notion that the strength of encoding an idea increases by activation from multiple sources of information (called convergence) and constraint satisfaction, and the notion that elements in a knowledge structure are more accessible to the extent that there is repetition and automaticity from past experiences.

It is the coherence assumption and the explanation assumptions that made the most discriminating predictions about the classes of inferences that are routinely made during comprehension. According to the coherence assumption, the classes that would have the processing status of being routine or automatic would be *referential* (1), *case structure role assignment* (2), *causal an-*

tecedent (7), and *theme* (12). These inferences are needed to link together constituents of the explicit text. According to the explanation assumption, the routine or automatic inferences would be superordinate goals (4) and causal antecedents (7). These inferences are generated as answers to *why* questions. The remaining categories of inferences would be strategic, off-line, or contingent on the outcome of the uncontroversial components and assumptions. Graesser et al. (1994) reviewed the empirical evidence for the constructionist theory and identified the predictions of alternative theoretical positions. It is a matter of debate how well the constructionist theory has survived after a decade of empirical research and a number of new theoretical models that have entered the arena, such as memory-based models (Lorch, 1998; O'Brien et al., 1998), the landscape model (van den Broek et al., 2002), and embodied theories of cognition (Glenberg, 1997; Kaup, Zwaan, & Lüdtke, this volume, 2005; Zwaan, Stanfield, & Yaxley, 2002).

It is informative to illustrate how the constructionist theory would generate predictions different from alternative theoretical predictions. Consider the following excerpt from the beginning of Ian Rankin's 1992 novel *A Good Hanging*.

> It was the perfect Murder.
>
> Perfect, that is so far as the Lothian and Borders Police were concerned. The murderer had telephoned in to confess, had then panicked and attempted to flee, only to be caught leaving the scene of the crime. End of story. (p. 1)

The following four inferences would potentially be made at particular points in the text.

(A) ***Superordinate goal***: "The murderer wanted to turn himself into the police" is an inference made from the clause *The murderer had telephoned in to confess.*

(B) ***Subordinate goal/action***: "The murderer dialed a telephone number" is an inference made from the clause *The murderer had telephoned in.*

(C) ***Causal antecedent***: "The murderer changed his mind" is an inference made from the clause *he then panicked.*

(D) ***Causal consequence***: "The murderer escaped" is an inference made from the clause *he then panicked.*

According to the constructionist theory, adult readers would generate A and C as routine or automatic inferences, but not B and D. Inferences A and C are answers to *why* questions, the signature question for explanation-based reasoning. So when asked "Why did the murder telephone in?" a plausible answer would be "In order to turn himself in to the police." When asked "Why did the murderer panic?" a plausible answer would be "Because he changed his mind and did not want to turn himself in to the police." Inference B is an answer to a *how* question ("How did the murderer telephone in?"), not a *why* question, so it would be mere ornamentation and strategically generated rather than be a routine inference. Inference D is an answer to a *what-happened-next* question ("What happened after the murderer panicked?"), not a *why* question.

The predictions are quite different for other theoretical frameworks. The minimalist hypothesis of McKoon and Ratcliff (1992) would predict that none of the inferences would be generated, whereas the script theory of Schank and Abelson (1977) would predict that all four of the inferences would be generated. Some theoretical models would offer predictions for some of these inference classes but not other classes. One can track each inference class and derive predictions for each theoretical position. For example, causal consequences (D) are predicted to be routine inferences by a prediction-substantiation model (DeJong, 1979) and script theory, but not routinely by Kintsch's construction integration model, the minimalist hypothesis, and the constructionist theory. Subordinate goals/actions (B) are predicted to be routine inferences by script theory and an embodied theory of cognition (Glenberg, 1997; Zwaan et al., 2002), but not by the minimalist hypothesis and the constructionist theory. It is important to acknowledge that we have specified all-or-none predictions for these positions for the sake of simplicity; clearly, these inferences vary in strength of activation rather than being generated all-or-none. For example, the constructionist theory does specify special conditions when causal consequence and subordinate goal/action inferences are generated (Graesser et al., 1994), whereas Schmalhofer, McDaniel, and Keefe (2002) have augmented Kintsch's CI model to accommodate the possibility of the prediction-substantiation mechanism. Nevertheless, the predictions that we have outlined offer testable claims about the relative strength and reliability of generating such inferences.

Predictions of the constructionist theory were tested in several empirical studies published in the 1990s. These studies collected word naming latencies and lexical decision latencies for test words that were presented quickly after sentences were read in the text (Long, Golding, & Graesser, 1992; Magliano, Baggett, Johnson, & Graesser, 1993; Millis & Graesser, 1994), reading times for sentences in text (Graesser & Bertus, 1998), and think-aloud protocols (Magliano, Trabasso, & Graesser, 1999). However, empirical tests in the arena of neuroscience are sparse, so this is one direction for future research. The classes of inferences presumably differ with respect to the areas of the brain that are activated and with respect to patterns of brain activity. For example, Griesel, Friese, and Schmalhofer (2003) reported that bridging inferences (i.e., categories 1 and 7 in Table 12–1) are accessed more rapidly in the left hemisphere, whereas predictive inferences (categories 4 and 8) are accessed more rapidly in the right hemisphere. There is some evidence that the predictive inferences start out being generated in the right hemisphere before being represented in the left hemisphere later on (Beeman et al., 2000). Brain imaging technologies (such as fMRI and ERPs) can be used to better inform us on the processing status of the different classes of inferences.

COHESION SIGNALS AND RELATIONS

A fundamental distinction can be made between *coherence* and *cohesion*. Coherence is a characteristic of the representation in the mind of the reader, whereas cohesion is a characteristic of the text. A reader perceives a text to be coherent to the extent that the ideas conveyed in a text hang together in a meaningful and organized manner. Coherence relations are constructed in the mind of the reader if the reader has adequate world knowledge about the subject matter and if there are adequate linguistic and discourse markers. Thus, coherence is an achievement that is a product of psychological representations and processes. In contrast, cohesion is an objective property of the explicit language and discourse. There are explicit features, words, phrases, or sentences that guide the reader in interpreting the substantive ideas in the text, in connecting ideas with other ideas, and in connecting ideas to higher level global units (e.g., topics, themes). Simply put, coherence is a psychological construct, whereas cohesion is a textual construct (Louwerse, 2002; Louwerse & Graesser, 2005).

Graesser, McNamara, and Louwerse (2003) identified several categories of cohesion signals and relations that exist in narrative and informational text. These cohesion signals and relations are summarized in Table 12–2. As in the case of inferences, this list of categories is not intended to be exhaustive or to be the theoretically most natural classification. Instead, it provides a representative landscape of what researchers need to worry about. As one moves from class 1 to 10, there is a general shift in the span of the text units (and the associated situation model) from local to global. That is, the span grows from a single word or phrase (classes 1 and 2), to a single clause or sentence (classes 3 and 4), to pairs or small sets of clauses or sentences (classes 5, 6, and 7), to paragraphs (class 8), and to sections of text (classes 9 and 10).

One of the interesting challenges for discourse researchers is to understand the coordination of text cohesion with a coherent situation model. There are some advantages to having a tight coupling between (a) cohesion signals and relations and (b) the ideal coherent situation model that the author intends to convey. For example, if the ideal situation model is a causal chain of four events (A ◊ B ◊ C ◊ D), then a considerate text would present the events in chronological order, with the same verb tense, and with causal conjunctive relations that connect some of the adjacent event pairs (such as those event pairs that some readers might not believe are causally related in the absence of a causal connective). Indeed, a tight coupling between cohesion and the situation model is desirable for low-knowledge readers because they rely on cohesion markers to direct their deeper comprehension (Britton & Gulgoz, 1991; McNamara, 2001; McNamara et al., 1996).

On the other hand, it is not practical and sometimes not even desirable to have a tight coupling between the cohesion markers and the situation model.

TABLE 12–2.
Landscape of Cohesion Signals and Relations

Type of Signal or Relation	*Brief Description*
1. Coreference	Two words or expressions in a text refer to the same person, thing, abstract concept, or idea.
2. Deixis	References to people, location, and time in a conversation among participants. For example, there are pronouns that refer to people (*I, you, we*), to location (*here, there*), and to time (*now, then, later*).
3. Given-new cues	The content of a sentence in a text can be segregated into given (old) information and new information. Given information has already been introduced, mentioned, or inferred from the previous text.
4. Punctuation	In addition, to periods (.), commas (,), colons (:), semi-colons (;) , question marks (?), and exclamation points (!), there are quotation marks ("").
5. Conjunctive relations	Conjunctive relations are text-connecting relations that normally link adjacent clauses or sentences. The subcategories of conjunctive relations include additive (*and, also, moreover*), temporal (*and then, when, before*), causal (*because, consequently, as a result*), intentional (*in order to, by means of*), adversative (*however, but, although*), and logical (*therefore, so*).
6. Verb tense and chronology	Events in text often unfold in a chronological order that matches the order of explicit mention. When the order of mention deviations from chronological order (including flashbacks and flash forwards), this is cued by shifts in verb tense and temporal expressions.
7. Scene changes	A scene is the spatial context that houses the agents in a story or the entities in an expository text. Scene changes are explicitly signaled (*meanwhile back at the ranch . . .*).
8. Topic sentences	The first sentence in a paragraph normally captures the main topic of the paragraph, with subsequent sentences embellishing the topic sentence.
9. Headers and highlighting	Headers, subheaders, and highlighted words help organize the text, direct the reader's attention, and cue discourse genre.
10. Signals of rhetorical structure	There are distinctive words and phrases associated with major subtypes of genres.

Consider the following five events that describe part of the mechanism of a cylinder lock, as described in Macaulay's *The Way Things Work* (1988):

Text 0:

(A) The key turns.

(B) The cam rotates.

(C) The lip of the cam pulls back the rod.

(D) The bolt that is connected to the rod moves into the door.

(E) The door opens.

In the original text, the five events in text 0 were accompanied by a picture and some surrounding text that made the comprehension experience flow more naturally; these five events are extracted here for the sake of making some points. One point is that it would be cumbersome if there were a relational, causal verb (such as *cause, enable, allow*) that connected each pair of events, as illustrated below in text 1:

Text 1:

The key's turning causes the cam to rotate. The rotation of the cam causes the lip of cam to pull back the rod. The pulling back of the rod by the lip of the cam causes the bolt that is connected to the rod to move into the door. The bolt's moving into the door allows the door to open.

Although text 1 has a distinct advantage of coreferential cohesion, the text is undesirable in several respects. The sentences are longer, sometimes to the point of potentially overloading working memory. The syntactic composition of some sentences is awkward, as in the case of the third sentence, which results in potential comprehension difficulties. There is a need to create gerund expressions (*the key's turning*) and nominalizations (*the rotation of the cam*) in order to accommodate the causal verb and to specify the events. Gerunds and nominalizations are syntactically dense constructions that might challenge readers with low reading ability. There is added redundancy because events B, C, and D need to be mentioned twice. This has the virtue of repetition, which is presumably helpful to learning, but has the liability of wordiness. Perhaps the repetition can be avoided by connecting only some of the adjacent pairs with causal verbs. However, that approach would require a decision on which adjacent pairs to connect and would have a looser coupling between cohesion and the situation model.

Text 2 articulates the same five events with conjunctive relations that specify time or causality:

Text 2:

(2) When the key turns, the cam rotates. As a result, the lip of the cam pulls back the rod. Consequently, the bolt that is connected to the rod moves into the door, so the door can open.

Despite the sacrifice of some referential cues, text 2 is clearly a much smoother and more concise articulation than text 1. However, there are a few difficulties with the use of conjunctive relations as a general solution to the specification of causal relations between events. One problem is that most of the conjunctions frequently used in English have undesirable features. Some of the conjunctions are not necessarily causal, such as *when, and then,* and *so. When* and *and then* may merely convey temporality, whereas *so* may suggest a logical derivation rather than causality (Louwerse, 2002). Such polysemous conjunctions fail to discriminatively pinpoint the causal relation. *Consequently* is patently causal, although it is debatable what sort of causal relation is implied (e.g., direct or indirect cause). *Because* is the prototypical causal conjunction, but it has the undesirable feature of reversing temporal order of events in articulation frames *X because Y*. For example, it is inappropriate to say *the key turns because the cam rotates* (A because B), even though the order of mentioning the events follows the chronological causal order in the situation model. Instead, it is appropriate to say *the cam rotates because the key turns* (B because A), where the order of mentioning events is opposite that of the chronological causal order.

Writers often remove information in order to cope with the complexity of mapping cohesion markers onto the intended situation model. This is accomplished by deleting some of the causal relations and by using noun phrases that elliptically delete fragments of the event being referred to. This is illustrated in Text 3:

Text 3:

(3) When the key turns, the cam rotates. The rotation causes the lip of cam to pull back the rod. Then the bolt moves into the door so the door can open.

The rotation in the second sentence elliptically deletes mentioning that it is the cam that rotates. There is no causal link between the pulling back of the rod and the bolt moving into the door, and no mention of the fact that the bolt is connected to the rod. Unfortunately, the removal of this content will likely create problems for low-knowledge readers because they will be unable to fill in the missing information and construct a coherent causal thread. The sentences are indeed shorter, which presumably alleviates working memory load and creates simpler syntactic constructions; both of these are allegedly bonuses for readers with low reading skill. However, the liability is that the integrity of the situation model suffers.

McNamara has documented an intriguing interaction between text cohesion and the world knowledge of the readers when they attempt to comprehend science texts (McNamara, 2001; McNamara et al., 1996). In a series of studies, McNamara manipulated text cohesion (high versus low), measured the prior knowledge that readers had about the topics (high versus low knowledge about the science topic), and administered tests that assessed different levels of meaning representation (recall of the explicit propositions versus answering questions about the deeper situation model). High-cohesion texts were best for low-knowledge readers, no matter what type of test was administered. This unsurprising result is compatible with most theories of comprehension and the folklore of teachers and text designers. Recall for high-cohesion texts was also a bit higher than, or equivalent to, low-cohesion texts for readers with high world knowledge. Again, this outcome is not particularly surprising. However, in tests of the deeper situation model, high-knowledge readers frequently benefited from text with low cohesion. The low-cohesion texts encouraged the knowledgeable readers to work harder and build more elaborated situation models. This result strongly suggests that it is important to tailor the cohesion of the text to the world knowledge of the reader. High-knowledge readers may benefit from more challenges and difficult texts that prevent them from being lulled into complacency by a well-crafted text that engenders an illusion of comprehension. Low-knowledge readers benefit from a high density of coherence relations.

It would be intriguing to test whether a Knowledge/Cohesion interaction occurs in evoked potentials, fMRIs, or other paradigms in cognitive neuroscience. The experimental procedure would be quite straightforward in the case of fMRI. Participants would be administered tests of individual differences on world knowledge, reading fluency, language decoding, working memory, and other measures of verbal ability (Perfetti, 1985, 1994). As they read texts that vary in cohesion, researchers would collect fMRI data and observe the extent to which areas of the brain are active for theoretically expected dimensions of the situation model. For low-knowledge readers, brain activities in these areas should be more pronounced for high-cohesion than for low-cohesion texts; the opposite trend should occur for high-knowledge readers. Of course, a fair test of the impact of cohesion should rule out auxiliary dimensions of language and the situation model. The computer tool described in the next section scales the texts on metrics that correspond to these potentially correlated dimensions.

Cohesion markers need to be systematically coordinated with the situation model, so it is extremely important to have a sufficiently detailed theoretical specification of the situation model. The content, format, and structure of the situation model are matters of substantial theoretical debate, but there is widespread agreement that the situation model is a multithreaded construct rather than a monolithic construct. This notion is emphasized in Zwaan's *event indexing model* (Zwaan, Langston, & Graesser, 1995; Zwaan, Magliano, & Graesser, 1995; Zwaan & Radvansky, 1998). According to this model, the reader monitors five conceptual dimensions during reading: The protagonist (agency), temporality, spatiality, causality, and intentionality (i.e., character goals). A break in continuity may occur on any one of these dimensions during reading of an event E_N in an incoming sentence and relating it to the event E_{N-1} in the previous sentence. *Protagonist* discontinuity occurs when event E_N

has a character that is different from the characters in the previous event E_{N-1}. *Temporal* discontinuity occurs when event E_N occurs much later in time than E_{N-1}, or there is a flashback. *Spatial* discontinuity occurs when the spatial setting of E_N is different from that of E_{N-1}. *Causal* discontinuity occurs when event E_N is not causally related to E_{N-1}. *Intentional* discontinuity occurs when the event E_N is part of a protagonist's plan that is different from the plan in the local discourse context. An incoming event in a text may have discontinuities on more than one of these five dimensions. Zwaan, Magliano, and Graesser (1995) reported that reading time for an explicit event in a literary story increased as a function of the number of dimensions with discontinuities and that each dimension had its unique impact on reading time. Discontinuities on these dimensions also predicted the extent to which pairs of events were associatively related, with weaker associations for pairs with more discontinuities (Zwaan, Langston, & Graesser, 1995).

The neuroscience literature should shed some light on whether discontinuities and the resulting inferences on the multithreaded situation model will systematically predict brain activities. Researchers in cognitive neuroscience have examined differences in the roles of the right and left hemispheres during comprehension at different levels of processing (Ferstl, Guthke, & von Cramon, 2002). Long and her colleagues (Long & Baynes, 2002; Long, Bayes, & Prat, 2005) reported that the propositional representation and the establishment of local coherence reside in the left hemisphere, whereas many aspects of the situation model and global discourse coherence reside in both hemispheres. Beeman et al. (2000) reported differences in the types of inferences processed in the two hemispheres. Participants listened to stories that stimulated inferences and then named inference-related words. The test words were presented to the right visual field (i.e., processed by the left hemisphere) or the left visual field (processed by the right hemisphere), and word priming effects were measured. The inferences needed for establishing cohesion showed priming when processed in the left hemisphere, whereas the predictive inferences had more involvement of the right hemisphere. Aside from the hemispheric differences, neuroimaging studies have suggested that the frontal cortex has a prominent function in creating coherence. Wharton et al (2000) used fMRI to investigate causal inferences that are needed to fill causal discontinuities; the bilateral dorsomedial frontal cortex was primarily involved in the construction of these causal inferences.

Individual differences will no doubt present a somewhat more complex picture of the brain activities associated with inferences, cohesion, and coherence. St. George, Mannes, and Hoffman (1997) used an electroencephalogram (EEG) to measure working memory capacity in readers. The inferences generated during reading were affected by working memory capacity. Readers with high working memory span were able to make both bridging inferences (needed to establish text coherence) and elaborative inferences (not needed for text coherence). Readers with low working memory span were able to make only the bridging inferences.

Many of the cognitive neuroscience studies have unfortunately been imprecise in specifying the classes of inferences and cohesion relations that were used in the text materials. One direction for future neuroscience research is to be somewhat more specific about text and content features, perhaps to the level of grain size shown in Tables 12–1 and 12–2.

COHMETRIX: A SOFTWARE TOOL THAT ASSESSES TEXTS ON COHESION AND LANGUAGE USING ADVANCES IN COMPUTATION LINGUISTICS

Recent advances in the field of computational linguistics have made it more feasible to automate the processing of language and text comprehension (Allen, 1995; Jurafsky & Martin, 2000). As a consequence of these advances, we can go some distance in accounting for discourse cohesion by identifying language and discourse patterns that are sufficiently well specified that they can be extracted by computers. We have recently developed a web-based software tool, called Coh-Metrix, that analyzes texts on hundreds of measures of cohesion, language, and readability (Graesser et al., 2004). The ultimate goal is to have a tool that replaces standard readability formulas by being sensitive to a range of cohesion relations, classes of inferences, and reader abilities (i.e., world knowledge). This section describes Coh-Metrix and gives examples of its metrics for some example texts.

We view Coh-Metrix as an important integration of research in discourse psychology and research in computational linguistics. In the past, researchers in computational linguistics were only minimally aware of contributions in discourse psychology. Computational linguists were primarily concerned with building automated natural language technologies that accurately process text and incorporate linguistic theories and or statistical algorithms; there was no direct concern with cognitive representations, psychological mechanisms, and neuroscience—the concerns of the discourse psychologist. At this point, the integration of these fields is so much in its infancy that we can only raise the open question of which modules in Coh-Metrix are psychologically plausible and which are merely engineering feats.

As we have discussed in this chapter, inference generation, cohesion, and coherence are fundamental to text comprehension. However, these components are not captured in common text readability formulas that focus almost exclusively on word length, word frequency, and sentence length. Coh-Metrix measures texts on a broad profile of language and cohesion characteristics. Consequently, we anticipate that Coh-Metrix will eventually replace the current readability formulas. Another salient feature of Coh-Metrix, particularly the future versions that we develop, is that it does not predict readability of the text on the basis of textual characteristics alone. Instead, it predicts how readable a text will be on the basis of its cohesion in combination with reader characteristics (such as world knowledge and general reading ability).

Coh-Metrix (http://csep.psyc.memphis.edu/cohmetrix) analyzes texts on over 50 types of cohesion relations and over 200 measures of language and discourse. It does so through modules that use lexicons, classifiers, syntactic parsers, shallow semantic interpreters, conceptual templates, latent semantic analysis, and other components that are widely used in computational linguistics (Allen, 1995; Jurafsky & Martin, 2000; Landauer, Foltz, & Laham, 1998). For example, Coh-Matrix taps into a large number of lexicons that are available for free, including WordNet (Miller, Beckwith, Fellbaum, Gross, & Miller, 1990), MRC Psycholinguistic Database (Coltheart, 1981), and the word frequency statistics collected by Francis and Kucera (1982). These lexicons collectively provide information about a word's syntactic class(es), semantic composition, alternative senses, concreteness, imagability, frequency of usage of words in the English language, and dozens of other characteristics. One module uses syntactic parsers (Abney, 1997; Sekine & Grishman, 1995) and a part-of-speech "tagger" (e.g., classifier) developed by Brill (1995). Many words can be assigned to more than one part of speech (e.g., *bank* can be an adjective, noun, or verb), so there needs to be some way of determining what syntactic class is relevant in the sentence context; these natural language technologies automatically assign the appropriate syntactic class. The syntactic parser also provides the foundation for scaling sentences on syntactic complexity, the density of noun phrases, referential cohesion, and many other characteristics. Another important component in Coh-Metrix is the Latent Semantic Analysis (LSA) module that measures the conceptual similarity between sentences, paragraphs, and texts on the basis of world knowledge (Kintsch, 1998, Landauer et al., 1998).

It is well beyond the scope of this chapter to define and discuss the various measures of Coh-Metrix. Instead, we present an example analysis that scales texts on referential cohesion, causal cohesion, and a few other measures. Consider the four texts that were presented earlier when we discussed how the causal chain of a cylinder lock would be articulated. Table 12–3 presents a subset of the Coh-Metrix measures for these four texts. The Flesch Kincaid Grade Level and the measure of average sentence length would lead one to the conclusion that Texts 0 and 3 are the easiest texts. They would presumably be assigned to poor readers or readers with low world knowledge. They have shorter sentences, which allegedly are less taxing on working memory. However, as we discussed earlier, this may be a misleading conclusion. Texts 0 and 3 have fewer cohesion signals and relations than do texts 1 and 2. When considering referential cohesion, texts 1 and 2 are substantially higher than texts 0 and 3. Regarding causal cohesion and the LSA metrics, text 1 is greater than text 0, and text 2 is greater than text 3; the mean scores for texts 1 and 2 combined exceed those of texts 0 and 3 combined. Therefore, if we used cohesion as a criterion measure rather than readability, we would recommend assigning texts 1 or 2 rather than texts 0 or 3 to beginning readers or to readers with low word knowledge. There obviously is a clash between the read-

TABLE 12–3.
Coh-Metrix Measures for Four Texts on the Cylinder Lock

	Four Texts			
Coh-Metrix measures	0	1	2	3
Readability measures				
Average sentence length	6.00	15.50	12.33	10.33
Average word length	3.70	3.56	3.78	3.71
Flesch Kincaid grade level	.80	4.31	3.21	2.80
Referential cohesion				
Adjacent sentences	.75	1.00	1.00	.50
2 sentence spans	.55	.88	.80	.40
Causal cohesion				
Ratio of causal cohesion particles to causal verbs	.50	.57	1.25	1.00
Latent semantic analysis				
All possible sentence pairs	.31	.48	.17	.13
Sentences to text	.49	.57	.38	.31

ability formulas and the cohesion metrics of Coh-Metrix. Regarding the readers who are more advanced, with more world knowledge, we would recommend texts 0 or 3, just the opposite of the recommendation of a reading expert who advocates readability formulas.

We should say a few words about our method of computing referential and causal cohesion. One of the two measures of referential cohesion in Table 12–3 was computed for adjacent sentences in the text. A pair of adjacent sentences was scored as referentially linked if (a) there was at least one noun shared by the two sentences (or what some researchers call argument overlap) or (b) the morphological stem of a noun in sentence A overlapped the stem of any content word in sentence B. The "b" alternative allows a referential link between *the cam rotated* in one sentence and *the rotation* in another sentence. Our first measure of referential cohesion was simply the proportion of adjacent sentence pairs that had referential links, as defined above. The second measure of referential cohesion was measured in the same way, except that we included sentence pairs that were within two sentences of each other, such as sentences 1 and 3 but not sentences 1 and 4.

Causal cohesion was measured as a ratio of (a) the number of words that signal causal cohesion and (b) the number of main verbs that are classified as causal. Examples of words that signal causal cohesion are conjunctions (e.g., *because, so, consequently*) and verbs that directly denote or assert a causal relation (e.g., *cause, enable, allow*). Verbs were scored as being causal (e.g., *turn, pull, move*) if WordNet identified them as being causal.

Global cohesion of a text was measured by Latent Semantic Analysis (LSA). LSA has recently been proposed as a statistical representation of a large body of world knowledge (Landauer et al., 1998). LSA uses a statistical method called "singular value decomposition" (SVD) to reduce a large Word-by-Document co-occurrence matrix to approximately 100–500 functional dimensions. The Word-by-Document co-occurrence matrix is simply a record of the number of times word W_i occurs in document D_j. A document may be defined as a sentence, paragraph, or section of an article. Each word, sentence, or text ends up being a weighted vector on the K dimensions. The "match" (i.e., similarity in meaning, conceptual relatedness) between two unordered bags of words (single words, sentences, or texts) is computed as a geometric cosine (or dot product) between the two vectors, with values ranging from 0 to 1. From the present standpoint, LSA was used to compute the similarity between two sentences, or between the entire text and a sentence. The first LSA measure was simply the mean cosine value of all possible pairs of sentences. The second LSA measure was the mean cosine value between each sentence and the text as a whole.

The measures in Table 12–3 clearly show that there are trade-offs among some of the measures of text quality. Texts with short sentences fit within the limited capacity working memory but run the risk of sacrificing referential and causal cohesion. Such trade-offs support the conclusion that there may be no such thing as the perfect text to convey a body of knowledge. Moreover, an ideal text depends on the characteristics of the reader. Readers with low reading ability and domain knowledge should be given texts with higher cohesion and longer sentences; good readers with high domain knowledge should be assigned texts with lower cohesion to encourage them to actively construct the meaning.

SUMMARY

This chapter has discussed how readers construct situation models while comprehending text. Readers construct different classes of inferences to fill out the situation model. The likelihood of constructing particular classes of inferences is systematic, just like other language modules (such as syntax) because members of a culture are exposed to very similar worlds and have very similar cognitive constraints. However, the alternative models of discourse comprehension make rather different assumptions about what classes of inferences are routinely constructed during comprehension. The construction of the situation model is heavily influenced by linguistic features and cohesion of the text. This chapter identifies many of the linguistic and discourse features that contribute to text cohesion and psychological coherence. We are convinced that the next stage of unraveling the mysteries of situation models, inferences, cohesion, and coherence will require breakthroughs in neuroscience and computational linguistics. Neuroscience will provide more convincing evidence on what cognitive representations are recruited during these comprehension processes. Computational linguistics will offer more precise analytical detail on text characteristics. A recent computer system we have developed, called Coh-Metrix, incorporates new modules and metrics in computational linguistics that allow us to analyze text on over 50 measures of cohesion and 200 measures of language. The question remains whether our metrics of cohesion in Coh-Metrix have any validity from the standpoint of psychological models and brain mechanisms. Both the discoveries and the devil lie in the details.

ACKNOWLEDGMENTS

This research was supported by the Institute for Education Sciences (IES R3056020018-02), the National Science Foundation (SBR 9720314, REC-0089271, REC 0106965, REC 0126265, ITR 0325428), and the Department of Defense Multidisciplinary University Research Initiative (MURI) administered by the Office of Naval Research under grant N00014-00-1-0600. Any opinions, findings, and conclusions or recommendations expressed in this material are those of the authors and do not necessarily reflect the views of the DoD, ONR, or NSF. We thank members of the Tutoring Research Group at the University of Memphis (visit http://www.autotutor.org) and the Cognitive Studies and Educational Practice lab at the University of Memphis (http://csep.psyc.memphis.edu).

REFERENCES

Abney, S. (1997). *The SCOL Manual (version 0.1b).* Unpublished manuscript, Tuebingen, Germany. Available at www.sfs.nphil.uni-tuebingen.de/\Tilde abney/

Allen, J. (1995). *Natural language understanding.* Redwood City, CA: Benjamin/Cummings.

Beeman, M. J., Bowden, E. M., & Gernsbacher, M. A. (2000). Right and left hemisphere cooperation for drawing predictive and coherence inferences during normal story comprehension. *Brain and Language, 71,* 310–336.

Bower, G. H., Black, J. B., & Turner, T. J. (1979). Scripts in memory for text. *Cognitive Psychology, 11,* 177–220.

Brill, E. (1995). Transformation-based error-driven learning and natural language processing: A case study in part-of-speech tagging. *Computational Linguistics, 21,* 543–566.

Britton, B. K., & Gulgoz, S. (1991). Using Kintsch's computational model to improve instructional text: Effects of repairing inference calls on recall and cognitive structures. *Journal of Educational Psychology, 83,* 329–345.

Coltheart, M. (1981). The MRC Psycholinguistic Database. *Quarterly Journal of Experimental Psychology, 33A,* 497–505.

DeJong, G. F. (1979). Prediction and substantiation: A new approach to natural language processing. *Cognitive Science, 3,* 251–273.

Ferstl, E. C., Guthke, T., & von Cramon, D. (2002). Text comprehension after brain injury: Left prefrontal lesions affect inference processes. *Neuropsychology, 16,* 292–308.

Francis, W. N., & Kucera, N. (1982). *Frequency analysis of English usage.* Houghton-Mifflin, Boston.

Gernsbacher, M. A. (1997). Two decades of structure building. *Discourse Processes, 23,* 265–304.

Glenberg, A. M. (1997). What memory is for. *Behavioral and Brain Sciences, 20,* 1–19.

Graesser, A. C., & Bertus, E. L. (1998). The construction of causal inferences while reading expository texts on science and technology. *Scientific Studies of Reading, 2,* 247–269.

Graesser, A. C., Gernsbacher, M. A., & Goldman, S. R. (2003). Introduction to the Handbook of Discourse Processes. In A. C. Graesser, M. A. Gernsbacher, & S. R. Goldman (Eds.), *Handbook of discourse processes* (pp. 1–24). Mahwah, NJ: Lawrence Erlbaum Associates.

Graesser, A. C., McNamara, D. S., & Louwerse, M. M. (2003). What do readers need to learn in order to process coherence relations in narrative and expository text. In A. P. Sweet & C. E. Snow (Eds.), *Rethinking reading comprehension* (pp. 82–98). New York: Guilford.

Graesser, A. C., McNamara, D. S., Louwerse, M. M., & Cai, Z. (2004). Coh-Metrix: Analysis of text on cohesion and language. *Behavioral Research Methods, Instruments, and Computers, 36,* 193–202.

Graesser, A. C., Millis, K. K., & Zwaan, R. A. (1997). Discourse comprehension. *Annual Review of Psychology, 48,* 163–189.

Graesser, A. C., Singer, M., & Trabasso, T. (1994). Constructing inferences during narrative text comprehension. *Psychological Review, 101,* 371–395.

Griesel, C., Friese, U., & Schmalhofer, F. (Submitted) What are the differences in the cognitive representations of predictive and bridging inferences?

Haberlandt, K. (1994). Methods in reading research. In M. A. Gernsbacher (Ed.), *Handbook of psycholinguistics* (pp. 1–31). San Diego: Academic Press.

Jurafsky, D., & Martin, J. H. (2000). *Speech and language processing: An introduction to natural language processing, computational linguistics, and speech recognition.* Englewood Cliffs, NJ: Prentice-Hall.

Just, M. A., & Carpenter, P. A. (1992). A capacity theory of comprehension: Individual differences in working memory. *Psychological Review, 99,* 122–149.

Kahneman, D., Slovic, P., & Tversky, A. (1982). *Judgements under uncertainty: Heuristics and biases.* Cambridge, UK: Cambridge University Press.

Kintsch, W. (1974). *The representation of meaning in memory.* Hillsdale, NJ: Lawrence Erlbaum Associates.

Kintsch, W. (1988). The role of knowledge in discourse comprehension: A construction-integration model. *Psychological Review, 95,* 163–182.

Kintsch, W. (1998). *Comprehension: A paradigm for cognition.* Cambridge, UK: Cambridge University Press.

Landauer, T. K., Foltz, P. W., & Laham, D. (1998). An introduction to latent semantic analysis. *Discourse Processes, 25,* 259–284.

Long, D. L., & Baynes, K. (2002). Discourse representation in the two cerebral hemispheres. *Journal of Cognitive Neuroscience, 14,* 228–242.

Long, D. L., Golding, J. M., & Graesser, A. C. (1992). Test on the on-line status of goal-related inferences. *Journal of Memory and Language, 31*, 634–647.

Lorch, R. F. (1998). Memory-based text processing: Assumptions and issues. *Discourse Processes, 26*, 213–221.

Louwerse, M. M. (2002). An analytic and cognitive parameterization of coherence relations. *Cognitive Linguistics*, 291–315.

Louwerse, M. M., & Graesser, A. C. (2005). Coherence in discourse. In P. Strazny (Ed.), *Encyclopedia of linguistics*. Chicago: Fitzroy Dearborn.

Macaulay, D. (1988). *The way things work*. Boston: Houghton Mifflin.

Magliano, J. P., Baggett, W. B., Johnson, B. K., & Graesser, A. C. (1993). The time course of generating causal antecedent and causal consequence inferences. *Discourse Processes, 16*, 35–53.

Magliano, J. P., Trabasso, T., & Graesser, A. C. (1999). Strategic processing during comprehension. *Journal of Educational Psychology, 91*, 615–629.

McKoon, G., & Ratcliff, R. (1992). Inference during reading. *Psychological Review, 99*, 440–466.

McNamara, D. S. (2001). Reading both high and low coherence texts: Effects of text sequence and prior knowledge. *Canadian Journal of Experimental Psychology, 55*, 51–62.

McNamara, D. S., Kintsch, E., Songer, N. B., & Kintsch, W. (1996). Are good texts always better? Text coherence, background knowledge, and levels of understanding in learning from text. *Cognition and Instruction, 14*, 1–43.

Miller, G. A., Beckwith, R., Fellbaum, C., Gross, D., & Miller, K. (1990). *Five Papers on WordNet*. Cognitive Science Laboratory, Princeton University, No. 43.

Millis, K., & Graesser, A. C. (1994). The time-course of constructing knowledge-based inferences for scientific texts. *Journal of Memory and Language, 33*, 583–599.

Myers, J. L., O'Brien, E. J., Albrecht, J. E., & Mason, R. A. (1994). Maintaining global coherence during reading. *Journal of Experimental Psychology: Learning, Memory, and Cognition, 20*, 876–886.

O'Brien, E. J., Rizzella, M. L., Albrecht, J. E., & Halleran, J. G. (1998). Updating a situation model: A memory-based text processing view. *Journal of Experimental Psychology: Learning, Memory, and Cognition, 24*, 1200–1210.

Perfetti, C. A. (1985). *Reading ability*. New York: Oxford University Press.

Perfetti, C. A. (1994). Psycholinguistics and reading ability. In M. A. Gernsbacher (Ed.), *The handbook of psycholinguistics* (pp. 849–894). San Diego: Academic Press.

Reichle, E. D., Carpenter, P. A., & Just, M. A. (2000). The neural basis of strategy and skill in sentence-picture verification. *Cognitive Psychology, 40*, 261–295.

Rips, L. J. (1983). Cognitive processes in propositional reasoning. *Psychological Review, 90*, 38–71.

Russell, B., & Whitehead, A. N. (1925). *Principia mathematica* (Vol. 1, 2nd ed.). New York: Cambridge University Press.

Schank, R. C., & Abelson, R. P. (1977). *Scripts, plans, goals, and understanding: An inquiry into human knowledge structures*. Hillsdale, NJ: Lawrence Erlbaum Associates.

Schmalhofer, F., McDaniel, M. A., & Keefe, D. (2002). A unified model for predictive and bridging inferences. *Discourse Process, 33*, 105–132.

Sekine, S., & Grishman, R. (1995). A corpus-based probabilistic grammar with only two nonterminals. In *Fourth International Workshop on Parsing Technologies* (pp. 260–270). Prague/Karlovy Vary, Czech Republic, 20–23 September 1995.

Singer, M., Graesser, A. C., & Trabasso, T. (1994). Minimal or global inference during reading. *Journal of Memory and Language, 33*, 421–41.

Singer, M., & Kintsch, W. (2001). Text retrieval: A theoretical exploration. *Discourse Processes, 31*, 27–59.

Snow, C. (2002). *Reading for understanding: Toward an R&D program in reading comprehension*. Santa Monica, CA: RAND Corporation.

St. George, M., Mannes, S., & Hoffman, J. E. (1997). Individual differences in inference generation: An ERP analysis. *Journal of Cognitive Neuroscience, 9*, 776–787.

St. John, M. F. (1992). The story gestalt: A model of knowledge-intensive processes in text comprehension. *Cognitive Science, 16*, 271–306.

van den Broek, P., Everson, M., Virtue, S., Sung, Y., & Tzeng, Y. (2002). Comprehension and memory of science texts: Inferential processes and the construction of a mental representation. In J. Otero, J. Leon, & A. C. Graesser (Eds.), *The psychology of science text comprehension*. Mahwah, NJ: Lawrence Erlbaum Associates.

van Dijk, T. A. (1972). *Some aspects of text grammars. A study in theoretical linguistics and poetics*. The Hague: Mouton.

Wharton, C. M., Thompson, J., Sevostianov, A., Graesser, A. C., Fromm, S. J., Courtney, S., Bowles, A., & Braun, A. R. (2000, April). *The neural basis of language and situation models*. Poster presented at the 2000 Annual Meeting of the Cognitive Neuroscience Society, San Francisco.

Winograd, T. (1972). *Understanding natural language*. New York: Academic Press.

Zwaan, R. A., Langston, M. C., & Graesser, A. C. (1995). The construction of situation models in narrative comprehension: an event-indexing model. *Psychological Science, 6*, 292–297.

Zwaan, R. A., Magliano, J. P., & Graesser, A. C. (1995). Dimensions of situation-model construction in narrative comprehension. *Journal of Experimental Psychology: Learning, Memory, and Cognition, 21*, 386–397.

Zwaan, R. A., & Radvansky, G. A. (1998). Situation models in language comprehension and memory. *Psychological Bulletin, 123*, 162–185.

Zwaan, R. A., Stanfield, R. A., & Yaxley, R. H. (2002). Do language comprehenders routinely represent the shapes of objects? *Psychological Science, 13*, 168–171.

13

Multidimensional Situation Models

David J. Therriault
University of Florida

Mike Rinck
Dresden University of Technology, Germany

WHAT'S IN A SITUATION MODEL?

The research landscape examining situation models in discourse has been transformed considerably in the last 20 years. Van Dijk and Kintsch (1983) originally included the concept of a situation model to address issues that were problematic for earlier versions of their theory (Kintsch & van Dijk, 1978). Specifically, van Dijk and Kintsch (1983) argued that situation models were necessary to explain issues of reference, coreference, coherence, perspective taking, translation, individual differences, memory, reordering effects, problem solving, updating knowledge, and learning. One might first notice the comprehensive nature of such a list. It is not surprising, then, that there is general agreement regarding the theoretical importance of situation models. What is surprising, however, as originally pointed out by Glenberg, Meyer, and Lindem (1987), is the lack of agreement regarding what constitutes a situational model and the types of information it might contain.

For the purposes of this chapter, we use the term *situation model* to refer to a discourse representation that captures aspects of a micro-world created by the reader (Johnson-Laird, 1983; van Dijk & Kintsch, 1983). In this sense, a situation model can include propositional information, but also information beyond that given in the text proper. For example, situation models can contain information related to the gist of the text, a reader's potential background knowledge, and inferences not explicitly stated in the text (Zwaan & Radvansky, 1998).

One theory of situation-model construction (i.e., the event-indexing model) suggests that readers comprehend information in the story world at an *event* level (Zwaan, Langston, & Graesser, 1995). In this sense, events are the building blocks of comprehension, capturing the nuances of situations described in narrative text. Readers are sensitive to specific dimensions when attending to these events: space, causality, intentionality, time, and protagonist/objects (Zwaan & Radvansky, 1998). The rationale for each of these dimensions is briefly reviewed below (we realize that there is a vast literature on situation model construction, but it is not our purpose to review that entire body here).

Managing our physical environment is critical to everyday functioning. It is not surprising, then, that readers might also form a spatial layout of a described text, referred to as the space dimension. Most of the early evidence documenting the existence of situation models is predicated on experiments showing that a reader's decisions about an object in a spatial layout is faster the closer that object is to a protagonist currently in focus within the text (Glenberg, Meyer, & Lindem, 1987; Morrow, Bower, & Greenspan, 1989; Morrow, Greenspan, & Bower, 1987; Rinck & Bower, 1995; Wilson, Rinck, McNamara, Bower, & Morrow, 1993). This suggests that readers are mentally keeping track of the protagonist's spatial movement in the story world. It is important to note, however, that in a typical experiment of this sort, subjects first memorize the layout of a building and then read a narrative, which is atypical of normal reading and of normal experience. There is evidence suggesting that readers, who do not have the benefit of a map, do not routinely represent complex spatial information (Hakala, 1999; Langston, Kramer, & Glenberg, 1998; Rinck, 2005; Zwaan & Oostendorp, 1993).

Trabasso and Sperry (1985) and Trabasso and Suh (1993) argue that in order to understand text, readers must represent the causal relations between events, objects, and protagonists and that this is the backbone of the situation model. The causation dimension can be described as the representation of causal relations indicated in text by the connectives *because* or *therefore*. It has been demonstrated that using such connectives increases the coherence of a final representation of events described in a sentence (Millis, Golding, & Barker, 1995). It should be noted, however, that explicit connectives are typically not needed to build causal structures in narrative, unless the content is very unfamiliar or disconnected.

Readers also keep track of goals of the protagonist. This is referred to as the intentionality dimension. Goal monitoring has been well documented (Suh & Trabasso, 1993; Trabasso & Suh, 1993; Lutz & Radvansky, 1997). As an example, Lutz and Radvansky (1997) demonstrated that when readers are presented with a statement such as *David is attempting to submit his chapter in a timely manner*, they store David's goal to submit the chapter and maintain this goal in memory until David is removed from the focus of the text or until the goal has been accomplished. Moreover, recent evidence suggests that objects relevant to a protagonist's active goal remain highly accessible, that the accessibility of objects relevant to a completed goal decays over time, and that objects relevant to a postponed goal are inhibited almost immediately (Rinck & Bower, 2004).

Temporal information is pervasive in language. All sentences contain absolute or relative information about the time course of events described in those sentences (Ter Meulen, 1995; Zwaan & Radvansky, 1998). For example, in English there are 12 different categories in the tense-aspect system: past, present, and future tenses combined with the simple, perfect, progressive, and perfect-progressive aspectual forms (Celce-Murcia & Larsen-Freeman, 1999). The regularity of such temporal markers underscores the importance of time information in building coherent situation models (Magliano & Schleich, 2000; Radvansky, Zwaan, Federico, & Franklin, 1998; Rinck, Hähnel, & Becker, 2001; Zwaan, 1996).

Finally, in a review of situation model research, Zwaan and Radvansky (1998) highlight the importance of protagonist and objects during situation-model construction. There is some argument that they may be the core around which situation models are built. Research consistently demonstrates that readers monitor the identity and traits of a protagonist (Albrecht & O'Brien, 1993, 1995; Cook, Halleran, & O'Brien, 1998; O'Brien, Rizzella, Albrecht, & Halleran, 1998). For example, Albrecht and O'Brien (1993) found that readers slow down when reading a description of actions that are inconsistent with a protagonist's trait (e.g., a vegetarian orders a hamburger). This provides evidence that readers are sensitive to these inconsistencies and therefore must have stored the protagonist's traits in memory.

The selection of the critical dimensions in the event-indexing model appears apt, given their support in the literature. We would suggest, however, that a coherent situation model is more than an aggregation of dimensions. Traditional situation model research examines single dimensions; but it is also important to explore the relative contributions of the individual dimensions and their potential interactions. Consequently, the purpose of this chapter is to synthesize research exploring multidimensional situational models—more specifically, to explore the necessity and dominance of particular indices, interactions between dimensions, and appraise possible additions to the event-indexing model (i.e., emotions and/or reader perspective). The concluding remarks in this chapter will attempt to evaluate the status of the event-indexing model with respect to multidimensional situational models.

STUDIES EXPLORING DIMENSIONAL DOMINANCE

Zwaan, Langston, and Graesser (1995) provided the first test of the event-indexing model using a verb clustering task. In their study, participants were presented with 10 unique verbs from narratives they had previously read. Participants were instructed to write down verbs that they thought belonged together, based on either their memory for the narrative or when the narrative was available for their inspection. In Experiment 1, participants read the narratives and completed the verb clustering task from memory and then completed the verb clustering task a second time with the narratives present. In both conditions, beta weights from the multiple regression analyses indicated that all five situational dimensions predicted verb clustering scores. This was taken as evidence that readers simultaneously monitor all five dimensions specified in the model.

In Experiment 2, participants first completed the verb clustering task when the narratives were available for inspection and then completed the task a second time from memory. Experiment 2 mirrored many of the same results as Experiment 1 with two exceptions. Interestingly, the protagonist and time dimensions did not significantly predict verb clustering scores in Experiment 2. One possible explanation offered for this was that by providing the text first, participants focused more upon the surface structure at the expense of forming a more coherent situation model.

Zwaan, Langston, and Graesser (1995) did not report any colinearity issues between dimensions, suggesting that they were more or less orthogonal. However, there was a significant correlation of note. Causality was significantly correlated with time (.38, $p < .001$). We interpret this correlation as reflective of the obvious temporal relationship between a cause and its effect (i.e., a cause must precede its effect), suggesting that the causal dimension can never truly be orthogonal to the superordinate time dimension.

Zwaan, Magliano, and Graesser (1995) explored how situational discontinuity (for natural literature) affected reading times on three of the event-indexing dimensions: time, space, or causality. Participants read two published short stories, and their time to read each sentence was recorded. Specific pieces of literature were selected in which temporality, spatiality, and causality approached orthogonal variation. That is, there were discrepancies between real world constraints and narrative structure. For example, in the narrative structures selected, an effect could be stated before its cause (causal discontinuity), events could be described as occurring at the same time in different locations (spatial discontinuity), and different events could be described as occurring in the same place at different times (temporal discontinuity).

Results from Zwaan, Magliano, and Graesser (1995) confirmed that readers slowed down considerably when encountering temporal and causal discontinuities. This was not the case for spatial discontinuities. Thus, these results provide some evidence that time and causality are more dominant than space. Interestingly, there were no significant correlations between the time, space, or causality dimensions. The authors suggest that this confirms the orthogonal nature of the dimensions in their particular materials.

Zwaan, Radvansky, Hilliard, and Curiel (1998) examined the extent to which readers monitor the five indices of the event-indexing model during narrative comprehension. The narratives used were coded for situational continuity, and participant reading times were recorded at the sentence and clause levels. Results indicated that reading times increased when temporal, causal, protagonist, and goal discontinuities were encountered. Spatial discontinuities did not elicit an increase in reading times. However, when participants were provided with a relevant map before they read the narratives, spatial discontinuities did increase reading times. This pattern of results was interpreted by Zwaan et al. (1998) as providing further evidence for the event-indexing model. Readers concurrently monitored all of the indices of the event-indexing model (with the exception of space).

Interestingly, the beta weights across three experiments (i.e., an indicator of how much reading time variance was accounted for by each dimensional variable) were greatest for time and causal dimensions. Discontinuities related to time and causation (overall) created the largest increases in reading times. Moreover, a significant correlation was obtained between time and causation across all experiments (Experiment 1: $r \nabla .36, p \leqslant .001$; Experiments 2 and 3: $r \nabla .55, p \leqslant .001$). We argue that this provides stronger evidence that causation is a subcomponent of the time dimension and highlights the importance of the time dimension (i.e., suggests the potential dominance of the time dimension over the other dimensions).

Magliano, Miller, and Zwaan (2001) investigated how various temporal and spatial shifts are understood in film. Participants identified the natural breakpoints of two segments of film by pushing a button. A priori, Magliano et al. identified three different types of film shifts: shifts in time, in movement, and in spatial region. Shifts in time and movement were sufficient to create a change in situation as decided upon by participants. However, shifts in region did not. Furthermore, there were differences in the monitoring levels of participants. Magliano et al. found that monitoring changes in time was more dominant in event understanding than monitoring changes in movement.

Rinck and Hähnel (2002) systematically compared the effects of spatial, intentional, causal, temporal, and emotional inconsistencies to each other. For each dimension, they created texts that contained critical information that was either consistent or inconsistent with information given earlier. Spatial information was related to the location of the protagonist, intentional information to his or her goals, causal information to causally related events in the narrative world, temporal information to the order of events, and emotional information to the feelings of the protagonist. Rinck and Hähnel (2002) found that for each dimension, inconsistent information yielded a reliable increase in reading times of the critical information. The size of this inconsistency effect, however, differed greatly: it was smallest for spatial information, intermediate for intentional and causal information, and largest for temporal and emotional information. However, this pattern has to be interpreted with caution because the different dimensions were assessed with the use of different texts.

Scott-Rich and Taylor (2000) explored the dominance of protagonist, time, and location shifts in narrative text at different levels of processing. They presented participants with narratives that included dimensional shifts (i.e., character, time, or location shifts) and asked readers to rate the cohesion (i.e., how well the sentence fits with the previous sentence), rate the coherence of the sentence (i.e., how well integrated the narrative is overall), or simply read the sentences (i.e., a measure of on-line processing). Shifts in each dimension produced comprehension difficulties, providing further evidence for the event-indexing model. Protagonist shifts were the most disruptive to comprehension. Furthermore, evidence is presented that the protagonist and spatial indices were more dominant than time. Inspection of Scott-Rich and Taylor's materials provides some insight into the discrepancy between this study and the previously reviewed literature. All of the experimental sentences included shifts of two of the three dimensions being examined. Thus, in their design, it is not possible to isolate the effects of a single shift type. There was also little variability in the type of time statements used (e.g., a day later or a week later).

A stronger experimental test of the event-indexing model was reported by Rinck and Weber (2003). In two experiments, participants read narratives containing target sentences that involved situational shifts. Independently of each other, continuity versus shifting of the protagonist, time, and location dimension were varied. Thus, all possible combinations of the three dimensions were created, from completely continuous to completely discontinuous. Despite these variations, the target sentence was identical in all combinations. In both experiments, reading times of the target sentences increased for protagonist shifts and temporal shifts, whereas the effect of spatial shifts was weak. Moreover, an interaction of protagonist shifts and spatial shifts was found: a shift on one of these dimensions sufficed to yield an increase in reading time that was just as large as the increase for a shift on both dimensions. These results support the processing load predictions of the event-indexing model and extend previous correlational results by experimental evidence.

Therriault, Rinck, and Zwaan (2006) directly tested the relative contributions of three situational dimensions when constructing situation models: space, time, and protagonist. In their study, participants were instructed to pay close attention to a single situational dimension (e.g., space) and then read a series of passages (always answering comprehension questions about the focus dimension). However, critical sentence-reading times were also analyzed for shifts in dimensions *not* focused on by the instructions (e.g., time shifts), providing information about the monitoring level of nonfocused dimensions. The study attempted to answer the question, when asked to pay attention to only one dimension, at which level do participants monitor the other dimensions? This inductive approach is conservative, in that the true contribution of nonhighlighted dimensions may be underestimated. Results from Therriault et al. (2006) indicated that time and protagonist were more dominant indices than space, as evidenced by increased reading times for character and temporal shift sentences, even when the reader's attention was focused on another dimension. There was also a slight advantage for time over protagonist—overall, temporal shifts increased reading time more than character shifts.

In summary, the above literature provides converging evidence for the dominance of particular dimensions. Ostensibly, the protagonist and time dimensions are crucial, and this was evident across all experiments in which they were included as factors (Zwaan, Langston, & Graesser, 1995; Zwaan, Magliano, & Graesser, 1995: Zwaan et al., 1998; Magliano et al., 2001; Rinck & Hähnel, 2002, 2003; Scott-Rich & Taylor, 2000; Rinck & Weber, 2003; Therriault et al., 2006), with the exception of the work by Scott-Rich and Taylor (2000). Thus it can be argued that these two dimensions are the most dominant of the ones studied so far.

Discontinuities on the intentionality dimension (protagonists' goals) elicited reliable increases in reading times (Zwaan, Langston, & Graesser, 1995; Zwaan et al., 1998). However, both of these studies were correlational in nature. More work is necessary to determine the relative contribution of the intentionality dimension. It is also difficult to understand goals without relying on protagonist information. Thus we concur with Zwaan, Radvansky, and Whitten (2002) that intentionality is probably a second-order dimension. Even if the orthogonal nature of intentionality can be firmly established, there is little evidence that it is as dominant a dimension as time or protagonist.

Discontinuities on the causality dimension also elicited reliable increases in reading time (Zwaan, Langston, & Graesser, 1995; Zwaan, Magliano, & Graesser, 1995: Zwaan et al., 1998). The causality dimension has often been portrayed as orthogonal from the time dimension. This seems odd, considering that causality is essentially defined by using events in time. That is, an effect cannot precede its cause. One could argue, based upon the correlations data from the reviewed articles, that the causality dimension is also a second-order dimension, that is, a subset of the larger time dimension. Indeed, Rinck and Hähnel (2003) found that temporal inconsistencies yielded reading time increases even when they were not accompanied by causal inconsistencies. In two experiments, they employed an inconsistency paradigm. The inconsistencies were temporal, in that a sentence was either consistent or inconsistent with the order of two events mentioned earlier. In one condition, these two events were causally related: one was the cause of the other. In the alternative condition, the two events were causally unrelated. For causally related events, the inconsistency effect was significantly larger than for unrelated ones. However, even for the latter, the effect was large and highly significant. Thus, readers seem to monitor temporal relations because these are important in and of themselves. Causal relations, on the other hand, cannot exist independently of temporal ones.

There is further evidence that causality can be explained with the use of time. Thüring, Grobmann, and Wender (1985) conducted an experiment in which subjects were instructed to pay attention to the causal (i.e., causal connections between events) or temporal (i.e., the exact dates between events) relations in a series of experiments. Subjects then read sentences that contained explicit and implicit causal and temporal relations.

An example of Thüring et al.'s (1985) materials is provided here:

Example 1: Temporal, explicit passage

In 1553 Henry VIII married Anne Boleyn from England.

In 1554 she gave birth to a daughter, called Elizabeth I.

So just one year after marriage, there was a successor to the throne.

Example 2: Temporal, implicit passage

In 1553 Henry VIII married Anne Boleyn from England.

She gave birth to a daughter, called Elizabeth I.

So just one year after marriage, there was a successor to the throne.

Example 3: Causal, explicit passage

Near the coast of Scotland the Spanish fleet got into a storm.

Most of the ships sank.

Hence, the position of England as a leading naval power was assured in the period that followed.

Example 4: Causal, implicit passage

(1) Near the coast of Scotland the Spanish fleet got into a storm.

Hence, the position of England as a leading naval power was assured in the period that followed.

To the researchers' surprise, subjects that were instructed to make temporal inferences also made causal inferences when reading the causal texts, although they had not been asked to do so (as indicated by increased reading times on the third sentences). Furthermore, subjects actually did better on verification judgments of sentences that employed implicit causal relations when they received the temporal rather than causal instructions. These results suggest that causality is a subset of a larger understanding of the temporal relations in the text.

Finally, there is only minimal evidence that spatial information is routinely monitored by readers. In the original test of the event-indexing model, Zwaan, Langston, and Graesser (1995) found evidence that readers monitor spatial information in narratives (in a verb clustering task). Scott-Rich and Taylor (2000) also found some evidence that location shifts coupled with other dimensions (i.e., time and characters) increased reading times. However, the majority of the literature suggests that space is not a dominant index of the situation model. Further follow-ups exploring space suggest that readers do not form a spatial mental model when reading normal narratives unless explicitly asked to do so or when they are given a map before reading a narrative (Hakala, 1999; Langston et al., 1998; Zwaan & Oostendorp, 1993). We are forced to conclude that space is not a dominant index, but that there may be specific situations when it is conducive to monitor spatial shifts (see also Rinck, 2005).

STUDIES EXPLORING DIMENSION INTERACTIONS

In addition to comparing the relative dominance of situation model dimensions, several studies were designed to investigate possible interactions of dimensions. These experimental studies complement the correlational ones reported originally by Zwaan and his colleagues (1995). One set of experiments (Rinck & Bower, 2000, 2004) employed the map-plus-reading paradigm introduced by Morrow, Bower, and Rinck. Participants first studied the layout of a fictitious research center with rooms and objects located in them, then read narratives taking place within the building. At several points, reading was interrupted by yes-no test probes, which tested the current accessibility of previously learned objects. In Experiment 2 of Rinck and Bower (2000), effects of spatial distance were measured by testing of the accessibility of objects located at differing distances from the protagonist's current location (e.g., 0 or 1 room away). Before presentation of the test probe, however, an intervening episode was inserted in the narrative. Story time distance was manipulated by stating that the intervening episode lasted for either minutes or hours. Discourse time (that is, time spent reading the inserted episode) was manipulated by describing the intervening episode either briefly or at length. Clear effects of story time distance and spatial distance on accessibility were found: objects were more accessible if they were located in the same room as the protagonist, and if the intervening episode was described as short. In contrast, discourse time distance did not affect accessibility at all, demonstrating the negligible role of surface variables compared with situation model variables. These results show that readers use information about both temporal and spatial distance to focus attention on the more important parts of the situation model they create during narrative comprehension. Most importantly for our current question is the fact that the effects of spatial distance and story time distance were perfectly additive.

A similar conclusion was drawn by Rinck and Bower (2004) regarding the possible interaction of spatial distance and goal relevance. In two experiments that also employed the map-plus-reading paradigm, spatial proximity of objects to the current location of the protagonist as well as relevance of these objects to the protagonist's current goal increased the objects' accessibility in memory. These two factors had additive effects on accessibility, so that close, relevant objects were most accessible, and distant, irrelevant objects were least accessible.

The lack of interactions in the above experiments may be due to the fact that accessibility of situation model entities (i.e., objects) was the main dependent variable. This is quite different from other studies, which addressed situational shifts directly. In these studies, evidence for interactions was repeatedly found. First, Rinck and Weber (2003) observed an interaction of protagonist shifts and spatial shifts: a shift on one of these dimensions sufficed to yield an increase in reading time that was just as large as the increase for a shift on both dimensions. They explained this observation by pointing out that the different combinations are not equally plausible: Although a protagonist shift and a spatial shift together involve more situational updating than single shifts, this situation is highly plausible because it involves a second character in a second location. In contrast, the single shifts involve unexplained protagonist movements: There is either a sudden new protagonist in the known location (protagonist shift only), or the known protagonist is suddenly appearing in a new location (spatial shift only). These implicit changes require inferences that take additional time, just as the double shift takes time for updating (see Rinck & Weber, 2003). This result was replicated in Experiment 2 of Therriault et al. (2006). Moreover, both studies also showed a three-way interaction of protagonist, time, and space shifts. This interaction was due to the fact that any single situational shift caused a large increase in reading time compared with the fully continuous baseline condition. A second or third additional shift caused only smaller increases. Moreover, the correlational study by Magliano et al. (2001) yielded evidence for interactions, too: some combinations of shifts were much more frequent in existing movies than other combinations. One has to keep in mind, however, that the assumption of independent dimensions inherent in the event-indexing model was made mainly for theoretical parsimony, because the early correlational studies had not yielded evidence for interactions. Now that this evidence is available, it should be accounted for. One way to do this would be to incorporate indices of frequency and/or plausibility for each combination of shifts, such that frequent and highly plausible combinations would yield smaller or even no increases in processing load.

ARE ADDITIONAL DIMENSIONS NECESSARY?

The event-indexing model specifies a core set of dimensions that readers monitor. It is important to evaluate if the model has captured the fundamental set of necessary dimensions. Thus far, the review of dimensional dominance suggests that space is not fundamental, at least in normal, narrative reading (although there are specific situations where the monitoring of the spatial situation can be easily demonstrated). Another proposed vital dimension of the situation model is the causality dimension (Trabasso & Sperry, 1985). However, we have argued, based upon the correlations data from the reviewed articles, that the causality dimension is a subset of the larger time dimension. If one is willing to entertain our arguments, the set of core dimensions in the event-indexing model has been reduced to protagonist, time, and possibly intentionality. However, it is important to consider whether there are other dimensions, previously unspecified, that warrant inclusion in the model.

Emotion is one potential candidate. The discourse literature provides ample evidence that readers can activate knowledge related to fictional characters' emotional states (de Vega, Diaz, & León, 1997; de Vega, León, & Diaz, 1996; Gernsbacher, Goldsmith, & Robertson, 1992; Gernsbacher & Robertson, 1992; Gernsbacher, Hallada, & Robertson, 1998; Gygax, Oakhill, & Garnham, 2003; Rapp, Gerrig, & Prentice, 2001). In a typical experiment of this sort, participants read emotion words that match or mismatch the context created by a narrative passage. Emotion words that do not match the context of the narrative consistently increase reading times. However, there is some debate about the specificity with which readers can predict particular emotions from context (see Gygax et al., 2003; Rapp et al., 2001).

It is interesting to note the different approaches researchers have taken in attempts to incorporate emotion into the event-indexing model. For example, Gernsbacher (1995) links readers' abilities to activate emotional information with the intentionality dimension of the event-indexing model. Consider the following passage taken from Gernsbacher et al. (1992):

> Paul had always wanted his brother, Luke, to be good in baseball. So Paul had been coaching Luke after school for almost 2 years. In the beginning, Luke's skills were very rough. But after hours and hours of coaching, Paul could see great improvement. In fact, the improvement had been so great that at the end of the season, at the Little League Awards Banquet, Luke's name was called out to receive the Most Valuable Player Award.

Gernsbacher (1995) argues that readers would store the goal information that Paul wants Luke to excel at baseball. It is the achievement or failure of this goal that readers would then use to gauge emotionality. Positive outcomes should lead readers to attribute positive emotions to Paul's character, and inconsistent outcomes should lead readers to attribute negative emotions to Paul's character.

Another approach to explaining emotional traits has been offered by Rapp et al. (2001). They suggest that readers use specific information from the protagonist dimension (i.e., character dispositions and traits) to evaluate story outcomes and make inferences regarding the states of characters. Consider the following example taken from Rapp et al. (2001):

> Peter was looking forward to the first day of the new semester. He was interested in seeing who his new professors would be. His first class was held in a lecture hall. He was well prepared for taking notes. Peter brought a new package of pens with him to class. A student sitting next to him asked to borrow a pen, and Peter said, "Take two."

Rapp et al. (2001) argue that the example paragraph would lead readers to infer that Peter is generous. Rapp et al. (2001) posit a link between such dispositional attributes (e.g., generosity) and the causal dimension of the event-indexing model. More specifically, they argue that readers focus upon dispositional, trait information (often emotional) and apply it to causal structures (i.e., whether Peter donates or not to a charity mentioned later in the passage).

An important theme in both Gernsbacher et al. (1998) and Rapp et al. (2001) is the second-order nature of the emotionality dimension. Ostensibly, emotions are tied to goals and protagonist traits. We would argue that emotional content derived from discourse is a by-product (an important one, to be sure) of interactions between dimensions. For example, Gernsbacher et al. (1998) argue that emotional states are discerned from the outcome of goals (intentionality), and Rapp et al. (2001) argue that emotional trait information is gleaned from the protagonist dimension and then applied (causally).

Another approach to studying emotion in discourse has been to view it as a type of mental perspective taking (de Vega et al., 1996, 1997). According to de Vega et al. (1997), literature often exploits the dissociation between protagonists' incorrect beliefs and the readers' privileged knowledge to create tension. Consider de Vega et al.'s (1997) example, Shakespeare's *Romeo and Juliet*, in which the patron knows that Juliet simulates her death but Romeo does not. In such a case, readers would need to keep two conflicting interpretations of the story world, namely their own and that of the protagonist, Romeo.

It will be challenging to find evidence for an independent emotional dimension given the research suggesting its reliance on more fundamental dimensions. Consequently, we would not promote including emotion as a new dimension. However, we are excited by the prospect of exploring emotion within the context of mental perspective taking. It follows, then, that another possible addition to the event-indexing model is perspective taking. We would posit that there are two main types: objective and mental. Objective perspective taking would entail the various *simulated* physical (perceptual) ways in which a reader could experience the described story world. For example, readers might be contemplating the process of scanning a horizon (Zwaan 1999a,b). In contrast, mental perspective taking would be the simulation of the more abstract beliefs, values, and emotions associated with described characters in the story world. Recently, perspective has been proposed as a fundamental tool for helping readers to organize information from a text (MacWhinney, 2005; Zwaan, 2004).

It is beyond the scope of this chapter to review the extensive literature on objective perspective taking that exists in pragmatics and rhetoric (e.g., see Duchan, Bruder, & Hewitt, 1995). We would like to point out, however, that there is empirical evidence supporting objective perspective taking. For example, Spivey and Geng (2000) have demonstrated that when listening to stories, participants can adopt particular visual orientations/perspectives (i.e., participants will make eye movements that mimic directionality described in the story world—looking up and down at absent objects). Furthermore, Zwaan and Stanfield (2001) and Zwaan, Stanfield, and Yaxley (2002) have shown that participants are sensitive to the verbally implied orientation and shape of objects.

Givón (1992) proposed that mental perspective taking is an integral part of communication. In mental perspective taking, the speaker must keep track of not only his own knowledge, but the listener's knowledge of the topic under discussion. A logical extension of this relates to discourse. One could argue that one prerequisite of comprehension is that readers keep track of their knowledge of the story world (privileged knowledge) coupled with various mental states of characters described in the story. More research is needed to explore this claim, but perspective appears to be a potential candidate for inclusion in the event-indexing model. One topic on the agenda of this research will be to determine whether objective perspective is a more fundamental situation model dimension than space. Obviously, objective perspective depends on spatial relations, and given the weak evidence for the importance of the spatial dimension, it will take extra effort to establish the role of perspective. Another topic will be to explore the relation of mental perspective and the protagonist dimension. Similar to the second-order nature of emotions, mental perspective may turn out to be dependent on the more fundamental protagonist dimension.

CONCLUSIONS

Our review of the literature suggests that the event-indexing model has become a useful tool in the exploration of multidimensional situation models. Evidence strongly suggests that readers encapsulate event information during comprehension. There are differences, however, in the nature of the dominance of certain dimensions. Comparable results in correlational and experimental studies indicate that time and protagonist dimensions are always monitored. Readers are sensitive to time because this dimension provides critical duration, order, progression, and causal information about how events unfold. Readers are sensitive to protagonists because this dimension conveys information related to the objects and entities that make up events—including traits, emotions, and possibly goal and perspective information.

We also put forward the argument that intentionality (goals) and causality are second-order dimensions and as such should not be considered separate dimensions in the model. Goals cannot be defined without resorting to protagonist identity, trait, and disposition information. Similarly, causation cannot be understood without reference to time. The strength of causal relationships is often based on the amount of time between a cause and its potential effect. Moreover, temporal relations between events are monitored by readers even when there is no obvious causal relation between the events.

Several experimental studies provide evidence for dimensional interactions. For example, shifts in single dimensions caused the largest increases in reading time compared with fully continuous conditions. Increasing the number of dimensional shifts further caused only slightly smaller increases in reading times. More research will be necessary to explore the nature of these interactions, but one potential direction would be to document the plausibility for each shift combination and its frequency in natural text.

Two additions to the event-indexing model were considered. Evidence was presented suggesting that readers can monitor emotional and perspective information when constructing situation models. However, emotion can be classified as a second-order dimension (because emotions are a by-product of protagonist information). More work is necessary to gauge perspective, but it too may have its base in protagonist relations (i.e., mental perspective) and spatial relations (i.e., objective perspective).

In this chapter we attempted to identify how important the individual dimensions of multidimensional situation models are in general. It should be noted, however, that the importance may depend on a number of factors that modify dominance and interactions. For example, differences in individual abilities such as visuospatial working memory or imagery ability may turn out to be crucial. Individual differences might also explain why the evidence in favor of the spatial dimension is rather weak: if spatial dimensions are spontaneously monitored only by readers with high visuospatial abilities, mixed results are to be expected (see Dutke & Rinck, submitted). So far, research on the role of situation models in text comprehension has often ignored individual differences. Consequently, there is much work left for the future.

Finally, the scope of the event-indexing model (and others) is currently limited to the comprehension of narrative text. It will be an interesting challenge to develop and test comparable models of expository text comprehension. So far, research efforts on narrative comprehension versus expository text comprehension have not had much theoretical overlap (but see Otero, Leon, & Graesser, 2002). This is unfortunate because in both cases, deep comprehension involves the creation of multidimensional situation models (often called "mental models" in research on expository text). Thus, a truly general theory of text comprehension should address both types of text. If one wishes to extend the event-indexing model in this direction, at least two questions will have to be answered. First, what is the expository equivalent of a narrative event? Maybe this could be an idea or an argument. Second, which dimensions are critical to the comprehension of expository text? Naturally, protagonist information including emotions, goals, and intentions will not be relevant in this area. However, temporal and causal relations should be as important as they are for narrative comprehension, and spatial information may be important, depending on the particular contents of the text (e.g., assembly instructions, route directions). Answering these questions will be an interesting and fruitful task for researchers interested in general aspects of comprehension.

REFERENCES

Albrecht, J. E., & O'Brien, E. J. (1993). Updating a mental model: Maintaining both local and global coherence. *Journal of Experimental Psychology: Learning, Memory, and Cognition, 19,* 1061–1070.

Albrecht, J. E., & O'Brien, E. J. (1995). Goal processing and the maintenance of global coherence. In R. F. Lorch & E. J. O'Brien (Eds.), *Sources of coherence in reading* (pp. 263–278). Hillsdale, NJ: Lawrence Erlbaum Associates.

Celce-Murcia, M., & Larsen-Freeman, D. (1999). *The grammar book: An ESL/EFL teacher's course* (2nd ed.). Heinle & Heinle.

Cook, A. E., Halleran, J. G., & O'Brien, E. J. (1998). What is readily available during reading? A memory-based view of text processing. *Discourse Processes, 26,* 109–129.

de Vega, M., Diaz, J. M., & León, I. (1997). To know or not to know: Comprehending protagonists' beliefs and their emotional consequences. *Discourse Processes, 23,* 169–192.

de Vega, M., León, I., & Diaz, J. M. (1996). The representation of changing emotions in reading comprehension. *Cognition and Emotion, 10,* 303–321.

Duchan, J. F., Bruder, G. A., & Hewitt, L. E. (Eds.). (1995). *Deixis in narrative: A cognitive science perspective.* Hillsdale, NJ: Lawrence Erlbaum Associates.

Dutke, S., & Rinck, M. (in press). Predictability of locomotion: Effects on updating of spatial situation models during narrative comprehension. *Memory & Cognition.*

Gernsbacher, M. A. (1995). Activating knowledge of fictional characters' emotional states. On macrostructures, mental models, and other inventions: A brief personal history of the Kintsch-van Dijk theory. In C. A. Weaver, S. Mannes, & C. R. Fletcher (Eds.), *Discourse comprehension: Essays in honor of Walter Kintsch* (pp. 141–156). Hillsdale, NJ: Lawrence Erlbaum Associates.

Gernsbacher, M. A., Goldsmith, H. H., & Robertson, R. R. W. (1992). Do readers mentally represent characters' emotional states? *Cognition and Emotion, 6,* 89–111.

Gernsbacher, M. A., Hallada, B. M., & Robertson, R. R. W. (1998). How automatically do readers infer fictional characters' emotional states? *Scientific Studies of Reading, 2,* 271–300.

Gernsbacher, M. A., & Robertson, R. R. W. (1992). Knowledge activation versus sentence mapping when representing fictional characters' emotional states. *Language and Cognitive Processes, 7,* 353–371.

Givón, T. (1992). The grammar of referential coherence a mental processing instructions. *Linguistics, 30,* 5–55.

Glenberg, A. M., Meyer, M., & Lindem, K. (1987). Mental models contribute to foregrounding during text comprehension. *Journal of Memory and Language, 26,* 69–83.

Gygax, P., Oakhill, J., & Garnham, A. (2003). The representation of characters' emotional responses: Do readers infer specific emotions? *Cognition and Emotion, 17*(3), 413–428.

Hakala, C. M. (1999). Accessibility of spatial information in a situation model. *Discourse Processes, 27*(3), 261–279.

Johnson-Laird, P. N. (1983). *Mental models.* Cambridge, MA: Harvard University Press.

Kintsch, W., & van Dijk, T. A. (1978). Toward a model of text comprehension and production. *Psychological Review, 85,* 363–394.

Langston, W., Kramer, D. C., & Glenberg, A. M. (1998). The representation of space in mental models derived from text. *Memory & Cognition, 26*(2), 247–262.

Lutz, M. F., & Radvansky, G. A. (1997). The fate of completed goal information. *Journal of Memory and Language, 36*, 293–310.

MacWhinney, B. (2005). The emergence of grammar from perspective taking. In D. Pecher & R. Zwaan (Eds.), *The grounding of cognition.* Cambridge, UK: Cambridge University Press.

Magliano, J. P., Miller, & Zwaan, R. A. (2001). Indexing space and time in film understanding. *Applied Cognitive Psychology, 15*, 533–545.

Magliano, J. P., Millis, K. K., Golding, J. M., & Barker, G. (1995). Causal connectives increase inference generation. *Discourse Processes, 20*, 29–49.

Morrow, D. G., Bower, G. H., & Greenspan, S. L. (1989). Updating situation models during narrative comprehension. *Journal of Memory and Language, 28*, 292–312.

Morrow, D. G., Greenspan, S. L., & Bower, G. H. (1987). Accessibility and situation models in narrative comprehension. *Journal of Memory and Language, 26*, 165–187.

O'Brien, E. J., Rizzella M. L., Albrecht, J. E., & Halleran, J. G. (1998). Updating a situation model: a resonance text processing view. *Journal of Experimental Psychology: Learning, Memory, and Cognition, 24*, 1200–1210.

Otero, J., Leon, J. A., & Graesser, A. C. (2002). (Eds.). *The psychology of science text comprehension.* Mahwah, NJ: Lawrence Erlbaum Associates.

Radvansky, G. A., Zwaan, R. A., Federico, T., & Franklin, N. (1998). Retrieval from temporally organized situation models. *Journal of Experimental Psychology: Learning, Memory, and Cognition, 24*, 1224–1237.

Rapp, D. N., Gerrig, R. J., & Prentice, D. A. (2001). Readers' trait-based models of characters in narrative comprehension. *Journal of Memory and Language, 45*, 737–750.

Rinck, M. (2005). Spatial situation models. In A. Mijake & P. Shah (Eds.), *Handbook of visuospatial thinking*. Cambridge, UK: Cambridge University Press.

Rinck, M., & Bower, G. H. (1995). Anaphora resolution and the focus of attention in situation models. *Journal of Memory and Language, 34*, 110–131.

Rinck, M., & Bower, G. H. (2000). Temporal and spatial distance in situation models. *Memory & Cognition, 28*, 1310–1320.

Rinck, M., & Bower, G. H. (2004). Goal-based accessibility of entities within situation models. In B. Ross (Ed.), *The psychology of learning and motivation* (Vol. 44, pp. 1–33).

Rinck, M., & Hähnel, A. (2002). *A comparison of spatial, temporal, intentional, causal, and emotional inconsistencies in short narratives.* Unpublished manuscript.

Rinck, M., & Hähnel, A. (2003). *The relation of temporal and causal information in situation models created from text.* Unpublished manuscript.

Rinck, M., Hähnel, A., & Becker, G. (2001). Using temporal information to construct, update, and retrieve situation models of narratives. *Journal of Experimental Psychology: Learning, Memory, and Cognition, 27*, 67–80.

Rinck, M., & Weber, U. (2003). Who when where: An experimental test of the event-indexing model. *Memory & Cognition, 31*, 1284–1292.

Scott Rich, S., & Taylor, H. A. (2000). Not all narrative shifts function equally. *Journal of Memory & Cognition, 28*, 1257–1266.

Spivey, M. J., & Geng, J. J. (2001). Oculomotor mechanisms activated by imagery and memory: Eye movements to absent objects. *Psychological Research/Psychologische Forschung, 65*(4), 235–241.

Stanfield, R. A., & Zwaan, R. A. (2001). The effect of implied orientation derived from verbal context on picture recognition. *Psychological Science, 12,* 153–156.

Suh, S., & Trabasso, T. (1993). Inferencing during reading: Converging evidence from discourse analysis, talk-aloud protocols, and recognition priming. *Journal of Memory and Language, 32,* 279–300.

Ter Meulen, A. G. B. (1995). *Representing time in natural language: The dynamic interpretation of tense and aspect.* Cambridge, MA: MIT Press.

Therriault, D. J., Rinck, M., & Zwaan, R. A. (2006). Assessing the influence of dimensional focus during situation model construction. *Memory & Cognition, 34*(1), 78–89.

Thüring, M., Grobmann, I., & Wender, K. F. (1985). Causal and temporal inferences and their effects on memory for discourse. In G. Rickheit & H. Strohner (Eds.), *Inferences in text processing.* Amsterdam: Elsevier.

Trabasso, T., & Sperry, L. L. (1985). Causal relatedness and importance of story events. *Journal of Memory and Language, 24,* 595–611.

Trabasso, T., & Suh, S. Y. (1993). Understanding text: Achieving explanatory power coherence through on-line inferences and mental operations in working memory. *Discourse Processes, 16,* 3–34.

van Dijk, T. A., & Kintsch, W. (1983). *Strategies of discourse comprehension.* New York: Academic Press.

Wilson, S. G., Rinck, M., McNamara, T. P., Bower, G. H., & Morrow, D. G. (1993). Mental models and narrative comprehension: Some qualifications. *Journal of Memory and Language, 32,* 141–154.

Zwaan, R. A. (1996). Processing narrative time shifts. *Journal of Experimental Psychology: Learning, Memory, and Cognition, 22,* 1196–1207.

Zwaan, R. A. (1999a). Embodied cognition, perceptual symbols, and situation models. *Discourse Processes, 28,* 81–88.

Zwaan, R. A. (1999b). Situation models: the mental leap into imagined worlds. *Current Directions in Psychological Science, 8,* 15–18.

Zwaan, R. A. (2004). The immersed experiencer: Toward an embodied theory of language comprehension. In B. H. Ross (Ed.), *The psychology of learning and motivation* (Vol. 44, pp. 35–62). New York: Academic Press.

Zwaan, R. A., Langston, M. C., & Graesser, A. C. (1995). The construction of situation models in narrative comprehension: an event-indexing model. *Psychological Science, 6,* 292–297.

Zwaan, R. A., Magliano, J. P., & Graesser, A. C. (1995). Dimensions of situation model construction in narrative comprehension. *Journal of Experimental Psychology: Learning, Memory, and Cognition, 21,* 386–397.

Zwaan, R. A., & Oostendorp, H. (1993). Do readers construct spatial representations in naturalistic story comprehension? *Discourse Processes, 16,* 125–143.

Zwaan, R. A., & Radvansky, G. A. (1998). Situation models in language comprehension and memory. *Psychological Bulletin, 123,* 162–185.

Zwaan, R. A., Radvansky, G. A., Hilliard, A. E., & Curiel, J. M. (1998) Constructing multidimensional situation models during reading. *Scientific Studies of Reading, 2,* 199–220.

Zwaan, R. A., Radvansky, G. A., & Whitten, S. N. (2002). Themes and situation models. In M. Louwerse & W. van Peer (Eds.), *Thematics: Interdisciplinary studies* (pp. 35–53). Amsterdam/Philadelphia: John Benjamins.

Zwaan, R. A., Stanfield, R. A., & Yaxley, R. H. (2002). Language comprehenders mentally represent the shapes of objects. *Psychological Science, 13*(2), 168–171.

14

Sentence and Discourse Representation in the Two Cerebral Hemispheres

Debra L. Long, Kathleen Baynes, and Chantel Prat
University of California, Davis

An important goal of research in language comprehension is to specify the nature of listeners' and readers' mental representations and the processes involved in constructing them. Psycholinguists study comprehension at three levels. At the word level, processes are necessary to encode the spoken or printed word and access its meaning in memory. At the sentence level, processes are devoted to the formation of structures that specify the syntactic and conceptual relations among words in a sentence. These processes help to encode propositions, abstract units that represent meaning. At the discourse level, processes form connections among successive propositions in discourse. These processes are involved in establishing referential connections, the knowledge that two text elements refer to the same entity, and coherence relations, the knowledge that ideas are related in terms of the situation or context to which a text refers.

Research on language representation in the brain suggests that the two cerebral hemispheres may process words, sentences, and discourse quite differently. The left hemisphere has high-quality phonological, orthographic, and semantic representations of words, and disruption of these processes is most frequently seen following damage to the left hemisphere (Blumstein, 1990; Bub & Kertesz, 1982; Caramazza & Hillis, 1990). The left hemisphere is also primarily responsible for syntactic processing (Baynes & Eliassen, 1998; Kaan & Swaab, 2002; Zaidel, 1990). The right hemisphere has fairly well-developed word recognition abilities, although it has little speech output and little ability to use phonological information in word recognition (Baynes, 1990; Baynes & Eliassen, 1998; Gazzaniga & Sperry, 1967; Zaidel, 1990). At the sentence level, the right hemisphere is poorer at syntactic analysis than is the left (Baynes & Gazzaniga, 1988; Zaidel, 1978, 1990). It relies heavily on word order information in parsing and has difficulty with complex syntactic structures—in particular, structures that require coordination of subject/object and direct object/indirect object relations.

In this chapter, we focus on cerebral asymmetries in the representation of discourse. Recent evidence suggests that the right hemisphere plays an important role in understanding language as a connected whole (Beeman, 1993; Brownell, Gardner, Prather, & Martino, 1995; Brownell, Potter, Bihrle, & Gardner, 1986; Delis, Wapner, Gardner, & Moses, 1983; Joanette, Goulet, & Hannequin, 1990; Meyers, 1994). Lesion studies of right-hemisphere-damaged patients have documented patterns of deficits at the discourse level. These patients often have difficulty making inferences, integrating ideas across sentences, and identifying main ideas and themes. Indeed, so many studies have documented discourse-level deficits in right-hemisphere-damaged patients that many researchers have argued that the right hemisphere is primarily responsible for processes involved in integrating ideas across sentences and making inferences (for an example, see Meyers, 1994). Few studies, however, have directly examined the left hemisphere's role in these processes. Most research on left-hemisphere language comprehension in neurological populations has focused on word- and sentence-level processes.

In one of the few studies investigating discourse understanding in both hemispheres, Zaidel, Kasher, Soroker, and Batori (2002) examined performance on the "Right Hemisphere Communication Battery" (Gardener & Brownell, 1986) in left-hemisphere- and right-hemisphere-damaged groups. The battery is composed of subtests that measure patients' understanding of indirect requests, metaphors, sarcasm, and humor, as well as their ability to consider alternative word meanings, make inferences, and recall the main idea of a story. Zaidel et al. (2002) found that both left-hemisphere- and right-hemisphere-damaged patients performed worse on all subtests than did age-matched controls; however, they found no differences in the performance of the two brain-damaged groups. In another study directly comparing discourse processing in the two hemispheres, Robertson and his colleagues investigated the integration of concepts across sentences. They found that the right hemisphere was more active than was the left when sentences introduced a noun with a definite article, an explicit cue to anaphoric reference (Robertson et al., 2000).

In the following sections, we describe our research examining sentence and discourse representation in the two hemispheres using the theoretical constructs and paradigms that are standard in psycholinguistics. We use these paradigms in divided visual-field and clinical studies to address one of the most basic questions in language comprehension research: How is discourse represented in memory? Our particular focus is on cerebral asymmetries in the representation of explicit information in discourse and asymmetries in the representation of contextually relevant semantic information.

HOW IS DISCOURSE REPRESENTED IN MEMORY?

Most theories of discourse processing claim that readers construct and store in memory at least two interrelated representations: a propositional representation and a discourse model (Gernsbacher, 1990; Graesser, Singer, & Trabasso, 1994; Greene, McKoon, & Ratcliff, 1992; Kintsch, 1988; Kintsch & van Dijk, 1978; McKoon & Ratcliff, 1990, 1992, 1998). A propositional representation contains the individual ideas (propositions) that are derived from each sentence and the relations among them (Kintsch, 1974). A proposition is a structured, coherent unit consisting of a predicate (e.g., verb, adjective, adverb) and one or more associated arguments (i.e., concepts that are related or modified by the predicate). The propositional representation is "locally" coherent; that is, propositions in each incoming sentence are mapped to propositions currently active in working memory, usually those from the immediately preceding sentence or two. The relations among propositions are often referential (Kintsch, 1974; McKoon & Ratcliff, 1980; Ratcliff & McKoon, 1978); propositions are connected when their arguments refer to the same entity. Propositions that cannot be connected by means of a referential link require one or more inferences to fill the gap.

The propositional representation serves as a foundation for constructing the discourse model. The discourse model is a representation of what the text is about and is "globally" coherent. Explicit text information is integrated with contextually relevant semantic knowledge to represent features of the real or imaginary world that the text describes. To construct a discourse model, readers must engage in active inferential processing to interpret and restructure text information in light of their prior understanding of the knowledge domain.

In a classic study, Bransford and Johnson (1972) demonstrated that readers could represent the explicit ideas from a sentence and yet not understand what the sentence was about. Consider the following sentence:

(1) The haystack was important because the cloth ripped.

Readers can easily derive and represent three propositions from this sentence: *the haystack was important*, *the cloth ripped*, and a causal link between the first two propositions. Although these propositions can be readily identified, the absence of contextually relevant, semantic information makes it difficult to construct the discourse model. This difficulty disappears when readers are given information about the situation to which the sentence refers. Readers who are told that the sentence refers to *skydiving* can construct a discourse model quite easily. They can map entities in the sentence to specific referents in the situation (e.g., *cloth* refers to parachute). They can also make inferences to specify the nature of the causal relation (e.g., the haystack was important because it cushioned the skydiver's fall).

Research in our laboratory suggests that the distinction between a reader's representation of explicit information in a text (the propositional representation) and the reader's representation of what the text is about (the discourse model) is also important with respect to how discourse is represented in the brain (Long & Baynes, 2002; Long, Baynes, & Prat, 2005). We have used a standard psycholinguistic paradigm for examining how discourse is represented in memory and adapted it to study discourse representation in the two hemispheres. This paradigm, called item-priming-in-recognition, is described in the next section.

ITEM PRIMING IN RECOGNITION MEMORY

The logic of the item-priming-in-recognition paradigm is that activation of a concept in memory facilitates recognition of other concepts to which it is linked (Long, Oppy, & Seely, 1997; McKoon & Ratcliff, 1980; Ratcliff & McKoon, 1978). The paradigm was developed by Ratcliff and McKoon (1978) to investigate the representation of sentences in memory. Participants received a series of study-test trials. During the study phase, they read a list of unrelated sentences. Table 14–1 contains two sample sentences and their propositional structure. Immediately after reading the last sentence in the list, participants received a recognition memory test. The test list contained single words, presented one at a time. Participants decided whether each test word had been in one of the sentences that they studied.

Ratcliff and McKoon (1978) manipulated the order of test words such that some of the items were arranged in prime-target pairs. The target, a word from the sentence (e.g., wind), was preceded by a prime word that was (a) in the same proposition as the target (e.g., clouds) (b) in the same sentence, but in a different proposition (e.g., horizon), or (c) in a different sentence (e.g., wine). Participants responded to all items (primes, targets, and fillers), and they had no information that some items were arranged in pairs. Ratcliff and McKoon (1978) found that the size of the priming effect depended on the relation between the prime and target in the propositional structure of the sen-

TABLE 14–1.
Sample Sentences and Their Propositional Structure (from Ratcliff & McKoon, 1978)

Sentence	*Propositions*
	P1(crossed, geese, horizon)
Geese crossed the horizon as wind shuffled the clouds	P2(shuffled, wind, clouds)
	P3(as, P1, P2)
	P1(mixed, host, cocktail)
The host mixed a cocktail but the guest wanted wine.	P2(wanted, guest, wine)
	P3(but, P1, P2)

Note: The propositions are listed according to standard notation (Kintsch, 1974). In each proposition (P), the predicate is listed first, followed by its arguments.

tence. The effect was largest when the prime and target were from the same proposition, suggesting that the concepts were linked strongly in memory.

We adapted this paradigm to investigate the propositional structure of discourse in memory, as well as the representation of semantic information relevant to constructing a coherent discourse model. We have also used the paradigm to investigate discourse representation in young, healthy adults and in special populations, including callosotomy patients and left-hemisphere-damaged aphasics.

HOW IS DISCOURSE REPRESENTED IN THE TWO CEREBRAL HEMISPHERES?

How are propositional representations and discourse models stored in the hemispheres? In a recent study, we considered three possibilities (Long & Baynes, 2002). One is that the propositional representation resides in the left hemisphere, whereas the discourse model resides in the right. This possibility is founded in previous research on the language comprehension abilities of the two hemispheres. The left hemisphere has much better syntactic processing abilities than does the right (Baynes & Gazzaniga, 1988; Zaidel, 1978, 1990). Syntactic analysis is an essential process involved in deriving propositions from sentences because propositions roughly correspond to syntactic constituents. Moreover, propositions are typically connected by means of referential relations; establishing these relations would seem to depend on knowledge about "who did what to whom" in a sentence. The right hemisphere, in contrast, may store the discourse model. Considerable evidence suggests that the right hemisphere is involved in integrating ideas among sentences and in making inferences, processes that are essential to constructing a coherent and referential discourse model (Beeman, 1993; Brownell et al., 1986, 1995; Delis et al., 1983; Robertson et al., 2000; Hough, 1990; Meyers, 1994; Rehak, Kaplan, & Gardner, 1992).

A second possibility is that both the propositional representation and discourse model reside in the left hemisphere. The two representations are strongly interrelated (Kintsch, 1988; Kintsch & van Dijk, 1978; McKoon & Ratcliff, 1990, 1992, 1998); their interdependence may result in similar storage. If the propositional representation resides in the left hemisphere, then the discourse model, which is based on this representation, may reside in the left hemisphere as well.

The final possibility is that the propositional representation and discourse model are distributed across the two hemispheres, even though the hemispheres may have different roles in constructing them. The hemispheres are strongly interconnected. Although the left hemisphere may be involved in deriving and connecting propositions, once the propositional representation has been constructed, it may be stored such that both hemispheres have access to it.

The challenge with respect to the first two possibilities would be in understanding the circumstances in which the right hemisphere might play a role in constructing the discourse model in the absence of access to the propositional representation on which it is based. At the very least, limited access to the propositional representation would place constraints on the means by which the right hemisphere is involved in constructing discourse-level relations. The challenge with respect to the third possibility would be in understanding the unique contribution of each hemisphere when the two hemispheres contain similar and redundant discourse representations.

We should note that the experiments that we have conducted were not designed to investigate the roles of the two hemispheres in *constructing* the propositional representation and discourse model; rather, they were designed to examine the hemispheric distribution of these representations once comprehension is complete. In one of these experiments, we used the item-priming manipulation in combination with a lateralized visual-field (VF) procedure (Long & Baynes, 2002, Experiment 1). Participants were all right-handed college students. They received a series of study-test trials in which a set of passages was presented for study, followed by a recognition test consisting of single words. Embedded in the recognition list were sets of prime-target pairs. Sample passages and prime-target pairs appear in Table 14–2. Each passage was two sentences long and contained a homograph (e.g., *mint*) that appeared as the final word of either the first or second sentence in the passage. Each test list contained three types of priming pairs interleaved among true and false filler items. *Propositional-priming* pairs consisted of a target (e.g., *structure*) that was preceded by a prime from the same proposition (e.g., *disaster*) or by a prime from a different proposition in the same sentence (e.g., *danger*). *Associate-priming* pairs consisted of a target that was either the appropriate (e.g., *money*) or the inappropriate (e.g., *candy*) associate of a homograph in the sentence and was preceded by a prime from the sentence containing the homograph (e.g., *townspeople*). Finally, *topic-priming* pairs consisted of a target that was the topic of a passage (e.g., *earthquake*) or was an unrelated word (e.g., *breath*) and was preceded by a prime from the final sentence of the passage (e.g., *architect*). It should be noted that the correct response to the associate and to the topic words was no. These items did not appear in the sentences. Primes were presented in the center of a computer screen; targets were briefly presented in either the left visual field/right hemisphere (LVF/RH) or the right visual field/left hemisphere (RVF/LH).

We used the priming manipulation to examine three aspects of readers' sentence representations. First, we examined the representations for evidence of propositional structure. If both hemispheres have access to sentence representations structured by means of propositional relations, then both should show a propositional priming effect, faster responses to targets that are preceded by primes from the same propositions relative to primes from different propositions in the same sentence. Second, we examined memory represen-

TABLE 14–2.
Sample Passages and Example Prime-Target Pairs (from Long & Baynes, 2002)

Priming Relation	*Prime*	*Target*
The townspeople were amazed to find that all the buildings had collapsed except the mint. Obviously, the architect had foreseen the danger because the structure withstood the natural disaster.		
Propositional priming pairs		
Same-proposition	disaster	structure
Different-proposition	danger	structure
Associate priming pairs		
Appropriate-associate	townspeople	money
Inappropriate-associate	townspeople	candy
Topic priming pairs		
Appropriate-topic	architect	earthquake
Inappropriate-topic	architect	breath
The guest ate garlic in his dinner, so the waiter brought a mint. The worried guest soon felt comfortable socializing with his friends.		
Propositional priming pairs		
Same-proposition	guest	garlic
Different-proposition	waiter	garlic
Associate priming pairs		
Appropriate-associate	dinner	candy
Inappropriate-associate	dinner	money
Topic priming pairs		
Appropriate-topic	friends	breath
Inappropriate-topic	friends	earthquake

tations for evidence that the hemispheres represented contextually relevant, semantic information. Specifically, we asked whether the representations contained information about the context-appropriate senses of ambiguous words and information about the themes or topics of the passages.

In all of our item-priming experiments, we conducted separate analyses of the propositional, associate, and topic conditions. Thus, we never compared responses across true and false items. The reaction-time results appear in Fig. 14–1. The priming patterns suggested both similarities and differences in how discourse was represented in the two hemispheres. Only the left hemisphere showed evidence for a representation that was structured propositionally. Participants showed propositional priming, but only when targets were presented in the RVF/LH. No propositional priming was found for targets presented in the LVF/RH. The priming patterns in the two hemispheres were similar, however, with respect to the representation of relevant, semantic information. Participants had difficulty rejecting both appropriate associates and topics irrespective of visual field. This suggests that information about the appropriate senses of ambiguous words and information about the topics of the passages were incorporated into readers' representations in both hemispheres. Participants had difficulty rejecting targets when they resonated with information contained in their memory representations.

Our propositional priming results suggest clear differences in how the two hemispheres represent propositions. The left hemisphere has a representation in which concepts in a sentence are organized structurally. Our results, however, tell us less about how discourse is organized in the right hemisphere. It may be that the right hemisphere made no connection among the explicit concepts in the sentences. That is, it may have had information that the concepts appeared, but may not have constructed links among them. Thus, we found no propositional priming effects because the primes and targets were unconnected in memory. Alternatively, the right hemisphere may have a representation of sentence structure that is more loosely organized than the one in the left hemisphere. That is, the right hemisphere may link concepts in a sentence, but it may not form closer connections among concepts within a clause than it does among concepts across clauses in the same sentence. If so, the right hemisphere might be sensitive to more distant, intersentential relations. That is, it may form connections among concepts within a passage, but it may not represent the structural relations among concepts within a sentence. Thus, we conducted a study to determine whether the right hemisphere represents any links among concepts within a passage.

We used the item-priming-in-recognition paradigm to examine propositional relations within and across sentences (Long et al., 2005, Experiment 1b). Participants read sets of passages and then received a recognition test consisting of single words. Four types of prime-target pairs were embedded in the test list. Sample passages and test items appear in Table 14–3. In the *same-proposition condition*, a target from one of the sentences (e.g., *hunter*) was preceded by a prime from the same proposition (e.g., *pheasant*). In the *different-proposition condition*, the target was preceded by a prime from a different proposition in the same sentence (e.g., *deer*). In the *different-sentence condition*, the target was preceded by a prime from a different sentence in the same passage (e.g., *birds*). Finally, in the *different-passage condition*, the target was preceded by a prime from a different passage in the same block of passages (e.g.,

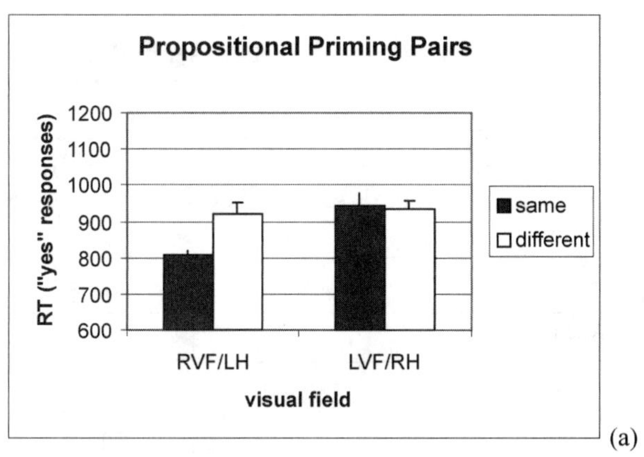

(a)

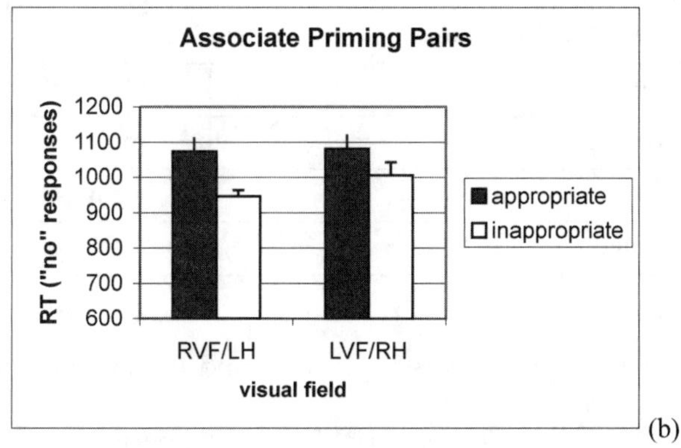

(b)

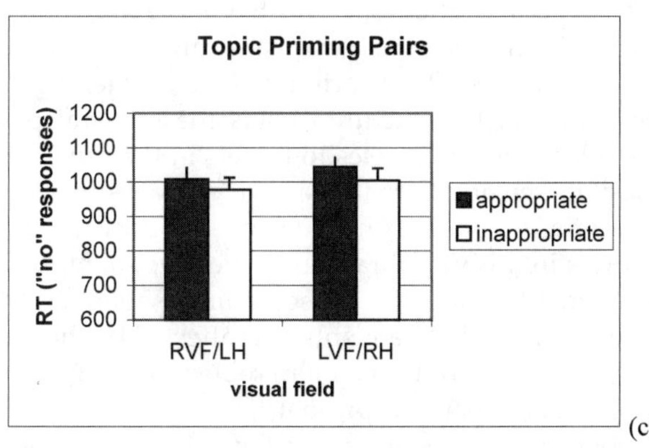

(c)

FIGURE 14–1. Item priming results from Long and Baynes (2002, Experiment 1). Mean response times (in milliseconds) to targets as a function of visual field: (a) "yes" responses to targets in propositional priming pairs, (b) "no" responses to targets in associate priming pairs, and (c) "no" responses to targets in topic priming pairs. Error bars depict standard errors.

TABLE 14–3.
Sample Passages and Example Prime-Target Pairs (from Long, Baynes, & Prat, 2003)

Priming Relation	*Prime*	*Target*
While the hunter (who was wearing an orange vest) stalked the pheasant, the deer ate leaves in the meadow. The birds sang as they roosted in the trees and watched the creatures below.		
Same-proposition	pheasant	hunter
Different-proposition	deer	hunter
Different-sentence	birds	hunter
Different-passage	apples	hunter
The children laughed at the silly sight. The elephant (that was large and gray) pulled the cart, while the monkey juggled the apples.		
Same-proposition	elephant	cart
Different-proposition	monkey	cart
Different-sentence	sight	cart
Different-passage	creatures	cart

apples). Primes were presented centrally, and targets were presented to the LVF/RH or to the RVF/LH.

We manipulated one other variable in this experiment, the syntactic structure of the sentences. In the Long and Baynes (2002) materials, concepts in the same-proposition condition always appeared as nouns in a simple noun-verb-noun (NVN) phrase. Thus, priming in our earlier experiment may have been affected by syntactic structure. That is, the left hemisphere may have exhibited particularly fast responses to targets in the same-proposition condition because of its sensitivity to the canonical NVN syntactic structure. In the current experiment, concepts in the same-proposition condition also appeared as nouns in a NVN phrase; however, we manipulated the syntactic structure such that the nouns were sometimes separated by an intervening clause. If priming in the left hemisphere is affected by the canonical structure of a sentence, then we should see more robust priming when the embedded clause is absent than when it is present.

The reaction-time results appear in Fig. 14–2. We found no effect of embedding a clause in the passage, so the results are presented collapsed across this variable. We found priming effects in the left hemisphere that reflected the linear distance between primes and targets in the propositional structure of the passages. Embedding a clause between the nouns in the same-proposition condition had no effect on priming. This addresses our concern that the

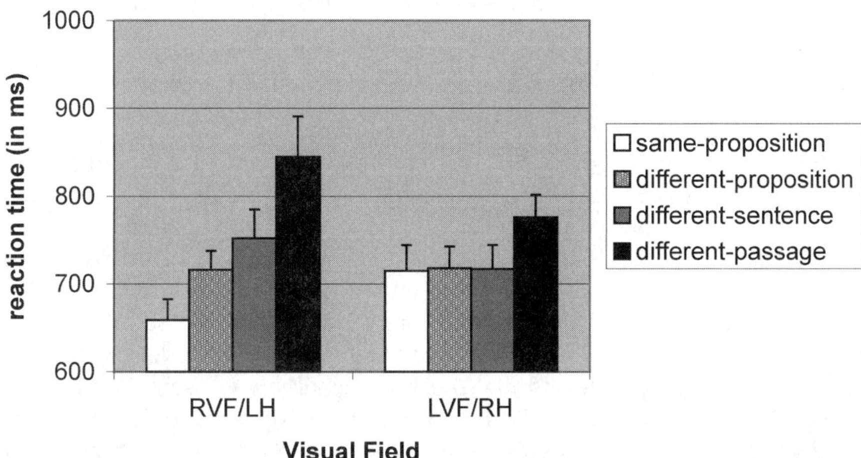

FIGURE 14–2. Item priming results from Long, Baynes, and Prat (2005, Experiment 1b). Mean response times (in milliseconds) to targets as a function of prime-target condition and visual field. Error bars depict standard errors.

propositional priming results that we observed in Long and Baynes (2002) merely reflected the left hemisphere's sensitivity to the canonical syntactic structure of sentences. In the current experiment, the primes and targets in the same-proposition condition were still part of a syntactic constituent, but the canonical NVN structure was disrupted by an embedded clause in the clause-present condition. Nonetheless, participants experienced the greatest facilitation in the same-proposition condition, and this facilitation did not differ by clause condition. Thus, it appears that the left hemisphere was sensitive to the underlying structural relations among the concepts in the sentences, not merely to their physical proximity.

With respect to priming in the LVF/RH, we found that the right hemisphere was insensitive to the structural relations among concepts within a passage. We found no reliable priming differences among the same-proposition, different-proposition, and different-sentence conditions. We did find, however, that participants responded faster in these three conditions than they did in the different-passage condition. Thus, the right hemisphere representation does appear to contain links among the explicit concepts within a passage. A target was retrieved more easily when it was preceded by a prime from the same passage relative to a prime from a different passage in the same block.

One explanation for the priming results in the right hemisphere is that the nouns within a passage were linked by virtue of the semantic information conveyed by the passage. That is, concepts such as *hunter, pheasant, deer,* and *birds* were associated in the right hemisphere because they were thematically related. Thus, responses were faster when primes and targets were from the same passage than when they were from different passages. Of course, it is also possible that the priming results in the RH may have nothing to do with how it represented the passages. Rather, priming may have reflected preexisting semantic relations between primes and targets on the test list. That is, primes and targets in the same-proposition, different-proposition, and different-passage condition may have been similarly related, whereas primes and targets in the different-passage condition may have been more distantly related.

We examined the possibility that our priming results reflected preexisting semantic relations among primes and targets by first examining association norms for connections among them (Long et al., 2005). We used the University of South Florida word association norms as our source (Nelson, McEvoy, & Schreiber, 1998) and found that most of our targets were not produced as associates to our primes. Of the 192 primes, 91% appeared in the norms, but only 4% of these primes had one of our targets produced as an associate. Given that our targets were rarely produced as associates to our primes, the association norms provided limited information about semantic relatedness. Thus, we conducted another experiment to investigate the role of preexisting semantic relations in our priming results (Long et al., 2005, Experiment 2).

We used a lexical-decision task in to examine the semantic relatedness among our primes and targets. Participants received blocks of trials in which they made word/non-word judgments about a series of letter strings. Embedded in each block were the prime-target pairs from Long et al. (2005, Experiment 1b), as well as the filler items and a number of non-words. Primes were always presented centrally; targets were presented briefly to the LVF/RH or the RVF/LH. Participants never saw the passages associated with the primes and targets. If preexisting semantic relations influenced priming at test, we should find facilitation to targets preceded by primes in the same passage relative to targets preceded by primes from different passages.

The reaction-time results appear in Fig. 14–3. The pattern of responses in this experiment was different from the pattern in our previous experiment. We did not find faster responses in the within-passage conditions than in the between-passage condition. Although we found no within-passage priming in this experiment, we do not believe that the concepts in the within-passage conditions were semantically unrelated. Rather, our results suggest that, in the absence of the contexts that the passages provide, the primes and targets are not sufficiently related to yield robust priming in a lexical-decision task.

In summary, we have found both similarities and differences in how discourse is represented in the two cerebral hemispheres. Both hemispheres represent contextually relevant, semantic information, including information about the appropriate senses of ambiguous words and information about the topics of passages. Moreover, both hemispheres represent explicit informa-

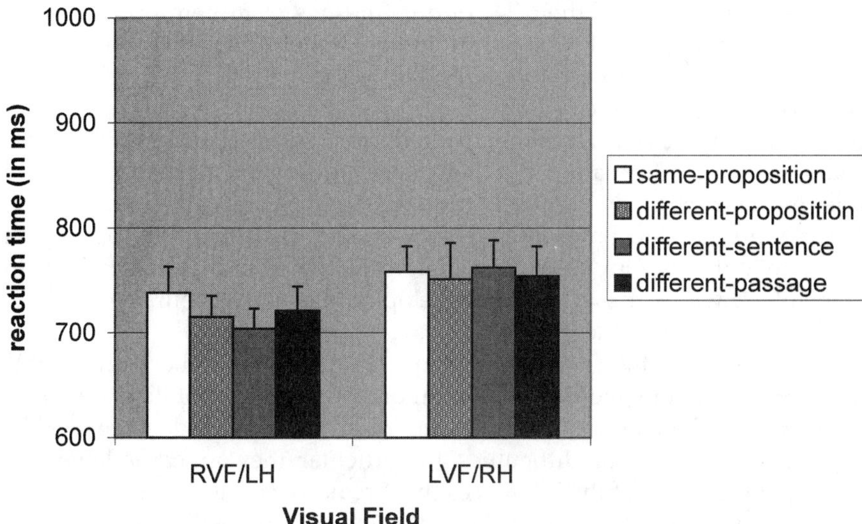

FIGURE 14–3. Lexical-decision results from Long, Baynes, and Prat (2005, Experiment 2). Mean response times (in milliseconds) to targets as a function of prime-target condition and visual field. Error bars depict standard errors.

tion from a text; however, they appear to organize this information differently. The left hemisphere contains a representation that is structured according to propositional relations. The right hemisphere also represents explicit concepts from a passage, but we found no evidence that these concepts are organized structurally. Rather, the right hemisphere represents concepts within a passage similarly, but distinct from concepts in other passages.

DISCOURSE REPRESENTATION IN SPECIAL POPULATIONS

One advantage of the item-priming-in-recognition paradigm is that it can be used to investigate memory for discourse in special populations, such as left-hemisphere-damaged aphasics, who often have difficulty with discourse comprehension tasks involving recall or question answering. The item-priming task requires only a simple judgment about whether a word appeared in a studied passage. In this section, we describe discourse representation in two populations, a group of callosotomy patients and a group of left-hemisphere-damaged aphasics.

Discourse Representation in Callosotomy Patients

We might conclude, on the basis of our findings from item priming in divided VF studies, that the left and right hemispheres represent contextually relevant, semantic information redundantly. One problem with this conclusion is that it ignores the fact that the two hemispheres interact during comprehension. The two cerebral hemispheres may ultimately store similar discourse-relevant information, but they may each play a unique and important role in constructing the representation. We investigated this issue by replicating the Long and Baynes (2002, Experiment 1) study in a group of callosotomy patients. Our goal was to determine whether input from the right hemisphere was necessary to the development of the discourse representation in the left hemisphere.

Previous research on right-hemisphere language comprehension suggests that the right hemisphere plays an important role in the ability to identify main ideas and themes. Individuals with right-hemisphere damage exhibit a range of comprehension difficulties. In particular, they appear to have difficulty making many of the inferences that are necessary to construct a coherent discourse model (Beeman, 1993; Brownell et al., 1986; Meyers, 1994). Thus, the priming that we found for topic-related words in Long and Baynes (2002) may have depended on comprehension activities that occurred in the right hemisphere. Alternatively, the hemispheres may have represented the topic-related information redundantly and in parallel.

Participants were three callosotomy patients (for details see Long & Baynes, 2002, Experiment 2). The materials and procedures were the same as those used by Long and Baynes (see Table 14–2 for the sample materials), with one exception. All test items were presented on the computer screen until participants made a response. All responses were made with the patient's right hand.

The patients' response latencies appear in Fig. 14–4, and their accuracy data appear in Fig. 14–5. The patients showed evidence for a discourse representation that was propositionally structured. They showed a propositional priming effect in both their reaction-time and accuracy data. The patients made numerous errors in the associate- and topic-priming conditions, so we analyzed only the accuracy data. All patients had difficulty rejecting the context-appropriate associates of the ambiguous words and the topic words, suggesting that they represented discourse-relevant semantic information.

These results suggest that the left hemisphere was able to construct a discourse representation in the absence of substantial right-hemisphere input. We are somewhat cautious about this conclusion, however, because it is based on the assumption that right-handed responses only reflect comprehension activities in the left hemisphere. Although this technique emphasizes the left hemisphere's contribution, it does not rule out some contribution from the right hemisphere. For example, Kingstone and Gazzaniga (1995)

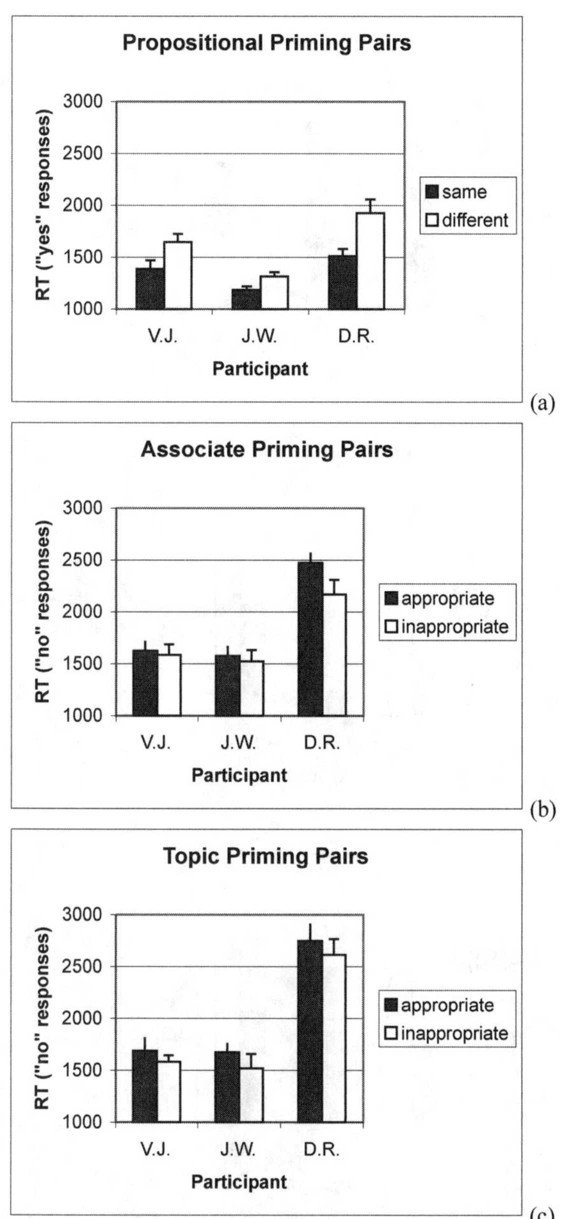

FIGURE 14–4. Item priming results from Long and Baynes (2002, Experiment 2). Mean response times (in milliseconds) to targets for each participant: (a) "yes" responses to targets in propositional priming pairs, (b) "no" responses to targets in associate priming pairs, and (c) "no" responses to targets in topic priming pairs. Error bars depict standard errors.

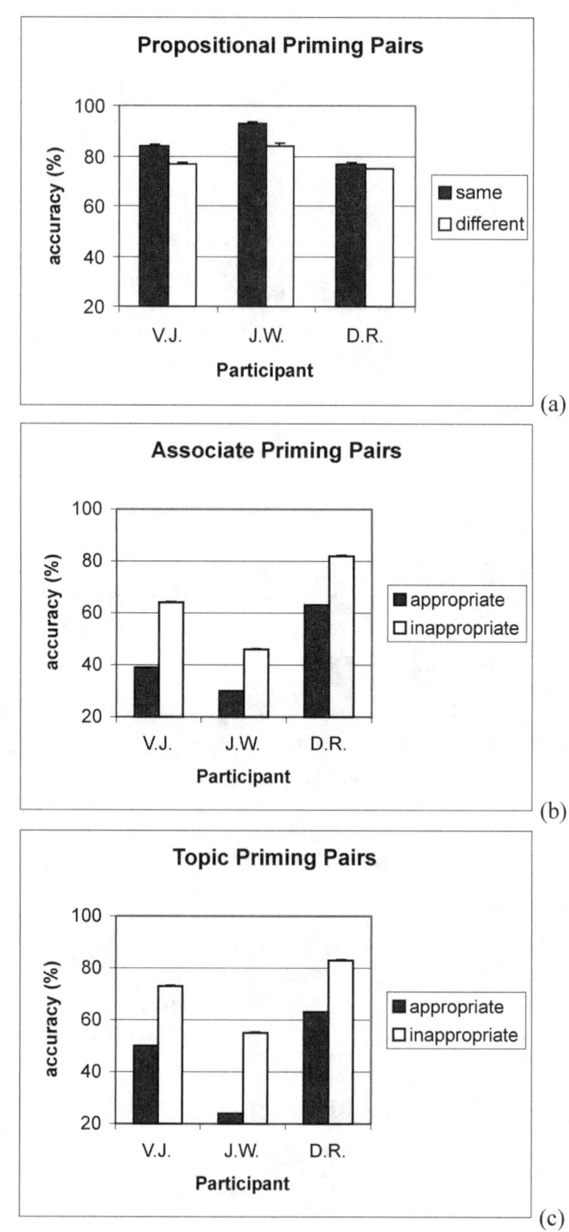

FIGURE 14–5. Item priming results from Long and Baynes (2002, Experiment 2). Mean accuracy rates (in percentages) to targets for each participant: (a) "yes" responses to targets in propositional priming pairs, (b) "no" responses to targets in associate priming pairs, and (c) "no" responses to targets in topic priming pairs. Error bars depict standard errors.

showed that the two hemispheres collaborated to combine literal information with a manual output, although the hemispheres were unable to combine higher-order information. Thus, we cannot completely exclude the possibility of some right-hemisphere input to our task, given that both hemispheres had access to the stimulus materials.

Discourse Representation in Left-Hemisphere-Damaged Aphasics

We used the item-priming-in-recognition paradigm to study discourse representation in a heterogeneous group of aphasics (Baynes, Long, Gillette, Dronkers, & Davis, 2002). We predicted that the representation of propositions would be impaired in these patients, given the left hemisphere's role in syntactic analysis and the importance of syntactic analysis in deriving and integrating propositions. Our primary question of interest was how impairments in the representation of propositions might affect the representation of information relevant to the discourse model.

One possibility is that failure to derive and integrate propositions would lead to deficits in the ability to represent contextually relevant semantic information, such as information about the context-appropriate senses of ambiguous words and information about the topics of passages. This possibility is founded on the assumption that constructing the discourse model involves refining and elaborating a propositional representation (Kintsch & van Kijk, 1978; McKoon & Ratcliff, 1990, 1992). If readers fail to represent propositions, then they should also fail to represent the discourse model. Thus, left-hemisphere-damaged patients should show no propositional priming, nor should they show priming in the associate and topic conditions.

A second possibility is that the left hemisphere may be essential for deriving and integrating propositions, but that the representation of the discourse model may not depend on an accurate propositional representation. Lexical processing in both the left and right hemispheres may support the representation of contextually relevant, semantic information. That is, both hemispheres may be able to link explicit concepts in the text with semantic information that has been activated by means of lexical-semantic priming (Beeman, 1993; Chiarello, 1991). If so, then left-hemisphere-damaged aphasics may show associate and topic priming, in the absence of reliable propositional priming.

Thirteen patients participated in our experiment. They were all right-handed, native speakers of English who had suffered a single left-hemisphere stroke. They represented a range of aphasia types, and all were at least one year post-stroke at the time that they participated in the experiment. Table 14–4 contains demographic information about the patients and their percentile scores on the vocabulary and comprehension subtests of the Nelson-Denny Reading Comprehension Test.

TABLE 14–4.
Patient Information (from Baynes, Long, Gillette, Dronkers, & Davis, 2002)

					Nelson-Denny	
ID	*Age*	*Educa.*	*Gender*	*Overall*	*Vocab.*	*Comp.*
BK	56	16	M	8.7	13.8	6.9
BW	63	12	M	NA	4.1	NA
CH	70	12	M	4.1	5.8	4.1
DS	50	16	M	5.1	9.3	4.1
EJ	78	18	M	14.2	16.9	9.4
EP	61	16	M	6.4	8.9	5.1
FY	78	12	M	4.9	9.3	4.1
GS	50	16	F	15.9	15.9	15.4
JS	61	12	M	4.5	5.1	4.7
LC	20	12	F	7.1	9.8	8.4
LW	54	13	M	6.8	6.9	6.1
WE	72	15	M	9.1	11	9.5
WT	66	20	M	4.3	7.9	4.1
Means	59.92	14.62		7.01	9.59	6.30

The materials and procedure were the same as those that we used with the callosotomy patients (Long & Baynes, 2002, Experiment 2), except that all participants in this study responded with their dominant hand. Their reaction-time and accuracy data appear in Figs. 14–6 and 14–7. Neither the reaction-time nor the accuracy data revealed reliable propositional priming. The patients made many errors to targets in the associate and topic conditions, so we analyzed only their accuracy data. The accuracy data revealed both associate and topic priming effects. Patients made more errors in response to context-appropriate associates of ambiguous words than to inappropriate associates and made more errors in response to appropriate than to the inappropriate topic words.

These results suggest that intact left-hemisphere mechanisms are necessary for reliable propositional priming, probably because of the role of syntactic analysis in deriving and representing propositions. Nonetheless, these patients appeared to represent relevant semantic information about the passages. Thus, they were able to represent aspects of the discourse model in the absence of a well-structured propositional representation. This finding is consistent with the idea that some discourse-relevant information may be supported by lexical processing in the two hemispheres (Beeman, 1993, 1998; Chiarello, 1991, 1998; Faust, 1998; Faust, Babkoff, & Kravetz, 1995; Faust & Kravetz, 1998). Words and phrases in the text may activate semantically related information by means of lexical-semantic priming. This information

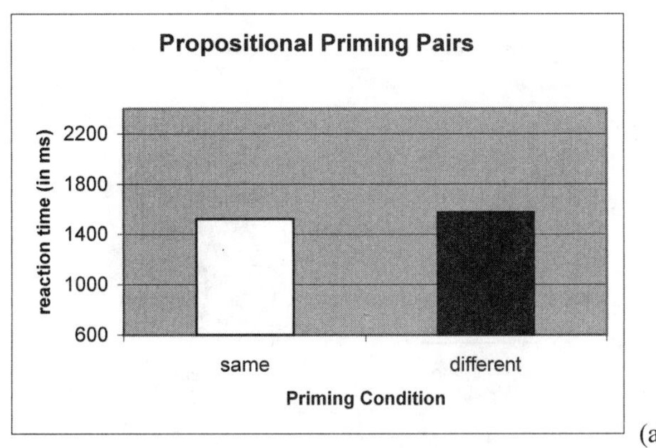

(a)

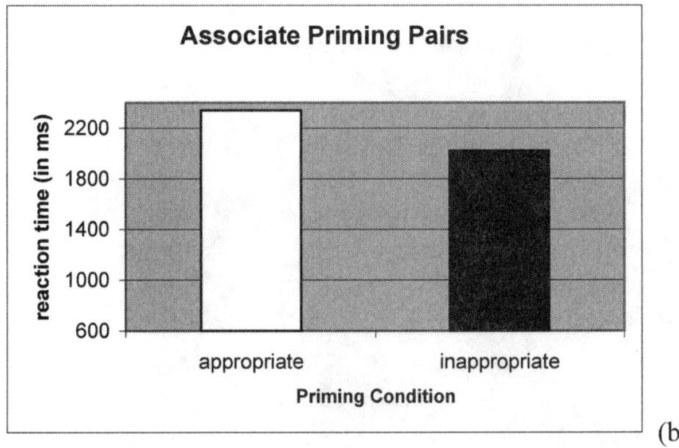

(b)

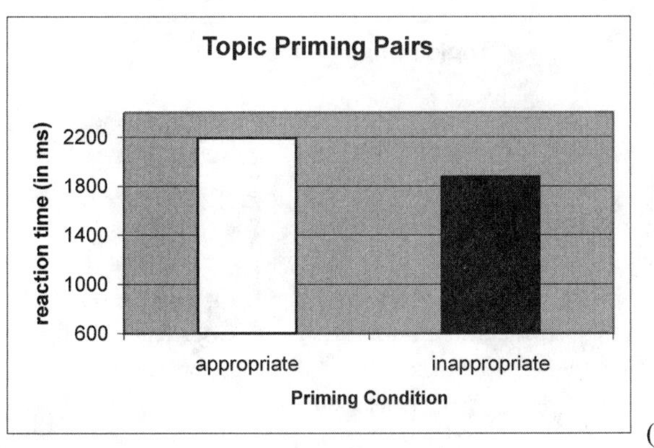

(c)

FIGURE 14–6. Item priming results from Baynes, Long, Gillette, Dronkers, and Davis (2002). Mean response times (in milliseconds) to targets as a function of visual field: (a) "yes" responses to targets in propositional priming pairs, (b) "no" responses to targets in associate priming pairs, and (c) "no" responses to targets in topic priming pairs.

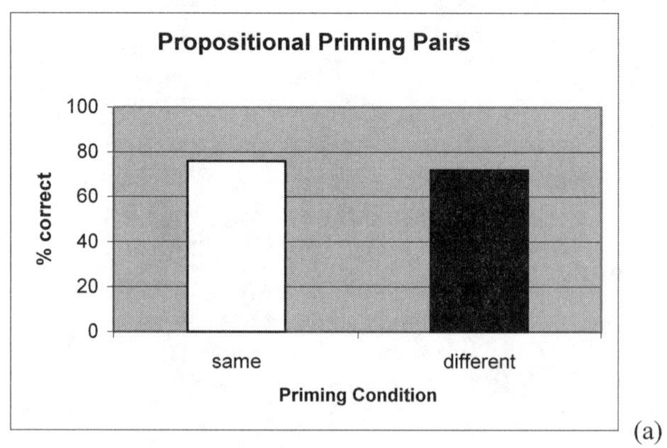

(a)

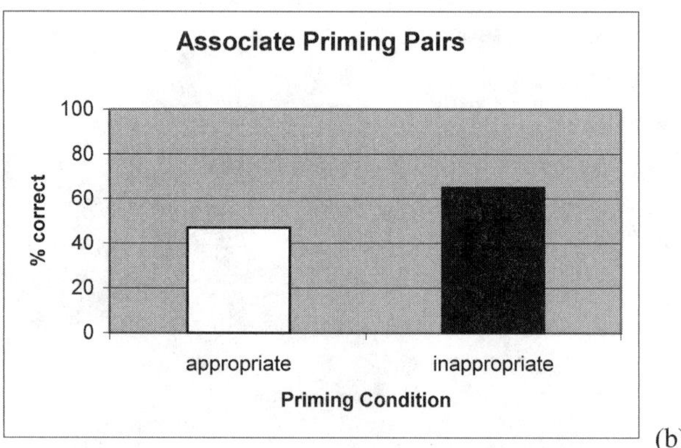

(b)

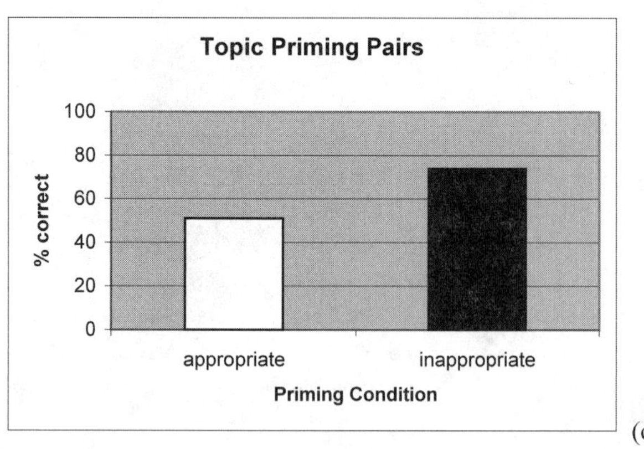

(c)

FIGURE 14–7. Item priming results from Baynes, Long, Gillette, Dronkers, and Davis (2002). Mean accuracy rates (in percentages) to targets: (a) "yes" responses to targets in propositional priming pairs, (b) "no" responses to targets in associate priming pairs, and (c) "no" responses to targets in topic priming pairs.

may then be linked to explicit text concepts and represented in memory, even though the representation lacks propositional structure.

CONCLUSIONS

Current theories of discourse processing make an important distinction between the representation of explicit information in a text (the propositional representation) and the representation of what the text is about (the discourse model). Our research suggests that this distinction is also important for understanding how discourse is represented in the brain. Our data consistently show that the left hemisphere organizes explicit text concepts in memory according to the propositional relations among them. In all of our experiments, we find reliable propositional priming. The one exception is in left-hemisphere-damaged aphasics. They show reliable associate and topic priming, but no evidence for propositional priming. It is likely that syntactic deficits in this group lead to difficulty in constructing structured representations of sentences.

In addition to a structured, propositional representation, the left hemisphere also appears to represent contextually relevant, semantic information, such as the context-appropriate senses of ambiguous words and thematic information about passages. Our study of callosotomy patients provides additional information about the representation of discourse-relevant information. We investigated the possibility that priming for topic-related words in both hemispheres may have depended on comprehension activities that occurred in the right hemisphere. The performance of the callosotomy patients suggests that this was not the case, however. They showed both associate and topic priming in their left hemispheres, in the absence of substantial right-hemisphere input. Thus, it appears that hemispheres represented topic-related information redundantly.

The performance of left-hemisphere-damaged aphasics in the item-priming task also extends our understanding of the representation of discourse-relevant information. These patients showed substantial associate and topic priming in the absence of well-structured sentence representations. These patients were able to extract the "gist" of these passages even though they were unable to represent appropriate connections among explicit concepts in the sentences.

Although we found that both hemispheres contained a representation of explicit information from a text, they appeared to organize this information differently. The left hemisphere was sensitive to within-sentence relations among explicit text concepts, whereas the right hemisphere was insensitive to these relations. The right hemisphere did appear to form connections among explicit text concepts; we found faster responses when a target was preceded by a prime from the same passage relative to a prime from a different passage. Our data tell us little, however, about the nature of these connections beyond the fact that they are not structural. These connections may reflect semantic and/or thematic relations among the topics, such that the right hemisphere was sensitive to the global change of topic across passages. This would be consistent with claims by Faust and her colleagues that the two cerebral hemispheres encode the meanings of sentences differently (Faust, 1998; Faust, Babkoff, & Kravetz, 1995; Faust & Kravetz, 1998). They argue that the left hemisphere has integrative syntactic and semantic mechanisms that encode a "message-level" representation, that is, a semantically integrated representation of the whole sentence meaning. The right hemisphere, in contrast, constructs an associative network representation consisting of the individual words in a sentence and the semantic relations among them.

Another possibility is that the right hemisphere may represent links among concepts that are episodic rather than semantic in nature. In our studies, concepts within a passage appeared on the screen at one time and in close physical proximity. If the right hemisphere has an episodic representation of the passages, then concepts that appeared together would have closer connections than concepts that appeared at other times (i.e., the other passages in the study phase). We are currently investigating the nature of the right-hemisphere connections among explicit text concepts by examining item priming in the context of scrambled passages. If the right hemisphere represents "message-level" relations among explicit text concepts, then we should find priming of within-passage concepts only when the concepts are presented in a meaningful passage. If, however, the right hemisphere forms purely lexical or episodic connections among the concepts, we should find priming of within-passage concepts both when the concepts are presented in a meaningful passage and when the concepts are presented in a scrambled passage.

In summary, the studies that we have described here address important gaps in our knowledge about discourse representation in the two hemispheres. Our research questions and hypotheses have been guided by important distinctions in current theories of discourse processing. In addition, we have adapted a standard paradigm from psycholinguistics that can be used in divided visual-field and clinical studies. This allows us to compare and integrate our findings across a range of materials and subject populations. Our results have implications for how the two hemispheres are likely to process linguistic input. Processes that depend on information about linguistic structure, such as resolving certain types of anaphor, are likely to be left-hemisphere functions. In contrast, processes that rely on lexical-semantic information may be performed in either hemisphere. Further study of discourse representation in the two hemispheres is likely to provide additional constraints on our hypotheses about the laterality of language processing and help to integrate research in neuropsychology and discourse processing.

ACKNOWLEDGMENTS

The research described in this chapter was supported by National Institute of Health Grant 1R01DC/NS04442-01.

REFERENCES

Baynes, K. (1990). Language and reading in the right hemisphere: Highways of byways of the brain? *Journal of Cognitive Neuroscience, 2*, 159–179.

Baynes, K., & Eliassen, J. C. (1998). The visual lexicon: Its access and organization in commissurotomy patients. In M. Beeman & C. Chiarrello (Eds.), *Right hemisphere language comprehension* (pp. 79–104). Mahwah, NJ: Lawrence Erlbaum Associates.

Baynes, K., & Gazzaniga, M. (1988). Right hemisphere language: Insights into normal language mechanisms? In F. Plum (Ed.), *Language, communication, and the brain* (pp. 117–126). New York: Raven.

Baynes, K., Long, D. L., Gillette, J., Dronkers, N., & Davis, C. (2002). Priming of discourse level relations in left-hemisphere injured patients. *Cognitive Neuroscience Society Abstracts.*

Beeman, M. (1993). Semantic processing in the right hemisphere may contribute to drawing inferences from discourse. *Brain and Language, 44*, 80–120.

Beeman, M. (1998). Coarse semantic coding and discourse comprehension. In M. Beeman & C. Chiarello (Eds.), Right hemisphere language comprehension: Perspectives from cognitive neuroscience (pp. 255–284). Mahwah, NJ: Lawrence Erlbaum Associates.

Blumstein, S. E. (1990). Phonological deficits in aphasia: Theoretical perspectives. In A. Caramazza (Ed.), *Cognitive neuropsychology and neurolinguistics: Advances in models of cognitive function and impairment* (pp. 33–54). Hillsdale, NJ: Lawrence Erlbaum Associates.

Bransford, J. D., & Johnson, M. K. (1972). Contextual prerequisites for understanding: Some investigations of comprehension and recall. *Journal of Verbal Learning and Verbal Behavior, 11*, 717–726.

Brownell, H., Gardner, H., Prather, P., & Martino, G. (1995). Language, communication, and the right hemisphere. In H. S. Kirshner (Ed.), *Handbook of neurological speech and language disorders* (pp. 325–349). New York: Marcel Dekker.

Brownell, H. H., Potter, H. H., Bihrle, A. M., & Gardner, H. (1986). Inference deficits in right brain-damaged patients. *Brain and Language, 27*, 310–321.

Bub, D., & Kertesz, A. (1982). Deep agraphia. *Brain and Language, 17*, 19–46.

Caramazza, A., & Hillis, A. (1990). Where do semantic errors come from? *Cortex, 26*, 95–122.

Chiarello, C. (1991). Interpretation of word meanings by the cerebral hemispheres: One is not enough. In P. J. Schwanenglugel (Eds.), *The psychology of word meanings* (pp. 251–278). Hillsdale, NJ: Lawrence Erlbaum Associates.

Chiarello, C. (1998). On codes of meaning and the meaning of codes: Semantic access and retrieval within and between hemispheres. In M. Beeman & C. Chiarello (Eds.), *Right hemisphere language comprehension: Perspectives from cognitive neuroscience* (pp. 141–160). Mahwah, NJ: Lawrence Erlbaum Associates.

Delis, D., Wapner, W., Gardner, H., & Moses, J. (1983). The contribution of the right hemisphere to the organization of paragraphs. *Cortex, 19*, 43–50.

Faust, M. (1998). Obtaining evidence of language comprehension from sentence priming. In M. Beeman & C. Chiarello (Eds.), *Right hemisphere language comprehension: Perspectives from cognitive neuroscience* (pp. 161–185). Mahwah, NJ: Lawrence Erlbaum Associates.

Faust, M., & Kravetz, S. (1998). Levels of sentence constraint and lexical decision in the two hemispheres. *Brain and Language, 62*, 149–162.

Faust, M., Kravetz, S., & Babkoff, H. (1993). Hemisphericity and top-down processing of language. *Brain and Language, 44*, 1–18.

Gardener, H., & Brownell, H. H. (1986). *Right hemisphere communication battery*. Boston: Psychology Service, VAMC.

Gazzaniga, M. S., & Sperry, R. W. (1967). Language after section of the cerebral commissures. *Brain, 90*, 131–138.

Gernsbacher, M. (1990). *Language comprehension as structure building*. Hillsdale, NJ: Lawrence Erlbaum Associates.

Graesser, A. C., Singer, M., & Trabasso, T. (1994). constructing inferences during narrative text comprehension. *Psychological Review, 101*, 371–395.

Greene, S. B., McKoon, G., & Ratcliff, R. (1992). Pronoun resolution and discourse models. *Journal of Experimental Psychology: Learning, Memory, and Cognition, 18*, 266–283.

Hough, M. S. (1990). Narrative comprehension in adults with right and left hemisphere brain-damage: Theme organization. *Brain and Language, 38*, 253–277.

Joannete, Y., Goulet, P., & Hannequin, D. (1990). *Right hemisphere and verbal communication*. New York: Springer-Verlag.

Kaan, E., & Swaab, T. (2002). The brain circuitry of syntactic comprehension. *Trends in Cognitive Sciences, 6*, 350–356.

Kingstone, A., & Gazzaniga, M. S. (1995). Subcortical transfer of higher order information: More illusory than real? *Neuropsychology, 9*, 321–328.

Kintsch, W. (1974). *The representation of meaning in memory*. Hillsdale, NJ: Lawrence Erlbaum Associates.

Kintsch, W. (1988). The role of knowledge in discourse comprehension: A construction-integration model. *Psychological Review, 95*, 163–182.

Kintsch, W., & van Dijk, T. A. (1978). Toward a model of text comprehension and production. *Psychological Review, 85*, 363–394.

Long, D. L., & Baynes, K. (2002). Discourse representation in the two cerebral hemispheres. *Journal of Cognitive Neuroscience, 14*, 228–242.

Long, D. L., Baynes, K., & Prat, C. S. (2005). The propositional structure of discourse in the two cerebral hemispheres. Brain and Language, 95, 383–394.

Long, D. L., Oppy, B. J., & Seely, M. R. (1997). Individual differences in readers' sentence- and text-level representations. *Journal of Memory and Language, 36*, 129–145.

McKoon, G., & Ratcliff, R. (1980). Priming in item recognition: The organization of propositions in memory for text. *Journal of Verbal Learning and Verbal Behavior, 19*, 369–386.

McKoon, G., & Ratcliff, R. (1990). Textual inferences: Models and measures. In D. A. Balota, G. B. Flores d'Arcais, & K. Rayner (Eds.), *Comprehension processes in reading* (pp. 403–421). Hillsdale, NJ: Lawrence Erlbaum Associates.

McKoon, G., & Ratcliff, R. (1992). Inference during reading. *Psychological Review, 99,* 440–466.

McKoon, G., & Ratcliff, R. (1998). Memory based language processing: Psycholinguistic research in the 1990's. *Annual Review of Psychology, 49,* 25–42.

Meyers, P. S. (1994). Communication disorders associated with right hemisphere brain damage. In R. Chapey (Ed.), *Language intervention strategies in adult aphasia* (pp. 514–534). Baltimore: Williams & Wilkins.

Nelson, D. L., McEvoy, C. L., & Schreiber, T. A. (1998). The University of South Florida word association, rhyme, and word fragment norms. Available at http://www.usf.edu/FreeAssociation/

Ratcliff, R., & McKoon, G. (1978). Priming in item recognition: Evidence for the propositional structure of sentences. *Journal of Verbal Learning and Verbal Behavior, 17,* 403–417.

Rehak, A., Kaplan, J. A., & Gardner, H. (1992). Sensitivity to conversational deviance in right-hemisphere-damaged patients. *Brain and Language, 42,* 203–217.

Robertson, D. A., Gernsbacher, M. A., Guidotti, S. J., Robertson, R. R. W., Irwin, W., Mock, B. J., & Campana, M. E. (2000). Functional neuroanatomy of the cognitive process of mapping during discourse comprehenison. *Psychological Science, 11,* 255–260.

Sanford, A. J., & Garrod, S. C. (1998). The role of scenario mapping in text comprehension. *Discourse Processes, 26,* 159–190.

Zaidel, E. (1978). Lexical organization in the right hemisphere. In P. Buser & A. Gougeul-Buser (Eds.), *Cerebral correlates of conscious experience* (pp. 177–197). Amsterdam: Elsevier.

Zaidel, E. (1990). Language functions in the two hemispheres following complete cerebral commissurotomy and hemispherectomy. In F. Boller & G. Grafman (Eds.), *Handbook of neuropsychology* (Vol. 4, pp. 115–150). Amsterdam: Elsevier.

Zaidel, E., Kasher, A., Soroker, N., & Batori, G. (2002). Effects of right and left hemisphere damage on performance of the "Right Hemisphere Communication Battery." *Brain and Language, 80,* 510–535.

15

Hemispheric Asymmetry in the Processing of Negative and Positive Emotional Inferences

Isabelle Tapiero, Virginie Fillon
University of Lyon 2, France

A lexical decision task combined with a visual split field methodology were used to study hemisphere differences in the generation of emotional inferences. Subjects read short passages that implied a character's emotional state, either with a negative valence (e.g., guilt) or with a positive valence (e.g., happiness). Although each whole passage implied an emotional state, the last sentence of each passage was intended to induce readers to generate an inference in relation to the character's emotional state implied (see Gernsbacher, Goldsmith, & Robertson, 1992). For each passage, and following the last but one word of the final sentence, participants performed lexical decisions on inference words presented directly to the left hemisphere (right visual field) or to the right hemisphere (left visual field). The test stimuli could refer to the emotion that matched the textual information (e.g., guilt/matching emotion word) or to an emotion with the perceived opposite valence (e.g., pride/mismatching emotion word). Results confirmed that the right hemisphere is sensitive to more than the relevant information and that this effect is modulated by the valence of the emotion word to infer (positive and negative). The findings showed evidence for the existence of hemisphere differences in the generation of emotional inferences and indicate that emotion has a critical role in the construction of a coherent situation model.

RICHNESS OF READERS' SITUATION MODEL

Theories on text comprehension assume that readers form a model of the situation described by the text (van Dijk & Kintsch, 1983). What is remembered at this level is the result of the interaction between information provided by the text and the reader's knowledge. Thus, attaining full comprehension depends not only on the understanding of words and syntax, but also on implicit information elicited by the text. This situational representation is rich and requires the generation of different types of inferences, and it has been widely shown that inferences occupy a crucial role in discourse comprehension. Indeed, they enable readers not only to maintain coherence by linking different parts of the text but also to elaborate on what is actually presented. Inference generation and the maintenance of coherence in text comprehension has received substantial attention (see, e.g., Gernsbacher, 1990; Kintsch, 1988, 1998; McKoon & Ratcliff, 1986, 1992; O'Brien, Shank, Myers, & Rayner, 1988; Tapiero & Otero, 2002). Research in that field has mainly focused on which inferences are made and the circumstances under which they are made (Graesser, Singer, & Trabasso, 1994). For instance, readers are enabled to capture information in relation to spatiality, causality, temporality, intentionality, and protagonists (Zwaan, Langston, & Graesser, 1995), and their mental representation is therefore based on these specific dimensions. Another class of inferences that has not received much attention, although it is crucial in text understanding, is emotion inferences. Research in emotion inferences indicates that readers infer characters' emotions while reading (DeVega, Leon, & Diaz, 1996; Gernsbacher, Goldsmith, & Robertson, 1992; Gernsbacher & Robertson, 1992; Gygax, Oakhill, & Garnham, 2003), and some of these studies (see Gernsbacher et al., 1992) indicate that these emotion inferences are quite specific. Thus, emotion is part of the readers' mental representation and plays a crucial role in comprehension process (Miall, 1989).

ONE SPECIFIC TYPE OF INFERENCES: THE EMOTION INFERENCES

In three experiments, Gernsbacher, Goldsmith, and Robertson (1992) investigated whether readers activate knowledge on emotions during story comprehension. According to these authors, a reader is supposed to activate, from explicit textual information, his/her knowledge about human emotions and thus is enabled to build a coherent representation of the characters' emotional states. The materials used in the three experiments were 24 stories that described information related to characters' goals and actions without explicitly mentioned their emotions in the text. Among these 24 stories, half described emotions with a positive valence (e.g., joyful), whereas the other half evoked a negative emotional state (e.g., sad). Although the whole passages implied an emotional state, the last sentence of each passage (i.e., target sentence) was intended to induce readers to generate an inference in relation to the character's emotional state implied. Participants' task was to read at a natural reading rate each story, and reading times for the target sentence were recorded (Gernsbacher et al., 1992, experiments 1 and 2). In a third experiment, participants had to read the same stories as in the first two experiments but had to name test words displayed immediately after the offset of the final word of the last sentence (Gernsbacher et al., 1992, experiment 3). The last sentence of each passage (i.e., target sentence, experiments 1 and 2) or the test words used for the naming task (experiment 3) referred to an emotion that matched the textual information or that mismatched the textual information (e.g., guilt/matching emotion word or pride/mismatching emotion word). Materials from experiment 2 differed from those used in experiment 1 by the nature of the mismatched information. Mismatching emotion words had the same valence as in the matching condition, but were different from the opposite emotion (e.g., sad/mismatching emotion word for guilt/matching emotion word).

In Table 15–1 a story example is given that includes or does not include the target sentence containing the emotional word with the different matching conditions for the emotion words (from Gernsbacher et al., 1992, experiments 1, 2, and 3).

Gernsbacher et al. (1992, experiments 1 and 2) found shorter reading times for target sentences that contained matching emotional terms than for target sentences that contained mismatching emotional terms. In addition, the authors showed that readers activate knowledge about human emotions during the process of reading (experiment 3). From these results they concluded that readers activate and mentally represent very specific emotions.

In line with these studies, Gygax et al. (Gygax, Oakhill, & Garnham, 2003; Gygax, Garnham, & Oakhill, 2004) investigated whether the emotion inferred by readers was specific or rather general. In a first study, participants had to read stories (the same stories as in Gernsbacher et al., 1992) and then had to provide emotional words that completed the last sentence of the passages. In a second study, participants had to read each story and to perform a rating task on the likelihood of the main character feeling several emotional responses. The authors' findings indicated that readers inferred from textual information a general feeling rather than a specific emotion: Participants referred more to the general ideas and stories' protagonists than to the specific emotional word that was expected. Gygax et al. (2003) carried out a third experiment in which emotional synonyms and similar emotions of coherent words were added to the matched emotional words. Their results indicated no difference in reading times between target sentences containing matching

TABLE 15–1.
A Story Example: "Suzanne"

"Suzanne had just returned from her regular visit to the nursing home. Today, there had been several problems and one elderly patient had died. Another had fallen in the stairs and broken her hip. [. . .] The sheer magnitude of the problems simply overcame Suzanne. A tear ran slowly down her cheek." *Target sentence (only for experiments 1 & 2)* "Her visit to the nursing home filled her with feelings of *Sadness/Joy/Guilt.*"

but different emotion words (similar and synonyms) and therefore confirmed that readers infer general emotional information, which is compatible with different emotions, rather than a specific emotion.

Thus, emotional information appears to be part of the readers' mental representation, and one goal of this chapter is to deepen our knowledge about emotion and about how it may affect stories' comprehension. However, investigating the "weight" of emotion in readers' mental representation requires accounting for what has been found on the specific processing of the two hemispheres regarding emotional information. Indeed, we think it necessary to investigate emotion by combining recent findings issued from research in cognitive psychology and in neuroscience. For that purpose, we chose to study the influence of emotional information on readers' representation by using a split visual field methodology. Our goal is to examine hemispheric differences in the processing of emotion, by taking into account the nature of the emotion inference generated (i.e., valence and specificity). We organize our chapter into three sections. First, we review some of the studies showing how language processing may be differentiated in the two hemispheres. Then we present the main hypotheses related to emotion and its hemispheric specialization. Finally, we describe in more detail our main assumptions and how we investigated the relation between emotion and hemispheric asymmetry.

HEMISPHERIC ASYMMETRY IN LANGUAGE PROCESSING

Linguistic Constraints and Levels of Representation

Although it has been widely demonstrated that the left hemisphere is dominant for language processing (comprehension and production), recent cognitive neuroscience studies utilizing the divided visual field (DVF) priming paradigm have shown that the right hemisphere is involved in some aspects of language comprehension. From these studies it has been suggested that the cerebral hemispheres process linguistic information in a different manner (e.g., phonological information and access and use of meaningful information).

Faust and Kravetz (1998) investigated, with a divided-visual field methodology, the levels of linguistic constraints of the two cerebral hemispheres and whether the hemispheres had an independent linguistic functioning. In a first experiment, subjects had to read sentences (one at a time) and then had to perform as fast and as accurately as possible a lexical decision task with words and pseudo-words, presented in the right (left hemisphere) or in the left (right hemisphere) visual field. Each sentence had a high or low level of linguistic constraint. For instance, *the cop caught the—*, followed by *thief*, was defined as a sentence with a high level of linguistic constraint, as *thief* is the most expected linguistic candidate for the completion. The authors also used sentences with a low level of constraint, such as *the car was opened by*—followed by *the thief*. This sentence, contrary to the previous one, has several potential candidates. Faust and Kravetz (1998) also constructed medium constraining sentences ("the lock was broken by a *thief*") as well as neutral sentences (i.e., baseline condition) ("the next word is *thief*"). Their main results indicated that the reaction times for target words presented in the right visual field (left hemisphere) increased from the highly constraining sentences to the medium constraining sentences, with longer reaction times for the low constraining sentences. When target words were presented in the left visual field (right hemisphere), reaction times for highly constraining sentences were significantly different from the other levels of constraints, but no difference occurred for the other levels of constraints (medium, low, and neutral). The left hemisphere appeared to be more sensitive to the variations of syntactic and semantic constraints than the right hemisphere. However, when the prime was only a word (and not a sentence), the facilitation of the left hemisphere was weaker. Thus, these findings indicated that the right hemisphere syntactically processes sentences poorly.

Consistent with these studies, and to investigate deeply whether differences occur between the two hemispheres for semantic and situational representation, Long and Baynes (2002) attempted to define the role of the two hemispheres in processing discourse and tried to show their relation with the two main levels of discourse representation (i.e., semantic and situational). Regarding the role of the two cerebral hemispheres, the authors assumed that although the semantic and situational levels of representation are strongly related, the left hemisphere should be used for the processing of the macrostructure, whereas the right hemisphere could be the basis for the situation model. In a first study, the authors used a divided visual field word recognition task and examined how discourse was represented. Participants read two consecutive sentences centered on a computer screen, each composed of one homograph, either at the end of the first sentence or at the end of the second one. Then the participants' task was to state as rapidly and accurately as possible whether the word presented at the right or at the left of the screen was present in the two sentences previously read. The recognition task was performed on several pairs of words; each pair was composed of a prime and a target. Three types of prime-target pairs of words were used: (1) a propositional prime-target, (2) an associated prime-target and (3) a thematic prime-target pair of words. In (1), the target was preceded with a prime, either issued from the same proposition, or from a different proposition. Although the first pair of prime-target words tested the propositional level of representation, the second and third pairs of prime-target words tested the situation model. According to Long and Baynes (2002), if the two hemispheres have a similar access to discourse representation, priming effects should be identical whatever the visual field position (left or right) of the target words.

Contrary to their expectations, data indicated that the two hemispheres differ in the way they represent discourse. The level of propositional representation (1) appeared to be stored only in the left hemisphere, with faster responses for target words issued from the same proposition only when the target is presented in the right visual field (left hemisphere). However, information that dealt with the contextually appropriate meaning of ambiguous words (2) as well as the theme of the passages (3) appeared to be represented in both hemispheres. In sum, the left hemisphere is crucial for discourse propositional representation, whereas the situation model is represented in both hemispheres (see also, Long, Baynes, & Prat in this volume for other evidence that supports this conclusion). In a second experiment, Long and Baynes (2002) investigated how the right hemisphere could contribute to the construction of the two levels of representation. More specifically, they attempted to determine whether the information processed by the right hemisphere was required for the development of the representation in the left hemisphere. With callosotomy patients, they used the same material and method as those described in their first experiment, but the presentation of the prime-target words was centered on the screen and only the left hemisphere was involved in that task (right-hand answers). Their data indicated that participants elaborated an appropriate propositional and situational discourse representation. Thus, although these findings showed evidence for the fact that the situation model is represented in the two hemispheres, the left hemisphere could elaborate "on its own" an appropriate discourse representation, and no evidence is found for a unique role in discourse comprehension of the right hemisphere. Consistent with Long and Baynes (2002), Griesel, Friese, and Schmalhofer (2003) went one step further relative to the idea that a discourse propositional representation is more strongly represented in the left hemisphere. In two experiments, they evaluated representational differences between two types of inferences: bridging and predictive inferences. In their first study, they used the tapping speed-accuracy trade-off method (see Schmalhofer & Glavanov, 1986) for estimating representational strengths and respective differences between these two types of inferences. Participants had to read two-sentence passage (from McDaniel, Schmalhofer, & Keefe, 2001) and then had to decide whether a test sentence had occurred (1) explicitly in a text (i.e., recognition test) or (2) was true or false regarding the situation described in the text (i.e., verification test). The test sentence constituted an explicit sentence, a paraphrase, a bridging inference, and a predictive inference (for the experimental conditions), and a false statement was presented for the control passages. According to the authors' assumptions, if bridging inferences are encoded only at the situational level, as predictive inferences are assumed to be, the proportion of yes responses in the bridging and predictive inference conditions should not differ in a significant way. If, however, bridging inferences are encoded as the paraphrases are, at the propositional level, the relative frequencies of yes responses in the bridging inference and paraphrases conditions should be similar. The main results showed that depending on the particular processing goal, a propositional elaboration may occur (for the verification test) or not (for the recognition task). Their second experiment was aimed at testing that a text representation should more strongly reside in the left hemisphere and that a situation model may be distributed across both hemispheres (see Long & Baynes, 2002). For that purpose, they used a lateralized-presentation technique by assuming that if bridging inferences are represented as part of the textbase, they should show shorter latency time as compared with predictive inferences when presented to the left hemisphere. Also, predictive inferences should show a facilitation effect for left visual field presentation (right hemisphere). The material was similar to that used in the first experiment, with two exceptions. First, there was no paraphrase condition, and second, the test sentences were replaced with word pairs to indicate the propositional contents of sentences that had to be verified. The first word of the pair was always presented at the center of the screen, and the second word was presented in the left or right visual field. The participants' task was to decide whether a proposition was true ("yes") or false ("no") in relation to the just-read text. The main results showed that bridging inferences appear to have a propositional encoding. Thus, these two studies confirm that text and situation representation are differentially represented in the two hemispheres and that bridging inferences, unlike predictive inferences, contain a propositional component.

HEMISPHERIC ASYMMETRY IN ACTIVATION OF SEMANTIC INFORMATION AND IN DRAWING INFERENCES

The Role of the Right Hemisphere in Maintaining Coherence

The different findings presented above (Long & Baynes, 2002; Griese, Friese, & Schmalhofer, 2003; Long, Baynes, & Prat, this volume) indicated that although the left hemisphere plays a crucial role in representing situational representation, the right hemisphere might have also some implication in that level of representation. Other recent data confirmed the influence of the right hemisphere for building situational representation. Indeed, one important aspect of hemispheric asymmetry is that semantic activation might be performed differently in the two hemispheres (Beeman, 1998; Beeman & Bowden, 2000; Beeman & Chiarello, 1998; Virtue, Linderholm, & van den Broek, 2000). For instance, Beeman and Bowden (2000) demonstrated that problem solvers do exhibit hemispheric differences in semantic activation related to solutions of insight-like problems. Specifically, the authors showed that the right hemisphere is more likely than the left hemisphere to maintain semantic activation of unusual interpretations of problem elements. In addition, recent works indicate that right-hemisphere-damaged patients have specific difficulties in answering true/false questions about inferable information, although they answer correctly questions about explicitly stated information (Beeman, 1993). They also have difficulties performing complex tasks, such as understanding humor or metaphors and idioms, controlling the prosody, and revising their interpretation. Finally, it has also been shown that the right hemisphere was involved in the pragmatics of communication behaviors (Eustache & Faure, 2000). All of these findings indicate that RH-damaged patients fail to activate some semantic information necessary to perform high-level language processing, such as drawing coherence inferences (Beeman, Bowden, & Gernsbacher, 2000), a cognitive activity that is crucial in the construction of a coherent situation model.

Beeman (1993) proposed two interpretations to explain the difficulty of right-hemisphere-damaged patients to elaborate and generate coherence inferences during text reading. These patients could have either a poor structural discourse organization or a weak activation of the necessary semantic information for the construction of coherence inferences. On one hand, difficulties in recognizing and constructing an appropriate structure for representing the text could affect the perception of coherence of a new input as well as the final integration of inferences to the representation. On the other hand, the lack in semantic processing could impair the selection of an appropriate inference to connect old and new information. Beeman (1993) tested these two hypotheses (i.e., structure and semantic activation) with right-hemisphere-damaged patients and normal elderly subjects and examined the interaction between the coherence inferences and the construction of the structure.

In his study, participants had to listen to stories for which the comprehension required the production of coherence inferences within the same episode and between episodes. Then, subjects had to answer explicit or inferring questions. The author's expectations were that right-hemisphere-damaged patients should have more difficulties answering inferring questions, whereas no difference should occur between the two subject groups for explicit questions. The main results are in favor of a lack of activation of the semantic information necessary for inference generation. Right-hemisphere-damaged patients had difficulties answering inferring questions compared with explicit questions, with no reliable difference between these two types of questions for elderly subjects. Moreover, and whatever the position of the inferences to generate (within or between episodes), the performances of patients (i.e., correct responses) were very low. Thus, these findings confirmed that the right hemisphere is widely involved in the generation of coherence inferences and that the difficulties encountered by right-hemisphere-damaged patients are not due to a poor elaboration or organization of the mental structure, because they are not affected by the conditions within and between episodes.

The Implication of the Right Hemisphere in the Generation of Causal Inferences

The findings we described above indicate that the right hemisphere is involved in the generation and maintain of some types of inferences (i.e., coherence inference). As we mentioned previously, there are many types of inferences (see Graesser, Singer, & Trabasso, 1994), and one of those that received a lot of attention is causal inferences (McKoon & Ratcliff, 1986). van den Broek (1990) proposed a process model of inference generation the Causal Inference Maker and adopted the criteria for causality as the principles that guide the inferential process. From a focal event (i.e., the newly read event), two types of inferences might be made: backward and forward (or predictive) inferences. Backward inferences connect a focal event to prior events, whereas forward inferences generate expectations about what will happen next in the text. Predictive inferences are not required for comprehension and are less constrained than backward inferences, but they are assumed to facilitate processing of later events. Therefore, forward inferences are supposed to be drawn only under specific circumstances (see Duffy, 1986; Graesser, Singer, & Trabasso, 1994; McKoon & Ratcliff, 1992). One critical parameter in the generation of predictive inferences is the degree of causal constraint. In a recent study, Virtue, Linderholm, and van den Broek (2000) investigated using a divided visual field methodology, the influence of two levels of textual constraint (High vs. Low) on the generation of predictive inferences, and how this influence could deepen our understanding of what we currently know about cerebral hemispheric asymmetries. Their main hypothesis was that the left hemisphere should have an advantage in processing predictive inferences, but this advantage should be dependent on the level of causal constraints: The right hemisphere should be faster in responding to low constraint predictive inferences than the left hemisphere. One reason for this might be that the right hemisphere has a coarse semantic coding compared with the left hemisphere that allows a precise selection of meaning through a relatively fine semantic coding. In their study (Virtue et al., 2000), participants had to read items (i.e., four sentences) on a computer screen, one sentence at a time in a self-paced manner. These sentences were constructed such that a predictive inference could be generated after reading the last sentence with two constraint versions (high and low). For both the high and low constraint items, the target words presented to the participants in the right (left hemisphere) or left visual field (right hemisphere) were words representing the inference. Neutral items that did not promote inferences (i.e., baseline condition) were paired with the same target as those presented in the inference items. The participants' task was to respond as rapidly and accurately as possible to the probe words and non-words.

As expected, the authors found that causal constraints differentially affect predictive inferences in the two hemispheres. Both hemispheres seemed to play a role in the generation of highly constrained predictive inferences, as data indicated similar levels of priming. However, the right hemisphere appeared to be more efficient at producing predictive inferences that are less constrained by the text, since the authors found a greater level of priming for the low constraint items in the right hemisphere than in the left. Thus, these findings confirmed the importance of the right hemisphere in the elaboration of situation models.

Beeman, Bowden, and Gernsbacher (2000) showed results consistent with what we discussed above (see Beeman, 1993; Virtue, Linderholm, & van den Broek, 2000). In three experiments, they investigated the activation of predictive and coherence inferences during stories' comprehension using a divided visual field methodology. While listening to stories, participants (i.e., healthy students) had to perform a naming task on inference-related test words (and unrelated test words) presented to the right (left hemisphere) or to the left (right hemisphere) visual field. At different points in the stories, the authors tested participants' ability to generate either predictive or coherence inferences and assessed inference-related activation in each hemisphere. According to the authors' view, concepts related to the inference are more likely to receive converging input from multiple words in the right hemisphere than in the left hemisphere. Indeed, the left hemisphere (LH) engages in fine semantic coding, strongly focusing activation on a single interpretation of a word and a few close associates, whereas the right hemisphere (RH) engages in coarse semantic coding, weakly and diffusely activating alternative meanings and distant associates (see Beeman, 1998; Beeman & Bowden, 2000). Therefore, inference-related priming should occur for the right hemisphere target words at an earlier point than for the left hemisphere. Data from these three studies showed priming for predictive inferences only for target words presented to the right hemisphere and not for the left hemisphere. In addition, the priming for coherence inferences was only reliable for target words presented to the left hemisphere when the data from experiments 1 and 2 were combined. Thus, although both hemispheres were involved in drawing inferences, inference generation was influenced by the specificity of processing in the right and left hemispheres. The left hemisphere appeared to play a larger role than the right hemisphere in selecting a coherence inference and incorporating it into the representation of the text, whereas information capable of supporting predictive inferences was more likely to be initially activated in the right hemisphere than in the left hemisphere. Therefore, these findings showed evidence for the fact that the two hemispheres differently process semantic information, although they also share information and are crucial to a deep understanding of the different phases in hemispheric processing (see Beeman, Bowden, & Gernsbacher, 2000). Complementary processing by the two hemispheres is necessary to comprehend complex discourse. But in general, the right hemisphere seems better suited to processing complex discourse connected by distant semantic associations than to processing single words or word pairs (see Beeman & Bowden, 2000).

CEREBRAL HEMISPHERIC ASYMMETRY AND EMOTION: IS THE RIGHT HEMISPHERE THE CENTER OF NEGATIVE EMOTIONS AND THE LEFT HEMISPHERE THE CENTER OF POSITIVE EMOTIONS?

Hemispheric asymmetries have been shown to have an influence in higher-level discourse processing. As we previously described, the right hemisphere has a critical role in the generation and maintenance of coherence inference (Beeman, 1993), in the causal constraints for the generation of predictive inferences (Virtue et al., 2000), as well as in the type of semantic coding of meaningful information (Beeman, Bowden, & Gernsbacher, 2000). Evidence of hemispheric asymmetries for emotional behavior and affect have also been demonstrated (see Davidson, 1995; Sutton & Davidson, 1997). Observations of patients with unilateral cortical lesions have indicated that damage to the left hemisphere was more likely to lead to a "catastrophic-depressive" reaction compared with comparable damage to the right hemisphere. Consistent with these observations, Gainotti (1988) showed that patients with left cortical lesions reacted dramatically relative to their difficulty in their oral production as well as to their failure to the neuropsychological tests. Conversely, the patients with right lesions showed a global indifference to their disease as well as to their failure to perform the tasks. Gainotti (1988) assumed that catastrophic reactions may be the result of emotional reactions to the disease, and euphoric reactions could be explained by the fact that the right hemisphere plays a critical role in the elaboration of emotional behavior.

Davidson, Ekman, Saron, Senulis, and Friesen (1990) conducted a study in which participants were exposed to two positive and two negative short films designed to induce approach-related positive emotion (i.e., happiness) and withdrawal-related negative emotion (i.e., disgust). Subjects' facial behavior and brain electrical activity were recorded. The authors assumed that the disgust period (EEG during periods of happy and disgusted facial expressions) should be associated with greater right-sided anterior activation compared with the happy periods, and that the happy periods should be associated with greater left-sided activation compared with the disgust periods. Consistent with their hypotheses, the data indicated a highly significant Hemisphere $\gtrsim$ Valence interaction and showed a greater right-sided activation during disgust compared with happiness in anterior region brain, whereas no differences in the central or parietal regions occurred. Davidson and Fox (1989) also explored the relation between individual differences in anterior activation asymmetries and affective style in young children and infants. Infants were divided into two groups on the basis of whether they cried or not in response to maternal separation. First, baseline measures of frontal and parietal activation from the two hemispheres were recorded (prior to the episode of maternal separation); then were recorded EEG measures of frontal activation asymmetry during this preceding baseline period. Results indicated that "crier" infants had greater right-sided and less left-sided frontal activation during the preceding baseline period compared with "non-crier" infants. Thus, these findings indicated that asymmetry in the frontal cortical regions is significantly associated with emotion and emotional reactivity and that these regions are specialized for approach and withdrawal processes. The left hemisphere appears to be specialized for the approach-related positive affect, whereas the right hemisphere is specialized for the withdrawal-related negative affect. Partly consistent with what has been previously stated, Davidson and Irwin (1999) supported the view of right-sided activation in several regions within the prefrontal cortex associated with negative emotion. However, they stressed the importance of conducting further systematic studies with patients who are predisposed to positive affect, since less evidence occurred on the prefrontal changes associated with positive affect.

Finally, although most clinical and laboratory observations suggest that the left prefrontal cortex is a biological substrate of approach behavior and positive affect, whereas the right prefrontal cortex is a biological substrate of withdrawal behavior and negative affect (Sutton & Davidson, 1997), it appears necessary to address the specific question of whether asymmetrical frontal activity is associated with affective valence, motivational direction, or some combination of valence and motivation. Indeed, Harmon-Jones pointed out recently (Harmon-Jones, 2003) the fact that affective valence and motivational direction are often confounded, since on many occasions, positive emotion is associated with approach-related motivation, and negative emotion is associated with withdrawal motivation. For example, with anger, evoking approach motivation although associated with negative valence, Harmon-Jones (2003) showed a relative left frontal activation, indicating that not all emotions behave in agreement with the presumed relationship between the valence of emotion and direction of motivation. Thus, the frontal asymmetry seems to be responsive to motivational direction and not affective valence, and this result should be taken into account when interpreting data on emotional valence and hemispheric specificities.

EXPERIMENT

Our study is aimed at showing the importance of emotion in the elaboration of the readers' situation model and therefore in the generation of inferences. We tested with a divided visual field methodology, the differential processing of the two cerebral hemispheres on the generation of emotional inferences. Hemispheric asymmetries were investigated regarding the nature of the inferences to be generated (i.e., valence and specificity). Subjects had to read short passages that implied a character's emotional state, either with a negative valence (e.g., guilt) or with a positive valence (e.g., joy) (see Gernsbacher et al., 1992). Participants performed a divided visual field priming task that immediately followed the last but one word of the last sentence of each passage. Probe words and non-words were presented in the left and right visual fields, and the words referred to the emotion that matched the textual information provided in the passage (e.g., guilt/matching emotion word) or to an emotion with an opposite valence (e.g., pride/mismatching emotion word). The participants' task was to respond as rapidly and accurately as possible by stating whether the probe items were a word.

First, and according to the theoretical approach that emphasizes the crucial role of the right hemisphere in the inference elaboration and the maintain of coherence, we assumed that the cerebral hemispheres should be sensitive in a different manner to the inference to be generated, regarding not only the specificity of the emotional information (matching/mismatching) but also in terms of the valence of this information (positive and negative). More specifically, and although both hemispheres should be involved in generating these inferences, the right hemisphere should show a greater facilitation effect for representing non-matching (contradictory) emotional inferences than the left hemisphere, which should be only sensitive to emotional inferences (coherent) that matched the information provided by the text. Indeed, the left hemisphere has been shown to be dominant for contextually relevant information (i.e., fine semantic coding). Also, it has been widely demonstrated that when subjects view words in the left visual field (right hemisphere), they respond faster to test words related to less frequent or contextually inappropriate meanings of ambiguous words. The right hemisphere is therefore supposed to maintain several semantic candidates because of its more diffuse semantic coding and should interpret in multiple ways the textual elements, contrary to the left hemisphere, which would select only one possible semantic interpretation. Thus, the multiple interpretations proposed by the right hemisphere should facilitate the selection by the left hemisphere of the most relevant information to build coherence (Beeman, 1993).

In addition, consistent with some observations that found hemispheric specificities for the representation of emotions (see Davidson, 1995; Gainotti, 1969), and assuming that there is agreement in the association between the valence of emotion and the direction of motivation (see Harmon-Jones, 2003), the right hemisphere should be more sensitive to negative emotional information compared to the left hemisphere, which might show facilitation effect only for positive emotional inferences.

Last but not least, we also expected that the two hemispheres showed different patterns of responses in relation to the valence of emotional information as well as the specificity of hemispheric semantic coding. If emotion is one component of the reader's situation model, its influence might be shown in this study. Regarding the valence of information, the diffuse semantic coding in the right hemisphere was expected only for negative information, and we predicted a greater priming effect with non-matching or contradictory information for negative information than for positive information. We did not predict such priming for non-matching information in the right hemisphere for positive information, for which the left hemisphere might be more sensitive. Conversely, we assumed that the facilitation of the left hemisphere for matching information should be greater for positive information.

Method

Participants. A group of 28 undergraduate students at the University of Lyon 2 (France) participated in this experiment. All participants were right handed according to the Edinburgh Inventory (Oldfield, 1971). All had normal or corrected to normal vision and participated for course credit (course in psychobiology).

Materials

Stories. Twelve experimental stories (half describing a positive emotional state and the other half a negative emotional state) were used for the purpose of this experiment. They were translated into French and revised from the materials originally used by Gernsbacher and collaborators (Gernsbacher, Goldsmith, & Robertson, 1992; Gernsbacher & Robertson, 1992). No explicit mention of the emotional state was presented. Each story ended with a target sentence, and following the reading of each passage, participants had to perform a lexical decision task with target items either presented on the right visual field (left hemisphere) or on the left visual field (right hemisphere). In Table 15–2 is presented Suzanne's story, with its target sentence (the last word of the target sentence was part of the divided visual field priming task).

To confirm that these stories induced the readers to activate the emotional states (positive or negative) inferred by the textual information, we carried out a preliminary experiment in which we tested the generation of characters' emotional states using the same design and procedure as used by Gernsbacher, Goldsmith, and Robertson (1992, experiments 1 and 2). Reading times of the last sentence of each passage were recorded, and the emotional word that ended the sentence either matched or mismatched the emotional state implied in the text (i.e., inconsistent emotional word with and without the same valence as the matching emotional word). Our main findings, re-

TABLE 15–2.
Example Passage Using the "Suzanne Story" with the Target Sentence

"Suzanne had just returned from her regular visit to the nursing home. Today, there had been several problems and one elderly patient had died. Another had fallen in the stairs and broken her hip. [. . .] The sheer magnitude of the problems simply orvercame Suzanne. A tear ran slowly down her cheek."
Target sentence
"Her visit to the nursing home filled her with feelings of ______"

garding the nature of the inferences to be generated, indicated that readers processed longer target sentences when the emotional word was in contradiction with the emotion implied in the text (non-matching conditions) than when the emotional word was coherent with the emotion implied in the text (matching condition) and thus confirmed the fact that readers represent characters' emotional states when reading stories. However, consistent with Gygax et al. (2003), we also showed that the inferences generated were not specific, since we did not observe any time differences between the coherent emotional word (matching condition) and the non-coherent but with the same valence emotional word (non-matching condition for a target word with the same valence). Thus, in the experiment reported here, we chose to use only emotional words opposite in valence in comparison with the information implied in the text.

Table 15–3 lists for each passage the characters' emotional states that subjects had to infer from textual information, with their respective valence, and their mismatching emotional word (written in italics).

In addition to the 12 experimental stories, there were 6 filler stories. The filler stories were written in the same style as the experimental stories (i.e., same number of sentences and of characters) and were also adapted from Gernsbacher et al. (1992). They were neutral and were not intended to induce readers to represent a particular emotional state. The order of presentation of the control and experimental passages was counterbalanced but remained the same for all participants.

TABLE 15–3.
Character Emotional States That Subjects Had to Infer from Textual Information with Their Respective Valence

Passage	*Positive*	*Negative*
Suzanne	*Joyful (mismatching)*	Sad (matching)
Eric	*Confident (mismatching)*	Shy (matching)
Angéla	*Sympathetic (mismatching)*	Envious (matching)
Alice	*Bold (mismatching)*	Afraid (matching)
Jacques	*Proud (mismatching)*	Guilty (matching)
Marc	*Caring (mismatching)*	Callous (matching)
Sarah	Joyful (matching)	*Sad (mismatching)*
Sébastien	Confident	*Shy (mismatching)*
Josiane	Sympathetic	*Envious (mismatching)*
Anna	Bold	*Afraid (mismatching)*
Paul	Proud	*Guilty (mismatching)*
Philippe	Caring	*Callous (mismatching)*

Note: Regular characters indicate the text version in which participants read the text and italics indicate the mismatching words associated with the text versions.

Probe Words Used in the Split Visual Field Priming Task. Twelve emotional target words that tested the emotional state implied in the stories were visually presented. They were displayed at the offset of the last but one word of the last sentence for the experimental texts, but interrupted the reading (middle of the passages) for the filler texts. Twelve other emotional words were added and used in the filler texts. These probe words were either positive or negative and forced participants to not only focus their attention on emotional words presented in the experimental texts. Eighteen neutral probe words (e.g., *week*) were also proposed. Each neutral word was extracted from the control and experimental passages, but any of them had an emotional valence. Controls for frequency, familiarity, and length (number of syllables) were done with Brulex software (Content, Mousty, & Radeau, 1990). Of these, 12 neutral words were used in the experimental texts, and 6 in the control texts. In addition, we constructed 48 pseudo-words by modification of two to four letters from words present in the control and experimental passages. Controls of words from which we operated modifications were also made for frequency, familiarity, and length. Thus, our pseudo-words were as close as possible to meaningful words. Thirty-six of 48 pseudo-words were used in the control texts to allow the testing of matching and mismatching emotional words in the experimental texts. The 12 remaining pseudo-words were used in the experimental texts (one per text).

In Table 15–4 is presented the four probe items (coherent word, contradictory, neutral and pseudo-word) associated with the target sentence for "Suzanne's story."

Procedure

Subjects were tested individually in a soundproofed room in a session lasting approximately 20 minutes. They were told that they were taking part in an experiment involving reading and comprehension of stories. They were informed that in addition to the reading, they would have to perform a lexical

TABLE 15–4.
Example of Target Sentence Associated with the Different Probe Words for "Suzanne's Story"

Target sentence:
"Her visit to the nursing home filled her with feelings of ______"

Probe words:
Matching word: Sadness
Mismatching word (contradictory): Joyful
Neutral word: week
Pseudo-word: toigine

decision task. Prior to the beginning of the experiment, participants were asked to sign an agreement (ethics committee) and had to fill out the Edinburgh Inventory (Oldfield, 1971). Subjects had to read each passage on the computer, one sentence at a time at a self-paced manner, and then had to perform the divided visual field lexical decision task. All participants were seated at a distance of 57 cm from the screen, with their head resting on a chin rest. The experimental session started with detailed instructions presented by the experimenter, and all participants started the session with a control text in order to be familar with the procedure (reading and lexical decision task).

The procedure for the divided visual field lexical task was adapted from the one used by Virtue and al. (2000). Subjects were asked to locate their finger of the left hand on the space bar and their index of the right hand on the keypad so that they were ready to read and to perform the lexical decision task. For each passage, after the offset of the last but one word of the last sentence, a fixation plus was presented in the center of the screen for 750 ms to focus participants' attention and to inform them of the next presentation of an item. Next, the probe words (*coherent*, *contradictory*, or *neutral*) or non-words were presented to the participants' left (right hemisphere) of right (left hemisphere) visual field for 170 ms. The fixation plus remained in the screen during the presentation of the probes. All words appeared approximately 3.5 degrees of visual angle to the left or the right of fixation. The center of each probe was 3.4 cm from the fixation center, and the inner edge of each word was at least 1.5 cm from the outer edge of the fixation point. Participants were instructed to press the index finger, as accurately and rapidly as possible, on the "1" button of the keyboard pad for a "Yes" response and on the "2" button for a "No" response. Each item presentation was followed with a white screen that disappeared when subjects pressed the key. For the control texts, the reading of the text was interrupted by the presentation of the probes either at the middle of the passage or at the end. After the presentation of the four probe items (i.e., matching word, mismatching word, neutral and pseudo-word), subjects were explicitly told that they would have a new passage to study. For each passage, we constructed four lists in order to counterbalance text presentation as a function of the probe items. Decision times and correct responses were automatically recorded, and we used Psyscope software (Cohen, MacWhinney, Flatt, & Provost, 1993) to control stimulus presentation and data collection.

Results

The ANOVA (SuperAnova, Abacus Concepts, 1989) presented here has been applied to the data collected, treating subjects as the random variable. The analyses were conducted on the correct decision times in milliseconds to the lexical decision task. The factors Matching of the emotional word (Coherent,

Contradictory), Text valence (Positive, Negative), and Hemispheric difference (Left hemisphere, Right hemisphere) were all within subjects' variables.

As expected, we observed a different pattern of responses for the two hemispheres as a function of the coherence of the emotional words in relation to the valence of information, $F(1, 27) \nabla 10.462$, $p \nabla 0.003$ (see Fig. 15–1).

The breakdown of this effect indicated that

- For coherent words (i.e., matching condition), although the decision times were shorter for positive words ($M \nabla 1440.86$ ms) than for negative words ($M \nabla 1503.46$ ms) in the left hemisphere, this difference was not reliable ($F \leqslant 1$). Conversely, for the right hemisphere, the decision times were shorter for negative words ($M \nabla 1383.22$ ms) than for positive words ($M \nabla 1529.25$ ms; $d \nabla 146.03$; $F(1, 27) \nabla 4.828$, $p \nabla 0.03$). These data confirmed our hypothesis according to which negative emotions are more rapidly processed in the right hemisphere than in the left hemisphere (see Davidson, 1995; Sutton & Davidson, 1997) but did not replicate findings already obtained on the specialization of the left hemisphere for positive emotion. It remains unclear why this effect did not occur, but it could be the case that some positive emotional states used in our stories did not permit this effect to occur. Further investigations have to be done to determine the reliability of this pattern.

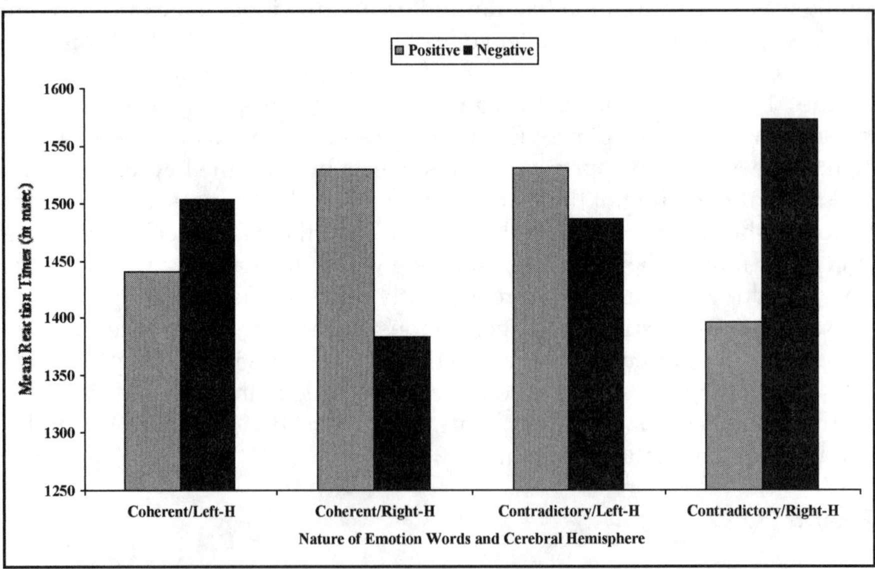

FIGURE 15–1. Mean decision lexical times for coherent and contradictory emotional words as a function of the valence of information and the hemispheric dissociation.

Moreover, the difference in the decision times between the two hemispheres tended to be significant for the coherent words in relation to the negative valence of information ($d \nabla 120.24$; $F(1,27) \nabla 3.274$; $p \nabla 0.08$). For the coherent words in relation to the positive valence, this difference did not reach the significance level ($F \leqslant 1$). Thus, the right hemisphere showed facilitation only for negative emotional information that matched the textual information, and this is consistent with our expectations.

- For contradictory words (i.e., mismatching condition), although we did not observe any reliable difference in the decision times between positive words ($M \nabla 1530.24$ ms) and negative words ($M \nabla 1485.65$ ms), in the left hemisphere ($F \leqslant 1$), a difference in the right hemisphere occurred with longer decision times for negative words ($M \nabla 1572.55$ ms) than for positive words ($M \nabla 1395.86$ ms; $d \nabla 176.69$; $F(1,27) \nabla 7.069$; $p \nabla 0.01$). Also, and contrary to what we observed in the matching condition, the difference in the decision times between the two hemispheres was only reliable for the positive words ($d \nabla 134.38$; $F(1, 27) \nabla 4.088$; $p \nabla 0.05$). Thus, the right hemisphere seemed to be less affected by the contradictory information than the left hemisphere, but unexpectedly, this effect occurred only for positive emotional words.

Finally, our data did not indicate, for the left hemisphere, any difference in the decision times between the coherent and contradictory emotional words ($F \leqslant 1$), whatever the valence of information. However, this difference occurred for the right hemisphere and was greater for negative words ($d \nabla 169.33$; $F(1,27) \nabla 8.117$; $p \nabla 0.008$) than for positive words ($d \nabla 135.38$; $F(1,27) \nabla 4.028$; $p \nabla 0.05$).

Thus, our findings indicated that the nature of emotional words (coherent, contradictory) and the valence of information (positive, negative) had a differential effect on the two cerebral hemispheres. According to our predictions, we showed the implication of the right hemisphere for both coherent and contradictory information, and this influence was a function of the valence of information. For coherent words (i.e., matching information), negative words were processed faster than positive words, whereas the reverse pattern occurred for non-coherent or contradictory words (i.e., faster processing for positive than for negative words). We partly confirmed our hypothesis relative to the effect of emotion on the processing of the two cerebral hemispheres. Indeed, the right hemisphere appeared to be more efficient at processing negative information and showed facilitation for the representation of negative coherent information. It also appeared to be less disrupted by contradictory information but only when emotional information was positive. Surprisingly, we did not confirm the well-known effect for positive information in the left hemisphere as well as the greater activation of the left hemisphere for coherent information, and more data have to be collected to determine the reasons for this lack of effect.

DISCUSSION AND CONCLUSION

The goal of this chapter was to deepen the knowledge we may have of emotion and its influence on readers' mental representation. We tested, using a split visual field methodology, the differential processing of the two cerebral hemispheres on the valence and the specificity of the emotion inferences to be generated. Subjects had to read short passages that implied characters' emotional state, either with a negative valence (e.g., guilt) or with a positive valence (e.g., happiness) (see Gernsbacher et al., 1992) and had to perform a decision lexical task on probe items that were presented either in the left or in the right visual fields. Probe words could refer to the emotion that matched or mismatched the textual information provided in the passages. Our main assumption was that the cerebral hemispheres should be sensitive in a different manner to the valence (positive, negative) and to the nature (coherent, contradictory) of emotional information. Consistent with previous observations (Beeman, 1993; Davidson, 1995) and according to our expectations, the right hemisphere showed facilitation for both coherent and contradictory information, differently from the left hemisphere, for which no priming occurred (even for coherent information). This finding confirmed the diffuse semantic coding of the right hemisphere and its dominance for multiple interpretations (see Beeman & Bowden, 2000; Beeman, Bowden, & Gernsbacher, 2000). Thus, the right hemisphere plays an important role in the construction of a coherent representation, and emotion is part of this representation.

In addition, although we found more facilitation in the right hemisphere for negative information when the emotional words matched the textual information, we only observed a priming effect for positive information when the emotional words mismatched the textual information. This finding is intriguing, as we expected the right hemisphere to be more specialized in negative information than in positive information. Thus, our data underlined an advantage of the right hemisphere in processing "complex" and "polysemantic" structures—that could be defined in our study as "contextual negative information" (i.e., positive contradictory and negative coherent), compared with a more "monosemantic" configuration that could be associated with "contextual positive information" (i.e., positive coherent and negative contradictory). Additional work has to be done to replicate these findings and to study in more depth the relation between the level of processing on which the right hemisphere operates and the valence of information, as it seemed that the representation of emotional information in stories' comprehension involves some changes in the specialization of the cerebral hemispheres.

Contrary to what we expected, the left hemisphere did not show any specialization for the valence of information. Some limitations of the present study may be at the origin of this finding. One of them concerns the definition of the emotional states implied in our stories. According to Gygax et al. (2003), we assume that readers represent general rather than specific emotions, and we are currently developing some studies to define the basic components of these general emotions and how these components may interact in readers' mental representation of emotions (see Gygax & Tapiero, 2003). Also, we did not control in our experimental material the association between valence of emotion and the direction of motivation. A third limitation is the possible confusion between the valence of information and the hemispheric specialization. Our procedure did not permit differentiation of the respective contributions of these two factors, and further research must be conducted to palliate this problem and to deeply understand the specific role of emotion in hemispheric asymmetry and how emotion is represented in the readers' situation model.

ACKNOWLEDGMENTS

We greatly thank Paul van den Broek for his suggestions regarding the development of this study. We are also very thankful to the anonymous reviewer for his helpful and relevant comments.

REFERENCES

Beeman, M. (1993). Semantic processing in the right hemisphere may contribute to drawing inferences from discourse. *Brain and Language, 44*, 80–120.

Beeman, M. (1998). Coarse semantic coding and discourse comprehension. In M. Beeman & C. Chiarello (Eds.), *Getting it right: The cognitive neuroscience of right hemisphere language comprehension* (pp. 225–284). Mahwah, NJ: Lawrence Erlbaum Associates.

Beeman, M., & Bowden, E. M. (2000). The right hemisphere maintains solution-related activation for yet-to-be solved problems. *Memory and Cognition, 28*(7), 1231–1241.

Beeman, M., Bowden, E. M., & Gernsbacher, M. A. (2000). Right and left hemisphere cooperation for drawing predictive and coherence inferences during normal story comprehension. *Brain and Language, 71*, 310–336.

Beeman, M., & Chiarello, C. (1998). *Getting it right: The cognitive neuroscience of right hemisphere language comprehension*. Mahwah, NJ: Lawrence Erlbaum Associates.

Cohen, J. E., MacWinney, B., Flatt, M., & Provost, J. (1993). Psyscope: An interactive graphic system for designing and controlling experiments in the psychology laboratory using Macintosh computers. *Behavior Research Methods, Instruments, and Computers, 25*, 257–271.

Content, A., Mousty, P., & Radeau, M. (1990). Brulex, une base de données lexicales informatisée pour le français écrit et parlé. [Brulex, a computerized lexical data base for written and oral French language.] *L'Année Psychologique, 90*, 551–566.

Davidson, R. J. (1995). Cerebral asymmetry, emotion, and affective style. In R. J. Davidson & K. Hugdahl (Eds.), *Brain asymmetry* (pp. 361–387). Cambridge, MA: MIT Press.

Davidson, R. J., Ekman, P., Saron, C. D., Senulis, J. A., & Frieson, W. V. (1990). Approach/withdrawal and cerebral asymmetry: Emotional expression and brain physiology. *Journal of Personality and Social Psychology, 58*, 330–341.

Davidson, R. J., & Fox, N. A. (1989). Frontal brain asymmetry predicts infants' response to maternal separation. *Journal of Abnormal Psychology, 98*, 127–131.

Davidson, R. J., & Irwin, W. (1999). The functional neuroanatomy of emotion and affective style. *Trends in Cognitive Sciences, 3*(1), 11–21.

de Vega, M., Leòn, I., & Dìaz, J. M. (1996). The representation of changing emotions in reading comprehension. *Cognition and Emotion, 10*, 303–321.

Duffy, S. A. (1986). Role of expectations in sentence integration. *Journal of Experimental Psychology: Learning, Memory and Cognition, 12*, 208–219.

Eustache, F., & Faure, S. (2000). *Manuel de neuropsychologie* [Textbook in neuropsychology]. Paris: Dunod.

Faust, M., & Kravetz, S. (1998). Levels sentence constraint and lexical decision in the two hemispheres. *Brain and Language, 62*, 149–162.

Gainotti, G. (1988). Emotions et spécialisation hémisphérique: Vers de nouvelles stratégies de recherche [Emotion and hemispheric specialization: Toward new research strategies]. *Bulletin de Psychologie, XXXIX*(377).

Gernsbacher, M. A. (1990). *Language comprehension as structure building*. Hillsdale, NJ: Lawrence Erlbaum Associates.

Gernsbacher, M. A., Goldsmith, H. H., & Robertson, R. R. W. (1992). Do readers mentally represent characters'emotional states? *Cognition and Emotion, 6*(2), 89–111.

Gernsbacher, M. A., & Robertson, R. R. W. (1992). Knowledge activation versus sentence mapping when representing fictional characters'emotionnal states. *Language and Cognitive Processes, 7*(3/4), 353–371.

Graesser, A. C., Singer, M., & Trabasso, T. (1994). Constructing inferences during narrative text comprehension. *Psychological Review, 101*(3), 371–395.

Griesel, C., Friese, U., & Schmalhofer, F. (2003). What are the differences in the cognitive representations of predictive and bridging inferences. In F. Schmalhofer, R. Young, & R. G. Katz (Eds.), *Proceedings of EuroCogSci03: The European Cognitive Science Conference 2003* (pp. 145–150). Mahwah, NJ: Lawrence Erlbaum Associates.

Gygax, P., Garnham, A., & Oakhill, J. (2004). Inferring characters'emotional states: Can readers infer specific emotions? *Language and Cognitive Processes, 49*(5), 613–638.

Gygax, P., Oakhill, J., & Garnham, A. (2003). The representation of characters'emotional responses: Do readers infer specific emotions? *Cognition and Emotion, 17*(3), 413–428.

Gygax, P., & Tapiero, I. (2003). *Divide and conquer: A study of the semantic structure of emotional inferences in reading comprehension*. Paper presented at the 8th Congress of the Swiss Society of Psychology, Berne, Switzerland.

Harmon-Jones, E. (2003). Clarifying the emotive functions of asymmetrical frontal cortical activity. *Psychophysiology, 40*, 838–848.

Kintsch, W. (1988). The role of knowledge in discourse comprehension: A construction-integration model. *Psychological Review, 95*, 163–182.

Kintsch, W. (1998). *Comprehension: A paradigm for cognition*. New York: Cambridge University Press.

Long, D. L., & Baynes, K. (2002). Discourse representation in the two cerebral hemispheres. *Journal of Cognitive Neuroscience, 14*(2), 228–242.

McDaniel, M. A., Schmalhofer, F., & Keefe, D. (2001). What is minimal about predictive inferences? *Psychonomic Bulletin & Review, 8*, 840–848.

McKoon, G., & Ratcliff, R. (1986). Inferences about predictable events. *Journal of Experimental Psychology: Learning, Memory and Cognition, 12*, 82–91.

McKoon, G., & Ratcliff, R. (1992). Inferences during reading. *Psychological Review, 99*, 440–466.

Miall, D. S. (1989). Beyond the schema given: Affective comprehension of literary narratives. *Cognition and Emotion, 3*, 55–78.

O'Brien, E. J., Shank, D. M., Myers, J. L., & Rayner, K. (1988). Elaborative inferences during reading: Do they occur on line? *Journal of Experimental Psychology: Learning, Memory and Cognition, 14*, 410–420.

Oldfield, R. C. (1971). The assessment and analysis of handedness: The Edinburgh Inventory. *Neuropsychologia, 9*, 97–114.

Schmalhofer, F., & Glavanov, D. (1986). Three components of understanding a programmer's manual: Verbatim, propositional, and situational representations. *Journal of Memory and Language, 25*, 279–294.

Sutton, S. K., & Davidson, R. J. (1997). Prefrontal brain asymmetry: A biological substrate of the behavioral approach and inhibition systems. *Psychological Science, 8*(3), 204–210.

Tapiero, I., & Otero, J. (2002). Situation models as retrieval structures: Effects on the global coherence of science texts. In A. C. Graesser, J. A. Leon, & J. Otero (Eds.), *Psychology of science text comprehension* (pp. 179–198). Mahwah, NJ: Lawrence Erlbaum Associates.

van den Broek, P. (1990). The causal inference maker: Toward a process model of inference generation in text comprehension. In D. A. Balota, G. B. Flores d'Arcais, & K. Rayner (Eds.), *Comprehension processes in reading* (pp. 423–445). Hillsdale, NJ: Lawrence Erlbaum Associates.

van Dijk, T. A., & Kintsch, W. (1983). *Strategies of discourse comprehension*. San Diego: Academic Press.

Virtue, S., Linderholm, T., & van den Broek, P. (2000, July). *Hemisphere differences in the processing of high and low constraint predictive inferences*. Poster presentation at the Tenth Annual Meeting of the Society of Text and Discourse, Lyon, France.

Zwaan, R. A., Langston, M. C., & Graesser, A. C. (1995). The construction of situation models in narrative comprehension: An event-indexing model. *Psychological Science, 6*(5), 292–297.

16

Beyond Language Comprehension: Situation Models as a Form of Autobiographical Memory

Joseph P. Magliano
Northern Illinois University

Gabriel A. Radvansky
University of Notre Dame

David E. Copeland
University of Southern Mississippi

A great deal of research has examined the role of situation models in text comprehension and memory (see Zwaan & Radvansky, 1998, for a review). This research suggests that there is an isomorphism between representations of narrative and real word events (Magliano, Zwaan, & Graesser, 1999). For example, narrative events are causally linked within a narrative time and space, in much the way that we understand real world events.

Presumably, the cognitive mechanisms that lead to understanding and memories of events operate independently of how they are experienced (Magliano, Miller, & Zwaan, 2001). As such, because they are representations of people's experiences of events in real or possible worlds, we view situation models as a form of autobiographical memory. That is, memory for encountered events, even when encountered through narratives, draws on the same cognitive machinery used to create autobiographical memories. If the same mental representations and processes are used in other circumstances where situation models are created, then they can all be viewed as a form of autobiographical memory. However, there has been relatively little research on this idea (Thompson, Skrowonski, Larsen, & Betz, 1996; Wagenaar, 1986). Although the work on situation models and text comprehension is important, it is also important to assess how well this theoretical framework can move beyond language comprehension to provide insights into cognition more generally.

Here we first provide a brief outline of situation models theory, followed by a discussion of some studies that show how this theory can be applied to areas beyond language comprehension. In particular, we discuss research assessing situation models in the context of comprehending narrative films and negotiating virtual reality interactions. In general, we explore the similarities and differences in the situation models constructed from these different experiences. Both forms of media may more closely resemble everyday experiences than do narrative texts, given their perceptual and analog nature. Furthermore, the goals that motivate one to engage in virtual reality environments are likely to differ somewhat from those that motivate one to read a narrative text. It is reasonable to expect that differences such as these would have an impact on situation model construction. However, if findings from narrative text are replicated for these media, this may suggest that many aspects of situation models for events may be independent of mode of experience and reflect a general representation for event understanding. As such, one reasonable first step in assessing the generalizability of situation model research in the context of narrative texts would be to determine whether traditional findings are replicated for other media, such as those that are described in this chapter.

SITUATION MODELS

Situation models are mental simulations of real or possible worlds (Johnson-Laird, 1983). These mental representations isomorphically capture the elements of a situation and relations among them that define it. There are a number of elements and relations that can be involved in the structure of a model, which can capture static and dynamic aspects of situations (Barwise & Perry, 1983; Wyer & Radvansky, 1998).

In terms of static components, a situation is defined and bounded by a *spatial-temporal framework*. This is the region of space that contains the situation and the stretch of time in which the situation is in force. Time is static in this sense because there is only one time period used to provide the framework to define an event. Within this spatial-temporal framework are *tokens* that represent entities, such as people, animals, objects, abstract concepts, and so forth. Associated with these entities can be various *properties*. These properties can include external physical characteristics, such as size, color, or weight, and internal properties, such as emotional state, goals, and sanity. Finally, there are *structural relations* among entities within a framework, such as spatial, social, and ownership relations. The likelihood that properties and relations are included in a situation model is a function of the degree to which they play a functional role in defining the interaction among situational elements. The more they are interacting or likely to interact, the greater the probability that they will be represented in the model.

In real or simulated situations, we are active participants. As such, the self becomes another entity in a situation model. One's internal and physical states are incorporated into our understanding of the situation. To explore the extent to which situation model theory can be applied to non-text domains, research must assess the role of this aspect in situation model constructions.

For the dynamic component, a series of spatial-temporal frameworks may be joined by a collection of *linking relations*. These linking relations can be things like temporal and causal relations and are grounded in the entities, because it is the entities that are moving through time and which have causal interactions with one another. In this case, time is dynamic because it represents the flow of changes across time in a developing situation.

There is a considerable amount of evidence consistent with the assumption that readers monitor multiple components, as specified by the event-indexing model (e.g., see Zwaan & Radvansky, 1998, for an extensive review). However, within a given context, some components are monitored more closely than others. With respect to the static elements, the spatial-temporal framework is monitored closely because it provides the context that defines the static situation (e.g., Radvansky & Zacks, 1991; Radvansky, Zwaan, Federico, & Franklin, 1998; Bower & Morrow, 1990). Beyond that, the entities and their structural relations are important because these provide the content for the static situation (Radvansky, Spieler, & Zacks, 1993; Radvansky & Copeland, 2001). Entity properties are of less importance unless they provide information about the functional relations among entities in the situation. As such these are at the lowest end of the hierarchy. Linking relations, such as time and causality, have no real definition in static situations because there is no change in time.

There is also a considerable amount of evidence that some dynamic components are monitored more closely than others. For example, during the first reading of a text, reading times increase when there are breaks in causal coherence (Zwaan, Magliano, & Graesser, 1995; Magliano, Trabasso, & Graesser, 1999; Magliano, Zwaan, & Graesser, 1999) and temporal contiguity (Zwaan, Magliano, & Graesser, 1995; Zwaan, 1996; Magliano et al., 1999; Therriault and Rinck, this volume) but not spatial contiguity (Zwaan, Magliano, & Graesser 1995; Magliano et al., 1999; Therriault and Rinck, this volume). Readers do appear to monitor shifts in spatial contiguity when they have a specific goal to do so (Zwaan & von Oostendorp, 1993), when there is a great deal of prior knowledge about the space (Rinck & Bower, 1995; Zwaan, Radvansky, Hilliard, & Curiel, 1998), or upon a second reading of a story (Zwaan, Magliano, & Graesser, 1995; Magliano et al., 1999). Presumably, causal and temporal contiguities are monitored more closely than space because those dimensions provide stronger cues for coherence in episodic memory (e.g., Zwaan et al., 1998). Indeed, causal connectivity and temporal connectivity are strong predictors of coherence judgments (Magliano et al., 1999). Furthermore, the degree of causal connectivity among story constituents is a primary predictor of recall and summarization (see van Den Broek, 1994, for an extensive review). It is important to note that both temporal and spatial relations are also indicative of the extent to which story constituents are connected in memory, but they do not carry as much variance as causal relatedness (e.g., Zwaan, Langston, & Graesser, 1995).

Some researchers have argued that situation models are structured around the narrative protagonist (Ozyurek & Trabasso, 1997; Scott-Rich & Taylor, 2000). For example, Scott-Rich and Taylor (2000) found that character shifts are more likely to lead to decreases in (a) judgments of coherence, (b) judgments of cohesion between narrative sentences, and (c) the accessibility of narrative entities than shifts in either time or location. They interpreted these results as indicating that narrative events are structured around the characters and they are monitored more closely than time or location. However, Rinck and Weber (2003) argued that Scott-Rich and Taylor (2000) confounded shifts in the situation components because they did not independently manipulate them across text versions. In a study to correct this, Rinck and Weber found that characters and time shifts are monitored more strongly than spatial shifts, and there was no evidence that characters were monitored more closely than time. This suggests that when the only linking relation is time, it may not play as large a role in the situation model relative to other components unless it has the support of a causal structure.

ISOMORPHISM BETWEEN SITUATION MODELS AND REAL WORLD EXPERIENCES

As mentioned previously, work on situation models has focused largely on the comprehension and memory of narrative texts. However, situation models should also capture events in the real world. For example, this is found in ideas about embodied cognition and perceptual symbols (Wilson, 2002; Zwaan, 2004; Barsalou, 1999). Before moving on, we consider the validity of such an analogical representational form.

Let's take an evolutionary view of human cognition for event comprehension and memory. Humans evolved from other species that were operating in and adapting to complex environments without the aid of human reason and cognitive complexity. Still, it is reasonable to assume that these creatures were able to mentally represent various aspects of their world, mentally manipulate that information, and store it for future use. What sort of mental representations were used?

The two most prominent candidates in current cognitive research on event comprehension and memory are abstract propositions and perceptual symbols (e.g., Barsalou, 1999). The traditional way of thinking about situation models created from text is that they are built up from a propositional textbase used as a scaffolding to create the situation model. Although this is a possible scenario in some cases, it seems implausible for non-human organisms. Instead, it seems more reasonable that these creatures are creating a mental representation derived from the perceptual information that is readily available. The derivation of abstract propositions is a more highly developed process.

Given this, the situation model is the more fundamental form of mental representation, whereas an abstract propositional representation is a more complex and fragile form of mental representation that is more prone to distortion and forgetting. These characteristics of the different memory representations are well documented in the literature (Fletcher, 1994). As such, we adopt the view that the characteristics of situation models observed in narrative comprehension research should extend to other aspects of cognition where situation models can be assumed to operate. This chapter serves as a tour of some of these areas beyond language comprehension.

BEYOND LANGUAGE COMPREHENSION

One test of situation model theory is to examine whether the same predictions and findings hold for events not conveyed in narratives. For example, do the components involving both static and dynamic elements of a situation (Zwaan & Radvansky, 1998) have a similar influence in other types of experience? To this end we discuss some studies that we have conducted that address this question. The first study involves a different narrative medium, namely film. The latter studies extend to virtual reality experiences (e.g., video games) in which one is a participant. As such, the "self" becomes an entity in a situation model. A domain-independent hypothesis predicts that the general influence of these components on processing is independent of medium or modality of experience (Magliano et al., 2001), although it is possible that their relative importance may vary.

Narrative Film

Compared with texts, there is relatively little research on narrative film comprehension (Baggett, 1979; Magliano, Dijkstra, & Zwaan, 1996; Magliano et al., 2001; Schwan, Hesse, & Garsoffky, 1998; Tan, 1996). Because both narrative texts and films are event-based, theories and findings derived from work on texts should generalize to film (Magliano et al., 1996, 2001). Although there are some similarities, there may be differences regarding the prominence of situation model components. In general, the predictions are that people should parse their understanding of events along the same boundaries as they do events presented in a text. However, given the visual nature of narrative film, it may be the case that spatial dimensions of the situation model take on a more prominent role in defining event boundaries than in narrative texts. As such, it may be the case that spatial shifts are routinely monitored in this medium, in contrast to narrative texts. Furthermore, the spatial dimension may take on a more prominent role than time (see Zwaan & Radvansky, 1998, for a review).

Spatial-Temporal Framework. Prior research on narrative discourse has shown that readers monitor the changes along boundaries of a temporal framework of a narrative more closely than spatial framework information (e.g., Zwaan, Magliano, & Graesser, 1995). Magliano et al. (2001) assessed whether this is also true for narrative film. Given the visual nature of film, changes in spatial location are more apparent. As such, viewers may find it easier to track spatial framework information in film. Alternatively, it may be that a dominance of time over space in narrative comprehension is medium independent.

To test these possibilities, Magliano et al (2001) used an event-partonomy task (e.g., Newtson, 1973; Newtson & Engquist, 1976). People viewed feature-length narrative films and made *situation-change judgments* by identifying points in the film that contained a change in the situation that the characters were facing. People were not told what constituted a change. One hour from each film was sampled for analyses. Each shot in that hour was coded, and the specific shots in which the participants made their judgments were identified. An *a priori* analysis of the film identified shifts in time, characters locations, and spatial region in the scenes. Note that this analysis of space differed from other discourse analyses (e.g., Zwaan, Magliano, & Graesser, 1995) in that it distinguished between two types of spatial shifts. One type of shift involved the movement to another location, and the second involved shifts to new regions of the narrative space that did not involve the movement of prominent characters.

The large number of shots (total of 2457) enabled a full Time (shift VS no shift) × Character movement (shift VS no shift) × Spatial region (shift VS no shift) analysis. We calculated situation-change scores by dividing the number of times a person indicated that there was a change by the total number of shots in that cell. For example, if there were 28 shots that had shifts in all three dimensions and a person indicated that there was a change in situation in 20 of these shots, the change score would be .71.

These situation change scores were submitted to a 2 × 2 × 2 repeated measures ANOVA. Consistent with situation model theory, it was found that people index film events along multiple components. There is evidence that these components are indexed independently, but only with respect to time and character movement. Change judgments were greater for shots that contained these shifts than for those that did not. However, change judgments did not increase when there was a shift to a new spatial region. A spatial region shift was only sufficient to create the impression of a new situation when it co-occurred with a temporal shift. There was also evidence for additivity, in which the more shifts that occurred, the greater the impact on the situation-change judgments.

Most importantly for this chapter, the importance of situational components may be medium independent. Shifts in time had a greater impact on perceptions that the situation had changed than either the movement of character or shifts of spatial regions. Furthermore, aspects of space that are linked to a character (i.e., movements) had a greater impact on the perception that the situation had changed than did the shifts to new regions.

Entities, Properties, and Structural Relations. The research in narrative film comprehension suggests that viewers do monitor and index entities, properties, and structural relations. We conducted a new analysis of the Magliano et al. (2001) data to assess whether viewers track characters in the story world. A regression analysis suggested that situation change judgments increased when new characters were introduced or established characters were reintroduced ($t(2442) = 13.801$, Beta $= .22$, $p = .001$). Furthermore, Magliano et al. (2001) showed that once these characters are introduced, viewers monitor their movements in the narrative world. Finally, using a similar paradigm, Magliano, Taylor, and Kim (in press) also found that viewers monitor the goals of multiple characters, but this was primarily the case for those characters that are prominent in the plot. These findings are consistent with picture story narration data (Trabasso & Nickels, 1992). Obviously, more research on this aspect of situation model construction is needed in the context of narrative film comprehension.

Linking Relations. One would expect that both readers and viewers infer causal relations between story events. There is a growing body of evidence for this expectation. Magliano, Taylor, & Kim (2005) conducted a reanalysis of the situation change data from Magliano et al. (2001). In this analysis, they assessed the extent to which situation-change judgments increased at shifts in the causal goal episodes (e.g., initiation events, the beginning and ending of goal-oriented action sequences) for primary and/or secondary characters that are interacting during the films. They found that situation change scores increase at shots that depicted shifts in the causal episodes associated with multiple characters in a scene, but only when those characters were central to the plot (i.e., primary characters).

In a similar study, Baggett (1979) had people either read a description of a feature length film or view a picture flip book constructed of movie frames. Judgments of the episode boundaries were the same for both. The correspondence in the perception of these episodes entails that both readers and viewers were inferring and monitoring causal relationships between story events because these episode boundaries are determined by changes in the causal structure (e.g., Trabasso, van den Broek, & Suh., 1989).

There is considerable evidence to suggest that causal relations drive story recall for narrative texts (van den Broek, 1994). There is also some evidence to suggest that the same is true for narrative film. For example, Van den Broek, Pugzles-Lorch, & Thurlow (1996) had participants view and then later recall a short film. They conducted a causal network analysis on a verbal description of the film. As expected, people recalled events more often that were causally central in the causal hierarchy.

Conclusion

There is a growing body of research on film understanding that is consistent with findings of studies investigating event indexing in the context of narrative text comprehension (see Zwaan & Radvansky, 1998, for an extensive review). For example, Magliano et al. (2001) found that viewers monitor shifts in time more closely than shifts in special regions, which is consistent with the text comprehension research (e.g., Zwaan, Magliano, & Graesser, 1995). In order to further bolster this assessment, we conducted new analysis of the situation-change judgments, using the discourse analyses from Magliano et al. (2001) and Magliano et al. (2005). Specifically, we conduced a series of hierarchical regression analyses in order to determine the unique variance accounted for by shifts in the spatial-temporal framework, shifts in the character entities, and shifts in the causal-goal episodes for primary characters. The second step of these analyses provides an assessment of the unique variance accounted for by variables associated with these different dimensions, while controlling for all other variables that were force entered in the first step. Shifts in the special-temporal framework (e.g., shifts in time and narrative region) accounted for approximately 7% ($F(2, 799) = 47.90$, $p = .05$); shifts in character entities (i.e., introduction of new characters, changes in location of existing characters) accounted for approximately 10% ($F(2, 799) = 66.59$, $p \leqslant .05$); and shifts the causal goal episodes (i.e. initiation events, beginning of actions sequence, ending of action sequences for primary protagonists and antagonists) accounted for approximately 12% ($F(6, 799) = 26.78$, $p = .05$). These findings are consistent with research on narrative text comprehension and indicate that situation character entities and the causal episodes in which they interact play a central role in situation model construction relative to the spatial-temporal framework.

It appears that the relative importance of the dimensions of situation continuity when a situation model is constructed is by and large medium independent, at least with respect to narratives. This finding bolsters the claim that the higher level processes involved in situation understanding are generalizable across experiences, whether they occur in text, film, or real life (Gernsbacher, Varner, & Faust, 1990).

Virtual Reality

Recently, we looked at people's performance in virtual reality situations. Of particular interest are flight and ground combat situations. In these tasks, people are asked to interact in some desktop virtual environment. Afterward, performance was coded with respect to the components as identified by situation model theory.

In addition to looking at performance in the virtual environment, in some cases we had a second person providing assistance in the role of a coach. That is, the coach viewed the subjects' performance on a second computer monitor in a separate room and could communicate over a headphone-microphone system. These conversations were recorded along with game play to a recording device and later scored. The coaches' comments are interesting because they can be used to help our understanding of the processing of situation information when we look at their impact on performance, the type of information that was provided, and when they occurred as the situation developed and unfolded.

In general, the more assistance that was provided by the coaches, the better was player performance. Thus, outside observers are sensitive to the ongoing structure of the situation, have an awareness of what information might be lacking in the player's developing situation model, and provided assistance that was useful.

Because of the structure of these situations, according to situation model theory we can expect that spatial location is going to play a more prominent role than in text comprehension. There is no real influence of temporal shifts in this case because people are moving continuously through time and not making temporal leaps. The fact that the person is an entity in the situation should also increase the salience of entity information, although characteristics of the self are likely to be more salient. Finally, it is reasonable to expect that personal goals within the situation will have a more driving effect on the representation and processing of the situation, because this is how the person is oriented with respect to the ongoing events. The following results are based on looking at performance in 5-s bins. That is, within a given 5-s period, what was the state of the situation, what were the aims of the person, and what sort of assistance was provided?

Spatial-Temporal Framework. In our environments, spatial shifts influenced processing in the ongoing event. For example, in the ground combat situation, when there was change in location, players were more likely to be hit by their enemies when they were present. Also, when we looked at coaches' comments, fewer comments were given when there was a change in spatial location (e.g., the soldier entered a new room) as compared with the case where there was no shift. This suggests that changing location in the virtual environment requires a person to update his or her mental representation, taking away mental resources that would otherwise be devoted to other aspects of situation processing. Comments provided during this time are more likely to be disruptive. Thus, the need to process a change in location is more likely to bring about a greater demand on cognitive resources, just as is seen in text comprehension research (e.g., Zwaan, Langston, & Graesser, 1995; Zwaan, Magliano, & Graesser, 1995).

Entities, Properties, and Structural Relations. An interesting component about these virtual reality situations is the inclusion of the self. The person is an active participant in the situation, rather than experiencing the event indirectly. This self-perspective is interesting because we can look at how the structure of the situation interacting with the self can affect performance.

In our simulations, people needed to monitor various aspects about their own status, such as whether they have been hit by the enemy or are running low on ammunition. Also, people needed to actively interact with the environment through some virtual representations of themselves, either as a fighter plane or as a soldier. The influence of monitoring the self in the situation was most highlighted in terms of the comments that were provided. Specifically, when the person was actively interacting with the environment, when they needed to direct more attention to their own status and to what they needed to do to accomplish their goals, people were provided with fewer comments relative to when they were less actively engaged with the environment.

In addition to the self, a person needed to also monitor other entities in the situation. In this case, these other entities could be active ones that were trying to harm the person, or were passive ones, such as targets that the person needed to destroy. In general, the more entities that a person needed to monitor, the more difficult it was to process information about the situation, and the less effective a person was at achieving his or her goals. Also, the more entities there were in the situation, the less likely the coach was to provide disruptive assistance. The only exception to this was that when there were increased numbers of passive entities, coaches increased the number of comments they provided that updated the person about the status of the current situation, such as whether a target had been hit or not.

Linking Relations. Although the virtual reality situations that we studied progressed steadily through time and involved different causal relations, we were not able to assess these at this point, because there were no clear breaks along either of these dimensions.

Conclusion

Work has begun showing that comprehension of a situation that one is interacting with—in this case, a virtual reality environment—parallels, to some degree, what is observed in the context of narrative text comprehension. It appears that processing is disrupted whether there are significant changes in a situation, similar to what is seen in reading times from people reading texts. Moreover, this seems to influence both the person involved in the situation as well as a person who is merely monitoring this event. This further bolsters the claim that the higher level processes involved in situation understanding are generalizable across experiences (Gernsbacher et al., 1990).

SUMMARY

Although the majority of the research that has tested situation model theory has been conducted in the context of narrative discourse, we believe that situation models are general mechanisms that are used to understand and remember many different types of events. Perhaps this claim is not surprising. As we have argued, it is reasonable to expect that a common set of cognitive mechanisms would operate in many different types of events that are experienced (e.g., texts, film, video games, and real life social interactions). However, this claim must be empirically addressed.

Furthermore, although similar mechanisms may operate to construct meaning across experiences, the nature of the situation models constructed may vary across different types of experiences. Again, such differences can only be revealed through research. In this chapter we presented two different event domains where this theoretical approach has been successfully applied, although more research is needed. This research demonstrates that situation models for different types of experience are similar in some respects. For example, we expect elements of an event that provide a basis for linking parts of the events together in memory, such as causal reasoning, are critical regardless of experience. In particular, the research reported here suggests that causal relationships are important for understanding events across all modalities of experience.

However, the relative importance of static components of a situation may vary across experiences. For example, the extent to which a person monitors location and time may depend on the modality of experience. For example, monitoring changes in location is very important for performing well in a virtual environment. This is in contrast to narrative understanding, in which there is clear evidence that changes in time are monitored more closely than location changes (e.g., Magliano et al., 2001). Additionally, in many types of events, we are participants. In these experiences, characteristics of the self are important to defining the unfolding situation and may be incorporated into a situation model. Again, this is a departure from narrative experiences in which we are side participants.

It seems likely that there are other domains of cognition that are open to the theoretical insights and tools that have been successfully applied in the area of language comprehension. So much of cognition is based on the comprehension and memory of events. There are a myriad of ways that people can experience events, and it seems reasonable that a common mental apparatus underlies the comprehension of all of them.

ACKNOWLEDGMENTS

The research reported in this chapter was partially supported by contracting grants awarded to the first and second authors from Sandia National Laboratories.

REFERENCES

Baggett, P. (1979). Structurally equivalent stories in movie and text and the effect of the medium on recall. *Journal of Verbal Learning & Verbal Behavior, 18*, 333–356.

Barsalou, L. W. (1999). Perceptual symbol systems. *Behavioral and Brain Sciences, 22*, 577–660.

Barwise, J., & Perry, J. (1983). *Situations and attitudes*. Cambridge, MA: MIT Press.

Bower, G. H., & Morrow, D. G. (1990). Mental models in narrative comprehension. *Science, 247*, 44–48.

Fletcher, C. R. (1994). Levels of representation in memory for discourse. In M. A. Gernsbacher (Ed.), *Handbook of psycholinguistics* (pp. 589–608). New York: Academic Press.

Gernsbacher, M. A., Varner, K. R., & Faust, M. E. (1990). Investigating differences in general comprehension skill. *Journal of Experimental Psychology: Learning, Memory, and Cognition, 16*, 430–445

Johnson-Laird, P. N. (1983). *Mental models*. Cambridge, MA: Harvard University Press.

Magliano, J. P., Dijkstra, K., & Zwaan, R. A. (1996). Generating predictive inferences while viewing a movie. *Discourse Processes, 22*, 199–224.

Magliano, J. P., Miller, J., & Zwaan, R. A. (2001). Indexing space and time in film understanding. *Applied Cognitive Psychology, 15*, 533–545.

Magliano, J. P., Taylor, H. A., & Kim, H. J. (2005). When goals collide: Monitoring the goals of multiple characters. *Memory & Cognition, 33*, 1357–1367.

Magliano, J. P., Trabasso, T., & Graesser, A. C. (1999). Strategic processing during comprehension. *Journal of Educational Psychology, 91*, 615–629.

Magliano, J. P., Zwaan, R. A., & Graesser, A. C. (1999). The role of situational continuity in narrative understanding. In H. van Oostendorp & S. R. Goldman (Eds.), *The construction of mental representations during reading* (pp. 219–245). Hillsdale, NJ: Lawrence Erlbaum Associates.

Newtson, D. (1973). Attribution and the unit of perception of ongoing behavior. *Journal of Personality and Social Psychology, 28*, 28–38.

Newston, D., & Engquist, G. (1976). The perceptual organization of ongoing behavior. *Journal of Experimental Social Psychology, 12*, 436–450.

Oezyuerek, A., & Trabasso, T. (1997). Evaluation during the understanding of narratives. *Discourse Processes, 23*, 305–335.

Radvansky, G. A., & Copeland, D. E. (2001). Working memory and situation model updating. *Memory & Cognition, 29*, 1073–1080.

Radvansky, G. A., Spieler, D. H., & Zacks, R. T. (1993). Mental model organization. *Journal of Experimental Psychology: Learning, Memory, and Cognition, 19*, 95–114.

Radvansky, G. A., & Zacks, R. T. (1991). Mental models and the fan effect. *Journal of Experimental Psychology: Learning, Memory, and Cognition, 17*, 940–953.

Radvansky, G. A., Zwaan, R. A., Federico, T., & Franklin, N. (1998). Retrieval from temporally organized situation models. *Journal of Experimental Psychology: Learning, Memory, and Cognition, 24*, 1224–1237.

Rinck, M., & Bower, G. H. (1995). Anaphora resolution and the focus of attention in situation models. *Journal of Memory and Language, 34*, 110–131.

Rinck M., & Weber, U. (2003). Who when where: An experimental test of the event-indexing model. *Memory and Cognition, 31*, 1284–1292.

Schwan, S., Hesse, F. W., & Garsoffky, B. (1998). The relationship between formal filmic means and the segmentation behavior of film viewers. *Journal of Broadcasting and Electronic Media, 42,* 237–249.

Scott-Rich, S., & Taylor, H. A. (2000). Not all narrative shifts function equally. *Memory & Cognition, 28,* 1257–1266.

Tan, E. S. (1996). *Emotions and the structure of narrative film.* Mahwah, NJ: Lawrence Erlbaum Associates.

Thompson, C. P., Skowronski, J. J., Larsen, S. F., & Betz, A. L. (1996). *Autobiographical memory: Remembering what and remembering when.* Mahwah, NJ: Lawrence Erlbaum Associates.

Trabasoo, T., & Nickels, M. (1992). The development of goal plans of action in the narration of a picture story. *Discourse Processes, 15,* 249–275.

Trabasso, T., van den Broek, P., & Suh, S. (1989). Logical necessity and transitivity of causal relations in the representation of stories. *Discourse Processes, 12,* 1–25.

van den Broek, P. (1994). Comprehension and memory of narrative text: Inferences and coherence. In M. A. Gernsbacher (Ed.), *Handbook of psycholinguistics* (pp. 539–588). New York: Academic Press.

van den Broek, P., Pugzles-Lorch, E., & Thurlow, R. (1996). Childrens' and adults' memory for television stories: The roles of causal factors, story-grammar categories, and hierarchical level. *Child Development, 67,* 3010–3028.

Wagenaar, W. A. (1986). My memory: A study of autobiographical memory over six years. *Cognitive Psychology, 18,* 225–252.

Wilson, M. (2002). Six views of embodied cognition. *Psychonomic Bulletin & Review, 9,* 625–636.

Wyer, R. S., & Radvansky, G. A. (1999). The comprehension and validation of social information. *Psychological Review, 106,* 89–118.

Zwaan, R. A. (1996). Processing narrative time shifts. *Journal of Experimental Psychology: Learning, Memory, and Cognition, 22,* 1196–1207.

Zwaan, R. A. (2004). The immersed experiencer: Toward an embodied theory of language comprehension. B. H. Ross (Ed.), *The psychology of learning and motivation* (Vol. 44) (pp. 35–62). New York: Academic Press.

Zwaan, R. A., Langston, M. C., & Graesser, A. C. (1995). The construction of situation models in narrative comprehension: An event-indexing model. *Psychological Science, 6,* 292–297.

Zwaan, R. A., Magliano, J. P., & Graesser, A. C. (1995). Dimensions of situation model construction in narrative comprehension. *Journal of Experimental Psychology: Learning, Memory, and Cognition, 21,* 386–397.

Zwaan, R. A., & Radvansky, G. A. (1998). Situation models in language comprehension and memory. *Psychological Bulletin, 123,* 162–185.

Zwaan, R. A., Radvansky, G. A., Hilliard, A. E., & Curiel, J. M. (1998). Constructing multidimensional situation models during reading. *Scientific Studies of Reading, 2,* 199–220.

Zwaan, R. A., & van Oostendorp, H. (1993). Do readers construct spatial representations in naturalistic story comprehension? *Discourse Processes, 16,* 125–143.

Author Index

Subject Index